Dear Student:

The aim of this textbook is to introduce you to the kinds of thinking, reading, and writing done in academic disciplines. Equally important, you'll see how your personal experiences contribute to your understanding of academic knowledge and practices. Part One aims to introduce you to a community of scholars and to ways participants in that community think, learn, read, and write. As you become involved in the practices of various disciplines you'll be writing in your journal and learning how to write summaries, syntheses, and analyses. Here are some samples of what you'll find in this part of the textbook.

PART I: READING AND WRITING IN ACADEMIC DISCIPLINES

Chapter 1 Social History

In an interview, Professor Lynn Weiner, a social historian, tells us how she learned to write in her field:

> ... As an undergraduate I took a history seminar in which we had to write essays over and over again. I didn't know how ... The teacher took us through each essay and said, "No, you have to learn how to make an argument ... You have to learn how to use evidence ... You have to show support for your claims." After college I was a research assistant to a historian writing a book and that was an apprenticeship. This historian sent me to various archives and libraries to find out the answers to specific questions for a book she was writing. That experience taught me that history is like a puzzle.

Chapter 2 Cultural Anthropology

Professor Mike Lieber guides us through Carol Stack's study of family relationships in an African-American community. As Professor Lieber explains the author's use of the term *sponsorship*, he is helping us learn how to read research in an academic discipline:

> The term sponsorship *helps us to understand that for this community, kinship is social, not genealogical. Who you live with and who takes care of you is more important than who is a blood relative. This term allows Stack to explore all the relationships in the community that people count as kin relations.*

Chapter 4 Philosophy

To learn about philosophy in Chapter 4, we discuss a particular form of philosophical argument called the "thought experiment." Through this discussion you can begin to make meaning within an academic discipline. While reading John Locke's essay on personal identity, you'll notice that he tells a story about a parrot who could speak and then asks whether we would say the parrot is rational or human. Stories such as these have come to be called "thought experiments" and they are sometimes used by philosophers to think through claims about what makes a person.

Chapter 8 Geology

Throughout the chapters you'll be asked to think about how your interests connect with the academic scholarship you've been reading. Here's what one student, Amit Garg, wrote.

> I have an interest in the field of geology, especially earthquakes, because I have relatives who live in Los Angeles ... [A] long time ago I did research on earthquakes. I want to know how much advancement we have made in this field in the past five to ten years. ... I am also curious about earthquakes because I experienced them during my childhood in India.

(Continued on inside back cover)

WRITING AND LEARNING
IN THE DISCIPLINES

WRITING AND LEARNING IN THE DISCIPLINES

Ann Merle Feldman
The University of Illinois at Chicago

HarperCollins*CollegePublishers*

Executive Editor: Anne Elizabeth Smith
Developmental Editor: Lynn M. Huddon
Project Editor: Edith Baltazar
Text Designer: Sarah Johnson
Design Supervisor and Cover Designer: Sandra Watanabe
Cover Illustration: Henri Matisse, *Conversation,* 1909. Scala/Art Resource, NY. Copyright ARS, NY. In Hermitage, St. Petersburg, Russia.
Art Studio: Academy ArtWorks, Inc.
Photo Researcher: Diane Kraut
Electronic Production Manager: Valerie A. Sawyer
Manufacturing Manager: Helene G. Landers
Electronic Page Makeup: BookMasters
Printer and Binder: RR Donnelley & Sons Company
Cover Printer: Phoenix Color Corp.

For permission to use copyrighted material, grateful acknowledgement is made to the copyright holders on pp. 601–603, which are hereby made part of this copyright page.

Writing and Learning in the Disciplines

Library of Congress Cataloging-in-Publication Data

Feldman, Ann Merle.
    Writing and learning in the disciplines / Ann Merle Feldman.
        p. cm.
    Includes index.
    ISBN 0-673-46070-3
    1. English language—Rhetoric. 2. Interdisciplinary approach in education. 3. Academic writing. 4. Study skills. I. Title.
PE1408.F43 1996
808'.042—dc20   95-43896
                                                        CIP

96 97 98 9 8 7 6 5 4 3

For Sally Israel Weingart and Louis David Weingart.

. . . *From my own unique place an approach is open to the whole world in its uniqueness, and for me it is open only from that place.* . . . *Every thought of mine, along with its content, is an act or deed that I perform—my own individually answerable act or deed.*

M. M. BAKHTIN

. . . *Hearing each other's voices, individual thoughts, and sometimes associating these with personal experience makes us more acutely aware of each other. That moment of collective participation and dialogue means that students and professor respect—and here I invoke the root meaning of the word, "to look at"—each other, engage in acts of recognition with one another, and do not just talk to the professor.*

BELL HOOKS

BRIEF CONTENTS

CONTENTS

PART I
READING AND WRITING IN ACADEMIC DISCIPLINES   9

The Social Sciences: A Focus on the Family   11

In this section you will learn about the family through a social history of the medieval family, two ethnographic studies of kinship relations, and a quantitative survey of nest-leaving.

The Humanities: A Focus on the Self   116

In this section you will learn about John Locke's notion of personal identity, read two of Elizabeth Bishop's short stories and a critical treatment of them, and examine a painting by the artist Henri Matisse.

The Sciences: A Focus on the Environment   240

In this section you will explore marine life through a study of the aggressive behavior of the sea anemone; explore the geological world by reading research on the damage to the Arctic tundra from oil development; and study the impact of a high-protein diet on osteoporosis in Alaskan Eskimos.

PART II
STRATEGIES FOR WRITING AND LEARNING   365

PREFACE

THE APPROACH OF THE TEXTBOOK

Students entering college frequently find academic practices a mystery. They bring to the academic context rich and extensive personal experience and a desire to succeed, but they do not know how to make use of these resources. Further, they often do not realize the important role that writing plays in the learning process or the support that the classroom can offer to a community of learners. I wrote this textbook, *Writing and Learning in the Disciplines,* to help students develop a sense of personal authority and identity within the academic context. In addition, it offers academic strategies that help students gain access to and participate more fully in the kinds of reading and writing used in different disciplines.

Writing and Learning in the Disciplines models the thinking, learning, reading, and writing that we do in academic work. Each of the nine discipline-based chapters begins with an interview with a professor who shares with students how his or her academic interests in the particular discipline developed and what each thinks students ought to know about that discipline. The professor then guides readers through a close, critical reading of a specialized text or texts in that discipline, which helps students see that academic disciplines rely on specialized methods for inquiry and for making meaning. Student journal entries and sample papers, as well as letters and peer and group activities, model academic thinking, writing, and learning while students make personal connections to what they read. The three-way interaction between the writing teacher, the professor, and the student thus creates a dialogic learning situation.

In addition, *Writing and Learning in the Disciplines* offers instruction in three crucial intellectual strategies: summary, synthesis, and analysis. Students use these every day but they become more complex in an academic context. They are essential to reading academic texts critically and to doing scholarly research. This multifaceted approach to academic writing contributes to making the writing of the research essay a genuine communicative activity. When students integrate personal interests with academic inquiry, when they learn strategies for conducting research, and when they have tools to develop their ideas in writing, they can participate more fully in academic practices.

ORGANIZATION OF THE BOOK

Writing and Learning in the Disciplines begins with an introduction, addressed to students, that offers an overview of the complexities of academic learning and asks students to think self-consciously about their participation in academic practice. The remainder of the book consists of four parts.

In **Part One: Reading and Writing in Academic Disciplines,** a series of chapters draws students into the meaning-making practices of nine academic disciplines divided among the social sciences, humanities, and sciences. The social sciences chapters—social history, cultural anthropology, and quantitative social research—focus on the family: a social history of the medieval family, an ethnographic study of kinship relations, and a quantitative survey of nest-leaving, respectively. The humanities chapters—philosophy, literary studies, and art history—focus broadly on notions of the self. Students first learn about philosopher John Locke's notion of personal identity, then read two of writer Elizabeth Bishop's short stories and a critical treatment of them, and lastly, examine a purportedly autobiographical work by artist Henri Matisse. The chapters in the sciences section—marine biology, geology, and nutrition—focus on the world around us. Students first explore marine life through a study of the aggressive behavior of the sea anemone, then explore the geological world by reading research on how oil development damages the Arctic tundra, and, finally, study the impact of a high-protein diet on osteoporosis in a group of Alaskan Eskimos.

The featured professors were chosen for their reputations as excellent teachers, researchers, and scholars who communicate well with students in their fields. Their very frank, human accounts draw the students into the field and provide a basis for continued interest. In the reading of the specialized text, the professor demonstrates the special methods and ways of thinking that contribute to making meaning in that field. The chosen readings were ones that might be assigned to undergraduates in that discipline. One or two texts cannot represent a discipline fully, of course, but these close readings introduce students to the thinking and learning in that discipline.

Following the readings are insights into how practitioners make meaning. For instance, in social history we learn how claims and evidence work to support a historian's argument. The literary studies chapter shows how a response to a literary work may rely on what the reader brings to the work, textual features, and critical readings of that work. The marine biology chapter describes how careful observation of the sea anemone contributes to defining a key term: *aggression*.

The Writing and Learning Activities placed throughout each chapter offer ways for students to connect their personal experience with the academic subject matter, through journal entries, group activities, and class presentations. The activities also help students think about the readings and practice some of the discipline's methods discussed in the chapter. The last section, called Developing Interests, invites students to further develop interests based on topics discussed in the chapter. Each chapter ends with an assignment to complete either a summary, synthesis, or analysis linked to the chapters in Part Two.

In order to demonstrate in Part One genuine writing in each of these disciplines, I chose to use a documentation style appropriate for each of the fields discussed: APA for the social sciences, MLA for the humanities, and CBE for the sciences (all discussed in detail in Chapter 15). The MLA documentation style was used throughout the rest of the text, unless otherwise noted, to provide consistency.

Part Two: Strategies for Writing and Learning introduces summarizing, synthesizing, and analyzing as strategies for writing and learning in the context of specific texts and specific disciplines. Although presented here in three separate chapters, in actual academic reading and writing the three strategies are seamlessly woven together. Once students have learned something about the issues and methods of specialized academic disciplines, they can practice any of these strategies.

The three chapters—Summarizing Discipline-Specific Texts, Synthesizing Discipline-Specific Texts, and Analyzing Discipline-Specific Texts—have parallel formats to allow students and instructors to easily find the information they need. Each chapter opens with a definition and examples of the strategy, followed by an illustration of the process of writing a summary, synthesis, or analysis by following the work of a student or other writer. Groups of key questions help the student focus. Each chapter provides one reading from each of three disciplines (three in all). Instructors may substitute their own readings for the selected ones. At the end of each of the three chapters is a writing assignment for practicing the particular strategy and a useful and comprehensive step-by-step guide to writing a summary, synthesis, or analysis, with activities and questions.

The chapters in **Part Three: Academic Skills for Writing and Learning**— Reading and Annotating Discipline-Specific Texts, Paraphrasing and Quoting, and Documenting Sources—are set up so that the instructor can introduce this material when appropriate, and students can refer to the chapters' guidelines easily. Chapter 13 should be used early in the semester to introduce students to the idea of active reading, to illustrate how to annotate their reading, and to show the many benefits of journals. In Chapter 14, examples drawn from sources in the earlier, discipline-centered chapters help students see how paraphrasing and quoting function. The chapter on documenting sources (Chapter 15) offers an updated explanation of in-text citations and the three documentation styles—APA, MLA, and CBE.

In **Part Four: Writing the Research Essay** we follow a student writer as he moves through the process of developing a research essay on the topic of the role of the young African-American father. For many students, the research essay is the most complex academic project they have done thus far in their academic careers. Developing such an essay—and a working claim—builds directly on what they have done throughout the book as they learned to relate personal interests to academic inquiry.

To make the project more manageable for students, I introduce three helpful tools for developing a research essay. The first is a *double-entry note-taking procedure* with which they can summarize strategically. The second tool is the *source focus chart,* which enables them to synthesize and analyze their sources, and evaluate how they will use them. Assembling a *focus outline,* the third tool, helps them organize their project, section by section.

The three strategies—summarizing, synthesizing, and analyzing—are now seen emerging as part of the writer's intellectual tool kit when writing a research essay. The student essay, which is annotated, also gives students a clear idea of the kind of essay they should be aiming for.

The **Appendix,** Directions for Further Research in the Social Sciences, Humanities, and Sciences, offers a lengthy, useful list of general references, academic indexes, and journals that can help students extend their newly developing interests.

The aim of this book is to demystify academe and encourage students to take a critical yet involved role in writing and learning about academic discourse. With access to knowledge, the tools to make meaning, and a sense of personal authority, our students will find writing and learning in college a truly transforming experience.

ACKNOWLEDGMENTS

My thanks go first to all the students in my classes, and especially to those whose writing is included in this textbook, for their continuing generosity and willingness to think together with me about what it means to learn in an academic community. Next, I wish to thank each of the faculty members included in *Writing and Learning in the Disciplines,* whose commitment to undergraduate education and to making their specializations knowable by others made this textbook possible. A number of graduate students and colleagues have helped me think through practical and theoretical concerns. Lynn Huddon's assistance on this project was invaluable. As a graduate student she field-tested and helped develop the textbook, and at HarperCollins continued to bring the project to fruition. Mary Kay Mulvaney helped to reconceptualize the project from an early draft and has developed wonderfully innovative approaches to using it in class. I am grateful that she has agreed to develop the Instructor's Manual. Bob Schwegler helped me think through the theoretical underpinnings of the book. Others who have helped and influenced me as well are Mary Sheridan-Rabideau, Karen Quinn, Mary Zajac, Annie Knepler, Jennifer Cohen, Phil Gitelman, Kathy Ruhl, Tina Kazan, Carrie Brecke, Gloria Nardini, Julie Lindquist, Raul Ybarra, Cordelia

Maloney, David Seitz, Nancy Downs, Daiva Markelis, Julie Bokser, Derek Chong, Doug Petcher, Alice Gillam, Anne Herrington, Charles R. Cooper, Amy Joyce, Eva Bednarowicz, Elizabeth Burmester, David Jolliffe, William and Debby Covino, Marcia Farr, Melanie Thompson, Gordon Brossell, Carol Severino, Kris Kowal, Tom Philion, Ginger Brent, John Mellon, Deborah Holdstein, Sarah Freedman, Clare Finley McCord, Elizabeth Chiseri-Strater, Bonnie Sunsteen, and Lillian Bridwell-Bowles.

I would like to thank the English Department at the University of Illinois at Chicago for the sabbatical during which I did much of the groundwork for this textbook and Donald G. Marshall, the head, for his continued support. I would also like to thank Jim Stukel who, as Executive Vice-Chancellor of the University of Illinois at Chicago, in 1986 funded a writing-in-the-disciplines project that gave me the impetus for this text. Nora Zukas and the research staff at the UIC Library provided invaluable assistance. The support of the English Department staff has been unwavering. Thanks go to Shirley Gilchrist, Bee Cabanban, Judy Gudgalis, Doris Cunningham, Dorothy Thomas, Ken McCallister, Taufik, Andy Sheils, and all those who work in the front office.

The participants in the Bryn Mawr Women in Higher Education Administration Summer Seminar in 1995 offered a lively and challenging group of interlocutors with whom to try out my ideas. I have also valued my continuing conversations with Dan Lindley and Joanne Olsen about self and other throughout this process. Tom Hamilton at the U.S. Geological Survey in Anchorage and Gary Pohl were very helpful in finding materials for the geology chapter.

Many individuals at HarperCollins helped this project get started and others kept it going. I thank Patricia Rossi, Jane Kinney, and Marisa L'Heureux and especially Constance Rajala and Anne Smith for their early encouragement. I also thank Anne Smith, who recently returned to English, for her continuing enthusiasm for *Writing and Learning in the Disciplines*. My thanks especially to the following reviewers: Evelyn Butler, San Diego State University; Alice Gillam, University of Wisconsin, Milwaukee; George Gopen, Duke University; Joan Graham, University of Washington; Malcolm Kiniry, Rutgers University; Karen Burke LeFevre, Rensselaer Polytechnic Institute; Sarah Liggett, Louisiana State University; Susan Peck MacDonald, University of California, San Diego; Ben W. McClelland, The University of Mississippi; Christina Murphy, Texas Christian University; Cheryl Peters, Houston Community College; Jeff Schiff, Columbia College; John Schilb, University of Maryland; John S. Shea, Loyola University of Chicago; Christopher Thaiss, George Mason University; John Trimbur, Worcester Polytechnic University; Margaret Kemmer Woodworth, Hollins College; Virginia Young, Central Missouri State University.

I thank my partner Michael E. Hurst for his boundless and energetic support and for our ongoing dialogue about all of our projects. I thank, too, our children Philip Matsuhashi, Amy Matsuhashi, Briana Hurst, and Taprine Moats for their good spirits and continual cooperation. Friends such as

Prem, Reed, Penny, and Jeff Glidden, Bob and Sandy Mintz, and Steve and Mary Silverstein make life exciting and rewarding. I could not have completed this project without my parents' help; Morton and Florence Feldman, along with my grandfather, Louis Weingart, and my two brothers, David and Joel, and their families, made it possible to do what seemed like several jobs all at once.

ANN MERLE FELDMAN

WRITING AND LEARNING IN THE DISCIPLINES

PARTICIPATING IN AN ACADEMIC COMMUNITY

When you enrolled in college, you entered a special community, an academic one. This textbook invites you to learn to participate in this community by introducing you to subjects such as geology, anthropology, history, and nutrition, and to some professors who teach these subjects. You will hear how their interests developed and learn how they think and work in these disciplines. You'll begin to ask yourself how your personal knowledge and experiences can contribute to learning about these disciplines. You will also practice using thinking strategies such as summarizing, synthesizing, and analyzing—everyday tools that take on special importance when you read and write about academic subjects. Most important, you will develop your own perspective on issues in one or more of these disciplines and identify topics of interest to explore.

THE PERSONAL AND THE ACADEMIC

Have you ever felt as though you were a visitor in a foreign land as you sit in a classroom? Consider this scenario: Your anthropology professor is introducing the topic of kinship relations. After listing several unfamiliar terms on the board—*sponsorship, matrilineal, genealogical order*—she asks students what they know about kinship relations and how these words relate to such relations.

Your immediate reaction is, "What am I supposed to say? I've thought a lot about relationships in my own family, but I would never use those words to describe them." You are caught between the worlds of academic knowledge and personal knowledge. On the one hand, you have a family and experiences that count in the study of anthropology. On the other hand, you probably have not thought about your family as an anthropologist would—as a system of kinship relations.

One of the challenges in an academic community is to build a bridge between the academic treatment of a subject, in this scenario kinship, and your personal connections to it. But you came to college to learn something new, so how could your past experiences contribute to that process? Interestingly enough, learning always depends on connecting new information to what is already known. Unfortunately, learning is sometimes portrayed as the process of pouring knowledge into an empty canister—your head. It is cast as a solitary activity: You read; you take notes; you memorize; you learn procedures. And then you demonstrate that you have learned by doing well on tests.

One of my students, Liza Beier, wrote in her journal about her dissatisfaction with the way she and other students had approached learning.

> *There is sort of a game we play when we enter a classroom. We listen to the teacher. We wait to hear his views. We notice the words he uses and then we incorporate them into our writing.*

Liza's strategy for learning involved taking in knowledge and then parroting it back. This is one way to learn and may even be a first step, but genuine learning must take you beyond imitation. I wrote this text because I believe that a significant part of learning comes from the process of actively participating in a community of learners, not just repeating what was heard in a lecture or read in a book. As you participate, you develop a sense of yourself as someone who has something to contribute to the whole community's learning process. Your contribution comes out of your personal knowledge and experience, or what I call *personal connections*. How much you identify and make use of these connections depends on how much you see yourself as the same as or different from others in the community. Exploring those similarities and differences in relation to the material you are studying makes learning a richer, more rewarding experience. You begin to learn and to understand your relationship to that material. As the words gradually become your own and the language you use reflects *your* thinking on the subject and not someone else's, learning becomes a process of reinventing yourself and even reinventing your academic community. When you connect your experience with what you are learning, you are participating in the academic community.

In the chapter on Writing the Research Essay, you will read about several students who were able to build an academic project from personal connections. One, Bruce Williams, for example, was doing reading on kinship in a poor African-American community. He had read several essays and research reports on the subject when he began to sense that something was missing. Then he realized that, as a young African-American father, he could bring substantial personal experience to the subject. Because he knew something about the role of fathers from his own experience, he began to "see" the topic differently. His final research essay, which appears in Chapter 16, resulted from the process of connecting his own experience with his readings in cultural anthropology and sociology.

PARTICIPATING IN AN ACADEMIC COMMUNITY

Participating in an academic community has its challenges. Each classroom you enter is different—different professors and students, different reading and writing assignments, different classroom interactions, and different subject matter. You are expected to learn the sometimes different languages and the different kinds of thinking that define the specific subject matters you have chosen to study. This can be overwhelming. This textbook will help you become involved in the academic community—and be more satisfied with your position in it—by showing you how your personal knowledge and experiences—your *connections*—can be put to use with different academic subjects.

As a student, you may yourself have to create an environment that provides the support that you need in order to learn. To do this, some students have formed study groups; conversations begun in class continue in the professor's office later. Still other students give presentations in their classes. The more you learn and grow, the fuller your participation will be.

SPECIALIZED THINKING

In the scenario referred to earlier, the student felt she had thought a lot about families, but she was dismayed by the special language to study kinship that the anthropology professor was using. As you engage in academic work, you will become more conscious of your own way of thinking and of the special kind of thinking required by academic disciplines. Philosopher Gilbert Ryle (18) calls the latter kind of thinking "specialist thinking," and one of the most important jobs a college or university has is to offer training and practice in different kinds of specialist thinking. One of the major aims of this textbook is to introduce you to this training and offer you practice in it.

Let's consider an example offered by Ryle, who contrasts the kind of thinking done by a wanderer with that done by an explorer, both of whom are lost. The wanderer wants to get back home, so she may look around at street signs, or try walking down one block and then another. As Ryle puts it, she is searching but not researching. In contrast, the explorer methodically develops a plan. She uses time-tested procedures, for example, using the sun to determine east or west, noting if street or building numbers are getting larger or smaller, or checking architectural or geographical landmarks. In short, by adopting a method and using tools, she works within a discipline.

Wandering and exploring both have their place in learning. By learning to explore a subject matter or discipline through its special methods you are making an important addition to your learning toolbox. A discipline is commonly defined as a branch of knowledge or as an orderly or prescribed pattern of behavior. When I use the term in this textbook, I am referring to the specific subjects that I cover in the first nine chapters. What underlies each of these subjects, though, is a method, or a way of thinking systematically about a branch of knowledge. For instance, in learning about philosophy (Chapter 4), you'll see how one philosopher, John Locke, used a special method called thought experiments to learn about personal identity. We all wonder about who we are, how we have changed over the years, and what we will be like in the future. The specialized approach of thought experiments gives philosophers a tool for thinking systematically about the problem of personal identity.

In this textbook you will become the explorer as you learn about the various areas you will be studying as disciplines. To understand these disciplines you will be required to engage in several kinds of specialist thinking and to recognize the tools and methods used in each subject area for exploring a topic or issue.

WRITING AND LEARNING IN SPECIALIZED DISCIPLINES

An important feature of any specialized discipline—whether it is academic or not—is how it uses language. For example, if you have a particular interest in rebuilding classic cars, you might subscribe to special-interest magazines and newsletters such as *Hot Chevy, Cars and Parts,* or *Hemmings' Motor News.* You might attend rallies and shows, or you might share information on the subject with others in your neighborhood or community. When you speak or write to someone with the same interests, you don't have to explain what a "straight six" is or why it takes two people to start a Model T. You might think of people with these interests—in this case, classic-car buffs—as a "special-interest group." Participants don't have to know each other personally; they don't even have to live in the same town. But they do have plenty in common, and their use of shared language is important in how they communicate with each other.

The special languages and specialized thinking of academic disciplines are reflected in different subject areas that look at one topic in more than one way. Let's take the topic of the family, for instance. Historians might look at the family by collecting pictures, diaries, and letters from a specific period in the past. Cultural anthropologists might conduct fieldwork with families in different communities here and around the world. Social science researchers might use the data from a large-scale survey to find out at what age and under what circumstances children leave the family home. Each of these subject areas has developed specific tools and a specialized language to answer the special questions it asks.

The nine different subject areas covered in this textbook are typically housed under the divisions of social sciences, humanities, and sciences, as they are in colleges and universities. These three categories reflect broad distinctions, even though some subject areas might fit in more than one category. For example, I have grouped social history, anthropology, and quantitative social research under the social sciences. These three disciplines all study society and behavior, but their methods, as noted above, vary greatly.

The humanities usually include disciplines that ask questions about the quality of our life and about how to interpret the creations and ideas of writers, artists, philosophers, and musicians. The chapter on philosophy discusses personal identity in relation to part of an essay by philosopher John Locke, exploring the question, "Who am I?" The chapter on literary studies introduces us to two short stories by Elizabeth Bishop, and the art history chapter gives us insight on the painting of Henri Matisse.

Researchers in the sciences observe the world in order to formulate an understanding that accounts for the evidence they see, or they develop experiments to test theories. This text offers three examples of the type of specialized thinking used in the sciences. In the marine biology chapter, the aggressive behavior of the sea anemone is studied; the geology chapter probes the effects of oil exploration on vast expanses of Arctic tundra; and in the chapter on nutrition the effects of a high-protein diet on the nutrition of a group of Alaskan Eskimos are examined.

PARTICIPATING IN SPECIALIZED DISCIPLINES

All of these specialized disciplines work in different ways to create knowledge. To introduce you to a discipline and how specialists work and think in their disciplines, I begin each chapter by interviewing a specialist. For instance, Professor Todd Newberry talks about how he became interested in science by doing odd jobs at the Museum of Natural History. Professor Lynn Weiner talks about the importance of studying the history of everyday people rather than that of kings and queens. Professor John Huntington talks about how he became interested in literary studies and it means to him. In telling you their stories, the professors appearing in this book are inviting you into their disciplines.

These same professors also provide an entrance into their disciplines by taking you along as they do a "reading" of a specialized text. Each discipline operates in different ways, but these differences may not be obvious to you simply by reading books, articles, and research reports in the discipline. The purpose of Professor Weiner, for instance, in guiding you through Philippe Ariès's research on the family is to show you how a historian—in this case a social historian—thinks and what she looks for as she reads. Certainly, you could never learn all about a discipline by doing just one reading, but by closely following Professor Weiner's comments and by reading the selected text in depth, you will begin to get a feel for the way practitioners in that discipline think and learn about a subject.

The next section in a chapter looks closely at how scholars make meaning in that discipline. For instance, in Chapter 3, Quantitative Social Research, you examine research exploring under what circumstances young people in parts of Latin America leave the family home. We argue about similar issues every day, but when we do so within an academic discipline we use special methods, almost all of which involve making a claim and supporting it with reasonable evidence. In this case, you learn about and discuss how the author uses evidence and data to support his or her claim.

The last portion of each of the first nine chapters is called "Developing Interests." It asks you to think about how your personal experience connects with the material you have been studying, and to consider what topics you might like to explore further.

SUMMARY, SYNTHESIS, AND ANALYSIS

As discussed earlier, part of participating in an academic discipline is being able to connect your own ideas and experiences to the specialized subjects you are reading about, and learning how to talk as the specialists do about their work. Chapters 10 through 12 offer three important strategies for using language in academic learning situations: summary, synthesis, and analysis. Although these are not the only strategies available, I believe they are at the heart of writing and learning about any subject matter or discipline.

You already summarize, synthesize, and analyze in everyday life to make sense of events around you. Using these skills in an academic setting with subject matter from an academic discipline is more complicated, however. The discussion following the scenario below illustrates how we use these, strategies daily.

Before you even set your lunch tray down on the table, your friend Jane began telling you about an event that had happened the day before. After getting on the train to go home after classes, she pulled out her psychology textbook to read a chapter due the next day. Highlighter in one hand and pencil in the other, she had shoved her backpack under the seat between her feet. She must have dozed off because when she jerked her head up she found that she had gone two stops past the one in her neighborhood. Pushing her book and pencils into her backpack, she ran off the train and crossed to the other side of the tracks to wait for the next train in the other direction.

Jane had caught her breath and looked into her backpack for her wallet, gasping out loud when she did not see it. She pulled all her books out hoping it would really be there, wedged at the bottom. Retracing her actions, she thought, "I had just gotten my change out for the train and I put my wallet right back in on top." She had a sinking feeling; what she feared was, in fact, the case. Her wallet was gone. The half-open backpack must

*have tilted back, allowing her wallet to fall out, or worse, someone behind
her had seen the wallet and made quick work of taking it. Now, blaming
herself for her carelessness, Jane moaned, "If only I hadn't fallen asleep . . .
If only I had thought to close up my backpack. I'm supposed to know these
things. I've lived in Chicago all my life and have taken public transportation
for years. I can't believe I did this."*

Because you take public transportation, too, you symphathized with
what had happened to your friend, thinking it could easily have happened
to you. Later that day you told another friend what had happened to Jane. In
repeating the story you are **summarizing,** offering a more concise, but accurate, version of the event Jane told you about. The next day two other
friends told you about related experiences on public transportation. When
you thought about several such experiences, you identified a pattern that
helped you see similarities and differences among these experiences, thus
creating a new understanding of the whole. This pattern-finding activity is
synthesizing.

As you thought about all these events, you took a position about how
you feel about this kind of event: In an urban environment crime is a fact of
life; sometimes it is random and being a victim is not necessarily one's
fault. Such thoughts constitute **analyzing,** examining the situation methodically and taking a position you can support.

In the academic community, these thinking strategies take on new importance as we use them to make meaning in specialized disciplines. You
will have more flexibility at some times than at others. In the everyday example above, in summarizing Jane's story for your friend you needed to
stick closely to the event just as Jane had narrated it to you. In synthesizing,
though, you had more freedom to think about the event in relation to similar events you had heard about or had experienced. And, finally, in analyzing, you were able to develop your own position. These strategies are used
similarly in academic work. I have demonstrated here how they work separately, but much of your class time will be spent examining how they work
together.

Throughout the text you'll have opportunities to practice summary, synthesis, and analysis. And as you read and learn in each of the disciplines,
you will begin to see how the three strategies relate to each other. And as
you become increasingly comfortable with them, you will be able to integrate them into your own writing, especially in the longer research essay
you will write as part of this course.

IDENTIFYING TOPICS

The purpose of this text is to guide you toward full participation in the academic community. My job as its author is not complete until you have
been guided through the process of finding a topic and developing that
topic into a research essay that becomes your contribution to work being

done in academic disciplines. In that project you will integrate everything you've learned so far. The topic you choose should grow out of a personal interest that has arisen from material you have read in a particular discipline. As you learn more about that topic you will come up with a working claim, which you will develop into an essay that supports and explains your claim to others. Where appropriate, you'll *summarize* the work of an author or authors, but you will also be looking for patterns—*synthesizing*—across all the readings you do. Most important, you will *analyze* the material you cover, taking a position on it and developing that position in your own voice.

WRITING AND LEARNING ACTIVITIES

Your writing classroom is a place where many of the usual challenges of joining an academic community can be overcome. The writing and learning activities you will engage in are all designed to build a sense of participation. The frequent journal entries allow you to mull over new material, review what you do and do not understand, reflect on your experience and knowledge, and observe your own learning process. Frequent group activities and class presentations provide the active part of learning that helps you make the knowledge your own. The formal writing assignments give you practice in summary, synthesis, and analysis. Finally the process of developing a research essay offers the opportunity to develop a major project of significance to you.

WRITING AND LEARNING ACTIVITIES

1. **Journal Entry:** Write about your first experiences in this school. What seems strange to you and what seems to be just as you expected? What is happening in your classes? Do you feel like a stranger in a strange land or do you feel comfortable? What contributes to that feeling?

2. **Writing Activity:** Write a letter to a friend, a high school teacher, a colleague at work, or a younger brother or sister. Tell him or her about your college experience. Talk about how you have changed recently and how you expect to change. Mention the classes you are taking and the subjects you are studying. Reflect on your learning process. What were your original goals for coming to college? Have these changed? What do you expect to do when you leave college?

3. **Research Activity:** Visit some different college classes with a friend. (First introduce yourself to the instructor and ask permission to sit in on the class.) Observe the way the class operates. How does the instructor conduct the class? What do the students do? What is the class studying? Do you understand the material? Why or why not? Does the subject of the class interest you? Why or why not? Ask your friend about his or her experience in the class. Write your impressions in your journal and report back to your class on what you found out.

READING AND WRITING IN ACADEMIC DISCIPLINES

C H A P T E R

1

SOCIAL HISTORY

In her book *Families*, Jane Howard says that whether we "call it a clan, call it a network, call it a tribe, [or] call it a family," each and every one of us needs one (260). She goes on to list what she considers some common features of good families. Among other things, she says, "Good families are affectionate" (271). Do you believe this is true? Is it true of all the families you have known? If it is true now, has it always been true? How do we know what a "good family" is? How might we measure "affection"? How do you think Ms. Howard arrives at this claim? Is the claim offered on the basis of her own experience? Did she test her claim by studying many families? Other cultures than her own? Does her research support the claim that a good family is affectionate?

One way to learn more about the family and the lives of ordinary people is to follow the work of a group of scholars who study social history. In this chapter I will interview Professor Lynn Weiner, a social historian who studies the history of motherhood, work, and the family in the United States. Professor Weiner will guide you through an excerpt from *Centuries of Childhood: A Social History of Family Life* by Philippe Ariès, which examines family life from the fifteenth to seventeenth century. In the section of this chapter entitled "Making Meaning in History," we learn how Ariès uses evidence to support his argument. Finally, I ask you to think about what *you* bring to the study of family. How do *your* interests and experiences shape your understanding of family?

INTERVIEWING A SOCIAL HISTORIAN

Professor Lynn Weiner, a social historian who teaches at Roosevelt University in Chicago, talks about her interest in the history of women and the family in the United States. In 1985 she published a book on the history of women workers in the United States called *From Working Girl to Working Mother: A History of the Female Labor Force in the United States 1820–1980*. Her article, "Reconstructing Motherhood: The La Leche League in Postwar America," won the 1994 Binckly-Stevenson prize for the best article in the *Journal of American History*. Her current project is a book on the history of motherhood in the United States.

What are your research interests and how do they fit into the field of social history?

I'm currently working on the social and cultural history of motherhood in the United States. What I'm really interested in is how the increasing number of mothers who work has changed the culture of family life. For example, I recently completed an article on the La Leche League. The La Leche League, an organization offering support to new mothers, expressly encourages breastfeeding over bottle feeding as a method of childrearing, and supports natural childbirth as well.

The La Leche League was founded in the 1950s and presents an important voice in how we think about motherhood. You see, I don't think there is only one way to be a mother or one way to have a family. There are many ways and there have been many ways historically. Soon after La Leche League was formed more mothers went out to work. What's interesting to me is the conflict that resulted between the idea that women should stay home with their babies and the idea that it's O.K. for a mother to work. I see the work of La Leche League, in a historical sense, as a paradox. On the one hand they encourage women to take control over their private, domestic lives but on the other hand they imply restrictions on women's other activities.

I am also studying the development of such social services for working mothers as day care, from its beginnings in the nineteenth century all the way into the present. This brings us to corporate day care, parental leave, and other kinds of social policy issues that we face at the end of the century.

What is the study of social history?

Social history is a subfield of history, which is the study of the past. There are a lot of different ways you can approach history. For example, you can do political history and look at past elected leaders and political parties; you can do military history and study wars and battles; and you can do social history, which is the study of ordinary peoples. And there are a lot of different ways you can do social history. You can look at specific ethnic or racial groups. You can look at different economic or social classes. You can look at different regions: rural or suburban or urban settings. Social history can subsume women's history or African-American history but most importantly, it's concerned with the lives of ordinary people.

How has the study of history changed over the years?

Historians used to write narrative history, a sweeping saga of some aspect of the past. But then they began to say, "Whose narrative is that? What or who is missing from the story?" So today, for example, if we talk about a wealthy southern planter in the mid-nineteenth century, we would also want to know about the slaves, the free blacks, the poor whites, and the women living in that community.

Now we're interested in a more holistic look, not just the elites but also the whole community. The study of history has burgeoned into many, many subfields and methods. We now define evidence in a much broader way than was commonly done in the past. Then, you might have looked at official government papers; today we look at oral histories, letters, diaries, and artifacts such as clothing and toys. We even analyze such pieces of popular culture as comic books and music videos.

Historians are interdisciplinary, bridging both the social sciences and the humanities. Some historians use methods that other social scientists use, such as quantification and statistical models; many other historians use the techniques of literary or cultural analysis. Some history departments are found in the social sciences cluster in universities but others are housed in the humanities.

What methods do you use in your own research?

Because my work, in part, looks at recent history I use a lot of oral history; I can talk to people. For instance, I talked to the founders of La Leche League, who are all now women in their sixties and seventies. In addition to that I read their newsletters and studied their institutional records, which is a more traditional method of research.

But research methods can even go beyond studying documents, census records, church records and so on. We should be thinking about the places where history took place: buildings, schools, houses. For instance, the Tenement House Museum in New York City was re-created to show the kind of living space an immigrant family might have lived in at the turn of the century. Think about it this way: If a historian was interested in you and your family where would they find traces of you in the past? Telephone books, real estate records, school records, school yearbooks, but also places you might have frequented like youth centers, shopping malls, or school classrooms.

What do you tell students about how to conduct an oral history?

Let's assume for instance that you're going to interview your grandmother. You should first do some preliminary work and find out some general facts about where she was born and grew up, what ethnic group she's from, what large historical events occurred during her lifetime. You may need to know a little about events in the 1940s and 1950s. Then you would think of some questions ahead of time: For instance, "Where were you born?" "What did your parents do?" and "What was it like going to school?"

When conducting the interview you should use a reliable tape recorder and take notes on the general conversation. The key is to show a genuine interest in the life of your subject and not to put words in her mouth or ask leading questions. For example, you wouldn't ask your grandmother, "Why did you hate school?" but rather, "Tell me how you felt about school." If your grandmother is not comfortable talking about a particular topic then you need to respect that and switch to another topic.

When you're finished, you'll need to transcribe the tape—which involves a lot of time. Then, if you were doing a larger family history, you would use appropriate portions of this conversation in the larger report. It's important to remember that an oral history provides one type of data, and you'll use it primarily to test other data but also to illustrate it and bring a human voice to your report.

How did you learn to write about social history?

I never really thought about this much but I suppose I learned through an apprenticeship. First, as an undergraduate I took a history seminar in which we had to write essays over *and over again. I didn't know how. They were my first Cs and I was shocked. The teacher took us through each essay and said, "No, you have to learn how to make an argument . . . You have to learn how to use evidence . . . You have to show support for your claims." After college I was a research assistant to a historian writing a book and that was the apprenticeship. This historian sent me to various archives and libraries to find out the answers to specific questions for a book she was writing. That experience taught me that history is like a puzzle. A story is revealed when you put pieces together, but depending on the kind of puzzle pieces you put together the story can shift and change.*

What kinds of courses do you teach?

I teach United States History survey courses where I try to introduce students to the content, excitement, and process of history. I also teach upper-level courses on particular topics and time periods, such as "America from 1880–1920" or "The U.S. from 1945 to the Present." Right now I'm developing a new course on great reform movements in U.S. history.

What do you think is especially important for students to learn when they study history?

To be a historian is to be very powerful. You are a historian when you read history critically and make your own conclusions about the past. Students need to learn not only the facts of history, such as that there was slavery in the United States, but that those facts have been and continue to be interpreted in different ways by different people.

Historians recently have been talking about something called "collective memory." It appears likely that each generation of Americans "remembers" the past in a unique way. People born in the 1950s almost all remember the assassination of President John F. Kennedy in a very powerful way. They frequently remember where they were and what they were doing at the instant they heard the news of his death. People born in the 1970s have no personal memory of Kennedy but may have a more powerful memory of the explosion of the space shuttle Challenger than do their parents. Historians are just now coming to understand that there is a generational memory or frame of reference that influences how whole groups of people remember the past. Students need to see themselves as active participants in the making and understanding of collective memory.

Finally, history teaches you how to think critically. Historians know that you have to be critical about reading because you have to look at all the evidence that a piece is built on. Everybody ought to be able to read the newspaper and not simply accept it at face value, but to say, "What's the source? Who's the writer? Who's their intended audience? What is the intent of the piece? Is it meant to sway you one way or another?" That is what a historian does and that's why learning to think as a historian is a very useful tool for any student preparing for any career.

Why do you study history?

I love studying history because it is empowering to learn about the past. I love to read history; it brings a human focus to things that are dead and gone, or at least sometimes forgotten. When you read something and you can re-create it in your mind, something that's 150 years old, the texture and richness of that life, I think it is really exciting. I find history to be an endlessly fascinating subject.

WRITING AND LEARNING ACTIVITIES

---

1. **Journal Entry:** Look up a definition of social history in a specialized historical reference source (see Directions for Further Research in the appendix), a college dictionary, or a general reference encyclopedia. Consider the differences and similarities among these definitions. Report to the class on what you found.

2. **Question Posing:** Write three questions you would ask Professor Weiner if you had the opportunity to talk with her.

3. **Peer Conversation:** With a partner, discuss your journal entries and questions for Professor Weiner. Respond also to the following questions: Were you reminded by something she said of another experience you've had at home, school, or work? Have you had experiences like those she discusses? Have you ever had the opportunity to interview someone?

4. **Research Project:** Look up the history major in your college catalog. Respond to the following questions: How is the discipline of history described? How does this description differ from Professor Weiner's description or from other definitions you've found? What are the required courses for this major? What are the possible areas of specialization? Next, interview someone who is a history major at your school. Why is this person studying history? What courses has she taken in this major? Is she specializing in any particular area of history? What does she plan to do with a degree in history?

5. **Writing Activity:** Based on your research, write a report about what it's like to major in history at your school. Present your report to the class.

6. **Developing Interests:** In her interview, Professor Weiner talked about a variety of topics and approaches that concern social historians. What interests you? Look through the *Encyclopedia of American Social History* for topics that interest you. Have you seen any historical documentaries or fictionalized accounts of historical events? Be prepared to tell the class about a historical topic that interests you and why.

READING RESEARCH ON THE HISTORY OF THE FAMILY

What can we learn about families of the past by looking at paintings and by reading letters, diaries, and advice books from those times? Such sources provide the data that allows the social historian to construct a picture of the family as it existed long ago. In this chapter, we will read an excerpt from Philippe Ariès's *Centuries of Childhood: A Social History of Family Life*, written in 1962. At the time Ariès began to study the family of the middle ages, social history was a relatively new field. Until that time, historians had been more interested in royalty and in military heroes and their victories than in what happened to the children of a poor shopkeeper. Ariès's method of learning about ordinary people's lives was to see how they were depicted in paintings, letters, and diaries of the time.

WRITING AND LEARNING ACTIVITIES

---

1. **Reading:** Read the Ariès excerpt along with Professor Weiner.
2. **Journal Entry:** As you read, make notes in your journal about your reading process. Write down any questions you have about the reading and any familiar or unfamiliar terms you encounter. Also, note any places in the readings where you make connections to your own experiences.
3. **Annotate the Text:** As you read, mark the text to help you follow the argument. Highlight key claims; you might use another color to identify data or evidence. Place question marks next to places that confuse you, and restate main points in the margins.

BUILDING A CONTEXT FOR READING RESEARCH IN SOCIAL HISTORY

Ariès's pioneering social history of the family might seem to provide good material for a novel or even a movie on the life of an apprentice in medieval France. But this excerpt is basically a research report. As such, we expect to learn some new ways of reading. Professor Weiner stressed the importance of asking what a scholar's data means and what might have been left out. As we follow her reading of Ariès's research we try to see what Ariès has learned about the medieval family. We will also track his method, constantly asking ourselves how he knows what he says he knows and whether his findings seem reasonable to us as readers.

As Professor Weiner looks over the text she relates it to her general knowledge in the field and to her experience. You too should look the text over and ask yourself how your school and family experiences, your reading, and movies you have seen help you to read the text. Even if the text seems quite scholarly and distant from your experience you may be surprised to find connections to it. Scholarly research can be quite specialized, and as you will see below, this work by Ariès is not something even Professor Weiner finds easy or familiar.

This work isn't precisely in my field and it is a difficult text. I also know it by its reputation. But, like any student, I need to create a context in which to understand this work. When this book was written, the idea of studying the family was relatively new. Before this time historians often studied kings, presidents, and military leaders. That's why this new type of social history encouraged us to ask, "How did ordinary people live?" Not the kings, but families in the middle ages. Then we have to ask: Which families is he talking about? What causes the change that he sees? Is it rooted in the economy and political change? For whom is the change significant and is it true?

Next Professor Weiner tells us something about how she typically reads.

As you can see, even before I read this piece I am making assumptions and guesses about what I will look for when I skim. I'll want to be careful not to read from a "presentist" position; that is, to assume the old family is bad and the new family is good. The title suggests a transition so I'll be looking for signs of it. I don't read only for content. I'm always critiquing, questioning, wondering whether the evidence supports the claim. When I read I keep flipping back and forth between the text and the notes.

The next step is to look for clues that help her build a context for reading.

I see that this is the second chapter in the book and it is titled "From the Medieval Family to the Modern Family," so he's talking about a transition in time. I see from the title page that the book was published in 1960 in French and then in 1962 in English. We always need to ask: Who wrote it? When was it published? What is it that we are looking at? Even before reading it I look at what follows the selection. Are there footnotes? They're very important in reading the text. Are there appendices? Is there a chronology? As I look I see that there are footnotes, not as many as I expected and—help!—most are in French. This puts the reader who doesn't read French in the uncomfortable position of doing detective work, trying to translate the footnotes for some clue to what the sources actually might contain.

WRITING AND LEARNING ACTIVITIES

1. **Journal Entry:** Professor Weiner tells us that social history is concerned with the study of ordinary people's lives. Write a journal entry describing how your views on education are similar to or different from those of other members of your family.

2. **Writing Activity:** Brainstorm about what you know about the history of the family. You can start with different portrayals or images of the family with which you are familiar. Consider your personal experiences, as well as information from books, movies, the media, and other classes. Report back to the class about the similarities and differences you have noticed in these different portrayals.

II

FROM THE MEDIEVAL FAMILY TO THE MODERN FAMILY

PHILIPPE ARIÈS

■ ■ ■

The preceding analysis of iconography has shown us the new importance assumed by the family in the sixteenth and seventeenth centuries. It is significant that in the same period important changes can be noted in the family's attitude to the child; as the attitude towards the child changed, so did the family itself.

Idea Group #①

Idea
Group
#1.
(continued)

An Italian text of the late fifteenth century gives us an extremely thought-provoking impression of the medieval family, at least in England. It is taken from an account of England by an Italian:[1] "The want of affection in the English is strongly manifested towards their children; for after having kept them at home till they arrive at the age of seven or nine years at the utmost [in the old French authors, seven is given as the age when the boys leave the care of the womenfolk to go to school or to enter the adult world], they put them out, both males and females, to hard service in the houses of other people, binding them generally for another seven or nine years [i.e. until they are between fourteen and eighteen]. And these are called apprentices, and during that time they perform all the most menial offices; and few are born who are exempted from this fate, for everyone, however rich he may be, sends away his children into the houses of others, whilst he, in return, receives those of strangers into his own." The Italian considers this custom cruel, which suggests that it was unknown or had been forgotten in his country. He insinuates that the English took in other people's children because they thought that in that way they would obtain better service than they would from their own offspring. In fact the explanation which the English themselves gave to the Italian observer was probably the real one: "In order that their children might learn better manners."

This way of life was probably common in the West during the Middle Ages. Thus a twelfth-century Mâcon knight called Guigonet, whose family Georges Duby was able to describe from a study of his will, entrusted his two young sons to the eldest of his three brothers.[2] At a later date, numerous articles of apprenticeship hiring children to masters prove how widespread was the custom of placing children in other families. It is sometimes specifically stated that the master must "teach" the child and "show him the details of his merchandise" or that he must "send him to school."[3] But these are exceptional cases. As a general rule, the principal duty of a child entrusted to a master is to "serve him well and truly." Looking at these contracts without first of all ridding ourselves of our modern habits of thought, we find it difficult to decide whether the child has been placed as an apprentice (in the modern meaning of the word), or as a boarder, or as a servant. We should be foolish to press the point: our distinctions are anachronistic, and a man of the Middle Ages would see nothing in them but slight variations on a basic idea—that of service. The only type of service which people could think of for a long time, domestic service, brought no degradation and aroused no repugnance. In the fifteenth century there was an entire literature in the vernacular, French or English, listing in a mnemonic verse form the rules for a good servant. One of these poems is entitled in French: "Régime pour tous serviteurs."[4] The English equivalent is "wayting servant"—which has remained in modern English with the word "waiter." True, this servant must know how to wait at table, make beds, accompany his master, and so on. But this domestic service goes with what we would nowadays call a secretary's duties: and it is not a permanent condition, but a period of apprenticeship, an intermediary stage.

Thus domestic service was confused with apprenticeship as a very general form of education. The child learnt by practice, and this practice did not stop at the frontiers of a profession, all the more so in that at that time and for a long time afterwards there were no frontiers between professional and private life; sharing professional life—an anachronistic expression in any case—meant sharing the private life with which it was confused. It was by means of domestic service that the master transmitted to a child, and not his child but another man's, the knowledge, practical experience, and human worth which he was supposed to possess.

5   All education was carried out by means of apprenticeship, and a much wider meaning was given to this idea than that which it took on later. Children were not kept at home: they were sent to another house, with or without a contract, to live there and start their life there, or to learn the good manners of a knight, or a trade, or even to go to school and learn Latin. In this apprenticeship we see a custom common to all classes of society. We have noted an ambiguity between the valet and the superior secretary-companion. A similar ambiguity existed between the child—or the very young man—and the servant. The English collections of didactic poems which taught manners to the servants were called "babees books." The word "valet" meant a young boy, and Louis XIII as a child would say in an outburst of affection that he would like to be "Papa's little valet." The word *garçon* denoted both a very young man and a young servant in the language of sixteenth- and seventeenth-century France: the French have kept it to summon café waiters. Even when, in the fifteenth and sixteenth centuries, people began to establish distinctions within domestic service, between subordinate services and nobler offices, it still fell to the boys of good families—and not to the paid servants—to wait at table. To appear well-bred it was not enough, as it is today, to know how to behave at table: one also had to know how to wait at table. Until the eighteenth century, waiting at table occupied an important place in the manuals of etiquette and treatises on good manners: a whole chapter in Jean-Baptiste de La Salle's *Civilité chrétienne,* one of the most popular books of the eighteenth century. It was a survival from the time when all domestic services were performed indiscriminately by children whom we shall call apprentices and by paid help who were probably also very young. The distinction between these two categories was established very gradually. The servant was a child, a big child, whether he was occupying his position for a limited period in order to share in the family's life and thus initiate himself into adult life, or whether he had no hope of ever becoming a master.

There was no room for the school in this transmission by direct apprenticeship from one generation to another. In fact, the school, the Latin school, which was intended solely for clerics, gives the impression of being an isolated and special case. It would be a mistake to describe medieval education in terms of the school: this would be to make a rule of an exception. The general rule for everybody was apprenticeship. Even the clerics who were sent to school were often lodged, like the other apprentices, with

Idea Group # 2

a cleric, a priest, sometimes a prelate, whose servants they became. Service was as much part of a cleric's education as school. For the poorer students it was replaced by college scholarships: we have seen that these foundations were the origin of the colleges of the ancient regime.

There were cases where apprenticeship lost its empirical character and took a more pedagogical form. A curious example of technical tuition originating in a traditional apprenticeship is given in a book that describes schools of hunting at the court of Gaston Phoebus, where pupils were taught "the manners and conditions necessary to him who wishes to learn to be a good hunter."[5] This fifteenth-century manuscript is illustrated by some very fine miniatures. One of them shows an actual class: the master, a nobleman so his dress indicates, has his right arm raised, his index finger levelled—a gesture punctuating a speech. In his left hand he is waving a stick, the indisputable sign of professorial authority, the instrument of correction. Three pupils, boys who are not very tall, are reading the big scrolls which they are holding in their hands and which they have to learn by heart: this is a school like any other. In the background, some old huntsmen are looking on. A similar scene shows a lesson in horn-blowing: "How to halloo and sound the horn." These were things learnt by practice, like riding, fencing and courtly manners. It may be that certain forms of technical education—tuition in writing for instance—developed from an apprenticeship which had already been organized on a scholastic pattern.

However, these cases remained exceptional. Generally speaking, transmission from one generation to the next was ensured by the everyday participation of children in adult life. This explains the mingling of children and adults which we have seen so often in the course of this study, even in the classes of the colleges, where one would have expected to find a more homogeneous distribution of the ages. Everyday life constantly brought together children and adults in trade and craft, as in the case of the little apprentice mixing the painter's colours;[6] Stradan's engravings of trades and crafts show us children in the workshops with older companions. The same was true of the army. We know cases of soldiers of fourteen; but the little page holding the Duc de Lesdiguières's gauntlet,[7] and those carrying Adolf de Wignacourt's helmet in the Caravaggio in the Louvre, or General del Vastone's in the great Titian in the Prado, are not very old either: their heads do not come up to their masters' shoulders. In short, wherever people worked, and also wherever they amused themselves, even in taverns of ill repute, children were mingled with adults. In this way they learnt the art of living from everyday contact. The social groups corresponded to vertical partitions which brought together different age groups.

In these circumstances, the child soon escaped from his own family, even if he later returned to it when he had grown up. Thus the family at that time was unable to nourish a profound existential attitude between parents and children. This did not mean that the parents did not love their children, but they cared about them less for themselves, for the affection they felt for them, than for the contribution those children could make to the common task. The family was a moral and social, rather than a sentimental, reality. In the case of very poor families, it corresponded to nothing more than the material installation of the couple in the midst of a bigger environment— the village, the farm, the "courtyard" or the "house" of the lord and master where these poor people spent more time than in their own homes (and sometimes they did not even have a home of their own but rather led a vagabond life); among the prosperous, the family was identified with the prosperity of the estate, the honour of the name. The family scarcely had a sentimental existence at all among the poor; and where there was wealth and ambition, the sentimental concept of the family was inspired by that which the old lineal relationships had produced.

Idea Group #3, (continued)

10   Starting in the fifteenth century, the reality and the idea of the family were to change: a slow and profound revolution, scarcely distinguished by either contemporary observers or later historians, and difficult to recognize. And yet the essential event is quite obvious: the extension of school education. We have seen how in the Middle Ages children's education was ensured by apprenticeship to adults, and that after the age of seven, children lived in families other than their own. Henceforth, on the contrary, education became increasingly a matter for the school. The school ceased to be confined to clerics and became the normal instrument of social initiation, of progress from childhood to manhood. This evolution corresponded to the pedagogues' desire for moral severity, to a concern to isolate youth from the corrupt world of adults, a determination to train it to resist adult temptations. But it also corresponded to a desire on the part of the parents to watch more closely over their children, to stay nearer to them, to avoid abandoning them even temporarily to the care of another family. The substitution of school for apprenticeship likewise reflects a rapprochement between parents and children, between the concept of the family and the concept of childhood, which had hitherto been distinct. The family centered itself on the child. The latter did not as yet live constantly with his parents: he left them for a distant school, although in the seventeenth century the advantages of a college education were disputed and many people held that education at home under a tutor was preferable. But the schoolboy's separation was not of the same character and did not last as long as that of the apprentice. The child was not as a general rule a boarder in college. He lived in a master's house or in a private lodging-house. Money and food were brought to him on market-days. The ties between the schoolboy and his family had tightened: according to Cordier's dialogues, the masters even had to intervene to prevent too many visits to the family, visits planned with the complicity of the mothers. Some schoolboys, from well-to-do homes, did not set off alone: they were accompanied by a preceptor, an older boy, or by a valet, often a foster-brother. The educational treatises of the seventeenth century laid great stress on the parents' duties in the choice of college and preceptor, and the supervision of the child's studies when he returned home at night. The sentimental climate was now entirely different ↓

Idea Group #4

and closer to ours, as if the modern family originated at the same time as the school, or at least as the general habit of educating children at school.

In any case the separation which was rendered inevitable by the small number of colleges would not be tolerated for long by the parents. Nothing could be more significant than the effort made by the parents, helped by the city magistrates, to found more and more schools in order to bring them closer to the pupils' homes. In the early seventeenth century, as Père de Dainville has shown,[8] a dense network of schools of various sizes was created. Around a college providing a full course of tuition and comprising the full range of classes, there was established a concentric system of a few humanities colleges (with no philosophy class) and a greater number of Latin schools (with just a few grammar classes). The Latin schools provided pupils for the higher classes in the bigger colleges. Certain contemporaries expressed alarm at this proliferation of schools. The multiplication of schools satisfied both the desire for a theoretical education to replace the old practical forms of apprenticeship and the desire of parents to keep their children near home as long as possible. A phenomenon which bears witness to a major transformation of the family: the latter fell back upon the child, and its life became identified with the increasingly sentimental relationship between parents and children. It will be no surprise to the reader to discover that this phenomenon occurred during the same period in which we have seen a family iconography emerge and develop around the couple and their children.

True, this extension of schooling, so important in its effects on the formation of the concept of the family, had no effect on a vast proportion of the child population, which continued to be brought up in accordance with the old practices of apprenticeship. Girls at first did not go to school. Apart from a few who were sent to "little schools" or convents, most of them were brought up at home, a neighbour's or a relative's. The extension of schooling to girls would not become common until the eighteenth and early nineteenth centuries. Efforts such as those made by Mme de Maintenon and Fénelon would have an exemplary value.

In the case of the boys, schooling was extended first of all to the middle range of the hierarchy of classes: the great families of the nobility and the artisan class remained faithful to the old system of apprenticeship, providing pages for grandees and apprentices for artisans. In the working class, the apprenticeship system would continue down to our own times. The tours of Italy and Germany made by young nobles at the end of their studies also stemmed from the old tradition: they went to foreign courts or houses to learn languages, good manners, noble sports. This custom fell into disuse in the seventeenth century, when it gave place to the academies: another example of the substitution for practical education of a more specialized and theoretical tuition.

The survival of the apprenticeship system at the two extremities of the social ladder did not prevent its decline; it was the school which triumphed by means of its increased numbers, its greater number of classes and its moral authority. Our modern civilization, built on a scholastic foundation, was now solidly established, and time would steadily consolidate it, by prolonging and extending school life.

⟩ *Idea Group #4*

15   The moral problems of the family now appeared in a very different light. This is shown very clearly in connection with the old custom which allowed one child in a family to be favoured at the expense of his brothers, generally the eldest son. It would appear that this custom was established in the thirteenth century,[9] to avoid the dangerous division of an estate whose unity was no longer protected by the practices of joint ownership and lineal solidarity, and which was threatened by the greater mobility of wealth. The privilege of the child favoured by its primogeniture or by its parents' choice was the basis of family society from the end of the Middle Ages to the seventeenth century, but not during the eighteenth century. In fact, starting in the second half of the seventeenth century, moralists and educational theorists disputed the legitimacy of this practice; in their view, it was inequitable, it was repugnant to a new concept of equal rights to family affection, and it was accompanied by a profane use of ecclesiastical benefices. One chapter in Varet's treatise, *De l'éducation des enfants,* is about "the equality which must be maintained among children."[10] There is another regrettable practice which has become common among the faithful and which is no less prejudicial to the fairness which parents owe their children, and that is the habit of thinking only of the establishment of those who by the order of their birth or by the qualities of their person please them most. [They "pleased" them because they served the family's future better than the rest. This was the concept of a family as a society in which personal feeling played no part, as a "house."] People are afraid that if they share their property equally among all their children, they will not be able to add to the glory and lustre of the family as much as they would wish. The eldest son will not be able to hold and keep the posts and offices which they are trying to obtain for him, if his brothers and sisters enjoy the same advantages as he. They must therefore be rendered incapable of challenging this right of his. They must be sent into monasteries against their will and sacrificed early in life to the interests of the one who is destined for the world and its vanity." It is interesting that the indignation aroused by false vocations and the privileges granted to the eldest son is totally absent when marriage is involved: there is no question of disputing parental authority in this field.

Idea Group #5

The text quoted above expresses a definite opinion. But Coustel, in his *Règles de l'éducation des enfants,*[11] displays a certain embarrassment, and he sees fit to employ all sorts of verbal precautions in condemning an old, widespread practice which seemed to be tied up with the permanence of the family. He recognizes the right of parents to have certain preferences: "It is not that parents are wrong to love those children most who are the most virtuous and who have more good qualities than the others. But I maintain that it may be dangerous to make too great a show of this distinction and this preference."

The Abbé Goussault, in his *Portrait d'un honnête homme* of 1692,[12] is more vehement: "There is not only great vanity in giving the better part of one's estate to the eldest son of the family, to maintain him in splendour and eternalize his name; there is even injustice. What have the younger sons done to be treated like this?" "There are some who, in order to establish certain sons beyond their means, sacrifice the others and shut them up in monasteries without consulting them on the matter and without seeing whether they have a vocation. . . . Fathers do not love their sons equally and introduce distinctions where Nature put none." For all his indignation Goussault nonetheless admits, as a concession to the common opinion, that parents "may have more love for certain of their children," but "this love is a fire which they must keep hidden underneath the ashes."

Idea Group #5. (continued)

Here we see the beginning of a feeling which would result in equality before the law and which, as we know, had already become widespread in the late eighteenth century. The efforts made in the early nineteenth century to restore the privileges of the eldest son encountered invincible repugnance on the part of the public: very few fathers, even in the nobility, used the right which they enjoyed by law to favour one of their children. Fourcassié cites a letter from Villèle in which the latter deplores this failure of his policy and prophesies the end of the family.[13] In reality this respect for equality among the children of a family bears witness to the gradual move from the family viewed as a "house" to the modern sentimental view of the family. People now tended to attribute a new value to the affection between parents and children. The theorists of the early nineteenth century, Villèle among them, considered this sentimental foundation too fragile; they preferred the concept of a "house," a real business company, in which private feelings had no place; they had also realized that the concept of childhood was at the bottom of this new family spirit. That is why they tried to restore the law of primogeniture, thus overthrowing the entire tradition of the religious moralists of the ancien regime.

Here we will note that the concept of equality among children was able to develop in a new moral and emotional climate, thanks to a greater intimacy between parents and children.

20   The story outlined here strikes one as that of the triumph of the modern family over other types of human relationship which hindered its development. The more man lived in the street or in communities dedicated to work, pleasure or prayer, the more these communities monopolized not only his time but his mind. If, on the other hand, his relations with fellow-workers, neighbours and relatives did not weigh so heavily on him, then the concept of family feeling took the place of the other concepts of loyalty and service and became predominant or even exclusive. The progress of the concept of the family followed the progress of private life, of domesticity. For a long time the conditions of everyday life did not allow the essential withdrawal by the household from the outside world.

•   •   •

NOTES FOR CHAPTER II:
FROM THE MEDIEVAL FAMILY TO THE MODERN FAMILY

1. *A Relation of the Island of England,* Camden Society, 1897, p. XIV, quoted in *The Babees Book,* edited by F. J. Furnivall, 1868.
2. G. Duby, op. cit., p. 425.
3. C. de Robillard de Beaurepaire, *Instruction publique en Normandie,* 3 vols, 1872. C. Clerval, *Les écoles au Moyen Age,* 1895.
4. *The Babees Book,* edited by F. J. Furnivall.
5. "L'école des veneurs," MS. Bibliothèque Nationale.
6. Conrad Manuel, Berne Museum.
7. Grenoble Museum.
8. Père de Dainville, "Effectif des collèges," *Populations,* 1955, pp. 455–83.
9. G. Duby, op. cit.
10. Varet, *De l'éducation des enfants,* 1661.
11. Coustel, *Règles de l'éducation des enfants,* 1687.
12. Goussault, *Portrait d'un honnête homme,* 1692.
13. J. Fourcassié, Villèle, 1954.

A CLOSE READING OF RESEARCH
ON A HISTORY OF THE FAMILY

Now that Professor Weiner has made some guesses about the chapter's content, she is ready to do a close, critical reading of the text. She will read to question the author and ask how his claims—what he is going to argue is acceptable or true—are supported by evidence. When a historian makes a claim about or proposes a theory to explain, for instance, how children were educated at some point in the past, that historian has presented an argument. Typically we think of an argument as an attempt to persuade an audience of a particular proposition. But an argument can also be thought of as an invitation to a dialogue with one's readers. Ariès proposes a view of how children were educated in the Middle Ages and how that process changed. Professor Weiner's response is to accept some of Ariès argument but to question other of his ideas.

Read the first section, paragraphs 1 to 9.

First, Professor Weiner asks how this portion of the chapter fits into Ariès's book. She reads,

The preceding analysis of iconography has shown us the new importance assumed by the family in the sixteenth and seventeenth centuries. (paragraph 1).

He hasn't helped us out much by summarizing what he covered in the previous chapter, as a textbook might do, but I'm guessing—because of the word iconography—that he used

paintings or some kind of visual art as the data from which to talk about the transition he refers to in the title of the chapter, "From the Medieval Family to the Modern Family." So I'm looking for clues to this transition and I find one in the next sentence. The word attitude *pops out at me. Ariès seems to be telling me—although I'm having to work pretty hard at this—that in this chapter he's going to talk about a change in attitude. When the attitude toward the child changes, the attitude toward the family changes.*

Professor Weiner glances ahead and sees that Ariès has used as an example the observations of an Italian in the fifteenth century. This is primary data, a first-hand report by someone who lived at that time. Secondary data would be someone else's summary of that report. Following is how she reads these examples and keeps them in perspective.

Whenever I see examples like this I stop myself. On the one hand I usually enjoy examples like these—they're entertaining and they give you a mental picture of a real person who had opinions about what was happening at that time. But I'm always looking for the connection, and in this case asking myself how does this example provide evidence for the claim that Ariès is making in this chapter.

We get a lot from this particular example. For one thing, the writer is an Italian who is evaluating the practices of another culture, those of England, as cruel. He gives us a definition of apprenticeship, characterizing it as the experience of all children between the ages of about 7 and 18 during which they are sent to someone else's house to provide service. Further, he thinks this "cruel" custom shows a "want" or a lack of affection on the part of the English toward their children. I'm guessing that Ariès chose this example because of its emphasis on affection, which in turn offers support for Ariès's concern with the family's attitude toward the child.

Looking for the generalizations through which Ariès makes his claims, Professor Weiner finds that he makes the claims by defining apprenticeship.

Ariès is starting to make some claims: the main idea of apprenticeship is service. We might think of it as domestic service. It doesn't matter. We might think of such service as a lowly job, but Ariès cautions us not to be "anachronistic," or, as I put it, "presentist," that is, applying our current values to past situations. Reading on, it looks as if the next move Ariès makes is to tie the idea of apprenticeship to the idea of education.

Professor Weiner notes that in the next several paragraphs Ariès extends his argument (or claim) that "All education was carried out by means of apprenticeship" (paragraph 5). At this point, Professor Weiner adopts a more critical, question-asking approach to her reading.

Up to this point Ariès has been telling us that all children—boys and girls—were "put out" in apprenticeship positions. But now I'm reading something different. He says, "it still fell to the boys of good families" (paragraph 5), to wait tables. I'm wondering where the girls come in. At this point I would start to look seriously at the footnotes to see how he's documenting these claims, but there aren't any footnotes for this section. He's writing this as if it were a narrative, a story, with no need to stop and tell us where these facts came from.

Ariès goes on to offer two examples that he says may be exceptions to the rule—the Latin school and the hunting school—then returns to his major claim that apprenticeship was the major form of education. Ariès uses examples from art works (paragraph 8) to argue that apprenticeship was woven into the very fabric of life. He claims that it was so important to the society that the culture was transmitted from generation to generation by the "everyday participation of children in adult life" (paragraph 8). What interests Professor Weiner is Ariès's next claim. At the end of this section, in paragraph 9, he concludes,

> The family scarcely had a sentimental existence at all among the poor; and where there was wealth and ambition, the sentimental concept of the family was inspired by that which the old lineal relationships had produced.

This is really an important claim that has been challenged recently. He says earlier in that paragraph that it wasn't that parents didn't love their children but, more accurately, they were all working for the larger good, the good of the community. But then he singles out the poor in particular as having no sentimental feelings toward their offspring. I have to ask again how Ariès can support that claim. Poor people are less likely to produce the kinds of evidence that rich people do. They wouldn't produce writings or diaries, because they were for the most part illiterate. Neither would their portraits be painted. Yet we see Ariès making class distinctions when he has shown us no specific evidence for it.

Read the next section, from paragraphs 10 to 14.

Professor Weiner skims the next section and notes that there are fewer examples. Here, she tells us, is where he describes the transition to the modern family.

With the first part of the first sentence, Ariès has my attention: "Starting in the fifteenth century, the reality and the idea of the family were to change . . . " (paragraph 10). The transition from the medieval family to the modern family, Ariès claims, is caused by "the extension of school education" (paragraph 10). This whole section is really important because he lays out, point by point, the reasons that the switch from apprenticeship to education is important. I would even outline the points he makes in paragraph 10 for myself:

Ariès's claim: *Education now took place in the schools.*
Evidence: *The schools were opened to more than clerics.*
Evidence: *Teachers wanted to separate children from adults.*
Evidence: *Parents wanted to be closer to children (not putting them out in apprenticeships).*

The result of all these changes was to create a family more like the one we know today. Ariès concludes this at the end of paragraph 10 when he says that the "sentimental" feelings of the family were more like ours today. He credits this change to new (new after the fifteenth century) ideas about sending children to school nearby for shorter periods of time rather than putting them out for long periods of time as apprentices.

Professor Weiner has now identified the transition Ariès promised us, but as she reads on she finds herself questioning some of the evidence he presents.

I would like to read this as a narrative, a good story, but questions about the argument that underlies the story keep popping up for me. For instance in paragraph 12, Ariès tells us that this major transition that he's been describing only applies to half the population—the boys. And reading further into the next paragraphs the extension of schooling applied first only to the middle class, not to the nobility or the poorer folks. Now I have to wonder how far we can generalize from his argument. In other words if the extension of schooling is true for the middle class how do we know who else this applies to?

At this point, I'd like to question his methodology. I wonder what kinds of evidence or data he could have collected to strengthen his argument. I would have been interested in looking at parish or church records and comparing last names to try to figure out what per-centage of children are placed out, or living with families with different names. Then I wonder how we could have found out more about which children were enrolled in schools in order to see if the class distinctions he makes affected large portions of the population.

Read the next section, paragraphs 15 to 19.

What does Ariès mean when he refers to the "moral problems of the family" (paragraph 15)? Professor Weiner tells us that this entire section is devoted to an explanation of primogeniture, the custom of giving the family's wealth or land to the oldest son.

Primogeniture becomes a moral problem for the family as it evolves because the members of the family and the society are very closely linked at this time. As the attitude between parents and children changed, families had to decide whether primogeniture was a cus-tom that could be considered morally acceptable.

In the beginning of paragraph 15 Ariès gives us a very brief history of primogeni-ture and then tells us that it was the custom until the seventeenth century but not dur-ing the eighteenth century. I want to read further to find out why that's important, but I'm also still questioning as I read. I realize that only a particular group in the society had enough money to be concerned about primogeniture, but Ariès doesn't tell us who that group is. It could be quite a small portion of the society and yet he's making a sweeping generalization.

Professor Weiner next shows us how Ariès uses primary data, in this case the voices of seventeenth-century writers, to tell us about the custom of primogeniture. He's using these examples, she reminds us, to bolster his argument that there is a new sentimentality between parents and children.

Now we get to some actual sources—I'm glad to see this—I was getting worried about some of Ariès's broad claims. His first source says he thinks that primogeniture is a "re-grettable practice" (paragraph 15). We get some interesting details of life at that time younger siblings, for instance, are sent away against their will. I think that Ariès adds this explanation in brackets to the quote in paragraph 15.

[They "pleased" them because they served the family's future better than the rest. This was the concept of a family as a society in which personal feeling played no part, as a "house."]

With it he wants to emphasize for us an idea about the family that was common during this time period—the idea of the family as a "house," that is, an economic institution rather than a sentimental union between parents and children. Ariès is explaining how the quote helps support his argument about the shift in the nature of family life.

The next two primary sources tell us a little more. Both admit that parents can like and favor one child but that they should keep these feelings hidden. Finally, Ariès tells us that later in the nineteenth century some people—I would imagine a very small group of nobility—wanted to reinstate the custom of primogeniture and the idea of the family as a "house" of business, but the idea didn't catch on because we now had a new concept of family, a sentimental one.

Read Ariès partial summary, from paragraph 20.

In the section that follows Ariès summarizes the argument he has made up to this point. Professor Weiner notices the difference in the language here from that of the preceding text. If Ariès were making a movie, this would be the long-distance, panoramic shot. He even refers to what precedes this section as a "story." Professor Weiner uses this summary to help her pull together some of her thoughts on the value of Ariès's work.

It seems to me that Ariès has become rather melodramatic here. This "story" means the "triumph" of the modern family. Now we have lost touch with the data—the details of day-to-day life. What Ariès presents us with are sweeping generalizations: When man (now there's a generalization right there!) had no privacy and was constantly a part of the community he could have no sentimental or emotional view of the family. When schooling became more popular and children lived at home, the family developed a sense of domesticity that contributed to a sense of the family as a unit. I still feel the tension between Ariès wanting to tell a story and my need for a good look at the supporting data.

Ariès's work has provided a fascinating look at ordinary peoples' lives during a time most of us know little about. I want to stress that even though I've been critical of Ariès's work, it doesn't mean I don't find it valuable and informative. Ariès's work in Centuries of Childhood *led the way to an entirely new approach in social history. A path-breaking book, it was credited with advancing the idea that childhood as a stage of life is historically constructed and not the same in every culture and every time. In my own work I might refer to Ariès as I think and write about families as they exist today. If it were possible, I might correspond with him about some of the questions I have on his interpretations or talk to him at a conference. This is how scholars build on each other's work.*

WRITING AND LEARNING ACTIVITIES

1. **Journal Entry:** What does Professor Weiner discuss as key words in Ariès's reading? Looking back at your journal, what other key terms did you find in the reading, and how do you define these? What key words did Professor Weiner's use and how did she define these?

2. **Group activity:** Think about your experiences with driver's education or vocational/technical training programs. In these types of programs, you learn

to do something by working with someone who knows the skill. Discuss the similarities and differences between these classes and the apprenticeships discussed by Ariès. Draw on the ideas of both Ariès and Professor Weiner, and report back to the class.

3. **Writing Project:** Investigate possible internships and volunteer projects in the field of history; check with the history department and Career Services. Report to the class about one program you find.

MAKING MEANING IN HISTORY

As you followed Professor Weiner's reading of Ariès's research, did you note how she seemed to engage him in a dialogue about the subject matter? This may have seemed surprising, since reading is often thought of as a process of taking in information rather than as an interchange between an author and reader. However, to participate fully as a student in the university you'll want to begin to see yourself as actively engaged in a dialogue rather than as a passive recipient of knowledge. But dialogue requires an understanding of the methodologies of the discipline, "how" historians work. How do they learn about the past? What are the facts of the historical situation and how can those facts contribute to a full picture of that situation? Professor Weiner's analysis enabled you to observe her process firsthand. The following sections discuss how Ariès makes meaning through the development of an argument.

UNDERSTANDING HISTORICAL ARGUMENTS

While reading Ariès's work, Professor Weiner remarked; "I would like to read this as a narrative, a good story, but questions about the argument that underlies the story keep popping up for me." The popular notion of history is that it tells a story. But in an academic setting, a historical text cannot be accepted simply as a narrative or a story. We must ask critical questions as we read. We must ask the storyteller, as Professor Weiner does, "Whose story is that? How do you know that's the way it was?" It then becomes the job of the historian to persuade us. This requires a dialogue between the reader and the writer. We observed this dialogic approach as Professor Weiner read the text. She consistently asked questions. When Ariès claimed in paragraph 9 that, "The family scarcely had a sentimental existence at all among the poor . . . ," Professor Weiner responded,

This is really an important claim that has been challenged recently. He says earlier in that paragraph that it wasn't that parents didn't love their children but, more accurately, they were all working for the larger good, the good of the community. But then he singles out the poor in particular as having no sentimental feelings toward their offspring. I have to ask again how Ariès can support that claim. Poor people are less likely to produce the kinds of evidence that rich people do. They wouldn't produce writings or diaries, because they were for the most part illiterate. Yet we see Ariès making class distinctions when he has shown us no specific evidence for it.

Throughout her reading, Professor Weiner emphasized that Ariès was building an argument. It might be helpful here to think of an argument as a dialogue within a specialized discipline. You may feel that because professors have authority they know the truth and your job is to receive it from them. Yet what Professor Weiner and all good teachers wish for their students is that the students develop the ability to engage them in dialogue, to reason with and even against them, and thus to develop a critical voice. You can gauge your involvement in an academic discipline by your ability to talk to other students and faculty about what you are learning.

One way for you to gain authority is to ask what standards or procedures are needed to evaluate a particular historical text. We have observed Professor Weiner reading Ariès, but imagine the two of them sitting at a table engaged in a dialogue, a conversation. She has a procedure for conducting a dialogue that she uses over and over again as she makes meaning in her discipline. It is a systematic procedure or method for making meaning, one that is crucial to participating in an academic discipline such as social history and to thinking about important issues in that field.

DEVELOPING ARGUMENTS TO MAKE MEANING

This particular way of making meaning—developing an argument—asks questions about a claim that someone makes. In 1958 a philosopher named Stephen Toulmin developed the procedure we discuss here. For him, an argument is a systematic method of conducting a dialogue or conversation. What keeps the dialogue going is that one of the participants has proposed a claim that the other person questions. The person setting up the argument expects that the listener will want to participate by asking questions and evaluating the responses, just as Professor Weiner did.

In everyday conversation you might imagine an argument with a friend who is angered by you telling her that it is her fault that her wallet was stolen because she shouldn't have set her backpack down under the seat and fallen asleep on the subway. She responds by telling you that she doesn't know when her wallet was stolen and that you should mind your own business. What we have here is an angry exchange. Toulmin's type of argument, however, asks you to imagine a different sort of dialogue. When a person makes a claim you may want to ask for her reasons for doing so. Once she gives them to you, you may want to question her further, to determine how strong or how appropriate those reasons are. She will work hard to answer your questions in such a way that you can accept her claim. In the end you both might agree that the claim should be revised in some way.

THE PARTS OF AN ARGUMENT

Now let's take a dialogue apart and look at its parts. If an argument relies on a systematic procedure, you should be able to identify the parts and how they function. They are the tools used to question the strength and the appropriateness of any claim and are described below.

Claim

The claim is the conclusion to the argument. It is the statement that says: "The following is acceptable or true." In an extended, highly specialized argument such as the one presented in the chapter from Ariès's book, you will find a major claim and many subclaims linked together. Sometimes claims are not stated explicitly but inferred. Whether you are planning to write a paper and thus develop your own claim, or you are reading a paper and analyzing someone else's claim, you have to always consider whether what is claimed is acceptable or true.

Evidence (Also Referred to as Data, Grounds, and Reasons)

You are probably most familiar with this part of the argument. Since grade school you have been asked to give reasons for your claims. We have many synonyms for *reasons* since different discourse communities rely on slightly different terms. Any of the terms listed above—*grounds, data, evidence,* and *reasons*—may be used to refer to this part of an argument.

Suppose you do not accept a claim or you would like to know how the speaker established it. Your first step would be to inquire about the evidence or grounds: "What have you got to go on?" In Toulmin's scheme the evidence is the specific facts that the speaker uses to support a claim.

The Warrant

This aspect of an argument may be new to you, but it is very important for developing an argument in an academic discipline. If you are not satisfied by the facts provided by the grounds, you can ask more probing questions, such as, "How did you get from your grounds to your claim?" This question asks the speaker to build a bridge—a warrant—from the grounds to the claim. This is a more difficult concept to understand since warrants are frequently unspoken. You could think of a warrant as a license or permit that authorizes you to say that the grounds do provide the necessary facts for the claim.

Specialized disciplines frequently use warrants connected to the methods used in those disciplines. For instance, in mathematics the warrant might be that a particular formula provides the appropriate method for achieving a particular result. In the law, conclusions are warranted by the results of previous cases. The historical method depends on finding an acceptable pattern of relevant information that allows the historian to build a picture of family life in those times. The warrant thus tells you that Ariès has proceeded in a methodologically sound way to convince you that his grounds or evidence does indeed support his claim.

The Qualifier

To consider the strength of the link between the grounds and the claim, you may want to add a qualifier. "Is the claim completely true in all situations or do we need to limit it in some way?"

The Rebuttal

If we cannot accept a claim completely, without a shred of doubt, we will want to describe the specific circumstances which tell us that the claim is not as strong as originally proposed. This explanation is called the rebuttal. The rebuttal is one of the most difficult aspects of an argument for students to feel comfortable with. If you are writing a paper in support of a claim you have made, then you must put yourself in the position of the questioner and imagine what challenges he or she will make to the strength or appropriateness of your claim. Ask yourself, "What is the other side to this argument?" or "What problems might someone else have with this argument?"

LAYING OUT AN ARGUMENT

The diagram below illustrates visually how all the parts of the argument described above fit together. In the next section is an imaginary dialogue between the two historians. Note how each of the parts of the argument are handled in a dialogue form.

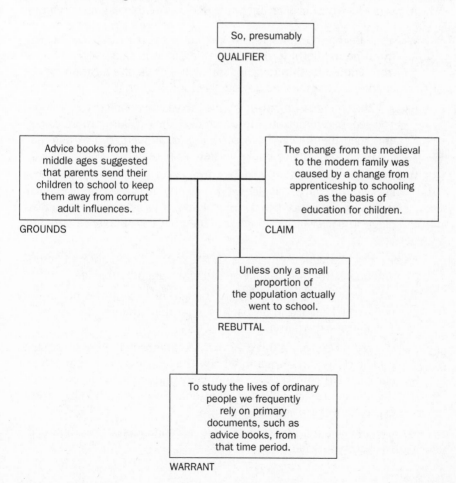

WRITING AND LEARNING ACTIVITIES

---

1. **Journal Entry:** Identify at least two more claims in the Ariès reading (other than those discussed by Professor Weiner). Explain why you chose those statements as claims.

2. **Group Activity:** Bring in an article from a newspaper or magazine. As a group, determine what argument is being made in the article and underline the claims you think the author is making.

3. **Peer Activity:** Based on your group work and journal entries, work with a partner to formulate your own definitions for a *claim* and *evidence* in an argument. Share these new definitions with the class.

AN IMAGINARY DIALOGUE
TO DEMONSTRATE AN ARGUMENT

Let's imagine a short dialogue between Professor Weiner and Philippe Ariès, which covers a bare outline of an argument Ariès makes in paragraphs 10 to 14.

WEINER: In this portion of your chapter you claim that the change from the medieval to the modern family was caused by a change from apprenticeship to schooling as the basis of education for the children. What reasons do you give for this change?

ARIÈS: The change was caused by the increasing popularity of schools. You see, parents wanted to watch over their children more closely and keep them away from corrupt adult influences. I've relied on contemporary advice books written for parents.

WEINER: So, your evidence comes from advice books. To study the lives of ordinary people we frequently rely on primary documents we find from that time period. This is accepted methodology in social history, so I can see how your evidence supports your claim.

ARIÈS: Yes, throughout my research I have relied on paintings, letters, and books from the middle ages that tell about family life.

WEINER: I have a further question, though. In those times not everybody could read. Did all parents send their children to school or was it just some parents?

ARIÈS: You have a point there. At first it was mostly the boys from the middle classes who went to school. The high and low end of the social class structure, that is, the nobility and the artisans, continued the apprenticeship model of education. Eventually, though, almost everyone went to school.

WEINER: Taking this information into account, don't you think this weakens your claim?

ARIÈS: Perhaps I should qualify my claim.

WEINER: Yes. I would argue in return that we can't be absolutely sure that the increased popularity of schooling caused a change in the family when schooling was only available to a small portion of the population. I recommend that you qualify your claim by saying something a bit more conservative, such as the increased popularity of schooling may have caused the family to change.

WRITING AND LEARNING ACTIVITIES

1. **Journal Entry:** In the dialogue above, underline the parts of the argument. What claims do the two each put forth in this dialogue? What are Professor Weiner's rebuttals to Ariès's claims? Write out the claims and the evidence for them.

2. **Peer Activity:** Write a dialogue between a history major and Ariès for the argument Ariès makes in paragraph 9 that "The family scarcely had a sentimental existence at all among the poor." What are the claims of each? How do they support their claims?

DEVELOPING INTERESTS
PERSONAL CONNECTIONS

Have Philippe Ariès's views of the family in the middle ages caused you to think any differently about families in general or your family in particular? In the middle ages in Europe, young men and women of your age or younger would be sent to other homes as apprentices as a way of entering the larger society. How do you suppose family life differed during that time in other parts of the world? In China? In Africa? In South America? How have things changed today?

What social structures allow you to enter the larger society? Focus on personal connections that you can develop out of issues that arise in social history. When you can draw from your own experience or identify questions that are important to you, you are more able to participate in the work of the discipline. Below are some activities that may help you to identify personal connections and interests.

WRITING AND LEARNING ACTIVITIES

1. **Research Activity:** Philippe Ariès used a research method based on paintings, letters, diaries, and advice books produced during the middle ages. Collect similar sources from your family and community. What do they tell you about family life? What do they suggest is most important? Develop a collage of these items and write a covering explanation.

2. **Journal Entry:** How is your family different from the families described by Ariès? What questions do you have that were not answered by Ariès's research? What would you like to know more about?

_____

◼◻ LINKED WRITING ASSIGNMENT

Writing a Summary of Work in Social History (see Chapter 10, Summarizing Discipline-Specific Texts). In the previous section, Developing Interests, you began to identify issues and ideas that you might want to explore further. Finding personal connections to the material you are studying is one important way to participate more fully in an academic community. You will also need to learn how some everyday thinking strategies, such as summarizing, help you to participate in the disciplines you are studying here. Chapter 10 introduces you to the process of writing a summary and offers a reading from social history for you to practice summarizing.

C H A P T E R

2

CULTURAL ANTHROPOLOGY

Have you ever heard the expression, "blood is thicker than water"? It suggests that the speaker values biological or "blood" kin over non-related kin. Have you ever thought about why people say this? Do only blood relatives make a family? Have you ever been faced with the dilemma of choosing between family and friends? How do members of your culture or other cultures define family relations? Who do you consider family? These questions reflect important issues that can affect our own lives. Anthropologists have developed special methods to learn about the ways different cultures think about such questions.

To introduce you to the field of anthropology, I interview Professor Michael Lieber, a cultural anthropologist who has done fieldwork in Micronesia. Professor Lieber will guide you through two readings of ethnographic reports of fieldwork, both of which examine the nature of kinship, or family relations, in two different cultural settings. We then examine some of the problems anthropologists face in describing the lives of particular social or cultural groups. Following this, I ask you to consider how your own experiences with kinship help you to identify interests you'd like to explore further.

AN INTERVIEW WITH
A CULTURAL ANTHROPOLOGIST

Professor Michael Lieber is a cultural anthropologist at the University of Illinois at Chicago (UIC). He teaches introductory courses in cultural anthropology and cybernetic systems as well as courses on such topics as ethnicity, gender, research methods, and folklore. His book, *More Than a Living: Fishing and the Social Order on a Polynesian Atoll*, published in 1994, describes how traditional fishing activity was organized and what happened to that organization as the social order underwent profound changes in the twentieth century. He has also gained national attention for *Coaching Outfield in Tee-ball in the Pee Wee Minors*, a manual that teaches parents how to coach outfield for Little Leaguers ages 5 to 10. It is now being translated into Spanish at the request of Mexican-American coaches.

What are some of the different types of anthropology and what is your specialty?

The word anthropology *means "the study of humankind"; the discipline focuses on human variability in all its aspects—biological variability, cultural variability (including languages), and variability through time (using archaeological techniques). I'm a cultural anthropologist with strong interests in biology. The principal method in my branch of the discipline is called ethnography—the first-hand observation of people in their own home setting. This involves living in their community, learning their language, ways of doing things, and ways of thinking about what they experience. This is what we refer to when we use the term* fieldwork.

Tell us how you got started doing fieldwork.

I started doing fieldwork when I was studying folklore, doing several field collections of stories and music. When I switched to anthropology, I participated in a summer field training school in Nevada, where I worked with the Shoshone people. I also worked as a field researcher for the Pennsylvania Department of Sanitation. In addition, I did my own independent research on African-American male verbal dueling, all between 1960 and 1965. When I heard about a research unit looking for students to do fieldwork in the Pacific for one of their projects, I applied and was accepted.

It was a comparative study of relocated communities, that is, situations where a whole community or part of a community had been moved from one island to another to live. Twelve of us were sent to study twelve different communities in places like Fiji, New Guinea, the Marshall Islands, and the Solomon Islands. I was sent to Kapingamarangi atoll, in Micronesia; with less than half a square mile of land, it was one of the most isolated of all the Pacific islands until the 1880s. An atoll is a low coral reef with islets perched on the flat part of the reef fronting a lagoon. In 1919, about a third of the population was taken to Pohnpei, a high island controlled by the Japanese colonial administration, after a disastrous two-year drought and famine. The community on Pohnpei had grown since then, and I spent seven months on Pohnpei and five months on Kapingamarangi gathering information to compare the two communities. I've been back several times since 1966, most recently in 1990.

While I was working on Pohnpei in 1965, I met Vern Carroll, the anthropologist who was studying the other Polynesian atoll, Nukuoro, 164 miles north of Kapingamarangi. We became fast friends, and, frankly, I learned much of what I know about anthropology from him.

What was the most important thing you learned from your mentor?

Two things. First, he taught me about culture. You see, culture is not a "thing" in people's heads that somehow "does" something on its own to people. Culture is a theory, a way of explaining why people do what they do in the patterned ways they do them, and why the patterns in one community are so different from those in another. Culture is a theory about human perception that says that people give shape to their experiences by conferring meaning on the things, people, and relations between them that comprise their universe.

Two communities can confer very different meanings on the same object. I look at a cow and see beef on the hoof. An orthodox Hindu looks at a cow and sees something resembling what would be a crucifix for a Christian. The difference between us is not what is happening in our optic nerves. The light patterns entering the pupils of our eyes are identical, yet we "see" different things. The difference between us is in the rules that we use to interpret sense data, and that's a cultural difference, a learned set of conscious and unconscious conventions that order our perceptions, lend them coherence, and make it possible for us to live in reasonably predictable universes.

The second thing my mentor did was to introduce me to the work of Gregory Bateson, who is largely responsible for introducing cybernetic theory into anthropology. Cybernetics is the study of systems that operate to achieve a goal and have the capacity to correct their own errors in the process. Organisms and ecosystems have this capacity as do well-designed machines. When your blood temperature gets too high, you automatically sweat, and the evaporation of sweat cools your skin surface and the capillaries just below the skin, eventually bringing your internal temperature down. This is an example of negative feedback, error correction that keeps a system stable. You can look at the operation of genes in a cell and the decision making at a community meeting as particular instances— special cases—of the same thing—information processing.

How does this apply to the differences you found between the two Kapingama-rangi communities in Micronesia?

What amazed me were the differences in the social organizations of these two communities. The atoll community, whose only contact with the outside world was three or four visits of a ship each year, had gone through radical changes in social organization. Meanwhile, the resettled community, right in the middle of an urban area with stores, movies, government offices, and surrounded by other ethnic groups had a social organization that was the same as the atoll community's organization fifty years before. It hadn't changed in all that time. You would have expected just the opposite—that the resettled community would have changed the most.

To understand this enigma, you need to understand a profound cultural difference between them and us. We understand the person to be an individual, a self-contained, self-reliant human being whose relationships with other people are based on his or her capabilities for occupying statuses—like doctor, husband, teacher, secretary, and so on—and performing the tasks (roles) expected of someone in that status. The individual is an egocentric way of defining personhood.

Kapingamarangi people define the person the other way around, starting with the relationship. It is the relationship that defines the person. The person is a relatum, one end of a relationship. They say that the difference between people and animals is that people know how to establish and maintain social relationships and animals don't. Dogs, for example, mate with their siblings and parents—they don't know who their relatives are; people do. For another example, we would call a funny person a "comedian," while they would refer to him or her as "a person who causes other people to laugh." We see humor as a property of the person, while they see it as a property of the relationship between persons. So, a person who acts like your mother is your mother, regardless of genealogy. We predict what people will do by knowing their statuses and roles; they predict what people will do by knowing their biographies—the histories of how they have conducted their relationships.

How did these differences result in changes for the Kapingamarangi people?

These two communities operated in very different contexts, even though they were governed by the same colonial administration. After World War II, the United States took over Micronesia and began programs of economic, social, and political development—schools, medical dispensaries, co-operatives, and democratic political institutions. The atoll was considered a municipality, and so it was a target for these programs, which the Kapinga had to staff and run themselves. To do that, Kapinga people had to take on western-style statuses and roles (teacher, student, nurse, chief magistrate, court judge, and so on) in order to interact with other Kapinga. So the atoll became a single community operating in two, differently organized universes—one of biographies and the other of statuses and roles. Thus people's expectations of one another in one universe were constantly being violated by the requirements of the other universe.

By contrast, the people in the resettled community on Pohnpei were not a municipality or a legal entity of any kind. They lived in a municipality with a municipal council, courts, police, businesses, schools, and the like. But their community was not a formal polity or a target for these programs. The Kapinga people on Pohnpei adopted statuses like student, teacher, customer, employee, and the like—but almost always to interact with people of different ethnic groups, not with each other. The relationship of each community with the American administration was different. Therefore, the political-social context of each community was different, and their adaptations to their contexts were different. You can see how the organization of social systems and their relations with their contexts is informed by local premises—cultural premises—about what it means to be a person.

Can you give us an example about how this might work a little closer to home?

You can see the same kind of thing in families. Take a family of a married couple and three children. Your own experience tells you that the oldest child has a different relationship with his or her parents than the second and third child do. The first child has been an only child but the next two children will have never been without siblings. The third child inherits very different parents than his or her elder siblings got. The parents are older, under much greater economic pressures, have much less time and attention to devote to him or her, and are dependent on the two older children to help raise this third child. So if this family lives together in the same house, can we say that these three kids have the same environment? Clearly not! The organization of each child's relationships with the same people is different. Therefore, the environmental context of each child's experience is different.

What is involved in taking field notes?

It's not all that different from taking notes in a lecture. You learn how to write fast, use abbreviations and little symbols (like for "that," "which," "and," and so forth), and to paraphrase the important things that someone is saying. You also have to learn when to stop the speaker and ask for clarification and when to let him or her go on, mark the unclear passage, and come back to it later. Part of that is a function of learning the local language, but another part of it is knowing when the speaker is developing a thought or a narrative, and listening to other people converse to find out the proper points at which they feel it is okay to interrupt a speaker. You can always go back to the person later and ask for an explanation, or you can ask someone else.

When I first started doing field research, tape recorders were expensive and unwieldy, so I had to depend on note taking, which meant always having a notebook of some sort with me, usually at least a 3-×-5-inch spiral notebook and a larger tablet or a 4-×-6-inch notebook. When I did formal interviews, I'd carry a tablet. When I went back in 1977, I used a mini-cassette recorder and a notebook. (I got a friend there to make accordion pockets for my shorts, so I could carry the recorder, extra batteries, pens, and notebooks and still have my hands free.) Even when I record a conversation, I still take notes, and those notes serve as a catalogue of what is on the tape. If I have to go back to the tape to transcribe, I know where to look. As I learned the language, more and more of my notes were in the local language, which I learned there.

What kind of papers do you write as an anthropologist?

I write about all kinds of topics, like adoption practices, land tenure, social organization, cultural change, death and grieving, leprosy epidemics, fishing practices, educational policy, ethnicity, and folklore. These topics can all be studied by use of ethnographic data to develop an argument about some point that is comparatively generalizable to many societies. That is, all of them focus on some issue using data from my particular field case to come to a general conclusion about the issue. It could be a theoretical issue, such as how to define ethnicity, or it could be some comparative generalization that needs attention, like the differences between high islands and low islands or the differences in kinship group organization where different ways of reckoning descent from an ancestor are used.

My own writing is heavy on processes—processes of group formation, processes by which local interpretations of situations shape the possibilities for personal or group action, processes of historical change, processes of transmitting the leprosy bacteria, and the like. I've even written about processes of confronting racial discrimination with curricular responses at UIC. What I write and how I write depends on the topic and the audience. Over the years I've tended to concentrate on writing for a general, literate audience, which means less jargon and more data, put as clearly as possible. And that means lots of editing and rewriting.

A lot of my papers have been written for symposia. These are conferences or meetings at which a number of anthropologists get together to work on papers and talk about the same topic. Each participant sends a draft of his or her paper to the whole group ahead of time, contributing data from the specific group he or she studied. For example, one year everyone might talk about kinship. We try to look at the similarities and differences among the data presented by each anthropologist in the group. After all, comparison is what anthropology is about, and in a symposium, people bring to a topic their data and their ideas. If data are missing in someone's paper, you can always ask the person about it on the spot. That way, the person's paper gets better in a rewrite and the discussion is enriched by having information that wasn't in the paper. You can't ask a paper a question, but you can ask a person. That's what makes symposia the best possible way to conduct cultural comparison.

Did your knowledge of anthropology help you to write your Tee-ball coaching manual?

Producing and writing that manual is a good example of applied anthropology. I started coaching baseball in 1989 when my 6-year-old's coach had fourteen kids and no help. He put me with the outfielders. The only baseball I knew was sandlot ball; I knew nothing about organized teams or coaching. My response to this exotic culture was to do what I had been trained to do: observe, interview, generalize about patterns, test the generalizations with more observations and interviews. One of the things I noticed during this process was that when a fly ball comes straight at a 5- to 10-year-old outfielder, the kid will always come in for the ball, with the result that the ball always lands behind the kid—what we call a Tee-ball home run.

I went to a physical anthropologist, Jack Prost, who specializes in the biology of vision to ask why this happens. He explained it as the zoom effect—the trajectory of any object coming straight at you is a zoom: It gets smaller as it goes up and larger as it comes down. That's all any of us see. But any 6-year-old has learned that an object that gets smaller is going further away. That's why kids go in after the ball. With this information, I developed a coaching system that concentrated on what kids do see clearly. The system worked, so I wrote it up as a manual for parents new to coaching. Word got out and I've been getting orders for it from all over the country and Canada, including a request to translate it into Spanish.

What kinds of problems does a cultural anthropologist try to solve?

Any problem that affects the lives of people in communities is a cultural anthropologist's business—economic problems, health care problems, crime, rape, domestic violence, international monetary policy, education, global warming, environmental degradation, ethnicity, drug addiction, rock and roll, what kinds of jokes people tell, what people call mental illness and what they do about it—you name it, and you'll find some anthropologist working on it. It's not because we claim some superior sensitivity, but because we're trained to do two things very well. First, we're trained to observe what people do and how they talk about what they do in the context of a particular social order. We look for PATTERNS *of behavior that typify community consensus on what gets done and how it gets done. Then we look for variations of the patterns—individual differences in doing things that give us an idea of the range of variability in patterned action. Then we're in a position to compare that with violations of the patterns of expected behavior—mistakes, crimes, and rebelliousness. In other words, we're trained to observe what constitutes systematic, predictable responses to both the mundane and the unusual events of everyday living. Second, we're trained to connect these observed patterns of response with patterns of perception that people learn as part of living together in a community. Culture is a theory of human perception—a set of procedures for inferring the unstated assumptions people make about how the things of their world are related. These assumptions, or premises, are the unchallenged truths that form the basis for interpreting situations—for making conclusions about what is going on and for deciding what to do about it.*

What is truth for one community may not be truth for another. And this fact leads to the next problem level that anthropologists deal with—what is human nature? How is a person like all other people, like some other people, and like no other person? What do we need to know to answer a question like this, and how do we get that knowledge? You can

measure the intellectual development of anthropology by the kinds of answers each gen-
eration of scholars tries to give to these questions. And these answers depend upon how
we do ethnography. The latest and greatest theory only sheds one kind of light in my field:
new questions that direct us to new kinds of ethnographic questions, enabling us to
make sense of patterns of response that were unclear before we asked those new
questions.

WRITING AND LEARNING ACTIVITIES

1. **Journal Entry:** Look up a definition of anthropology in a specialized reference
   source (see Directions for Further Research in the appendix), a college dictionary, and a reference encyclopedia. Consider the differences and similarities
   among these definitions. Report to the class on what you found.

2. **Writing Activity:** Write three questions you would ask Professor Lieber if
   you had the opportunity to talk with him.

3. **Peer Conversation:** With a partner, discuss your journal entries and questions for Professor Lieber. Respond also to the following questions: Were
   you reminded by something he said of another experience you've had at
   home, school, or work? What do you know about anthropology? Where have
   you gotten your ideas about anthropology? Have you ever visited or lived in a
   community very different from your own? What did you notice or learn from
   that experience?

4. **Research Project:** Look up the description of anthropology courses or for the
   major in your college catalog. Respond to the following questions: How is the
   discipline described? How does this description differ from Professor
   Lieber's description or from other definitions you've found? What are the required courses for the anthropology major? What are the possible areas of
   specialization? Next, interview someone who is majoring in anthropology.
   Why is that person studying anthropology? What courses has he or she
   taken? Is he or she specializing in any particular area? What does he or she
   plan to do with a degree in this area? Finally, attend one class with the student and take notes about how it is similar to or different from other classes.

5. **Writing:** Based on your research, write a report on what it's like to major in
   anthropology.

6. **Developing Interests:** In this interview Professor Lieber talks about how culture is a way of explaining why people do the things they do and believe in
   certain ways. For two days, observe what you consider to be a cultural pattern. What aspects of that culture would you like to learn more about?

READING ETHNOGRAPHIC REPORTS
OF FIELDWORK ON KINSHIP

Professor Lieber went to Micronesia to study what happens when people
from a particular culture are relocated to another home. One of the kinds
of social relations he studied were family relations, or kinship, and how

resettlement affected them. These same relationships can be studied in contemporary American culture. The two ethnographic reports Professor Lieber will read are similar to ones you would likely find if you did research on kinship relationships at the library.

The first report of fieldwork we will read is a portion of *All Our Kin: Strategies for Survival in a Black Community,* written by Carol Stack in 1974. It describes kinship relations among poor, urban African-Americans in the Cleveland, Ohio area referred to as "The Flats." The second report, written by Ruth Horowitz, is from *Honor and the American Dream: Culture and Identity in a Chicano Community,* published in 1983. It explores extended family relationships in a Hispanic community in west side Chicago. Both descriptive reports present the results of fieldwork and thus are called ethnographies. As we learned in our interview with Professor Lieber, ethnographic research depends on a detailed inquiry into a specific community by a participant-observer, someone who has observed as well as participated in the life of that community.

SETTING THE CONTEXT
FOR ETHNOGRAPHIC REPORTS

An ethnographic report of fieldwork is usually a highly detailed description of life in a particular culture. The introduction to the report is especially important because that's where the ethnographer tells us about the fieldwork and the specific problems he or she set out to solve. I asked Professor Lieber to comment on the introductions to help build a context for learning about ethnographic research.

Carol Stack's Introduction to *All Our Kin*

The first thing Professor Lieber did when he picked up the Stack book was to turn to the introduction to find out about the background and orientation for this particular ethnography. He explained:

The introduction is where you get the significant information telling you when the fieldwork was done, where it was done, for how long, or at how many different sites. It is also where the author tells you what he or she wants to do, what's about to happen, and what issues he or she is addressing.

Carol Stack begins her introduction by asking the very question that she feels must be on her readers' minds: "how a young white woman could conduct a study of black family life" (ix). Here is a case of how an anthropologist can learn about a specific culture through participant-observation. However, Stack must ask: How good is my description? What roles can an ethnographer assume? How might my own cultural biases influence my understanding of the African-American community I am studying?

Stack goes on to tell us that rather than entering this community through its "elders," the largely male group of politicians and religious leaders who could have introduced her around, she began to get to know women in the community through a student of hers at the university who had grown up in The Flats. This student gave Stack an entrance to the community by introducing her to two families the student knew well.

It might seem from all that has been said so far that an anthropologist simply observes a culture and "writes up" a description of it. In fact, participant-observation is a two-way street; the anthropologist changes the culture in some way just by being present in it, and the anthropologist is affected by the experience as well. Stack ends her introduction by telling us (xiv):

> The three years I spent in The Flats opened and reassembled my life ways and my understanding of womanhood, parenthood, and the American economy. Likewise, I brought perceptions and biases to the study that joggled and molded the views of those closest to me.

Ruth Horowitz's Introduction to *Honor and the American Dream*

Ruth Horowitz begins her introduction with a description of a Chicano community celebrating the opening of a new park in their neighborhood. She describes young women "wearing summer outfits of pastel pants and halter tops," strolling along, pretending to ignore the young men "[l]ounging easily on cars,. . . [passing] around bottles of Boone's Farm Strawberry wine," joined by small children "hopping up and down," among mothers exchanging gossip about neighborhood events (3). This celebration tells a story quite different from an event at the same location several months earlier in which members of the community had protested violently against the mayor's refusal to respond to their concerns for better schools. Horowitz uses this contrast to establish the themes she will explore in her report of her participant-observation of this community.

Between 1971 and 1974, Ruth Horowitz, fluent in Spanish, worked at getting contacts in the community, returning to it later in 1977. She faced much the same problem as Carol Stack as an outsider, "Jewish, educated, small, fairly dark, . . . and only a few years older than most of those I observed" (6). She hung out on street corners with gang members and spent time with groups of young women talking about makeup and their social lives. She was "adopted" by families and spent much time at dinners and other gatherings. She told the people she observed that she was doing research on the community; as such she was a part of but at the same time apart from this community.

At the end of her introduction, Ruth Horowitz describes how each chapter contributes to the cultural study of this Chicano community located on 32nd Street in Chicago. She tells us that in Chapter 4, "Expanded Family and Family Honor," she will explore the roles of members in the expanded families in this community. The roles of fathers, mothers, brothers, sisters, aunts, uncles, and even godfathers (*compadres*) have traditional expectations that are affected by the economy and the life in their community.

Interestingly, Horowitz does not use the word *kinship*. Even though Stack talks about kinship and Horowitz talks about the expanded family, the two studies provide sources for contrasting views of family relationships. As you read further and at the same time examine your own family relationships, you will begin to see how all of these sources contribute to a richer understanding of the sameness and the diversity of cultures.

WRITING AND LEARNING ACTIVITIES

1. **Journal Entry:** In their introductions, both Carol Stack and Ruth Horowitz express their concern for how cultural differences between themselves (as Caucasian researchers) and the communities they were observing might influence their descriptions of African-American and Hispanic communities. Write a description of a situation in which you or someone you know felt different from others. The situation might have occurred in your home community, at a church or synagogue, at work, at school, or anywhere else. What made you feel different in that particular situation?

2. **Group Activity:** Meet in a group of three to five students and assign one member of your group to report back to the class. Share the situations you described in the journal writing activity above. Choose one that seems interesting and talk about the possible reasons for the differences. Consider the following questions: How do the participants become aware of the differences? Were they differences in experience? Were they differences that arose from different types of education, or from living in different communities?

READING TWO REPORTS OF FIELDWORK

In these ethnographies both Horowitz and Stack write about what they saw and experienced during their fieldwork, as they observed what people said and did during routine periods in their lives. They work at connecting their observations with the particular concept they are exploring, and they illustrate their conclusions with anecdotes, quotations, or even possibly numerical data or diagrams (as Stack does) that highlight a particular issue. In the following sections Professor Lieber will guide us through the two readings. As he reads, he looks for the detailed description that characterizes ethnographic fieldwork. In addition, he looks for broader statements that clarify the ethnographers' understanding of the communities they describe. He also relates what each says to his own ethnographic work.

Reading "Personal Kindreds"

WRITING AND LEARNING ACTIVITIES

1. **Reading:** Read Chapter 4, "Personal Kindreds," from Stack's book. Pay close attention to the issues Professor Lieber brings up as he reads. How does Stack describe the community she is observing? How does she tell the story of her research?

2. **Journal Entry:** As you read, make notes in your journal about your reading process. Write down any questions you have about the reading and any familiar or unfamiliar terms you encounter. Also, note any places in the readings where you make connections to your own experiences. Think about how the research of this discipline is different from that of other disciplines.

3. **Annotate the Text:** As you read, mark the text to help you follow the argument. Use one color highlighter to identify key claims, another to identify striking examples. Place question marks at points where you are confused. Restate main points or write questions in the margins.

IV
PERSONAL KINDREDS
"ALL OUR KIN"
CAROL STACK

■ ■ ■

Billy, a young black woman in The Flats, was raised by her mother and her mother's "old man." She has three children of her own by different fathers. Billy says, "Most people kin to me are in this neighborhood, right here in The Flats, but I got people in the South, in Chicago, and in Ohio too. I couldn't tell most of their names and most of them aren't really kinfolk to me. Starting down the street from here, take my father, he ain't my daddy, he's no father to me.[1] I ain't got but one daddy and that's Jason. The one who raised me. My kids' daddies, that's something else, all their daddies' people really take to them—they always doing things and making a fuss about them. We help each other out and that's what kinfolks are all about."

Throughout the world, individuals distinguish kin from nonkin. Moreover, kin terms are frequently extended to nonkin, and social relations among nonkin may be conducted within the idiom of kinship. Individuals acquire socially recognized kinship relations with others through a chain of socially recognized parent-child connections (Goodenough 1970). The chain of parent-child connections is essential to the structuring of kin groups.

Although anthropologists have long recognized the distinction between natural and social parenthood (Malinowski 1930; Radcliffe-Brown 1950; Goodenough 1970; Carroll 1970), until recently most ethnographic data has not clarified those social transactions involving parental rights. This omission has led to the persistent belief that each person is a kinsman of his natural mother and father, who are expected as parents to raise him (Scheffler 1970). Much of the controversial and misleading characterizations of kinship and domestic life can be attributed to this assumption and to the lack of ethnographic data that interprets the meaning people give to the chain of parent-child connections within a particular folk culture.

At birth a child in any society acquires socially recognized kinship relations with others. Who is socially recognized as kin depends largely upon the cultural interpretation of the chain of parent-child connections. Young black children in The Flats are born into personal networks that include some "essential kin,"[2] those people who actively accept responsibility toward them, and some "relatives" who do not actively create reciprocal obligations.

5   My experience in The Flats suggests that the folk system of parental rights and duties determines who is eligible to be a member of the personal kinship network of a newborn child. This system of rights and duties should not be confused with the official, written statutory law of the state. The local, folk system of rights and duties pertaining to parenthood are enforced only by sanctions within the community. Community members clearly operate within two different systems: the folk system and the legal system of the courts and welfare offices.[3]

MOTHERHOOD

Men and women in The Flats regard child-begetting and childbearing as a natural and highly desirable phenomenon. Lottie James was fifteen when she became pregnant. The baby's father, Herman, the socially recognized genitor, was a neighbor and the father of two other children. Lottie talked with her mother during her second month of pregnancy. She said, "Herman went and told my mama I was pregnant. She was in the kitchen cooking. I told him not to tell nobody, I wanted to keep it a secret, but he told me times will tell. My mama said to me, 'I had you and you should have your child. I didn't get rid of you. I loved you and I took care of you until you got to the age to have this one. Have your baby no matter what, there's nothing wrong with having a baby. Be proud of it like I was proud of you.' My mama didn't tear me down; she was about the best mother a person ever had."

Unlike many other societies, black women in The Flats feel few if any restrictions about childbearing. Unmarried black women, young and old, are eligible to bear children, and frequently women bearing their first children are quite young.

A girl who gives birth as a teen-ager frequently does not raise and nurture her firstborn child. While she may share the same room and household with her baby, her mother, her mother's sister, or her older sister will care for the child and become the child's "mama." This same young woman may actively become a "mama" to a second child she gives birth to a year or two later. When, for example, a grandmother, aunt, or great-aunt "takes a child" from his natural mother, acquired parenthood often lasts throughout the child's lifetime. Although a child kept by a close female relative knows who his mother is, his "mama" is the woman who "raised him up." Young mothers and their firstborn daughters are often raised as sisters, and lasting ties are established between these mothers and their daughters. A child being raised by his grandmother may later become playmates with his half siblings who are his age, but he does not share the same claims and duties and affective ties toward his natural mother.

A young mother is not necessarily considered emotionally ready to nurture a child; for example, a grandmother and other close relatives of Clover Greer, Viola Jackson's neighbor, decided that Clover was not carrying out her parental duties. Nineteen when her first child, Christine, was born, Clover explains, "I really was wild in those days, out on the town all hours of the night, and every night and weekend I layed my girl on my mother. I wasn't living home at the time, but Mama kept Christine most of the time. One day Mama up and said I was making a fool of her, and she was going to take my child and raise her right. She said I was immature and that I had no business being a mother the way I was acting. All my mama's people agreed, and there was nothing I could do. So Mama took my child. Christine is six years old now. About a year ago I got married to Gus and we wanted to take Christine back. My baby, Earl, was living with us anyway. Mama blew up and told everyone how I was doing her. She dragged my name in the mud and people talked so much it really hurt." Gossip and pressure from close kin and friends made it possible for the grandmother to exercise her grandparental right to take the child into her home and raise her there.

10   In the eyes of the community, a young mother who does not perform her duties has not validated her claim to parenthood. The person who actively becomes the "mama" acquires the major cluster of parental rights accorded to the mothers in The Flats. In effect, a young mother transfers some of her claims to motherhood without surrendering all of her rights to the child.

Nothing in the conception of parenthood among people in The Flats prevents kinsmen of a child's socially recognized parents from having claims to parenthood (Goodenough 1970, p. 17). Kinsmen anticipate the help they may have to give to young mothers and the parental responsibilities they may have to assume toward the children of kinsmen. The bond between mothers and children is exceedingly strong, and the majority of mothers in The Flats raise their own children. Statistical data on residence patterns and kin relationships of 1,000 AFDC children in Jackson County was gathered from AFDC case histories. Of the 188 AFDC mothers surveyed, 30 percent were raising their own children, 5 percent were raising younger siblings, and 7 percent were raising their grandchildren, nieces, or nephews.

Just how a "mama" provides a child with concerned relatives can best be viewed in terms of Fischer's (1958) notion of sponsorship.[4] Fischer, in his discussion of residence, calls attention to the question of who is an individual's immediate sponsor in a residence group. This term refers to the sponsorship of individuals rather than of couples, a flexible means of providing information on residence over an individual's lifetime. The term can also be applied to the creation of personal kinship networks for the new-born child. Determining who becomes one of the immediate sponsors of a child's network clarifies its initial formation, the kinship links that are effective, and the shape of the network.

In The Flats the recognized mother, the "mama" (80 percent are the natural mothers), determines the child's kinship affiliations through females. She is one of the immediate sponsors of a child's personal kinship network. A black child's "mama's" relatives and their husbands and wives are eligible to be members of the child's personal kinship network. How the relationship between a child's natural mother and his or her socially recognized genitor determines a child's kin affiliations through males is described below. When a child is raised by close female relatives of his mother in a more-or-less stable situation, the immediate sponsor of the child's personal network is the "mama." This reckoning of relatives through the immediate sponsor is especially useful when a child's residence changes during his lifetime. Even if a child is raised by a person who is not a blood relative (described below), he usually becomes a part of the network of his "mama."

FATHERHOOD

People in The Flats expect to change friends frequently through a series of encounters. Demands on friendships are great, but social-economic pressures on male-female relationships are even greater. Therefore, relationships between young, unmarried, childbearing adults are highly unstable. Some men and childbearing women in The Flats establish long-term liaisons with one another, some maintain sexual unions with more than one person at a time, and still others get married. However, very few women in The Flats are married before they have given birth to one or more children. When a man and woman have a sexual partnership, especially if the woman has no other on-going sexual relationships, the man is identified with children born to the woman. Short-term sexual partnerships are recognized by the community even if a man and woman do not share a household and domestic responsibilities. The offspring of these unions are publicly accepted by the community; a child's existence seems to legitimize the child in the eyes of the community.

15   But the fact of birth does not provide a child with a chain of socially recognized relatives through his father. Even though the community accepts the child, the culturally significant issue in terms of the economics of everyday life is whether any man involved in a sexual relationship with a woman provides a newborn child with kinship affiliations. A child is eligible to participate in the personal kinship network of his father if the father becomes an immediate sponsor of a child's kinship network.

When an unmarried woman in The Flats becomes pregnant or gives birth to a child, she often tells her friends and kin who the father is. The man has a number of alternatives open to him. Sometimes he publicly denies paternity by implying to his friends and kin that the father could be any number of other men, and that he had "information that she is no good and has been creeping on him all along." The community generally accepts the man's denial of paternity. It is doubtful that under these conditions this man and his kin would assume any parental duties anyway. The man's failure to assent to being the father leaves the child without recognized kinship ties through a male. Subsequent "boyfriends" of the mother may assume the paternal duties of discipline and support and receive the child's affection, but all paternal rights in the child belong to the mother and her kinsmen. The pattern whereby black children derive all their kin through females has been stereotyped and exaggerated in the literature on black families. In fact, fathers in The Flats openly recognized 484 (69 percent) of 700 children included in my AFDC survey.

The second alternative open to a man involved in a sexual relationship with a mother is to acknowledge openly that he is responsible. The father can acknowledge the child by saying "he own it," by telling his people and his friends that he is the father, by paying part of the hospital bill, or by bringing milk and diapers to the mother after the birth of the child. The parents may not have ever shared a household and the affective and sexual relationship between them may have ended before the birth of the child.

The more a father and his kin help a mother and her child, the more completely they validate their parental rights. However, since many black American males have little or no access to steady and productive employment, they are rarely able to support and maintain their families. This has made it practically impossible for most poor black males to assume financial duties as parents. People in The Flats believe a father should help his child, but they know that a mother cannot count on his help. But, the community expects a father's kin to help out. The black male who does not actively become a "daddy," but acknowledges a child and offers his kin to that child, in effect, is validating his rights. Often it is the father's kin who activate the claim to rights in the child.

Fatherhood, then, belongs to the presumed genitor if he, or others for him, choose to validate his claim. Kinship through males is reckoned through a chain of social recognition. If the father fails to do anything beyond merely acknowledging the child, he surrenders most of his rights, and this claim can be shared or transferred to the father's kin, whose claim becomes strengthened if they actively participate as essential kin. By failing to perform parental duties the father retains practically no rights in his child, although his kin retain rights if they assume active responsibility.

20   By validating his claim as a parent the father offers the child his blood relatives and their husbands and wives as the child's kin—an inheritance so to speak. As long as the father acknowledges his parental entitlement, his relatives, especially his mother and sisters, consider themselves kin to the child and therefore responsible for him. Even when the mother "takes up with another man," her child retains the original set of kin gained through the father who sponsored him.

A nonparticipating father also shares some of his rights and duties with his child's mother's current boyfriend or husband. When a man and woman have a continuing sexual relationship, even if the man is not the father of any of the woman's children, he is expected by the mother and the community to share some of the parental duties of discipline, support, and affection.

A child's father's kin play an active role in the nurturing of children, and as a result they have the right to observe and judge whether a woman is performing her duties as a mother. If a young woman is unable to care for her child, nothing prevents a father's close female relatives from claiming parental rights. When 188 AFDC mothers listed in order of rank who they would expect to raise each of their children (total of 1,000 children) if they died, one-third of the women listed their own mother as their first choice and one-third listed either their child's father or the father's mother as the first choice. The remaining one-third (second through fifth choice) were close kin to the mother (her mother's sister, her own sister or brother, and her daughter). In crisis situations, such as a mother's death or sickness, a child's kin through his mother and father are equally eligible to assume responsibilities of jural parenthood.

The chain of sponsored parent-child connections determines the personal kindreds of children. Participants in active units of domestic cooperation are drawn from personal kinship networks. How a particular individual, say a mother, works to create the active networks which she depends upon for the needs of her children, depends largely on sponsorship or parental links. Commonly, the mother's personal domestic network includes the personal networks of her children, who are half siblings with different fathers. Each child will grow up into a slightly different personal network from his brothers and sisters. Mothers expect little from the father; they just hope that he will help out. But they do expect something from his kin, especially his mother and sisters. Mothers continually activate these kin lines, and since the biological father's female relatives are usually poor, they too try to expand their network. The exchanges and daily dependencies get very complicated, but they constitute the main activity of daily life for these women.

Daily life is also complicated as individuals expand their own personal networks, in part by recruiting friends into their own domestic networks. When friends live up to one another's expectations, they are identified as kin. Friends often participate in the personal networks of others within the idiom of kinship, and some kin exhibit the interactive patterns of friends.

25   Domestic arrangements and strategies among the black poor in The Flats usually assure that children are cared for and that kin and friends in need will be helped. Participants in cooperative networks are primarily drawn from personal kindreds. R. T. Smith (1970, p. 68) has stated that although there is a tendency among "lower classes" to keep kin links open, this does not mean that large cooperating groups of kinsmen are found among the "lower classes." But I found, to the contrary, stable domestic net-

works of cooperating kinsmen among the poorest black people. These kinship networks have stability because the needs of the poor are constant. Friendships, on the other hand, change more often, and friends drop in and out of one another's networks while assuming a stable position in their own kinship network. From the individual's viewpoint, he is immersed in a domestic circle in which he can find help (Stack 1970).

Similar to patterns found in The Flats, American middle-class children are born into a network of relatives which in principle is infinite. Relatives on both sides of the family are kin, and there is no clear-cut limit to the range of one's kinsmen. But cognatic reckoning by itself cannot distinguish between essential kin and others within the system.[5] The choice of which relatives an individual draws into her personal kindred is by no means mechanical.

How individuals cast their net to create personal kinship networks depends upon the culturally determined perceptions of jural parenthood: the rules and criteria for including and excluding persons connected by blood and marriage to a particular kinsman, and the interpersonal relations between these individuals. These criteria determine which individuals acquire socially recognized kinship relations with others.[6]

Personal kindreds of adults are ego-centered networks of essential kin. These networks are not residential units or observable groups, and they change participants, for example, when friends "fall out" with one another. From the individual's viewpoint personal kindreds comprise the people who are socially recognized as having reciprocal responsibilities. These people become acting and reacting participants for some focal purpose (Fox 1967, p. 167).

Young children exercise little choice in determining with whom they have kinship relations. They are born into a network of essential kin which is primarily the personal kindred of the kinfolk responsible for them. As children become adults they expand, contract, and create their own personal networks.

Geographical distance, interpersonal relations, or acknowledgment of paternity discourage some relatives from actuating claims of responsibility. These relatives effectively drop out of the individual's personal kinship network, and all of the people linked through them also tend to drop out. Thus, an important criterion affecting the size and shape of the personal kinship network of adults is whether the relative who drops out of the network is genealogically close or distant. Sometimes close kinship links, like that of a parent, are broken. A father, for example, may claim that he doesn't "own the baby," thereby refusing to acknowledge paternity. When a close link such as that of a father is broken, it has a profound effect on the shape of the personal kindred.

30   The following chart shows the genealogical categories in American kinship (consider the "child" as EGO). If a child's grandparents through his father, for example, break a link, all those individuals related through the

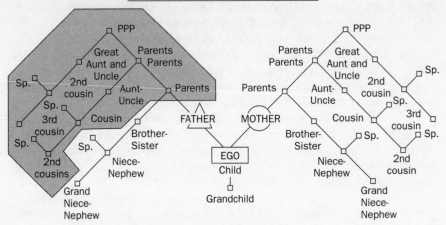

CHART A: GRANDPARENTAL LINK BROKEN

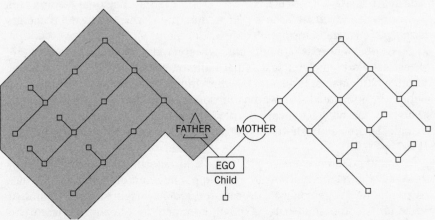

CHART B: PARENTAL LINK BROKEN

grandparents effectively drop out of the child's personal kinship network. Chart B shows the shape of a network in which a father has broken a kinship link.

Because any relative can break a link, personal kindreds can take any number of shapes. But the networks are skewed roughly in proportion to the nearness of the kinship links which are ineffective. In principle, the dropping of a father from a network affects the shape of the network in the same way as if other more distant relatives on either side were to drop out. But the effect of dropping a close relative is obviously much more profound.

FRIENDSHIP

Men and women in The Flats know that the minimal funds they receive from low-paying jobs or welfare do not cover their monthly necessities of life: rent, food, and clothing. They must search for solutions in order to survive. They place their hopes in the scene of their life and action: in the closed community, in the people around them, in kin and friends, and in the new friends they will make to get along. Friendships between lovers and between friends are based upon a precarious balance of trust and profit. Magnolia describes this balance, "I don't have nothing great and no more than nobody else. It doesn't matter. I'm happy with my kids and I'm happy with the friends that I got. Some people don't understand friendship. Friendship means a lot, that is if you can trust a friend. If you have a friend, you should learn to trust them and share everything that you have. When I have a friend and I need something, I don't ask, they just automatically tell me that they going to give it to me. I don't have to ask. And that's the way friends should be, for how long it lasts. But sometimes when you help a person they end up making a fool out of you. If a friend ain't giving me anything in return for what I'm giving her, shit, she can't get nothing else. These days you ain't got nothing to be really giving. You can't care for no one that don't give a damn for you."

Even in newly formed friendships, individuals begin to rely upon one another quickly, expecting wider solutions to their problems than any one person in the same situation could possibly offer. As a result the stability of a friendship often depends upon the ability of two individuals to gauge their exploitation of one another. Everyone understands that friendships are explosive and abruptly come to an end when one friend makes a fool out of another. Life, therefore, as Abrahams shows, is "conceived of in terms of a series of encounters with a large number of individuals" (1970, p. 120). As Ruby says, "You got to go out and meet people, because the very day you go out, that first person you meet may be the person that can help you get the things you want."

Individuals in The Flats continually evaluate their friendships by gossip and conversation. They talk about whether others are "acting right" or "doing right by them." They define personal relationships in terms of their dual expectations of friends and kin. When friends more than adequately share the exchange of goods and services, they are called kinsmen. When friends live up to one another's expectations, their social relations are conducted as kin. For example, if two women of the same age are helping one another, they call their friend "just a sister," or say that "they are going for sisters." Anyone in the community with whom a person has good social dealings can be classified as some kind of kin. When a friendship ends because individuals "let one another down," this concludes both their expectations of one another and their kin relationship. In addition, a person defined as a kin, for example, a "sister," does not usually bring to the relationship her own personal genealogical entailments. Her mother is not necessarily her "sister's" mother and her father's father is not her "sister's" grandfather. Losing a fictive relative, therefore, does not dramatically affect the shape of personal networks as does the dropping of a close kinship link.

35   The offering of kin terms to "those you count on" is a way people expand their personal networks. A friend who is classified as a kinsman is simultaneously given respect and responsibility.

When a mother has a boyfriend, the community expects that he will assume some parental duties toward her children. This is especially true if the couple are "housekeeping," sharing their domestic tasks. A father surrenders many of his rights and responsibilities to the mother's husband or current boyfriend. The attitude and behavior of the boyfriend toward the children defines his relationship to them. Clover compares her last two boyfriends and how they dealt with her children. "I stopped going with Max because he took no time for my kids; he just wanted them out of our way. I took it for a while, 'cause I got things from him, but when he hit my boy I called it quits. If he can't care, he can't bully my kids. But Lee, he was something else. He was so nice to my kids that the babies cried when he left the house. Sometimes I had to yell to keep the kids from bothering him and get some time for myself. After we was housekeeping for about six months, Lee said to the boys that they should call him their 'play daddy.' Lee and I quit last year and I'm sorry we did, 'cause the kids really miss him. But he still comes over, especially when I'm out, and they still call him their 'play daddy.' "

Fictive kin relations are maintained by consensus between individuals, and in some contexts can last a lifetime. If Lee maintains his interest in Clover's boys, he may remain their "play daddy" throughout their adult life.

Children very often establish close and affectionate ties with their aunts and uncles, for example, with their mother's sister's "old man" and their mother's brother's "old lady." These aunts and uncles, on the basis of their original consensual relationship, can remain in a child's personal network for a long time. Personal kinship networks are enlarged by the inclusion of these affines who may keep the relationship active. Ruby recently visited her Uncle Arthur, one of her Aunt Augusta's "old men," in the hospital. "Uncle Arthur and I was always good friends," says Ruby, "even when he and Aunt Augusta weren't getting on. He was staying with Augusta, my grandmother, and me when I was just a kid, and he always treated me like something real special. Now he is just as nice to my kids when he comes over to see them. I really feel sad that he's old and sick; he has high blood, and I think he may die." Ruby is also attached to her Uncle Lazar, who started going with her mother's youngest sister when her aunt was just fifteen. "My aunt has been married twice since, but Uncle Lazar just remained a part of our family. He's fifty-eight now and he's been a part of our family ever since I can remember. He always has been staying with our family too. Right now he's staying in the basement below Aunt Augusta's apartment and she cooks for him and her old man. He'll always be my uncle and he and my aunt never did get married."

Just as these "aunts" and "uncles" remain in the personal kinship networks of their nieces and nephews, best friends may remain in each other's domestic network on the basis of original friendship even if the friendship has ended. Sometimes when nonkin become a part of a family and are given a fictive kin term, no one remembers just how the tie began. Billy tried to remember how cousin Ola became a part of her family. "My mama once told me," said Billy, "but I hardly remember. I think cousin Ola was my mama's oldest sister's best friend and they went for cousins. When my mama's sister died, Ola took her two youngest children, and she has been raising them up ever since."

40   In the above examples, social relations are conducted within the idiom of kinship. Members of the community explain the behavior of those around them by allowing behavior to define the nature of the relationship. Friends are classified as kinsmen when they assume recognized responsibilities of kinsmen. Those kin who cannot be counted upon are severely criticized. Harsh evaluation of the behavior of others accounts for some of the constant ups and downs in the lives of friends and kin. Expectations are so elastic that when one person fails to meet another's needs, disappointment is cushioned. Flexible expectations and the extension of kin relationships to nonkin allow for the creation of mutual aid domestic networks which are not bounded by genealogical distance or genealogical criteria. Much more important for the creation and recruitment to personal networks are the practical requirements that kin and friends live near one another.

Members of domestic networks in The Flats are drawn from kin and friends. Of the two, the kin network is more enduring because all of an individual's essential kin are "recognized as having some duties toward him and some claims on him" (Fox 1967, p. 167). Friendships end and that is to be expected; new friendships can be formed. But the number of relatives who can be called upon for help from personal kinship networks is limited. As a result a cluster of relatives from personal kinship networks have continuing claims on one another. Some observers of daily life in black communities regard the friendship network as the "proven and adaptive base of operations" in lower-class life (Abrahams 1970, p. 128). But the adaptive base of operations of the poorest black people can be attributed to personal kindreds as well as to networks of friends.

·   ·   ·

NOTES FOR CHAPTER 4. PERSONAL KINDREDS

1. Schneider (1968) maintains that distinctions between terms of reference (father) and terms of address (pa, pop, daddy) increase ethnographic error because they are synonyms which are equally referential and are equally names of categories. Schneider's observation clearly is not adequate for dealing with the terminology from the above passage. The kinship term *father* in the passage refers to the *socially recognized genitor*. "Daddy," which informants themselves put in quotations by intonation, refers to an essential kin such as the man who raises a child. Black people in The Flats, then, distinguish between the "pater" (essential kin), the jural father (the socially recognized genitor), and the "genitor." This perception of fatherhood does not fit into the long-accepted dichotomy between "pater" and "genitor" (Radcliffe-Brown 1950).

2. The following distinction between relatives, kin, and essential kin will be used throughout the study: (a) *relatives:* in cognatic reckoning the universe of cognates is in principle unlimited in the number of genealogical categories (not

persons) it contains. A relative is any person who is genealogically defined within the cognatic web; (b) *kin:* some relatives (at least) and some others who are members of the culturally specific system of kinship categories which have behavioral entailments with respect to one another; (c) *essential kin:* at least some of the above kin and others who activate and validate their jural rights by helping one another, thereby creating reciprocal obligations toward one another.

3. I wish to thank Ward Goodenough for clarifying this point, and for other valuable suggestions.

4. I am grateful to Jan Brukman for suggesting this idea.

5. On this point in particular, and many others throughout this chapter, I wish to thank F. K. Lehman.

6. Professor Charles Valentine and Betty Lou Valentine provided extensive comments on this chapter at an early stage in the writing. I am extremely grateful for their generous help and criticism.

BIBLIOGRAPHY
Literature Cited

Abrahams, Roger. 1970. *Positively Black.* Englewood Cliffs, N. J.: Prentice-Hall.

Carroll, Vern, ed. 1970. *Adoption in Eastern Oceania.* Honolulu: University of Hawaii Press.

Fischer, J. L. 1958. "The Classification of Residence in Censuses." *American Anthropologist* 60:508–517.

Fox, Robin, 1967. *Kinship and Marriage.* Baltimore: Penguin Books.

Goodenough, Ward H. 1970. *Description and Comparison in Cultural Anthropology.* Chicago: Aldine Publishing Company.

Malinowski, Bronislaw. 1930. "Parenthood—The Basis of Social Structure." In *The New Generation,* eds. V. F. Calverston and Samuel D. Schmalhausen, pp. 113–168. New York: Macauley.

Radcliffe-Brown, A. R. 1950. Introduction. In *African Systems of Kinship and Marriage,* eds. A. R. Radcliffe-Brown and C. D. Forde. London: Oxford University Press.

Scheffler, Harold W. 1970. "Kinship and Adoption in the Northern New Hebrides." In *Adoption in Eastern Oceania,* ed. V. Carroll, pp. 369–383. Honolulu: University of Hawaii Press.

Smith, Raymond T. 1970. "The Nuclear Family in Afro-American Kinship." *Journal of Comparative Family Studies* 1(1):55–70.

Stack, Carol B. 1970. "The Kindred of Viola Jackson: Residence and Family Organization of an Urban Black American Family." In *Afro-American Anthropology: Contemporary Perspectives,* eds. N. E. Whitten and John F. Szwed. New York: The Free Press, pp. 303–312.

Use of Informants' Narratives. Professor Lieber began reading the text, smiling at the anecdote offered in Stack's first paragraph: a quote from Billy, a member of the community she worked with, "We help each other out and that's what kinfolks are all about" (paragraph 1). Professor Lieber tells us,

She just nailed what kinship is about in this African-American community.

Identifying Key Concepts.   Following this narrative definition of kinship, Carol Stack tells us what key concept she will be exploring in her fieldwork. She referred to the work of other anthropologists on kinship in the 1960s and 1970s. Professor Lieber goes on to explain:

In paragraphs 2 and 3 Carol Stack is referring to a hot debate going on between the group of people who say that genealogical ties are what kinship is all about and the group of people who say that social ties are what kinship is all about. So the theory of kinship itself is in question and here she is addressing it right off the bat. By jumping quickly to the bibliography and reading her notes we can see that she is using the work of anthropologists such as Ward Goodenough and Vern Carroll. So what Carol Stack is doing here is a cultural analysis of kinship—what it means in The Flats.

Professor Lieber pointed out to us that Stack uses the fourth paragraph of the introduction to state her position—that is, what she has learned from her fieldwork about kinship in the community she studied. But the information is not only found in the text. To understand this position fully, a careful reader must turn to end note 2 in the portion of the text reproduced below. (Notes provide an opportunity for a researcher to add additional information to his or her report.)

> Young black children in The Flats are born into personal networks that include some "essential kin,"[2] those people who actively accept responsibility toward them and some "relatives" who do not actively create reciprocal obligations (paragraph 4).

In note 2 (pp. 57–58) Stack gives us three identifications of kin: (1) a blood relative, a relative who is part of the child's social system; (2) a group composed of relatives and others who have some level of obligation; and (3) the most important for Stack, "essential kin," relatives and others who have strong reciprocal relationships, that is, people who share goods, labor, empathy, and the performance of tasks essential to maintain the domestic group. We also see where the name for this chapter, "Personal Kindreds," comes from. Whereas some anthropologists look at kinship from a purely biological perspective (blood relatives), Stack's fieldwork with this African-American community illustrates that the meaning of a biological tie can vary from one community to another. In this case, the biological parent-child tie confers eligibility for a certain kind of social relationship, but it does not assume that the relationship automatically follows. This distinction or lack of it between genealogy (biological or blood ties) and social ties has been of major interest to anthropologists, and we will see as Professor Lieber continues to read how important it is to Stack's argument.

The remainder of Stack's chapter is divided into three sections: Motherhood, Fatherhood, and Friendship. In these sections Stack offers us the evidence for her claim about kinship in the African-American community where she did her fieldwork. As you follow Professor Lieber's reading of the chapter, you will see how Stack uses the information from her informants, statistical data, and the work of other anthropologists to develop her description of kinship relations.

Developing Terminology to Characterize Kinship Relations.   In The Flats, Carol Stack reports, getting pregnant and having a baby is nothing to be ashamed of. She tells us what one young pregnant girl's mother said to her daughter,

> "I had you and you should have your child. I didn't get rid of you. I loved you and I took care of you until you got to the age to have this one. Have your baby no matter what, there's nothing wrong with having a baby. Be proud of it like I was proud of you" (paragraph 6).

Carol Stack's ethnographic study shows us how a kinship network will emerge for this new baby. If the mother is unable to care for the child, another relative, usually female, will care for him or her, thus earning the designation "Mama." This caring relationship begins a kinship network built on a concept of "sponsorship," a term that Stack adapted for her own purposes from earlier work done by Fischer, another anthropologist (see paragraph 12) who used the term to study residences, or where people lived. Professor Lieber thinks the term is very helpful:

The term sponsorship *helps us to understand that for this community, kinship is social, not genealogical. Who you live with and who takes care of you is more important than who is a blood relative. This term allows Stack to explore all the relationships in the community that people count as kin relations. Then she can say later, as she does in paragraph 26 that the network of sponsors forms a "personal kindred," a group of people who recognize their responsibility toward one other.*

Using Quantitative Data to Support Conclusions from Fieldwork.   In the section on fatherhood, Stack continues to describe how shared responsibility for children creates links and networks of essential kin. The biological father of the child can declare that he is responsible for the baby and validate his place in the child's network by helping as much as possible. If the father actively becomes part of the child's network, he brings with him a much broader group of potential sponsors in female relatives, such as his mother and his sisters. Professor Lieber points out to us that Stack uses quantitative data to support her observations about fatherhood responsibilities in The Flats.

Look here (points to paragraph 16)! It really is great the way the numbers can back up what Stack observed. It is so fascinating because we can see Stack breaking down a cultural myth. Stack can tell us that claims about African-American fathers not admitting paternity are grossly exaggerated, because in this poor urban community 69 percent of the fathers in her survey did openly recognize their children. Stack goes on to explain that what is important for the child is whether or not the father can open another network of sponsors for the child through the father's essential kin. If the biological father does not activate his kinship, the child may be sponsored by a "play daddy," perhaps the mother's boyfriend, who will assist in raising the child. The point is that "daddy" is the one who acts like daddy!

In Stack's final section, on friendship, she balances the importance of shifting and changing friendships with the central and longer lasting kinship relations.

Next we will examine family relationships in a quite different urban Chicano community.

WRITING AND LEARNING ACTIVITIES

1. **Journal Entry:** Record your impressions about the community Stack observed. Did you learn anything new from her fieldwork report?

2. **Interview Activity:** Keeping Stack's definitions of relatives, kin, and essential kin (Note 2 on pp. 57–58) in mind, interview friends and family and make notes about the various kinship networks that exist. Report your findings to your class.

3. **Examining the Text:** Meet in small groups and collaborate on the following: Look over the Notes and Bibliography for Stack's work. What type of information does she include in the notes? What types of references does she rely on for her research? What are the publication dates of the books and journals she uses? Are you familiar with any of the authors? Pick out two journal articles and two books that you might like to read. Report back to the class on what you have found.

Reading "The Expanded Family and Family Honor"

In reading Carol Stack's ethnographic description Professor Lieber worked to understand kinship relations in the specific community she was observing. Now, Professor Lieber will read Ruth Horowitz's ethnography to see how what she observed on 32nd Street in Chicago might contribute to our growing understanding of the concept of kinship.

WRITING AND LEARNING ACTIVITIES

1. **Reading:** Read the excerpt from Horowitz's Chapter 4, "The Expanded Family and Family Honor." Pay close attention to the issues Professor Lieber brings up. How does Horowitz describe the culture she is observing? How does she tell the story of her research?

2. **Journal Entry:** As you read take notes in your journal about your reading process. Write down any questions you have about the reading and any familiar or unfamiliar terms you encounter. Also, note any places where you

make connections to your own experiences. Think about how the research in this discipline differs from that in other disciplines.

3. **Annotate the Text:** As you read, mark the text to help you follow the argument. Use one color highlighter to identify key claims and another to identify striking examples. Place question marks at points where you are confused. Restate main points or write questions in the margins.

IV
THE EXPANDED FAMILY AND FAMILY HONOR
RUTH HOROWITZ

■ ■ ■

Three months prior to Ana's cotillion, or *quinceañera* (fifteenth birthday celebration),[1] everything appeared to be ready. Sponsors to pay for almost all aspects of the religious ceremony and the party afterward had been found. Relatives, *compadres* (godparents), and friends had been enlisted to help: an uncle was paying for the food, an aunt was paying for the liquor, a grandmother was buying her dress, baptismal godparents were buying the cake, and two of their daughters were going to "stand up" (serve as an attendant) for the church procession. Other relatives and friends were enlisted as godparents to pay for the flowers, a *cojín* (pillow) to kneel on in the church, a *diadema* (diadem or tiara), the bands, the photographs, and several other incidentals. As Ana had chosen to have the dinner and dance in the gym of the local community center, she did not have to rent a hall. An order for two hundred invitations had been placed at the engravers with the names of all the attendants printed on an inserted sheet.

In addition to finding enough relatives and friends of the family to pay for the affair, Ana had found the requisite fourteen young couples, *damas* (women) and *chambelaones* (men), to stand up in matching dresses and tuxedos. This is frequently a difficult task, as each of the young women has to buy her own dress (generally $45 to $100), which Ana, like most celebrants, picked out of a catalog of bridesmaid dresses. The cost of the rented tuxedo is often $40. A cotillion is an expense for everyone. Ana had already stood up for two of the young women, who were returning the favor, and she was scheduled to participate in four more. Finding fourteen couples who could afford and would agree to stand up for the affair was difficult. In addition, she wanted to exclude from the males any potential troublemakers. As it was, two of the young women were standing up with their brothers, who were in different gangs, and another's escort was in a rival gang, but none were known as troublemakers at parties.

Problems began several weeks before the affair. An aunt's family dropped out, claiming they could not afford to pay for the band because they had to attend the funeral of a relative in Mexico. Excuses such as this are common, but the day was rescued when Ana's mother agreed to try to pay for the band herself.

One week prior to the cotillion Ana discovered that her mother had hired only a Mexican *ranchera* (Mexican country music) band and not a rock group. Ana did not want a cotillion without a rock group, and a local band was finally located forty-eight hours before the party. Then one of the couples decided that they could not afford to pay for the clothes and dropped out. Another couple broke up and an escort had to be found on short notice. While anxious about having only thirteen couples, Ana claimed it was better than seven or eight, as some had. Her problems were not over. An aunt informed her mother that she had seen Ana kissing her boyfriend, and her mother threatened to cancel the event because she did not want to endure the questions about Ana's virginity that public knowledge of her activities might engender. If the affair had been cancelled, the strength of the family network might have been questioned.

5   A cotillion is a public affirmation both of a young woman's virginity and of her kin's ability to work together to pay for such an event. Not all fifteen-year-olds have cotillions. Many families cannot afford them. Moreover, rumors often claim that a young woman holding a cotillion is trying to prove that she is still a virgin when she no longer is one. On the other hand, failing to have a cotillion is frequently considered a good indication that the young woman is no longer a virgin and may even be pregnant.

The evening before the affair required major organization, as beans and rice had to be prepared for two to three hundred guests and the gym had to be decorated. Retiring at two in the morning, everyone was awake by six. Clothes had to be ironed for her six brothers and sisters and both Ana and her older sister had to buy shoes the day of the affair. Her family congratulated themselves for having chosen to buy fried chicken rather than spending the considerable effort to cook the more traditional *mole* (a spicy baked chicken in sauce), though a few guests later commented on its absence.

Ana marched down the church aisle in her long white dress and veil on the arm of her uncle, following the thirteen couples and the new godparents. As she knelt with her boyfriend before the priest, Ana and the others resembled a wedding party. She did not kiss him but quietly left her flowers at a side altar and prayed there to the Virgin Mary. Her mother was pleased that seventy-five guests attended the church ceremony and that close to two hundred attended the party, many of whom brought presents. Wandering around the room while the photographer took pictures, one could hear compliments about the open bar, the dresses Ana had chosen, and the Mexican band.

Several of the members of the Lions gang arrived after dinner, having learned of the party from their member Ten Pen, whose sister stood up for Ana. On their best behavior and wearing their good clothes, they sat quietly drinking and, when the rock band played slow tunes, got up to dance. No incidents occurred, unlike several weeks before, when a groom fought at his own wedding and was arrested when the fight continued outside the hall. Ana's cotillion was dubbed a success by all. After the party, the photographs were admired over and over.

This event symbolizes much of what is valued in the Chicano family: the close, interdependent family network and the family's success in finances, in containing the sexual activities of the daughter so that she not only remains a virgin but is perceived as such, and in following the proper forms of social interaction. Expectations based on symbols of the expanded family, male domination, virginity, motherhood, and formalism determine the meanings of social relationships within and outside the family. The family relationships should be strong, the males should be dominant, the unmarried women must remain virgins, and the married women should center their lives around motherhood. Courtesy toward and respect for others, particularly elders, is expected of everyone. Some expectations closely resemble those found in Mexican villages;[2] others are affected by United States institutions. In either case, situations of normative ambiguity create dilemmas for concrete action, and the economic status of community residents creates problems for which new cultural resolutions are constantly devised and tested.

10   While familial social relationships have been somewhat altered, traditional arrangements remain strong. According to Bott (1971: 265) "geographical mobility *alone* should be enough to disrupt the sort of close-knit networks one finds in homogeneous working-class areas, and such disruption should be accompanied by greater jointness in the husband-wife relationship."[3] On 32nd Street the move from other areas of the United States or from Mexico has not greatly altered traditional arrangements. The worlds of the men and the women remain largely segregated and traditionally oriented yet interdependent. This is attributable to a number of factors: relatives often came together or followed one another; close networks were expanded to include *compadres* (children's godparents), who were often friends and/or neighbors; and the cultural symbols that give meaning to social relationships were frequently stronger than many of the forces of change. It is situations where the circumstances (ecological, social, or economic) have changed that highlight the strengths and weakness of the collective expectations. What *should* be done may become unclear, be revised, or be reaffirmed. Let us look at these dilemmas and the evolving solutions.

A COHESIVE FAMILY

The kinship network on 32nd Street can best be termed an "expanded family" in the model described by Gans (1962). While many relatives of varying generations tend to live nearby and interact continuously, each household is comprised of a nuclear family unit. A similar structure is found throughout the Chicano population regardless of social class and is the expected standard for families.[4] In Mexico, particularly among the urban poor, the ties of kinship have been augmented to include *compadres* (fictive kin) through treating the godparents of the children as part of the expanded family network.[5] While there is some indication that the importance of fictive kin as an extension of family relationships is lessening in some areas of the United States today,[6] in other communities it remains important.[7] On 32nd Street, the relationship between the godparents of a child's baptism and the child's parents remains particularly important for many families. *Padrinos* (godfathers) and *madrinas* (godmothers) are remembered on mother's and father's day and celebrate birthdays and many holidays with their godchildren. The interaction among generations and the closeness among age groups serve in part to maintain cultural continuity in Mexico and in the United States.

The expanded family is the normative familial form for all classes, whether or not it includes fictive kin in the United States as in Mexico. An important aspect of the expanded family network is one of continuous exchanges that are not governed by laws of supply and demand. Not only is the relationship with friends who have engaged in these exchanges strengthened by being named *compadres,* but the mutual obligations further strengthen the relationship of the entire expanded family unit both as a symbol of their cohesiveness and because they need each other. The content of the exchanges varies slightly by social class among Chicanos (Sena-Rivera, 1979). While the extent of economic interdependence and the exchange of personal services vary by social class, the family in all social classes remains the primary source of emotional and social support and is a major source for feelings of self-worth.[8] Sena-Rivera argues that economic interdependence is strongest for the most affluent and the least affluent families, that "interdependence in personal services is universal . . . but . . . follows socio-economic class lines (actual necessity rather than performance as an end in itself)" (ibid., p. 127). On 32nd Street the exchange of economic and personal services is frequently necessary for survival. Exchanges of money and individual skills are frequently made among kin and fictive kin. Turning for help to outside agencies such as public welfare or a public employment agency is regarded as a failure of a family's solidarity and worth. Ana's mother, for example, feared a public disgrace for the family when an aunt's family could not assist by paying for the band at the cotillion.

Having a large, close family that can be augmented by *compadres* who can and will readily help in time of need is very highly valued. Being seen as a cohesive family transcends economic success.[9] In such a family on 32nd Street and in other Chicano communities members lend each other money, locate a car mechanic, and help out in innumerable other situations.[10] "We can hardly keep track of all the money that goes around between us anymore. We just assume it's about equal," a young couple declared while discussing the state of their finances and their families' aid.

Much tension and weight are placed on the family relationship, which sometimes cannot support the demands made on it. At times these demands may lead to conflicts. With the lack of economic resources available to a nuclear family unit, its financial situation can easily become overextended, as when Ana's uncle dropped out, leaving her mother with additional expenses that were more than she could afford. This situation strained the family's relationship for several months until Ana's uncle was again able to help them. Economic pressures can disrupt the ongoing flow of resources and social relationships.

15   Being a cohesive family does not mean that members do not have problems. Amelia's family is close and they help each other frequently by exchanging favors and with mutual social and emotional support. Amelia is one of nine children (aged eight to thirty). Though her mother frequently drinks heavily, which embarrasses her, the children were very close to their mother and were upset at her first absence, when, as a local representative, she went to Washington for a conference. When one of the daughters married and moved into the basement apartment, her sister felt the double bed was too large for one person and had a younger sister sleep with her. A second married sister lives upstairs, another lives ten blocks away, and the sons all live within a few blocks. All the sons and daughters congregate almost daily at their mother's home. Amelia considers her family to be a cohesive one. They constantly help each other, just as Ana's family did in providing aid to make her cotillion successful, and reaffirming their image as a strong family.

Those families who do not have relatives or *compadres* on whom to rely must turn to public welfare in time of financial problems or must ask for support, thereby publicly acknowledging their humiliation. The neighborhood is attuned to such events, and news of them is quickly shared.[11] One of the members of the Lions gang frequently attempted to invite himself to dinner at other homes. The other gang members often refused and laughed at his attempts, ridiculing him for his inability to obtain readily a meal from the usual sources—relatives. While eating at relatives' homes is common, no one *asks* to do so; relatives or *compadres* are expected to offer meals to anyone at their homes at mealtime. A person who can survive without money for a long period by going from relative to relative, is viewed as having a cohesive family. A responsible individual does make some attempt to reciprocate, though no accounting is kept and the help received may not be reciprocated for a long period of time. However, even within the family, overdependence can lead to tension, as there is little money to go around.

Compadres and relatives usually make up an emotional and social support group. Women move freely back and forth between homes—cooking together, talking, taking care of one another's children, shopping, and going out together for entertainment. They have frequent Tupperware, makeup, toy, and clothes demonstrations at relatives' or *compadres'* homes. A young woman described one such party:

They're lots of fun. We girls get together and play lots of games, talk, laugh a lot, and buy too many things. Our husbands don't always like that when we have to pay up. Everyone dresses up to come and we laugh and gossip a lot.

Holidays, birthdays, and other special occasions are usually celebrated with *compadres,* relatives, and their children. A special dinner is prepared, and people eat in several shifts if no table is large enough to accommodate all the guests. Attending a Thanksgiving dinner, which includes not only turkey and sweet potatoes but rice, beans, and chili sauce, at the Mendoza home with two sets of *compadres* (each of the three families had seven children, then all below seventeen years old), guests ate in three or four shifts. The children played and ran in and out, while the women discussed problems of child rearing in the kitchen and then joined the men to dance to Latin music.

Not everyone is pleased with the close familial ties. For those who wish to do things differently, close ties may be viewed as prying, not helpful. Tina, a twenty-five-year-old mother of two boys, explained:

I hate living around the corner from my mother-in-law. She always wants to know what's happening over here. It's my family and I'll run it as I choose. I like some of my relatives but having them all over here asking for things constantly is too much.

Several months later I bumped into Tina after she had moved from the eastern to the western side of the community. She declared that living so near her mother-in-law had become too unpleasant and she had moved at the first opportunity. Tina gave her sister-in-law all her old dishes and furniture when she moved into the downstairs apartment. Both declared that they were happier in their new apartments in the same building. While a close family is highly valued, privately it displeases those who wish to be different.

20   The strong network of intergenerational relationships provides a means by which traditions can be readily passed on. Few child-rearing manuals are used, and intergenerational aid encourages traditional practices. Young girls spend time helping their mothers and learning the mothering role. Girls frequently take on household responsibilities and care for their younger siblings before becoming mothers themselves.[12] At ten or twelve, girls frequently are party to discussions among their mothers' friends and between their mothers and grandmothers about family life and relationships. The intergenerational interaction and the strong emotional support these relationships provide are a solid basis for the maintenance of traditional sex role relationships within the family, upon which the code of honor is based.

MANHOOD

Manhood is expressed through independence, personal strength, control over situations, and domination. This image of manhood, particularly in relationship to femininity, has been traced by some scholars to the culture of Spain, where the desire for precedence in interpersonal relationships and authority over the family are important symbols of manliness.[13] Others trace it to the culture of the Aztecs, where women were expected to be subordinate and submissive to men, while a third group argues that male domination was a result of colonialism.[14] Though the traditional symbols of manhood have not changed substantially in the transition to 32nd Street and have significant implications for men's relationships as fathers, husbands, sons, and brothers,[15] male domination as worked out within the family does not weaken the critical position of the mother.

The role of the Mexican father/husband has been described as one of domination and control over his wife and daughters. Studies of Mexican towns demonstrate that men are seen as people who cannot be "gotten around."[16] Fathers are seen as rigid, closed, and distant.[17] Sons become independent at an early age.[18] Some of these descriptions are similar to those of relationships for fathers and husbands in the 32nd Street community while others are not. The symbols of manhood articulate many of the salient meanings of social relationships within the family. The father/husband, as the dominant member of the household, must maintain the honor of his wife and daughters. To dishonor them reflects not only on them but also on his ability to maintain his self-respect as an independent and dominant individual. He alone must be responsible for supporting his family and must not publicly appear to become dependent on a working wife. The husband/father as the family head and the son as an independent young man both expect to be served by the women in the household and to come and go as they please. Sara, an eighteen-year-old, explained:

> My brother, he comes rushing in and sits down at the table expecting a hot dinner no matter what time it is, just like my father. . . . You know he gets it every time and we have to make it.

No one found it extraordinary that one wife, who worked an early shift (7:00 A.M. to 3:00 P.M.), was expected to prepare dinner for her husband, who finished his shift at 11 P.M. and arrived home to eat at 4:00 A.M., after several hours of drinking. If she was asleep he woke her, and she had to cook and still get their seven children ready for school and be at work by 7:00 A.M. A spotless house was also expected and provided.

Though the men can demand and usually receive services (cooking, cleaning, and so forth) of the women when they want, the men are dependent on the women to provide these services. Men are taught that cooking, washing clothes, and cleaning are women's and *not* men's work. For example, when one male youth pulled out the ironing board to iron his pants, his sisters took it away from him and laughed and teased him for wanting to do "woman's work." They all thought him strange and talked about him behind his back. His father even gave him a lecture. A man who does "woman's work" must be unable to find a woman to do that work, and therefore less than a man, or must be unduly controlled by his woman. This male dependence actually gives a woman a significant source of power.

Within this cultural context, men are caught in what appears to be an unresolvable dilemma. A working wife is a public indication that the husband is unable to support his family and therefore lacks control in the family and dominance over his wife, who could become economically independent. But the alternatives to an employed wife are few and not much better. A hungry and poorly clothed family does not enhance a man's reputation, nor does depending on support from the expanded family for any length of time without reciprocation. Caught in this dilemma, many husbands prefer to let their wives work and explain their actions within the traditional cultural context. By stating that they are still in control, that they *let* their wives work, and then only to pay for incidental expenses while the men remain the main breadwinners, their actions are legitimized. For example, while two men in their thirties were sitting in a bar discussing whether wives should work, one said to the other, "I would never let my wife work while I got this good job, but a lot of guys are getting laid off now and my wife didn't get bad money before we got married." The second responded, "I got her working now 'cause we need a new washer and dryer to help her out. Now she has to go to the laundromat." Both men criticized another man whose wife was working though he had a well-paying job and the couple had a "good home." Only if a man explains that he is still in control is a working wife considered legitimate. The fact that women work is still articulated in terms of male domination, and the women infrequently use their employment to change the husband-wife relationship.

VIRGINITY

25 The Virgin Mother is among the most salient religious symbols in Mexico. She is more important than the adult Christ in many Mexican religious ceremonies. For example, *el día de la Virgen de Guadalupe* (December 12) is an important celebration both in Mexico and on 32nd Street, when even men who rarely attend church go to mass.[19] In Mexico City women walk on their knees the several miles from the downtown to the Virgin in Guadalupe's shrine. The sexual purity of women—the faithfulness of a wife to her husband or the virginity of an unmarried woman—is symbolized by the Virgin Mother. The honor of a man is besmirched if a daughter is not a virgin at marriage or a wife is unfaithful. His honor is inexorably tied to that of his family. In Mexican villages, the role of an honorable woman, both as a mother and as a daughter, is that of a *mujer abnegada,* a self-sacrificing, dutiful woman (Diaz, 1966: 78). While the symbol of the Virgin Mother is used in evaluating women's relationships on 32nd Street, some expectations have changed from those of the traditional Mexican village.

According to Mexican tradition, maintaining a young woman's public image as a virgin requires that she be accompanied on social occasions by a chaperone (usually an older or younger relative). On 32nd Street, chaperonage of unmarried women has largely been eliminated though wives are often accompanied by their young children when visiting or shopping. The result is that everyone is aware that most women can escape the watchful eyes of their kin. Consequently, maintenance both of a woman's virginity or faithfulness and of community perception of that state are difficult. Most families are concerned with the movements of their daughters but cannot completely restrict their activities, though a few families do attempt to retain tight control.

Brothers and other relatives act as unofficial chaperones for young women. They will often stop young women from drinking, watch their sisters if they are with young men, or tell all their friends to stay away. For example, at a party sixteen-year-old Sara asked me:

> Please tell me if you see my brother because I can't drink with him around, he'll beat me. Me and my sisters are not supposed to drink, he doesn't like that. You know when we go to dances on the north side, we got to sneak 'cause if he ever found out he would follow us around and we'd never get to go anywhere.

The importance that parents give to a daughter's identity as a virgin is revealed in the following example. Alicia, when she was fourteen, hid her pregnancy from her parents until her sixth month. Her parents sent her to an aunt and uncle in Mexico to whom she was supposed to give the child. Realizing how much she wanted to keep the baby, her aunt persuaded Alicia's parents to let her keep the child. When she returned home seven months pregnant, Alicia was not permitted to leave the house. Anytime a visitor arrived, she hid, first under the bed and then, when she became too big, under the sink in the kitchen. Labor pains started when she was hiding in the garage. Later her parents almost took over the upbringing of her son, taking him as a deduction on their income tax even after Alicia went to work and referring to him as their son, though everyone knew who the parents were.

Parents are faced with what seems to many an unresolvable dilemma. If they follow the traditional honor-based code and refuse to allow their daughter to go out unsupervised, then her virginity remains publicly unquestioned and the honor of her family is upheld. The wider society and many of the local institutions, whether organized by members of the wider society or by local residents, provide legitimation for allowing a young woman some degree of freedom. Both the schools and the churches sponsor dances that are sparsely supervised. Local community groups also sponsor dances with American rock bands. Parents are invited to attend yet discouraged from participating or actually attending by the type of music and the dim lighting. This local legitimation of more freedom for young women places parents in a problematic situation. Freedom heightens the risk of the daughter losing her virginity or being perceived as having lost it. But if they closely supervise her activities, they risk alienating her. Again a situation of normative ambiguity exists and the resolution must be situationally negotiated between parents and their daughters.

30   The parental dilemma is exacerbated by the expectation that men will take what they can from women. Men are defined as dominant and women defined as submissive; consequently, only male relatives can be trusted with women. One father succinctly expressed these views:

> You know what all men are after. . . . It's natural for them to go out and get it anyway they can. I don't trust any of the young punks around here. They take it and run. There are too many unmarried pregnant girls around here. The young girls don't know how to handle themselves.

Parents are confronted directly with the dilemma when young women ask permission to attend a party or dance with friends. Parents often employ the tactic of nondecision. They postpone any decision until the last moment. Then, when their daughter is ready to go out, they deny her permission. Other times the responsibility is shifted back and forth between mother and father and then changed again at the last moment. This lack of resolution can result in dissatisfaction on both sides. Many young women stop asking. "I just go where I please without asking permission. She [her mother] would just stare at me in silence when I asked, so what's the point in asking?" a nineteen-year-old explained. By going out on their own, young women risk being appraised as nonvirgins.

Parental permission for their daughter to go out affects the public evaluation not only of the parents but of their daughter. If she is permitted to attend parties, she is at a much greater risk of being appraised as a nonvirgin even if she actually retains her virginity. Parents frequently increase the risk of such erroneous perceptions by failing to take a strong stand if their daughter sneaks out. It is the public perception of her sexual purity that reflects upon the parents. If she is perceived as a nonvirgin, then her family's honor is questioned. Only complete parental control over her behavior minimizes the risk of her being perceived as a nonvirgin or of actually losing her virginity. As such control is difficult to maintain in modern urban society, it is more an ideal than a reality.

MOTHERHOOD

Motherhood is the most culturally acceptable identity available to women. The role of independent career woman is not culturally acceptable. Women must be either wives, sisters, or mothers to men. Motherhood is seen not as a last resort but rather as a highly honored role. The Mexican image of the Virgin Mother, loving and dependable, the person with whom the child satisfies desires for nurturing and acceptance, is the 32nd Street model of motherhood.[20] Motherhood is the basis of the strongest bonds of blood ties.[21] These bonds are much stronger than those of husbands and wives or fathers and children.

The husband-wife bond is based on procreation and expression of love but little on companionship. The expectation that men will dominate in all situations makes it difficult to develop companionable relationships between men and women even in marriage, as sociability usually develops between equals. (Moreover, any time a man and a woman who are not related through blood ties are together, it is expected that they will become sexually involved, because men dominate women and, lacking equality and the possibility of friendship, the only reason they would be together is as sexual partners.)[22] Most socializing occurs in single-sex groups, and the expanded family network fulfills companionship functions. But children's ties with their mothers are natural and lifelong:[23] they never become distant with age, as do ties with their fathers, who discipline and control them. While the dynamics of the father-child interaction is in part determined by the child's willingness to obey him and demonstrate respect for him, mothering places no such conditions on the parent-child relationship.

35   Loyalty and support for his mother was demonstrated by a young man who had become addicted to heroin and entered a methadone program only after stealing from his mother:

> I used to steal all the time from my brothers and sisters and went through my old man's coat pockets many times . . . even stole his watch once and pawned it, but you know when I took some bread [money] from my old lady, then I knew I had to do something. Taking from your old lady's real bad.

The mother remains the central and most stable feature in a son's life. He depends on her for nurture and emotional support and she on him for support and the ultimate protection of her honor. As a son his honor is dependent on hers; any aspersion cast on her honor reflects on his own.

The traditional expectation that a woman's unique role is to be a mother with many children creates a conflict for those young women who have interests outside the home. Some reject motherhood. One nineteen-year-old college student, the eldest of seven, despised the traditional female role of daughter and mother:

> I had to change diapers for my three youngest brothers and sisters. They were such a mess and were so much trouble. I hate them for it. I wish my mother didn't have them. What did she need so many kids for anyway? It would have been a lot better without the last two. They were always crying and wanting attention . . . comb their hair, wash them, feed them, change their diapers, and put them to sleep. . . . They're my mother's kids. She should be responsible for them. I'm not their mother . . . if my mother gets married again and has another kid I'll die. One time I told her I wasn't going to have any kids. She really got angry and said God will punish me. It was up to Him, not me. She didn't speak to me for a week. I'm not going to have any kids. They're just trouble.

Celia's oldest sister, a student, added another problem to the list:

> It wouldn't be good for my mother to have more kids. They cost money and it would be like the dog; everyone would get excited for a while and then

bored and not want to take care of it. [Celia objected here.] I don't want to take care of it. I'd move out.

The views of the two students are not generally accepted and often considered immoral. They violate all expectations of femininity and the family. Though it is becoming more common for young women to desire to limit family size, in part because of the expense of bringing up children, older people and many younger ones see this not only as tampering with "God's will" but also as comparing things that cannot be compared: economics and family. These young women are openly denying the importance of motherhood and appear to equate the family's worth with that of money. For most, social and economic success are not valued above motherhood. Problems arise only for those young women who are beginning to strive for success in the wider society. The exclusion of motherhood is still regarded as deviant.

It is clear what the important symbols of family life are: solidarity, male domination, virginity, motherhood, and respect. In the context of an urban community within a highly industrialized and educated society, some of the expectations derived from these symbols become distorted, are ambiguous, or are in conflict. While some of the problematic situations can be resolved within the traditional culture, for other situations all solutions seem less than perfect. Much of the ambiguity and conflict is found in the expectations concerning sex role behavior and child-parent relationships.

In the urban context youths are granted many freedoms and hold few responsibilities. These expectations are validated and supported by the media, by the schools, and even to some extent by the Catholic church. The situation places continual pressure on parents to allow their children more freedom while encouraging youths to demand those freedoms. Moreover, women are encouraged to work, particularly because of financial need.

40   The cohesive family with its strong network of relatives and *compadres* provides economic supports to help deal with financial realities, emotional supports to deal with normative ambiguity and conflict, and social supports and mechanisms to maintain the traditional symbols of sex role relationships and nearly traditional behavior patterns. With the support of the expanded family, actors negotiate difficult situations of normative ambiguity and conflict. Sometimes the process is painful, emotionally charged, and the consequence unsatisfactory to both parties; a son is physically punished or a daughter is locked in her room. Members of the expanded family may provide advice and emotional support or may invite the unruly son or daughter of a relative or *compadre* to live with them. Families do their best to keep members out of the social welfare and justice systems.

Youths are caught between the traditional model of social relationships and the Chicago urban reality: the streets, the school, the media, and the job scene. With the freedom they take or are given, the youths are faced with many dilemmas as they venture beyond the confines of the communal and familial order. The subsequent chapters explore their attempts to resolve a variety of dilemmas as they interact outside their homes.

•   •   •

NOTES FOR CHAPTER 4.
THE EXPANDED FAMILY AND FAMILY HONOR

1. A *quinceañera* is a young woman's fifteenth birthday celebration and is often referred to as a cotillion. It is a special birthday for a young girl in both Mexico and the United States and symbolizes her transition from childhood to adulthood. Traditionally, she then had to be chaperoned and guarded in her behavior. In the small villages of Mexico she is often given some new clothes, while on 32nd Street some of the girls have affairs for several hundred guests, such as the one described in the text.

2. See, for example, Diaz (1966), Foster (1967), Nelson (1971), and Romanucci-Ross (1973).

3. Several empirical studies support Bott's hypothesis. In England, Young and Willmot (1957) studied the problems of wives who moved from the Bethnal Green neighborhood where many of their kin lived and found that only forty years later networks of friends and kin developed again in Dagenham (Willmott, 1963). Studies of the United States such as Handel and Rainwater (1964) and Rainwater and Handel (1964) found that geographic mobility brought an increase in home-centeredness and less sex role segregation between husband and wife in working-class families.

   Mobility has not affected familial sex roles in this way in the 32nd Street community, nor have lack of propinquity and urbanization affected the strength and importance of family ties. There is evidence that propinquity is not necessary to maintain the cohesion of extended kinship, and urbanization does not entirely destroy it (Coult and Habenstein, 1962; Litwak, 1960). Both studies found extended kinship among people who lived in different places and in urban areas.

4. For similar findings in other Chicano communities see Alvirez and Bean (1976), Murillo (1971), Sena-Rivera (1979), Sotomayor (1972), and Temple-Trujillo (1974).

5. Mintz and Wolf (1950), in an historical analysis of *compadrazgo,* have documented its changes of function and content since the sixth century. According to Gibson (1966) *compadrazgo* was widely adopted in Mexico during the colonial period, when an epidemic caused significant depopulation and *compadres* became accepted as substitute parents.

   Lomnitz (1977), in her study of a Mexico City shantytown, found that the function of the *compadre* relationship from the rural situation and from the "ideal model" had been strengthened and broadened in the shantytown. Rural *compadres* were never cited as necessary for emergency help and close friendship but were "respected" persons. However, through participant-observation, Lomnitz found in the shantytown that not only has the number of *compadre* relationships increased (for example, *compadres* are chosen for saint days, upon graduation from primary school, and so on), but *compadres* are frequently picked from neighbors and friends and are part of the reciprocal obligation network which is necessary for economic survival:

   > The *compadrazgo* institution is being used in the shantytown to make preexisting reciprocity relations more solid and permanent. . . . I agree with Safa (1974: 61–64) in that

cooperation between equals is a result of necessity born of the social structure. If one lacks a powerful godfather one must make do with *compadres* (Lomnitz, 1977: 162).

Compadrazgo is a way of legitimizing mutual assistance among neighbors and is judged in its "intensity and trustworthiness of reciprocal exchange" (Lomnitz, 1977: 173).

6. Keefe, Padilla, and Carlos (1979) and Sena-Rivera (1979) argue that *compadrazgo* is decreasing; however, Carlos (1973) has found that with urbanization and modernization that *compadres* still play an important role in Mexico and the relationship remains strong.

7. See Madsen (1964), Moore (1970), and Rubel (1966) for illustrations of its continued importance.

8. See Keefe, Padilla, and Carlos (1979), Murillo (1971), Rubel (1966), and Sena-Rivera (1979) for similar findings in other studies of Chicanos.

9. This "familism" in which individuals subordinate their needs to the collective can be traced back to Aztec culture (Mirandé and Enríquez, 1979).

10. Alvirez and Bean (1976) argued that many Chicano families pool their resources, and Carlos (1973) has found that fictive kin help each other by finding jobs, lending money, and giving preferential treatment in business.

11. On some occasions, such as a fire or death, it might be permissible to accept emergency public aid, but it is still better if friends and family help out.

12. A fourteen-year-old girl explained:

> I stay home until at least one o'clock in the summer every day to wash the kitchen and bathroom floors, otherwise they get dirty and sticky and the little kids crawl around on them all the time. In the winter during school, I do it before I go in the morning. Sometimes I'm late for school. We clean the whole house twice a week and my other sisters do the cooking and the washing.

13. See Pitt-Rivers (1966) for an analysis of male honor in Spain.

14. See Hayner (1966) and Paz (1961), who argue that Aztec women were submissive to men. However, Mirandé and Enríquez (1979) argue that Aztec women had roles beyond wife and mother and that complete male domination occurred through external forces such as those imposed by colonialization (Baca Zinn, 1975; Sosa Riddell, 1974).

15. Similar patterns have been found in other Chicano communities (Flores, 1971; Nieto-Gomez, 1974; Vidal, 1971).

16. Nelson (1971: 51) describes this phenomenon in her study of a Mexican village. In his analysis of psychological studies of the Mexican, Peñalosa (1968) found that they described the father-son relationship as distant and respectful and the father-daughter relationship as distant and conflict-free.

17. Diaz (1966), Fromm and Maccoby (1970), and Nelson (1971) so describe the fathers in the Mexican villages they studied. Rubel (1966) and Goodman and Beman (1971) describe similar findings in Chicano communities.

18. Diaz (1966) found that mothers expected their sons to become independent early in their lives in Tonalá, Mexico.

19. The Virgin of Guadalupe symbolizes piety, virginity, and saintly submissiveness. She is the supreme good (Mirandé and Enríquez, 1979). Peñalosa (1968) argues that "guadalupanismo," that is, the highly emotional, devout veneration of the Virgin of Guadalupe, is very strong in Mexican culture (see Bushell, 1958; Madsen, 1960).

20. See Fromm and Maccoby (1970) and Nelson (1971) for analyses of the Virgin Mother.

21. This traditional Mexican situation is similar to that of the Aztecs, who considered the mother the heart of the house, solely responsible for child rearing and cleaning, dedicated to her husband, and remaining respectable in the eyes of the community (Mirandé and Enríquez, 1979: 14).
22. Gans (1962) describes a very similar situation among Italians living in the United States.
23. This has been documented in other Chicano communities (Murillo, 1971).

BIBLIOGRAPHY

Alvirez, David, and F. D. Bean
   1976 "The Mexican American Family." In C. H. Mindel and R. W. Habenstein (eds.), *Ethnic Families in America,* pp. 271–292. New York: Elsevier.
Baca Zinn, Maxine
   1975 "Political familism: Toward sex role equality in Chicano families." *Aztlán: Chicano Journal of the Social Sciences and the Arts* 6:13–26.
Bott, Elizabeth
   1971 *Family and Social Network.* New York: Free Press.
Bushnell, John H.
   1958 "La Virgen de Guadalupe as surrogate mother." *American Anthropologist* 60:261–265.
Coult, Allen, and R. Habenstein
   1962 "The study of extended kinship in urban society." *Sociological Quarterly* 3:141–145.
Diaz, May N.
   1966 *Tonalá: Conservatism, Authority and Responsibility in a Mexican Town.* Berkeley: University of California Press.
Foster, George
   1967 *Tzintzunztán.* Boston: Little, Brown.
Fromm, Erich, and Michael Maccoby
   1970 *Social Character in a Mexican Village.* Englewood Cliffs, N. J.: Prentice-Hall.
Gans, Herbert
   1962 *The Urban Villagers.* New York: Free Press.
Goodman, M. E., and A. Beman
   1971 "Child's-eye-views of life in an urban barrio." In N. Wagner and M. Haug (eds.), *Chicanos: Social and Psychological Perspectives,* pp. 109–122. Saint Louis: C. V. Mosby Company.
Handel, G., and L. Rainwater
   1964 "Persistence and change in working-class life-styles." In A. B. Shostak and W. Gomberg (eds.), *Blue-Collar World,* pp. 36–41. Englewood Cliffs, N. J.: Prentice-Hall.
Hayner, Norman
   1966 *New Patterns in Old Mexico.* New Haven: College and University Press.
Keefe, S. E., A. M. Padilla, and M. L. Carlos
   1979 "The Mexican-American extended family as an emotional support system." *Human Organization* 38:144–152.
Litwak, Eugene
   1960 "Geographic mobility and extended family cohesion." *American Sociological Review* 25:385–394.
Lomnitz, Larissa Adler
   1977 *Networks and Marginality.* Trans. by Cinna Lomnitz. New York: Academic Press.

Madsen, William
  1960 *The Virgin's Children.* Austin: University of Texas Press.
  1964 *The Mexican Americans of South Texas.* New York: Holt, Rinehart, and Winston.
Mintz, S. W., and E. R. Wolf
  1950 "An analysis of ritual co-parenthood." *Southwestern Journal of Anthropology* 6:341–635.
Mirandé, A., and E. Enríquez
  1979 *La Chicana.* Chicago: University of Chicago Press.
Moore, Joan
  1970 *Mexican Americans.* Englewood Cliffs, N.J.: Prentice-Hall.
  1978 *Homeboys.* Philadelphia: Temple University Press.
Murillo, Nathan
  1971 "The Mexican-American family." In N. N. Wagner and M. J. Haug (eds.), *Chicanos: Social and Psychological Perspectives,* pp. 97–108. Saint Louis: C. V. Mosby.
Nelson, Cynthia
  1971 *The Waiting Village: Social Change in Rural Mexico.* Boston: Little, Brown.
Nieto-Gomez, Anna
  1971 "Chicanas identify." *Regeneración* 1(10):9–13.
  1974 "La Feminista." *Encuentro Feminil* 1:34–37.
Paz, Octavio
  1961 *The Labyrinth of Solitude.* Trans. by Lysander Kemp. New York: Grove.
Peñalosa, Fernando
  1967 "The changing Mexican-American in Southern California." *Sociology and Social Research* 51:405–417.
  1968 "Mexican family roles." *Journal of Marriage and the Family* 30:680–689.
  1973 "Toward an operational definition of the Mexican-American." In Gilberto Lopez y Rivas (ed.), *The Chicanos,* pp. 91–106. New York: Monthly Review Press.
Pitt-Rivers, Julian
  1966 "Honour and social status." In J. Peristiany (ed.), *Honour and Shame,* pp. 19–78. Chicago: University of Chicago Press.
Rainwater, L., and G. Handel
  1964 "Changing family roles in the working class." In A. B. Shostak and W. Gomberg (eds.), *Blue-Collar World,* pp. 70–75. Englewood Cliffs, N. J.: Prentice-Hall.
Romanucci-Ross, Lola
  1973 *Conflict, Violence and Morality in a Mexican Village.* Palo Alto: National Press Books.
Rubel, Arthur
  1966 *Across the Tracks.* Austin: University of Texas Press.
Seña-Rivera, Jaime
  1979 "The extended kinship of the United States: Competing models and the case of la familia chicana." *Journal of Marriage and the Family* 41:121–129.
Sosa Riddell, Adaljiza
  1974 "Chicanas and el movimiento." *Aztlán: Chicano Journal of the Social Sciences and the Arts* 5:155–165.
Sotomayor, Marta
  1972 "Mexican American interaction with social systems." *Social Casework* 52:316–322.

Temple-Trujillo, Rita E.
  1974 "Conceptions of the Chicano family." *Smith College Studies in Social Case-work* 45:1–20.
Vidal, Mirta
  1971 *Women: New Voice of La Raza.* New York: Pathfinder.
Willmott, P.
  1963 *The Evolution of a Community.* London: Routledge and Kegan Paul.
Young, M., and P. Willmott
  1957 *Family and Kinship in East London.* London: Routledge and Kegan Paul.

Use of Informants' Narratives.   Professor Lieber notices that both Stack and Horowitz began their chapters with a narrative description of the community they were studying, after which each author summarized her perspective, explaining the meaning she derived from her observation of the particular culture and citing the scholars upon whose work she depended.

This [Horowitz's chapter] is like Stack. It's about sponsors: an uncle pays for the food and an aunt pays for the liquor. Horowitz gives the narrative first and then highlights what these events mean in this culture.

Horowitz, in paragraphs 9 and 10 of the first section, offers a road map for the remainder of the chapter. The cotillion, Horowitz explains, symbolizes both the organization of and the strong values of the Chicano family. What makes these values interesting for Horowitz is that to uphold them members of the Chicano family must adapt expectations about family relationships brought from their villages in Mexico to the current context in the United States.

Identifying Horowitz's Conceptual Approach.   Horowitz says in the beginning of her chapter that in order to understand the relationships among the Chicano families on 32nd Street it is necessary to understand the problems that arise as people moved from Mexico to Chicago. How did this move influence husband-wife relationships? Do families now rely more on social ties than genealogical ones? Professor Lieber noted that in paragraph 10 one scholar named Bott, cited by Horowitz, suggested that,

. . . geographical mobility should weaken relations with one's genealogical kinsmen, at the same time strengthening the husband-wife relationship. Horowitz, however, is saying that on 32nd Street this geographic mobility has not changed the nature of relationships in the culture. People have been assimilated into kinship positions, so that in this new situation in the United States people create as little change as possible. This is precisely what I found in the Kapinga community resettled on Pohnpei. So, it looks like Horowitz wants to study ambiguous situations where circumstances have changed, in particular to study dilemmas between traditional expectations based on home life and expectations derived

from living in the United States, particularly in urban settings. Now she's set up the chapter and we know what it's supposed to be about.

Professor Lieber suggests here that Horowitz's conceptual approach to studying the family in this Chicano community is to look at the dilemmas or problems that result from the community's relocation.

Developing Terminology to Characterize the Expanded Family. Professor Lieber notes that Horowitz has adopted the term *expanded family* from the sociologist Herbert Gans. As he reads he notices many similarities with the way that Stack describes kinship in her ethnography, but also some differences.

Horowitz says that each family is composed of a nuclear family unit; many relatives live nearby and the compadre are included in the kinship network as well. As I read I can't help but wonder what the relationship is between a single household and all the participants in the network.

All the members of the expanded family, whether genealogically related or not, have important obligations to one another. The women especially visit back and forth and help each other out; it's not just an economic exchange but a moral one. I love this quote from one of her informants about the exchange within their expanded family, "We can hardly keep track of all the money that goes around between us anymore. We just assume it's about equal" (paragraph 13). This suggests that everyone expects there to be some kind of balance, but only in the long run.

Solving Family Dilemmas.   The very values that hold the Chicano family on 32nd Street together cause dilemmas or problems, which families must solve. These problems are quite different from the ones Stack describes in The Flats. Professor Lieber points out that just one of the many dilemmas discussed by Horowitz is the value placed on virginity.

The first thing that you have to notice when Horowitz talks about virginity in paragraphs 25 and 26 is the difference from The Flats—virginity simply had no value in that community. Here, on 32nd Street and in Mexico, the Virgin Mother is one of the most important religious symbols. The sexual purity of women must be maintained at all costs. Events such as the cotillion described at the beginning of the chapter are intended to present the young woman as a virgin. Often brothers and friends serve as chaperones, a custom retained from Mexico. The concept of honor that Horowitz describes has its cultural roots in Europe. What we see here is its Mexican form.

For the young women living in the middle of urban Chicago where freedom is valued by the young and by schoolmates, the members of the expanded family face a difficult dilemma indeed in maintaining a young woman's virginity or at least the appearance of it.

WRITING AND LEARNING ACTIVITIES

1. **Journal Entry:** Horowitz's fieldwork report is different from Stack's in some ways and similar in others. Write about the similarities and differences in your journal.

2. **Peer or Group Activity:** Discuss as a group the new terms you learned in this report and try to define those terms in your own words. Talk about whether they have a meaning in your day-to-day life that is different than the academic meaning.

3. **Writing Activity:** Working in groups, pairs, or on your own, write up an introductory guide to the terminology used in fieldwork on kinship based on the two articles you have read. In your own words describe what each term means, how it is used, and why it is important.

4. **Interview:** Talk to someone from a culture different than your own. Ask him or her about kinship relations and some of the same topics covered in the reports of fieldwork you just read.

5. **Examining the Text:** Meet in small groups and collaborate on the following: Look over the Notes and Bibliography for Horowitz's work. What type of information does she include in the notes? What types of references does she rely on for her research? What are the publication dates of the books and journals she uses? Are you familiar with any of the authors? Pick out two journal articles and two books that you might like to read. Report back to the class on what you have found.

MAKING MEANING IN ANTHROPOLOGY
MAKING A "VIDEO" OF A CULTURE

A writer in anthropology faces the peculiar problem of describing for readers a particular social group or culture by way of his or her own experience with that group. We could almost say that the anthropologist is trying to produce a video of the culture. Does where the writer stands as she figuratively holds and aims the camera make a difference in the resulting picture? Yes, it does. And *what* she "films" as she goes about her fieldwork—what she chooses to record in her voluminous notes—is also important.

The anthropologist's special method allows him or her to interpret and describe individuals as they live, love, learn, resist, change, and cope within a group or a culture. Learning about a group's culture, a concept for which there is no easy definition, is achieved through fieldwork—living and participating in a culture for a long period of time. We can see and understand a culture only through the actions of its members, making fieldwork a complicated knowledge-making activity. The fieldworker lives in the community, observes and participates in its social life, and interprets how the actions of the participants create and re-create meaning. And finally, the fieldworker faces the difficult task of writing an ethnographic report of fieldwork—the editing of miles of tape to produce the final, compact picture of a culture—that will help a reader to see and understand a community's cultural universe and its participants.

DOING ANTHROPOLOGY

To understand the work of anthropology we want to look closely at how members of this discipline think systematically about the problems they face in studying cultures. Anthropology is a social science, so the anthropologist first observes and then explains what he or she has observed. Professor Lieber demonstrated how Carol Stack began by observing a community, with special attention to family relationships; she focused on how sponsorship functions in that community. Other anthropologists will look at these same issues in other cultures and describe how they are similar or different. It is in this way that anthropologists contribute to our growing understanding of the concept of culture.

In their writing, anthropologists work to communicate accurately what they have learned from their fieldwork. In a 1988 book called *Tales of the Field: On Writing Ethnography,* John van Maanen talks about the problems and challenges of writing about fieldwork. Both fieldwork and the writing about it are problem-oriented. Carol Stack and Ruth Horowitz conducted fieldwork to look at specific aspects of family life, and both communicated their findings to their audience. Each of their chapters began with anecdotes that offered us, the reader, a taste of the community life they were about to describe. One special advantage of anthropological research is, because it is conducted on site, in the actual community, anthropologists can ask the individuals they are observing about what they are doing, thus adding more depth to the research.

ANTHROPOLOGY AS "BEING THERE" AND "BEING HERE"

Clifford Geertz, a well-known anthropologist, reminds us that the world that we once called, "primitive, tribal, [or] traditional" is now called "emergent" or "modernizing" (131). Increasingly, we have begun to see the same people we might have once called different as now a part of a global economy and world culture. When we think of people as different in some way we must guard against the tendency to write about them in language that distances the observer from a common humanity. Here is a paragraph, for instance, from a paper that uses language to poke fun at the way anthropologists describe others. The title of this 1956 paper by Horace Miner is "Body Ritual Among the Nacirema" (Nacirema spells American backward).

> The daily body ritual performed by everyone includes a mouth rite. Despite the fact that these people are so punctilious about care of the mouth, this rite involves a practice which strikes the uninitiated stranger as revolting. It was reported to me that the ritual consists of inserting a small bundle of hog hairs into the mouth, along with certain magical powders, and then moving the bundle in a highly formalized series of gestures.

Can you see how easily our most common practice, brushing our teeth, can appear comic when described as if by someone from another culture, indeed, maybe from another world? Anthropologists urge us to remember this example as we try to describe the cultural practices of people whom we see as quite different from us, whether neighbors on our block or neighbors across an ocean. Carol Stack, for instance, helped us to examine the nature of the differences she saw in the community she examined. As you continue to think and learn about anthropology you will want to remember how important it is to consider why you see differences when you are observing.

"BEING HERE" AND WRITING ABOUT OURSELVES

One way to better understand the challenges posed by ethnographic fieldwork is to try your hand at observing and reporting on a culture and community you have participated in for many years—your own. The activities at the end of the chapter ask you to examine your own experience as an observer as well as a participant and to try your hand at "writing up" some fieldwork. Here are some excerpts from students' journals as they began those activities.

> My family and I are rarely together—my Dad works nights and my Mom works days while my brother and I go to school. I think we interact the best every morning. My mother is the first to wake up—around 6:30. She sets up the coffee and her curling iron, washes her hair, and will sometimes blast her favorite country music station, US 99. Then around 7 o'clock she wakes up my brother and gives him breakfast while he's playing Nintendo. I get up after hearing Randy Travis about five times and listening to "Sh-h-h-h, your father's sleeping!" Then begins the fight over our one bathroom. We argue about who gets the sink, where's the brown comb. I'm yelling at my brother in Ukrainian because there's stuff I can say in Ukrainian, but not in English. In the middle of all this I might see my Dad standing in the hallway in his pajamas. He tries to get up for a little while in the morning to check up on us: What's new, how's school, how's hockey practice. I really admire him for trying to keep up with our lives, but at 8:15 in the morning it gets pretty crazy. God help us if one of us wakes up in a bad mood!
>
> NATALIE ACEVEDO

> When it comes to my family interacting, I think we do best at work. My father owns a restaurant and it is the family business. Everyone works there; I started working at the restaurant when I was in the sixth grade but I have been at the restaurant ever since I can remember. When I was a baby my grandmother took care of me there. Everybody had a job to do. As we got older we learned not to be so dependent on them [parents] because often times it got very busy. My sister and I learned to answer the phones and help in other ways. Being at the restaurant felt like being at home. We

talked about all kinds of things, mostly about education. My parents constantly urged us to study hard and get good grades.

ANNA HONG

For me, 32nd Street is a reality. I was born in Mexico. Half of my family is here and half is there. I'm part of a society in transition and there can be many levels of transition even within the same family. My mother-in-law is very traditional; the man should be strong and free and the woman should take care of the family. My wife, on the other hand, is more educated and no longer accepts those traditions. I also can identify with Stack when she describes how members of a very poor community depend on each other economically as a network. In my block there is a mechanic who does electrical work and we often trade off. My father-in-law lets me have an apartment very cheap and in exchange I work on his car. So, to use the same word, we have a reciprocal relationship.

FERNANDO ESCOBAR

DEVELOPING INTERESTS

These three students all began to examine their family life more closely after discussing the issues raised in this chapter. Finding points of connection between your experiences and the questions raised by anthropologists provides a gateway to academic research. Other activities below will help you identify interests you might like to pursue further.

WRITING AND LEARNING ACTIVITIES

1. **Journal Entry:** Write about either an important event you experienced with your family recently or about some routine aspect of your family life. Choose a situation in which you can describe interactions among family members. What makes your family similar or different from others? How does your position in the family change your perspective?

2. **Group or Peer Activity:** In a group of from three to five students or with a peer, share your family stories. Appoint one person to take notes and report back to the class. A. First, read the stories out loud to each other. Each person should ask questions about areas you'd like to know more about. For instance, in response to Anna Hong's journal entry above, you might ask about what specific jobs members of the family held and what happened when one person got sick. B. Next, consider these stories in light of the issues raised by Stack and Horowitz. Make a list of questions you could ask about kinship relations and then see how those questions would be answered by the members of your group.

3. **Writing Activity:** Choose an activity or event like the toothbrushing example above. Write a short description of the event as an outsider observing it for the first time.

4. Research Activity: Listed at the end of this book in the appendix, Directions for Further Research, are annotated sources for research in anthropology. Go to your library and browse through some of them. You might take a look at the *Atlas of Mankind* or the *Illustrated Encyclopedia of Mankind.* You might also want to look through the *Journal of Ethnology* or *Current Anthropology.* Write in your journal about which topics interest you and why.

▣ LINKED WRITING ASSIGNMENT

Writing a Synthesis of Work in Cultural Anthropology (see Chapter 11, Synthesizing Discipline-Specific Texts). In the previous section, Developing Interests, you began to identify issues and ideas that you might want to explore further. Finding personal connections to the material you are studying is one important way to participate more fully in an academic community. You will also need to learn how some everyday thinking strategies, such as synthesizing, help you to participate in the disciplines you are studying here. Chapter 11 introduces you to the activity of synthesizing and offers readings from cultural anthropology for you to practice synthesizing material from several sources.

3

QUANTITATIVE SOCIAL RESEARCH

A re you still living at home? Perhaps you are living in a college dormitory, sharing an apartment with friends, living with relatives, or living with your husband or wife. If you have left your childhood home, how did you come to make the decision to leave? How has the process of leaving home—or nest-leaving as it is referred to in the social sciences—occurred for others you know? How are the attitudes and practices associated with nest-leaving influenced by a person's culture or family expectations, by marriage and divorce, or by the economy? Social researchers explore such questions by conducting research on how an individual's behavior is shaped by the social groups he or she belongs to. These groups—from families to countries—are always changing and social researchers try to develop research methods to uncover patterns in these changes.

In this chapter Professor Michael Maltz speaks about his research in the field of criminal justice and why social research is important. He then guides us through a reading of a report on nest-leaving research. Next we look at how social researchers make meaning, what questions they ask, and what methods they use. Finally, I ask you to think about what nest-leaving means to you.

AN INTERVIEW WITH
A SOCIAL SCIENCE RESEARCHER

Michael Maltz is a professor in the Criminal Justice Department at the University of Illinois at Chicago, and is also affiliated with the Department of Information and Decision Sciences. He researches patterns of criminal activity and has written an award-winning book on recidivism, the study of the circumstances under which criminals repeat a crime. He teaches courses on both criminal justice and research methods.

Tell us how you became interested in social research.

I started out in engineering. In high school I had done well in English and math and physics; however, the jobs were in math and physics and not in English, so I went to engineering school for my bachelor's degree and continued on to a Ph.D. About halfway through my Ph.D. I decided that I wasn't really that keen on engineering, but I figured I might as well finish what I'd started.

My first job out of graduate school was working for an aerospace corporation, building and designing guidance systems for missiles, which helped me decide that I didn't want to spend the rest of my life building things to kill people. So I turned it into a summer job and spent a year in Denmark teaching and doing research in engineering at the Technical University of Denmark. When I came back I started working for an engineering consulting firm. One of our projects was working with the Boston Police Department to redesign their communication system, computer system, and record-handling system. That's basically the way I got into criminology and criminal justice. You see, I was originally brought on board to work with the communication system because my training is in electrical engineering, but then I got more interested in the social aspects of the project rather than the equipment they were using. And that's how my career shifted to criminal justice.

Why is criminal justice considered social research?

What we are dealing with in criminal justice is basically the relationship of the individual to the state in a very profound sense—and also in a very practical sense, because the state can send someone to prison, the state can decide to kill a person. So it's social in the sense that society says these are the rules, and they are the rules you should live by.

How can social research influence the relationship between the state and individuals?

Well, there's so much that we don't know. For instance, do the police prevent crime? Some say yes and some say no. And I say that's the wrong question. I'd say, under what conditions do what actions of the police prevent or deter what kinds of crime? So what we have to do is take these broad concepts of, say, police preventing crime, and keep breaking them up into little pieces so that we know what it is they do that causes things to improve—or get worse, for that matter. And what we do for one class of people is not going to work for another. If we pass a law saying "You should not do thus and such," some people will say "Oh, there is a law, therefore I shouldn't do it." Other people will say, "Hey, there's a law I can break." It depends upon whether they are, what you might call, "risk preferrers" or "risk avoiders." And each person is different.

Can you tell us something about your recent research?

One of the questions that has always plagued correctional officials is, what works in terms of correcting people? We know that when people leave prison some of them commit crimes again and some of them don't. The term recidivism means recommitting crime, and that's a social problem that's difficult to measure. One can say, "Sure, you can measure it very easily because all you've got to do is follow a person's career and if that person commits another crime, well then that person has recidivated." But, let's face it, people do not say, "Hey, I committed another crime," and let you know they have done it. So what we have to do is look at official records. And what we have in official records are arrests and convictions.

If correction officials want to try out a particular rehabilitation program, they need to know whether it is working; whether, for example, people who go through the program go out and commit more crimes. I consider myself a toolmaker. I try to find or make a tool to measure recidivism. It's what we call methodology: I'm developing a new method that other people can use. I make the yardstick. How you measure with it and what you use it for is not my primary concern. If you want to see if giving convicts peanut butter sandwiches every other day works, you are welcome to use my yardstick to see if it does.

How might scholars in the field of psychology look at the same questions you do?

We're all concerned in some way with the relationship of individuals to state and the impact of the social structure we live with. Suppose a kid commits a crime. We can ask why did this kid commit a crime? Well, it may be because he is developmentally disabled, or because he got involved with lousy friends or peer group relations. Those are two different possibilities. In fact, both possibilities may be at work. From a psychological perspective, you could use psychology to study what happened within the psyche of that individual so that a propensity to commit crime developed. From a sociological perspective, you could look at the social environment and study the impact of the peer group, the high school, friends on the street. That's a social structure: semipermanent relationships among people that may be very much of an influence and cause people to commit crime. So if you are looking at causes for things happening, sometimes you look only at the individual; sometimes you look at the individual in the context of the social structure.

How often do you find yourself analyzing research and writing about your analyses?

These days, I analyze others' research more than I do my own, unfortunately. You get to a certain stage in your career and people in the field know about your research and they say, "Hey, this guy seems to know what he's talking about in this area. Let's send him all these articles we're thinking about publishing so he can tell us whether they're any good." So they descend on me. I see manuscripts in the mail: "Mike, take a look at this one, at that one, see if they're any good." Younger colleagues, and older colleagues for that matter, ask, "Mike, what do you think of the ideas in here? Do you think there are any holes in my arguments?" And so, what I end up doing is spending a lot of my time analyzing other people's work.

How can undergraduates begin to develop analyses of social research?

To some extent it means relying on what you already know. A lot of what gets published isn't worth the powder to blow it to you know where. A lot of bull gets published, and if you accept everything that is written in a journal just because somebody has a couple of degrees, what you are doing is not using your own brain. A lot of the stuff that I read is worthless. No matter how statistically significant it is, it's substantively insignificant.

Because I'm so critical of things I read, I tell students, "Don't be embarrassed to use your own ideas. You read something and if it sounds like bull to you, say it sounds like bull because of A,B,C,D, and E. Don't just say it for some empty reason but give your own reasons. Maybe the researcher doesn't really have a true picture of everything. A white *person talking about African Americans based on data from the Census Bureau might not realize that the African-American cultural experience causes people to behave in a certain way. There are so many people who use questionnaires to collect data and think that people in every single cultural context will respond in exactly the same way. That's not the case. Your experience counts. If your cultural context is different from the cultural context of the person collecting the data, then you may have a valid point to make.*

WRITING AND LEARNING ACTIVITIES

1. **Journal Entry:** The research discussed in this chapter is characterized in several ways: social science research, sociology, or sometimes quantitative research. Look up these terms in a specialized reference source (see Directions for Further Research in the appendix), a college dictionary, and a general reference encyclopedia. Consider the differences and similarities among the definitions. Report your findings to the class.

2. **Writing Activity:** Write three questions you would like to ask Professor Maltz if you had the opportunity to talk with him.

3. **Peer Conversation:** Discuss your journal entries and questions for Professor Maltz with a partner. Respond also to the following questions: Were you reminded by something he said of another experience you've had at home, school, or work? Have you experienced a shift in your interests like the one Professor Maltz experienced?

4. **Research Project:** Look up in your college catalog the description for the social research or sociology major. How is the discipline described? How does the description differ from Professor Maltz's description or from other definitions you've found? What are the required courses for that major? What are the possible areas of specialization? Next, interview some students who are majoring in sociology or social research. Why are they studying in this area? What courses have they taken? Are they specializing in any particular area? What do they plan to do with a sociology degree? Finally, attend a class with another student. Take notes on what you observe in the class and ask the student questions about what you observed.

5. **Writing:** Based on your research, write a report describing what it's like to major in social research or sociology at your school.

6. **Developing Interests:** Look through newspapers and popular magazines for reports of social research. What aspects of human social behavior do you have questions about? What research would you like to see conducted?

READING SOCIAL RESEARCH ON NEST-LEAVING

Suppose you wanted to know when and for what reasons young adults leave home in contemporary society? The piece that Professor Maltz will read with us, "Leaving the Parental Home: Patterns in Six Latin American Countries," by Susan De Vos, explores this question from a sociological perspective. The author used survey information to learn about patterns of nest-leaving. This research report is typical of much quantitative research found in a university library. It is divided into sections, each of which contains specific kinds of information about the study. Students often avoid quantitative research reports because they seem filled with uninterpretable numbers, graphs, and tables. Professor Maltz offer some strategies for reading and understanding these types of reports.

PLANNING TO READ SOCIAL RESEARCH ON NEST-LEAVING
Making Personal Connections

In many academic areas research is very specialized and a researcher might spend years looking at one problem. Professor Maltz has not read much research in this area so when he looks at the title, "Leaving the Parental Home: Patterns in Six Latin American Countries," he immediately wonders how he might relate to the information in the piece on a personal and professional level. He thought about his own children leaving home and also about a recent visit to Latin America. In whatever you read, you too will want to ask yourself what personal connections you can make to the subject.

This is something I might be interested in because I've got two kids who have supposedly left the nest. Actually, one has and the other is still working on it. I spent some time in Costa Rica this past summer. Here's a story about a joke I told in Costa Rica that bombed. It will tell you something important about cultural context. You know that old joke about when life begins? The priest, the minister, and the rabbi are all discussing when life begins. The priest says, "Life begins at conception." The minister says, "No. Life begins at the end of the first trimester when the fetus might be considered viable." The rabbi says, "No, both of you have it all wrong. Life begins when the kids move out and the dog dies."

That joke says something about my own background in terms of nest-leaving. I think it's a great joke and I agree with the rabbi. But the joke bombed entirely in Costa Rica because in that culture the children often want to stay with Momma and Poppa. The family I was living with had seven daughters, all of whom were very tightly tied to the mother, although the father was there in the usual support role. They could not understand the joke. So it's obvious that there are differences between what I consider to be the appropriate nest-leaving behavior and what they considered appropriate.

WRITING AND LEARNING ACTIVITIES

1. **Survey the Report:** Follow Professor Maltz as he takes a first pass through the reading.
2. **Journal Entry:** As you read the report and follow Professor Maltz's initial reading of it, take notes in your journal. What do you learn from looking over a research report before reading it closely?

Surveying the Text

Next Professor Maltz looks quickly through the entire research report. He explains that this procedure, surveying the text, is as important as the close reading he will do next. A quantitative research report offers certain types of information in each of its sections. Sometimes it is better to jump around and look for specific information. Here are the steps Professor Maltz follows as he surveys the text.

1. *I look for the author to see if I know the person or what he or she has written.*
2. *Then, I look to see what journal it's in; I want to see if I've heard of it.*
3. *I look at the date of the article. I need to know if the research is current in order to evaluate it.*
4. *The next thing I do is count the number of pages. I want to be able to plan to read it in one fell swoop and if I only have fifteen minutes and it's a thirty-page document then I'm not going to be able to.*
5. *After that I notice how the article is divided up. I see these sections:*
   Abstract (not labeled, but printed in italics)
   Introduction (also not labeled)
   Sociodemographic Factors in Leaving Home
   The Study (including data, method, variables, and findings)
   Discussion and Conclusion
   Notes
   References

As Professor Maltz surveys each of the sections, he finds some to be more important than others. As he proceeds, he stops to explain some technical terms and something about the research methods used in this report.

The Abstract.   Professor Maltz notices that this is a cross-sectional study.

There are two kinds of data you can collect for a study like this: longitudinal data or cross-sectional data. They are big words but the idea is really very simple: Longitudinal data means that you are studying the same group over time, over a long period. That's why it is called longitudinal—you take the long view. But De Vos is not doing that. She is looking at cross-sectional data to see how things change from country to country at the particular time the data was collected. From that she infers what must have happened in the past.

Professor Maltz next reads that the data comes from the World Fertility Survey.

This is a secondary analysis. The World Fertility Survey was collected in the mid-1970s for other reasons. They throw in lots of questions and I expect that those questions that might shed some light on nest-leaving were not originally put in there for the purpose of studying nest-leaving. She isn't following a group of people as they mature and leave home—that would be a longitudinal study.

Continuing on, Professor Maltz finds that the topic of the study will be the "sociodemographic determinants" of leaving home in six countries, but he also notes the purpose for the study.

I suppose I am going to learn about the "age, sex, marital status, urban/rural residence, education, and work status" of those who leave their parents' house in these six countries. The purpose of the study seems to be to get some basic idea (that's what they mean by "baseline") of what's going on so that future studies can take it from there.

Introduction and Sociodemographic Factors in Leaving Home.   Here the author does what is sometimes called a literature review. She tells you about all the other research that has been done up to this point on that topic. Some of the topics covered in the review concern marriage as a reason for leaving home, a concern for the age at which one leaves home, and how leaving home differs for males and females. By checking the in-text citations against the list of articles referenced at the end of the article you can find out the full titles of the works she is referring to and where they were published. In surveying the text, Professor Maltz simply glances through the section looking for what he calls key words.

Hmmm, lot's of new terms here but I think I can figure them out from the context. Neolocal residence. Hm-m-m. Neo means new. New local residence? I think it means that your new residence is close to your old residence. Now, stem family. . . . it looks like that's a situation in which young married couples do not leave home but stay in their parents' home instead. I'll have to come back to this on my second time through this report.

Data.   Professor Maltz quickly notices one thing about this section.

Huge numbers, lots of data here. That's why we need statistics. But even though there is lots of data. I hope De Vos will consider individual cases. When I have a large data set I always look at individual cases to bring me back to reality.

Method.   Professor Maltz doesn't slow down at all for this section. Even though he is a statistics expert and this section and the findings section discuss the statistics used in the research, he doesn't want to pay much attention to them.

I'm not that interested in this section. It has to do with what statistical techniques are used to determine which relationships are valid and which aren't. Normally, an article written by someone from a reputable university contains a minimally acceptable methodology. I'm not interested in what's under the hood. I'm interested in where the car is going.

Variables.   The variables in a study provide actual behaviors or situations through which the concept of nest-leaving can be described and measured. In this case the two most important variables are "being a child of the household head" and marital status.

I usually take a look at the variables since all the results are based on these behaviors or situations. Take something like education. It may be that some countries have better data than others. In fact, I notice here that it says there is no education data from Mexico; so anything that relates to Mexico will not have anything to do with education. Hmmm, urban versus rural for a place of residence. Is that a good dichotomy? What does it mean if you live in a suburb? In this country if you live in a suburb you've got some money. In other places, like Mexico, the slums are often located outside the city, so these distinctions can be tricky.

Findings.   This section contains the specific results of the statistical tests and can easily confuse you if you don't know statistics. As Professor Maltz surveys the report, he looks only for information that might tell him the results of the study. In addition, he always looks for statements that suggest that one thing causes another thing. He finds just such a statement and assures us that during his, next, more detailed reading, he will be looking for evidence that marriage indeed was the cause of leaving home.

> . . . marriage is probably the most important reason for leaving home. It is also consistent with the notion that marriage is associated with increased responsibility and independence (paragraph 22).

I would dispute that statement because De Vos is suggesting a causal relationship. She is saying that the reason one leaves home is that one gets married. It could be that the reason one gets married is that one has left home and is living alone and doesn't like it. Association does not imply causality.

Discussion and Conclusion.   Professor Maltz spends a good deal of time on the discussion section even though he is only surveying the text.

The next thing I do, even though I'm only quickly surveying the report, is read the discussion and conclusion section fairly carefully. It's only about a page and a half long, but it will tell me what she found. When I go back to read the paper more thoroughly I'll have her conclusions in the back of my mind and I can evaluate them as I go.

She talks about marriage as being the major reason for leaving the parental home. It would have been interesting to see figures of married versus unmarried. The other important finding is that young adults didn't stay in the home past 22 for the most part. I will definitely want to come back to this conclusion when I go through the report a second time. She goes on to tell us that parents want their sons to stay in the house because sons can contribute financially. I wonder if this conclusion really comes out of her data.

When he finishes surveying the text, Professor Maltz sits back and thinks about his process. This was the first time, he told us, that he had paid so much attention to what he did daily in his own work.

I guess I go back and forth a lot when I read this kind of research report, because I have to figure out if I believe the conclusion. I ask myself, "Could this conclusion be a reasonable outcome of her data?" The example I gave about male children being more likely to contribute and parents wanting sons to stay in the household longer, could not come out of her data. Maybe that's true. She's interested in this topic and she may have spent some time in Latin America. In fact, the next thing I would do is take a look at her list of references and see what else she has written.

WRITING AND LEARNING ACTIVITIES

1. **Reading:** Read De Vos's study of nest-leaving.
2. **Journal Entry:** Make notes about your reading process in your journal. Write down any questions you have about the reading and any familiar or unfamiliar terms you encounter. Also, note any places where you make connections to

your own experiences. Think about how the research of this discipline is different from that of other disciplines you have encountered in this class or other classes.

3. **Annotate the Text:** Mark the report to help you follow the research. Use highlighters to mark key points. Restate the researcher's claim in the margins. Put question marks where you don't understand something or where the text contradicts your personal experience.

LEAVING THE PARENTAL HOME: PATTERNS IN SIX LATIN AMERICAN COUNTRIES
SUSAN DE VOS

■ ■ ■

Using cross-sectional data from household files of the World Fertility Survey, this study explores sociodemographic determinants of leaving the parental household among young adults in Colombia, Costa Rica, the Dominican Republic, Mexico, Panama, and Peru in the mid-1970s. The article describes the relationships between being a child of a household head on the one hand and age, sex, marital status, urban/rural residence, education, and work status on the other, thus providing a baseline for future studies of the family life course of Latin Americans.

In many cultures an individual's transition from a family of orientation to a family of procreation involves leaving the parental household. In the West, young adults have tended to leave their family households of origin either prior to or at marriage (Goldscheider and Da Vanzo, 1985; Hajnal, 1982; Young, 1977). The preference here appears to be for separate living when housing is available and affordable (see Glick and Lin, 1986; Heer, Hodge, and Felson, 1985; Kiernan, 1986).

We know little about "leaving home" in Latin America, however.[1] Similar to our understanding of the European family before the 1960s, most of what we know applies only to an ideal followed by some wealthy families (Balmori, Voss, and Wortman, 1984). The ideal traditional Hispanic family in the New World was supposed to be patriarchal and extended, but people with more modest means had to accommodate such ideals to economic contingencies. However, we do not know how this has been done. Although we know that young adults, especially males, have not been expected to go through a period of service in someone else's household, and that conjugal couples tend to establish separate households except at young and old ages (De Vos, 1987), we do not know the typical age at which young adults are no longer members of their parents' household; nor how leaving the

---

From *Journal of Marriage and the Family* 51 (August 1989): 615–626.

parental household is related to marriage, gender, or urban/rural residence. Finally, we do not know how leaving a parental household might differ by education or work status.

This study establishes a baseline with which future changes or more detailed studies can be compared, by describing sociodemographic correlates of leaving home among young adults in six Latin American countries in the mid-1970s. The intent is to begin development of a "typical" family life course in Latin America and to see how it may be related to social change. Since it is the young who most often face new social developments, the leaving-home stage is particularly sensitive to social change, and it is particularly important to establish it with clarity.

SOCIODEMOGRAPHIC FACTORS IN LEAVING HOME

Since neolocal residence appears to be the norm among most age groups, the major reason for leaving the parental household in Latin America is most probably marriage and the added responsibility and independence it entails. Still, there is some evidence, both historical and for contemporary society, of married young adults forming at least temporary stem families (e.g., Deere, 1978; Lomnitz and Lizaur, 1978). It stands to reason that this pattern is most likely when it is in the interest of both parents and children to continue sharing living arrangements even when the child marries (see Thornton and Fricke, 1987)—for instance, when a married child is still financially dependent on his or her parents or where there is a potential or actual transfer of property (as when a son would inherit a right to the farm or family business). Where such interest does not exist—for instance, where second and higher-order siblings are not needed to maintain a family enterprise—marriage probably heralds a household separation. Were children to stay, they would remain under the control of the parental head.

5   Age is probably independently important because a temporary stem family will split over time for such reasons as an increasing need for space (see Deere, 1978). While grandparents may be able to accommodate one or even two grandchildren in their abode, they are less likely to be able to accommodate three or four. Also, never-married young adults might leave over time for such reasons as domestic conflict, the inability of a parent to continue caring for the young adult, national service, ideas about economic opportunities elsewhere (see Goldscheider and Da Vanzo, 1985; Young, 1977), or simply to manage their own affairs. Finally, the risk of parents dying increases with age.

It is reasonable to expect leaving home to differ between males and females because sons and daughters are usually expected to perform different household tasks (Le Vine and Le Vine, 1985; Tienda, 1979). While female tasks tend to involve "domestic duties," male tasks are usually oriented toward supporting the household economically. Whereas daughters may be considered an economic drain, sons may be seen as productive resources. As a result, parents may be less inclined to "let go" of sons. In fact, a daughter may leave at a rather early age to become a household servant (perhaps to send back some of her pay to her family in a rural area), whereas such a departure would be uncommon for a son (see, e.g., Arizpe, 1977; Butterworth and Chance, 1981; Cross-Beras, 1980; Jelin, 1977).

Young adults are probably more likely to remain for a longer time in a parental household in rural as opposed to urban areas because of the different economies of the two areas and the relationship between the economy and household structure. The potential labor contribution of a young adult to the parental household may be higher in rural areas, especially if the family owns or has rights to land (see Tienda, 1979) and is therefore motivated to try to "hang on" to children. In contrast, even when young adults in urban areas find remuneration, it is harder for parents to control it. Although some urban youths are employed in family-owned businesses, it is more common for labor to be "sold" in a market.

Insofar as a majority of young people in Latin America have not gone past about eight years of school, education cannot be as important a reason for staying at home there as in the United States (Goldscheider and Da Vanzo, 1985). Even so, education in Latin America can be associated with leaving home. First, some people over 15 years are, of course, still in school and living at home. A more important point is that education helps indicate social status, and young adults in different strata may behave differently. For instance, parents in higher strata may be better able to afford keeping children at home, whereas parents in lower strata may have to let children fend for themselves as soon as they are able. The idea of a dependent adolescent period is also more consistent with a middle-class value system.

To the extent that residence and education are changing with each new cohort, those factors could also help indicate social change. Young people in particular are moving from rural to urban areas and are getting a better education. Thus, if the likelihood of remaining in the parental home is greater among residents of the major metropolitan areas and among people with more education, this may suggest a general trend toward staying at home for a longer time.

THE STUDY

Data

10   The data for this study come from the household files of the World Fertility Survey and were gathered in the middle 1970s in Mexico, Costa Rica, the Dominican Republic, Panama, Colombia, and Peru.[2] Samples are nationally representative of the de jure household populations. We include only never-married or currently married (including "in union") individuals, thus omitting the small proportion of formerly married persons[3] and those who are married but whose spouse is absent. The final samples of persons from 15 to 29 years of age in the six countries contain 18,089, 6,513, 13,832, 5,489, 14,755, and 9,856 individuals, respectively. (For more on the data, see De Vos, 1985, or Kabir, 1980).

Method

The ideal way to study the "leaving home" stage is to use longitudinal data (e.g., Goldscheider and Da Vanzo, 1985; Hill and Hill, 1976). The next best is to use retrospective data (e.g., Young, 1977). When these approaches are not feasible, information on a person's duration in his or her present state still enables one to use survival analysis. Unfortunately, we are limited to cross-sectional data that provide information on an individual's current state only. We must therefore formulate a synthetic cohort and assume that a person has permanently left the parental household if that person is not a child of the household head.

Although these assumptions enable us to use multivariate techniques, it is first important to examine bivariate relationships. To do this, we look at frequency distributions, the Cramer's V measure of association[4] (Loether and McTavish, 1974: 192–202), Pearson's R, and a bivariate logit association. The former two measures can be used for discrete variables, while the latter two are appropriate for measuring associations between two-category or continuous variables.

Since our major interest is in net, multivariate effects, we estimate additive models in a stepwise manner. We first fail to control, and then control, marital status, and finally add a variable for work status in Colombia and Mexico (the two countries for which information on work status is available). The purpose of the first two steps is to ascertain whether (and by how much) a factor that is significant before controlling for marital status is also significant afterward, because people with various characteristics tend to marry at different ages (McCarthy, 1982).

Logit regression is used for the multivariate analyses because the dependent variable is dichotomous (being a child/not a child), and logit regression solves the problem of heteroscedasticity in an error term that would occur with OLS. In the logit model, the dependent variable is the log of its likelihood: log $(P/1\text{-}P)$ (Hanushek and Jackson, 1977). Following common practice, we transform the estimated effects from their log to their antilog form to make them more interpretable. We use the GLIM software package (Baker and Nelder, 1978).

The Variables

15 **Being a Child of the Household Head**   Since the household files list an individual's "generation" relative to the household head, we dichotomize our sample according to whether or not the person is in the child's or grandchild's generation. Spouses of a child (or grandchild) are also considered "children." All others are "nonchildren" (including "nonrelatives" of the household head).[5]

Marital Status   Young adults are either never-married or currently married. People in consensual unions are considered "married" even if not "officially" so. Conversely, people who were reported as married but were not living with a spouse (even on a de jure basis) are not considered "currently married" but "married, spouse absent" (De Vos, 1985). They, and people reported as formerly married, are excluded.

Age   Age is coded in completed single years.

Sex   The coding of sex is straightforward.

Residence   Except in the Dominican Republic, residence is coded in three categories: the major metropolitan area, other urban areas, and rural areas (see United Nations, 1986). In the Dominican Republic, data limitations required the use of the less informative urban/rural dichotomy.

20 *Education*   Education has four categories: less than primary school, primary school, some secondary school, and secondary school or more. This codification appears to be more accurate than single years (De Vos, 1985) and provides as much explanatory power as a six-category variable. Education data were absent in the Mexican file.

Work Status   Information on work status was only available for Mexico and Colombia. In Mexico, people were simply listed as "working" or "not working." In Colombia, they were "working," a "student," or "not working."[6]

Findings

Marital Status   As predicted, marital status was an important determinant of whether or not a young adult 15–29 years of age was still living in the parental household in all six countries. In the bivariate case, marital status was strongly related to whether someone was still living at home ($V = 0.56$–0.68; Table 1). While over 80 % of the never-married young adults were children of the household head, 26 % or fewer married young adults were still living in the parental household. In the Dominican Republic, in fact, this was less than 11 %. In the multivariate case, married individuals were 0.05–0.13 as likely to still be a child of the household head (Equations 2, Table 3). This is consistent with the findings of Goldscheider and Da Vanzo (1985) for the United States and of Young (1977) for Australia, in that marriage is probably the most important reason for leaving home. It is also consistent with the notion that marriage is associated with increased responsibility and independence.

Controlling for marital status changed the effects of age, sex, residence, and education; thus it is important to examine effects before as well as after controlling for marital status (compare Equations 1 and 2 of Table 3).

The Effect of Age   In Latin America, most dependent children live in a parental household but leave that household during young adulthood. Although children may actually be stepchildren of the household head (legally or not), there is no indication that child fosterage is as common, say, as in parts of Africa (e.g., Isiugo-Abanihe, 1985). From an unweighted average of roughly 97 % at the age of 10, to roughly 11 % at the age of 34, there is a clear decline in the proportion of individuals 10–34 years of age who live in a parent's household in the six Latin American countries (Table 2). This pattern is graphed in Figure 1. It seems clear that the six countries are quite similar.

TABLE 1.   Percentage of Persons Aged 15–29 Reported as a Child of the Household Head, by Various Characteristics, and Bivariate Associations: Six Latin American Countries in the Mid-1970s

VARIABLE	COLOMBIA[a]	COSTA RICA	DOMINICAN REPUBLIC	MEXICO	PANAMA	PERU[a]
Sex						
Male	67.5	73.4	65.9	67.5	71.4	70.9
Female	53.0	57.5	44.9	55.0	53.8	60.0
Cramer's V	.15	.17	.21	.13	.18	.11
Pearson's R	−.16	−.17	−.22	−.13	−.19	−.12
Marital status						
Single	81.4	86.9	79.8	87.9	85.6	83.0
Married	13.5	18.6	10.5	20.6	17.3	25.8
Cramer's V	.64	.67	.66	.68	.67	.56
Pearson's R	−.65	−.67	−.67	−.68	−.67	−.56
Urban status						
Capital city	55.5	62.3	51.4	57.0	58.5	61.9
Other urban	61.2	69.1		60.3	67.5	64.7
Rural	60.0	66.1	60.3	63.9	66.6	70.1
Cramer's V	.04	.05	.09	.06	.09	.07
Education						
Less than primary graduate	54.0	54.7	53.8		51.4	54.5
Primary graduate	57.5	66.5	57.4		57.8	59.8
Some secondary	71.2	76.4	68.4		73.4	75.3
Secondary graduate	61.1	64.4	54.7		60.3	70.9
Cramer's V	.15	.16	.09		.18	.18
Working status						
Working	56.1			87.9		
Student	91.4					
Not working	46.0			20.6		
Cramer's V	.33			.68		
Total	60.0	65.6	55.7	61.2	63.1	64.2

	SAMPLE SIZE					
Sex						
Male	7,080	3,311	7,102	8,953	2,905	4,867
Female	7,673	3,216	6,730	9,136	2,590	4,989
Marital status						
Single	10,264	4,490	9,016	10,910	3,685	6,816
Married	4,491	2,037	4,816	7,192	1,810	3,040
Urban status						
Capital city	2,018	1,971	7,092	4,602	2,453	3,183
Other urban	7,436	1,350		4,761	696	3,748
Rural	5,300	3,206	6,740	8,739	2,346	2,925
Education						
Less than primary graduate	6,972	1,652	10,073		944	2,930
Primary graduate	2,421	2,246	1,188		1,428	1,672
Some secondary	4,103	1,571	1,428		2,094	2,749
Secondary graduate	1,258	1,058	1,143		1,029	2,504
Working status						
Working	6,977			10,900		
Student	2,988					
Not working	4,790			7,189		
Total	14,755	6,527	13,832	18,089	5,495	9,856

SOURCE: World Fertility Survey, Household File.

NOTE: The term *child of the household head* includes anyone, including in-laws, in the child's or grand-child's generation vis-à-vis the head of the household. The chi-squares for all the relationships are significant ($p < .05$).

[a]Figures for Colombia and Peru are based on weighted counts.

TABLE 2. Percentage of Persons Reported as a Child of the Household Head, by Age, and Bivariate Correlations Between Age (15–29) and the Likelihood of Being a Child of the Head

Age	Colombia[a]	Costa Rica	Dominican Republic	Mexico	Panama	Peru[a]
10	97	98	94	98	98	98
11	97	98	94	98	98	97
12	96	97	91	98	97	95
13	94	97	92	97	97	96
14	92	96	90	95	95	92
15	91	93	85	93	91	91
16	87	92	83	90	91	87
17	82	84	81	88	85	85
18	77	83	71	81	83	82
19	70	80	67	76	75	79
20	65	74	59	67	71	72
21	62	64	55	62	69	70
22	54	60	48	54	54	62
23	47	55	41	45	51	56
24	42	43	35	42	42	52
25	39	41	28	35	40	44
26	30	32	26	28	33	36
27	26	34	20	30	28	35
28	23	30	17	24	23	29
29	17	20	14	21	18	19
30	22	20	12	20	17	23
31	15	17	8	11	9	16
32	13	13	5	16	12	14
33	11	11	9	10	16	15
34	10	12	6	11	14	11
Pearson's R	−0.48*	−0.47*	−0.47*	−0.52*	−0.50*	−0.45*
Logit effect of age (15–29)	0.78*	0.76*	0.77*	0.74*	0.76*	0.78*
			Sample Size			
10	1,642	734	1,810	2,246	695	1,154
11	1,367	685	1,536	1,970	613	962
12	1,731	724	1,702	2,147	645	1,212
13	1,569	702	1,487	1,961	622	1,007
14	1,524	621	1,482	1,929	579	978
15	1,334	637	1,363	1,800	562	958
16	1,368	606	1,277	1,688	518	945
17	1,271	575	1,272	1,616	453	940
18	1,291	598	1,320	1,626	519	938
19	1,061	508	1,074	1,314	410	662
20	1,150	487	1,132	1,377	359	719
21	879	423	714	1,024	349	660
22	963	407	891	1,315	341	736
23	847	385	828	1,206	327	618
24	824	390	747	1,021	299	554
25	883	360	792	1,113	304	596
26	728	301	622	1,041	257	500
27	722	299	559	820	286	443
28	726	319	606	967	282	497
29	561	218	483	777	223	418
30	840	307	685	1,084	312	533
31	350	167	277	560	193	305
32	569	264	476	762	226	441
33	486	225	361	703	229	328
34	451	196	368	606	221	316
Total	25,137	11,138	23,864	32,673	9,824	17,418

Source: World Fertility Survey, Household File.

Note: Logit effects are transformed to their multiplicative (natural antilog) form.

[a]Figures for Colombia and Peru are based on weighted counts.

*Significant at $p < .05$.

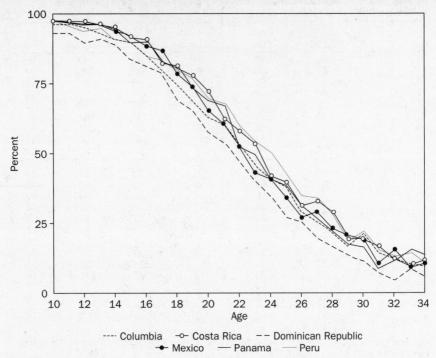

Figure 1. Percentage of Persons in Child's Generation, by Age, in Six Latin American Countries

25   The age at which half the individuals no longer live in a parent's household is 22 in the Dominican Republic, 23 in Colombia and Mexico, 24 in Costa Rica and Panama, and 25 in Peru. (The Pearson's *R* correlation between age [15–29] and being a child of the household head is within the narrow range of −0.45 and −0.52. The bivariate logit is 0.74–0.78.) This pattern is roughly similar to the historical sample for Rhode Island in which LeBourdais and Goldscheider (1986) found that "half the men who reached age 16 between 1920 and 1939 were still living with their parents at age 26." The proportion of women who still lived with their parents was 37% (p. 143).

The multivariate effect of age is shown in Table 3. Before marital status is controlled, the effects are very similar to the bivariate ones. Controlling additionally for marital status greatly decreases this effect (to 0.85–0.88), although it still remains important. Presumably, such factors as parental mortality, greater housing needs, the desire to control one's own life, and a general expectation that older young adults leave parental households even if not yet married are important.

It was speculated that work status could help to explain why age would be correlated with living separately from parents, as a working young adult could afford to live on his or her own. This expectation was not supported by the data. In Colombia, work status explains only a little of the age effect; in Mexico, it explains even less (Table 3).[7] It is still reasonable to speculate,

TABLE 3. The Effect of Age, Sex, Residence, Education, Marital Status, and Work Status on the Likelihood of Being a Child of the Household Head

VARIABLE	COLOMBIA[a]			COSTA RICA		DOMINICAN REPUBLIC		MEXICO			PANAMA		PERU[a]	
	1	2	3	1	2	1	2	1	2	3	1	2	1	2
Age	0.77	0.87	0.90	0.75	0.86	0.74	0.88	0.74	0.87	0.86	0.74	0.85	0.76	0.86
Sex														
Male	1.00	1.00	1.00	1.00	1.00	1.00	1.00	1.00	1.00	1.00	1.00	1.00	1.00	1.00
Female	0.47	0.66	0.46	0.40	0.51	0.31	0.65	0.47	0.54	0.68	0.32	0.54	0.67	0.88
Residence														
Capital	1.00	1.00	1.00	1.00	1.00	1.00	1.00	1.00	1.00	1.00	1.00	1.00	1.00	1.00
Other urban	1.58	1.75	1.62	1.33	1.63	1.82		1.09	1.21	1.21	1.44	1.76	1.35	1.49
Rural	2.10	2.73	2.45	1.24	1.74	2.63		1.33	2.50	2.52	2.15	3.07	3.80	5.27
Education														
<Primary graduate	1.00	1.00	1.00	1.00	1.00	1.00	1.00				1.00	1.00	1.00	1.00
Primary graduate	1.21	1.29	1.27	1.20	1.23	1.54	1.32				1.13	0.94	1.69	1.66
>Primary <secondary	2.05	2.06	1.68	1.61	1.68	2.40	1.70				2.42	2.02	5.05	2.86
Secondary graduate +	2.87	2.12	1.79	2.21	1.92	2.71	1.46				3.41	2.59	6.63	4.63
Marital status														
Never married	1.00	1.00	1.00	1.00	1.00	1.00	1.00	1.00	1.00	1.00		1.00		1.00
Currently married	0.06	0.06	0.06	0.06	0.06	0.05	0.05	0.06	0.06	0.05		0.07		0.13
Work status														
Working			1.00							1.00				
Student			3.07											
Not working			2.24							1.60				

NOTE: Effects are reported as (natural multiplicative) antilogs. Thus in Colombia, females aged 15–29 are only 0.47 as likely as males aged 15–29 to be a child of the household head, when age, residence, and education are controlled. The chi-squares for all the relationships are significant ($p < .05$).

*Figures for Colombia and Peru are based on weighted counts.

however, that the search for work or better-paying work increases with age and explains part of the relationship of age to leaving home.

Sex   Consistent with our reasoning that males would stay in the parental household longer than females because they are more highly valued economically, sex was found to be an important correlate of whether young adults were still living at home. In the bivariate case (Table 1), females were only slightly less likely to be a "child" of the head of the household ($V = .11-.21$); but in the multivariate case when age was controlled (but before controlling for marital status) females were only 0.3–0.5 times as likely as males to still be a "child" of the household head (Equations 1 of Table 3). Marital status explains part of the effect, since at any age more females tend to be married than males, but a significant effect remains (Equations 2). This was found also by Goldscheider and DaVanzo (1985) for the United States, although they did not attempt to explain why the effect existed.

In Colombia and Mexico, work status explained part of the sex differential, as could be expected, since people who were reported as "working" were predominantly male (figures not shown). But even after all the controls were calculated, the sex differential remained highly significant (compare Equations 1, 2 and 3 of Table 3).

30 ***Urban/Rural Residence***   Consistent with the idea that parents in rural areas may find it more beneficial to "hang on" to children, and with the idea that stem families are more common in rural areas because some families control the use of limited land, residents of rural areas were much more likely to be living in households headed by their parents than were urban residents. In the bivariate case, residents of rural areas were about as likely to live with parents as were residents of other areas (Table 1; $V = .04-.09$), but this was largely due to the different demographic compositions of the areas. After age, sex, and education (except in Mexico) were controlled, there was substantial disparity between rural and urban residents (Table 3). Further controlling for marital status enhanced the effect of residence (Equations 2). In Peru, for instance, residents of rural areas were more than five times as likely as residents of Lima to be living in the parental household. For Colombia and Mexico, residence did not change substantially when work status was controlled.

Education   The expectation that education would be positively related to the likelihood of still living in a parental household was supported. In the bivariate case, there was a positive relationship between living at home and having an education up to completion of secondary school, but among secondary school graduates there appeared to be a slight decline in this tendency, probably because they would be older, on average (Table 1). After age, sex, and residence were controlled, however, this curvilinearity was ironed out (controlling for age would take away the aforementioned problem). Young adults with a secondary education or more were most likely to be living in the parental household, in the five countries with education data

(Mexico did not have such data) (Table 3). Persons in this group would be most likely to live in middle-class families that believed in such notions as an "adolescence" and would also be best able to afford maintaining a young adult child's residence.

Although the effect of education was reduced after marital status was controlled (compare Equations 1 and 2 of Table 3), it stayed highly significant. The reduction is not surprising, given that age at marriage rises with education (McCarthy, 1982). In Colombia, the effect of education was reduced after work status was controlled, but this was primarily due to the variable's incorporation of information on school attendance.

Work Status   As might be expected if one assumed a preference for independent living, work had an important negative relationship with the likelihood of living in the parental household in Colombia and Mexico, the two countries with data on work status. This relationship was not evident in the bivariate association, mainly because females do not "work." When other factors were controlled, however, the likelihood of living at home was 0.45 in Colombia and 0.63 in Mexico if one worked, as opposed to not working.

Although controlling for work status substantially reduced the effect of sex (compare Equations 2 and 3 in Table 3), work did not help explain much of the effects of age, residence, or marital status. This is probably because young people are motivated to work whether or not they live in rural or urban areas, and irrespective of their marital status.

DISCUSSION AND CONCLUSION

This study has examined the effects of several sociodemographic variables on the likelihood that young adults (mainly 15–29 years old) were still living in a parental household in several Latin American countries in the mid-1970s. The short-term purpose has been to provide an initial survey and baseline by which future studies could be compared. The long-term goal is to help document the family life course of individuals in Latin America and to describe how such a life course fits into the larger social structure. To some extent, this process entails comparison with other societies. Although relatively little research has been done on the "leaving home" stage in Latin America, I would suggest that the situation might not be too different from that in the United States earlier in this century, as described by LeBourdais and Goldscheider (1986).

The data used in the present study indicate that being married was the major reason for no longer living in the parental home, which is consistent with the idea that marriage in Latin America is associated with the acquisition of new responsibilities and independence. When variables of age, sex, residence, and education were controlled, married individuals were only 0.06–0.13 times as likely to be children of the household head as were never-married young adults. At the same time, some married young adults were still living in the parental household, which may be seen as evidence of a stem-family system; but since most middle-aged married males headed their own households (De Vos, 1987) this arrangement was probably temporary. (This interpretation is reinforced by the finding that age is significant even after marital status is controlled.)

A second major finding is that half the young adults were no longer living in the parental household by their early twenties. The median age was a minimum of about 22 years, in the Dominican Republic, and a maximum of about 25 years, in Peru. In a multivariate analysis, young adults were between 0.85 and 0.88 times as likely to be living in the parental household with each year of increase in age. Age is important because married people might not "split off" from a parental household until their own children are born, while never-married young people might leave home when they are deemed old enough to fend for themselves, despite being unmarried, to "explore" the world or to serve in the military.

Factors associated with sex, urban/rural residence, education, and work are also important. Females were less likely to remain in the parental household because male children are considered more likely to contribute economically to the household, and parents want sons to stay in the household longer. Household economics (as well as values) also differ significantly between urban and rural areas. Family businesses that transfer resources between generations, such as farms, are more prevalent in rural areas, and young adults are more likely to be tied to a parental household there. Unpaid family labor is also more common in rural areas. Education was negatively related to leaving home. Parents of educated children (e.g., of the middle class) adhere more to the Western notion of adolescence and have the resources with which to carry it out. Finally, young adults who were reported as "working" were more likely to live apart from a parent.

In "developing" societies such as these, residence and education might help indicate social change because there has been significant rural-to-urban migration and because education is being upgraded. If the data had shown a tendency toward less or more co-residence with urban living and increased education, we would have had an indication that leaving home was related to social change in the same way. These analyses indicate, however, that individuals in more "developed" social sectors (residents of the major metropolitan areas or those with more education) had contradictory tendencies toward living independently. On the one hand, urban residents tended to be less likely to be living in the parental household; on the other, people with more education tended to be more likely.

40   This leads me to wonder whether the "development" paradigm is applicable to change in Latin America. Others have questioned the paradigm, with regard to urbanization in particular, noting that many characteristics of urbanism in Latin America appear to differ from what was expected, given a simple application of "development" theory (see, e.g., Butterworth and Chance, 1981). On the other hand, education is one of the strongest correlates of modernity that we know of (see, e.g., Inkeles, 1983). It may be among the better educated, then, that a movement toward staying in the

parental home longer is occurring, although this speculation needs confirmation by a study of the situation at different times. Also, there has been some suggestion that class disparities are growing in Latin America and that one should not expect all change to occur in the same direction. My findings could also be consistent with that view.

While the present findings also point to similarities among the Latin American countries, differences should be noted. The most striking, perhaps, are those between the Dominican Republic and Peru, the two least socioeconomically developed of the six countries. A stem-family arrangement appeared most common in Peru, where over one-quarter of the married young adults were still living in parents' households, compared to less than 11 % in the Dominican Republic. It is probably of import that the Dominican Republic, although influenced by Hispanic culture, is also influenced by a Caribbean culture, whereas much of Peru has been Andean in nature. "National" differences should not be overemphasized, however, because cultural lines do not coincide with national boundaries. These data have been exceedingly frustrating in their lack of information on ethnicity. Still, given what the data have disclosed, this is a modest limitation indeed.

NOTES

The author is grateful for the permission of the statistical offices in Colombia, Costa Rica, Dominican Republic, Mexico, Panama, and Peru to use World Fertility Survey data to study household structure in Latin America. The project was funded in part by NICHD Center Grant HD18788. Beverly Rowe, former head of the Computer and Archive Division of the World Fertility Survey, graciously facilitated access to the data. Cheryl Knobeloch provided assistance in data handling; Kerry Richter, research assistance; and Barbara Corry, editorial assistance. Anonymous reviewers provided helpful comments on earlier versions of the article. Facilities of the Center for Demography and Ecology of the University of Wisconsin–Madison, funded by NICHD Center Grant HD05876 and the Hewlett Foundation, are also gratefully acknowledged.

1. In fact, we know little about the family in Latin America. A paucity of information forced Goode (1970) to omit the region from his study of the family worldwide. Nor has the situation improved much since then, although there is potential for information on the household to provide insights into the family (see Torrado, 1981). Works such as those edited by Das and Jesser (1980) have made important inroads but also underscore how little we know.

2. Except for Peru, which could be considered a "less developed" area, these countries tend to be part of "middle developed" Latin America (Miró and Potter, 1981). Diverse in many respects, they may help to represent Latin America as a whole.

3. Formerly married individuals were found to be much more likely than married individuals to be in the "child's" generation vis-à-vis the household head in all six countries. Since they would be more likely to move back into a parental household after having left it during marriage, these cases were omitted. Individuals in the sample are also "at risk" of having moved in and

out of the parental household but are assumed by the study to be much less likely to have done so.

4. Cramer's V is defined as $\sqrt{\frac{\chi^2}{N^t}}$, where t is the smaller of the two quantities, (number of rows − 1) or (number of columns − 1). Although there is no measure of association between nominal variables that has the ideal properties held by Pearson's R, Cramer's V does have the advantage that its maximum value is normed at 1.0 even for tables that are not square. The values of Cramer's V should be interpreted as showing the relative strength of the association between two variables on a scale of zero to one.

5. Although the situation is rare, it should be pointed out that headship (or being the wife of the head) is not synonymous with no longer living with a parent. If a parent turned over headship to the child, then the child could be considered a household head even if he/she still lived with a parent.

6. For Colombia, a two-category work status variable comparable to the one for Mexico had much less explanatory power than when the "student" category was left separate. There is little reason to make the variable comparable to the Mexican one because the Mexican data file does not have information on education.

7. "Work status" had little impact in Colombia primarily because younger individuals were more likely to be students.

REFERENCES

Arizpe, Lourdes. (1977). "Women in the informal labor sector: The case of Mexico City." *Signs* 3: 25–37.

Baker, R. J., and J. A. Nelder. (1978). *The GLIM System Release 3 Generalised Linear Interactive Modelling Manual,* Oxford, England: The Royal Statistical Society and Numerical Algorithms Group.

Balmori, Diana, Stuart F. Voss, and Miles Wortman. (1984). *Notable Family Networks in Latin America.* Chicago: University of Chicago Press.

Butterworth, Douglas, and John K. Chance. (1981). *Latin American Urbanization.* Cambridge, England: Cambridge University Press.

Cross-Beras, Julio A. (1980). "The Dominican family." Chapter 8 in Man Singh Das and Clinton J. Jesser (eds.), *The Family in Latin America.* New Delhi: Vikas Publishing House.

Das, Man Singh, and Clinton J. Jesser (eds.). (1980). *The Family in Latin America.* New Delhi: Vikas Publishing House.

Deere, Carmen Diana. (1978). "The differentiation of the peasantry and family structure: A Peruvian case study." *Journal of Family History* 3: 422–438.

De Vos, Susan. (1985). "Using World Fertility Survey data to study household composition: An example of Latin America." *CDE Working Paper* 85–22, Center for Demography and Ecology, University of Wisconsin–Madison.

De Vos, Susan. (1987). "Latin American households in comparative perspective." *Population Studies* 41: 501–517.

Glick, Paul C., and Sung-Ling Lin. (1986). "More young adults are living with their parents: Who are they?" *Journal of Marriage and the Family* 48: 107–112.

Goldscheider, Frances Kobrin, and Julie Da Vanzo. (1985). "Living arrangements and the transition to adulthood." *Demography* 22: 545–563.

Goode, William. (1970). *World Revolution and Family Patterns,* New York: Free Press.

Hajnal, John. (1982). "Two kinds of preindustrial household formation systems." *Population and Development Review* 8: 449–494.

Hanushek, Eric A., and John E. Jackson. (1977). "Models with discrete dependent variables." Chapter 7 (pp. 179–216) in *Statistical Methods for Social Scientists.* New York: Academic Press.

Heer, David M., Robert W. Hodge, and Marcus Felson. (1985). "The cluttered nest: Evidence that young adults are more likely to live at home now than in the recent past." *Sociology and Social Research* 69: 436–441.

Hill, Daniel, and Martha Hill. (1976). "Older children and splitting off." Chapter 4 in *Five Thousand American Families; Patterns of Economic Progress* (Vol. 4). Ann Arbor: Institute for Social Research, University of Michigan.

Inkeles, Alex. (1983). *Exploring Individual Modernity.* New York: Columbia University Press.

Islugo-Abanihe, U. C. (1985). "Child fosterage in West Africa." *Population and Development Review* 11: 53–73.

Jelin, Elizabeth. (1977). "Migration and labor force participation of Latin American women: The domestic servants in the cities." *Signs* 3: 129–141.

Kabir, Mohammad. (1980). *The Demographic Characteristics of Household Populations,* WFS Comparative Studies No. 6. The Hague, Netherlands: International Statistical Institute.

Kiernan, Kathleen E. (1986). "Leaving home: Living arrangements of young people in six West-European countries." *European Journal of Population* 2: 177–184.

LeBourdais, Celine, and Frances Kobrin Goldscheider. (1986). "The decline in age at leaving home, 1920–1979." *Sociology and Social Research* 70: 143–145.

LeVine, Sarah, and Robert A. LeVine. (1985). "Age, gender, and the demographic transition: The life course in agrarian societies." Pp. 29–42 in Alice S. Rossi (ed.), *Gender and the Life Course.* New York: Aldine.

Loether, Herman J., and Donald G. McTavish. (1974). *Descriptive Statistics for Sociologists.* Boston: Allyn and Bacon.

Lomnitz, Larissa A., and Marisol Perez Lizaur. (1978). "The history of a Mexican urban family." *Journal of Family History* 3: 392–409.

McCarthy, James. (1982). *Differentials in Age at Marriage.* WFS Comparative Studies No. 19. Voorburg, Netherlands: International Statistical Institute.

Miro, Carmen A., and Joseph E. Potter. (1980). *Population Policy: Research Priorities in the Developing World.* London: Frances Pinter.

Thornton, Arland, and Thomas Fricke. (1987). "Social change and the family: Comparative perspectives from the West, China, and South Asia." *Sociological Forum* 2: 726–749.

Tienda, Martin. (1979). "Economic activity of children in Peru: Labor force behavior in rural and urban contexts." *Rural Sociology* 44: 370–391.

Torrado, Susana. (1981). "Estrategias familiares de vida en America Latina: La familia como unidad de investigacion censal (primera parte)" ["Family living strategies in Latin America: The family as a unit of investigation in the census (first part)"]. *Notas de Poblacion* No. 26, pp. 55–106.

United Nations. (1986). *Rural-Urban Residence and Fertility: Selected Findings from the World Fertility Survey Data.* Prepared by the Population Division, Department of International Economic and Social Affairs (ESA/P/WP/95). New York: United Nations.

Young, Christabel M. (1977). "Ages, reasons and sex differences for children leaving home." Chapter 6 in *The Family Life Cycle.* Australian Family Formation Project Monograph 6. Canberra: Australian National University.

A CLOSE READING OF A RESEARCH REPORT ON NEST-LEAVING

As Professor Maltz surveyed the research report, he moved quickly over certain sections and spent more time on others, looking for trouble spots, for questions he would want to answer for himself.

When I read something like this, the question in the back of my mind to the author is, "How do you know?" And then, "How do you know you know?" I tell my students, if you read a paper and you can find holes in it, that may mean that the paper is well written. The papers that you can't find any holes in are often the ones that are so mushy and amorphous that you really can't analyze them.

During the second, thorough reading Professor Maltz identifies four major areas that trouble him and about which he has questions: (1.) De Vos doesn't adequately define the key concept of leaving home; (2.) De Vos doesn't adequately consider the gender variable; (3.) the survey questions in her study may not have considered the cultural context adequately; and (4.) the study is limited by cross-sectional data.

Problem 1: De Vos Doesn't Adequately Define the Key Concept of Leaving Home

As Professor Maltz reads the research report for a second time, he asks himself, "What's the big idea De Vos is exploring here?"

Almost anyone would agree that leaving home is a transition, but in the context of this research report we need to know in very specific terms what that transition means. In this sort of social research one of the most important activities is taking a general concept like leaving home and determining specific behaviors that define it. In the broadest sense, when reading this research report we should have some idea of what "leaving the parental home" or nest-leaving means. As I read the introductory section and the one labeled "Sociodemographic Factors in Leaving Home," I should be getting a clear picture of the basic concept or idea at work here.

In the first sentence of her introduction, De Vos talks about an "individual's transition from a family of orientation to a family of procreation" (paragraph 1). From this paragraph it seems that she defines leaving home in terms of marriage, that is, moving from the family in which you are the child to a family in which you are making (or procreating) the child.

Professor Maltz is drawn back to the portion of the discussion he mentioned earlier where De Vos claims,

> Females were less likely to remain in the parental household because male children are considered more likely to contribute economically to the household, and parents want sons to stay in the household longer (paragraph 38).

Now I start to question the whole thrust of the article. Does she assume that leaving home is an act of dependence or independence? Leaving home can have two different meanings. If you send your daughters out to work for another family, you are not letting go of them. When you get married and stay with your family have you become more independent? Per-

haps not. One could also look at the transition from leaving one's home to marriage as moving from one kind of dependence to another or moving from one nest to another. At this point I have to ask whether she's not confusing the act or behavior of leaving home with the idea of becoming more independent. The act and the concept may be two different things. In social research we would ask, "How is she operationalizing the concept of leaving home?" I'm not sure I have the answer.

You can see how important it is to question the ideas on which studies in social research are based. It might be useful to ask about any research report: Do I understand how the researcher has defined and explained the research question?

Problem 2: De Vos Doesn't Adequately Consider the Gender Variable

Who are the people included in this study? In the section labeled "Data," De Vos tells us that she only included those who are currently married and couples who are not married but are living together. She leaves out those who are divorced or whose spouse is not living in the house. The small superscript 3 tells us that more information is included in the notes at the end of the report. Here's the text of that end note:

> [3]Formerly married individuals were found to be much more likely than married individuals to be in the "child's" generation vis-à-vis the household head in all six countries. Since they would be more likely to move back into a parental household after having left it during marriage, these cases were omitted. Individuals in the sample are also "at risk" of having moved in and out of the parental household but are assumed by the study to be much less likely to have done so (see pages 105–106).

Professor Maltz feels she's being contradictory here:

In the section on sociodemographic factors, De Vos reported that daughters were sometimes sent off to be servants. But these girls come back to the household after they spend a couple of years with other families, I imagine. The note suggests she has not counted these individuals in her sample or that the percentage of girls who leave to be servants is very small. I wish she had given me some more specific information. If she's eliminating people from her sample I want to know what the percentage is.

This problem suggests gender-specific differences that might influence the results in her study. It's as though she wants her data to look like a certain kind of tree and she's cutting off the branches to make it look like that tree.

In the final data analysis Professor Maltz would rather De Vos had used gender as the main variable instead of marriage. Married or not, as we can see, is sometimes difficult to define but sex is a dichotomous variable that means either one or the other. He asks,

Why doesn't she use gender in her first analysis instead of marriage? You know she's talking about sons staying home and daughters going off at certain ages, and she doesn't use

gender right up front. If I had this set of data I would draw lots of figures or graphs on the computer. I would compare home-leaving by gender for each country. Then I would do the same with the other variables. When you see a big difference between two different variables you go back to the books to see if you can figure it out.

Problem 3: Survey Questions in the Study May Not Have Considered the Cultural Context Adequately

As Professor Maltz read the list of variables in paragraphs 15–21, he went back to his story of the joke that no one laughed at in Costa Rica. The problem there, he said, was with the cultural context. His audience did not have the same cultural values and so didn't find his joke funny. That same phenomenon could be at work in this study.

I just noticed a major problem with this study on the variable of work status; she only has data available for two countries, Mexico and Colombia. Even if she did have data for more countries, I'd have to question the meaning of the data. You see, some kinds of data can be collected by asking questions with concrete answers: Are you a male or female? What is your age? What year did you leave your house? But data on work requires some careful question design. Individuals might not be working for reasons of illness, pregnancy, not wanting to work, not being able to work, unemployed, or being laid off.

A lot depends upon how the question was worded. And again, it may mean different things to different people. If you ask somebody, "Are you working?" and just use that phrase, it may mean something entirely different in different cultures. In one country it may mean, "Do you have a job?" and in another country, it may mean, "Did you work today?" The cultural context is very important and I wonder if the questionnaire has taken all these things into account. I am especially concerned because this study examines six different countries.

Problem 4: Study Is Limited by Cross-sectional Data

The fourth limitation Professor Maltz finds in this study is identified by the researcher herself when she says,

> The ideal way to study the "leaving home" stage is to use longitudinal data. . . . The next best way is to use retrospective data. . . . Unfortunately, we are limited to cross-sectional data that provide information on an individual's current state only (paragraph 11).

Professor Maltz explores the limitations of cross-sectional survey data as he examines Figure 1, referred to in paragraph 24. De Vos explains that for this study she formulated a "synthetic cohort" (a cohort is a group of similar subjects). That is, she's taken the very large number of subjects included in the survey and graphed the number of 10-year-olds living with their families and the number of 34-year-olds living with their parents. This figure shows that when this survey was done in the mid-seventies, only 10 percent of the 34-year-olds were living with their families but that 98 percent of the 10-year-olds were. From this cross-sectional look at the situation in the mid-seventies we must assume that 24 years earlier, most of the 34-year-olds were living with their families. That assumption might be true, but then again, it might not. Professor Maltz proposes a design for a new, longitudinal study:

You could do a retrospective-prospective longitudinal study. You'd need to go back into the records of 25 years ago in each of these countries; ten-year-olds were, by and large, in school. Schools keep good records, so you could take a random sample of 2,000 ten-year-olds and find these people today wherever they are. In Latin American countries people don't move very much and even if someone does move, the neighbors usually know where that person is. Interview those individuals and follow them into the future. You would thus be able to solve a lot of the problems we have been talking about. You can look at divorced individuals. You can ask: How much school did you complete? Where did you live? Did you stay with your family? Did you live somewhere else? That would make for a fascinating study.

WRITING AND LEARNING ACTIVITIES

1. **Journal Entry:** How is this research report different from other academic and nonacademic reading you have done? What does it tell you about quantitative social research?

2. **Group Discussion:** What are the key ideas about home-leaving that were introduced in this reading? Key terms? How does this research fit with your own ideas about home-leaving?

3. **Examining the Text:** Look over the reference list at the end of the research report. Write down the names and publication dates of at least three different journals used in the report. Write down the names of two books used in the report. Write down the titles of the oldest and the most recent references used. What can you tell about this discipline from looking at the references? Write three questions you'd like to ask the author of the research report about the references she relied on.

4. **Writing Project:** Find two or three individuals who have recently left their family home. Interview them about the process. Use some of the ideas from the reading to generate questions. For instance, did they leave home because they got married? What does this person think being independent from his or her parents means? How did his or her culture and economic circumstances influence the decision? Write a report on your interviews and present the information to your class in a brief oral presentation.

MAKING MEANING IN THE SOCIAL SCIENCES

As Professor Maltz read Susan De Vos's research report on nest-leaving he called on both his personal and professional knowledge to help him make meaning from the text. First he called on his personal knowledge from having two nest-leavers himself and from his experiences with cultural differences. Recall his anecdote about the joke he told in Costa Rica that simply was not funny to the family he was staying with. He learned from the unexpected and disappointing response to his joke that people's cultural background has a marked influence on how they see and understand their world. He also called on his knowledge and expertise as a social researcher. In the initial interview with Professor Maltz we learned how his academic career evolved, how he became involved in social research, and something about his research interests in the field of criminal justice. Even a seasoned professional relies on personal experience as well as on the knowledge of his or her specialized academic discipline to make sense of a research report.

WHAT QUESTIONS DO SOCIAL RESEARCHERS ASK?

Social researchers are interested in learning about how an individual's behavior is shaped by the social groups he or she belongs to. We already know a good deal about individuals in society and the nature of social groups, but since our world is constantly changing, social researchers continue to ask questions about the nature of the changes. How do they affect our values, our attitudes, and our expectations? Social researchers might study the changing relationships between our political structure and the economy, health care, religious institutions. All of these changes affect people's lives and behavior. How do social researchers get ideas for their research? Often when you're familiar with an area, one you've been thinking about for a long time, you get "hunches" about what's going on. Frequently, social researchers combine their knowledge about their field with ideas or hunches that suggest a new turn or interesting new version of a familiar question.

WHAT METHODS DO QUANTITATIVE SOCIAL RESEARCHERS USE?

Social researchers do three things. First, they collect data about the social world. This data might come from a number of sources: written accounts of observations, questionnaires, surveys, and interviews. Second, these data are organized to find out what they mean and why they are important. Third, the researcher will take the procedure a bit farther to generalize about the meaning of the data. He or she will try to develop a theory that explains human behavior in a particular situation. We can think of this procedure as having three parts, but we must remember that research can be messy. Sometimes you start out with a question and collect and analyze your data, only to find out that you wanted to ask a slightly different question. Or perhaps the data doesn't explain the theory the way you thought it would.

We saw this process at work in the research report we just read. Susan De Vos used already available survey data to look at nest-leaving in six Latin American countries. To organize the data, De Vos decided to look at specific behaviors or situations, such as marital status or whether the person is the head of a household or the child of the head of the household. De Vos was reluctant to offer a theory about nest-leaving, but she did suggest that getting married was the main reason for leaving home. In her discussion section, she thought carefully about the meaning of her results—how might the economy and cultures of the six countries influence nest-leaving behavior? As is the case in much sociological research, this study raised more questions than it answered.

IS SOCIAL RESEARCH A SCIENCE OR A CRAFT?

If you just look at the standard sections of a quantitative research report—the abstract, introduction, literature review, data, methods, results, and discussion—you might be tempted to think that social science research is merely collecting and analyzing data and writing about the results in the format of the report. However, some parts of the research process involve precise techniques, such as designing a survey in such a way that the questions will be asked in a way that the respondent understands. Sociologist C. Wright Mills urges us to think of social research as more than technique, though; he would like us to think of it as a craft (195). He encourages us to use what he calls the "sociological imagination" (19).

The sociological imagination is a tool that can be used by anyone planning to do research or reading research and thinking about it. It is a thinking tool, one that helps you connect your personal experiences and observations with your research interests. Developing a sociological imagination reflects some of the same processes as developing writing abilities. Mills suggests that as researchers think about sociological problems, they should simultaneously keep a journal that reflects their life experiences. For instance, researchers who want to study family interaction might write in their journals about their own family's interaction at the dinner table. Or they might visit friends at dinnertime. As the researcher designs a research project, the intuitions and hunches drawn from these personal experiences will be almost as important a contribution as other research studies. It may seem obvious but it is important to stress that we are people who live in social groups and our day-to-day problems are those that sociologists want to study. A researcher's journal serves as a resource for ideas for writing and research.

HOW PERSONAL CONNECTIONS PROVIDE A STARTING POINT FOR WRITING

If we take Mills's advice, we should start our analysis of De Vos's research by looking at our own personal histories. Leaving home is something that happens to most of us sooner or later. In the next journal activity you are asked to tell the story of when you or someone you knew left home. Do not think about sociological issues but tell the story as you remember it. Two students tell their stories.

I can still remember that day when my sister left home for college. In fact, I don't think I'll ever forget that day. It was the end of August and the start of school was just around the corner. Of course I was excited because I was a sophomore in high school and when my sister left, I was the oldest kid in the house. Even though I didn't mind the thought of my sister leaving, I knew that I'd miss her sometimes. Our house was full of boxes packed with all her things to move out to Purdue University in West Lafayette. It seemed as though she was moving away forever. The morning quickly came when we packed up the van and drove her two hours to her new home. We moved all her things into a small hot dorm room. We all talked for a little while and left after a teary good-bye.

BRIAN BOLL

I find myself once in a while thinking about leaving home. I think for me, it is a way of becoming totally independent and having more responsibility in my life. It is very hard to live in my house right now because it is overflowing with relatives from Spain. Even though it is only temporary, the lack of privacy and the limited space really get to me sometimes. If I received enough money from financial aid to move into a dorm, I would seriously consider it, especially if I had a friend to dorm with. There have been some times this year when I and a few of my friends considered moving out of our homes and getting an apartment, but I just keep telling myself that my relatives will leave in just a few short months and I'll have my privacy back again.

RAQUEL GRYS

WRITING AND LEARNING ACTIVITY

---

1. **Journal Entry:** Tell the story of how you or someone you know left the family home. Think about why the event is important to you and why you chose to write about it. Try to re-create the scene. Be specific in your description of the participants in the event and what the event meant to each of them.

DEVELOPING INTERESTS

These personal stories hold in them the seeds of sociological research. What story did *you* tell? To discover your own interest in this discipline, shift the perspective away from the particulars of your story and use a wide-angle lens to see it as part of a bigger picture. Ask how your story fits into the social world we all live in. In the next activity you will meet in small groups to look over each of your stories and list all the reasons for leaving home. As you all study the list you may see trends, groups of reasons that seem to fit together, or you may see many different reasons. What interests you? What would you like to know more about? How do your personal experiences lead you to find an area that interests you?

WRITING AND LEARNING ACTIVITIES

1. Group Activity: In small groups of about three to five students tell or read each others' stories. Ask one person in your group to act as a scribe and write down a list of reasons for each home-leaving story. How do these reasons differ from those presented in De Vos's research? How does your story differ from the data presented in the De Vos report?

2. Writing Activity: Over the next few days talk to people you see regularly about when they left home and why. For people who are still living at home, ask them if they expect to leave and what they think about doing so. Record your own impressions. How do these persons' stories make you look at yourself differently. What interests you in what they are saying?

■-⊒ LINKED WRITING ASSIGNMENT

Writing an Analysis of Work in the Quantitative Social Sciences (see Chapter 12, Analyzing Discipline-Specific Texts). In the previous section, Developing Interests, you began to identify issues and ideas that you might want to explore further. Finding personal connections to the material you are studying is one important way to participate more fully in an academic community. You will also need to learn how some everyday thinking strategies, such as analyzing, help you to participate in the disciplines you are studying here. Chapter 12 introduces you to the activity of analyzing and offers readings from quantitative social science for you to practice developing an analysis.

C H A P T E R

4

PHILOSOPHY

Have you ever wondered what makes you the person you are? How are you different from the "you" of ten years ago? How will the you ten years in the future be different from the you of today? Do you ever feel like you're split into several people: one of you a student and the others are defined by your neighborhood, family, work, or friends? Here's what Sandra Cornejo told another student:

> . . . here at school sometimes I have a hard time being myself because I still do not have a sense of the "real" me. Before I started attending college I was pretty sure who I was and what I was supposed to be as a daughter, sister, friend, and student. Now that I'm here in college, I'm unsure of myself and the decisions I am making and find it difficult to fit in. From the time I was a baby until now, everything that I am and have done revolved around the way my parents have taught and showed me. That's where the conflict starts. My dad wants me tied down to the family, but I want to learn new things and experience life as an independent woman.
>
> SANDRA CORNEJO

What Sandra Cornejo is struggling with has a lot to do with philosophical issues of personal identity. In this chapter you'll meet a philosopher who will tell you about her research and about her own experiences learning to write. You'll read from the work of philosopher John Locke on personal identity. Most importantly, you'll start to think about what issues of that subject interest you and in what directions you might take them.

116

AN INTERVIEW WITH A PHILOSOPHER

Professor Marya Schechtman is a philosopher at the University of Illinois at Chicago. She teaches the general introductory undergraduate course in philosophy as well as an introduction to the philosophy of consciousness and reasoning. She also teaches such topics as the philosophy of psychology, metaphysics, and existentialism. Her article in the *Journal of Philosophy*, "Personal Identity and Personal Memory," reflects her research interests.

What is your special interest in studying and doing research in philosophy?

My research interests involve the philosophical question of personal identity. There are many different ways in which this question can be asked, but it is usually posed as the question of what makes someone the same person throughout his or her life. Although this may seem like an easy question to answer, as it turns out, it is really quite difficult. When you consider that a person changes dramatically in both physical and psychological makeup over the course of a lifetime, and you realize how little a person of 50 has in common with her 10-year-old self, it's not easy to explain what it is that has remained the same. And why it carries the tremendous importance that we seem to attach to personal identity.

Today, there are two basic views about what makes someone the same person over time. One is that it is having the same body, in which this is defined not as having a body that stays exactly the same, but one that changes gradually and continuously. The other is that it is having the same psychology or consciousness that makes someone the same; this, too, however, is defined in terms of gradual change and continuity rather than exact sameness.

My own sense is that both of these views have some truth to them. There is one set of concerns about personal identity in day-to-day life in which we identify the person with his or her body and another set in which the person is associated with his or her psychological life. My research has tried to define the differences between these two contexts and to develop the idea of psychological continuity. I find the contexts in which a psychological account is appropriate more interesting since they help us to understand, for instance, why people should be held morally responsible for their actions. Perhaps I should first talk about philosophy in more general terms to show how the study of personal identity fits into the field.

Yes, tell us more about what philosophy is.

It is almost impossible to really answer the question "What is philosophy?" because philosophy is so many things to so many people. One of the most important things to realize is that philosophy, unlike many disciplines, is not defined primarily by its subject matter, but by its methods. Anything and everything can be, and often is, the subject of philosophical investigation. What the philosopher is supposed to do, first and foremost, is to articulate and call into question the most basic, ordinary, commonsense presuppositions we all share. Most of these presuppositions are so deeply ingrained by our culture and upbringing that we are not even aware that they are assumptions, or that there is any other way of looking at things.

If philosophy does have a subject matter, it is the study of the nature of the world and its inhabitants at the most basic level. Other special disciplines investigate their objects from within a particular framework or context. They are able to assume that certain objects of investigation exist, that truths can be found in particular ways (through observation or mathematical proof, for instance), and that certain conclusions reached in the past can be taken as a starting point. None of this is true for philosophy, which seeks to push inquiry back as far as it can go. Philosophers can ask all sorts of different questions, but the common thread that makes all of this work philosophical is that nothing is taken for granted and everything is open to questioning.

What are the major divisions in the study of philosophy?

The major divisions are the following: metaphysics, epistemology, aesthetics, logic, ethics, and social and political philosophy. Metaphysics asks basic questions about the nature of the universe—the questions that are usually thought of as philosophical, such as "What kinds of things are there in the world? Matter? Soul? Mind?" "Does God exist?" "Are all of our actions predetermined, or do we have free will?" My own interests in the question of what underlies the identity of persons over time (and the related question of what persons essentially are) are considered to fall within metaphysics.

Epistemology is the study of how we know things. It asks questions such as "Does knowledge come from the senses alone, from reason alone, or from some combination of the two?" "What is required for us to really know something?" "What is certainty? Do we ever have it? How much evidence do we need to have and of what kind, before we are certain?" Aesthetics is the study of art and artistic expression. It asks questions such as "What is art?" "What is beauty?" "How do we know when something is beautiful? Are there objective standards of beauty or is it purely subjective?" "How do works of art express ideas?" Logic is the abstract and symbolic attempt to systematize the rules of reasoning, and in its advanced form looks very much like certain branches of mathematics.

Ethics and social and political philosophy ask questions about the interactions between persons. "How ought I to behave?" "What makes something morally right?" "Why should people act morally, and when, if ever, can self-interest override morality?" "What justifies some people having political power over others?" "What legitimates governments, and what form of government is most rational?"

In addition, recent philosophical work has given rise to new areas that are generally called philosophy of "something or other." The something-or-other blank is filled in by some specialty—philosophy of physics, philosophy of psychology, philosophy of literature, and so on. Finally, there is the history of philosophy, in which philosophers work on the texts of some particular figure or on some particular period in the history of philosophy.

Why is it important to study philosophy?

Philosophical investigation gives us a chance to step back and recognize our most basic assumptions as assumptions, as views and practices that can be changed if we decide it would be better to do so. Socrates, one of the earliest philosophers, described himself as a gadfly, one who annoyed ordinary citizens by making them recognize as seemingly insoluble problems things that it had never occurred to them could be difficulties. And this, I think, is really philosophy's main purpose. This can lead to a lot of jokes. When I tell people what I do they often ask me if I worry about whether I exist, and so on. Undoubt-

edly philosophy does sometimes take an exaggerated and comic form, but it can play an essential role in intellectual and cultural breakthroughs of tremendous importance.

How does this relate to your own research?

An example of what I have in mind here can be seen in the sort of concerns that led me to my own discipline. My interests basically came out of what is traditionally called philosophy of mind. This area of philosophy asks what mind is; whether our minds are distinct from our bodies, or in some way the same as them; whether minds are the same thing as brains; whether we are essentially machines; and so on. This has been a very difficult set of questions to address, because it expresses a tension between two basic world views in modern Western culture.

On the one hand, we have our ordinary everyday view of ourselves as creatures who think, who act freely, who are responsible for what we do, who make choices and decisions, and who shape our lives and interactions with others. On the other hand, we have a view of physics as the ultimate science, which should, in theory, eventually explain everything. That is, we believe that everything that exists in the world is subject to the laws of physics, and governed by them. But the laws of physics are often seen as mechanistic laws, and we, too, are part of the world. On the one hand, then, we believe that we make free choices and decisions, that we act for reasons and with purpose, but on the other we believe that everything we are and do is determined by the movement of molecules according to mechanistic laws. This conflict is very deep, and not easy to resolve.

Most of us believe in both of these world views to a certain extent, and under ordinary circumstances the conflict does not arise. On reflection, though, the conflict does become clear; and it is not just a problem about science, but about how we think about ourselves, about what it is to be a person, and about what our role in the world is. My own work concerns not just the question of what makes someone the same person over time, but also what it is to be a person, and this is an important part of the conflict. We do not have a clearly articulated idea of what it is to be a person, or why it is important to be one. Getting clear on these issues might help in considering questions about whether persons are the sorts of things which could be governed by the laws of physics; whether computers are decisively different from persons, or could, if complex enough, count as persons, and so on.

What do you remember about your writing experiences as an undergraduate?

I don't remember any particular turning points; it was just a long, slow evolution that is still going on. Writing philosophically is often difficult for students, because it is unlike many other kinds of writing. Quotations from texts, or facts uncovered through research, do not play a central role in most philosophy papers, which are instead analysis and argumentation. To learn to write philosophy is to learn how to write an argument without relying too heavily on another text or set of facts.

The first thing I had to master in learning how to write a compelling argument, I guess, was how to include enough material. I learned this by handing in papers that did not contain enough support for the claims I was trying to make, and getting them back with comments showing what was missing. I was able to figure out pretty quickly what was enough support for my argument, but the next stage took longer. That stage, which is almost as important as the first, was learning how not to put in too much material. For a philosophy paper to be effective, the argument that it presents has to flow and be clear, and so it is very important not to put in superfluous material, which could distract or mislead the reader.

There are several reasons I often tended to put in more material than I needed. One is that it just seemed to me that there couldn't be anything wrong with saying what was true. So when I had some insight that I thought was especially clever, I couldn't resist trying to put it in, even though it didn't really fit. Another is that I often was just not clear enough on the argument I was trying to make to know what was essential to it and what wasn't. It is interesting that often I would think that I had a completely clear vision of what I wanted to say, but wouldn't realize until I started trying to express it in writing that I was confused at many points. Another reason I would often say too much in papers was that it took a while to realize that I was never going to resolve all the philosophical issues that had remained unresolved for thousands of years. I always felt that I had to have the definitive word on whatever I was writing about, and so would force solutions that I could not actually defend.

It was a series of extremely good professors in college—both literature and philosophy professors—who helped me to improve my writing. They helped me learn to think more clearly, and to know better what I wanted to say, but this was just a small part of what helped. I now clarify sketchy or confused ideas by trying to put them in writing far more often than I start with a clear idea that I simply put down on paper. Writing out an argument in philosophy, like writing down a calculation in mathematics, is a way of working out the details that one cannot work out in one's head.

Mostly I learned to write by writing papers for courses and getting comments back showing me what I could have omitted, and how I could have structured things more clearly. I learned to organize and present my arguments more concisely, and to leave out details that were unnecessary. Furthermore, I learned to choose manageable projects. I realized that I did not have to decisively refute the giants in the history of philosophy, or conclusively prove something about the nature of the universe—I only had to express clearly the insights I had about some piece of the puzzle. I also learned that it can be just as important to honestly explain in writing where one's analysis breaks down or gets into trouble and why, as to offer some neatly tied package with no loose ends. In fact, papers that describe the puzzlements or dead ends of the author have been among the most important and influential papers in the discipline.

How did graduate school influence your writing?

When I became a teaching assistant and began to grade undergraduate papers, it was easier for me to see flaws in someone else's writing on material with which I was familiar but in which I had no particular emotional investment, as I did in my own. After grading a number of papers and remarking on a number of stylistic or structural problems with the writing, I would return to editing my own work and see for the first time that I was making the same mistakes but in a more subtle form (and not even always more subtle!). This helped me immeasurably in tightening up my own writing.

Also, in graduate school I worked with an advisor who gave a lot of thought to his writing and to style, and who took writing to be an essential part of philosophical study. He believed that although philosophy is often thought to be like the sciences, in that the writing must be clear but need not be beautiful or have any particular style, this was a dis-cipline in which writing style was of the utmost importance in communicating the philo-sophical content of one's ideas, and that one should self-consciously consider how one wants to write. (Some philosophers, notably Heidegger, Nietzsche, Wittgenstein, and Kierkegaard, have believed this, but many do not.) This advisor got me to thinking a great deal about style. Also, as it became easier for me both to read and write in philosophy, I became more aware of the prose of the various philosophers I read, and of how much more effective a well-written article was than one which was merely competently written. This, too, led me to try to refine my style.

It is still true that in college and graduate school, as well as now, the single most im-portant thing in learning to write has been feedback. I never had any writer's block and never had any difficulty producing at least the maximum number of pages called for by any assignment, but I have a terrible time editing. When I started writing philosophy I would write all at once; I could produce a paper off the top of my head in a single sitting. I was, however, at a loss as to how to tighten it up, or cut it if it was too long. I'm afraid (now that I'm on the other side, and know what it's like to receive them) that I handed in a number of papers as completed work that should have been first drafts. But each time I did I learned something about how I might have improved what I had, and so the next time I was able to refine my original draft a bit more. I am still helped a great deal by suggestions from my colleagues and referees' reports from journals. And I certainly view myself as still learning to write in my field.

WRITING AND LEARNING ACTIVITIES

1. **Journal Entry:** Look up a definition of philosophy in a specialized philosophy reference source (see Directions for Further Research in the appendix), a college dictionary, or a general reference encyclopedia. Consider the differ-ences and similarities among the definitions. Report to the class on what you found.

2. **Writing Activity:** Write three questions you would like to ask Professor Schechtman if you had the opportunity to talk with her.

3. **Peer Conversation:** With a partner, respond also to the following questions: Were you reminded by something she said of another experience you've had at home, school, or work? Have you ever considered any of the issues Pro-fessor Schechtman discusses here?

4. **Research Project:** Look up the description for philosophy courses or for that major in your college catalog. Respond to the following questions: How is the discipline described? How does the description differ from Professor Schechtman's description or from other definitions you've found? What are the required courses for this major? What are the possible areas of special-ization? Next, interview someone who is majoring in philosophy at your school. Why is that person studying this subject? What courses has he or she taken? Is he or she specializing in any particular area? What does he or she plan to do with a degree in this area? Finally, attend one class with the stu-dent and take notes about how it is similar or different from other classes you have taken.

5. **Writing:** Based on your research, write a report describing what it's like to major in philosophy at your school.

6. **Developing Interests:** In her interview, Professor Schechtman describes a wide range of issues that could be considered philosophical. For two days, notice everything that goes on around you and make journal entries about issues and events that you now see in a philosophical way. Would you like to learn more about some of these issues?

READING A PHILOSOPHICAL DISCUSSION OF PERSONAL IDENTITY

Professor Marya Schechtman will guide us through a reading of the portion of Locke's "Essay Concerning Human Understanding" in which he builds a definition of personal identity. As Professor Schechtman explained in her interview, questions such as the ones Locke addresses are of critical importance in thinking about issues we face today. We even see issues of personal identity explored in popular television shows such as *Quantum Leap* and the two *Star Trek* series. Locke's work is frequently included in anthologies for undergraduate philosophy courses but students find it difficult to understand and faculty find it difficult to teach. Think of Locke's work as a source of important ideas rather than a model for a style of writing you would want to emulate. Before reading the text closely, Professor Schechtman builds a context for this work since it was written hundreds of years ago. She also prepares to read by looking the entire essay over quickly. You'll notice that the text is divided into short sections subtitled in italics. Various editions of Locke's work include numbered sections; I have omitted the numbers and some sections not essential to his argument.

BUILDING A CONTEXT FOR READING

Can you tell us something about John Locke's philosophical position?

John Locke belonged to a group of British philosophers known as empiricists. The empiricists held quite different ideas from the rationalists such as René Descartes who believed that knowledge is obtained primarily through rational reflection. The empiricists, on the other hand, held that knowledge comes primarily from sensory experience, not from rational thought, in other words, from introspection.

Locke was a systematic philosopher, interested in building a large system that answered a number of philosophical questions. So he was not just talking about one issue or problem. Over the course of his work, Locke covered a tremendous amount of territory. He talked about how we know things, what kinds of different things are in the world, and how we should run our government. He wanted everything to fit together. He talked about memory and the nature of the physical world. His worry about personal identity was part of a more general worry about what it meant for complex, changing objects to continue to exist.

What makes "Of Identity and Diversity" so difficult for us to understand today?

Locke was writing in the late 1600s. This piece, "Of Identity and Diversity," was added four years after he wrote the original "Essay Concerning Human Understanding." What I've been told by Locke scholars is that he put it in partly to answer worries about trans-migration of soul. People were really concerned that they might have gotten a soul that did something really bad (a sullied soul) and that even though they lived perfectly good Christian lives they were bound to go to hell and be severely punished. So Locke wrote this to reassure people that if they didn't remember doing something, they couldn't be held accountable for it.

Why are Locke's views on personal identity important to us today?

For the most part, Locke's view is actually very modern. What's not modern about it is his emphasis on the soul. To study personal identity, Locke brought together two areas usually studied separately: metaphysics and ethics. He was concerned with both the metaphysical question of what is it that makes someone the same person over time and ethical questions about moral responsibility.

Issues of responsibility, compensation, and self-interested concern seem to depend on facts about personal identity. A person can, that is, be held responsible for only her own actions, only be compensated for her sacrifice by rewards that go to her, and has a special kind of interest in her own life.

In other words, to be responsible for something, you have to be the person who did it. Is it fair for me to work after school so I can go on vacation but not fair for me to work after school so my sister can go on vacation? Yes, because the same person who does the work should get the reward. Or the person who commits the crime should be the same one who gets punished.

Personal identity, in today's society, has become a big puzzle. We have two ideas about identity and two identity questions. There is the simple check-cashing question of identification (or re-identification) which asks "Are you the same person we saw at the U2 concert last week?" This is a question that you typically wouldn't ask about yourself, unless you were wondering, for instance, "Was it you or I who paid for dinner last week?" The second identity question asks a characterization question and concerns what we have come to call an "identity crisis." The problem is not that you don't remember, but from where you stand now you don't recognize yourself. You're really asking, "Who am I?" You might ask yourself about the relation between your past and your present by wondering. "Am I the same person who made 'Shrinky Dinks' out of nonbiodegradable materials but who now boycotts corporations that use environmentally destructive packaging?" Or, you might ask yourself about who you are in the present. When faced with a moral dilemma about whether or not to support women's entry into combat in the military, you are forced to ask yourself, "Is this what I really believe?"

WRITING AND LEARNING ACTIVITY

---

1. **Journal Entry:** Look over the text along with Professor Schechtman. Notice the headings in italics. Make notes in your journal about new ideas and new vocabulary.

SURVEYING THE TEXT

Before beginning her close reading of the text, Professor Schechtman quickly surveys the text as a whole. As she does so she uses the headings in italics to guide her.

What I always look for in a piece of philosophy is the argument, because a philosophical essay is going to be an argument—it's that simple. If you look at subject headings you can get an idea of where the essay is going. Let's see, I'm starting with the sections on personal identity [paragraphs 4–6]. I think the main argument will be there. Then he calls a later section Consciousness Makes Personal Identity. *So now I know the claim he's working towards.*

Professor Schechtman moves rapidly through the piece sorting out the important sections from the unimportant ones. Here are some of her comments. Notice how she questions the text when she notices he's using two terms: *person* and *self*.

Later on, where there are no subject headings I assume he's working out the details of the issue he names in the section called Personal Identity in Change of Substances. *But then I notice that a later section says* Self Depends on Consciousness. *And so here I wonder why he is saying this again. It seems to be the same subject heading as the other one. So when I get here I'm going to try to figure out what it is that's different about self, because I notice here that it says "self" and the other one says "person." So is self different from person?*

The section on Objects of Reward and Punishment *seems to come out of the blue, but I'm guessing that he is going to try to tie in notions of moral rewards and punishments with notions of personhood. Later he talks about* person *as a forensic term, which means having to do with the law. This section is probably going to tie in with the stuff about moral responsibility. In the last section,* The Difficulty from Ill Use of Names, *I'm assuming he's going to tie things up by warning us that his argument is dependent on using language accurately. This is commonly done in philosophical arguments. On the whole I'd say this piece is going to be difficult because it seems very repetitive and the arguments aren't clearly identified.*

WRITING AND LEARNING ACTIVITIES

1. **Group Activity:** What do group members think personal identity consists of? If someone's organs are donated after they die, is he or she living on in some way? What do you think the term *consciousness* means?

2. **Research Activity:** Look in general encyclopedias and specialized philosophy reference texts (see Directions for Further Research in the appendix), for explanations of the terms *personal identity, consciousness,* or *mind.* In addition, consider movies you've seen and books you've read that address issues of one's personal identity, soul, or consciousness. Write a report telling what you've found.

FROM *OF IDENTITY AND DIVERSITY*
JOHN LOCKE

Identity Suited to the Idea.—It is not therefore unity of substance that comprehends all sorts of identity, or will determine it in every case; but to conceive and judge of it aright, we must consider what idea the word it is applied to stands for: it being one thing to be the same substance, another the same man, and a third the same person, if person, man, and substance, are three names standing for three different ideas; for such as is the idea belonging to that name, such must be the identity; which, if it had been a little more carefully attended to, would possibly have prevented a great deal of that confusion which often occurs about this matter, with no small seeming difficulties, especially concerning personal identity, which therefore we shall in the next place a little consider.

Same Man.—An animal is living organized body; and consequently the same animal, as we have observed, is the same continued life communicated to different particles of matter, as they happen successively to be united to that organized living body. And whatever is talked of other definitions, ingenious observation puts it past doubt, that the idea in our minds, of which the sound man in our mouths is the sign, is nothing else but of an animal of such a certain form: since I think I may be confident, that, whoever should see a creature of his own shape or make, though it had no more reason all its life than a cat or a parrot, would call him still a man; or whoever should hear a cat or a parrot discourse, reason, and philosophize, would call or think it nothing but a cat or a parrot; and say, the one was a dull irrational man, and the other a very intelligent rational parrot. A relation we have in an author of great note, is sufficient to countenance the supposition of a rational parrot. His words are:

> I had a mind to know, from Prince Maurice's own mouth, the account of a common, but much credited story, that I had heard so often from many others, of an old parrot he had in Brazil, during his government there, that spoke, and asked, and answered common questions, like a reasonable creature: so that those of his train there generally concluded it to be witchery or possession; and one of his chaplains, who lived long afterwards in Holland, would never from that time endure a parrot, but said they all had a devil in them. I had heard many particulars of this story, and assevered by people hard to be discredited, which made me ask Prince Maurice what there was of it. He said, with his usual plainness and dryness in talk, there was something true, but a great deal false of what had been reported. I desired to know of him what there was of the first. He told me short and coldly, that he had heard of such an old parrot when he had been at Brazil; and though he believed nothing of it, and it was a good way off, yet he had so much curiosity as to send for it: that it was a very great and a very old one; and when it came first into the room where the prince was, with

a great many Dutchmen about him, it said presently, What a company of white men are here! They asked it, what it thought that man was, pointing to the prince. It answered, Some General or other. When they brought it close to him, he asked it, D'ou venez-vous? It answered, De Marinnan. The Prince, A qui estes-vous? The parrot, A un Portugais. The Prince, Que fais-tulà? Je garde les poulles. The Prince laughed, and said, Vous gardez les poulles? The parrot answered, Oui, moi, et je sçai bien faire; and made the chuck four or five times that people use to make to chickens when they call them. I set down the words of this worthy dialogue in French, just as Prince Maurice said them to me. I asked him in what language the parrot spoke, and he said in Brazilian. I asked whether he understood Brazilian; he said no: but he had taken care to have two interpreters by him, the one a Dutchman that spoke Brazilian, and the other a Brazilian that spoke Dutch; that he asked them separately and privately, and both of them agreed in telling him just the same thing that the parrot had said. I could not but tell this odd story, because it is so much out of the way, and from the first hand, and what may pass for a good one; for I dare say this prince at least believed himself in all he told me, having ever passed for a very honest and pious man: I leave it to naturalists to reason, and to other men to believe, as they please upon it; however, it is not, perhaps, amiss to relieve or enliven a busy scene sometimes with such digressions, whether to the purpose or no.

Same Man.—I have taken care that the reader should have the story at large in the author's own words, because he seems to me not to have thought it incredible; for it cannot be imagined that so able a man as he, who had sufficiency enough to warrant all the testimonies he gives of himself, should take so much pains, in a place where it had nothing to do, to pin so close not only on a man whom he mentions as his friend, but on a prince in whom he acknowledges very great honesty and piety, a story which, if he himself thought incredible, he could not but also think ridiculous. The prince, it is plain, who vouches this story, and our author, who relates it from him, both of them call this talker a parrot: and I ask any one else who thinks such a story fit to be told, whether—if this parrot, and all of its kind, had always talked, as we have a prince's word for it this one did—whether, I say, they would not have passed for a race of rational animals; but yet, whether, for all that, they would have been allowed to be men, and not parrots? For I presume it is not the idea of a thinking or rational being alone that makes the idea of a man in most people's sense, but of a body, so and so shaped, joined to it; and if that be the idea of a man, the same successive body not shifted all at once, must, as well as the same immaterial spirit, go to the making of the same man.

Personal Identity.—This being premised, to find wherein personal identity consists, we must consider what person stands for; which, I think, is a thinking intelligent being, that has reason and reflection, and can consider itself as itself, the same thinking thing, in different times and places; which it does only by that consciousness which is inseparable from thinking, and, as it seems to me, essential to it; it being impossible for any one to perceive without perceiving that he does perceive. When we see, hear, smell, taste, feel, meditate, or will anything, we know that we do so. Thus it is always as to our present sensations and perceptions: and by this every one is to himself that which he calls self; it not being considered, in this case, whether the same self be continued in the same or divers substances. For, since consciousness always accompanies thinking, and it is that which makes every one to be what he calls self, and thereby distinguishes himself from all other thinking things: in this alone consists personal identity, i.e., the sameness of a rational being; and as far as this consciousness can be extended backwards to any past action or thought, so far reaches the identity of that person; it is the same self now it was then; and it is by the same self with this present one that now reflects on it, that that action was done.

5 *Consciousness Makes Personal Identity.*—But it is further inquired, whether it be the same identical substance? This, few would think they had reason to doubt of, if these perceptions, with their consciousness, always remained present in the mind, whereby the same thinking thing would be always consciously present, and, as would be thought, evidently the same to itself. But that which seems to make the difficulty is this, that this consciousness being interrupted always by forgetfulness, there being no moment of our lives wherein we have the whole train of all our past actions before our eyes in one view, but even the best memories losing the sight of one part whilst they are viewing another; and we sometimes, and that the greatest part of our lives, not reflecting on our past selves, being intent on our present thoughts, and in sound sleep having no thoughts at all, or at least none with that consciousness which remarks our waking thoughts; I say, in all these cases, our consciousness being interrupted, and we losing the sight of our past selves, doubts are raised whether we are the same thinking thing, i.e., the same substance or no. Which, however reasonable or unreasonable, concerns not personal identity at all: the question being, what makes the same person, and not whether it be the same identical substance, which always thinks in the same person; which, in this case, matters not at all: different substances, by the same consciousness (where they do partake in it) being united into one person, as well as different bodies by the same life are united into one animal, whose identity is preserved in that change of substances by the unity of one continued life. For it being the same consciousness that makes a man be himself to himself, personal identity depends on that only, whether it be annexed solely to one individual substance, or can be continued in a succession of several substances. For as far as any intelligent being can repeat the idea of any past action with the same consciousness it had of it at first, and with the same consciousness it has of any present action; so far it is the same personal self. For it is by the consciousness it has of its present thoughts and actions, that it is self to itself now, and so will be the same self, as far as the same consciousness can extend to actions past or to come and would be by distance of time, or change of substance, no more two persons, than a man be two men by wearing other clothes today than he did yesterday, with a long or a short

sleep between: the same consciousness uniting those distant actions into the same person, whatever substances contributed to their production.

Personal Identity in Change of Substances.—That this is so, we have some kind of evidence in our very bodies, all whose particles, whilst vitally united to this same thinking conscious self, so that we feel when they are touched, and are affected by, and conscious of good or harm that happens to them, are a part of ourselves; i.e., of our thinking conscious self. Thus, the limbs of his body are to every one a part of himself; he sympathizes and is concerned for them. Cut off a hand, and thereby separate it from that consciousness he had of its heat, cold, and other affections, and it is then no longer a part of that which is himself, any more than the remotest part of matter. Thus, we see the substance whereof personal self consisted at one time may be varied at another, without the change of personal identity; there being no question about the same person, though the limbs which but now were a part of it, be cut off.

But the question is, "Whether, if the same substance, which thinks, be changed, it can be the same person; or, remaining the same, it can be different persons?"

Whether in the Change of Thinking Substances.—And to this I answer: First, This can be no question at all to those who place thought in a purely material animal constitution, void of an immaterial substance. For, whether their supposition be true or no, it is plain they conceive personal identity preserved in something else than identity of substance; as animal identity is preserved in identity of life, and not of substance. And therefore those who place thinking in an immaterial substance only, before they can come to deal with these men, must show why personal identity cannot be preserved in the change of immaterial substances, or variety of particular immaterial substances, as well as animal identity is preserved in the change of material substances, or variety of particular bodies: unless they will say, it is one immaterial spirit that makes the same life in brutes, as it is one immaterial spirit that makes the same person in men; which the Cartesians at least will not admit, for fear of making brutes thinking things too.

But next, as to the first part of the question, "Whether, if the same thinking substance (supposing immaterial substances only to think) be changed, it can be the same person?" I answer, that cannot be resolved, but by those who know what kind of substances they are that do think, and whether the consciousness of past actions can be transferred from one thinking substance to another. I grant, were the same consciousness the same individual action, it could not: but it being a present representation of a past action, why it may not be possible that that may be represented to the mind to have been, which really never was, will remain to be shown. And therefore how far the consciousness of past actions is annexed to any individual agent, so that another cannot possibly have it, will be hard for us to determine, till we know what kind of action it is that cannot be done without a reflex act of perception accompanying it, and how performed by thinking substances, who cannot think without being conscious of it. But that which we call the same consciousness, not being the same individual act, why one intellectual substance may not have represented to it, as done by itself, what it never did, and was perhaps done by some other agent; why, I say, such a representation may not possibly be without reality of matter of fact, as well as several representations in dreams are, which yet whilst dreaming we take for true, will be difficult to conclude from the nature of things. And that it never is so, will by us, till we have clearer views of the nature of thinking substances, be best resolved into the goodness of God, who, as far as the happiness or misery of any of his sensible creatures is concerned in it, will not, by a fatal error of theirs, transfer from one to another that consciousness which draws reward or punishment with it. How far this may be an argument against those who would place thinking in a system of fleeting animal spirits, I leave to be considered. But yet, to return to the question before us, it must be allowed, that, if the same consciousness (which, as has been shown, is quite a different thing from the same numerical figure or motion in body) can be transferred from one thinking substance to another, it will be possible that two thinking substances may make but one person. For the same consciousness being preserved, whether in the same or different substances, the personal identity is preserved.

10   As to the second part of the question, "Whether the same immaterial substance remaining, there may be two distinct persons?" which question seems to me to be built on this, whether the same immaterial being, being conscious of the action of its past duration, may be wholly stripped of all the consciousness of its past existence, and lose it beyond the power of ever retrieving it again; and so as it were beginning a new account from a new period, have a consciousness that cannot reach beyond this new state. All those who hold pre-existence are evidently of this mind, since they allow the soul to have no remaining consciousness of what it did in that pre-existent state, either wholly separate from body, or informing any other body; and if they should not, it is plain experience would be against them. So that personal identity reaching no further than consciousness reaches, a pre-existent spirit not having continued so many ages in a state of silence, must needs make different persons. Suppose a Christian Platonist or a Pythagorean should, upon God's having ended all his works of creation the seventh day, think his soul hath existed ever since; and would imagine it has revolved in several human bodies, as I once met with one, who was persuaded his had been the soul of Socrates; (how reasonably I will not dispute; this I know, that in the post he filled, which was no inconsiderable one, he passed for a very rational man, and the press has shown that he wanted not parts or learning;) would any one say, that he, being not conscious of any of Socrates' actions or thoughts, could be the same person with Socrates? Let any one reflect upon himself, and conclude that he has in himself an immaterial spirit, which is that which thinks in him, and, in the constant change of his body keeps him the same: and is that which he calls himself: let him also suppose it to be the same soul that was in Nestor or Thersites, at the siege of Troy (for souls being, as far as we know anything of

them, in their nature indifferent to any parcel of matter, the supposition has no apparent absurdity in it), which it may have been, as well as it is now the soul of any other man: but he now having no consciousness of any of the actions either of Nestor or Thersites, does or can he conceive himself the same person with either of them? Can he be concerned in either of their actions? attribute them to himself, or think them his own, more than the actions of any other men that ever existed? So that this consciousness not reaching to any of the actions of either of those men, he is no more one self with either of them, than if the soul or immaterial spirit that now informs him had been created, and began to exist, when it began to inform his present body, though it were ever so true, that the same spirit that informed Nestor's or Thersites' body were numerically the same that now informs his. For this would no more make him the same person with Nestor, than if some of the particles of matter that were once a part of Nestor, were now a part of this man; the same immaterial substance, without the same consciousness, no more making the same person by being united to any body, than the same particle of matter, without consciousness united to any body, makes the same person. But let him once find himself conscious of any of the actions of Nestor, he then finds himself the same person with Nestor.

And thus may we be able, without any difficulty, to conceive the same person at the resurrection, though in a body not exactly in make or parts the same which he had here, the same consciousness going along with the soul that inhabits it. But yet the soul alone, in the change of bodies, would scarce to any one but to him that makes the soul the man, be enough to make the same man. For should the soul of a prince, carrying with it the consciousness of the prince's past life, enter and inform the body of a cobbler, as soon as deserted by his own soul, every one sees he would be the same person with the prince, accountable only for the prince's actions: but who would say it was the same man? The body too goes to the making the man, and would, I guess, to everybody determine the man in this case; wherein the soul, with all its princely thoughts about it, would not make another man: but he would be the same cobbler to every one besides himself. I know that, in the ordinary way of speaking, the same person, and the same man, stand for one and the same thing. And indeed every one will always have a liberty to speak as he pleases, and to apply what articulate sounds to what ideas he thinks fit, and change them as often as he pleases. But yet, when we will inquire what makes the same spirit, man, or person, we must fix the ideas of spirit, man, or person in our minds, and having resolved with ourselves what we mean by them, it will not be hard to determine in either of them, or the like, when it is the same, and when not.

Consciousness Makes the Same Person.—But though the same immaterial substance or soul does not alone, wherever it be, and in whatsoever state, make the same man; yet it is plain, consciousness, as far as ever it can be extended, should it be to ages past, unites existences and actions, very remote in time into the same person, as well as it does the existences and actions of the immediately preceding moment: so that whatever has the consciousness of present and past actions, is the same person to whom they both belong. Had I the same consciousness that I saw the ark and Noah's flood, as that I saw an overflowing of the Thames last winter, or as that I write now; I could no more doubt that I who write this now, that saw the Thames overflowed last winter, and that viewed the flood at the general deluge, was the same self, place that self in what substance you please, than that I who write this am the same myself now whilst I write (whether I consist of all the same substance, material or immaterial, or no) that I was yesterday; for as to this point of being the same self, it matters not whether this present self be made up of the same or other substances; I being as much concerned, and as justly accountable for any action that was done a thousand years since, appropriated to me now by this self-consciousness, as I am for what I did the last moment.

Self Depends on Consciousness.—Self is that conscious thinking thing, whatever substance made up of (whether spiritual or material, simple or compounded, it matters not), which is sensible or conscious of pleasure and pain, capable of happiness or misery, and so is concerned for itself, as far as that consciousness extends. Thus every one finds, that, whilst comprehended under that consciousness, the little finger is as much a part of himself as what is most so. Upon separation of this little finger, should this consciousness go along with the little finger, and leave the rest of the body, it is evident the little finger would be the person, the same person, and self then would have nothing to do with the rest of the body. As in this case it is the consciousness that goes along with the substance, when one part is separate from another, which makes the same person, and constitutes this inseparable self; so it is in reference to substances remote in time. That with which the consciousness of this present thinking thing can join itself, makes the same person, and is one self with it, and with nothing else; and so attributes to itself and owns all the actions of that thing as its own, as far as that consciousness reaches, and no further; as every one who reflects will perceive.

Objects of Reward and Punishment.—In this personal identity is founded all the right and justice of reward and punishment; happiness and misery being that for which every one is concerned for himself, and not mattering what becomes of any substance not joined to, or affected with that consciousness. For as it is evident in the instance I gave but now, if the consciousness went along with the little finger when it was cut off, that would be the same self which was concerned for the whole body yesterday, as making part of itself, whose actions then it cannot but admit as its own now. Though, if the same body should still live, and immediately from the separation of the little finger have its own peculiar consciousness, whereof the little finger knew nothing; it would not at all be concerned for it, as a part of itself, or could own any of its actions, or have any of them imputed to him.

15　　　This may show us wherein personal identity consists: not in the identity of substance, but, as I have said, in the identity of consciousness; wherein if Socrates and the present mayor of Queenborough agree, they are the same person: if the same Socrates waking and sleeping do not partake of the same consciousness, Socrates waking and sleeping is not the same person. And to punish Socrates waking for what sleeping Socrates thought, and waking Socrates was never conscious of, would be no more of right, than to punish one twin for what his brother-twin did, whereof he knew nothing, because their outsides were so like, that they could not be distinguished; for such twins have been seen.

But yet possibly it will still be objected, suppose I wholly lose the memory of some parts of my life, beyond a possibility of retrieving them, so that perhaps I shall never be conscious of them again; yet am I not the same person that did those actions, had those thoughts that I once was conscious of, though I have now forgot them? To which I answer, that we must here take notice what the word I is applied to; which, in this case, is the man only. And the same man being presumed to be the same person, I is easily here supposed to stand also for the same person. But if it be possible for the same man to have distinct incommunicable consciousness at different times, it is past doubt the same man would at different times make different persons; which, we see, is the sense of mankind in the solemnest declaration of their opinions; human laws not punishing the mad man for the sober man's actions, nor the sober man for what the mad man did, thereby making them two persons: which is somewhat explained by our way of speaking in English, when we say such an one is not himself, or is beside himself; in which phrases it is insinuated, as if those who now, or at least first used them, thought that self was changed, the selfsame person was no longer in that man.

·   ·   ·

Consciousness Alone Makes Self.—Nothing but consciousness can unite remote existences into the same person: the identity of substance will not do it; for whatever substance there is, however framed, without consciousness there is no person: and a carcass may be a person, as well as any sort of substance be so without consciousness.

Could we suppose two distinct incommunicable consciousnesses acting the same body, the one constantly by day, the other by night; and, on the other side, the same consciousness, acting by intervals, two distinct bodies; I ask, in the first case, whether the day and the night man would not be two as distinct persons as Socrates and Plato? And whether, in the second case, there would not be one person in two distinct bodies, as much as one man is the same in two distinct clothings? Nor is it at all material to say, that this same, and this distinct consciousness, in the cases above mentioned, is owing to the same and distinct immaterial substances, bringing it with them to those bodies; which, whether true or no, alters not the case; since it is evident the personal identity would equally be determined by the consciousness, whether that consciousness were annexed to some individual immaterial substance or no. For, granting that the thinking substance in man must be necessarily supposed immaterial, it is evident that immaterial thinking thing may sometimes part with its past consciousness, and be restored to it again, as appears in the forgetfulness men often have of their past actions: and the mind many times recovers the memory of a past consciousness, which it had lost for twenty years together. Make these intervals of memory and forgetfulness to take their turns regularly by day and night, and you have two persons with the same immaterial spirit, as much as in the former instance two persons with the same body. So that self is not determined by identity or diversity of substance, which it cannot be sure of, but only by identity of consciousness.

Indeed it may conceive the substance whereof it is now made up to have existed formerly, united in the same conscious being; but, consciousness removed, that substance is no more itself, or makes no more a part of it, than any other substance; as is evident in the instance we have already given of a limb cut off, of whose heat, or cold, or other affections, having no longer any consciousness, it is no more of a man's self, than any other matter of the universe. In like manner it will be in reference to any immaterial substance, which is void of that consciousness whereby I am myself to myself: if there be any part of its existence which I cannot upon recollection join with that present consciousness, whereby I am now myself, it is in that part of its existence no more myself, than any other immaterial being. For whatsoever any substance has thought or done, which I cannot recollect, and by my consciousness make my own thought and action, it will no more belong to me, whether a part of me thought or did it, than if it had been thought or done by any other immaterial being anywhere existing.

20   I agree, the more probable opinion is, that this consciousness is annexed to, and the affection of, one individual immaterial substance.

But let men, according to their diverse hypotheses, resolve of that as they please; this very intelligent being, sensible of happiness or misery, must grant that there is something that is himself that he is concerned for, and would have happy; that this self has existed in a continued duration more than one instant, and therefore it is possible may exist, as it has done, months and years to come, without any certain bounds to be set to its duration; and may be the same self by the same consciousness continued on for the future. And thus, by this consciousness, he finds himself to be the same self which did such or such an action some years since, by which he comes to be happy or miserable now. In all which account of self, the same numerical substance is not considered as making the same self; but the same continued consciousness, in which several substances may have been united, and again separated from it; which, whilst they continued in a vital union with that wherein this consciousness then resided, made a part of that same self. Thus any part of our bodies vitally united to that which is conscious in us, makes a part of ourselves: but upon separation from the vital union by which that consciousness is communicated, that which a moment since was part of ourselves, is now no more so than a part of another man's self is a part of me: and it is not impossible but in a little time may become a real part of another person. And so we have the same numerical substance become a part of two different persons; and the same person preserved under the change of various substances. Could we suppose any spirit wholly stripped of all its memory or consciousness of past actions, as we find our minds always are of a great part of ours, and sometimes of them all; the union or separation of such a spiritual substance would make no variation of personal identity, any more than that of any particle of matter does. Any substance vitally united to the present thinking being, is a part of that very same self which now is; anything united to it by a consciousness of former actions, makes also a part of the same self, which is the same both then and now.

Person as a Forensic Term.—Person, as I take it, is the name for this self. Wherever a man finds what he calls himself there, I think, another may say is the same person. It is a forensic term, appropriating actions and their merit; and so belongs only to intelligent agents capable of a law, and happiness, and misery. This personality extends itself beyond present existence to what is past, only by consciousness, whereby it becomes concerned and accountable, owns and imputes to itself past actions, just upon the same ground and for the same reason that it does the present. All which is founded in a concern for happiness, the unavoidable concomitant of consciousness; that which is conscious of pleasure and pain, desiring that that self that is conscious should be happy. And therefore whatever past actions it cannot reconcile or appropriate to that present self by consciousness, it can be no more concerned in, than if they had never been done; and to receive pleasure or pain, i.e., reward or punishment, on the account of any such action, is all one as to be made happy or miserable in its first being, without any demerit at all; for supposing a man punished now for what he had done in another life, whereof he could be made to have no consciousness at all, what difference is there between that punishment, and being created miserable? And therefore, conformable to this, the apostle tells us, that, at the great day, when every one shall "receive according to his doings, the secrets of all hearts shall be laid open." The sentence shall be justified by the consciousness all persons shall have, that they themselves, in what bodies soever they appear, or what substances soever that consciousness adheres to, are the same that committed those actions, and deserve that punishment for them.

I am apt enough to think I have, in treating of this subject, made some suppositions that will look strange to some readers, and possibly they are so in themselves. But yet, I think they are such as are pardonable, in this ignorance we are in of the nature of that thinking thing that is in us, and which we look on as ourselves. Did we know what it was, or how it was tied to a certain system of fleeting animal spirits; or whether it could or could not perform its operations of thinking and memory out of a body organized as ours is: and whether it has pleased God, that no one such spirit shall ever be united to any one but such body, upon the right constitution of whose organs its memory should depend; we might see the absurdity of some of these suppositions I have made. But, taking as we ordinarily now do, (in the dark concerning these matters,) the soul of a man for an immaterial substance, independent from matter, and indifferent alike to it all, there can, from the nature of things, be no absurdity at all to suppose that the same soul may at different times be united to different bodies, and with them make up for that time one man, as well as we suppose a part of a sheep's body yesterday should be a part of a man's body tomorrow, and in that union make a vital part of Meliboeus himself, as well as it did of his ram.

The Difficulty from Ill Use of Names.—To conclude: Whatever substance begins to exist, it must, during its existence, necessarily be the same: whatever compositions of substances begin to exist, during the union of those substances the concrete must be the same; whatsoever mode begins to exist, during its existence it is the same; and so if the composition be of distinct substances and different modes, the same rule holds: whereby it will appear, that the difficulty or obscurity that has been about this matter rather rises from the names ill used, than from any obscurity in things themselves. For whatever makes the specific idea to which the name is applied, if that idea be steadily kept to, the distinction of anything into the same, and divers, will easily be conceived, and there can arise no doubt about it.

25   *Continued Existence Makes Identity.*—For, supposing a rational spirit be the idea of a man, it is easy to know what is the same man, viz., the same spirit, whether separate or in a body, will be the same man. Supposing a rational spirit vitally united to a body of a certain conformation of parts to make a man, whilst that rational spirit, with that vital conformation of parts, though continued in a fleeting successive body, remain, it will be the same man. But if to any one the idea of a man be but the vital union of parts in a certain shape, as long as that vital union and shape remain in a concrete no otherwise the same, but by a continued succession of fleeting particles, it will be the same man. For, whatever be the composition whereof the complex idea is made, whenever existence makes it one particular thing under any denomination, the same existence continued, preserves it the same individual under the same denomination.

A CLOSE READING OF A PHILOSOPHICAL DISCUSSION ON PERSONAL IDENTITY

Now that Professor Schechtman has looked over the text and provided some context for us, she will do a close reading of the text. As she reads each portion, she will ask herself how it contributes to the argument that Locke is making. Often, to make clear what Locke is saying, she will paraphrase his work and then elaborate a bit to show why it is more or less important to the argument. As you read pay close attention to the relationship between Locke's text and Professor Schechtman's explanation of it so that you can talk about these ideas in your own words.

WRITING AND LEARNING ACTIVITIES

1. **Reading:** Read sections of the excerpt from Locke's essay in the order indicated below.

2. **Journal Entry:** As you read make notes in your journal about your reading process. Write down any questions you have about the reading and any familiar or unfamiliar terms you encounter. Also, note any places in the readings where you make connections to your own experiences.

3. **Annotate the Text:** As you read, mark the text to help you follow the argument. Use one color highlighter to identify key claims, and another color to identify thought experiments. Place question marks next to places that confuse you and restate main points in the margins.

Read *Identity Suited to the Idea*, paragraph 1.

What is our idea of identity? Locke is saying that if person, man, and substance are different names standing for different ideas, then they're going to have different identity criteria. He goes on to suggest that it could prevent a great deal of confusion if we define per-son correctly. What Locke is going to do is to develop an argument in which he first defines "man" and shows how "man" is different from "person." Then he'll tell us how being a person doesn't depend on our "substance." This idea of substance is a very difficult notion and I'll talk more about it later.

Read *Same Man*, paragraphs 2 and 3.

Locke makes his claim at the beginning of paragraph 2 that an animal is a living organized body. The term man *stands for the idea of a living organized body that looks like a man; if it looks like a parrot we call it a parrot. He offers this story of the parrot to show us that the term* man *applies to a certain kind of physical, biological creature. If the parrot exhibits rational behaviors, you wouldn't say that parrot is a human being; you would say that it is a rational parrot. So, Locke is using this story to argue against the common philosophical view that* man *means rational being. This type of argument—the story of the rational parrot—is what we call a thought experiment. Locke is known for his use of them and you will see several more as we read his essay. [Note: In the next section of the text (pages 144–145) we will discuss thought experiments as a method for argument in philosophy.]*

Locke continues in the section also called Same Man *(paragraph 3) to explain that when we think of man we don't only think of a rational being but we think of a body, "so and so shaped, joined to it [the rational being]" as well. To be the same man, then, is to have the same body. Locke emphasized the fact that even though a body is not made up of precisely the same matter from moment to moment we can still speak of it as being the same body, and so the same man.*

Read *Personal Identity*, paragraph 4.

We already know from the previous section what man is and what sameness of man is. Here Locke is going to define person, *which he does—a "thinking intelligent being that* has reason and reflection, and can consider itself as itself, the same thinking thing, in different times and places." This is an important quote and an important theme because the criterion of personal identity is, once again, having "reason and reflection." I'm assuming that consciousness is going to be what makes for sameness of person because that is what all those section headings say. He's saying that you don't even have to raise the question of whether you've got the same stuff (substance) or not. His major claim is that personal identity equals consciousness.

Read *Consciousness Makes Personal Identity*, paragraph 5, and *Personal Identity in Change of Substances*, paragraphs 6–7.

It is important to remember that in the contemporary discussion, philosophers talk about the problem of personal identity in terms of two major possibilities: on the one hand, personal identity could consist in psychological continuity. On the other hand, it could be bodily continuity. Locke is difficult to read because he uses a third term that reflects the times in which he wrote. That third term is soul. For Locke both the body and the soul are types of substances; the body is called material substance and the soul is called immaterial substance. The reader must remember then, that soul, thinking substance, and immaterial substance are used interchangeably and mean the same thing.

Locke builds his argument by showing that substance, whether material or immaterial, is irrelevant to being a person. In Consciousness Makes Personal Identity, he points out that our consciousness is frequently interrupted and we cannot remember everything right back to our birth, so we might wonder whether or not we are the same substance. Locke argues that it doesn't matter whether or not we are the same substance. Even if you wore a very small clothing size ten years ago and a much larger size today as you became an adult you are the same person because your consciousness can unite "those distant actions into the same person, whatever substances contributed to their production" (paragraph 5).

In the next section he points out that your hand is only your hand as long as you are conscious of what happens to it. Again, what matters is the consciousness, not the material substance.

Read *Whether in the Change of Thinking Substances*, paragraphs 8–11.

Locke opens this rather long section with a two-part question in the paragraph before, which asks us to think about whether immaterial substance (which also means the same thing as soul and thinking substance) is critical for personal identity. Here's the question:

> Whether, if the same substance, which thinks, be changed, it can be the same person; or, remaining the same, it can be different persons? (paragraph 7)

He's trying to prove his claim by eliminating all the likely possibilities. At the time he was writing, many people believed that the identity of the person was bound up with his soul. The answer to Locke's first question is yes: personal identity is preserved if the *soul is changed. Sameness or difference of soul is completely irrelevant to sameness or difference of person. Next, Locke considers the second part of the question: Can you have one soul and be two different persons? The answer, again, is yes.*

One way of understanding what he's talking about here is to think of the doctrine of reincarnation, which says basically that first you have a life, then your soul is completely wiped clean of its memories and comes back in a different body. Locke thinks that in each incarnation you would be a different person and so there can be two different persons with one soul.

Locke's strategy for this portion of his argument is to offer another thought experiment. He says he once met a very respectable man who held a high office and who was considered to be very rational, but who was sure that his soul had been the soul of Socrates. Locke asks us to consider whether this man should be considered the same person as Socrates? The answer to this question is no. You can imagine someone who claims to have Socrates' soul, but you wouldn't think that person was Socrates unless he could remember Socrates' experience and reason as Socrates did. In other words, without Socrates' consciousness he could not be Socrates.

Read *Consciousness Makes the Same Person*, paragraph 12, and *Self Depends on Consciousness*, paragraph 13.

Locke continues to press his claim by refining the idea of how we should define a person. Locke means very literally that if your consciousness can extend beyond the bounds of your body, then you, the person, can extend beyond the bounds of your body. He doesn't say whether he thinks this ever really happens.

It is important to notice that Locke introduces the word self *here and connects it to the idea of* person. *By talking about* person *from the first person perspective of* self *we are able to talk about how we care about "pleasure and pain, . . . [and] happiness or misery" (paragraph 13).*

I find his thought experiment here rather compelling. You would normally think that if your little finger is cut off, your consciousness stays with you and you have simply lost your little finger. But if you could imagine a fairy tale in which a person's consciousness was put in her little finger, you'd worry about tracking what happened to the little finger and not the rest of the body. Further, if the body had performed some crime the day before, then the little finger should be punished because it's the part that has the consciousness. Locke continues on with this topic in the next section.

Read *Objects of Reward and Punishment*, paragraphs 14–16.

In these paragraphs, Locke explores the idea of a person as a unit of responsibility and morality. As in the story of the little finger above, the little finger should be punished if consciousness resides in the little finger. Locke further illustrates this by proposing that we shouldn't punish a waking Socrates for a crime he committed while sleeping since waking and sleeping Socrates do not share the same consciousness. Locke is making the point that having the same body as someone who committed a crime or did a heroic act isn't enough to make you the appropriate object of punishment or reward, but having the same consciousness is.

He's trying again to distinguish between man and person. Locke reminds us that we usually assume the same man is the same person. However, we're usually using the term loosely because typically sameness of human body and sameness of consciousness go together. But if it were, in fact, possible for these two things to come apart, then we would think that rewards and punishments went with the consciousness and not with the body.

Read *Consciousness Alone Makes Self,* paragraphs 17–21.

At the opening to this section, Locke restates his claim: If there is no consciousness, there is no person. Then, with another thought experiment, Locke asks us to imagine two distinct consciousnesses acting on the same body, one by day and one by night. It would be like imagining a case of multiple personalities. In such a case we would conclude that there are really two people even though there is only one body. We can reverse the case and imagine one consciousness acting by intervals on distinct bodies by imagining, for instance, that every odd day we woke up in another body. Locke tells us, the fact that we forget things and remember them later shows that consciousness is separate from soul and so sameness of consciousness is different from sameness of soul. It's the sameness of consciousness that underlies our judgments.

Locke recognizes that in our casual, everyday thinking, we assume that one consciousness and one soul go together but, in fact, we have no way of knowing it. What we do know is that where the person goes, the consciousness goes. Earlier he defined a person as a thinking intelligent being who has reason and reflection. Here he reiterates this idea and emphasizes that an important part of being a person and of having the right kind of consciousness is viewing yourself as a self that continues to exist and viewing yourself as a self whose temporal parts hook up. This helps us understand why this kind of consciousness is necessary for responsibility: You know that you are the one who did this action and that you are now being punished or rewarded for that reason.

Read *Person as a Forensic Term,* paragraphs 22–23.

In the section Locke introduces the idea of person as a forensic, or legal, term. He emphasizes that we care about things that affect our conscious well-being and that we don't care about substances that don't. Furthermore, consciousness is concerned for its own state—what it is to be conscious or self-conscious is to care that you be happy rather than miserable.

Locke is going over material he has covered before but extending it a bit here. He has already reminded us that we assume that soul, body, and consciousness go together. His argument suggests that they don't necessarily go together and, in fact, could be separated. From a forensic point of view, Locke argues that it isn't fair to punish someone for something he or she has no consciousness of doing. But if he or she does have consciousness of doing it then it is fair to punish them even if they are in a different body or have a different soul. For instance, if I work really hard and save all my money to go on a vacation, it's not fair to send someone else on a vacation as a reward for my work. Locke is telling us that we have a sense of individual justice and we are happy or sad because our consciousness can care about itself and its state.

Read *The Difficulty from Ill Use of Names*, paragraph 24, and *Continued Existence Makes Identity*, paragraph 25.

Here Locke comes back to the issue he introduced at the beginning of this piece: that to understand personal identity we must understand what the word person *stands for. Person is a being with a self-conception and as long as that self-conception and consciousness continue, that person is the same person. That is, you must explain—or name— what it is whose identity is in question (denomination means name). Then it will be easier to answer that a person is a thinking, intelligent being that considers its self as a self, has certain capacities, and that these capacities come from consciousness. Once again, it's sameness of consciousness and not anything else that makes a person.*

WRITING AND LEARNING ACTIVITIES

1. **Journal Entry:** Look over the notes you took while reading Locke's essay. How was the experience of reading this essay similar to or different from other reading you have done? Write about the similarities and differences.

2. **Group Activity:** In a group or with a peer develop a description of a hypothetical or real situation that is related to the problem of personal identity. To do so, think about experiences you have had at home, at work, or at church or synagogue, or about books you have read or movies you have seen. Does Locke's essay help you to explain personal identity? Is consciousness a key ingredient in the situation you developed?

3. **Writing Activity:** Professor Schechtman, in her interview, explained that the philosophical method allows us to question ideas that we normally might not even think about. How has John Locke's essay helped us to question an idea that we might have taken for granted? Write a letter to a friend explaining what you have been studying in college and explain what you have learned from reading John Locke.

4. **Developing Interests:** Again think about books you have read, movies you have seen, or incidents you have witnessed. Write in your journal about how the philosophical problem of personal identity can be seen in these everyday experiences and events.

MAKING MEANING IN PHILOSOPHY
PARTICIPATING IN AN ACADEMIC DISCIPLINE

Writing and learning about philosophy doesn't mean simply taking in information about the subject matter; rather, it means participating in a new and unfamiliar discipline. It means learning to think and ask questions like a philosopher. All of us spend our lives as members of many different kinds of communities—neighborhoods, church groups, political interest groups, jobs, hobby clubs, and of course, school communities. In each community we share with the others in it a particular kind of talk and learning. You might even think that in the context of each of these groups you are a slightly different "you." When you enter the university you find yourself learning to participate in many new academic disciplines largely through your different classes, one of which might be philosophy.

Since each academic discipline has a special kind of inquiry or learning and special uses of reading, writing, and speaking, you need to recognize how scholars in each discipline use language to make meaning. To use philosophy as an example, you began this process as you read Professor Schechtman's interview and read a portion of John Locke's essay along with her. In the activities at the end of the interview you examined what it's like to be a philosophy major or you looked up the term *philosophy* in a specialized dictionary. In your journal or in another piece of writing you tried to talk about personal identity using some of these new ideas and this new language. At first the language seemed unfamiliar and strange, but, as you continued to become familiar with the discourse of philosophy you were able to be more critical, asking questions, even doubting whether something really made sense to you. Eventually you were able to ask, "What does this mean to me?" Once you can do that in any discipline, you will feel much more a part of that discipline because you will have connected this new knowledge with your own learning processes.

Joseph Harris, who teaches writing at the University of Pittsburgh, has written about what this idea of an academic community means and, in particular, how he learned that he had changed as a result of participating in a new, academic community. He explains,

> I was raised in a working-class home in Philadelphia, but it was only when I went away to college that I heard the term *working class* used or began to think of myself as part of it. (11)

It was in an academic classroom that Harris first heard a description of the socioeconomic status that he had grown up in and that had been his reality. But, by the time he had begun to think about this in his college classroom, Harris tells us, he was no longer only a part of that working-class community. He had now joined a new community and was, in some ways, a different person. This can sometimes be a bittersweet process—leaving behind parts of your old self as you learn, viewing yourself differently now. By writing this article about how his academic experiences had changed his view of himself, he was able to comment on the process and to influence the academic community in return.

At some point in your life you probably asked yourself the question, "Who am I?" Now, in the context of this particular discipline—the group of students and professors who study philosophy—you are being asked to think about it again, in a new language and with new methods. Already, in Professor Schechtman's interview and in your reading of John Locke you may have encountered new ideas and new ways of talking about these ideas. Making meaning in philosophy poses quite a challenge to the student entering the university. On the one hand, learning about, in this case philosophy, means learning a new way to see the world and a new way to talk about what you've seen. On the other hand you face the challenge of learning to talk about philosophy and doing it in a voice you can still call your own.

WRITING AND LEARNING ACTIVITIES

1. **Journal Entry:** Write about a specialized community you belong to or know of outside of school, such as church or work. What is the nature of your involvement with this community? How do members communicate with each other? Do they have a newsletter or meetings? What is the common subject matter of this group? What do you remember about how you came to join this group? What was difficult and what was easy during that process?

2. **Writing Activity:** Write a letter to a new member (real or imaginary) of the community you described above. Write about how *you* came to be a part of that group and what the newcomer should anticipate.

FINDING THE ARGUMENT IN PHILOSOPHICAL WRITING

As Professor Schechtman prepared to read John Locke's essay she had told us, "What I always look for in a piece of philosophy is the argument because a philosophical essay is going to be an argument—it's that simple." The field of philosophy is composed of many subdisciplines and these sometimes use different types of argument in different ways. Philosopher Stephen Toulmin sees two competing methods of arguing. One method depends on logic to set arguments out in a very simple form: a major premise, a minor premise, and a conclusion. The truth is proved through a sequence of statements such as the following:

> All humans are mortals.
> Aristotle is a human.
> Therefore, Aristotle is mortal.

Rather than think of argument as a series of logical steps that make an argument good or bad, Toulmin urges us to think of argument as a more informal, practical form of reasoning that takes into account the situation in which argument occurs.

He encourages us to think about argument as a dialogue or a conversation. Suppose we make a statement and claim that the statement is true. For instance, a student here at the University of Illinois at Chicago, an urban campus, claims that public transportation is the best way to get to school. Someone may challenge her claim, in which case she must be able to justify it. During this interchange she offers facts to support her claim. These facts are called a variety of names: data, evidence, grounds, or reasons. Another student might now object that the facts offered are not appropriate and ask her how she got from her data to her claim. As a result of this conversation, the first student might have to qualify her claim in some way—to say that it applies only under certain conditions, for example. The setting of conditions under which the claim must be met is called the rebuttal.

The train of reasoning involved in this sort of argument is shown in the following dialogue as two students pursue their exchange about the best way to get to school, by exploring reasons and qualifications for a claim. Here Maria is challenged by Clara to support and qualify Maria's claim that public transportation is the best way to get to school.

MARIA: I always take the train or a bus to school; public transportation is the only way to go. [Maria states her central claim.]

CLARA: Why do you say that? [Clara begins to question Maria's claim.]

MARIA: Well, it's cheap. I buy a monthly pass and I never have to think about gas, tolls, parking, or even the wear and tear on my Mom's car. [Maria offers one reason—the low cost—for using public transportation.]

CLARA: But is the cost the only concern? If I carpool with three friends it costs much less than that monthly pass. Besides, the train isn't very safe. A friend of mine had her wallet stolen right out of her bag. [Clara wonders whether or not using cost is the best way to support the claim. She also adds another consideration—safety.]

MARIA: Well, all right. Unless you can set up a carpool that really works, I still think public transportation is the best bet. [Maria is willing to qualify her claim, because Clara's rebuttal made sense in certain circumstances.]

This conversation offers a simple example of how an argument can be worked out between two people. One person didn't "win" the argument and frequently no one does. By forwarding claims which may at first seem like ordinary opinions, we can probe the underlying reasons for those opinions and then think about which reasons offer the best support.

WRITING AND LEARNING ACTIVITIES

1. **Group Activity:** Bring to your group meeting an example of reasoning from outside of class (consider material from newspapers, pamphlets, advertisements) and, as a group, work out the parts of the argument by developing a conversation like the one above. Choose the most interesting conversation and present it to the class.

2. **Journal Entry:** Write about some of the disagreements you've had with others. Choose one and write about the reasons for one person's claim. Do they seem appropriate? What problems do you see with those reasons? Should the claim be qualified in any way?

THOUGHT EXPERIMENTS AS A FORM OF ARGUMENT

As you read through Locke's essay you probably noticed how he told story after story to argue for his view of what constituted a person. First there was the story about the parrot who could speak. If the parrot behaves in a rational way, would you say the parrot is rational or would you say it is human? Or, if the mayor of Queenborough claims that his soul was the soul of Socrates, should we consider him to be Socrates? Such stories have come to be called thought experiments and they constitute a common form of philosophical argument, especially for thinking about personal identity.

In her interview, Professor Schechtman told us that philosophy's main purpose was to call into question "the most basic, ordinary, commonsense presuppositions we all share." These basic ideas are so much a part of our culture and our upbringing that we almost never question them. Philosophers want to help us to see as difficulties problems that we may not have seen as difficulties before. Thought experiments are one tool they use to achieve this purpose.

What is a thought experiment? In her 1988 book *Real People,* Kathleen Wilkes, (7) a philosopher, offers the following description of the thought experiment method (2–12). She asks us to suppose we want to test a philosophical claim. To do this, we ask a "what if . . . ?" question, where we have to imagine a hypothetical situation, one that would not normally occur in the real world. We are asking our audience to imagine a different world, or in Wilkes's words, a "possible world." In that world everything is just as it is in our world except for one crucial feature, such as Locke's talking parrot. If we are trying to define how a man is different from a person, we can use this thought experiment to develop reasons (or using Toulmin's scheme above, data, grounds, or evidence) for saying that even if a parrot were rational we would not call it a man.[1]

A closer look at the two terms in the label "thought experiments" helps us to understand this method. The term *thought* refers to the armchair philosopher using her imagination—the experiment can't actually be carried out in the real world (Do you know of a rational parrot?) so the philosopher must use her imagination. [However, Locke did claim the parrot story was a true one.] The term *experiment* reflects a link to the methodology of the sciences. In the sciences, an experiment offers the scientist a laboratory, a workspace if you will, in which she can observe some aspect of nature. By creating a minienvironment and changing one aspect of that environment the scientist can test a claim made by a theory. For instance, in Chapter 7, Marine Biology, we read about a scientist who observed the

---

[1]We should add that even though in her book Wilkes provides this very helpful description of thought experiments, she uses it to argue that thought experiments should *not* be used to study philosophical issues of personal identity. Wilkes strongly encourages philosophers to try to answer the question, "what actually happens when . . ." rather than "what might happen if . . ."

aggressive behavior of a type of sea anemone in the laboratory. She used an excised tentacle from one anemone to touch another one in order to create the aggressive behavior she wanted to learn more about. In this situation, a *thought* experiment was unnecessary; the scientist created a mini-environment in the real world and made the necessary changes in it to test her theory.

Thought experiments are used in several disciplines: the sciences, philosophy, and literature. In children's fiction a story can set up an entirely (or almost entirely) believable background situation and alter one feature of the story. In that "possible world" you could explain, quite reasonably, as Rudyard Kipling does in his "Just so" stories, how the elephant lost his tail. The author's purpose is to entertain and we as readers are willing to suspend disbelief or go along with the story. The author has achieved his or her purpose to entertain the reader: the most important part of such a story is to have fun.

However, in philosophy the situation is quite a bit different. Thought experiments are frequently used to help us define terms or concepts. For example, Locke uses them to understand what is necessary and sufficient to be considered a person. Determining the background situation is critical. In philosophical thought experiments the "possible world" is our world, except for one important difference (Wilkes, 8). When we accept a claim as believable on the basis of a thought experiment, we are also accepting the background situation as possible. So, in Locke's "little finger" thought experiment, we believe that the world in that experiment is just like the world as we know it and the only difference is that our consciousness is in our little finger. The importance of such experiments for philosophy, some believe, is that they cause us to reexamine our intuitions and our beliefs, and in so doing help us to uncover those assumptions about, say, personal identity, that might have remained unexamined.

In scientific as well as in philosophical research, the laboratory situation or as Wilkes calls it (7), the background conditions, must be described carefully and offer everything we need to know to evaluate the strength of our claim. The purpose of a thought experiment in scientific research is the same as a real-life experiment: to show that one, and one change only, in the experimental situation creates a difference that will then prove a theory or a claim right or wrong.

An important part of thinking about thought experiments is examining our intuitions and beliefs about what constitutes personal identity. In so doing, we may uncover what Professor Schechtman called "the most basic, ordinary, commonsense presuppositions we all share," and then proceed to think about whether they still make sense to us.

WRITING AND LEARNING ACTIVITIES

1. Journal Entry: Look for examples of thought experiments (or, "What might happen if . . . ?" situations) in other academic disciplines, in everyday life, on television, in books you read, or in movies. Write about one such hypothetical situation. What point was being made? What was the purpose of the thought experiment?

2. **Group Activity:** Meet in small groups and exchange the report on thought experiments that you have written. Choose the most interesting and develop a full explanation of it to present to the class.

DEVELOPING INTERESTS

You have now read a portion of John Locke's essay and gotten to know something about Professor Schechtman's views on philosophy. These are the first steps to getting involved with an area of academic inquiry, but you probably won't feel as though you are really participating in the process of inquiry until you can talk about your own ideas in this area. Through your journal entries and group discussions you have probably already begun to develop the personal connections which provide the points of connection between your experiences and knowledge and what you've been studying.

The work of Patricia Mann helped several of my students find connections between their personal experience and our academic study of personal identity. Mann, in her article, "Personal Identity Matters," takes the personal identity issue out of the realm of the "possible worlds" of thought experiments and into our kitchens to ask what the issue of personal identity means for family members and particularly for women. A problem of personal identity arose, Mann tells us, when women became socially enfranchised and began leaving the home to work. Many women thought it was reasonable to assume that men would take over some of the household duties, that "as a matter of basic reciprocity, men would assume substantial domestic roles as women took on major economic obligations for the family" (285). This has not happened. Instead, Mann tells us, women experience a double identity when they "spend crucial working hours thinking about the problems of a child, or when they are unable to leave work concerns behind at the end of a day, in order to fully respond to personal needs of spouses and children" (311).

> The traditional woman has become a full person by adding a public selfhood to a private female personhood. She has become, immediately, two selves though they reside in one body. . . . The problems of personal identity for women arise insofar as the reasons for acting which applied to the former female subsumed nurturer no longer work as sufficient reasons or causes for the family activities of the new socially enfranchised female self. In the same ways, the purposes and reasons for acting which motivated traditional male public selves also fail to provide sufficient reasons for public achievements to the socially enfranchised woman. Since this new female self is not identical with either, or both, of the previous selves from which she has originated, a sense of coherent personhood and agency eludes her. Such a coherent sense of female personhood

will be possible only when her personal services within the family, as well as those of men, can be comprehended, as alternative choices, with acts of ratio- nal purposive behavior in the public sphere. (311–312).

In the following conversation, two students—Raquel Grys and Sandra Cornejo—connect Mann's ideas to their personal experience. From these personal connections they will eventually be able to identify a topic for a re- search essay.

RAQUEL: Mann's reading relates to me because before my parents were separated, I remember the gendered roles in my family be- tween my mother, father, brother, and myself. Society believes that if women want to work, they have to still manage all the "duties" a woman must do without the man's help. My mother worked, and took care of the house and my brother and myself, while my father just worked and helped around the house once in a while. She re- ally had to be more than two people, but it's a no-win situation be- cause you just can't do it. This, however, has changed. Now we all share the housework and my father does a lot more than before be- cause he had to learn that my mom had many things to do. I think it was my father's identity that really changed. I'm just not sure what I want to write about though, what I want to focus on from my own experience.

SANDRA: I used to accept that the role of a woman was to go to school, go home, help your mother with the house chores, and so on. Now that I'm attending college I am beginning to find that there is so much more out there for women. Maybe you would want to focus on women and families, Raquel?

RAQUEL: Yes, I think that's right. Women and families. To be more spe- cific, I guess I would say that what I'm really interested in is how society views women's roles as working mothers and wives.

SANDRA: When I read Mann, I guess I thought about women's roles but I also thought of my own role in the family. When I'm here at school, I have a hard time being myself because I still do not have a sense of the "real" me. Before I started attending college I was pretty sure who I was and what I was supposed to do as a daughter, sister, friend, and student. Now that I'm here in college, I am un- sure of myself and the decisions I am making and find it difficult to fit in. From the time I was a baby until now, everything that I am and have done revolved around the way my parents have taught and showed me. That's where the conflict starts. My dad wants me tied down to the family, but I want to learn new things and experi- ence life as an independent woman.

RAQUEL: I too feel college has brought a lot of new experiences, but I like most of them. I feel a lot more independent and more respon- sible now that I am in college. In college there is no one to tell you when to turn in something or how to budget your time, so I have learned to be more organized in my life and to handle responsibility. I know that this new freedom can cause conflict between college kids and their parents. So, Sandra, maybe you could write about the struggle for independence from the family which people face when they go to college?

SANDRA: Yes, but it's not just independence that I'm thinking about here, but identity. I think that I would like to explore how one finds one's identity when the family is still dominating or controlling you. As I said my family had a lot of influence on who I was as a child and they still influence me as a young adult. I wonder, how can a person break free to be an individual without hurting anyone in the family?

WRITING AND LEARNING ACTIVITIES

1. **Journal Entry:** Have you ever felt as though you have two selves? When and why does this occur? Do you know women who work and take care of a family? Is the division of labor equal or unequal? How do you think this influences one's personal identity?

2. **Question Posing:** Write three questions that the excerpt from Mann's article suggests to you about personal identity. What other situations could cause you to question your personal identity?

3. **Journal Entry:** What other aspects of personal identity has this chapter made you think about? Write about several situations that involve this issue of personal identity. Which of these would you like to learn more about?

■-┥ LINKED WRITING ASSIGNMENT

Writing a Summary of Work in Philosophy (see Chapter 10, Summarizing Discipline-Specific Texts). In the previous section, Developing Interests, you began to identify issues and ideas that you might want to explore further. Finding personal connections to the material you are studying is one important way to participate more fully in an academic community. You will also need to learn how some everyday thinking strategies, such as summarizing, help you to participate in the disciplines you are studying here. Chapter 10 introduces you to the process of writing a summary and offers a reading from philosophy for you to practice summarizing.

```
┌─────────────────────────────────────────┐
│   C  H  A  P  T  E  R                    │
│                                          │
│            5                             │
│                                          │
│   LITERARY STUDIES                       │
│                                          │
└─────────────────────────────────────────┘
```

5
LITERARY STUDIES

Does literature offer a mirror to life? In their responses to two short stories by Elizabeth Bishop that we will read in this chapter, students grapple with ideas that reflect both their understanding of the stories as literature and the life experiences they bring to their reading.

> GINA MARIE ROSSI: *The two main characters of the stories, Lucy and the little girl, are similar because they are both going through a personal struggle. Lucy is struggling with her religion and her soul whereas the little girl is struggling with trying to accept and understand her mother.*

> MICHELLE DAHILIG: *But it wasn't just an emotional struggle. In "The Baptism," there was the physical death of Lucy. In "In the Village" it was essentially a death, because the girl lost her mother. Her mother's mental illness didn't allow her to be a mother to the girl.*

> SALVADOR GONZALEZ: *"The Baptism" seemed to be written from a distance, with a colder kind of writing. Bishop seemed to write with more emotion in "In the Village," as though she was willing to expose more of herself and her past experiences.*

In this chapter, we explore the subject of literary studies and introduce you to reading literary works and literary criticism. Professor John Huntington speaks about the importance of literary studies and the changes in the field over the last twenty years. In a close reading of two short stories by Elizabeth Bishop and in reading an excerpt from literary criticism of Bishop's work, Professor Huntington helps us to see how literary scholars approach this specialized discipline. You will learn how you can rely on what you know about yourself, the literary text, and literary criticism to make meaning in this discipline. Finally, I ask you to identify your own interests in reading and responding to literary works.

INTERVIEWING A LITERATURE SCHOLAR

Professor John Huntington teaches courses on Shakespeare, the Renaissance, critical theory, and cultural studies at the University of Illinois at Chicago. He recently edited a book of essays on H. G. Wells, and has published a book on science fiction short stories called *Rationalizing Genius: Ideological Strategies in the Classic American Science Fiction Short Story.*

When did you discover you had an interest in literature?

I was not a very good student in high school. In fact, for a while, around the ninth and tenth grade I did very poorly and nearly flunked out of school. Luckily, though, I did very well on standardized tests, so my teachers felt I had the ability but wasn't using it. I always thought that I would become a mathematician or physicist because math and science came most easily to me. But early in my freshman year of college I chose to major in literature. I had always loved reading and I thought literature was addressing questions about life that interested me more than math and physics did. I was not very good at it, though, particularly because I didn't pay very much attention to my own writing. I didn't do particularly well in college until the end. I remember quite vividly a noncredit writing course in which we were asked to bring in papers we had written so that the group could discuss them. I brought a paper that I had done well on, but I remember being very struck by the group's close study of the options one had to consider in writing even a single sentence. This kind of response is more common nowadays, especially with our interest in the teaching of writing, but back in the early sixties it was the only time I'd ever had a critique of that sort. The other thing that really changed me as a writer was learning German after my sophomore year. Then I tried to write English with the elaborateness of German. I produced some terrible prose, but I became more conscious of my prose and how it sounded.

What do you remember about your college English classes?

I was rather disappointed with my English courses because the professors were so interested in formal issues, such as the ways images were handled and the style of the writing. I wanted to discuss what was true about life in the works we read. Now I see myself back then as being naive, but I still feel that that is an important motive for wanting to go into literary studies. I improved slowly through my college years. At the end of my undergraduate career a professor asked me what I was going to do. This was before the Vietnam-War era, and I said that I was going into the army. He said, "Why don't you go to graduate school?" So I did, and it was in graduate school, I think, that I really figured out what was going on.

I do remember one very humiliating experience there. Once I handed in a forty-page paper that the professor said was full of bits and pieces and didn't have a point. I just hadn't understood that writing had to be an argument with a point. Now, as a teacher, I see the kind of paper I had written as an "exam paper": you just write down everything you know to be true. I had written that paper for a teacher I admired very much and ever since, I've been quite hard on myself about wanting to show that there is a reason for an essay, not just that I know a lot.

How has literary studies evolved over the course of your career?

When I started out, literary studies was quite secure in its sense of what it was and where it fit into the humanities. Literary scholars recognized specific works of literature that we should learn to appreciate and read accurately. The art of reading was the art of interpretation: reading accurately, carefully, and with sensitivity. Over the last two or three decades, however, we have come to recognize that it was naive to believe that one simply reads for the true meaning of a text. We now recognize that there are all kinds of complexities at work and literature is never "disinterested." What I mean by "interestedness" is that a writer is always writing something for a reason and out of some personal belief, and any reader's enthusiasm comes out of his or her own interested position. So that, if we go back to my early reason for wanting to be a literature major, I think literary studies has gone back to asking questions about the truth values of a piece of literature and about how it means what it means. Approaches like feminism have made us very much aware of how literature shapes us and makes us believe one thing rather than another.

One of the influential essays in criticism was W. K. Wimsatt's "The Intentional Fallacy." He argued that we never can really know exactly what the writer intends. All we know is what the text seems to say. That rejection of intention led us to ignore considerations of interestedness in literature. Today, the pendulum has swung in the other direction; we might not be able to know precisely what the writer intended, but we accept that the writer "intended" something, and that his or her intent has a purpose in the social sphere.

What are your research interests and how have they changed?

In some ways my research has followed some of the changes in the field as a whole. Nearly twenty-five years ago, I wrote a dissertation on George Chapman, an English poet and playwright who was a contemporary of Shakespeare's and the first translator of Homer. He's a famously difficult poet; he boasted of his obscurity. I did a reading of some of his poems—the sort of study that was expected at that time. I read a lot of Latin translations of Plato and a lot of scholarly research on neo-platonism. We knew that Chapman had read Marsilio Ficino who, in the fifteenth century, translated and commented on Plato's work. I defended my readings of Chapman by showing how something that Ficino has written could help us understand Chapman. That was a fairly conventional kind of dissertation project for that time.

Just about the time I was finishing my dissertation, a group of biology students asked for a science fiction course, and the head of the department told them that if they could get someone to teach it they could have the course. I volunteered. That spring I had a class of 40; the next year I had a class of 300. I had started reading science fiction myself a few years earlier. It tapped into my own earlier interests in physics and math. About a week before the course started I got together with a group of students and we drew up a fairly heavy reading list, including: H. G. Wells and Jules Verne, Karel Capek, Olaf Stapledon, Arthur C. Clarke and Isaac Asimov, Robert Heinlein, Ursula Le Guin, and others. This change in my teaching caused a radical change in my scholarly interests. I started researching H. G. Wells and wrote my first book on him. I looked at his writing but also thought a lot about his socialism and Utopianism.

That led me to my interest in popular writing—that I didn't particularly admire as literature but which was very popular. My next book was on pulp science fiction, popular stories of the '30s, '40s, and '50s. I wanted to explore what made this writing interesting to its readers, not whether it was or wasn't good literature. These stories remained popular right into the '70s. In fact, quite commonly one of my students would tell me his dad had seen what he was reading and said that he had read that story when he was younger. I wondered why people kept reading these stories. What are the concerns of the group of people who read and love these stories?

For instance, there was a story called "The Cold Equations" in which a man on a very small spaceship finds a young woman who has stowed away to visit to her brother. The man argues that the spaceship doesn't have enough fuel to land with her added weight and that she's got to get off which, of course, means certain death. After a lot of pleading and arguing the girl does step out of the door of the spaceship and everyone sees that physics and its cold equations are not kind. In my book on science fiction short stories, called Rationalizing Genius, *I argued that the whole story was set up to kill this young woman but also to justify the divorce of science from ethics.*

What are you working on now?

I've gone back to the Renaissance but with a much more sociological perspective than before. Now I'm looking at Chapman as a nonaristocratic poet in an era of largely aristocratic poets. He really was just a poor man writing poetry who argued that poets make a very important contribution in spite of the fact that they may have no money or political power.

Tell us something about the current debates in literary studies.

Currently, literary studies is involved in an important debate about its place in the humanities. Some scholars are trying to hold onto the older, formalist school in which we appreciate and dignify literature for itself. Others are paying increasing attention to studying literature for its ideological content. When I say ideological content I mean the presumptions that a text rests on, the ideas that inform a text, especially the unexamined ones. Literature is very instrumental in instilling these presumptions.

I was just reading some Louis L'Amour westerns and the picture that these novels present of how men and women should relate to each other is really quite extraordinary. The good woman quietly supports the male hero, with a frying pan and a shotgun, and then marries him in order to cook for him on the lonely ranch. Though from the male point of view the picture might appear reasonable, as a realistic way of life it will hardly bear examination. One can explain such a drama of passionless servitude as the distillation of the western genre as it develops through the twentieth century, but this portrayal still carries a powerful ideological message about the place of women and their importance. Someone who reads a lot of these stories could believe that that's the way it ought to be without ever being told so. So a reader who takes an ideological perspective would question the depiction of reality presented in L'Amour's books. The modern mode of literary studies questions and frequently attacks the ideology behind a work.

One other change that I've noticed is the increasing self-consciousness of the discipline and the rise of theory. In my training days, you picked a time period and a literary genre to work with and these guided your graduate work. Theory had a small esoteric corner of the field that no one paid much attention to. Now scholars train to be theorists, and English departments are hiring theorists.

We hear a lot in the popular press about the canon and what should be read by college students. How has literary studies changed with respect to the canon?

Some people have the idea that there exists a list of the greatest books and that this list has always been the same. As a matter of fact, the canon has always shifted quite dramatically and books that now are thought to be undoubtedly in the canon were out of the canon fifty years ago and others that were then honored are now forgotten. Moby Dick, *for instance, was ignored for the first half-century after its publication.* Uncle Tom's Cabin, *after a period of immense popularity a century ago, was looked down on in the middle of this century and is only recently again being recognized as an important book.*

I think our recognizing the interestedness of literature has led to a challenging of the canon. We have come to see that there are exclusions from the canon of works by women and minorities. Literary scholars have begun to recognize, too, that some works have been considered part of the canon for ideological reasons. For instance, D. H. Lawrence's writing has been considered an important contribution to the canon. Yet Lawrence forwards a male, patriarchal point of view which for many years was not questioned. He isn't admired today in the way he was before Kate Millet challenged his presentation of reality in her book Sexual Politics. *She argued that Lawrence was presenting a reality that celebrated a mystical, masculine core of energy that all of civilization finally depends on and that women are good only in so far as they see themselves in relation to that. I don't mean to say that you shouldn't read Lawrence, but you would want to consider his ideological perspective, then balance him with other readings. Such reevaluation of works of literature is how the canon gets expanded.*

In what areas can students specialize in literary studies?

The study of literature in English departments has traditionally been organized according to time periods: Medieval (twelfth to fifteenth centuries), Renaissance (from about 1500 to the English Revolution of the 1640s), Restoration and Eighteenth century (from the end of the English Revolution in 1660 to the French Revolution of 1789), nineteenth-century American, nineteenth-century British, and modern and contemporary (usually the last quarter of the century). Courses in the major might offer study by genre as in "the novel," or "epic poetry." Or, one can combine history and genre and study "the modern novel," or even Elizabethan poetry. It is also possible to study the works of a single author.

When as a graduate student I had to take a course in literary studies it was a course in how to do bibliography, not a course in theory. We needed such a course then, because any paper we wrote would be an interpretation of a single work and as such had to take into account all previous interpretations. The dream at that time was that you could read and interpret everything important that had been written and then literature would be over. There's a lot more to reading than we used to be aware of.

What are some current approaches to literary criticism?

Professors twenty-five years younger than me are now trained in a very different way. I was trained to study all of English literature and to stay focused on whatever text I was reading. This approach, sometimes called a formalist approach, teaches you how to do a "close reading" to understand the meaning of the text. New professors are much more interested in the theoretical and the critical issues.

Several approaches to criticism have developed in recent years. The Psychoanalytic school tends to say that the text is really a manifest statement of some deeper, more latent issue in the author or in the culture and asks how we get to that concealed truth, which the text is, in part, trying to hide. The Reader Response school focuses on how the text is received by its audience. Feminist scholarship has gone through an evolution in the last thirty years, from a critique of the masculine basis of much canonic literature, through the recovery of literature written by women (what Elaine Showalter called "gynocriticism"), to a kind of cultural studies in which all sorts of texts are analyzed to understand more intricately the ways women have been represented in literature and the affect of such representations on social conditions. Then, there is what's called Marxist, but I almost prefer to call it either the Sociology of Literature or Cultural Studies. This approach views literature in terms of social issues and the messages it is sending to society. Another area, which doesn't fit into a category so neatly, is called New-Historicism. It argues that the traditional studies that we've been talking about have isolated literature in an artificial way. Imaginative literature or fiction should be seen as linked very much to other kinds of writing, and it shouldn't be separated from histories and court cases and all kinds of other things that are happening at the same time. New-historicist scholars want to resituate imaginative literature back into the social and historical context of a particular time period.

Would you say something about deconstruction?

Deconstruction refers to a way of reading that focuses on how meaning is always constructed or forced. A very influential presence in this area of literary studies is Jacques Derrida. Even people who haven't read him are still influenced by him, just as Freud influenced people who hadn't read Freud half a century ago. For deconstructionists there is no truth or meaning in the text that you can gesture toward and have it simply emerge. This group is interested in finding points of strain and seeing how the illusion of truth or meaning is created. It means that more and more there is an awareness that interestedness (to use the term I've been stressing here) is at the heart of literary studies and the making of meaning within literary studies. The authors are interested; the critics are interested; even the reader is interested. Everybody has a perspective that is motivated by their own beliefs, experiences, and knowledge. Even scholars who write about the interestedness of literature are interested themselves since they will probably receive some benefit from their publication—perhaps a raise or perhaps they will earn tenure.

When literary scholars read, what textual features do they pay attention to?

Some concerns are at the level of the sentence; we look at the tone and structure of the sentence. Is it mocking? Is it serious? Is it casual? Is it careful? Plot, in its simplest sense, asks us to look at who succeeds and who fails and why. What sort of message does that send? Though I think character is an illusion, it is sometimes a useful device to think about what kind of a person this is. What are the person's values and motivation? What is their social function? How is the illusion of that character created through their words in the dialogue of that story? As we read we typically consider issues of form and genre. We ask, how does one's experience of other works of literature prepare one to read this work? You see, one is always comparing what one reads now to what one has read in the past. For instance, when we read about two beautiful people arguing at the beginning of a story we may expect them to get married at the end. Or, if the first part of a play is comical, we typically don't expect the characters to die in the end.

Then, at a broader level, we think about the structure of a whole work, the way parts echo or contradict each other. We look at the way themes are modified throughout the course of the work. At an even larger level of magnification we ask questions about life and culture. What is the value of this work? What was the world like at the time it was written? How might understanding the political or social issues of that day help us to understand the work? What is its message for life?

How do literary scholars write critical texts about literature?

When I began writing about literature a very clear model of good prose was held up by almost everybody: it should be clear and it shouldn't take a professional to read it. This writing—which is sometimes dismissed these days as belletristic—could almost be placed next to imaginative fiction. For instance, the same author, say E. M. Forster, could produce essays on the one hand and novels on the other. Recently, a different kind of writing—for example, the work of Derrida—one in which difficulty is equated with seriousness, has become acceptable. I have very mixed feelings about this. I certainly can get drawn in and write in that way; sometimes I find myself believing that the harder a piece of writing is to understand, the more profound it must be. The "difficulty" of an essay in literary studies could be because it is explaining some complicated ideas, or it could be the result of poor prose or unclear thought. Distinguishing one from the other can be difficult.

Putting the difficulty issue aside, though, writing about literature today can be quite adventuresome. Some of the most successful and stunning people in the field are really quite daring in their approaches. One big shift in attitude is that scholars can be much more personal in their writing. I was just reading Jane Tompkins' 1992 book on the western. She relies on her own memories of the movies she saw as a child and how she reacted to them. Twenty-five years ago my personal response was seen as irrelevant, but nowadays it is seen as inescapable and even a point from which to begin the study of a particular text.

Why is it important to study literature?

I don't have an easy answer to that question. I know that literature is influential and therefore is important, but I wouldn't say now what I might have said twenty-five years ago: that you will be a better person for reading Shakespeare. I would say that you will understand more about a certain society if you read the literature of that time period and culture. We need to think too about why people get pleasure from reading literature, and I think we have to come back to the idea of interestedness. By reading literature you may learn something about yourself as an "interested reader." It may be that the literature that we get pleasure from is the literature that somehow reinforces our view of ourselves or our world. We connect to it in some way.

Today not many people come to Shakespeare naturally; they usually come to enjoy it in an educational context. There is definitely a cultural process at work making Shakespeare important and we should take a close look at how that happens. Even a book as popular as Toni Morrison's Beloved presents difficulties and may need some backgrounding—for instance, about the facts of slavery—to be fully appreciated. The reasons I started studying literature are not my reasons for continuing to study literature. The reading of literature clearly is doing something and anything that's doing something ought to be understood.

WRITING AND LEARNING ACTIVITIES

---

1. **Journal Entry:** Look up a definition of literature or literary analysis in a specialized humanities reference source (see the appendix, Directions for Further Research), a college dictionary, or a general reference encyclopedia. Consider the differences and similarities among these definitions. Report your finding to the class.

2. **Writing Activity:** Write three questions you would like to ask Professor Huntington if you had the opportunity to talk with him.

3. **Peer Conversation:** Discuss your journal entries and questions for Professor Huntington with a partner. Respond also to the following questions: Were you reminded by something he said of another experience you've had at home, school, or work? What does the notion of "interestedness" discussed by Professor Huntington mean to you? Share an example of interestedness in your everyday life or in your reading.

4. **Research Project:** Look up the English or literature major in your college catalog. Respond to the following questions: How is the discipline described? How does this description differ from Professor Huntington's description or from other descriptions you've found? What are the required courses for the English or literature major? What are the possible areas of specialization? Next, interview someone who is majoring in literary studies. Why is he or she studying literature? What courses has this person taken? Is he or she specializing in any particular area? What does this person plan to do with this degree? Finally, attend one class with the student and take notes about how it is similar to or different from other classes.

5. **Writing Activity:** Write a report, based on your research, describing what it's like to major in English or literary studies at your school.

6. **Developing Interests:** Read in the *New York Times Book Review* reviews of several new works of fiction. Do any pique your interest? Would you be interested in reading any of those new works? Do you consider all of these to be "literature"? Why or why not? How do you define literature and popular fiction? What do you see as the difference between literature and popular fiction?

A CLOSE READING OF SHORT STORIES

READING SHORT STORIES

In reading any works of literature—in this case, short stories—our first task is to learn what is going on in the story. As Professor Huntington mentioned above, in the 1960s it was a common critical practice to ask what the text means. Now, however, literary scholars want to know how the text's meanings are constructed and how the text might be understood by different readers. Students are often assigned the task of developing an interpretation of a text, that is, writing an argument that supports his or her understanding of what the text is about. Understandings may vary, since different readers bring different experiences and different ideas to the reading. An interpretation is judged not by how close it comes to some absolute, "correct" reading (there is no such thing), but by how it accounts for the story's details, how it explains the language and structure of the text, and how it uses evidence from the text to convince the audience of its plausibility.

Professor Huntington states that there is a specific process to reading a short story (which he will demonstrate in his discussion of two short stories by Elizabeth Bishop). The first step he recommends is reading the story several times. The first readings clarify the basic elements of the story: the characters, movement of the plot, time and place, and any references to unfamiliar dialect, history, or geography. Later readings begin to focus on the rhetorical dimensions of the text and try to understand how the text creates its effect. *Reading in slow motion* is the wording given this process in an influential book by Reuben Brower and Richard Poirier written in 1962.

Professor Huntington also recommends that you pay attention to moments or points in the text that continue to confuse you even after you have put the basic elements of the story in order. It is important not to avoid or cover up confusion but to recognize it and try to understand it, because it is often in moments of apparent contradiction or crisis that the text is performing its most significant work. Often your own personal "interestedness" can guide you in noticing how a text slides over a difficult issue or poses an interpretive problem. For example, a person who has trouble being heard in her family may be particularly sensitive to the way a voice (like the narrative voice in "The Baptism," the first story you will read in this section), while seemingly neutral, in fact takes sides.

Pay attention to how the text orders information. The title is, of course, a very important beginning sign, but it can often pose as many problems as it solves. Italics and quotation marks can also seem to identify important information. How does the text distinguish (or blur) the author's voice from those of the characters? Make notes in the margins identifying repeated phrases, related ideas or images, moments of confusion. Use asterisks to mark points that you think particularly important and question marks to indicate points you need to come back to. See if you can connect ideas, images, or quotes in different parts of the text.

About Elizabeth Bishop

Elizabeth Bishop was born in Worcester, Massachusetts, on February 8, 1911. When Bishop was eight months old her father died, and her mother never recovered from his death. For the next five years, Bishop's mother was in and out of mental hospitals and rest homes, moving between Boston, Massachusetts, and her home town of Great Village, Nova Scotia. During this time, Elizabeth Bishop went to live with her grandparents in Nova Scotia, when her mother was permanently institutionalized in a sanitarium in Dartmouth, Nova Scotia in 1916. She went on to boarding school and then to Vassar College, where her literary career began. After college, she spent most of her time wandering between New York, Key West, and occasionally Nova Scotia, during which time she struggled with alcoholism.

Bishop, best known for her poetry, won numerous prizes and awards for her work, including the Pulitzer Prize for Poetry for her collections,

Poems: North & South and *A Cold Spring* in 1955. Her short stories in many ways seem to be influenced by her "poetic eye," with their attention to detail and abbreviated and highly descriptive language. Images from Bishop's childhood in Nova Scotia appear repeatedly in her work—the blue, blue sky; the ice cold water; cows; maple syrup; Protestant hymns.

Much of Bishop's work is somewhat autobiographical, although Bishop does not write extensively about the events of her childhood until about 1952, when she had established a relatively permanent residence in Brazil with her lover, Lota de Macedo Soares.*

Professor Huntington tells us enthusiastically why he chooses to teach Bishop's stories often.

I love to teach Bishop's stories because of the extraordinary intricacy of certain problematic moments in the text. Once you see it you have to do something with it, but you don't know what. The stories make you think in a literary way. Bishop's stories put pressure on the reader to make meaning with her. She does it responsibly; she's not trying just to confuse the reader. She's trying to put the reader in a situation that demands an act of interpretation.

WRITING AND LEARNING ACTIVITIES

1. **Reading:** Practice reading in slow motion. Read the two stories at least twice, the first time to get a general sense of the stories: the plot, characters, location, time period, and any dialect or speech patterns of the characters. Read more carefully the second time. What details do you notice the second time that you didn't notice before? Record these in your journal. As you read also write down in your textbook what strikes you as interesting about the two stories.

2. **Journal Entry:** As you read, jot down notes about your reading process in your journal. Make guesses about what might be going on. Think about your own personal experiences and those of others to help you understand what you are reading about. Note places in the text where you are confused or surprised. Record the way characters talk to each other, the things you see in the stories, and objects and ideas that appear to be connected.

3. **Annotate the Stories:** Put question marks at places where the stories confuse you, especially after several readings. Make notes in the margin about personal experiences the stories remind you of. Underline ideas, images, or quotes that seem related, though in different parts of the stories.

---

*This synopsis of Elizabeth Bishop's life is taken from a recent (1993) biography by Brett C. Millier. Recent biographies of Elizabeth Bishop suggest that some moments in "In the Village," one of the stories you'll read, reflect moments in the author's own life. This story recounts her mother's final visit to Great Village, Nova Scotia in 1916; shortly after, her mother was permanently institutionalized in a sanitarium, where she would die in 1934 without ever seeing her daughter Elizabeth again.

THE BAPTISM

ELIZABETH BISHOP

■ ■ ■

It was November. They bent in the twilight like sea plants, around their little dark center table hung with a cloth like a seaweed-covered rock. It seemed as if a draft might sway them all, perceptibly. Lucy, the youngest, who still did things for her sisters, rose to get the shawls and light the lamp. She sighed. How would they get through the winter?

"We have our friends!"

Yes, that was true and a consolation. They had several friends. They had old Mrs. Peppard and young Mrs. Gillespie and old Mrs. Captain Green and little Mrs. Kent. One of them was bound to drop in almost every afternoon.

When the weather was fine they themselves could make a call, although they preferred to stay at home. They were more in command of conversation when they sat close together around their own table. Antiphonally, they spoke to their friends of the snowstorm, of health, of church activities. They had the church, of course.

5   When the snow grew too deep—it grew all winter, as the grain grew all summer, and finally wilted away unharvested in April—old Mr. Johnson, who had the post office now, would bring the newspaper on his way home.

They would manage, but winter was longer every year. Lucy thought of carrying wood in from the woodshed and scratching her forearms on the bark. Emma thought of hanging out the washing, which was frozen before you got it onto the line. The sheets particularly—it was like fighting with monster icy seagulls. Flora thought only of the difficulties of getting up and dressing at six o'clock every morning.

They would keep two stoves going: the kitchen range and an airtight in the sitting room. The circulatory system of their small house was this: in the ceiling over the kitchen stove there was an opening set with a metal grill. It yielded up some heat to the room where Lucy and Emma slept. The pipe from the sitting-room stove went up through Flora's room, but it wasn't so warm, of course.

They baked bread once a week. In the other bedroom there were ropes and ropes of dried apples. They ate applesauce and apple pie and apple dumpling, and a kind of cake paved with slices of apple. At every meal they drank a great deal of tea and ate many slices of bread. Sometimes they bought half a pound of store cheese, sometimes a piece of pork.

Emma knitted shawls, washcloths, bed socks, an affectionate spider-web around Flora and Lucy. Flora did fancy work and made enough Christmas presents for them to give all around: to each other and to friends. Lucy was of no use at all with her fingers. She was supposed to read aloud while the others worked.

10   They had gone through a lot of old travel books that had belonged to their father. One was called *Wonders of the World*; one was a book about

Palestine and Jerusalem. Although they could all sit calmly while Lucy read about the tree that gave milk like a cow, the Eskimos who lived in the dark, the automaton chess player, etc., Lucy grew excited over accounts of the Sea of Galilee, and the engraving of the Garden of Gethsemane as it looks today brought tears to her eyes. She exclaimed "Oh dear!" over pictures of "An Olive Grove," with Arabs squatting about in it; and "Heavens!" at the real, rock-vaulted Stable, the engraved rocks like big black thumbprints.

They had also read: (1) *David Copperfield,* twice; (2) *The Deer-Slayer;* (3) *Samantha at the World's Fair;* (4) *The Autocrat of the Breakfast Table.*

Also two or three books from the Sunday School library, which none of them liked. Because of the source, however, they listened as politely as to the minister's sermons. Lucy's voice even took on a little of his intonation, so that it seemed to take forever to get through them.

They were Presbyterians. The village was divided into two camps, armed with Bibles: Baptists and Presbyterians. The sisters had friends on both sides.

Prayer meeting was Friday night. There was Sunday School and church on Sunday, and Ladies' Aid every other week at different friends' houses. Emma taught the smallest children in Sunday School. Lucy and Flora preferred not to teach, but to attend the class for adults held by the minister himself.

15   Now each was arranging the shawl over her shoulders, and just as Lucy lit the lamp, old Mrs. Peppard came to call. She opened the back door without knocking, and said, "Anybody home?" This was the thing to do. She wore a very old mud-brown coat with large black frogs down the front and a black, cloth-covered hat with a velvet flower on it.

Her news was that her sister's baby had died the day before, although they had done everything. She and Emma, Flora, and Lucy discussed infant damnation at some length.

Then they discussed the care of begonias, and Mrs. Peppard took home a slip of theirs. Flora had always had great luck with house plants.

Lucy grew quite agitated after Mrs. Peppard had gone, and could not eat her bread and butter, only drank three cups of tea.

Of course, as Emma had expected because of the tea, Lucy couldn't sleep that night. Once she nudged Emma and woke her.

20   "Emma, I'm thinking of that poor child."

"Stop thinking. Go to sleep."

"Don't you think we ought to pray for it?"

It was the middle of the night or she couldn't have said that. Emma pretended to be asleep. In fact, she was asleep, but not so much that she couldn't feel Lucy getting out of bed. The next day she mentioned this to Flora, who only said "Tsch—Tsch." Later on they both referred to this as the "beginning," and Emma was sorry she'd gone back to sleep.

In prayer meeting one Friday the minister called for new members, and asked some of those who had joined the church lately to speak. Art Tinkham stood up. He talked for a long time of God's goodness to him, and said that now he felt happy all the time. He had felt so happy when he was

doing his fall plowing that he had kept singing, and at the end of every fur-
row he'd said a Bible verse.

25   After a while the minister called on Lucy to give a prayer. She did it,
quite a long one, but at last her voice began to tremble. She could scarcely
say the Amen, and sat down very quickly. Afterwards her sisters said it had
been a very pretty prayer, but she couldn't remember a word of it.

Emma and Lucy liked the dreamy hymns best, with vague references in
them to gardens, glassy seas, high hills, etc. Flora liked militant hymns; almost her favorite was "A Mighty Fortress."

Lucy's was: "Sometimes a light surprises the Christian while he sings."
Emma's: "There is a green hill far away without a city wall."

Lucy was not yet a church member. Emma and Flora were, but Lucy
had been too young to join when they had. She sometimes asked her sisters
if she were good enough.

"You are too good for us, Lucy."

30   "That's not what I mean," Lucy said.

At night she felt that Emma's prayers were over all too quickly. Her own
sometimes lasted almost an hour, and even then did not seem quite long
enough. She felt very guilty about something. She worried about this so
much that one day she almost convinced Flora that she must have been
guilty of the gravest misdemeanor as a young girl. But it was not so.

It got to be Christmastime. The snow was up to the windowsills, practically over, as if they inhabited a sinking ship. Lucy's feeling of guilt grew
heavier and heavier. She talked constantly about whether she should join
the church or not.

At Christmas an elderly missionary, Miss Gillespie, young Mr. Gillespie's
aunt, came home from India on furlough. The Ladies' Aid had special meetings
for her. At them this tall, dark brown, mustached woman of sixty-four talked,
almost shouted, for hours about her lifework. Photographs were handed
around. They represented gentle-faced boys and young men, dressed in
pure-white loincloths and earrings. Next, the same boys and young men
were shown, in soiled striped trousers and shirts worn with the tails outside.
There were a few photographs of women, blurred as they raised a hand to
hide their faces, or backed away from the camera's Christian eye.

Emma and Flora disliked Miss Gillespie. Flora even said she was
"bossy." But Lucy liked her very much and went to see her several times.
Then for three weeks she talked about nothing but going as a missionary.
She went through all the travel books again.

35   Flora and Emma did not really think she would ever go, but the thought
of living without her sometimes horrified one or the other of them. At the
end of the third week she stopped speaking of it and, in fact, became very
untalkative.

Lucy was growing thinner. The skin of her forehead seemed stretched
too tightly, and although she had never had a temper in her life, Flora and
Emma could see that it was sometimes an effort for her not to speak crossly
to them.

She moved very slowly. At supper she would eat half a slice of bread and put the other half back in the bread dish.

Flora, who was bolder to say things than Emma, said: "She makes me feel that I'm not as good as she is."

Once when Lucy went out to get wood from the woodshed she didn't come back for fifteen minutes. Emma, suddenly realizing how long it had been, ran outside. Lucy, with no coat or shawl, stood holding on to the side of the house. She was staring at the blinding dazzle the sun made on the ice glaze over the next field. She seemed to be humming a little, and the glaring strip made her half shut her eyes. Emma had to take hold of her hand before she would pay any attention. Speaking wasn't enough.

40   It was the night of the day after this that the strange things began to happen.

Lucy kept a diary. It was written in pencil in a book that said "Jumbo Scribbler" in red letters on a tan cover. It was really a record of spiritual progress.

"*January 3rd.* This morning was clear again so Flora did some of the wash and we hung it in the garden, although it was hard to with the wind. For dinner we had a nice stew with the rest of the lamb and the carrots Mr. Jonson brought in. I say a nice stew, but I could not touch a bite. The Lord seems very far away. I kept asking the girls about my joining but they did not help me at all."

Here Lucy copied out three Bible verses. Sometimes for several days the diary was made up of nothing but such quotations.

"*January 16th.* It was 18 below zero last night. We had to get Father's old buffalo robe from the spare room. I didn't like the smell, but Emma didn't mind it. When the lamp was out I prayed for a long time, and a little while after I got into bed I felt that face moving toward me again. I can't make it out, but it is very large and close to mine. It seemed to be moving its lips. Is it reproachful?"

45   Four days after this Lucy began crying in the afternoon and cried almost all evening. Emma finally cried a little, too. Flora shook her by the shoulder, but left Lucy alone.

Emma wished that she and Flora slept together instead of she and Lucy, so that they could talk about Lucy together privately.

Flora said: "What has she ever done wrong, Emma? Why should she weep about her soul?"

Emma said: "She's always been as good as gold."

"*January 20th.* At last, at last, I know my own mind," she began, "or rather I have given it up completely. Now I am going to join the church as soon as I can. But I am going to join the *Baptist* church, and I must not tell Flora and Emma beforehand. I cannot eat, I am so happy. Last night at four o'clock a terrible wind began to blow. I thought all the trees were breaking, I could hear the branches crashing against the house. I thought the chimney would come down. The house shook, and I thought about the House founded on the Rock. I was terribly frightened. Emma did not wake up. It went on for hours in the dark and I prayed that we would all be safely delivered. Then there was a lull. It was very black and my heart pounded so I thought I was dying. I couldn't think of a prayer. Then suddenly a low voice began to talk right over the head of the bed. I couldn't make out the words, they weren't exactly words I knew, but I seemed to understand them. What a load dropped from my mind! Then I was so happy I woke Emma and said: 'Emma, Emma, Christ is here. He was here just now, in this room. Get up and pray with me.' Emma got out of bed and knelt, then she said the floor was cold and wanted to pull the rug over under our knees. I said: 'No, Emma. Why do we need rugs when we have all Christ's love to warm our hearts?' She did not demur after that, and I prayed a long time, for Flora, too. When we got back in bed I told Emma about the voice I had heard."

50   The next day Lucy called on the Baptist minister and told him she had decided to join his church. He was very severe, older than the Presbyterian minister, and Lucy felt at once that he was a much better man.

But a problem came up that she had not considered. She now believed ardently in the use of total immersion as practiced by the Baptists, according to their conception of the methods of John the Baptist. She could not join without that, and the river, of course, was frozen over. She would have to wait until the ice went out.

She could scarcely bear it. In her eagerness to be baptized and her disappointment she forgot she had intended not to tell her sisters of her change of faith. They did not seem to mind so much, but when she asked them, they would not consider changing with her.

She was so overexcited they made her go to bed at five o'clock. Emma wrapped up a hot stove lid to put at her feet.

"*January 25th.* I felt very badly last night and cried a great deal. I thought how Mother always used to give me the best of everything because I was the smallest and I took it not thinking of my sisters. Emma said, 'For mercy's sake, Lucy, stop crying.' I explained to her and she became much softened. She got up and lit the lamp. The lamplight on her face made me cry afresh. She went and woke Flora, who put on her gray wrapper and sat in the rocking chair. She wanted to make me something, but I said No. The lamp began to smoke. The smoke went right up to the ceiling and smelled very strong and sweet, like rose geranium. I began to laugh and cry at the same time. Flora and Emma were talking together, but other people seemed to be talking too, and the voice at the head of the bed."

55   A few days later Lucy became very sad. She could neither pray nor do anything around the house. She sat by the window all day long.

In the afternoon she pointed at the road which went off toward the mountains between rows of trees, and said: "Flora, what does it matter where the road goes?"

Emma and Flora were taking apart Emma's blue silk dress and making a blouse. A moth crawled on the windowpane. Emma said, "Get the swatter, Lucy."

Lucy got up, then sat down and said again: "What does it matter?"

She got out the scribbler and wrote in it from memory all the stanzas of "Return, O heavenly Dove, return."

60   After supper, she seemed more cheerful. They were sitting in the kitchen evenings now, because it was warmer. There was no light but one lamp, so the room was quite dark, making the red circle around the stove lids show.

Lucy suddenly stood up.

"Emma, Emma, Flora. I see God."

She motioned toward the stove.

God, God sat on the kitchen stove and glowed, burned, filling all the kitchen with a delicious heat and a scent of grease and sweetness.

65   Lucy was more conscious of his body than his face. His beautiful glowing bulk was rayed like a sunflower. It lit up Flora's and Emma's faces on either side of the stove. The stove could not burn him.

"His feet are in hell," she remarked to her sisters.

After that, Lucy was happy for a long time and everything seemed almost the way it had been the winter before, except for Lucy going to the Baptist church and prayer meeting by herself.

She spoke often of joining. It had happened once or twice that when people had wanted to join the church in the winter a hole had been broken in the ice to make a font. Lucy begged the minister that this might be done for her, but he felt that it was unnecessary in her case.

One had been a farmer, converted from drinking and abusing his wife. He had chopped the ice open himself. Another had been a young man, also a reformed drunkard, since dead.

70   Flora said: "Oh, Lucy, wait till the ice goes out."

"Yes," Lucy said in bitterness, "and until my soul is eternally lost."

She prayed for an early spring.

On the nineteenth of March, Flora woke up and heard the annually familiar sound, a dim roaring edged with noises of breaking glass.

"Thank goodness," she thought. "Now, maybe, Lucy won't even want to be baptized."

75   Everyone had heard the cracking start, off in the hills, and was at the bridge. Lucy, Emma, and Flora went too. The ice buckled up in shining walls fifteen or twenty feet high, fit for heavenly palaces, then moved slowly downstream.

Once in a while a space of dark brown water appeared. This upset Lucy, who had thought of the water she would be baptized in as crystal-clear, or pale blue.

The baptism took place on the twenty-fourth. It was like all the others, and the village was even used to such early ones, although they were usually those of fervent young men.

A few buggies were on the bank, those of the choir, who stood around in coats and hats, holding one hymnbook among three or four people. Most of the witnesses stood on the bridge, staring down. One boy or young man, of course, always dared to spit over the railing.

The water was muddy, very high, with spots of yellow foam. The sky was solid gray cloud, finely folded, over and over. Flora saw the icy roots of a tree reaching into the river, and the snowbanks yellow like the foam.

80   The minister's robe, which he wore only on such occasions, billowed until the water pulled it all down. He held a clean, folded handkerchief to put over Lucy's mouth at the right minute. She wore a robe, too, that made her look taller and thinner.

The choir sang "I am coming, Lord, coming now to Thee," which they always dragged, and "Shall we gather at the river where bright angel feet have trod?" After the baptism they were to sing something joyful and faster, but the sisters did not remain to hear it.

Lucy went under without a movement, and Flora and Emma thought she'd never come up.

Flora held Emma's heavy coat all ready to put around her. Rather unconventionally, Emma sat in the buggy, borrowed from Mrs. Captain Green, so as to drive off home as soon as Lucy reached the bank. She held the reins and had to keep herself from taking up the whip in her other hand.

Finally it was over. They put the dripping Lucy in the middle. Her hair had fallen down. Thank goodness they didn't live far from the river!

85   The next day she had a bad head cold. Emma and Flora nursed her for a week and then the cold settled in her chest. She wouldn't take to bed. The most they could get her to do was to lie on the couch in the kitchen.

One afternoon they thought she had a high fever. Late in the day, God came again, into the kitchen. Lucy went toward the stove, screaming.

Emma and Flora pulled her back, but not before she had burned her right hand badly.

That night they got the doctor, but the next night Lucy died, calling their names as she did so.

The day she was buried was the first pleasant day in April, and the village turned out very well, in spite of the fact that the roads were deep with mud. Jed Leighton gave a beautiful plant he had had sent from the city, a mass of white blooms. Everyone else had cut all their geraniums, red, white, and pink.

1937

IN THE VILLAGE

ELIZABETH BISHOP

A scream, the echo of a scream, hangs over that Nova Scotian village. No one hears it; it hangs there forever, a slight stain in those pure blue skies, skies that travelers compare to those of Switzerland, too dark, too blue, so that they seem to keep on darkening a little more around the horizon—or is it around the rims of the eyes?—the color of the cloud of bloom on the elm trees, the violet on the fields of oats; something darkening over the woods and waters as well as the sky. The scream hangs like that, unheard, in memory—in the past, in the present, and those years between. It was not even loud to begin with, perhaps. It just came there to live, forever—not loud, just alive forever. Its pitch would be the pitch of my village. Flick the lightning rod on top of the church steeple with your fingernail and you will hear it.

She stood in the large front bedroom with sloping walls on either side, papered in wide white and dim-gold stripes. Later, it was she who gave the scream.

The village dressmaker was fitting a new dress. It was her first in almost two years and she had decided to come out of black, so the dress was purple. She was very thin. She wasn't at all sure whether she was going to like the dress or not and she kept lifting the folds of the skirt, still unpinned and dragging on the floor around her, in her thin white hands, and looking down at the cloth.

"Is it a good shade for me? Is it too bright? I don't know. I haven't worn colors for so long now . . . How long? Should it be black? Do you think I should keep on wearing black?"

5   Drummers sometimes came around selling gilded red or green books, unlovely books, filled with bright new illustrations of the Bible stories. The people in the pictures wore clothes like the purple dress, or like the way it looked then.

It was a hot summer afternoon. Her mother and her two sisters were there. The older sister had brought her home, from Boston, not long before, and was staying on, to help. Because in Boston she had not got any better, in months and months—or had it been a year? In spite of the doctors, in spite of the frightening expenses, she had not got any better.

First, she had come home, with her child. Then she had gone away again, alone, and left the child. Then she had come home. Then she had gone away again, with her sister; and now she was home again.

Unaccustomed to having her back, the child stood now in the doorway, watching. The dressmaker was crawling around and around on her knees eating pins as Nebuchadnezzar had crawled eating grass. The wallpaper glinted and the elm trees outside hung heavy and green, and the straw matting smelled like the ghost of hay.

Clang.

Clang.

Oh, beautiful sounds, from the blacksmith's shop at the end of the garden! Its gray roof, with patches of moss, could be seen above the lilac bushes. Nate was there—Nate, wearing a long black leather apron over his trousers and bare chest, sweating hard, a black leather cap on top of dry, thick, black-and-gray curls, a black sooty face; iron filings, whiskers, and gold teeth, all together, and a smell of red-hot metal and horses' hoofs.

Clang.

The pure note: pure and angelic.

The dress was all wrong. She screamed.

15 The child vanishes.

Later they sit, the mother and the three sisters, in the shade on the back porch, sipping sour, diluted ruby: raspberry vinegar. The dressmaker refuses to join them and leaves, holding the dress to her heart. The child is visiting the blacksmith.

In the blacksmith's shop things hang up in the shadows and shadows hang up in the things, and there are black and glistening piles of dust in each corner. A tub of night-black water stands by the forge. The horseshoes sail through the dark like bloody little moons and follow each other like bloody little moons to drown in the black water, hissing, protesting.

Outside, along the matted eaves, painstakingly, sweetly, wasps go over and over a honeysuckle vine.

Inside, the bellows creak. Nate does wonders with both hands; with one hand. The attendant horse stamps his foot and nods his head as if agreeing to a peace treaty.

20 Nod.

And nod.

A Newfoundland dog looks up at him and they almost touch noses, but not quite, because at the last moment the horse decides against it and turns away.

Outside in the grass lie scattered big, pale granite discs, like millstones, for making wheel rims on. This afternoon they are too hot to touch.

Now it is settling down, the scream.

25 Now the dressmaker is at home, basting, but in tears. It is the most beautiful material she has worked on in years. It has been sent to the woman from Boston, a present from her mother-in-law, and heaven knows how much it cost.

Before my older aunt had brought her back, I had watched my grandmother and younger aunt unpacking her clothes, her "things." In trunks and barrels and boxes they had finally come, from Boston, where she and I had once lived. So many things in the village came from Boston, and even I had once come from there. But I remembered only being here, with my grandmother.

The clothes were black, or white, or black-and-white.

"Here's a mourning hat," says my grandmother, holding up something large, sheer, and black, with large black roses on it; at least I guess they are roses, even if black.

"There's that mourning coat she got the first winter," says my aunt.

30 But always I think they are saying "morning." Why, in the morning, did one put on black? How early in the morning did one begin? Before the sun came up?

"Oh, here are some housedresses!"

They are nicer. Clean and starched, stiffly folded. One with black polka dots. One of fine black-and-white stripes with black grosgrain bows. A third with a black velvet bow and on the bow a pin of pearls in a little wreath.

"Look. She forgot to take it off."

A white hat. A white embroidered parasol. Black shoes with buckles glistening like the dust in the blacksmith's shop. A silver mesh bag. A silver calling-card case on a little chain. Another bag of silver mesh, gathered to a tight, round neck of strips of silver that will open out, like the hatrack in the front hall. A silver-framed photograph, quickly turned over. Handkerchiefs with narrow black hems—"morning handkerchiefs." In bright sunlight, over breakfast tables, they flutter.

35   A bottle of perfume has leaked and made awful brown stains.

Oh, marvelous scent, from somewhere else! It doesn't smell like that here; but there, somewhere, it does, still.

A big bundle of postcards. The curdled elastic around them breaks. I gather them together on the floor.

Some people wrote with pale-blue ink, and some with brown, and some with black, but mostly blue. The stamps have been torn off many of them. Some are plain, or photographs, but some have lines of metallic crystals on them—how beautiful!—silver, gold, red, and green, or all four mixed together, crumbling off, sticking in the lines on my palms. All the cards like this I spread on the floor to study. The crystals outline the buildings on the cards in a way buildings never are outlined but should be—if there were a way of making the crystals stick. But probably not; they would fall to the ground, never to be seen again. Some cards, instead of lines around the buildings, have words written in their skies with the same stuff, crumbling, dazzling and crumbling, raining down a little on little people who sometimes stand about below: pictures of Pentecost? What are the messages? I cannot tell, but they are falling on those specks of hands, on the hats, on the toes of their shoes, in their paths—wherever it is they are.

Postcards come from another world, the world of the grandparents who send things, the world of sad brown perfume, and morning. (The gray postcards of the village for sale in the village store are so unilluminating that they scarcely count. After all, one steps outside and immediately sees the same thing: the village, where we live, full-size, and in color.)

40   Two barrels of china. White with a gold band. Broken bits. A thick white teacup with a small red-and-blue butterfly on it, painfully desirable. A teacup with little pale-blue windows in it.

"See the grains of rice?" says my grandmother, showing me the cup against the light.

Could you poke the grains out? No, it seems they aren't really there any more. They were put there just for a while and then they left something or other behind. What odd things people do with grains of rice, so innocent and small! My aunt says that she has heard they write the Lord's Prayer on them. And make them make those little pale-blue lights.

More broken china. My grandmother says it breaks her heart. "Why couldn't they have got it packed better? Heaven knows what it cost."

"Where'll we put it all? The china closet isn't nearly big enough."

45   "It'll just have to stay in the barrels."

"Mother, you might as well use it."

"*No,*" says my grandmother.

"Where's the silver, Mother?"

"In the vault in Boston."

50   Vault. Awful word. I run the tip of my finger over the rough, jeweled lines on the postcards, over and over. They hold things up to each other and exclaim, and talk, and exclaim, over and over.

"There's that cake basket."

"Mrs. Miles . . . "

"Mrs. Miles's sponge cake . . . "

"She was very fond of her."

55   Another photograph—"Oh, that *Negro* girl! That friend."

"She went to be a medical missionary. She had a letter from her, last winter. From Africa."

"They were great friends."

They show me the picture. She, too, is black-and-white, with glasses on a chain. A morning friend.

And the smell, the wonderful smell of the dark-brown stains. Is it roses?

60   A tablecloth.

"She did beautiful work," says my grandmother.

"But look—it isn't finished."

Two pale, smooth wooden hoops are pressed together in the linen. There is a case of little ivory embroidery tools.

I abscond with a little ivory stick with a sharp point. To keep it forever I bury it under the bleeding heart by the crab-apple tree, but it is never found again.

65   Nate sings and pumps the bellows with one hand. I try to help, but he really does it all, from behind me, and laughs when the coals blow red and wild.

"Make me a ring! Make me a ring, Nate!"

Instantly it is made; it is mine.

It is too big and still hot, and blue and shiny. The horseshoe nail has a flat oblong head, pressing hot against my knuckle.

Two men stand watching, chewing or spitting tobacco, matches, horseshoe nails—anything, apparently, but with such presence; they are perfectly at home. The horse is the real guest, however. His harness hangs loose like a man's suspenders; they say pleasant things to him; one of his legs is doubled up in an improbable, affectedly polite way, and the bottom of his hoof is laid bare, but he doesn't seem to mind. Manure piles up behind him, suddenly, neatly. He, too, is very much at home. He is enormous. His rump is like a brown, glossy globe of the whole brown world. His ears are secret entrances to the underworld. His nose is supposed to feel like velvet and does, with ink spots under milk all over its pink. Clear bright-green bits of stiffened froth, like glass, are stuck around his mouth. He wears medals on his chest, too, and one on his forehead, and simpler decorations—red and blue celluloid rings overlapping each other on leather straps. On each temple is a clear glass bulge, like an eyeball, but in them are the heads of two other little horses (his dreams?), brightly colored, real and raised, untouchable, alas, against backgrounds of silver blue. His trophies hang around him, and the cloud of his odor is a chariot in itself.

70   At the end, all four feet are brushed with tar, and shine, and he expresses his satisfaction, rolling it from his nostrils like noisy smoke, as he backs into the shafts of his wagon.

The purple dress is to be fitted again this afternoon but I take a note to Miss Gurley to say the fitting will have to be postponed. Miss Gurley seems upset.

"Oh dear. And how is—" And she breaks off.

Her house is littered with scraps of cloth and tissue-paper patterns, yellow, pinked, with holes in the shapes of *A, B, C,* and *D* in them, and numbers; and threads everywhere like a fine vegetation. She has a bosom full of needles with threads ready to pull out and make nests with. She sleeps in her thimble. A gray kitten once lay on the treadle of her sewing machine, where she rocked it as she sewed, like a baby in a cradle, but it got hanged on the belt. Or did she make that up? But another gray-and-white one lies now by the arm of the machine, in imminent danger of being sewn into a turban. There is a table covered with laces and braids, embroidery silks, and cards of buttons of all colors—bit ones for winter coats, small pearls, little glass ones delicious to suck.

She has made the very dress I have on, "for twenty-five cents." My grandmother said my other grandmother would certainly be surprised at that.

75   The purple stuff lies on a table; long white threads hang all about it. Oh, look away before it moves by itself, or makes a sound; before it echoes, echoes, what it has heard!

Mysteriously enough, poor Miss Gurley—I know she is poor—gives me a five-cent piece. She leans over and drops it in the pocket of the red-and-white dress that she has made herself. It is very tiny, very shiny. King George's beard is like a little silver flame. Because they look like herring- or maybe salmon-scales, five-cent pieces are called "fish scales." One heard of people's rings being found inside fish, or their long-lost jackknives. What if one could scrape a salmon and find a little picture of King George on every scale?

I put my five-cent piece in my mouth for greater safety on the way home, and swallowed it. Months later, as far as I know, it is still in me, transmuting all its precious metal into my growing teeth and hair.

Back home, I am not allowed to go upstairs. I hear my aunts running back and forth, and something like a tin washbasin falls bump in the carpeted upstairs hall.

My grandmother is sitting in the kitchen stirring potato mash for tomorrow's bread and crying into it. She gives me a spoonful and it tastes wonderful but wrong. In it I think I taste my grandmother's tears; then I kiss her and taste them on her cheek.

80   She says it is time for her to get fixed up, and I say I want to help her brush her hair. So I do, standing swaying on the lower rung of the back of her rocking chair.

The rocking chair has been painted and repainted so many times that it is as smooth as cream—blue, white, and gray all showing through. My grandmother's hair is silver and in it she keeps a great many celluloid combs, at the back and sides, streaked gray and silver to match. The one at the back has longer teeth than the others and a row of sunken silver dots across the top, beneath a row of little balls. I pretend to play a tune on it; then I pretend to play a tune on each of the others before we stick them in, so my grandmother's hair is full of music. She laughs. I am so pleased with myself that I do not feel obliged to mention the five-cent piece. I drink a rusty, icy drink out of the biggest dipper; still, nothing much happens.

We are waiting for a scream. But it is not screamed again, and the red sun sets in silence.

Every morning I take the cow to the pasture we rent from Mr. Chisolm. She, Nelly, could probably go by herself just as well, but I like marching through the village with a big stick, directing her.

This morning it is brilliant and cool. My grandmother and I are alone again in the kitchen. We are talking. She says it is cool enough to keep the oven going, to bake the bread, to roast a leg of lamb.

85   "Will you remember to go down to the brook? Take Nelly around by the brook and pick me a big bunch of mint. I thought I'd make some mint sauce."

"For the leg of lamb?"

"You finish your porridge."

"I think I've had enough now . . . "

"Hurry up and finish that porridge."

90   There is talking on the stairs.

"No, now wait," my grandmother says to me. "Wait a minute."

My two aunts come into the kitchen. She is with them, wearing the white cotton dress with black polka dots and the flat black velvet bow at the neck. She comes and feeds me the rest of the porridge herself, smiling at me.

"Stand up now and let's see how tall you are," she tells me.

"Almost to your elbow," they say. "See how much she's grown."

95   "Almost."

"It's her hair."

Hands are on my head, pushing me down; I slide out from under them. Nelly is waiting for me in the yard, holding her nose just under in the watering trough. My stick waits against the door frame, clad in bark.

Nelly looks up at me, drooling glass strings. She starts off around the corner of the house without a flicker of expression.

Switch. Switch. How annoying she is!

100 But she is a Jersey and we think she is very pretty. "From in front," my aunts sometimes add.

She stops to snatch at the long, untrimmed grass around the gatepost.
"Nelly!"
Whack! I hit her hipbone.

On she goes without even looking around. Flop, flop, down over the dirt sidewalk into the road, across the village green in front of the Presbyterian church. The grass is gray with dew; the church is dazzling. It is high-shouldered and secretive; it leans backwards a little.

105   Ahead, the road is lined with dark, thin old elms; grass grows long and blue in the ditches. Behind the elms the meadows run along, peacefully, greenly.

We pass Mrs. Peppard's house. We pass Mrs. McNeil's house. We pass Mrs. Geddes's house. We pass Hills' store.

The store is high, and a faded gray-blue, with tall windows, built on a long, high stoop of gray-blue cement with an iron hitching rail along it. Today, in one window there are big cardboard easels, shaped liked houses—complete houses and houses with the roofs lifted off to show glimpses of the rooms inside, all in different colors—with cans of paint in pyramids in the middle. But they are an old story. In the other window is something new: shoes, single shoes, summer shoes, each sitting on top of its own box with its mate beneath it, inside, in the dark. Surprisingly, some of them appear to be exactly the colors and texture of pink and blue blackboard chalks, but I can't stop to examine them now. In one door, great overalls hang high in the air on hangers. Miss Ruth Hill looks out the other door and waves. We pass Mrs. Captain Mahon's house.

Nelly tenses and starts walking faster, making over to the right. Every morning and evening we go through this. We are approaching Miss Spencer's house. Miss Spencer is the milliner the way Miss Gurley is the dressmaker. She has a very small white house with the doorstep right on the sidewalk. One front window has lace curtains with a pale-yellow window shade pulled all the way down, inside them; the other one has a shelf across it on which are displayed four summer hats. Out of the corner of my eye I can see that there is a yellow chip straw with little wads of flamingo-colored feathers around the crown, but again there is no time to examine anything.

On each side of Miss Spencer's door is a large old lilac bush. Every time we go by, Nelly determines to brush off all her flies on these bushes—brush them off forever, in one fell swoop. Then Miss Spencer is apt to come to the door and stand there, shaking with anger, between the two bushes still shaking from Nelly's careening passage, and yell at me, sometimes waving a hat in my direction as well.

110   Nelly, leaning to the right, breaks into a cow trot. I run up with my stick.
Whack!
"Nelly!"
Whack!
Just this once she gives in and we rush safely by.

115   Then begins a long, pleasant stretch beneath the elms. The Presbyterian manse has a black iron fence with openwork four-sided pillars, like tall,

thin bird cages, bird cages for storks. Dr. Gillespie, the minister, appears just as we come along, and rides slowly toward us on his bicycle.

"Good day." He even tips his hat.

"Good day."

He wears the most interesting hat in the village: a man's regular stiff straw sailor, only it is black. Is there a possibility that he paints it at home, with something like stove polish? Because once I had seen one of my aunts painting a straw-colored hat navy blue.

Nelly, oblivious, makes cow flops. Smack. Smack. Smack. Smack.

120   It is fascinating. I cannot take my eyes off her. Then I step around them: fine dark-green and lacy and watery at the edges.

We pass the McLeans', whom I know very well. Mr. McLean is just coming out of his new barn with the tin hip roof and with him is Jock, their old shepherd dog, long-haired, black and white and yellow. He runs up barking deep, cracked, soft barks in the quiet morning. I hesitate.

Mr. McLean bellows, "Jock! You! Come back here! Are you trying to frighten her?"

To me he says, "He's twice as old as you are."

Finally I pat the big round warm head.

125   We talk a little. I ask the exact number of Jock's years but Mr. McLean has forgotten.

"He hasn't hardly a tooth in his head and he's got rheumatism. I hope we'll get him through next winter. He still wants to go to the woods with me and it's hard for him in the snow. We'll be lost without him."

Mr. McLean speaks to me behind one hand, not to hurt Jock's feelings: *"Deaf as a post."*

Like anybody deaf, Jock puts his head to one side.

"He used to be the best dog at finding cows for miles around. People used to come from away down the shore to borrow him to find their cows for them. And he'd always find them. The first year we had to leave him behind when we went up to the mountain to get the cows I thought it would kill him. Well, when his teeth started going he couldn't do much with the cows any more. Effie used to say, 'I don't know how we'd run the farm without him.'"

130   Loaded down with too much black and yellow and white fur, Jock smiles, showing how few teeth he has. He has yellow caterpillars for eyebrows.

Nelly has gone on ahead. She is almost up the hill to Chisolms' when I catch up with her. We turn in to their steep, long drive, through a steep, bare yard crowded with unhappy apple trees. From the top, though, from the Chisolms' back yard, one always stops to look at the view.

There are the tops of all the elm trees in the village and there, beyond them, the long green marshes, so fresh, so salt. Then the Minas Basin, with the tide halfway in or out, the wet red mud glazed with sky blue until it meets the creeping lavender-red water. In the middle of the view, like one hand of a clock pointing straight up, is the steeple of the Presbyterian church. We are in the "Maritimes" but all that means is that we live by the sea.

Mrs. Chisolm's pale frantic face is watching me out the kitchen window as she washes the breakfast dishes. We wave, but I hurry by because she may come out and ask questions. But her questions are not as bad perhaps as those of her husband, Mr. Chisolm, who wears a beard. One evening he had met me in the pasture and asked me how my soul was. Then he held me firmly by both hands while he said a prayer, with his head bowed, Nelly right beside us chewing her cud all the time. I had felt a soul, heavy in my chest, all the way home.

I let Nelly through the set of bars to the pasture where the brook is, to get the mint. We both take drinks and I pick a big bunch of mint, eating a little, scratchy and powerful. Nelly looks over her shoulder and comes back to try it, thinking, as cows do, it might be something especially for her. Her face is close to mine and I hold her by one horn to admire her eyes again. Her nose is blue and as shiny as something in the rain. At such close quarters my feelings for her are mixed. She gives my bare arm a lick, scratchy and powerful, too, almost upsetting me into the brook; then she goes off to join a black-and-white friend she has here, mooing to her to wait until she catches up.

135   For a while I entertain the idea of not going home today at all, of staying safely here in the pasture all day, playing in the brook and climbing on the squishy, moss-covered hummocks in the swampy part. But an immense, sibilant, glistening loneliness suddenly faces me, and the cows are moving off to the shade of the fir trees, their bells chiming softly, individually.

On the way home there are the four hats in Miss Spencer's window to study, and the summer shoes in Hills'. There is the same shoe in white, in black patent leather, and in the chalky, sugary, unearthly pinks and blues. It has straps that button around the ankle and above, four of them, about an inch wide and an inch apart, reaching away up.

In those unlovely gilded red and green books, filled with illustrations of the Bible stories, the Roman centurions wear them, too, or something very like them.

Surely they are my size. Surely, this summer, pink or blue, my grandmother will buy me a pair!

Miss Ruth Hill gives me a Moirs chocolate out of the glass case. She talks to me: "How is she? We've always been friends. We played together from the time we were babies. We sat together in school. Right from primer class on. After she went away, she always wrote to me—even after she got sick the first time."

140   Then she tells a funny story about when they were little.

That afternoon, Miss Gurley comes and we go upstairs to watch the purple dress being fitted again. My grandmother holds me against her knees. My younger aunt is helping Miss Gurley, handing her the scissors when she asks. Miss Gurley is cheerful and talkative today.

The dress is smaller now; there are narrow, even folds down the skirt; the sleeves fit tightly, with little wrinkles over the thin white hands. Everyone is very pleased with it; everyone talks and laughs.

"There. You see? It's so becoming."

"I've never seen you in anything more becoming."

145   "And it's so nice to see you in color for a change."

And the purple is real, like a flower against the gold-and-white wallpaper.

On the bureau is a present that has just come, from an uncle in Boston whom I do not remember. It is a gleaming little bundle of flat, triangular satin pillows—sachets, tied together with a white satin ribbon, with an imitation rosebud on top of the bow. Each is a different faint color; if you take them apart, each has a different faint scent. But tied together the way they came, they make one confused, powdery odor.

The mirror has been lifted off the bureau and put on the floor against the wall.

She walks slowly up and down and looks at the skirt in it.

150   "I think that's about right," says Miss Gurley, down on her knees and looking into the mirror, too, but as if the skirt were miles and miles away.

But, twitching the purple skirt with her thin white hands, she says desperately, "I don't know what they're wearing any more. I have no *idea!*" It turns to a sort of wail.

"Now, now," soothes Miss Gurley. "I do think that's about right. Don't you?" She appeals to my grandmother and me.

Light, musical, constant sounds are coming from Nate's shop. It sounds as though he were making a wheel rim.

She sees me in the mirror and turns on me: "Stop sucking your thumb!"

155   Then in a moment she turns to me again and demands, "Do you know what I want?"

"No."

"I want some humbugs. I'm dying for some humbugs. I don't think I've had any humbugs for years and years and years. If I give you some pennies, will you go to Mealy's and buy me a bag?"

To be sent on an errand! Everything is all right.

Humbugs are a kind of candy, although not a kind I am particularly fond of. They are brown, like brook water, but hard, and shaped like little twisted pillows. They last a long time, but lack the spit-producing brilliance of cherry or strawberry.

160   Mealy runs a little shop where she sells candy and bananas and oranges and all kinds of things she crochets. At Christmas, she sells toys, but only at Christmas. Her real name is Amelia. She also takes care of the telephone switchboard for the village, in her dining room.

Somebody finds a black pocketbook in the bureau. She counts out five big pennies into my hand, in a column, then one more.

"That one's for you. So you won't eat up all my humbugs on the way home."

Further instructions:

"Don't run all the way."

165   "Don't stop on the bridge."

I do run, by Nate's shop, glimpsing him inside, pumping away with one hand. We wave. The beautiful big Newfoundland dog is there again and comes out, bounding along with me a ways.

I do not stop on the bridge but slow down long enough to find out the years on the pennies. King George is much bigger than on a five-cent piece, brown as an Indian in copper, but he wears the same clothes; on a penny one can make out the little ermine trimmings on his coat.

Mealy has a bell that rings when you go in so that she'll hear you if she's at the switchboard. The shop is a step down, dark, with a counter along one side. The ceiling is low and the floor has settled well over to the counter side. Mealy is broad and fat and it looks as though she and the counter and the showcase, stuffed dimly with things every which way, were settling down together out of sight.

Five pennies buys a great many humbugs. I must not take too long to decide what I want for myself. I must get back quickly, quickly, while Miss Gurley is there and everyone is upstairs and the dress is still on. Without taking time to think, quickly I point at the brightest thing. It is a ball, glistening solidly with crystals of pink and yellow sugar, hung, impractically, on an elastic, like a real elastic ball. I know I don't even care for the inside of it, which is soft, but I wind most of the elastic around my arm, to keep the ball off the ground, at least, and start hopefully back.

170   But one night, in the middle of the night, there is a fire. The church bell wakes me up. It is in the room with me; red flames are burning the wallpaper beside the bed. I suppose I shriek.

The door opens. My younger aunt comes in. There is a lamp lit in the hall and everyone is talking at once.

"Don't cry!" my aunt almost shouts to me. "It's just a fire. Way up the road. It isn't going to hurt you. Don't *cry!*"

"Will! Will!" My grandmother is calling my grandfather. "Do you have to go?"

"No, don't go, Dad!"

175   "It looks like McLean's place." My grandfather sounds muffled.

"Oh, not their new barn!" My grandmother.

"You can't tell from here." He must have his head out the window.

"*She's* calling for you, Mother." My older aunt: "I'll go."

"No. *I'll* go." My younger aunt.

180   "Light that other lamp, girl."

My older aunt comes to my door. "It's way off. It's nowhere near us. The men will take care of it. Now you go to sleep." But she leaves my door open.

"Leave her door open," calls my grandmother just then. "Oh, why do they have to ring the bell like that? It's enough to terrify anybody. Will, be *careful.*"

Sitting up in bed, I see my grandfather starting down the stairs, tucking his nightshirt into his trousers as he goes.

"Don't make so much noise!" My older aunt and my grandmother seem to be quarreling.

185   "Noise! I can't hear myself think, with that bell!"

"I bet Spurgeon's ringing it!" They both laugh.

"It must have been heat lightning," says my grandmother, now apparently in her bedroom, as if it were all over.

"*She's* all right, Mother." My younger aunt comes back. "I don't think she's scared. You can't see the glare so much on that side of the house."

Then my younger aunt comes into my room and gets in bed with me. She says to go to sleep, it's way up the road. The men have to go; my grandfather has gone. It's probably somebody's barn full of hay, from heat lightning. It's been such a hot summer there's been a lot of it. The church bell stops and her voice is suddenly loud in my ear over my shoulder. The last echo of the bell lasts for a long time.

190   Wagons rattle by.

"Now they're going down to the river to fill the barrels," my aunt is murmuring against my back.

The red flame dies down on the wall, then flares again.

Wagons rattle by in the dark. Men are swearing at the horses.

"Now they're coming back with the water. Go to sleep."

195   More wagons; men's voices. I suppose I go to sleep.

I wake up and it is the same night, the night of the fire. My aunt is getting out of bed, hurrying away. It is still dark and silent now, after the fire. No, not silent; my grandmother is crying somewhere, not in her room. It is getting gray. I hear one wagon, rumbling far off, perhaps crossing the bridge.

But now I am caught in a skein of voices, my aunts' and my grandmother's, saying the same things over and over, sometimes loudly, sometimes in whispers:

"Hurry. For heaven's sake, *shut the door!*"

"Sh!"

200   "Oh, we can't go on like this, we . . . "

"It's too dangerous. Remember that . . . "

"Sh! Don't let her . . . "

A door slams.

A door opens. The voices begin again.

205   I am struggling to free myself.

Wait. Wait. No one is going to scream.

Slowly, slowly it gets daylight. A different red reddens the wallpaper. Now the house is silent. I get up and dress by myself and go downstairs. My grandfather is in the kitchen alone, drinking his tea. He has made the oatmeal himself, too. He gives me some and tells me about the fire very cheerfully.

It had not been the McLeans' new barn after all, but someone else's barn, off the road. All the hay was lost but they had managed somehow to save part of the barn.

But neither of us is really listening to what he is saying; we are listening for sounds from upstairs. But everything is quiet.

210   On the way home from taking Nelly to the pasture I go to see where the barn was. There are people still standing around, some of them the men who got up in the night to go to the river. Everyone seems quite cheerful there, too, but the smell of burned hay is awful, sickening.

Now the front bedroom is empty. My older aunt has gone back to Boston and my other aunt is making plans to go there after a while, too.

There has been a new pig. He was very cute to begin with, and skidded across the kitchen linoleum while everyone laughed. He grew and grew. Perhaps it is all the same summer, because it is unusually hot and something unusual for a pig happens to him: he gets sunburned. He really gets sunburned, bright pink, but the strangest thing of all, the curled-up end of his tail gets so sunburned it is brown and scorched. My grandmother trims it with the scissors and it doesn't hurt him.

Sometime later this pig is butchered. My grandmother, my aunt, and I shut ourselves in the parlor. My aunt plays a piece on the piano called "Out in the Fields." She plays it and plays it; then she switches to Mendelssohn's "War March of the Priests."

The front room is empty. Nobody sleeps there. Clothes are hung there.

215   Every week my grandmother sends off a package. In it she puts cake and fruit, a jar of preserves, Moirs chocolates.

Monday afternoon every week.

Fruit, cake, Jordan almonds, a handkerchief with a tatted edge.

Fruit. Cake. Wild-strawberry jam. A New Testament.

A little bottle of scent from Hills' store, with a purple silk tassel fastened to the stopper.

220   Fruit. Cake. "Selections from Tennyson."

A calendar, with a quotation from Longfellow for every day.

Fruit. Cake. Moirs chocolates.

I watch her pack them in the pantry. Sometimes she sends me to the store to get things at the last minute.

The address of the sanatorium is in my grandmother's handwriting, in purple indelible pencil, on smoothed-out wrapping paper. It will never come off.

225   I take the package to the post office. Going by Nate's, I walk far out in the road and hold the package on the side away from him.

He calls to me. "Come here! I want to show you something."

But I pretend I don't hear him. But at any other time I still go there just the same.

The post office is very small. It sits on the side of the road like a package once delivered by the post office. The government has painted its clapboards tan, with a red trim. The earth in front of it is worn hard. Its face is scarred and scribbled on, carved with initials. In the evening, when the Canadian Pacific mail is due, a row of big boys leans against it, but in the daytime there is nothing to be afraid of. There is no one in front, and inside it is empty. There is no one except the postmaster, Mr. Johnson, to look at my grandmother's purple handwriting.

The post office tilts a little, like Mealy's shop, and inside it looks as chewed as a horse's manger. Mr. Johnson looks out through the little window in the middle of the bank of glass-fronted boxes, like an animal looking out over its manger. But he is dignified by the thick, beveled-edged glass boxes with their solemn, upright gold-and-black-shaded numbers.

230   Ours is 21. Although there is nothing in it, Mr. Johnson automatically cocks his eye at it from behind when he sees me.

21.

"Well, well. Here we are again. Good day, good day," he says.

"Good day, Mr. Johnson."

I have to go outside again to hand him the package through the ordinary window, into his part of the post office, because it is too big for the little official one. He is very old, and nice. He has two fingers missing on his right hand where they were caught in a threshing machine. He wears a navy-blue cap with a black leather visor, like a ship's officer, and a shirt with feathery brown stripes, and a big gold collar button.

235   "Let me see. Let me see. Let me see. Hm," he says to himself, weighing the package on the scales, jiggling the bar with the two remaining fingers and thumb.

"Yes. Yes. Your grandmother is very faithful."

Every Monday afternoon I go past the blacksmith's shop with the package under my arm, hiding the address of the sanatorium with my arm and my other hand.

Going over the bridge, I stop and stare down into the river. All the little trout that have been too smart to get caught—for how long now?—are there, rushing in flank movements, foolish assaults and retreats, against and away from the old sunken fender of Malcolm McNeil's Ford. It has lain there for ages and is supposed to be a disgrace to us all. So are the tin cans that glint there, brown and gold.

From above, the trout look as transparent as the water, but if one did catch one, it would be opaque enough, with a little slick moon-white belly with a pair of tiny, pleated, rose-pink fins on it. The leaning willows soak their narrow yellowed leaves.

240   Clang.

Clang.

Nate is shaping a horseshoe.

Oh, beautiful pure sound!

It turns everything else to silence.

245   But still, once in a while, the river gives an unexpected gurgle. "*Slp,*" it says, out of glassy-ridged brown knots sliding along the surface.

Clang.

And everything except the river holds its breath.

Now there is no scream. Once there was one and it settled slowly down to earth one hot summer afternoon; or did it float up, into that dark, too dark, blue sky? But surely it has gone away, forever.

It sounds like a bell buoy out at sea.

250   It is the elements speaking: earth, air, fire, water.

All those other things—clothes, crumbling postcards, broken china; things damaged and lost, sickened or destroyed; even the frail almost-lost scream—are they too frail for us to hear their voices long, too mortal?

Nate!

Oh, beautiful sound, strike again!

1953

READING "THE BAPTISM"

As he reads "The Baptism," Professor Huntington follows the process he outlined earlier. He focused on several passages that interested him, coming back to take a closer look at each one. Here's a passage that he came back to and reread several times. Mrs. Peppard has come in and told about the death of her sister's baby, and she and the sisters then talked about infant damnation (the belief that a child who dies without being baptized is damned forever).

> Lucy grew quite agitated after Mrs. Peppard had gone, and could not eat her bread and butter, only drank three cups of tea.
>
> Of course, as Emma had expected because of the tea, Lucy couldn't sleep that night. Once she nudged Emma and woke her.
>
> "Emma, I'm thinking of that poor child."
>
> "Stop thinking. Go to sleep."
>
> "Don't you think we ought to pray for it?"
>
> It was the middle of the night or she couldn't have said that. Emma pretended to be asleep. In fact, she was asleep, but not so much that she couldn't feel Lucy getting out of bed. The next day she mentioned this to Flora, who only said "Tsch—Tsch." Later on they both referred to this as the "beginning," and Emma was sorry she'd gone back to sleep. (paragraphs 18–23)

This passage interests me; I ask myself: "Is there anything funny or confusing about this passage?" Finally, after pacing back and forth a bit I realize that I'm wondering whether Emma was really asleep or not. Later in the same passage it says that she had "gone back to sleep" and that she was sorry. I'm confused, but as I read and reread I begin to think that there is some kind of cover-up going on here that I have to explain. You see, I know from my own experience that I've pretended to be asleep to avoid having a conversation in the middle of the night.

Emma seems impatient; she claims to be asleep but she also has to be awake enough to know what happened, and she does apologize to Flora for going back to sleep. The story says Lucy couldn't sleep because of the tea. Do I believe that, or is it something else? I think it's Lucy's concern about infant damnation and what it might mean to her.

But what we see here is that the other sisters have an interest in not paying attention to Lucy's religious anxieties—what they really want to do is go to sleep. The sisters just want to have a nice, quiet life and Lucy disrupts that life. One can feel a dynamic here. I'm beginning to think that I have to look more closely at the dynamic among the sisters, even possibly how the older sisters manipulate Lucy. How does Bishop create this dynamic? How has she made me question this?

Look, for instance, at the paragraph beginning, "It was the middle of the night." In the story it is not in quotation marks so we have to wonder who is speaking here. The narrator is using her own voice but she is speaking someone else's thoughts and even—here and in other places—using the language of someone else. The line, "Emma pretended to be asleep . . . " could be just the narrator, but, in the sentence following you can hear the narrator changing Emma's mind, "In fact, she was asleep. . . ." And then at the end of the paragraph, she figures out a way to be both asleep and not asleep when she says she was "sorry she'd gone back to sleep." This is confusing, even contradictory, but it is not inconsistent. What I hear is the voice of someone squirming to avoid responsibility.

By looking at the dialogue among the three sisters that Bishop offers, Professor Huntington has identified a confusion about the dynamics of the three sisters' relationships. By looking at another dialogue in the story he wonders if he can find more support for the idea that the two sisters seem to dominate Lucy. Here's another passage (paragraphs 28–30) that Professor Huntington returns to, reading in "slow motion":

> Lucy was not yet a church member. Emma and Flora were, but Lucy had been too young to join when they had. She sometimes asked her sisters if she were good enough.
> "You are too good for us, Lucy."
> "That's not what I mean," Lucy said.

When I read this, I said to myself, "I hate to admit it, but I have done this in conversations with someone I know: attempt to compliment someone, but really, at the same time, trying to dismiss them." That's what Emma and Flora are doing. This an attempt to shut her up, to quiet her. It's a deflection from the issue that concerns Lucy, which is whether or not she is virtuous enough to become a member of the church. The sisters turn the question into something else and Lucy protests.

Professor Huntington wonders what this subtle focus on the dynamic among the sisters might mean. The story seems, at first, to be about Lucy, yet we're finding out a lot about the relationship between her and the other two sisters. In the next passage Bishop's narrator tells us something about what goes on in Lucy's mind. As we typically have to do in Bishop's stories, though, we have to engage in a very careful reading process to unravel the confusion we might feel when reading a passage such as the one below.

At night she felt that Emma's prayers were over all too quickly. Her own sometimes lasted almost an hour, and even then did not seem quite long enough. She felt very guilty about something. She worried about this so much that one day she almost convinced Flora that she must have been guilty of the gravest misdemeanor as a young girl. But it was not so. (paragraph 31)

Who is saying, "But it was not so?" Perhaps it is the other sisters, who want to quiet Lucy. Lucy seems to be feeling guilty about something, perhaps about the privileges she's been given as the youngest child. Or, perhaps she is remembering some event in her past. When I taught this story in one class, a graduate student who had some therapeutic training suggested that this sounded like the memory of an abused child who, though she is the victim, can think of the experience only by depicting herself as the guilty person.

The older sisters care for Lucy as the youngest child, but they also hold her there in that position. Now that I have some idea of what I'm looking for, I can reread the opening to the story again with new understanding. The sisters are presented as thoroughly intertwined sea plants; even so Lucy is identified as, ". . . the youngest, who still did things for her sisters . . . "

Professor Huntington wants us, as we read, to stay alert to how we can uncover meanings that weren't available to us on our first reading. Part of the problem in our early readings of this story, Professor Huntington suggests, is that it seems to present an unbiased picture of the three sisters. But once you start reading closely and looking at the inconsistencies, you begin to see that the narrator herself is taking the older sisters' side. Huntington calls our attention to the language with which the baptism is described.

Lucy went under without a movement, and Flora and Emma thought she'd never come up.

Flora held Emma's heavy coat all ready to put around her. Rather unconventionally, Emma sat in the buggy, borrowed from Mrs. Captain Green, so as to drive off home as soon as Lucy reached the bank. She held the reins and had to keep herself from taking up the whip in her other hand.

Finally it was over. They put the dripping Lucy in the middle. Her hair had fallen down. Thank goodness they didn't live far from the river! (paragraphs 82–84)

All this makes the older sisters sound impatient. Surely the sisters knew she would come up. The line, "thought she'd never come up," is colloquial hyperbole (exaggeration); similarly, the word "finally" is logically redundant and tells us about the mood of the speaker. They are doing their duty and trying to take care of their younger sister. But they have very little patience or understanding for her desire to be baptized. Even the ending of the story pays more attention to the older sisters' response to the funeral than to thoughts about Lucy's death. They felt it was a pleasant day and the people of the village had all come out for the funeral. Social propriety had been preserved and this pleased the older sisters.

In his reading of "The Baptism," Professor Huntington found a pattern in the specific passages he looked at that helped him to understand the relationship among the sisters and how the older sisters might not want to deal directly with whatever is troubling Lucy.

The question of what is troubling Lucy remains; further readings and thought about this story might help a reader to argue several lines. One reader might argue that Lucy suffers from mental illness or religious fanaticism. Another might argue that the relationship among the sisters is typical of family politics: the older siblings try to suppress the eccentricities of the younger sibling in order to make life easier for themselves. This is by no means a complete reading but it does begin to get at the way I usually go through a text again and again, trying to understand the story in relation to my own experiences and to locate and explain confusions.

WRITING AND LEARNING ACTIVITIES

1. **Journal Entry:** What memories of personal experiences did this story evoke in you?

2. **Reading:** Read the story again, looking for patterns. Does Bishop repeat words, colors, feelings, or ideas in the story? Why do you suppose she titled the story, "The Baptism"? Review the notes you made about your reading process in your journal. Is there anything that helps you to understand the story more fully? Do you notice any recurring themes or patterns of ideas in the story? Continue to make notes in the margins as you read.

3. **Journal Entry:** As Professor Huntington read "The Baptism" he focused his discussion on some "confusing moments" he had noticed as he read. Make note of any such moments you found. Find at least three specific passages and write about what you found confusing. What do you think Bishop is doing during these moments in the text?

READING "IN THE VILLAGE"

As Professor Huntington reads through "In the Village" he points out how Bishop's use of tense and point of view can confuse a reader. Sometimes the story reflects the child's point of view and sometimes it reflects the perspective of an adult looking back. The narrative, he tells us, has a layered quality that asks the reader to be alert for shifts and jumps in the story line.

This is a long story, filled with episode after episode. This episodic quality allows us to look closely at a few passages that work over the themes that occur and reoccur throughout the story. We experience being a child and being left out. The real event of the story— her mother's leaving to be institutionalized—is hidden from the child. This moment is terribly important, a moment that will live with her forever, and there's a lot of pain attached to it. The child also remembers pleasure, the pleasure of being with her mother and the hope that her mother will come home with her.

The themes that run through "In the Village" differ from those in "The Baptism," but noticing differences can sometimes help us to see similarities as well.

The big difference, the interesting difference, is that "In the Village" offers the child's point of view. Here the child is eager to find out things but she can't reach them. She's trying to get at what's going on. But that means finding out about that scream, which is at the same time a source of terror. The mother in "In the Village" is another troubled, Lucy figure. In "The Baptism" Lucy seems repressed, her troubles hidden—from us and from Lucy. Lucy, like the child's mother, is a difficult figure, one who presents problems for others.

In some ways these stories deal with similar family structures and similar issues of knowledge and remembrance. The sisters hide their irritation with Lucy in "The Baptism" and the adults hide the mother's condition from the child in "In the Village." In both, Bishop seems concerned with repressed and hidden thoughts—with what has not been said— and how people deal with those thoughts.

Professor Huntington points to a long passage that illustrates how carefully Bishop has drawn the child's mind in this story.

> The purple dress is to be fitted again this afternoon but I take note to Miss Gurley to say the fitting will have to be postponed. Miss Gurley seems upset.
>
> "Oh dear. And how is—" And she breaks off.
>
> Her house is littered with scraps of cloth and tissue-paper patterns, yellow, pinked, with holes in the shapes of *A, B, C,* and *D* in them, and numbers; and threads everywhere like a fine vegetation. She has a bosom full of needles with threads ready to pull out and make nests with. She sleeps in her thimble. A gray kitten once lay on the treadle of her sewing machine, where she rocked it as she sewed, like a baby in a cradle, but it got hanged on the belt. Or did she make that up? But another gray-and-white one lies now by the arm of the machine, in imminent danger of being sewn into a turban. There is a table covered with laces and braids, embroidery silks, and cards of buttons of all colors—big ones for winter coats, small pearls, little glass ones delicious to suck.
>
> She has made the very dress I have on, "for twenty-five cents." My grandmother said my other grandmother would certainly be surprised at that.
>
> The purple stuff lies on a table; long white threads hang all about it. Oh, look away before it moves by itself, or makes a sound; before it echoes, echoes, what it has heard! (paragraphs 71–75)

What Miss Gurley does happens again and again in the story. People start saying something but stop in order to protect the child from the knowledge that something is terribly wrong with her mother. As the child looks around Miss Gurley's house, we hear her drifting into her own reality—"did she make that up?" She drifts into nursery rhymes: Miss Gurley sleeps in her thimble and the kitten sleeps as if in a cradle on the treadle of the sewing machine. These dreams also suggest the child's fears as she worries about kittens getting hanged or being sewn into a turban. But in the next paragraph the child's thoughts turn from dreams to reality as the thinks of her two grandmothers.

By the next paragraph the child has drifted back to her dream world as the material for the dress, with long white threads hanging on it, "echoes what it has heard!"—the scream. In telling herself to "look away before it moves by itself," she has very childishly made animate what would be inanimate, as if the cloth has absorbed and knows and remembers what it has heard and now can echo it. Part of this story is about the issues of remembering and not remembering at the same time. She's so afraid of that scream and yet it is her last memory of her mother.

Sounds are important in this story, and a particularly important one is the "Clang" of the blacksmith at work. In the segment below (paragraphs 9–15), Bishop has interwoven the sounds of happy memories—Nate and shoeing horses—with the sound of her mother's scream. We are left wondering what to make of the simple sentence, "The child vanishes."

Clang.
Clang.
Oh, beautiful sounds, from the blacksmith's shop at the end of the garden! Its gray roof, with patches of moss, could be seen above the lilac bushes. Nate was there—Nate, wearing a long black leather apron over his trousers and bare chest, sweating hard, a black leather cap on top of dry, thick, black-and-gray curls, a black sooty face; iron filings, whiskers, and gold teeth, all together, and a smell of red-hot metal and horses' hoofs.
Clang.
The pure note: pure and angelic.
The dress was all wrong. She screamed.
The child vanishes.

The "clang" is a kind of substitute for the scream. A happy, joyful version, which brings with it those things that are mortal. The unhappiness of her mother's last days at home is carried in the clang of the blacksmith. In technical terms, this is metonymy, remembering one thing by remembering something adjacent to it but not precisely the same. In this case the scream is quite different from the clang, but it is remembered by the clang.

Clang.
Clang.
Nate is shaping a horseshoe.
Oh, beautiful pure sound!
It turns everything else to silence.
But still, once in a while, the river gives an unexpected gurgle. "*Slp,*" it says, out of glassy-ridged brown knots sliding along the surface.
Clang.
And everything except the river holds its breath.
Now there is no scream. Once there was one and it settled slowly down to earth one hot summer afternoon; or did it float up, into that dark, too dark, blue sky? But surely it has gone away, forever.
It sounds like a bell buoy out at sea.
It is the elements speaking: earth, air, fire, water.
All those other things—clothes, crumbling postcards, broken china; things damaged and lost, sickened or destroyed; even the frail almost-lost scream—are they too frail for us to hear their voices long, too mortal?
Nate!
Oh, beautiful sound, strike again!

What's beautiful about this section (paragraphs 240–253) is how complicatedly contradictory it is. The line, "Now there is no scream" suggests relief that the scream isn't bothering her, but the clang recalls the scream and so in the end she asks for the sound to strike again. The clang is like a bell buoy out at sea; something that both warns you where the rocks are but it is also a sign that you're coming near port, you're coming near the shore. The list of "All those other things—clothes, crumbling postcards," and so on, reflect Bishop's attempt to hold it all together by remembering and covering up at the same time.

Both stories might be seen as being about controlling eccentricity and what you do with someone who's different, who makes a lot of noise, or who doesn't fit in. But the stories are so different in other ways that it becomes interesting to look, for instance, at point of view. In "The Baptism" it is the narrator who seems to side with Lucy's sisters sometimes, whereas in "In the Village" the point of view is limited to the child's perspective— the person the irritated adults are trying to save from knowledge. And also in "The Baptism," Lucy's eccentricity is granted a kind of possible dignity as having a religious revelation, which seems to be missing in "In the Village." The mother and her scream are merely incomprehensible and uncontrollable.

WRITING AND LEARNING ACTIVITIES

1. **Journal Entry:** What memories of personal experiences did "In the Village" evoke in you?

2. **Reading:** Read both stories again, looking for patterns. Does Bishop repeat words, colors, feelings, or ideas across both stories? Think about the title. What about the role of men in both stories? They are absent for the most part, but when they do appear why do you think they are portrayed the way they are? Review the notes you made about your reading process in your journal. Is there anything that helps you to understand both stories more fully? Continue to make notes in the margins as you read and reread these stories.

3. **Journal Entry:** As Professor Huntington read "In the Village" he focused his discussion on some "confusing moments" he had noticed as he read. Make note of any such moments you found. Find at least three specific passages and write about what you found confusing. What do you think Bishop is doing during these moments in the text?

A CLOSE READING OF LITERARY CRITICISM
READING CRITICISM

The *Penguin Dictionary of Literary Terms and Literary Theory* of 1992 defines literary criticism as "the art or science . . . devoted to the comparison analysis, to the interpretation and evaluation of works of literature" (page 207). Reading literary criticism goes hand in hand with reading literature. In the previous section Professor Huntington illustrated a method of reading in slow motion, during which we read and reread to identify and interpret confusions. Dealing with those confusions help us to build our understanding of the piece itself as well as move us toward developing our own interpretation of it. Once you have formulated some of your own ideas about a literary work, the most sensible next step is to read what others in the field of literary studies think about this work, what is called literary criticism.

Professor Huntington tells us that literary criticism used to be, to use Terry Eagleton's phrase, a "conspiracy of eloquence" (43):

This collaboration between the critic and the author was part of the work of literary studies; their task was seen as promoting literature and helping us to see what it means. In my interview I talked about the revolution that has taken place in literary studies. Now literary scholars are less interested in explaining the rhetoric of a literary work than they are in seeing what the work is doing.

You may feel that in his or her reading a work, a literary critic has said everything there is to say. In fact, however, you still need to consider the criticism in light of your own reading of the story. There is almost always something more you can say. Sometimes you may disagree with a critic and, of course, you must then argue convincingly for *your* reading. The purpose of criticism, however, is to help you extend your thinking about the work and consider different ways of understanding it. You might even consider yourself as conversing with the author and the critic about how to understand a particular work or writer.

You read a piece and then read it again. The second time you have the memory of the first reading, and thus you are looking at it differently. You are not the same "you" that read it the first time. You find different things the second time around because you're looking for different things. By treating the criticism as yet another reading of the work, you can build on and in general rethink your earlier readings, correcting and reversing your earlier understanding as necessary.

ABOUT THE CRITICAL TEXT

In this section, Professor John Huntington guides us in a close reading of excerpts from a critical text by David Kalstone titled *Becoming a Poet: Elizabeth Bishop with Marianne Moore and Robert Lowell.* Kalstone died before his book was completed, but two other scholars, Robert Hemenway (best known as the biographer of Zora Neale Hurston) and James Merrill (an important contemporary poet and friend of both Bishop and Kalstone), prepared the book for publication. In an early draft of his preface Kalstone explained that he intended to study Elizabeth Bishop as one of a very important group of American poets of the period from the mid-1930s until the mid-1960s. Relying on then newly available letters and biographical information he showed "how a tissue of valued personal connections supported a poetry both intelligent and open to unruly private energies" (pp. ix–x). Kalstone came to understand Bishop as a writer and especially as a poet by exploring—through her extensive correspondence with them—her relationships with her mentor, Marianne Moore, and her closest fellow poet, Robert Lowell. What makes this a *literary* biography is Kalstone's emphasis on understanding Elizabeth Bishop as an important poet by studying her life and her letters.

The brief portions of Kalstone's book included here offer readings of Bishop's work, biographical information, and material drawn from Bishop's correspondence with Moore and Lowell. These will help you make even more sense of the short stories you read in the previous section. The first pages included here focus on the story "The Baptism," published in 1937, and the remainder on "In the Village," published much later in 1953. In Chapter 11, Synthesizing Discipline-Specific Texts, there is another story by Bishop, "Gwendolyn," and an excerpt from Kalstone's critical work that relates to that story.

WRITING AND LEARNING ACTIVITIES

---

1. **Reading:** Read the excerpts from Kalstone's critical text. As you read, think back about the two stories you have read. Does Kalstone help you to think about them differently? Or does he strengthen your current understanding of the stories? Does anything he says confuse you?

2. **Journal Entry:** As you read, record your thoughts in your journal. What strikes you as interesting about this critical excerpt? How do your own personal experiences contribute to your understanding of the reading?

3. **Annotate the Readings:** Use question marks to identify places where the information confuses you, especially after several readings. Make notes in the margins about experiences or connections to other items you have studied. Underline ideas and examples that seem important and helpful.

ABOUT "THE BAPTISM"
DAVID KALSTONE

■ ■ ■

By the fall of 1934, Bishop was living in Greenwich Village at 16 Charles Street, in an apartment Mary McCarthy—they had become friends at Vassar—found for her. Jobs were hard to come by (it was mid-Depression) and she worked briefly, earning fifteen dollars a week, at the U.S.A. School of Writing, a shady and sad correspondence school for hopeful—and hopeless—writers. (She had a small income left her by her father but found a "real need for a little more money than I had.") "We were puritanically pink," Bishop writes. "Perhaps there seemed to be something virtuous in working for much less a year than our educations had been costing our families." That "we" suggests how much, despite her desperate shyness and the illnesses suffered throughout childhood, the Vassar years had given Bishop a spirited "modern" confidence. New York, in some ways, accelerated this feeling, and she was intensely aware of its power. As she had written in her notebook, New York and perhaps New York alone in this country offered "sudden intuitions into the *whole* of contemporaneity." With Margaret Miller, who was a painter, she was looking at modern painting and came to love particularly the work of Paul Klee. She was reading Wilenski's *The Meaning of Modern Sculpture* and despaired of finding terms half as precise and useful in contemporary literary criticism. She heard Gertrude Stein lecture in the New School that fall (and in fact knew Stein's work in college—was particularly interested in Stein's medical studies). And, of course, like many writers her age, she was an admirer (though never as openly as some an imitator) of Auden. His poems "colored our air and made us feel tough, ready, and in the know, too." One of the pieces she was working on in that first year, a masque called *The Proper Tears* (a fable about scientists and humanity), owes as much to Auden's *Paid on Both Sides* as it does to the seventeenth-century masque masters, Jonson and Fletcher, whose works she was studying assiduously at the New York Public Library. She had read Auden constantly in college and she would continue to read him:

> His then leftist politics, his ominous landscape, his intimations of betrayed loves, war on its way, disasters and death, matched exactly the mood of our late-depression and post-depression youth. We admired his apparent toughness, his sexual courage . . . Even the most hermetic early poems gave us the feeling that here was someone who *knew*—about psychology, geology, birds, love, the evils of capitalism—what have you?

Bishop's confidence—a modernist spunk—was close to the surface when she came down to New York from Vassar. Yet she seemed, and was always to feel, both in and out of her generation. Her school and college friends called her Bishop or The Bishop, a bow to the independent and cheerfully authoritative air she must have projected. In 1936, when Moore, who had addressed her for two years as Miss Bishop, picks up a note of distress in her letters and asks to call her Elizabeth, she replies with what seems almost a stab of relief for the intimacy: "As first names go, I am really quite fond of my own and should be delighted to be called by it—because so few people do." Moore's life touched on some of Bishop's private and particular strengths which remained in abeyance, rooted in an imagination nourished by the nineteenth-century cast of her first six years. These were resources not immediately available to her, or which came coupled with reserves of guilt and confusion—linked to her sense that she had always been a guest in others' houses. In this year of her mother's death she does not write directly about her childhood experience in the journal which has been preserved. But she does, in many of the entries, take a melancholy view of herself:

> My friendly circumstances, my "good fortune," surround me so well and safely, and only *I* am wrong, inadequate. It is a situation like one of those solid crystal balls with little silvery objects inside: thick, clear, appropriate glass—only the little object, me, is sadly flawed and shown off as inferior to the setting.

Emotional contradictions are everywhere in this her first New York journal: alongside the outgoing modernism and receptivity to the city are strong suggestions of guilt, reserve, withdrawal, and at times the sense that she was later to identify as homesickness. Contrary qualities which would one day come together as strengths in her writing were initially dispersed—and in her best work of this early period she made this dispersal of energies her subject.

Mary McCarthy once said of Bishop's writing, "I envy the mind hiding in her words, like an 'I' counting up to a hundred waiting to be found." The analogy is apt even down to the expectant concealed child. What one often hears "hiding" in Bishop's poems—especially the early ones she wrote in and about New York—is an instinctual self resisting a nervous seductive adult persona she associates with city life. The language of these early poems allows us to take them almost as Renaissance dialogues of soul and body. The prepositions in the title "From the Country to the City" (1937) are not just spatial, measuring a return from a weekend, but also suggest an epistle addressed from one realm to the other with the force of an interior drama. " 'Subside,' it begs and begs": this is the body's erotically tinged plea against the urban brain "throned in 'fantastic triumph' " (the latter a phrase borrowed from Aphra Behn's "Love Arm'd").

5   "The Man-Moth" and "Love Lies Sleeping," poems of the same period, involve similar messages and pleas from submerged figures resisting the encroachments of the febrile adulthood of the city: the single silent tear extracted from the man-moth bears witness to his plight and is a last extorted vestige of purity. The speaker of "Love Lies Sleeping" intercedes on behalf of city dwellers whose speechless representative is the dead staring protovisionary at the end of the poem. As that figure's head has fallen over the side of the bed, his vision inverted, so the man-moth sits in the underground train, always "facing the wrong way." A submerged self in these works is variously imagined and identified. But it is clear that in the poetry and prose Bishop wrote after she left college she was drawn to fables that gave body to a divided nature; alongside a hectic modernity one senses a shadowy space left for the absent or unrealized figures of a buried or inaccessible childhood. They may be elusive even in dreams. In "Sleeping Standing Up" (1938), the adult dreamer, freed to experience thoughts "recumbent in the day," can get only as close as the "armored cars of dreams" will permit. A curious image but one which suggests how rigidly separate she feels not only from the images of childhood but also from the modes of experiencing them:

> —Through turret-slits we saw the crumbs or pebbles that lay
>   below the riveted flanks
>   on the green forest floor,
> like those the clever children placed by day
>   and followed to their door
>   one night, at least; and in the ugly tanks
>
>   we tracked them all the night. Sometimes they disappeared,
>   dissolving in the moss,
>   sometimes we went too fast
>   and ground them underneath. How stupidly we steered

until the night was past
and never found out where the cottage was.

The dreaming adults succeed only in overrunning the traces of their earlier lives, not in finding the "cottage" the traces might lead to. When Bishop first used the Nova Scotia of her childhood as a setting for a short story, "The Baptism" (1937), it was with an eerie sense of a youthful life vanishing, withdrawing before her eyes. In "The Baptism" three young sisters, orphaned, face their first Nova Scotia winter on their own. The almost unspoken fact of the story is that the mother and father have only recently died. The parents' elided disappearance is taken for granted, as if it were perfectly natural for three young women to be living alone in a tiny remote village without some adult presence, some relative to oversee them.

Lucy, the youngest, becomes increasingly obsessed with a guilt whose sources she cannot identify and almost convinces her sisters that "she must have been guilty of the gravest misdemeanor as a young girl." One night she hears the voice of Christ above her bed and another evening has a vision of God burning, glowing, on the kitchen stove. "His feet are in hell." The growing ecstasy and alienation from her sisters ends in her decision— they are Presbyterians—to become a member of the Baptist church. She is only heartsick that for "total immersion" she must wait until the ice leaves the river. At the first thaw she is baptized, catches cold, develops fever, and dies.

Childhood images that Bishop was to look back on with affection in later works—the religious engravings in the family Bible, the singing of hymns around the piano—turn up here in a more dangerous context. Reading one of their father's old travel books, *Wonders of the World,* Lucy becomes overstimulated by a depiction of the Nativity: "the real, rock-vaulted Stable, the engraved rocks like big black thumbprints." Readers will anticipate the return of those images a good ten years later in "Over 2,000 Illustrations and a Complete Concordance." In that later poem Bishop remembers the engraving with yearning for simple belief in the domestic warmth it recalled. Lines of the engraving beckon magically to the eye, move apart "like ripples above sand,/dispersing storms, God's spreading fingerprint." But in 1936 and for the obsessive Lucy of "The Baptism" the "big black thumbprint" seems to mock, if not besmirch, the scene. The engravings draw her away from her family, deeper into her mania, until finally, terrifyingly, the child disappears. The narration is reasonable, plain; nothing departs far from the ordinary but the obsessive child. (Bishop was trying to produce an effect something like Hans Christian Andersen's, she told Moore.)

Early deaths—several in Nova Scotia—are subjects to which Bishop was frequently drawn, as if scrutinizing the horizon for her own childhood. "The Farmer's Children," a story probably begun in the late 1930s but not published until 1948, deals with two boys who die of exposure, frozen to death in a barn; "Gwendolyn" (1953) recounts the death of a valued young playmate; and the poem "First Death in Nova Scotia" (1962) is about the laying out of a child, her dead Uncle Arthur. One of the books she borrowed from Moore, read and reread in 1935, was the diary of Margery Fleming, a Scottish girl, born in 1803, who wrote her journal as part of her tutelage in her sixth, seventh, and eighth years, and was dead before she was nine.

ABOUT "IN THE VILLAGE"
DAVID KALSTONE

■ ■ ■

What shines through "In the Village" is the child's puzzled and persistent attentiveness to the outside world, a mystery to which her adult counterpart returns again and again. The story sets the two sides of Bishop's girlhood—one numb and threatened, the other receptive and full of natural promise—next to each other without comment or connection. Unlike "Gwendolyn," the story refuses explanation, resists the innate desire of fiction to suggest a scheme of causes and effects. Most of "In the Village" is told as by the child, and objects hold intense interest for her precisely because of what remains unspoken and unexplained—what must be pieced out and, shadowlike, apprehended about her parentage and the early disappearance of her mother. In a shop window, for example, she notices "something new: shoes, single shoes, summer shoes, each sitting on top of its own box with its mate beneath it, inside, in the dark. Surprisingly, some of them appear to be exactly the colors and texture of pink and blue blackboard chalks, but I can't stop to examine them now." The speed with which a perilous detail—the absent mate—is only grazed, then the eye diverted by surface for its own sake, is typical of the way this story negotiates troubled waters. Bishop is concerned here with the unresolved, the undetermined nature of childhood perception as a clue to survival; questions of guilt and innocence of the sort that obsessed her in "Gwendolyn" become largely irrelevant.

"In the Village" bears out Bishop's remarks about the difficulty of "telling the truth" in prose. However childlike the prose, these memories of her mother's disappearance require complicated narrative strategies and evasions, now the present tense, now the past, now the third person, now the first. The strategies themselves, her way of receiving her story, eventually become its subject. We are—she is—to be confused at a climactic moment. In the very first scene, in understated pasts, we have been shown the mother as she is being fitted for a dress—a purple dress, because, after two years, she is thinking, hesitantly, of coming out of mourning. She has been home and away, hospitalized several times, and her daughter, at this point referred to as "the child," unused to having her at home, watches from the doorway.

> The dress was all wrong. She screamed.
> The child vanishes.

In two sentences separated as paragraphs, and with a quiet shift to the present tense, the "child" vanishes literally from the doorway, and figuratively from the story, to be replaced by a narrative "I" who takes responsibility for putting together the pieces of her life and trying to survive the scream. Sometimes the "I" sees her story in a removed past, but, especially at a crucial juncture—the moment when the *mother* vanishes, never to be seen again, ever, in her life by her daughter—it is all vividly present.

There has been a fire one night in a neighbor's barn. The young girl is aware of confusion in her own house, "she," the mother, calling for the grandmother, etc.; but all the child is ever to know of it is what, even at the moment of the writing, she presents through the whispered overheard scramblings of the adults to shield her:

> But now I am caught in a skein of voices, my aunts' and my grandmother's, saying the same things over and over, sometimes loudly, sometimes in whispers:
> "Hurry. For heaven's sake, *shut the door!*"
> "Sh!"
> "Oh, we can't go on like this, we . . . "
> "It's too dangerous. Remember that . . . "
> "Sh! Don't let her . . . "
> A door slams.
> A door opens. The voices begin again.
> I am struggling to free myself.
> Wait. Wait. No one is going to scream.

The sense of menace from overheard incomplete conversations of her childhood is one about which Bishop had written in letters to Lowell. Here it is so vividly relived that the present tense seems not only to be that of intensely remembered childhood but, at certain instants, the present tense of the moment of writing. "Now I am caught in a skein of voices . . . I am struggling to free myself . . . Wait. Wait. No one is going to scream." She had chosen to elide a similar climactic moment in "Gwendolyn": "If I care to, I can bring back the exact sensation of that moment today, but then, it is also one of those that from time to time are terrifyingly thrust upon us." In "Gwendolyn" the statement seems too rationally realized; in "In the Village" volition plays no part. The child is caught in a skein of voices; so is this particular adult writer at the moment of writing, and the story refuses to tell the two of them apart. What ordinary narrative devices will satisfy the needs of such moments? Bishop once wrote in her journal:

> I think when one is extremely unhappy—almost hysterically unhappy, that is—one's time sense breaks down. All that long stretch in Key West, for example, several years ago—it wasn't just a matter of not being able to accept the present, that present, although it began that way, possibly. But the past and the present seemed confused, or contradicting each other violently and constantly, and the past wouldn't "lie doon." (I've felt the same thing when I tried to paint—but this was really taught me by getting drunk, when the same thing happens, for perhaps the same reasons, for a few hours.)

5   In trying to paint, Bishop experienced a confusion of present and past—a reminder, perhaps, that observation served a psychological as well as a scientific purpose. The observant child of "In the Village," so enthralled by details of Nate the blacksmith's shop and the intimate pastoral of her village even when she is suffering the violence and shame of loss, becomes a model for the adult telling her story. The story appears to do away with the usual censorship of fiction, the shaping to "explain," sculpting the story to reveal cause and effect. (Not that it doesn't have its own concisions, evidences of writerly choices.) Bishop attends much more to the "skein of voices" than to the logic of cause and result. Scenes and sounds from the blacksmith shop at the back of the garden are woven with choric frequency through moments of crisis. The clang of the anvil precedes the mother's scream.

> *Clang.*
> The pure note: pure and angelic.
> The dress was all wrong. She screamed.
> The child vanishes.
> Later they sit, the mother and the three sisters, in the shade on the back porch, sipping sour, diluted ruby: raspberry vinegar. The dressmaker refuses to join them and leaves, holding the dress to her heart. The child is visiting the blacksmith.
> In the blacksmith's shop things hang up in the shadows and shadows hang up in the things, and there are black and glistening piles of dust in each corner. A tub of night-black water stands by the forge. The horseshoes sail through the dark like bloody little moons and follow each other like bloody little moons to drown in the black water, hissing, protesting.
> Outside, along the matted eaves, painstakingly, sweetly, wasps go over and over a honeysuckle vine.

5   A tense writer would have lingered over those bloody moons, drowning, hissing, protesting. Coming as they do after the scene of the mother's scream, some details do in part refract the young girl's anger and helplessness. But that is not the point for Bishop. Feeling is deflected, refigured as the child becomes absorbed in the outside world, here Nate's blacksmith shop. The scream is never totally banished from this story, but it is repositioned by Bishop's insistence on the present tense. It is not simply a question of reproducing the past with some immediacy, as in the sudden overpowering recall of a moment, in Proust. With Bishop it is also the "surround" that she tries to recapitulate, the things we failed to notice in our concentration on pain—the equivalent of the backdrop of a conversation, audible to us only when we play it back on a recording. Writing, she attends not to a single obsessive tone but to the "skein of voices." The past is changed as it is reframed in the present, and the use of observation and present-tense description is to let the known tune be heard not only in a new key but as one instrument in a richer orchestra. Explanation becomes irrelevant as the present refigures the past.

The entrance into a narrative present coincides with the description of the blacksmith shop. James Merrill reminds me that this is an early exposure to a kind of art—the dangerous fire that is to throw them into panic later in the story is in Nate's shop perilously mastered, turned into a game which still bears traces of violence ("hissing, protesting"). By the end of the story, pain and receptivity to the outside world have practically merged.

> Clang.
> *Clang.*
> Nate is shaping a horseshoe.
> Oh, beautiful pure sound!
> It turns everything else to silence.
> But still, once in a while, the river gives an unexpected gurgle. "*Slp,*" it says, out of glassy-ridged brown knots sliding along the surface.
> *Clang.*
> And everything except the river holds its breath.
> Now there is no scream. Once there was one and it settled slowly down to earth one hot summer afternoon; or did it float up, into that dark, too dark, blue sky? But surely it has gone away, forever.
> It sounds like a bell buoy out at sea.
> It is the elements speaking: earth, air, fire, water.
> All those other things—clothes, crumbling postcards, broken china; things damaged and lost, sickened or destroyed; even the frail almost-lost scream— are they too frail for us to hear their voices long, too mortal?
> Nate!
> Oh, beautiful sound, strike again!

Voices are evanescent, and this writer's task seems to be almost a musical one, accommodating them to one another—the triumphant clang of the anvil, the almost-lost scream. At moments it is finally hard to tell them apart: the "it" that sounds like a bell buoy at sea might be, according to the grammar of the piece, either Nate's forging or the mother's cry of pain. The "it" that speaks with the four elements' tongues may also be, syntactically, either. "In the Village" employs a pictorial and musical art for traditionally narrative purposes. It positions and repositions the scream in a flow of language and landscapes which eventually almost absorb it. With the questions and intensives of the final lines one can almost hear the writer's effort and wished-for relief: "But surely it has gone away, forever"; "are they too frail for us to hear their voices long, too mortal?"

"In the Village" stands as a prologue to the descriptive poetry Bishop would write in Brazil. It was not simply that the two village worlds—Brazil and Nova Scotia—often fused in her imagination. Memories were to be dealt with—perhaps the rigidity of "Gwendolyn" taught her this lesson—not by elegy or by looking for narrative cause and effect in the past but by enlarging the frame, the "surround," in which the past is summoned back to a refiguring present. Writing fiction that served to define the limits of fiction, Bishop found the means to reenergize her poetry.

•   •   •

NOTES
Abbreviations

In the source notes the following abbreviations have been used:

For the correspondents:
EB   Elizabeth Bishop
MM   Marianne Moore
RL   Robert Lowell

For the manuscript holdings:
(H)   Houghton Library, Harvard University
(R)   The Rosenbach Museum and Library,
       Philadelphia, Pennsylvania
(V)   Vassar College Library
(W)   Washington University Libraries,
       St. Louis, Missouri:
       Olin Libraries Special Collections

Where there is no indication of manuscript location, the letter is in private hands.

Passages quoted from Elizabeth Bishop's poems are taken, unless another source is given in the notes, from *The Complete Poems, 1927–1979* (New York: Farrar, Straus and Giroux, 1983).

Letters begun on one day and completed on a later one are given both dates: January 8/20, 1964.

Notes on "The Baptism"

1. "a little more money than I had": EB, "The U.S.A. School of Writing," *Collected Prose*, p. 35.
1. "puritanically pink": Ibid.
1. "colored our air": EB, "A Brief Reminiscence and a Brief Tribute," *Harvard Advocate* (Auden issue, 1975), p. 47; repr. *Elizabeth Bishop and Her Art*, ed. Lloyd Schwartz and Sybil P. Estess (Ann Arbor: University of Michigan Press, 1983), p. 308.
1. "His then leftist politics": Ibid.
2. "so few people do": EB to MM, September 15, 1936 (R).
2. "My friendly circumstances": EB, journal (V).
4. "I envy the mind": Mary McCarthy in a symposium, "I Would Like to Have Written . . . ," *New York Times Book Review,* December 6, 1981, p. 68; repr. *Elizabeth Bishop and Her Art*, p. 267.
5. "The Baptism": Robert Giroux (Ed.). *Elizabeth Bishop: The Collected Prose.* New York: Farrar, Straus, Giroux, 1984, pp. 159–70.
8. like Hans Christian Andersen's: EB to MM, October 18, 1936 (R).

Notes on "In the Village"

1. "shoes, single shoes": Bishop, "In the Village," *Collected Prose,* p. 262.
2. "The child vanishes": Ibid, p. 253.
3. "a skein of voices": Ibid, p. 270.

4. "terrifyingly thrust upon us": "Gwendolyn," *Collected Prose,* p. 224.
4. "when one is extremely unhappy": EB, journal, 1950 (V).
5. "The pure note: pure and angelic": "In the Village," p. 253.
7. "Nate is shaping a horseshoe": Ibid, p. 274.

READING CRITICISM ON ELIZABETH BISHOP AND "THE BAPTISM"

Professor Huntington finds Kalstone's text to be a "graceful and somewhat elliptical piece of criticism."

Kalstone combines the research and the reading. He knows Bishop's journals; he knows the letters to Robert Lowell; he knows her biography; and he's able to move back and forth among those things. When he wrote this book little was publicly known about Elizabeth Bishop's life, although much of this material is now commonplace. Brett Millier's 1993 biography, especially, offers extensive information about Bishop's childhood and about her life at the time she was writing these stories.

What I admire in Kalstone's work is that the text itself is never forced and distorted by this other knowledge about Elizabeth Bishop's life; it's more of an amplification. For instance, let's look at the absent parent motif that comes up in both of our stories here. In "The Baptism," for instance, the three sisters live together with no parents and no mention of them. Relating this motif to Bishop's biography helps you to see how really important the motif is in "The Baptism," even though it is unemphasized in the story itself.

Professor Huntington looks over the first two pages of the excerpt (paragraphs 1–2) and reminds us that the Kalstone book is exploring Bishop's growth as a poet.

He's interested in seeing the work as a development rather than interpreting it in and of itself. By walking hand in hand with the real biography and then turning to the literary works, he manages to make plausible his accounting of the works. One of the problems of pure biography is sometimes that the literary works will be looked to as a biographical source, which is a very dangerous thing to do since the works are fictionalized. You usually want to go in the other direction—from the biography to the works, not from the works to the biography. Thus, you wouldn't want to say that Elizabeth Bishop lived alone with her two sisters in a cottage, which is what's portrayed in "The Baptism." Rather, you'd find something of interest about her life from her letters and see how she worked with that in a story.

Kalstone then tells us,

Moore's life touched on some of Bishop's private and particular strengths which remained in abeyance, rooted in an imagination nourished by the nineteenth-century cast of her first six years (paragraph 2).

Professor Huntington finds this an important statement, one which might even suggest the thesis of Kalstone's critical approach.

Kalstone suggests that there's a rich source of strength and of material for art that Bishop wasn't able to get at in her early work. It's only in her work done in the 1950s and 1960s that she learned to tap that strength. But the "nineteenth-century cast of her first six years" sounds like something out of Dickens—living with her grandparents, where, despite their good intentions, she felt lonely and alienated. But where also she learned to appreciate and get pleasure from books in a somewhat formal atmosphere. It was in her fifth or sixth year that her mother was permanently hospitalized. Kalstone goes on in the next two sentences to explain that she could not retrieve the resources that her childhood might provide. The absence of any mention of her mother's death in her journals suggests that the memories of her mother and of her own childhood were at that time—in the late 1930s when Bishop was still under thirty—too painful and confused for her to be able to think clearly about them. We read about these events in "In the Village," but Bishop could not confront them directly in "The Baptism."

Kalstone continues to find sources for understanding Elizabeth Bishop's development as a poet in what others say about her and in poems she has written. Mary McCarthy's comment about the "mind hiding in her words" suggests to Kalstone a submerged child self nervously at odds with an adult self (paragraph 4). Kalstone searches Bishop's poems for connections to this view of herself. He mentions two poems, "The Man-Moth" and "Love Lies Sleeping," in which Bishop seems to be crafting ways to signal a submerged self.

From these works, he's teasing out the issue of finding a way of recalling and handling important but painful experience. These issues concern all of her work, including "The Baptism." If we go back to the sentence I quoted earlier about "Bishop's private and particular strengths which remained in abeyance," we can see Kalstone tracing how Bishop herself struggled with a sense of the difficulty of finding a way of handling deep and difficult feelings. A challenge for becoming a poet, is learning how to tap those images and not feel them as being locked away.

When Professor Huntington talked about reading literature, he pointed out that it was very important for the reader to be aware of points of confusion that do not dissipate after several readings. Similarly, we can follow David Kalstone as he works through questions or confusions he has about Bishop's development as a poet. Bishop's development as a poet depended on her struggle with "not steering" or controlling the material she was writing about. Professor Huntington calls attention to Kalstone's statement,

> The dreaming adults succeed only in overrunning the traces of their earlier lives, not in finding the "cottage" the traces might lead to (paragraph 6).

Kalstone offers a very powerful and concise summary of the way in which Bishop's early work can be seen as pointing to but also avoiding "the absent or unrealized figures of a buried or inaccessible childhood" (paragraph 5). In this context Kalstone finds "The Baptism" important as the first time Bishop writes a story about her childhood home, Nova Scotia. He points at the start to the absent figures of the sisters' parents, and he even develops with delicate precision the careful way Bishop makes this odd situation feel "perfectly natural."

In the paragraph beginning with "Lucy, the youngest . . . " (paragraph 7), Kalstone offers a summary of "The Baptism."

He leaves ambiguous things that are ambiguous in the story. He quotes from the story to tell us that "she must have been guilty of the gravest misdemeanor"; however, where this guilt comes from is unclear in the story and remains unclear. I'm curious, though, why he inserts "His feet are in hell" and doesn't explain why it's there. It's almost as though he's giving us a flavor of the story. He reports that Lucy joined the Baptist Church in response to her "growing ecstasy and alienation from her sisters." In my reading, I emphasized her alienation, but I see that Kalstone is content to just touch on it.

Following this summary, Kalstone explores some of the religious artifacts that appear in "The Baptism" and also appear later in other of her works.

> Childhood images that Bishop was to look back on with affection in later works—the religious engravings in the family Bible, the singing of hymns around the piano—turn up here in a more dangerous context (paragraph 8).

Kalstone is sensitive to how a detail in one work can show up with a very different emotional suggestion in another. The childish perception that an engraving of a rock can look like a thumbprint is somehow related to Lucy's religious intensity, but it seems to be a consoling image in the poem, "Over 2000 Illustrations and a Complete Concordance." How the image can work both ways and what it meant to Bishop might well be the subjects of further meditations.

Professor Huntington and Kalstone emphasize different aspects of "The Baptism." The former felt that the narration, while appearing simple and "plain," as Kalstone refers to it, was actually quite complex. He hears a polite irritation in the older sisters that suggests more of a disturbance in the sisters' relationship than Kalstone suggests. Sometimes these differences emerge from the reader's "interestedness"; that is, Professor Huntington's experiences as a person and as a literary scholar have suggested a slightly different way to read than Kalstone's have. This illustrates how as a reader of fiction or criticism you must evaluate the writer's support for his or her claim. And as *you* write about both a piece of fiction and the criticism of it, you must come to an understanding of your own reading and the readings of others.

WRITING AND LEARNING ACTIVITIES

1. **Journal Entry:** What sort of picture do you have of Elizabeth Bishop from this criticism? Do you feel that you understand her better? Is she like you or unlike you? In what ways? What questions would you ask her if you were able to speak with her?

2. **Journal Entry:** What aspects of "The Baptism" did Kalstone discuss? Were there aspects of the story that you did not or that Professor Huntington did not discuss? Do you now understand the story differently than you did before? Do you have any sense of how Kalstone's interestedness might have

contributed to his work? How might your own interestedness influence your understanding of both Bishop and Kalstone?

3. **Group Activity:** Identify points of disagreement between members in your group and either Professor Huntington or Kalstone's reading of the stories. Discuss these differences and try to explain why each group member has the perspective he or she does.

4. **Writing:** Write a letter to a friend explaining what you have been working on in literary studies and what you have learned about reading literature and literary criticism. Use Elizabeth Bishop's story, "The Baptism," as an example. Explain what you have learned about it and how you now read it differently than you might have in high school.

READING CRITICISM ON "IN THE VILLAGE"

In his critical discussion of "In the Village," Kalstone extends many of the same themes he initiated in his discussion of "The Baptism." He continues to identify the "contrary qualities" in Bishop's work and to show how her willingness to examine them results in stories such as "In the Village." Professor Huntington points out that Kalstone is a very graceful writer who doesn't put trumpets around his thesis. Nevertheless, there are sentences, such as the one below, that can be carefully isolated as thesis statements.

> The story sets the two sides of Bishop's girlhood—one numb and threatened, the other receptive and full of natural promise—next to each other without comment or connection (paragraph 10).

Kalstone seems to be referring back to his earlier suggestion that her imagination was "nourished by the nineteenth-century cast of her first six years." The "puzzled and persistent attentiveness"—another rending of the contradictory heart of the story's style—is one of the things he appreciates in the story or wants to bring out. Bishop doesn't "steer" the story; she just sets memories side by side, again and again. Kalstone suggests,

> . . . the story refuses explanation, resists the innate desire of fiction to suggest a scheme of causes and effects (paragraph 10).

The richness and the complexity of the reading experience itself is important, in part, generated by the author's refusal to steer it to order it. Kalstone reminds us of this quality a number of times. This isn't a story that is going to explain something. Its intent is to depict the density and the complexity of the young girl's experience—the numbness and the threateningness of it—and the receptiveness of the young girl as well to everything that happened.

Reading Kalstone's critical work can help the reader sort out how Bishop has achieved this effect in this story. Kalstone, at the bottom of (paragraph 10), points out how the child notices the shoes in a store window, one on top of the shoe box and the other, its mate, hidden in the dark. But the child hurries on not wanting to "examine them now."

This, Kalstone says, is often the way Bishop's story negotiates "troubled waters." This example captures both the child's fascination with the surface of things, the colors and tex-

tures, but also hints at the anxiousness the child feels. Once again, Kalstone gives a typi-
cal example, which stands for the numerous other examples, but then doesn't give us the
numerous other example he could invoke.

In the paragraph beginning " 'In the Village' bears out Bishop's remarks about the difficulty of 'telling the truth' in prose" (paragraph 11), Kalstone begins to discuss the way in which Bishop creates this autobiographical short story: by creating confusions for the young child and for us, the readers. She is working through the challenge of "telling the truth" by using complex story-telling strategies to give the prose a childlike quality.

Poetry doesn't have to resolve things. Prose, however, has to "tell the truth." To do this,
Bishop moves from episode to episode and shifts tense, as in the passage below.

> The dress was all wrong. She screamed.
> The child vanishes.

The simultaneity of the act of telling the story and the memory of the event get layered on
each other. In paragraph 13, Kalstone goes on to explain that the sentence, "I am strug-
gling to free myself" is both the writer as an adult who is speaking and the child in the
story. Twice in this discussion, he invokes material from outside the story (from Bishop's
other works). He talks about the letters to Lowell, and later he quotes from Bishop's jour-
nal about the loss of the sense of time when you're terribly unhappy. This biographical in-
formation is helpful in that it helps Kalstone build his argument and persuade his readers.

Professor Huntington points us next to Kalstone's discussion of "In the Village" in paragraphs 14–15.

Another writer, Kalstone tells us, might have wanted to make something more of all this
extravagant imagery of moons "drowning, hissing, protesting." But what Bishop is inter-
ested in is "the skein of voices" she wrote about in her letters to Robert Lowell (paragraph
13) that surrounds her and that cushions the memory and gently deflects it without blunt-
ing or distorting it. Kalstone's art shows how these techniques of understated backdrop
contribute to that earlier conception of threat and promise that are always next to each
other in the story.

After Kalstone quotes the last lines of the story, he says something like what I did in
my own reading of the story. He gets quite specific: You can't tell what the referent of the
pronouns are. As he puts it, "The 'it' that sounds like a bell buoy at sea might be, accord-
ing to the grammar of the piece, either Nate's forging or the mother's cry of pain" (para-
graph 16). With this grammatical detail Kalstone confirms his opening sense of the story's
technique of setting the "numb" and the "receptive" sides of Bishop's childhood "next to
each other without comment or connection" (paragraph 10).

Professor Huntington glances at the concluding paragraph of this excerpt and suggests that it is a very helpful summary of the argument Kalstone has been trying to make.

> Memories were to be dealt with . . . not by elegy or by looking for narrative
> cause and effect in the past but by enlarging the frame, the "surround," in
> which the past is summoned back to a refiguring present.

What I like about this selection from Kalstone's book is the way he keeps the thesis about the juxtaposition of numbness and psychology of memory—how can the artist deal with her traumatic experiences?—and traces it in the details of technique—the shifts in tense, the "skein" of voices, the "surround," the ambiguous pronouns.

I should observe that in this selection we do not see how critics might argue with each other. Kalstone doesn't cite other literary critics in building his argument. One might say that Kalstone's argument is not with other readings but with the absence of readings. Though he is sparing of evaluative words (such as "good," or "important"), clearly his purpose is in part to make us realize how significant Bishop's accomplishment in "In the Village" is.

WRITING AND LEARNING ACTIVITIES

1. **Journal Entry:** After reading Kalstone's critical treatment of both stories, write about how one's personal history can contribute to writing fiction. How did it work for Elizabeth Bishop? How might it work for you? What sort of interestedness would you bring to writing a poem or a story?

2. **Journal Entry:** What aspects of "In the Village" did Kalstone discuss? What aspects of the story did you or Professor Huntington not discuss? Do you now understand the story differently?

3. **Writing:** Write about a theme that seems to be common to both stories. What, if anything, do Kalstone or Professor Huntington say about that aspect of the stories? Does the theme you have identified come from your own personal connections to the stories? If not, where does it come from?

MAKING MEANING IN LITERATURE
WHAT IS A LITERARY INTERPRETATION?

In literary studies, meaning is something you create as you read a work of fiction, not an objective truth that is hidden in the text waiting for you to find it and dig it out. As you read and reread, your understanding of that work changes and develops into an interpretation of the work. Recall when Professor Huntington began to read the two stories. He read and reread the text and worked on making personal connections that helped him to make sense of what he had read in the text, to interpret it.

For instance, let's look back at the first passage Professor Huntington looked at in "The Baptism" (page 180). This is when Lucy became agitated after Mrs. Peppard's visit and couldn't stop thinking about the baby who had died and their discussion of infant damnation. He was drawn back to that passage during his several readings because it confused him. The confusion did not go away until he had spent some time thinking about it. To make meaning from the passage he relied on his knowledge of religious issues, particularly infant damnation. He also relied on a close and observant reading of both the dialogue, and the narrator's explanation, and on his own "interested" perspective.

Critical texts about literature, another important source for learning about literature, also contribute to the meaning-making process in special ways. Frequently, the critic brings another perspective to the reading, as we learned from David Kalstone's critical reading of Elizabeth Bishop's stories during his examination of her development as a poet. He was specifically interested in how, over the years, she increasingly drew on her own past as a source for her work, beginning with "The Baptism" and again much later in "In the Village." Some critics might examine the "interestedness" of the writer, the work's social context, the ways in which characters and settings are represented, the historical features of the work, or how the work makes us read it in a certain way.

Any reading you do of a literary work or of criticism about that work produces an interpretation. Whether you casually talk with your friends about a book you've read, or produce several drafts of an essay on a book or story, you are interpreting. How will your readers or listeners judge your interpretation of that particular passage, stories, or group of stories? Unlike a legal case, your interpretation does not have to be the single best one chosen by a judge or jury. A legal argument must show how all other possible interpretations of the law are incorrect, but a well-developed literary interpretation, although indeed an argument, may offer one of many acceptable interpretations. In a book that looks at the art of argument in many different fields, Stephen Toulmin and his colleagues explain that arguments for literary interpretations should lead the listener or reader to say, "Now I see what you mean—now I understand your point of view and can recognize what you perceive in this work as a result of adopting that point of view" (Toulmin, Rieke, and Janik, 365). You want your interpretation to be seen in that way, understandable and plausible.

The most important element in producing a persuasive interpretation is the grounds or evidence with which you support your view. Evidence can come from a variety of sources: from features of the text, readings from other critical interpretations, the historical or social context of the work, biographical information about the writer, and even information from the reader's own personal experience.

SOURCES FOR RESPONDING TO LITERATURE

Where does the evidence for a literary interpretation come from? The three starting points for responses to works of literature are: yourself, the text, and critical treatments of the text. These sources cannot be seen as separate, however, nor does one precede the other. Rather, your responses and the features of the text interact and inform each other. When a person reads critical treatments of the text, his or her initial responses are challenged. Everything a particular person brings to a reading informs the ways in which that person makes meaning from it, which would be different from any other person's. Louise Rosenblatt, who has written about the teaching of literature, calls the highly personal relationship between readers and texts a "transaction." She goes so far as to say that what you see as

Elizabeth Bishop's stories is nothing so much as ink spots on a page until you read it and make meaning from it. When you read a literary work, Rosenblatt argues, "the text brings into the reader's consciousness . . . special meanings" (30) that communicate only to that reader. If, for instance, in reading "The Baptism" you remember something about a childhood religious experience, your understanding of the story will be formed from the transaction between the particular features of the story and your memory.

Both the reader and the text exist in particular social circumstances. The society in which Elizabeth Bishop wrote "The Baptism" had special beliefs and assumptions—some of them hidden and unquestioned—that informed her writing process. You as a reader are part of a society with perhaps different beliefs, customs, and assumptions. Today we call these often unquestioned beliefs a society's ideology. On the other hand, your personal beliefs—your ideology—may reflect values that differ in some ways from those of the society in which you live. When you read, then, you bring to the text everything about who you are, what you have experienced, and what you believe, as well as some of your society's values.

The critic, too, writes and responds from a specific ideological position within a community of literary scholars. Professor Huntington explained that at the time he entered literary studies, most literary scholars agreed that it was not necessary to study the author's intentions in writing. We can see how that has changed just by looking at Kalstone's interest in what Bishop's letters suggest about what she intended in her short stories. Stanley Fish, in thinking about what makes an interpretation acceptable, recognizes that literary scholars, in thinking about a work, rely on a frequently unspoken set of assumptions that are "a part of everyone's knowledge" (342). Kalstone, for instance, assumes that relying on Bishop's letters to her friends and colleagues offers an acceptable approach to literary scholarship. Part of learning about literary studies is gaining some sense of what literary scholars consider to be acceptable ways of making meaning, although what you bring to the reading process is equally important.

I encourage you to think of your reading as a transaction that "evokes" an interpretation from all of these aspects of the reading experience. As you develop your ability to read works of fiction and critical texts about them, you will find yourself increasingly able to reflect on the process, that is, to be self-critical, to move back and forth between the material you find interesting and important in the works, the criticism, and the elements of yourself that inform your developing interpretation.

The Self as a Source for Response

What you bring to the reading of a literary work is so important that I want to take some time here to focus on developing this aspect of your interpretation. I have designed a series of activities to get you to focus specifically on making personal connections to the material you read. These connections come from asking yourself the question, "What does this mean to me?" Developing an answer to that question will help you write a meaningful interpretation. Although these initial responses may or may not appear in the final drafts of your papers, they are extremely important in the process of making meaning from texts.

Student Gina Marie Rossi developed a personal connection that helped her to understand the child in "In the Village."

> *In "In the Village," the child's mother comes back from Boston to stay with her as the mother continues to mourn the death of her husband. The mother has suffered a severe mental collapse and the child was confused, uncomfortable, and "unaccustomed to having her back" (paragraph 8). The child has a distinct outlet in her visits to the town's blacksmith, Nate. When the child hears him working, Bishop writes, the noises he makes produce a bursting sound which fill the child's world. "Clang. Clang. Oh, beautiful sounds, from the blacksmith's shop at the end of the garden!" (paragraphs 9–11). Visiting Nate offers her a break from her reality, giving her somewhere to go to forget about life for a little while. I think everyone has to have an outlet. When my aunt gets angry at my cousins or my uncle she goes into their living room and plays the piano. People in the house could be screaming and fighting, but she just remains at the piano like nothing else matters. The child in the story needs an outlet because she doesn't understand the situation she is in.*   Gina Marie Rossi

---

WRITING AND LEARNING ACTIVITIES

1. **Journal Entry:** Think about your personal ideology. Write about who you are: your beliefs about religion, your relationships with family and friends, your education, your ethnic group. Do any of these beliefs differ from those of your parents, friends, or people you work with?

2. **Journal Entry:** In this journal entry, write about how your personal experience offers a way to understand the Bishop stories. In an earlier activity you identified three moments in each story that confused you or that you questioned in some way. How do your personal experiences and elements of your personal ideology help you to interpret the stories?

3. **Writing a Letter:** Write a letter to a family member or a close friend telling him or her what kind of reading you have been doing in your writing class. Explain what you have learned about yourself by reading Bishop's stories.

The Text as a Source for Response

As Professor Huntington pointed out earlier, when literary scholars read, they pay close attention to features of the text such as plot, characters, and tone of the narrator or the dialogue. You may ask: But what about the date it was written, the social and political context of the work, knowledge of the author's life and what he or she read or thought about? Literary interpretations do take into account background information such as this; some works might require more background information than others to gain a full understanding. Even though Bishop's stories were published in this century—"The Baptism" in 1937 and "In the Village" in 1953—they reflect a social context and an ideological perspective different from your own. As you focus on the text you've been reading and pay special attention to some of the features that Professor Huntington mentioned above, you may identify clues from the text that contribute to your meaning-making process.

We can see how these textual features—or, as they are frequently called, textual conventions—help us to make meaning by going back over Professor Huntington's reading of "The Baptism" and "In the Village." He paid close attention to the tone of the narrator and of several of the characters, wondering whether Lucy's sisters sounded impatient or asking why Miss Gurley, the seamstress, doesn't finish her question about the child's mother. Do you recognize these characters as people you might encounter? Why or why not? Do these stories conform to your idea of what stories should be? What ideas do these stories seem concerned with? What images, colors, or words come up again and again? How do the specific textual features you notice help you to make sense of the stories; how do they help you to make sense of your life and your culture?

WRITING AND LEARNING ACTIVITIES

1. **Journal Entry:** In an earlier activity you identified three moments in each story that confused you or that you questioned in some way. In the previous activity you looked at these moments for personal connections. Now review those moments again, focusing on what you can learn by looking at the textual features of the stories. Look over the notes you made about both stories. What textual features stand out to you? Make a list. Are you surprised or confused by them? Write about how you can explain that confusion. How do you suppose your response reflects your own perspective as drawn from your personal experiences?

2. **Group Activity:** Meet in small groups and share your responses to particular passages. How does one group member's response differ from another's? If someone does have a different understanding of the same passage, what is the basis of the difference?

3. **Journal Entry:** Write in your journal about how your ideas have changed and developed since you first identified those passages. How have subsequent readings changed your understanding of the passages? How did meeting with others in small groups change your understanding?

Criticism as a Source for Response

Students learning about criticism find that there are several "schools" of criticism, similar to the ones Professor Huntington identified: reader response, feminist, neo-historical, Marxist, deconstructionist, and cultural studies, to name a few. However, if your aim is to truly gain a better understanding of works of literature, you have to learn how participants in these schools think. You will want to continue using the reading method we've been relying on: look for confusions, places where, after reading the text several times, you still have questions about why the critic says what she or he does. The questions listed below will guide you in this process. They were developed by Donald G. Marshall, a literary scholar who has thought a great deal about how to bring students into the process of making meaning in literary studies (84–85).

WRITING AND LEARNING ACTIVITIES

1. **Journal Entries:** Listed below are four sets of questions developed by Donald Marshall. Look back over the criticism you read by David Kalstone. Respond to the following questions.

   a. List the critic's key terms. Which does he or she define, and how? Are these definitions different from the terms' ordinary meanings? What do the differences suggest about the author's way of thinking? Some terms may be defined implicitly—for instance, by the kinds of examples grouped under them. Try to make these definitions explicit. If some terms are left undefined, does that omission suggest anything about the critic's thinking?

   b. What are the critic's main concerns? What problems or questions is the critic aware of posing, and how does he or she hope to answer them in the essay? Why are those particular problems important to the critic (answer may be explicit or implicit)?

   c. What is the critic's method? Does the critic tell you *how* he or she is reading the text? What moves does the critic make in arguing the answers?

   d. How does the critic deal with specific literary works? What interpretive points are made, and what issues constitute the focus? What does the interpretation overlook? You must distinguish here between what you believe a critic could say if it were not irrelevant to a specific argument or topic and what you think the critic can't see because of his or her particular way of thinking. How does the critic's way of dealing with an actual example relate to the presuppositions, topic, and method of the essay?

2. **Group Activity:** Meet in small groups and discuss your responses to one of the above sets of questions. How do group members' responses differ? How did you resolve those differences?

3. **Class Presentations:** Each small group should prepare a presentation for the class on one aspect of Kalstone's criticism. Prepare a handout and present your results to the whole class.

DEVELOPING INTERESTS

Have you enjoyed reading the works of one particular author? Would you like to read more stories by Elizabeth Bishop or other short stories by another author? Would you prefer to learn about the lives of authors or read their works or both? What other types of writing would you like to explore:

drama, poetry, novels, essays, letters? Below are some activities that will help you identify interests you would like to explore further.

WRITING AND LEARNING ACTIVITIES

1. **Reading Activity:** Take a look through the current issue of the *New York Times Book Review* (found in the Sunday *New York Times*). Read the reviews of recent fiction and find one work you would like to read.

2. **Journal Entry:** Think back over reading you have done earlier and now in college. Think about your English classes or about a person who you've talked to about your interest in reading. What seems most important in those memories. What might you like to learn and write more about?

▪▫ LINKED WRITING ASSIGNMENT

Writing a Synthesis Essay on Literary Works (see Chapter 11, Synthesizing Discipline-Specific Texts). In the previous section, Developing Interests, you began to identify issues and ideas that you might want to explore further. Finding personal connections to the material you are studying is one important way to participate more fully in an academic community. You will also need to learn how some everyday thinking strategies, such as synthesizing, help you to participate in the disciplines you are studying here. Chapter 11 introduces you to the activity of synthesizing and offers readings from literary studies for you to practice synthesizing material from several sources.

```
C  H  A  P  T  E  R
6
ART HISTORY
```

When you look at a painting what do you see? How does what you see reflect your experiences and your culture? Is what you see changed by learning about the artist or about what others say about the work? Take a look at the painting by Matisse on the front cover and on page 222 of this text. What story does this painting tell? How does it make you feel? Here are the initial responses of some students to this painting and to these questions.

I don't know why it's called Conversation, because it seems as if no conversation is taking place!

The mother, sitting in the chair, has called the son into the room to discuss his behavior. The son has a look of innocence and the mother has the look of assurance that she is right.

This painting doesn't look too professional; in fact, it looks like a fifth-grader could have painted it.

The woman in the long, black fitted dress has just returned home early from France and her husband, still in his formal striped silk pajamas, wants to know why.

I'm wondering why they are in their pajamas in that sad blue room while it is so beautiful outside.

These first responses to Matisse's painting begin the process of "reading" a work of art. To introduce you to the field of art history, I interview Professor Ingrid Rowland, who explains that all art is a form of expression, and that when we "read" a work of art we learn how and what it communicates to us. To illustrate how art historians think and write, Professor Rowland guides us through Jack Flam's discussion of Matisse's *Conversation*. Next, we explore how art historians make meaning, how artists communicate through their work, and how we perceive their message. In the final section, I ask you to explore how your experiences can help you to develop new interests in art history.

AN INTERVIEW WITH AN ART HISTORIAN

Professor Ingrid Rowland, an art historian at the University of Chicago, teaches courses in ancient Greek, Roman, and Etruscan art; the Italian renaissance and baroque art; ancient Greek culture; and the classical tradition. In the following interview I ask Professor Rowland to tell us about her career as an art historian; a path that led her through some unexpected twists and turns. Professor Rowland publishes widely in both Italian and English. The Vatican will soon publish *The Correspondence of Agostino Chigi: An Annotated Edition*. Her essays—such as "Mother of the World," "Feast of Pliny," and "Character Witnesses"—appear frequently in the *New York Review of Books*.

Tell us how you became an art historian.

The path was not a straight one. I was trained as a classicist, which is why my Ph.D. is actually in Greek literature with a minor in classical archaeology. When I look back on my studies it was two women professors, Phyllis Bober and Julia Gaisser, and a male professor, Kyle Phillips, who encouraged me. But the story really goes all the way back to when I was fourteen.

I joined an Explorer Scout post a couple of years before girls actually were allowed to be Explorer Scouts. This troop did amateur archaeology in California, and their site happened to be virtually in my backyard. I started excavating California Indian artifacts at the age of fourteen and loved it. I decided at that point to do pre-Columbian archaeology with a scientific bent. My father is a scientist so I'd always thought that science was the highest human endeavor, even though it was quite clear that I drew and wrote quite well. In high school I was planning to become a scientific archaeologist. I knew all the different kinds of pre-Columbian figurines and went off to college feeling very sure of my future direction.

As sure as I was, my direction shifted again when, in my first year of college, I ran into a professor of classical archaeology whose personal charm was irresistible. He'd do things like write Greek words such as Dikaiosyne *on the blackboard, and after that we always wanted to know what it meant. He was giving us subliminal suggestions about Greek and Latin and what terrific languages they were. It worked on me. I entered graduate school planning to study classical archaeology.*

Is there a single event that you feel turned you toward art history as your field of specialization?

Yes. I went to Rome my first summer in graduate school, and the first day in Rome I was taken into Borromini's church of St. Ivo. It was one of those incredible experiences in which everything comes together at once and you emerge from the experience with a new understanding of yourself and your relation to things and people.

The experience of this structure hits you so fast it is probably a metaphor for the way that divine inspiration occurs. It almost knocks the breath out of you even if, as in my case, you've never seen or heard anything about this structure. I walked in and gasped. I have brought so many people in there and it seems to produce this response consistently.

We have a note written by Borromini in which he explains that he's trying to illuminate a reciprocity between the human soul striving to understand God and God coming down and meeting the human soul halfway. The way he shows this through form is by making the church incredibly vertical so that you walk in and you're forced automatically to look up. The walls are stripped down, forcing your gaze upwards toward an incredible dome inlaid with stars and all kinds of imagery that has to do with the Temple of Solomon. The way he plays with light suggests the holy spirit coming in as literal illumination. It is one of the brightest places in Rome.

I realized suddenly how art could give messages that were conceptual as well as aesthetic. Suddenly that allowed me to articulate all kinds of things not only having to do with art but also with literature. At that point I couldn't get enough of Baroque architecture. As a consequence of visiting that church I began teaching myself art history and architecture, when I was supposedly in Rome to learn how to be a classical archaeologist and visiting classical sites. Instead, I spent most of my time visiting Baroque churches. I came back to Bryn Mawr supposedly still as a graduate student in Greek literature, but I had shifted my studies toward antiquity in the Renaissance.

What interested you most about this period?

One of the characters I ran into in Rome was the artist Raphael's most important private patron, Agostino Chigi who lived from 1466 to 1520. Agostino Chigi—I was fascinated to learn—used to hold dinner parties for the Pope in a little portico that he had on the Tiber. He would serve meals to people on golden plates embossed with their coats of arms. After the meals he'd throw the plates into the Tiber and everyone was deeply impressed with how filthy rich he was. But it turned out that he had nets stretched under the surface of the water, which allowed him to gather up the plates after the party was over. This man seemed to me the opposite of a graduate student; he never doubted himself for a moment. I became obsessed with him and started studying about him for my preliminary graduate exams.

How do you study someone who lived so long ago?

While I worked at the American Academy in Rome I had a fair amount of free time and spent it looking at art or working in the Vatican library where I discovered Chigi's letters. The letters were totally illegible—in Italian with Latin jargon—and they looked like Arabic. It wasn't surprising that nobody had done anything with them. I applied for a fellowship to study these letters. The only reason I could do this is because his little brother's grandson in the seventeenth century did a transcription of about half the letters. It took me a week or so to be able to read anything, but after several years I was able to understand almost everything.

One letter is actually a letter in which Chigi, who is a banker, is on the road with Cesare Borgia (Lucretia Borgia's brother) and Machiavelli, who is running Borgia's campaign. The letter says something like this, "Dear Dad, I just told Cesare Borgia I'd loan him 3000 ducats. Please send money. I think you owe me 1500 in this account and 1500 in that account. I've sent these two servants out. They both have scars on their foreheads so you know who they are. Please put the money on their persons. . . ." The letter goes on and then says, "If we don't do this, it will be the death of me or at least I'll be the most ridiculed man in the world."

I finished my book on these letters two years ago and I'm waiting for the Vatican Press to publish it. With this book, I now have a basis for further work in art history, since my degree is not in that field. I'm still really excited about this work: it's power, politics, and money. Such good stories come out of work in art history and I love to tell stories.

Are there any common misconceptions about the study of art history?

I always thought when I was in college that art history must be sitting around looking at slides. And I think there still is such a strand in the teaching and practice of art history. A lot of women used to go into art history so that when they got married to their doctors they could select the right antiques to furnish their stately homes. This trend, in which you determine the value of art, is called connoisseurship.

How would you define the study of art history?

Art history starts out with the idea that art transmits or communicates all sorts of information, not just that a piece of art is pretty. Even being pretty is, in itself, a message of sorts. Also, I think that art is an expression of curiosity by individuals who tend to think and express themselves through form rather than through the written word. The language of form is as eloquent and often follows the same kinds of structures as written communication. Through specific techniques applied to specific materials the artist creates form. The form is the way the artist has envisioned some particular content, perhaps a woman bathing or Napoleon crossing the Alps.

Rhetoric—the art of persuasion—is practiced almost across the board. It is something that you do with the spoken word, it is something you do with behavior, but it is also something you do with the visual arts. In any painting (or in any other work of art), the painter places things in a particular way for a reason, to make it mean something. Art history involves isolating and studying the visual component of this expression. The art historian studies the works of art and the documents surrounding them, such as letters or contracts. These, fueled perhaps by a hunch, help the art historian construct the "story" of the work and if appropriate, to offer a persuasive, well-argued account of the work.

What are the traditional divisions in art history?

Geographically and chronologically there have always been a number of divisions in art history; for instance, you have an east and west division. The study of China and Japan, for instance, require that you study different languages. The Renaissance is divided usually between the northern area of Europe where you have the Germanic languages and the southern area where you have the Romance languages.

Then, in the west, we have the basic chronological periods: the ancient world, medieval world, Renaissance, Baroque. The time frames for these periods are always getting compressed. We teach a survey course here for beginning students in which I cover everything from The Venus of Willendorf (35,000 years ago) up to the Renaissance. In ten weeks I'm teaching 35,000 years. The Renaissance art course covers from approximately 1200 to 1600 and then you have modern after that. So there's incredible acceleration, some of which I attribute to the arrogance of the twentieth century. People will even divide the twentieth century into decades on the assumption that things happen more quickly now.

When you teach these survey courses what do you want students to learn?

One of the things that strikes me about both the ancient world and the Renaissance is the international nature of the culture itself; the culture is extremely cosmopolitan. So what I try to show students is that the twentieth century is not the first century that's had to confront problems of industrialization. That was going on in ancient Greece. The Greece that we deal with in terms of classical Greek literature extends from the time of Homer at the very beginnings of literacy to the time when Greece had achieved the status of an international trading power. It's true we're talking about a low technological level, but the culture did have industrial processes; it was an industrial society living off exports and imports.

Remember, the Mediterranean wasn't only mainland Greece. It included Italy and today's Turkey. It was a much larger and more open culture than we tend to think. As long as we speak English and are educated in the university system, we will have been influenced by this culture. The ancient world conditions us because the university system was itself conditioned by the ancient world. So I try to show the students why, as a culture, we have certain attitudes and where they may have come from and how people have dealt with these problems in the past.

How did you learn to write about art history?

The way that I learned to write about art was really through teaching and having to talk about what people see when they look at a painting. I'm influenced by what I know about art and the world, but I'm also influenced by my personal response. I ask myself, "How do I talk about what I see?" Suppose you find yourself standing in front of a crowd of people and a painting of, say, something as unlikely as a boat going through a woman's knees. You have to ask yourself, "How am I going to talk about that?" It has taken me years to learn to make people see pictures through words. The best advice I can give to students when they write about art is very simple. First, use your eyes. Next, use your head. After you write, go back over it and make sure you used both your eyes and your head.

Did your teachers have any particular influence on you?

I was deeply influenced by Professor Kyle Phillips, who would always make his students describe exactly what they saw and do it without having read anything about it previously. I learned that you don't walk up to an Etruscan sculpture and say, "This is primitive." The term primitive is often given to works outside European and Oriental traditions. It frequently refers, somewhat negatively, to these works of art as naive or simple. We argue today more frequently that we should see these works as expressing a straightforward statement of an enthusiasm for life. The label primitive still carries quite a bit of cultural baggage. So, to label something as primitive is to simply apply what someone else—a teacher or a textbook—told you it was. What Kyle Phillips wanted us to do is just, as I said above, use our eyes. You take the work at face value and nothing else. By doing that you learn what it is you are actually seeing. After you have seen what you have seen, then start to make judgments about it. You try to rid yourself of prejudices as much as possible.

What do you try to pass along to your students?

In my classes I try to do two things at once. First, I want to show students the influence of culture and social history on art in every way possible. But in order to train one's self to recognize that influence you must learn to write about art by eliminating or shaving away possible cultural and social influences. It sounds contradictory, but unless you can describe what you see, you can't see how social and cultural influences change how we see a work. When you call a work of art primitive you are bringing to bear an attitude, a conclusion from a social history that is a part of you. In studying art history, you train yourself to recognize when that is working and when it isn't.

What are the most important questions an art historian can ask about a piece of art?

Why does the work look like that? Who is the work for? How does the work make meaning and for whom? The most fundamental questions give you the best answers, which is why I love it when students ask me these questions. Students have a way of kicking me right back into these fundamental positions and making me clean up my typical and tired answers. Students can still ask us what it is all about in a very trenchant way and remind us, as professionals, why we were originally very excited about all this stuff. A lot of what I've written comes originally from questions that students have asked me.

WRITING AND LEARNING ACTIVITIES

1. **Journal Entry:** Look up a definition of art history in a specialized reference source (see the appendix, Directions for Further Research), a college dictionary, and a general reference encyclopedia. Consider the differences and similarities among these definitions. What other related definitions did you find? Report to the class on what you found.

2. **Writing Activity:** Write three questions you would ask Professor Rowland if you had the opportunity to talk with her.

3. **Peer Conversation:** With a partner, discuss your journal entries and questions for Professor Rowland. Respond also to the following questions: Were you reminded by something she said of another experience you've had at home, school, or work? Do you have any idea of what areas you'd like to study in college?

4. **Research Project:** Look up the art history courses or the major in your college catalog. Respond to the following questions: How is the discipline described? How does this description differ from Professor Rowland's or from other definitions you've found? What are the required courses for the art history major? What are the possible areas of specialization? Next, interview someone who is majoring in art history. Why is he or she studying art history? What courses has he or she taken? Is this person specializing in any particular area? What does he or she plan to do with an art history degree? Finally, attend one class with the student and take notes about how it is similar to or different from other classes.

5. **Writing Activity:** Based on your research, write a report describing what it's like to major in art history.

6. **Developing Interests:** Visit an art museum and spend some time looking at an exhibit of your choice. Or look over some art books from your public or university library. First, simply look at the works. Make notes in your journal about your first responses to the works. Were you interested or bored? Were you pleased or offended? Did you find them beautiful or ugly? Did they con-

fuse you or help you to see something more clearly? Next read the titles and the descriptive notes next to each picture. Write in your journal about what interests you and what you would like to know more about.

READING ABOUT HENRI MATISSE AND *CONVERSATION*

The very first thing to do when entering the world of art history is to look at the work of art under discussion. Take some time to look at a painting, for example, with your own eyes, uninfluenced by others, before you listen to what others have to say about it.

WRITING AND LEARNING ACTIVITIES

1. **Responding to a Piece of Art:** Look at the picture of *Conversation* on the cover of this book and write in your journal a description of it in your own words. What do you think is happening? Why do you think it is called *Conversation?* Could you be a figure or character in this painting? Why or why not? What story does this painting tell? How does it tell it? What do you think Matisse was trying to communicate with this picture? How does it make you feel? What is there about it that makes you feel this way? How is it alike or different from other artwork you have seen? If you had a poster of this piece of art, where would you hang it and why would you choose that particular location rather than another?

2. **Journal Entry:** Write a letter to a friend who has not seen this painting. Practice careful and thorough description by telling your friend about the painting.

Your own initial response to this painting is very important, because as you continue to read and learn what others think of this work you will want to reconsider this initial response. In this section Professor Rowland guides you through an excerpt from a book on Matisse by art historian Jack Flam, *Matisse: The Man and His Art 1869–1918,* published in 1986. Jack Flam is a professor of art history at Brooklyn College and at the Graduate Center of the City University of New York. This book is a large, impressive volume, filled with striking color plates of Matisse's work. As we follow Professor Rowland in her reading of two portions of Flam's book we will see how Flam works as an art historian first to construct a "picture" of Matisse as a person and as an artist, and then to build a "story" that will help us to understand Matisse's painting, *Conversation.*

BUILDING A CONTEXT FOR READING

Professor Rowland's first response to this excerpt was to tell us how much she enjoys Matisse's work.

Matisse is so accessible; he's somebody that I love to look at because he takes you so many different places. I haven't really done anything systematic or scholarly with his art at all. It's something I've enjoyed since I was a kid. I'm just so dazzled by the visual forms. Even now, I'm relieved that I don't have to have studied Matisse to enjoy his work. I'm still able to look at his work in a state of childlike wonder.

Even though Professor Rowland had not studied Matisse, she remembered a bit more about an anecdote she had told above. Her professor, Kyle Phillips, had taken a group of students to look at Etruscan art—art produced in an ancient country in what is now Italy—which is frequently labeled as primitive. The term *primitive* is often used to refer to work from a variety of cultures, typically those outside European and Asian civilizations. Henry Moore tells us that for many people, the term *primitive* means "crudeness and incompetence, ignorant groupings rather than finished achievements." But Moore sees primitive works instead as embodying an "intense vitality." The people who created these works express "a direct and immediate response to life," which illuminates their "powerful beliefs, hopes, and fears" (146).

Approaching the Greek and Etruscan art, Professor Phillips said, "Now look at this. Looks primitive to you, doesn't it?" And everyone in the class nodded, thinking that that was the right answer. Then he said, "What if I told you it was really done by Matisse?" And we all gasped, "Oh!" We suddenly realized how the term primitive *makes us think of things that are ancient and unstudied. So when we see something that doesn't look like what we see out our window, depicted by someone like Matisse, it can have the vitality and simplicity of something "primitive" but still be challenging to look at and think about. Matisse's work is frequently seen as childlike or primitive. I know that it has a lot more to it, so I'm going to enjoy the opportunity to delve into his work here and explore how sophisticated Matisse actually is.*

As Professor Rowland holds this hefty art book in her hands, she tells us that initially she does two things: looks at the acknowledgments in the beginning of the book and at the pictures.

When I get a book I always go right to the acknowledgments to find out who the author's friends are. I want to know who is talking to who in the art world. I know you're not supposed to do that but you can tell by a person's friends how they think. You're not supposed to care whether they're nice or not, but I think the humanities have to do with people, so I'm always comforted if somebody turns out to be friends with people I like and admire. And so much of my historical work concerns associations between people: who knows who, who are friends. It also gives you some indication of whether somebody is working in isolation or as part of a larger community.

Next, with art books I usually look at the pictures. I want to see what the authors think is interesting and whether they see it in an interesting way. Also, if there are endnotes instead of footnotes I'll always read them at the end almost as though they are a separate text. In this case I'm looking to see what kinds of additional information Jack Flam wants us to have.

WRITING AND LEARNING ACTIVITY

1. **Preparing to Read:** Look over the excerpt from Flam's book below. How does the Introduction differ from the discussion of *Conversation?* Look over the notes. What kind of information does Flam provide there? What sorts of books are listed in the references?

A CLOSE READING OF JACK FLAM'S TEXT

This reading is composed of two very different portions. The first comes from Flam's Introduction and provides an analytic framework for his approach to Matisse. The second portion illustrates the kind of work Flam does throughout most of the rest of the book. That is, he explores how individual paintings or works of art reflect his understanding of Matisse's work.

WRITING AND LEARNING ACTIVITIES

1. **Journal Entry:** As you read, make notes about your reading process in your journal. Write down any questions you have about the reading and any familiar or unfamiliar terms you encounter.

2. **Annotate the Text:** As you read, make notes in the margins of the excerpt. Underline key points, bracket new terms, paraphrase key points in the margins, and add question marks at points you don't understand. Write a question about what you don't understand in the margins. Try to restate the important points where you find them.

FROM THE INTRODUCTION
JACK FLAM

▨ ▨ ▨

The life of Henri Matisse was filled with paradoxes. That a man who at the age of twenty had never even considered a career as an artist would become one of the greatest artists of his time is only one of them. But it is a crucial one. His late and slow development, as we shall see, was a function of his caution, and his caution was in turn a requisite of his boldness. In a curious way, Matisse was at once the most radical and the most conservative great artist of the twentieth century. Stubbornly tied to the visible world, he generally hesitated to depart very far from it. Yet when he did depart from it, he did so with such absolute conviction that he seemed to be reinventing nature as much as extending the art of painting; to be recreating rather than depicting the world around him.

As late as 1896—when he was in his twenty-seventh year and had already spent five years studying art in Paris, the center of virtually all advanced artistic movements of the previous half-century—he remained unaffected not only by the work of Vincent Van Gogh and Paul Cézanne but even by the masters of impressionism. In 1896 he was still working in a manner that would have been considered conservative the day he was born; yet by the turn of the century he had a deeper understanding of Cézanne than any other painter had achieved and was on the verge of becoming the acknowledged leader of the Parisian avant-garde. Eventually students came from all over the world to work with him, to get the basic tenets of modernism at firsthand from the man who was supposed to be the most modern of masters. Yet he himself expressed an abiding mistrust of modernist conventions, even as he pushed his work toward greater and greater abstraction. He advised his students to draw from the model, restrain their color, and use the plumbline, as Ingres had done a century before. And even in his own work he frequently hesitated and tried different, often contradictory modes of seeing and rendering within a short time, sometimes alternating between straightforward naturalism and near-abstraction during the course of a single day.

Underlying this alternation of modes, paradoxically, was his profound conviction, inherited from Cézanne, that great painting was not merely a matter of stylization or technique but the result of deeply held convictions about vision in relation to life. The means of expressing these convictions—including a very deep sense of doubt—were numerous and varied, and had at all costs to be kept free from convention. So even as Matisse invented new forms, he was constantly impelled to repudiate his own inventions in order to move beyond them and to keep his art in touch with the direct experience that was his most powerful and reliable source of inspiration.

The battle and the battlefield were private ones. Unlike Pablo Picasso, to whom he later was constantly compared, he struggled slowly and painfully to acquire the rudiments of his craft. He was no prodigy, and in the long run it was his necessarily dogged and cautious persistence that allowed him to outdistance all of his contemporaries and to produce original and influential art of high quality to the very end of his long life. A great innovator, he nevertheless kept a clear distance between himself and the world around him. The historical topography of the twentieth century, its extraordinary inventions and horrors, are remarkably absent from his art. And unlike the protean Picasso, who literally picked up parts of the world around him and incorporated them piecemeal in his art, Matisse worked with clearly delimited subject matter and technique. He practiced the traditional plastic arts—painting, drawing, sculpture—with traditional materials: oil paint, artists' graphic tools, clay. Even the cutout compositions that occupied him during the last decade of his life were executed with carefully prepared papers, and he eschewed the variation of materials and textures and the disrupted space characteristic of cubist collage. The art, like the man, is as remarkable for what it was able to refuse as for what it was able to accept and make use of.

5   The descriptions of the man by his contemporaries are strikingly consistent.[1] He radiated an extraordinary sense of energy, almost of violence,

held in check beneath a manner of great reserve. The persona that he presented to the world was carefully composed: neatly dressed, his rather squarish face framed by his carefully trimmed hair and beard, he spoke with measure, gravity, and lucidity. "The professor," his friends called him, not without affection, but also not without irony. His blue eyes were quick and alert, penetrating, full of curiosity. Yet even here one sensed that something was being held back. As he stared out through his thick gold-rimmed spectacles, the strong lenses shielding his myopic eyes seemed to suggest the psychological distance from which he observed the world around him. And with one significant exception, this was also the way he portrayed himself in his work: neatly dressed and trimly bearded, often wearing a coat and tie, his eyes framed and covered by the glasses, so that he seems to look out at the world from behind a mask.

The depth of his feelings, passions, and loyalties were rarely expressed outside his work; and his work—not only the works themselves, the steady flow of drawings, paintings, and sculptures that came from his hands, but the very act of working—was in effect the true center of his life. Hardly a single memoir that mentions him fails to remark on his extraordinary capacity for work or on the relationship between this capacity and his sense of removal from the world around him. Even people closest to him remarked on "his inability to relax, his killing labor, his absolute incapacity, if only for the space of a tear or a smile, to sit down with his neighbor."[2]

His enormous capacity and intense need for work were rooted in an anxiety that appears to have settled on him in his earliest years and from which he found refuge only in his work. "Matisse the anxious, the madly anxious."[3] The characterization was made in 1904, at a moment of severe stress, but it holds true for his whole life. A kind of cosmic anxiety, a profound sense of the meaninglessness of life coupled with a nearly religious passion to accept and praise the whole of existence, was the driving force behind his work and the source of both its extreme tension and its remarkable transcendence. The polarities of his personal anxiety determined the polarities of his artistic temperament: respect for authority and the need to rebel; powerful sensuality and severe restraint; intense feeling and spartan self-control. In his work this duality was expressed over and over in the constant struggle between the physical and the spiritual, between the instinctual and the intellectual, between the formal polarities of color and drawing, surface and depth. In the continuous conflict that every artist faces in the need to choose between life and work. Matisse constantly chose his work.

Matisse's greatest assets were a powerful intelligence and an unrelenting courage, which drove him to look hard and without flinching at himself and at the world around him. He appears early in his career to have realized that he was not a man of particularly great imagination in the ordinary sense, but that his visual imagination, when stimulated by direct perception of the world around him, was very strong. Throughout his life he kept that imagination alive and nourished by working directly from nature. The direct stimulation of the real world united his extraordinary powers of perception and organization and provided tangible matter on which his imagination could act. By the time he had reached his early thirties, his exploration of the visible world had become inseparable from his exploration of self, and the medium of painting had become the means through which both endeavors were effected. The intensity of his sensory awareness, controlled and focused by his exceptional intellectual clarity and self-discipline, served as the basis for the invention of a new poetics based on the act of seeing—a poetics of vision. More than any other modern painter, Matisse opens our eyes to the possibilities and inferences of vision and teaches us that imagination can start in the eye as well as in the mind.

Matisse's constant contact with nature also allowed him to use his extensive knowledge of past art without losing or compromising his originality, and to work in very different stylistic modes—not only at different times in his career but often on the same day. The different modes of his art were based on different modes of vision, which in turn were based on different states of consciousness. Painting for Matisse was a means of knowing, a philosophical activity. (And by "painting" I mean here both the act of painting as a means of confronting reality and the contemplation of painting as a medium that has its own history and that at given moments in that history seems to have certain self-generated needs and tendencies.) The art of Matisse is based on a dialogue between the nature of painting as a medium with its own history and needs and the nature of painting as a descriptive or representational art. This is the central dialectic of early modernism, and no one seems to have understood it better than Matisse.

•   •   •

10   How, then, do we speak of these paintings? What is the nature of their symbolic language and how is it expressed? We start with the assumption that in a representational painting things are placed where they are and rendered as they are for a reason (albeit an unconscious one); that painting is a form of thinking. We also must realize that in the work of such a painter as Matisse, who is essentially a classicist, powerful feeling is contained and guided and controlled by the order and calm of form. The apparent neutrality of the subject matter provides a necessary foil for the form that embodies it, yet at the same time the relative neutralization of the subject by the form often creates an even stronger, metaphorical kind of signification, in which the interaction of form and subject creates a new reality that goes far beyond the sum of its parts. Finally, we must keep in mind that painting is a tabular art. Paintings enter our consciousness as whole entities in which the overall design is apparent at the outset—unlike books and musical compositions, which are apprehended gradually, part by part. While looking at a painting we may focus first here, then there, but the parts are seen in relation to a constantly present whole. The amount of time needed simply to "have looked at" a painting is relatively short, and any further time that is needed to "see" a painting is more or less left to the will or discretion of the viewer. But while paintings are tabular, our means of discussing them is lin-

ear; we can talk about only one thing at a time, and our discussion of a specific painting is always framed in narrative.

With such a painter as Matisse this dichotomy is especially problematic, as virtually all of his imagery is based on a rigorously nonnarrative aesthetic. His paintings are constructed as objects of contemplation, physical gatherings of spiritual force that can be looked at over and over again for extended periods of time without yielding the core of their meaning or all of their energy, in the manner of icons. For Matisse, as for Mallarmé, the essence of a work of art had by its very nature to be beyond the reach of description or definition; the inner core of the work remains ineffable. My procedure, then, is not to "explain" Matisse's symbolism but to point out some of the ways it may be approached and to provide an intellectual context for the history of its development. For Matisse's paintings not only are not "easy" but are specifically and willfully "difficult"; that is, their difficulty is built into their very structure and is an integral part of their meaning. Matisse's paintings do not employ an iconography that is based on fixed meanings for certain objects that are placed within a fixed narrative situation. They do not, in other words, employ a difficult *iconography,* based, for example, on obscure philosophical or literary texts. Rather, they employ imagery in which a certain ambiguity is built right into the structure of the image, and in which the facture, paint surface, color, and linear inflection are as crucial to meaning as is what is actually represented. Thus while the apparent subject matter of his paintings often seems easy, their "deep subject matter," or total meaning, is often dizzyingly complex. Like the poetry of Mallarmé and the painting of Cézanne, Matisse's painting contains a strong element that goes against the smoothly commonsensical, readily risks the pictorial equivalent of semantic breakdown, and provides the modern pictorial temperament with a powerful paradigm. Matisse, like Mallarmé, is "incomparably sensitive to those moments in human experience when familiar meanings dissolve and vacancy, or a dizzying blur of potential meanings, takes their place."[4]

Within the context of such subtlety of thought and expression, the distinctions that are usually drawn between form and subject or between form and content are often misleading or meaningless. For in the same way that content does not exist without form, form does not exist without content. We might, in fact, say that every aspect of Matisse's painting is an aspect of its content.

For the purposes of discussion, however, such distinctions must often be made if analysis is to proceed without becoming overwhelmed by the ambiguities we have set out to analyze. Moreover, a sometimes arbitrary separation of formal and representational content will allow us to approach a third, more elusive kind of content: a picture's metaphorical or symbolic content. We understand a painting's metaphors by seeing how its formal and representational contents interact and relate to each other; and this is in effect where the "deep meaning" of any work comes from—the point at which our ability to understand a painting's relationship with the outside world merges with painting's existence as a medium in and of itself. Here the visual, associational, and synthetic aspects of our own sensibilities also merge, or are brought together by the work of art. Or to put it differently, this is where our linguistic or verbal understanding of the world merges with our truly nonverbal understanding of the world.[5]

The bulk of Matisse's oeuvre, with its repetitive use of objects, models, places, and situations, appears to follow a developmental pattern not unlike that of Marcel Proust in *Â la recherche du temps perdu*. As in Proust's work, we are constantly made to realize that our observations of what is happening depend on where and when we are when we perceive what we do. An event presented as unique cannot occur again in precisely the same way; yet events and configurations do follow certain patterns, and the complex act of their recording simultaneously involves a careful rendering of the surface of things and a symbolic projection of an inner state of consciousness that reveals a deeper reality. This reality, for all its dependence on descriptions of the outer world, is revealed as much by the medium of the description as by the event described. We are thus constantly made aware of time's flux and of the truths that are independent of time's flux. The sensual and the rational, the apparent and the underlying are in each individual image united into a single reality, and each individual image in turn provides part of a broader context that enriches and is enriched by all of the others. It is within this larger context that the extraordinary accomplishment of Matisse's oeuvre can be most fully appreciated. And it is within this larger context that we can begin to understand to what a great degree his life and his oeuvre are inseparable.

246. *Conversation*, 1908–c. 1910/12? Oil on canvas, 177 × 217 cm. The Hermítage Museum, Leningrad.

ABOUT *CONVERSATION*
JACK FLAM

■ ■ ■

Another painting that seems to have a direct relationship to the circumstances of Matisse's life at this time is *Conversation* (fig. 246). Although the exact date of this painting remains in question, I feel reasonably sure that it was started in 1908, around the same time as *Harmony in Red,* though the last touches may not have been done until the late spring of 1912. Alfred Barr felt that the painting was done early in 1909, as a pendant to *Harmony in Red,* which is the same size, and which had also been begun as a blue painting.[6] Pierre Schneider, following the dating of Marguerite Duthuit, dated *Conversation* to the spring of 1911.[7] Since it had not been exhibited or shown to collectors until 1912,[8] this date seemed reasonable to me—until I examined the painting carefully in Leningrad; then it became apparent that certain aspects of the composition and rendering fix the origins of the painting in 1908.

The painting appears quite clearly to have been done at two distinct times. The intense cracking around both of the figures indicates that Matisse had rubbed out a dry paint film with a strong solvent before undertaking major revision. The figure of the woman was originally somewhat smaller than it is now, and her right shoulder was set farther forward to give a greater effect of foreshortening. This pose is related not only to the upper torso of the woman in *Harmony in Red* but also to the figure at the right in *Bathers with a Turtle* [see *Bathers with a Turtle,* in Chapter 12, page 510] (as well as to the right-hand figure in a watercolor study done for *Bathers by a Stream* in the spring of 1909). Moreover, the scumbled modeling of the woman's head in *Conversation,* and the rendering of her ear are characteristic of other paintings of this period, including *The Game of Bowls, Harmony in Red,* and *Nymph and Satyr.*

The blue color harmony, the heavy laying of the paint, and the symbolic juxtaposition of the window view and the interior of the room also connect *Conversation* to *Harmony in Red.* Finally, although the window depicts the front of Matisse's property at Issy-les-Moulineaux, the view through the window may originally have depicted the garden at the Hôtel Biron.[9] The pentimenti indicate that the window was originally slightly larger than it now is, the corner of the room above the woman's head was shown, and the grillework seems to have been repainted after everything else around it. The style, the composition, and the brushwork all suggest that the painting was started in 1908 or 1909. There are two likely reasons that Matisse did not exhibit the painting or show it to his regular collectors until 1912: he did not consider it finished until then and the subject matter was so intimate and personal that he hesitated to make it public earlier.

Conversation represents Henri and Amélie Matisse confronting each other early on a spring morning. Henri is dressed in striped pajamas and Amélie in a black-and-green bathrobe, one that she actually owned.[10] The two figures face each other with unnerving intensity. He stands stock-still,

This painting started out differently & was painted over again why?

with his hands in his pockets, upright, rigid, frozen, as if incapable of speech or action. Across from him sits his wife, larger than life, returning his stare with the dignity and aplomb of a queen. Neither of these persons is about to budge; each is enveloped by the dense silence of the blue room and each exudes stubbornness and will. The only indication of any communication is subtly embedded in the almost electrical connection between the woman's black sleeve and the black arabesques of the window grille-work, as if to suggest movement or articulation: speech. But even this articulation is cut off by the blue void. The stiff vertical form of the man stands apart from it, cut off from it, apparently incapable even of acknowledging its existence. In this sense, the painting represents a kind of antithesis to a similar gesture in Van Eyck's *Virgin with the Chancellor Rolin* in the Louvre, in which the hand of the Christ child forms a bridge between the sacred and profane worlds. Here we see something like the opposite of incarnation, the opposite of communication. The title, given to the painting when it was first exhibited in 1912, is ironic—even more than ironic, for it underlines an enormous absence, as if to suggest the earliest meaning of the word *conversation* in French, "relation, rapport, manner of life."[11]

5   The image seems vaguely familiar, reminiscent of something more specific than the blue enamel of Byzantine icons or early-Renaissance windows to which it has been compared.[12] For *Conversation* alludes to a work so apparently remote from the domestic theme of a man and wife confronting each other across an abyss of silence that the allusion, once grasped, astonishes and alarms us. The composition of *Conversation* is clearly based on the ancient stele of Hammurabi (fig. 247), which was brought to the Louvre at the beginning of the century, and which Matisse had seen often during his visits to the Near Eastern rooms there. King Hammurabi stands before the seated god Shamash, who dictates the law while the king stands in an attitude of reverent attention. The pose of the seated god, the position of the arms, and the strict profile are all echoed in the figure of Amélie Matisse; the figure of her husband echoes the rigid verticality of the king. Once we have become aware of this relationship, the resonance of Matisse's image is compounded. *Conversation* is less a conversation than a monologue. The seated woman "lays down the law." The standing man looks at her intensely but is noncommittal. Outside the window, the world springs back to life: the grass and trees are a vivid green, and red flowers burst like flames from their beds (an ironic echo of the sun god's flaming shoulders, carrying the light of inspiration?). Beyond the grass and trees and flowers, the pink walls that surround the property suggest the antithesis of the silent blues of the room. As we look more closely at the image before us, we are startled to see that the grillework at the window spells out *"NON"*—a word that asserts its negation in both directions, from left to right and from right to left, from the seated woman toward the standing man, only to be engulfed by the engulfing blue. The large *NON* also reads as an emblem for the viewer, an assertion of negation that sets its own limits at the plane of the window, where private life stops and the garden bursts into bloom. As we behold the

247. Upper portion of the stele of Hammurabi, c. 1760 B.C. Basalt, overall height about 224 cm. Musée du Louvre, Paris.

family drama before us, the *NON* becomes emblematic of the space and substance of the room, of the whole painting's thesis and antithesis of layered irony. This extraordinary image of isolation is intensified by the realization that this is the first of Matisse's paintings in which two people actually face each other. And we see that despite the "conversation" articulated by the window grillework, the artist, standing stiffly with his hands (expressively unexpressive) in his pockets, is reduced to a bar of stripes, a completely closed form, impassive, incommunicado, as if incapable of any action except looking.

•   •   •

NOTES
Introduction

1. Interesting descriptions of Matisse may be found in Puy 1939, p. 120; Duthuit 1950, p. 99; Stein 1933, p. 137; Stein 1947, p. 15; Alice B. Toklas, "Some Memories," in *Homage to Matisse, Yale Literary Magazine* 123 (1955): 15–16; Fernande Olivier, *Picasso et ses emis* (Paris, 1933), pp. 107–9. In a brief autobiographical sketch published in *Formes,* no. 1 (January 1930), p. 11, Matisse described his main activity as "extremely regular work, every day, from morning until evening."

2. Duthuit 1950, p. 99.
3. Henri-Edmond Cross to Théo van Rysselberghe, September 7, 1994, cited in Bock 1977, p. 274.
4. Malcolm Bowie, *Mallarmé and the Art of Being Difficult* (Cambridge, 1978), p. 5.
5. I suspect that the ignoration of this merging results in the frequent conflict between purely formal interpretations of paintings and iconographical interpretations. The formalists suspect that the iconographers either cannot or will not look at the significance of the form because they feel that verbal knowledge is in fact the only, or in any case the truest, way of knowing. The iconographers tend to feel that the formal structure of representational painting must be "got past," as it were, if one is to apprehend the intellectual construct of the work of art—as if the two were separate.

Notes to "*About* Conversation"

6. Barr 1951, p. 126. Matisse told Barr that he started it before *Dance* (Alfred Barr Papers, Museum of Modern Art Archives, New York).
7. Schneider 1975, pp. 76–82. See also Schneider 1984, pp. 14–24.
8. The painting was first shown at the second post-impressionist exhibition in London, October 5–December 31, 1912 (no. 28 in the catalogue). Shchukin evidently first saw the painting that summer; he expressed interest in it in a letter to Matisse dated August 22 (Barr 1951, p. 555).
9. The view through the window is of the front lawn and entrance gate at Issy—not, as Pierre Schneider says (1975, pp. 76–82; 1984, pp. 14–24), of the studio; the studio was at the back of the property. Such is the recollection of Pierre Matisse (in conversation, New York, March 30, 1983) and I was able to confirm his statement during a visit to the house on May 2, 1985. In fact, the flower plantings and driveways depicted in the painting correspond exactly to those indicated in the surveyor's drawings prepared at the time Matisse purchased the property (municipal records, Issy-les-Moulineaux). The pentimenti of the painting indicate that the window view was repainted sometime after the paint used for the first rendering had dried. It is thus possible that the window view was originally of the garden at the Hôtel Biron, and was changed when the picture was reworked at Issy.
10. Marguerite Duthuit, interviewed in Paris, November 26, 1979.
11. *Le Petit Robert,* 1976 ed.
12. The relationship to Byzantine enamels is discussed in Schneider 1975 and in Schneider 1984, pp. 14–24. This relationship was first suggested by Sarah Stein; see Walter Pach, *Queer Thing, Painting* (New York, 1938), p. 117.

REFERENCES

Barr 1951	Barr, Alfred H., Jr. *Matisse, His Art and His Public.* New York, 1951.
Bock 1977	Bock, Catherine C. "Henri Matisse and Neo-Impressionism, 1898–1908" Ph.D. dissertation, University of California, Los Angeles, 1977.
Duthuit 1950	Duthuit, Georges. *The Fauvist Painters.* New York, 1950.
Puy 1939	Puy, Jean. "Souvenirs." *Le Point* 21 (1939): 16–37 [112–33].
Schneider 1975	Schneider, Pierre. "The Striped Pajama Icon." *Art in America,* July–August 1975, pp. 76–82.

Schneider 1984   Schneider, Pierre. *Matisse*. New York, 1984.

Stein 1933   Stein, Gertrude. *The Autobiography of Alice B. Toklas*. New York, 1961. First published 1933.

Flam's Introduction

Read the section from paragraph 1 to paragraph 7.

When Jack Flam writes about Henri Matisse, he takes into account what is known about the life of the artist, the times he lived in, the cultural context, and attitudes about art in those times. Most importantly, he takes a close look at Matisse's art itself.

Flam is working here out of a general framework in which he presents Matisse, the artist and the person, as highly intelligent, highly disciplined, and in pursuit of something for which he sees no right answer. He is trying to present Matisse not only as visually rich— which he has always been recognized as—but also as intellectually rigorous, an artist who thinks carefully about what he is doing in relation to his own work and the work of other artists who have gone before him. Later, as I read on, I will be looking at how Flam's discussions of particular paintings fit his more general descriptions of Matisse the artist.

The first section of Flam's introduction weaves together biographical information about Matisse with a discussion of his relationship with the Impressionists, painters such as Van Gogh and Cézanne who, in the late 1800s, painted vivid scenes with dabs of color that evoked natural light and a sensory impression of reality. Professor Rowland is interested in the way Jack Flam presents the biographical information about Matisse.

One of the big issues in art history is whether or not to deal with biography. I'm very interested in biography. In fact, women traditionally have done biography, which was disparaged for much of the twentieth century by male historians, who said that biography was a less important form of scholarship. Then in 1979 Lawrence Stone, who was British (and a man!), wrote an article called "The Return of Narrative," after which people in art history thought it was all right to do narrative biographies again; in other words now it was all right to write about the lives of artists.

Jack Flam approaches his biography of Matisse by noting the paradoxes in his life and by insisting that Matisse was "at once the most radical and the most conservative great artist of the twentieth century" (paragraph 1).

This is a wonderful way to present Matisse. Radical means getting at the roots of something and almost always presupposes tradition. What Flam is getting at here is the way Matisse worked with the problem of form and content. The content is what the painting

means and how it feels and this content or meaning is expressed through form. Flam ar-
gues that Matisse is using the technical aspects of painting that contribute to form—
color, line placement, application of paint—to create a message that transforms reality
and asks us to see with our minds and not just our eyes. We will see this when we look at
Conversation. *Flam says,*

> More than any other modern painter, Matisse opens our eyes to the possibilities
> and inferences of vision and teaches us that imagination can start in the eye as
> well as in the mind (paragraph 8).

The paradox Flam suggests also emerges as he describes Matisse's habit of
relentless work. In his introduction Flam offers the following physical description of Matisse, that he then says we will see reflected in *Conversation.*

> He radiated an extraordinary sense of energy, almost of violence, held in check
> beneath a manner of great reserve. The persona that he presented to the world
> was carefully composed: neatly dressed, his rather squarish face framed by his
> carefully trimmed hair and beard, he spoke with measure, gravity, and lucidity.
> "The professor," his friends called him, not without affection, but also not with-
> out irony. His blue eyes were quick and alert, penetrating, full of curiosity. Yet
> even here one sensed that something was being held back. As he stared out
> through his thick gold-rimmed spectacles, the strong lenses shielding his my-
> opic eyes seemed to suggest the psychological distance from which he ob-
> served the world around him (paragraph 5).

Flam is illustrating the discipline he sees in Matisse, an artist who understands that disci-
pline is necessary to make a contribution. Yet Flam also sees a "cosmic anxiety," between,
on the one hand, the "meaninglessness of life," and on the other, a passion for life. This
contradiction made him see life differently and search to find ways to reflect that knowl-
edge in his painting. This is what Flam means when he says that "painting for Matisse
was a means of knowing, a philosophical activity" (paragraph 9).

Read paragraphs 10–14.

In this section Jack Flam poses the question of how we can "speak"
about these paintings: to study art we must develop a language with which
to speak about it. Through what is known as a "critical tradition," art historians and other scholars have developed a specialized language for speaking about works of art and helping us to go beyond our initial intuitive response in understanding the work of art.

In an earlier segment of Flam's work (not included here) he cautions us
about these critical traditions, which encourage us to see the artist as the
critics want us to. Matisse's work, Flam points out, has suffered in just
this way. Critics have told us that his work is "festive, gay, and simple-
mindedly optimistic," and until recently we have accepted this limited
description. Flam's approach in this volume is to change this preconceived
notion of Matisse's work. Flam must solve the problem of how to talk about
a new understanding of Matisse's work he wants to communicate to us.

Professor Rowland sees, in the problem Flam faces, a wonderful opportunity for students.

A student can take this two ways. One is listen to everything that has been written before or in the future, by Jack Flam or anyone else. The other is to take all that into consideration, but construct your own analysis. Flam tells us that he should only be a guide; the real point of all this is to look with your own eyes.

I think the only way you can see new things is by going against everything that's been said before. The whole point of Matisse's paintings is that they are acts of communication and in talking about them they become a communicative surface. They keep communication alive; nobody will ever say the definitive thing about them. And Matisse himself never felt that any of his paintings made a definite statement. I try to live by this rule myself. When I was younger I wanted answers; I wanted one interpretation, the interpretation. But the older I get, the more indefinite things seem to be and the more pleased I am by that.

In the first paragraph of this section Professor Rowland identifies what she calls Jack Flam's manifesto, the statement that sums up his central claim about Matisse's work.

We start with the assumption that in a representational painting things are placed where they are and rendered as they are for a reason (albeit an unconscious one); that painting is a form of thinking (paragraph 10).

Unfortunately, in a subsequent sentence, which should help explain his claim, Flam offers us a very difficult, complicated sentence.

The apparent neutrality of the subject matter provides a necessary foil for the form that embodies it, yet at the same time the relative neutralization of the subject by the form often creates an even stronger, metaphorical kind of signification, in which the interaction of form and subject creates a new reality that goes beyond the sum of its parts (paragraph 10).

I think this sentence is too complicated. It's the kind of writing I just can't stand. Fortunately I haven't seen Flam do too much of it. It simply doesn't get you anywhere. Later, he says much more simply that "content does not exist without form, form does not exist without content" (paragraph 12).

Flam is searching for the language here to speak about representational art, art that attempts to imitate nature. To the extent that Matisse is a representational artist, he chooses, consciously or unconsciously, how the painting will work to present us some aspect of nature. Both the content and the way it is articulated, form, work to communicate the meaning of the painting.

In Matisse's paintings you don't have Napoleon crossing the Alps; what you do have is an interior with something seemingly banal, a morning conversation. But that should not necessarily make us think that the issues addressed by the painting are banal just because it is not Napoleon crossing the Alps. So, by choosing not to portray Napoleon, the importance of the forms in getting across the message of the painting is intensified dramatically. This is what Flam means when he says that the painting creates a "new reality that goes far beyond the sum of its parts" (paragraph 10).

Viewing a painting, Flam reminds us, is different from reading a book: the viewing experience occurs holistically, all at once. Talking about a painting or work of art, though, presents a different challenge: we must construct a narrative or tell a story.

When Flam reminds us that painting is a "tabular art" he is referring to the "easel tradition." Twentieth-century European and American art assumed that painting is something that occurs on small bounded surfaces that were originally attached to easels. Artists chose a subject for their painting—such as a bowl of fruit or a vase full of flowers—because it could be represented on this small form. Matisse, on the other hand, is not doing that. He is painting a world and it happens to end up on a limited square of canvas.

But more importantly, when Flam says, "the discussion of a specific painting is always framed in narrative," (paragraph 10) he means explaining a painting means telling a story. Otherwise people would stop reading about art. Any time you talk about visual material you need to create suspense. Flam suggests that he is going to tell a story. So we then have the choice of buying his story, not buying his story, or telling a different story. The point of the story is partly enjoyment and partly to transmit certain essential truths, that is, to make meaning, to make the world we live in.

Flam's Discussion of *Conversation*

Read the discussion of *Conversation*, paragraphs 15–19, and study the accompanying art reproductions.

Jack Flam's first paragraph in this section, Professor Rowland tells us, is typical of art history: the writer attempts to place him- or herself in the historical context by connecting him- or herself to previous scholarship, in this case on Matisse. The list of notes tells us who Flam is reading. But what is more important to Professor Rowland is the fact that Flam tells us that he actually saw the painting where it hung in Russia. Sometimes, art historians work from photographs, which limits what they can say with confidence about a work of art.

Flam then goes on to talk about some technical aspects of the painting. He uses terms like *scumbled* (a technique in which the painter softens the colors by rubbing) and *pentimenti* (in which the painter uses layers of color) to describe the way the artist has worked with color and how he revised previous versions of the painting. When Flam compares, for instance, the woman's ear in *Conversation* with similar ears in other paintings done at about the same time, he makes a traditional art historical assumption: that we can learn from similarities and differences among paintings produced at about the same time.

Professor Rowland asks us to look at this painting to see how Matisse works with form and content, or how Matisse, as an artist, chooses to depict objects or nonobjects. We speak of syntax in writing as the set of relationships within a sentence that allows it to make meaning. Art historians think of syntax as the principles by which you assemble a painting.

For instance, there is no perspective in the picture. The figures and the window in the picture are not being lined up in a spatial way that follows any of the rules that have been laid down since the Renaissance. There is no perspective structure, with lines receding toward a vanishing point. Instead the figures and the view out the window seem to belong to the same plane.

Matisse is always so striking because he'll use these bright colors. It looks superficially pretty but then you realize there is much more going on there. It hits you like a ton of bricks: the color reproduction, the way that he treats the wall itself, the placing of the two figures and the window, the way he lays down paint on something that is supposedly uniform. That wall has probably been made a vivid color that was not its color at all in real life. It is made in some ways as striking and vibrant as the view out the window. All of these things are being shifted and brought to your attention by the use of color.

By ignoring perspective Matisse has made this picture look childlike or naive. The trees look like lollipops and the male figure's pajamas look like flat stripes. Yet what's going on in this picture is not naive at all. Let's see what Flam says is really going on.

The most critical aspect of Flam's reading here is the biographical story he tells, which begins, "*Conversation* represents Henri and Amélie Matisse confronting each other early on a spring morning" (paragraph 18).

It is quite shocking that Flam sees this as Matisse and his wife. It has suddenly become a biographical issue. How do we know it is Matisse? The way Flam writes about them is compelling—he makes us want to believe it. For instance, he brings up some historical evidence: Amélie's bathrobe, the view from the window of the hotel (see note 9). If students are going to write about this painting, it's almost better that they not read this first because I would want them to develop their own response and then test it against Flam's framework or compare it to Flam's response.

We have to stop and ask ourselves, how does this story connect to the evidence Flam offers and how does it connect to our understanding of Matisse as an artist? As readers, we have to ask ourselves whether he is offering a personal response or a professional judgment. This is exactly the challenge I face in my own work of reconstructing personalities from the Renaissance, and it's the only way that you get people excited.

Professor Rowland looks at some specific aspects of the painting and Flam's description of them.

If you look closely at the painting you'll see that the female figure is, as Flam puts it, "larger than life." If she stood up she would tower over the male figure. Flam finds an "almost electric connection" between her sleeve and the grillework of the window that suggests communication. This brings us to a discussion of the title of the painting. Is there a conversation? We will have to keep coming back to this question and reevaluating it.

What do we think the title, *Conversation*, means? What communication do we think occurs in the painting? How we answer these questions has a lot to do with whether we accept Flam's interpretation of the grillework.

When I look at the grillework, I see the "NO," and the next figure looks like an "X." It doesn't look like "NON" to me. I'm a handwriting expert and I say "close, but no cigar." Besides, if we accept Flam's initial analytic framework, then he's shooting himself in the foot—this interpretation is too obvious, too literal, gives the whole thing away. It forces us into a particular interpretation, which is not what Matisse was trying to do in his art work. The paradox is gone.

Flam brings an interesting piece of evidence to his narrative in his discussion of the Louvre's Hammurabi stele. (*Stele* is the Greek word for a tall, slender tablet.) Professor Rowland reminds us here of the story of Hammurabi.

Hammurabi, a Babylonian king, made the first legal code, which provided a way of ordering society. With this code, law became a concept that was higher than a simple arbitrary whim on the part of Hammurabi. But, he needed some way to base it on principles that weren't arbitrary and that went beyond himself. He said that this legal code was more than simply the desires of an individual; it was a way of creating a harmonious universe. He strengthened his power by subordinating himself to a higher principle derived from the god Shamash. In a way it was like Moses coming down from Mt. Sinai, because the laws he brought down are grounded not in Moses himself but in a higher power.

Professor Rowland then questions the connections Flam makes between the Hammurabi stele and the relation between the two figures in the painting. Flam argues that "The seated woman lays down the law" (paragraph 19).

"Laying down the law" won't quite work because it's not at all the same kind of thing as we see in the stele. With the Hammurabi stele we're talking about divine inspiration and justification for everything that Hammurabi is going to achieve. Sitting down in comfort is a sign of power that goes back not only to the Near East but is also in all kinds of rituals and western traditions. I would have thought a lot more about the window itself and the relationship between the two figures. I think that in a sense what we're getting in this painting is a statement about the gap between Shamash and Hammurabi. This gap is not just one of communication or conversation, but rather it is the gap on which the border between divinity and humanity rests.

I suppose you could make an argument that the space between these two could be bridged by Shamash's hand. The window, the space in between the two figures in Conversation, *could symbolize all sorts of things. It could be distraction, it could be opportunity, it could be words flying out the window—it's got all sorts of possibilities. But there's no question that the area is visually loaded.*

Professor Rowland has demonstrated how Flam moved back and forth from his own personal response to his framework for understanding Matisse. In addition, she jumped into the fray to contribute her analysis of Flam's reading.

Flam is throwing out some pretty wild ideas. What you will get out of his argument is how intelligent and how rewarding Matisse is and how much Matisse has to offer to you. I don't think Flam is primarily interested in whether you buy the "NON" in the grillework or the code of Hammurabi. What he's really trying to do is an analysis on an amazing person who's produced some amazing art, and in that sense it's an extraordinarily worthwhile piece of writing to work with.

WRITING AND LEARNING ACTIVITIES
---

1. **Journal Entry:** Look over the notes you made while reading Jack Flam's work on Matisse. How was reading this different from other reading you have done, inside school or out? Write about the differences.

2. **Journal Entry:** Bring several art reproductions to class. First, write about your personal responses using the activity questions on page 215 as a guideline.

3. **Group Activity:** Choose one piece of art to discuss. Compare your responses. Discuss how some of your responses come from your personal experience and others from what you can see in the work of art. Report to the class on the variety of meanings you can develop for the work.

4. **Writing Activity:** Write an imaginary dialogue about their interpretations of *Conversation* that might go on between Professor Rowland and Jack Flam, based on your reading of Flam and Professor Rowland's response.

MAKING MEANING IN ART HISTORY
THE ELEMENTS OF A WORK OF ART

Professor Rowland stressed how important it is to be able to "see pictures through words." Writing allows you to make certain for yourself what you have seen and also allows you to share it with someone else. What you see when you look at a painting has everything to do with how you look at it, what in it you choose to look at, the relationship between yourself and the painting, who you are, and how your experiences have helped you to look. No piece of art tells its own story; when you choose to look, you choose to question, and from the answers to your questions a story may emerge about what that work means.

What does the work of art contribute to this process? We can look at any piece of art as the result of specific techniques employed by the artist to create the image that we see. Jack Flam reminds us that painting, like writing, is a "form of thinking." Even if the artist is not consciously aware of his or her intentions, "things are placed where they are . . . for a reason" (paragraph 10). Art historians—like the participants of other specialized disciplines discussed in other chapters—have a special language with which to talk about the techniques artists use to create a work. That specialized language includes terms Flam uses, such as color, surface, perspective, space, medium, light, space, and, especially, form and content. Defined frequently in art history textbooks, they form the basis for much of the study of the visual arts. Flam argues, though, that the distinctive features we might identify about any painting, including *Conversation,* are only useful in that they help us to build and then share a story about the work. As Flam says, "our discussion of a specific painting is always framed in narrative" (paragraph 10).

Look back at your initial responses to this painting, as well as at some students' initial responses at the beginning of this chapter. The students had to have noticed, even if unconsciously, certain formal aspects of the painting in order to tell the stories or ask the questions they did. Many students responded to the title: were the two figures conversing or not? To some, the body language, the placement of the figures in the painting, their eye contact, evoked a feeling of tension. Other students remarked on the colors, noting the contrast between the dark room and the bright scene outside the window. The contrast of the straight lines that define the male figure with the curving lines of the seated woman was also noted. The student who said the painting looked like the work of a fifth-grader was echoing a common response to the so-called primitive quality of Matisse's work. Here, that image results, in part, from the artist's decision to portray a lack of depth in the painting. Such a response also reveals in the student an assumption about what "good art" is and what it should look like.

The terms *form* and *content* are frequently used in discussions of art. We can say that the subject matter of the Matisse painting is a man and a woman in a relationship. But to understand the meaning or the content of the work of art we must understand the way in which the language of form, "surface meaning," allows us to figure out for ourselves the painting's "deep meaning." As you saw from reading Jack Flam's analysis and Professor Rowland's response, there may be more than one reasonable description. As we engage in this meaning-making process we are doing no less than constructing the world we live in, since what we see in Matisse's world directly reflects what we see in our own.

Let's think for a moment about the dominant person in this painting. Which do *you* think is dominant? Who do Jack Flam and Ingrid Rowland think is dominant? How do we develop the "deep meaning" of this painting for ourselves? To some extent, the answer to this last question can be found by studying the language of form. What is there about the way that the two figures are constructed on the painted surface that helps us to think about this problem? In their initial responses, students noticed the very different postures of the two figures. If one is seen as the mother, with a mother's sense of assurance, would she be the dominant figure? Flam sees them as being in a stand-off of sorts: "Neither of these persons is about to budge." Professor Rowland helps us to see what Flam meant by the wife being larger than life. If she stood up, as Professor Rowland pointed out in the previous section, she would "tower over the male figure." We might also notice that the male figure is cut off at both the top and bottom of the painting.

One way to explore this question further is to go beyond the language of form to the social context of the artist. Flam tells us that when Matisse visited the Louvre, as he frequently did, he must have been influenced by the stele (a pillar) that illustrated two figures, King Hammurabi and the seated god, Shamash. How does this influence the meaning of this painting for Flam? How does Professor Rowland's story of the relationship between Hammurabi and Shamash influence your understanding of the relationship between the two figures in the painting?

WRITING AND LEARNING ACTIVITIES

1. **Writing:** Describe the scene in the painting and give a brief character description for each figure and provide some background. Then develop a conversation between them. If you think they are not speaking, write about their thoughts.

2. **Journal Entry:** Write a second response to the painting. What do you see now that you didn't see before? Look back at the questions on page 215.

3. **Writing:** Reread your second response. Compare it to Jack Flam's and Professor Rowland's. How are they similar and how different? Are you convinced by their analyses or do you have questions about something they said?

4. **Discussion:** Reread Professor Rowland's Hammurabi story. How does her telling of it influence the way you see the figures in Matisse's painting? How does her use of the stele differ from Flam's?

WHAT SHAPES THE WAY YOU SEE ART?
Seeing, Recognizing, and Gazing

Each specialized discipline uses language in a particular way to focus attention on the questions or problems of the particular area. Art historians pay special attention to the words used to describe how an artist "looks" at his or her subject, and in turn, how the viewer "looks" at the work of art. Until now we have used the verb *to see* to describe this act of looking, but it is important to specify how that meaning of *to see* can change when different language is used to characterize how we look at art.

In his book, *Ways of Seeing,* John Berger wrote that "the way we see things is affected by what we know or believe . . . we only see what we look at. To look is an act of choice" (8). This view of "seeing" as choice reflects an interest in how vision works in producing and understanding art. We, as casual observers, might assume that the artist paints what is seen, a precise copy of reality. When we see the piece of art, we evaluate it on the basis of how well we think the artist has copied reality.

Two very different assumptions then, underlie how we look at art. First, we can view seeing as strictly perceptual: a what-you-see-is-what-you-get approach. But, this approach runs into trouble when we try to explain Matisse's so-called primitive style. From what we have read we understand that he was technically quite talented and certainly capable of painting a couple such as the one in *Conversation* in a much more realistic way, yet he chose not to. Second, art historian Norman Bryson characterizes the activity of seeing as recognition. Our sight is not merely perceptual; it is informed by who we are, what we have experienced, what we know, and how we choose to see. When we gaze at a piece of art, we, as interested participants in society, take in the features of the painting and "talk back" as viewers. We recognize the familiar symbols and wonder about the meanings of elements we don't recognize. We ascertain meaning in relation to how well we recognize the relation of the elements of the work to one another, or the relation of the artist to the work, or the relation of the work to its culture's way of seeing. Look back at the student responses in the introduction to this chapter. How do you suppose those students' experiences and perspectives guided their responses?

This notion of seeing as recognition has a mirror-like quality, since we can also ask about figures within the painting. How shall we interpret the gaze of the two figures in *Conversation?* How are they seeing each other? What about Matisse's gaze as he painted the work? Matisse, as Flam suggested, viewed painting as a way of knowing; looking at art with a recognizant gaze can also be a way of learning about ourselves and our world, as well as the work of art.

Representing Reality

Would you say that Matisse's painting, *Conversation,* represents reality? What did Flam mean when he said that Matisse "teaches us that imagination can start in the eye as well as in the mind" (paragraph 8)? We have included below two other visual images to consider. One is a photograph of Henri and Amélie Matisse, the other an abstract oil painting of two figures by Max Ernst called *The Couple*. In the case of a photograph we are particularly tempted to say that the visual image is a facsimile or a replication of reality, quite the opposite of the Ernst painting, which is so clearly an abstract rendering of two figures.

Yet can we be sure that even a photograph is a representation or copy of reality? How does where the photographer stands and his selection of what he considers relevant change what you see in the photograph? How does the way *you* look at the photograph change what it means for you? We know it is Henri and Amélie Matisse in the photograph, but suppose for a moment that this couple is someone's parents or grandparents. How do we look at the photo differently? From what we have learned thus far about *Conversation,* how does seeing the three images next to each other change your understanding of them? When you look at *The Couple* next to *Conversation,* how does one painting help you to understand the other?"

Looking at these three visual images at the same time helps us to see how art—even photographs—can be viewed as a representation of a culture through its symbols. Can you guess or assume something about the couple in the photograph? Why did the photographer pose them in this way? Could this couple be your grandparents? If not, why not? What do they symbolize about the culture they come from, and how might their culture be different from your own?

Matisse and Mme Matisse in the studio at Issy-les-Moulineau, May 1913, with the unfinished *Bathers by a River* (pl. 193). Photograph by Alvin Langdon Coburn.

The Couple or *The Couple in Lace* 1923. Oil on canvas, 101.5 × 142 cm. Boymans van Beuningen Museum, Rotterdam.

Now look at Ernst's *The Couple*. Since this is a black-and-white reproduction, we cannot comment on the original oil colors. But you can ask the same questions about how the couple is posed. How are they looking at each other? What does Ernst seem to be saying through this painting about his view of how, as a culture, we define a couple?

When we "see" a piece of art, we are processing it through our retinas as well as actively responding to a piece of art that reflects the consciousness of the culture in which it was created. Did the artist intend to make a copy of reality or did he intend to express an understanding of the context he or she lived in? Artists do not create their works in a dream world apart from life. As art historian David Freedberg insists, "The picture is reality; it is not bad, or misleading, or deceiving, or even weak copy. It need not lose its aura, provided we see that its poetry or its clumsy prose lies not in its distance from the real, but rather in the possibility it offers for the integration of the unashamed creativity of the eye with the blunt receptiveness of the senses" (440).

WRITING AND LEARNING ACTIVITIES

1. **Journal Entry:** Write an initial response to the photograph of Henri and Amélie Matisse and to the Ernst painting, using the questions listed in Activity 1 on page 215.

2. **Group Activity:** Compare your initial responses to the photograph and to the Ernst reproduction. Ask for clarification on why each group member saw them as they did. Discuss how differences reflect your personal experiences and cultural identity.

3. **Writing a Letter:** Write a letter to Jack Flam or Ingrid Rowland telling him or her what you think is most interesting, provocative, or meaningful about the painting *Conversation*. How does your perspective compare to Flam's and Rowland's? Did yours differ from theirs? If so, how? Did you notice the same things?

4. **Class Presentation:** Bring in reproductions of two works that represent "reality" differently, yet depict a similar theme or issue. Explain to the class the similarities and differences you see between them.

DEVELOPING INTERESTS

Has this discussion of art history encouraged you to think about what you see in new ways? What would you like to learn more about? Would you like to study an artist whose work you admire, or think more about photography and how it does or doesn't reflect reality? What are you surrounded by every day that you could think of as art?

WRITING AND LEARNING ACTIVITIES

1. Journal Entry: Write answers to the questions in the last paragraph. Of all that has been discussed in this chapter, what interested you most? What would you like to learn more about?

2. Research Activity: Visit a local art museum or an art exhibit on your campus. What questions do you find yourself asking about the piece of art you are observing? How does this work differ from what you have studied in this chapter? Do any artists live in your community? What famous artists share the same ethnic or cultural background as you? Where could you view their art?

3. Class Activity: Stage an art exhibit as a class. Bring in a print of your favorite work of art and tell the class how you first discovered it, why it is important to you, what you know about it, and what more you'd like to learn about it or the artist who created it.

LINKED WRITING ASSIGNMENT

Writing an Analysis of Work in Art History (see Chapter 12, Analyzing Discipline-Specific Texts). In the previous section, Developing Interests, you began to identify issues and ideas that you might want to explore further. Finding personal connections to the material you are studying is one important way to participate more fully in an academic community. You will also need to learn how some everyday thinking strategies, such as analyzing, help you to participate in the disciplines you are studying here. Chapter 12 introduces you to the activity of analyzing and offers readings from art history for you to practice developing an analysis.

C H A P T E R

7

MARINE BIOLOGY

What makes us want to learn about marine life? Maybe we see or hear about something that surprises us or sparks our curiosity. For example, most people think of the anemone as a beautifully colored inhabitant of a coral community whose tentacles sway gracefully with the ocean's movement. As we will learn in this chapter, though, the harmless-looking sea anemone can attack other anemones that attempt to encroach on its territory. Here's what one student wrote in his journal about the first time he saw one.

> I lived in Florida for almost ten years. While living there I picked up the sport of snorkeling during a camping trip on an island in the Gulf of Mexico. The island we camped on was a base for an old Civil War prison. That island and the surrounding ones were called the Dry Tortugas. Snorkeling is amazing. While I'm under the water I am floating in another world. I see all kinds of animals and plants. It was on this trip that I saw my first sea anemones. There were large groups attached to the reef where I was diving. At that time I wasn't sure if it was coral or a flower of some kind. I wanted to touch it because it looked so beautiful and soft. But we were warned not to touch anything because there are a lot of animals and plants under the water that seem harmless, but could actually be very harmful.
>
> NEIL KHANT

To introduce you to the discipline of marine biology, I interview Professor Todd Newberry who tells us about his lifelong interest in observing the natural world. To get a closer look at research in marine biology, Professor Newberry guides us through a research report by Professor Lisbeth Francis that describes the aggressive behavior of an anemone called *Anthopleura elegantissima.* During his reading, Professor Newberry pays special attention to how scientists observe their environment and interpret their observations. Next, I introduce you to the ways specialized terms are used in the sciences and to the importance of asking questions. In the last section, I introduce a reading on sea anemones aimed at a more general audience to help you to develop further interests in marine biology.

AN INTERVIEW WITH A MARINE BIOLOGIST

Todd Newberry is a professor of marine biology at the University of California at Santa Cruz. After a 30 year career in teaching and research, he has retired to spend more time teaching graduate students and writing about his research. He frequently taught an introductory class in ecology, evolution, and biodiversity which involved substantial fieldwork and report writing. He has also taught many upper-division courses on invertebrate zoology and several interdisciplinary seminars on such topics as the experience of death and the experience of place. As you will learn in the interview below, Professor Newberry's research focuses on ascidian tunicates or, more commonly, sea squirts. He has published many essays on the growth, sexual reproduction, and systematics of these marine animals. He has also published essays on natural history and on our prospects as humans in the natural world.[1]

What early experiences do you suppose led you to eventually become a marine biologist?

Even as a kid I was interested in nature, maybe out of a juvenile shyness around people; maybe because discovering "free nature" at all seemed so unlikely in industrial northeastern New Jersey and was thus so rewarding in consequence—like being let in on a splendid secret whose unobserved clues lay open and abundant everywhere. First it was stars, then rocks, then birds. My parents never really shared my interest, but they supported me—it was respectable (no pockets full of ants and the rest), even if eccentric—and generously though in mostly an amused and indulgent way. I passed countless days in the American Museum in New York City. I recall how well curators there treated me, gave me little (but, to me then, big) jobs to do, and actually made me feel part of the huge place even though I was very much a youngster. Still, something was happening: I was sharpening my observational skills and investigative stamina.

How then with such varied interests did you become a marine biologist?

Near the end of my undergraduate years, I realized that I was going to be a biologist. I would study bird behavior—the great naturalists Tinbergen and Lack were active at Oxford then. But something, I'm still not sure what, made me hesitate about doing professionally what I had been doing for so long as an amateur—bird-watching. Maybe I just

---

[1]Some of the material in this interview appeared in an essay by Professor Newberry called "Fieldtrips" in *The Threepenny Review,* Volume 41, Spring, 1990, pp. 11–12.

didn't want to make a career of a refuge! Tentatively, I turned instead toward the sea. Why? The seafaring background of one of my uncles? Memories of summers at the shore? I'm not really sure. And I would go to California. Again, why? Because it just felt right: Whatever else, it was time to clear out of New Jersey!

In graduate school I felt I had been set free on a new planet. I seemed to change career plans with every new course. But the many options that drew me were still all of one sort of biology, natural history. When my turn came to decide on my doctoral research, Donald Abbott, at Stanford's marine lab, agreed to take me on. He was probably the finest marine naturalist in America then, and he was a teacher without peer. That settled it: I really was going to be a marine biologist! It still could as easily have been birds. The lesson, I think, is that in such decisions one's heart is one's best compass, and one's head is merely for navigating by it.

What area do you specialize in?

Usually a biologist's "specialty" combines a topic and a taxon (a kind of organism). Dr. Abbott worked on the taxon called sea squirts and so do I. Sea squirts are a poorly known but diverse, abundant group of marine animals (some 3,000 kinds), at first sight mostly blobs or enigmatic shapes fixed to marine surfaces. They are often confused with sponges, but the closer you look the more different the two groups appear. Biologists debate whether sponges are really animals at all—not some entirely separate major group of organisms by themselves—but sea squirts have several traits we associate even with animals like ourselves: for example, a rudimentary "thyroid gland," a tail-stiffening spinal cord in the swimming "tadpole" larva, and a "brain" with curious resemblances to the vertebrate brain.

Like Abbott, I study mostly two topics. First, many sea squirts form colonies of interconnected bodies, and I investigate their "rules of assembly"—that is, the large-scale growth processes and environmental influences that generate and mold the shapes of these colonies. And second, the taxonomy (the "systematics") of sea squirts—that is, their diversity and the evolution that has produced it—which remains a great puzzle. Deciphering it involves interpreting tiny or obscure traits that often are hard to detect even in carefully preserved and well-dissected specimens. This practical difficulty has discouraged most systematists from messing with sea squirts at all.

I work on both problems—colonial form-generation and systematics—because I think they each pose significant biological questions the answers to which apply much more widely than just to sea squirts; that is, I think these animals can tell us important things about widespread patterns of animal development and evolution generally. But I also study sea squirts because working with them is so much fun, pure and simple. Behind their bland or even ugly appearance, such beauty!

Why do you think it's important to study biology?

Well, we're alive. We are organisms and we should know something about ourselves as organisms, not just about ourselves as "people." Also, we are in a real environmental mess, one that is rapidly worsening and which stems largely from ecologically unsustainable technologies. Sooner or later we are going to have to be ecologically thoughtful, whatever that means, even if that is politically and economically painful. Nature itself will insist. Biology can give us a feel for what is the matter.

Finally, the living world, the sheer diversity of organisms that is now slipping away, is so extraordinary: what a pleasure to know about it! Biology—natural history—is our window on that world. For students, a lot of what is learned in school and college has to be taken on faith from books and professors. But I like to think that in the biology courses I teach, marine biology and natural history, you actually can see or touch what is going on. A lot of the living world has a size or duration or frequency that lets you gain a direct, observational acquaintance with what Evelyn Hutchinson once called "the ecological theater and the evolutionary play." Being able to observe (by whatever senses) so immediately, so intimately, seems a wonderful way to get involved in science.

What kinds of things do first-year students typically learn in an introductory course in biology?

Biology is an immensely verbal science. Where physics, say, uses common words but in treacherously unfamiliar ways, biology has a vast terminology of its own. Maybe this comes from biology's lack, until recently, of much quantification; words have done the work that numbers do in chemistry, physics, and astronomy. Whatever the reason, introductory biology is virtually a language course. New words become the vehicles by which whole concepts—natural selection, gene-action, metabolism and homeostasis, the ecological niche, the biological species concept, and so many others—are raised and explored.

One way to organize an introductory course around the fewest possible grand schemes is to try to decipher patterns in terms of the processes that produce them—genetic patterns, developmental ones, physiological, behavioral, ecological, and evolutionary ones. This approach implies another, that of "levels of organization"—essentially the variety of patterns and processes I have just mentioned. Either way, what you end up with after a year is a sense of life processes, from invisibly small (genetic) ones to unmanageably long ("deep time" evolutionary) ones, and some feeling for the diversity of living entities that these processes produce—organelles, cells, organisms, species, ecosystems. All this and an awful lot of new words: an ambitious year!

At the University of California at Santa Cruz you're right on the Pacific Ocean. What do you tell students as they head out on field trips?

I tell my students that the first thing they'll experience when they try to observe Nature is a standoff of sorts. Outdoors, you stare at Nature and Nature just stares back. The most important way to end the standoff is to ask questions. Questions are crucial; observations and measurements and the rest are merely ways of expressing them. Posing good questions is a remarkably difficult skill, just in itself.

I might take my students out to a rocky shelf along the ocean at low tide. I tell them: get your feet down into low tide. Then get your face down to where your feet are. Get your eyes into low tide, into the habitats that today's tide makes accessible. Get horizontal. Get wet. Get close up—hand-lens range. Eschew vistas. Your hand lens will help you: you cannot see a vista through a hand lens. Most invertebrates are little animals. Poke into crannies, where little creatures find protection from surf or scouring, from desiccation, and from many predators. Remember, other creatures live in their worlds as much as we live in ours. Choose any animal that intrigues you and study it in its neighborhood. From your animal's anatomical and behavioral traits, what do you think it might know about the world around it? Does your animal show a response to shadow, to a sudden noise, to sudden changes of temperature, to the smell or air-movement (which?) of your breath? Interview your animal, and its habitat, by posing questions it can answer promptly and by detecting its answers keenly.

How do the students document what they see?

I tell them: make notes on the basic body designs you notice. Don't make schematic diagrams; make real field sketches of the different kinds of animals you are comparing. Be strict but dare to be naive. Try to get those insights about your animal's world down in your notes right there, on the spot, like a reporter, not later when they will be mere recollections. You are in nature, where all is details. Never trust your memory in such a complicated place as the outdoors. Nothing crumbles faster than memories; the notes that fix them are the world's best glue.

One of the most important things students need to learn is to separate observations (data) from interpretations. We can say, most simply, that observations tell us about Nature, while interpretations observe one's own observations. Interpretations usually have a derivative, editorial quality. But sometimes interpretations can be surprisingly hard to recognize for what they are and can parade disguised as observations. Just asking yourself, "How do you know?" often strips off the disguise. One of my teachers, Dr. C. B. van Niel once told me, "When I've told someone something and he asks me that awful question, 'And . . . how do you know?', if I start to point to the organism, what I said was probably an observation. If, instead, I start to sweat, it was surely an interpretation."

What kind of reports do students do for your upper-level biology classes?

Both in my introductory course and in my upper-level classes, I have students do actual fieldwork and write formal research reports on it, or I have them read actual research reports and critique them. My aim is to instill some self-confidence in my students so that they need not forever depend on textbooks or popularizations for news that they can gather on their own or read in its originally reported form. I press this agenda because scientists are investigative reporters: we investigate and we report. Students can start learning this double-craft right away. So in my classes students write reports about their investigations—either investigations of someone else's research and how that other scientist has reported it, or, best of all, investigations of nature itself. Either way, I hope my students learn two conventions of the trade: (a) the "orthodox format," in which material is presented in research reports, because this convention helps readers figure out what an author is trying to tell them, and (b) those conventions of writing itself that let an author speak, above all, clearly.

Would you tell us something about how you learned to write?

I've been writing since I could hold a pencil, and I'm still learning how. I've always loved writing and I've always loved reading; they're two sides of the same coin, I think. I read voraciously. I gulp it in. I start off each day with the New York Times—it's a way of life! I get many magazines—The New Yorker, Harper's, The Atlantic, Science, Nature, The N.Y. Review of Books, The Nation. I usually stuff a magazine in my pocket and read it on and off during the day, sometimes to relax, sometimes to get my brain going. Of course I read for content, but also I read to learn the craft of writing from as many other writers as I can.

And I read and reread books of all sorts—one or two a week. This is alongside technical reading: research reports and reviews, new chapters or books in and around my specialty. If you read on this scale, something happens: even reading billboards, you're going to see new ways of putting things clearly and persuasively. And you're going to see—once you catch onto it—how a good writer "plays" with a reader, "works" a reader, to make a point and drive it home, whether it's in a billboard or a research report or a novel.

When I write, I try to read my own drafts as though I were reading someone else's. This isn't easy but it's crucial. There are ways of getting the distance to do it—for example, putting drafts aside to cool for a week or at least while you do something entirely different for a day or so. Subconsciously you will still be mulling over what you were trying to say. When I go back to my manuscript, I ask myself, "What's he driving at? What does he mean?" And then, to answer those questions, I revise the draft, usually straight through and usually twice over. We all have to learn not to have love affairs with our own words; we have to learn how to let them go, how to revise.

Finally, editors and readers can help tremendously. Shrewd ones try to misunderstand what you are getting at; if an editor can misunderstand you, there's sure to be someone else out there who will, too. A reader is a good one if she makes you have to think one more time about what you are putting permanently onto that most magical of surfaces, paper.

WRITING AND LEARNING ACTIVITIES

1. **Journal Entry:** Look up a definition of biology or marine biology in a college dictionary, a dictionary of biology, and a reference encyclopedia (see the appendix, Directions for Further Research). Consider the differences and similarities among the definitions. Report to the class on what you found.

2. **Question Posing:** Write three questions you would like to ask Professor Newberry if you had the opportunity to talk with him.

3. **Peer Conversation:** Discuss your journal entries and questions for Professor Newberry with a partner. Respond also to the following questions: Were you reminded by something he said of another experience you've had at home, school, or work? Have you had experiences like the fieldwork he discusses?

4. **Research Project:** Look up the biology major in your college catalog. Respond to the following questions: How is the discipline of biology described? How does this description differ from Professor Newberry's or from other definitions you've found? What are the required courses for this major? What are the areas of specialization? Next, interview someone who is a biology major. Why is he or she studying biology? What courses has he or she taken in it? Is he or she specializing in any particular area? What do they plan to do with a degree in biology?

5. **Writing Activity:** Write a report about what it's like to major in biology and present it to your class.

6. **Developing Interests:** Browse through some popular science magazines such as *Discover Magazine, Natural History,* and *National Geographic,* to find ideas and topics that interest you. Make a list of questions about things you would like to know more about.

A MARINE BIOLOGIST READS RESEARCH ON THE SEA ANEMONE

Scientific research papers can seem to be written in a foreign language. Just looking at the title of an article may convince you that it is beyond you. In this section Professor Newberry will guide us through a reading of one of Professor Lisbeth Francis's research papers on the sea anemone. You will get an insider's tour in which you learn how to read "between the lines," as well as learn something about the research process in biology and about how the results are written up as research reports.

Francis, the author of the research report included in this chapter, spent years observing sea anemones and reading what others had discovered. Both her observations and her reading led to the questions that guided her own research. Her paper, "Intraspecific Aggression and Its Effect on the Distribution of *Anthopleura elegantissima* and Some Related Sea Anemones"— shortened here to include only the information on the *Anthopleura elegantissima*—describes the aggressive behavior of this type of sea anemone.

Look through the entire research report before reading Professor Newberry's overview.

INTRASPECIFIC AGGRESSION AND ITS EFFECT ON THE DISTRIBUTION OF *ANTHOPLEURA ELEGANTISSIMA* AND SOME RELATED SEA ANEMONES

LISBETH FRANCIS

■ ■ ■

Contiguous aggregations of the west coast sea anemone *Anthopleura elegantissima* are composed of individuals from a single clone, the products of asexual reproduction. In the field, adjacent clones of anemones are observed to be isolated from each other by anemone-free spaces; and in the laboratory a group of anemones of mixed clonal origins will reaggregate into isolated uniclonal groups. (Francis, 1973). In the field I have also observed that individuals of the large solitary form of *Anthopleura elegantissima* also remain isolated from adjacent members of the species. Contacts between genetically different individuals of this species initiates in one or

---

Biology Department, University of California, Santa Barbara, California

both individuals an elaborate behavior pattern that usually results in damage to one or both animals. This is aggressive behavior according to the definition of Carthy and Ebling (1964), "An animal acts aggressively when it inflicts, attempts to inflict, or threatens to inflict damage on another animal. The act is accompanied by recognizable behavioral symptoms and definable physiological changes" (1). This behavior has never before been reported for this species, and my purpose here is to describe this specialized aggressive behavior.

MATERIALS AND METHODS

Animals and Collecting Methods

In synthesizing a description of the aggressive response, I observed individuals of both the solitary and the aggregating form of the anemone *Anthopleura elegantissima* (most recently described by Hand, 1955). The animals were observed and/or collected intertidally on the California coast between Pacific Grove and Santa Barbara, California.

The specimens of *Anthopleura elegantissima* used in the experiments were small to large sized individuals (from 1 to 5 cm across the expanded oral disc) of the aggregating form and large individuals (from about 5 to about 8 cm across the oral disc) of the solitary form of the anemone. These animals were collected intertidally within ten miles of the Hopkins Marine Station at Pacific Grove, California and between Gaviota and Santa Barbara, California. The very small sub-adult anemones used in one set of experiments were collected at Arroyo Hondo, an area just south of Gaviota. These animals were collected in October of 1971 in a mussel bed where they were attached to mussels and interspersed pebbles. . . . These anemones were removed from the rocks on which they were found by gently working a thin spatula under the edges of the pedal discs.

Laboratory Holding Conditions

. . . The anemones were kept in bowls supplied with flowing sea water. The anemones were fed intermittently except during experiments, when food was withheld.

Conditions Under Which Aggression Was Observed

5 Contact between two genetically different anemones, not mere proximity, appears to be the condition necessary for the initiation of the aggressive response.

In my early experiments anemones collected from different clones were brought into contact in the laboratory by first allowing some of the animals to attach to pieces of glass or stone, and then moving these portable animals to within contact distance of other anemones. More recently the anemones were stimulated to initiate the aggressive response by repeatedly touching the experimental animal on the tip of a tentacle with a tentacle excised from a non-clonemate. This was done in a manner designed to simulate natural contacts between anemones. Contacts between anemones and excised tentacles were as brief as possible (lasting less than a second), and sufficient time (2–3 minutes) was allowed for the retracted tentacles of the experimental animal to re-extend between successive contacts. A single set of repeated contacts was always restricted to the tentacles of one quarter section of the anemone. Stimulation was discontinued when the acrorhagi of the anemone began to inflate rapidly, signaling the beginning of the inflation stage of the aggressive behavior. If the behavior did not then proceed to completion, additional stimulations were given. The total number of stimulations needed to elicit a complete aggressive response (including the movement of application) is designated the aggressive threshold. Stimulation was discontinued if the reaction was not elicited within a preset number of contacts.

An excised tentacle was used for up to ten successive contacts with the same anemone, and the tentacle was kept in cool sea water between contacts. (I found for *Anthopleura elegantissima* that tentacles used for many more than ten intraspecific contacts and even those rubbed repeatedly and with considerable force among the tentacles and against the column of a non-clonemate were still completely effective at eliciting aggression upon contact with any non-clonemate. This was true as long as the surface of the tentacles was kept free of any superficial clinging material.)

PROCEDURES, OBSERVATIONS, AND RESULTS

Anthopleura elegantissima

Description of the Aggressive Behavior.   Although, as a matter of convenience, tentacles excised from another anemone were used to stimulate anemones during most laboratory experiments, it was found that contact with any of the external surfaces of a non-clonemate including the column, uninflated acrorhagi, or the intact surface of the pedal disc elicited aggression in laboratory maintained anemones.

I have also observed the behavior occurring naturally in tidepools during daytime low tides, especially as the tide begins to rise, bringing cool aerated water into the stagnant pools and submerging anemones previously exposed to the air. Aggression is common among these expanded anemones as they are jostled together by the movement of the water.

10   The following description of the aggressive response of *Anthopleura elegantissima* is, then, a composite description based on my numerous observations of the behavior rather than a description of a single episode.

For convenience I have separated the aggressive behavior of *Anthopleura elegantissima* into five stages: (1) stimulation (or initiation), during which the tentacles of the two anemones repeatedly come into contact and withdraw from contact; (2) inflation, during which the acrorhagi commence to become turgid; and (3) the movement of application, during which the inflated acrorhagi are pushed toward the source of stimulation; (4) application of ectoderm, during which damage is inflicted on another anemone; and (5) recovery, during which the anemone returns to its normal posture. The various stages, which correspond roughly with those described by Bonnin (1964) for the aggressive behavior of *Actinea equina,* are illustrated in Figures 1 through 7 and are described in full below.

When an expanded anemone is moved toward and first makes contact with another expanded anemone, the tentacle tips are usually the first parts to make contact. Typically, if two clonemates meet in this way their tentacles will at first withdraw from the contact and will then re-extend. This may happen several times in succession until finally the tentacles cease withdrawing and remain more or less in contact. If the anemones then move toward each other, their tentacles interlace without apparent further interaction.

If anemones from different clones come within contact range of each other, the reaction is very different. Tentacle contact between anemones from different clones is followed by rapid withdrawal of those tentacles involved and often of some nearby tentacles as well. The retracted tentacles then slowly re-extend until contact is again made between the two anemones. The tentacles withdraw again from contact, and the process of contact and withdrawal is repeated until the next stage of the behavior begins. During the period of repeated tentacle contact the acrorhagi (also called marginal spherules) closest to those tentacles involved in the contacts often become visible as white (or rarely pinkish) spherules beneath the outer cycle of tentacles (Fig. 1c). In unaroused anemones the acrorhagi, which are more or less numerous depending on the individual, are often difficult to see as they are usually quite small and lie hidden beneath the tentacles and in the fosse (a channel between the collar of the column and the tentacles).

The inflation stage of the aggressive behavior begins as the tentacles of the aggressor withdraw from the area of stimulation after repeated contact with a non-clonemate. As the tentacles begin to re-extend after the last contact, the anemone often assumes a more upright posture. This may be accomplished by contraction of the circular muscles of the column and/or relaxation of the longitudinal muscles. There is usually also some swelling of the capitulum at the base of the stimulated tentacles, perhaps the result of relaxation of the circular muscles just below the stimulated tentacles and contraction of those muscles below the remaining tentacles. At this time the acrorhagi associated with the stimulated tentacles become distended, changing in appearance from shriveled white spherules to transparent rounded cones with white tips (Fig. 1d). The gastrovascular cavity of these anemones extends into the hollow tentacles and acrorhagi, and it is possible that the contractions of the circular muscles described above serve to force water from the columnar portion of the gastrovascular cavity into these acrorhagi, causing them to become distended.

Sometimes there are, in addition to the above movements, peristaltic contractions that begin at the base of the elongated anemone and travel up

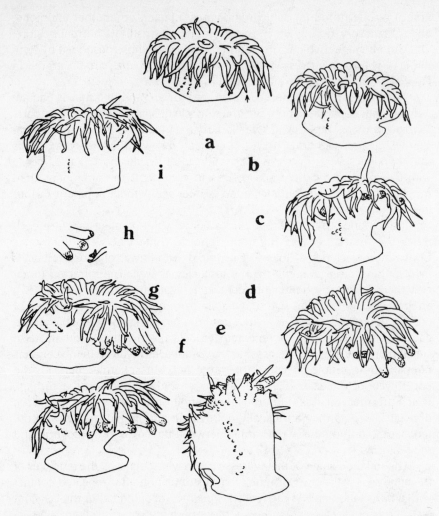

Figure 1. The positions of a specimen of *Anthopleura elegantissima* (the aggregating form) were traced from photographs taken during one aggressive episode. (a) The anemone is shown at rest (before contact with the non-clonemate); the arrow indicates the region that will come into contact with the non-clonemate. (b) Initiation: the anemone is shown just after contact with the non-clonemate; the relative retraction of the tentacles and a slight swelling of the capitulum (to the right) may be noted. (c) Inflation: the white tips (stippled) of the inflating acrorhagi have become visible in the area adjacent to the tentacles receiving the stimulation; the shape of the column is notably different from that shown in Figure 1a. (d) Inflation: the acrorhagi in the area of stimulation are strongly inflated, appearing white at the tips (stippled) and transparent at the bases. (e) Movement of application: the inflated acrorhagi are drawn upward and back away from the source of the stimulus. (f) Movement of application: the acrorhagi are sweeping downward and may, as in this case, continue downward to the position shown in Figure 1g, or the movement may stop in the position shown here with the anemone leaning over the adjacent non-clonemate. (g) Movement of application: the acrorhagi have reached the bottom of their downward sweep and are being wiped against the body of the victim. (h) Release of ectoderm: acrorhagial ectoderm has been released from one of the acrorhagi which is now transparent (unstippled) at the tip

the column. These muscular contractions (probably of the circular muscles) may serve to force water into the expanding acrorhagi.

Along with an increase in the turgidity of the involved acrorhagi during the inflation period, there is usually a progressive increase in the number of acrorhagi that are inflated. Recruitment progresses in both directions around the capitulum so that more and more acrorhagi on either side of the originally stimulated tentacles become involved. Typically four to twelve ✗ acrorhagi become fully turgid during a single aggressive episode.

Acrorhagial inflation has never before been reported for this species; and except in rare, unexplained cases full inflation of the acrorhagi seems ✓/ to occur only during the aggressive response.

The movement of application is a rather rapid movement for an anem- ③ one requiring between 30 and 120 seconds for the complete movement.

As the expanding acrorhagi begin to distend, the swollen edge of the capitulum is extended upward drawing the turgid acrorhagi upward and away from the original site of contact with the other anemone. This movement probably involves elongation of the longitudinal columnar muscles adjacent to the area of acrorhagial inflation. The anemone may remain in this position for a few seconds. Then the area of the oral disc between the mouth and the stimulated tentacles begins to elongate. This might be effected by relaxation of radially arranged muscles of the oral disc in this region and contraction of other muscles of the column and oral disc which would cause additional gastrovascular fluid to be forced into the area. As the oral disc changes shape the swollen edge of the capitulum moves downward, and the expanded acrorhagi point outward or somewhat downward. This motion, which is perceived as a smooth downward sweep of the expanded acrorhagi, sometimes stops as the acrorhagi reach the position shown in Figure 1f (the aggressor is leaning over the spot where the victim normally should be). More often, the downsweeping movement continues until the acrorhagi are on a level with the pedal disc or actually touching the substratum. During this time inflation of the acrorhagi often continues, and more acrorhagi at both edges of the inflated area continue to be recruited.

20   The full movement of application sequence may be repeated one or more times, or the anemone may slowly recover its normal posture after only one movement of application.

If during the downward motion of the movement of application the ④ white tip of one or more of the aggressor's fully inflated acrorhagi (i.e., acrorhagi so turgid that their bases appear transparent) comes into contact with a non-clonemate, the white surface layer can be observed to pull loose from the acrorhagus and adhere to the body of the non-clonemate (Fig. 1h).

Figure 1. (*continued*) where the ectoderm is missing; the ectoderm is shown clinging to a tentacle of the victim. (i) Recovery: the acrorhagi have deflated but the anemone has not yet fully recovered its preaggression posture: the column is still somewhat elongated and the capitulum is still swollen and somewhat elevated in the area proximal to the area of stimulation.

Fully expanded acrorhagi that had released part of their white surfaces as described above were sectioned using freeze sectioning and standard paraffin embedding techniques. In the region from which the white material was released the entire ectoderm layer was absent, and only the endoderm and mesogleal layers remained. *In vivo,* the tips of such acrorhagi appear transparent where the ectoderm is missing.

(5) During the slow return to a normal posture following the aggressive response, the anemone first rises from the arched over position (Fig. 1g) to an upright posture. The acrorhagi frequently lose their turgidity as the anemone returns to the upright position (Fig. 1i). If the anemone does not again come into tentacle contact with a non-clonemate, the acrorhagi eventually deflate and within a matter of hours the animal slowly returns to its more usual posture.

The anemone to which acrorhagial ectoderm has been applied (the victim of an aggressive episode) may respond by returning the aggression; more frequently, however, it will at first retract its tentacles, shorten its column, and contract the large sphincter at the top of the column. The damaged anemone may then move away from the aggressor; or sometime, after re-extending the tentacles and column and relaxing the sphincter, it may lean away, thus avoiding contact that would trigger another attack by the aggressor.

25 In other cases, apparently after having had insufficient time to attach its foot to the substratum or after having received severe damage as a result of repeated attacks, the victim may release its hold on the substratum. In the field, such an animal would certainly be carried away by the waves and might conceivably resettle elsewhere. In the laboratory, animals that have released their foothold after being attacked and damaged by a non-clonemate have subsequently resettled and recovered when they were removed to a separate bowl.

The tissue of the victim in the area of applied acrorhagial ectoderm shows obvious signs of damage and deterioration within about a day. This is especially evident for the tentacles, which contract and remain contracted as soon as acrorhagial ectoderm is applied. Within a few days, the obviously necrotic tissue in the damaged area is sloughed off along with the whitish patches of foreign acrorhagial ectoderm.

Tentacles to which acrorhagial ectoderm was applied were fixed, embedded in paraffin, sectioned, cleared, and stained (Masson's Trichrome dyes). In these sections it was possible to see the threads of the large atrich nematocysts (in this species, peculiar to the acrorhagi) penetrating the tentacle tissue.

•   •   •

DISCUSSION

The aggressive response of some members of the family Actiniidae is another example of a surprisingly specialized and complex behavior pattern displayed by sea anemones, animals having "primitive" systems for nervous integration and often assumed, therefore, to display a very limited behavioral repertoire.

•   •   •

. . . Several characteristics of the aggressive response are distinctive within the repertoire of anemone behavior. One of these is the peculiar manner in which the response is initiated. For *Anthopleura elegantissima* the initiating stimulus involves repeated contact of the tentacles with some part of a nonclonemate conspecific or some other anthozoan. In describing the aggressive response of *Actinea equina* Bonnin (1964) has noted that a definite time lapse between successive contacts during stimulation seems important in reaching the threshold for the response. Too rapid or massive stimulation usually results in complete retraction of the anemone without eliciting an aggressive response. The same seems to be true for *Anthopleura elegantissima.*

30   The aggressive behavior of these anemones is also remarkable in being a very specialized behavior that functions under very particular and limited circumstances (see also Bonnin, 1964) and that involves the use of specialized movements and equipment. Contact and retraction of the tentacles during initiation of the behavior does not appear to be particularly specialized (the animals respond in a similar way to mild mechanical or electrical stimulation of the tentacles); however some of the movements during the inflation stage of the behavior (e.g., the puffing up of one edge of the capitulum and the associated acrorhagi) and during the movement of application (e.g., the asymmetrical elongation of the oral disc and the downsweeping movement of the inflated acrorhagi) are quite distinctive movements of the aggressive behavior. The acrorhagi are specialized "organs" which have been observed to function only during aggression (Äbel, 1954; Bonnin, 1964) and apparently the acrorhagial atrich nematocysts are also used only during aggression.

From the evidence presented on the specificity of the aggressive response of *Anthopleura elegantissima,* it is apparent that the behavior is not directly involved either in defense against predators or capture of prey. Aggression is elicited only by contact with conspecifics and other Anthozoans. Bonnin (1964) found the same to be true for *Actinea equina.*

For *Anthopleura elegantissima* the aggressive response seems to have a clear function in intraspecific interactions. Briefly summarized, the pertinent evidence, presented in this and a previous paper (Francis, 1973) is as follows: (1) Within clonal groups of the aggregating form of *Anthopleura elegantissima* the individuals are in close contact with their neighbors and the tentacles of the adjacent animals are interlaced. In the field, adjacent clones of these anemones are isolated from each other by anemone-free spaces; and in the laboratory a group of anemones of mixed clonal origins will reaggregate into isolated uniclonal groups (Francis, 1973). (2) The specificity of the aggressive response is directly related to that shown in the segregation and separation phenomena seen both in the laboratory and in the field. Contact between clonemates does not elicit aggression and is commonly seen both in the laboratory and in the field. Contact between non-clonemates elicits aggression and is not maintained between these anemones either in the laboratory or in the field. (3) The response of the victim of an aggressive episode is such as to affect its separation from the non-clonemate aggressor. The damaged anemone may move away from the aggressor, or sometimes it may merely lean away. In the laboratory, anemones that were severely damaged as a result of repeated aggressive episodes have been observed to release their hold on the substratum; in the field, such animals would certainly be swept away in the surf. All of these responses tend to remove the victim from contact with the attacking non-clonemate. (4) The evidence also shows that aggression does occur at the boundary between two clonal groups. In the field, anemones collected from an interclonal border showed aggression-related damage while their clonemates that were collected from the center of the clonal groups showed no such damage. In the laboratory numerous aggressive episodes were observed over a three week period as two clonal groups that had been brought into artificially close proximity interacted at their common boundary (Francis, 1973). This suggests that aggression is important in the formation and maintenance of anemone-free zones between adjacent non-clonemates in this species.

. . .

The direct effects of the aggressive behavior of *A. elegantissima* would be sufficient to account for clone specific segregation and at least minimal separation between clones; and although other factors may be involved, the aggressive response undoubtedly functions as part of an intraspecific territorial behavior in this species.

Assuming that the aggressive response of acrorhagus-bearing members of the family Actiniidae is monophyletic in origin, and knowing that no function outside of aggression is known for the acrorhagi (Äbel, 1954), we may speculate on the evolutionary advantages and history of this highly specialized behavior.

. . .

35   . . . What might be the origin of and selective advantage(s) for intraspecific territoriality involving mutual repulsion among genetically unlike members of a species? I would suggest that an anemone that repulses all members of the species except clonemates may gain space on the substratum for its genotype. This could be a decided advantage to the genotype possessing this characteristic, especially if there were competition among members of the species for space itself or for the available food in a given area. As long as the adverse effects of this characteristic, such as the inability to form inter-clonal aggregations and thereby reduce water loss (Roberts, 1941) and the energy loss involved in the repulsion of non-clonemates, were not too great any anemone that developed some form of genetically determined interclonal "repulsiveness" would have a competitive advantage over its inoffensive neighbors. This genotype and the post-larval progeny inheriting the characteristic would be assured of adequate

"living space" and would therefore have an increased probability of survival and reproductive success. It may have been in this way that the evolutionary precursor of the aggressive response became fixed in the common ancestor of these anemones.

It seems apparent to me that an aggressive behavior that arose through intraspecific competition would be of value only to the individual anemones that display the behavior and not to the species as a whole. (Of course a characteristic theoretically need not be of advantage to the species in order to be selected for, because selection is believed to operate at the level of the individual.) Once aggression and armament are adopted and convey their temporary advantage to the aggressor, an evolutionary trend toward more potent weapons and more effective ways of using them seems very likely. Among the acrorhagus-bearing anemones the specialized nematocysts carried on specialized protuberances (the acrorhagi) and the relatively effective behavior pattern that brings these weapons into play may have evolved in this way.

It is also possible that the aggressive response evolved through interspecific interactions with other anthozoans and served to counter direct competition for space and food by other large sessile coelenterates. This hypothesis is appealing in that it provides a selective advantage to the species as well as to the individual in the origin and development of an aggressive response.

·   ·   ·

Before this question of evolution can be dealt with further, we clearly need more information, especially on the interspecific aspects of the aggressive response of acrorhagus-bearing Actiniids.

I thank Dr. James J. Childress for critically reading this manuscript, the staff and students of the Hopkins Marine Station, the UCSB Marine Institute and Biology Department, the Gatty Marine Laboratory, and the Plymouth Laboratory for help, encouragement and the use of their facilities during the research, and the NIH (predoctoral fellowship to the author) for financial support during part of the study.

LITERATURE CITED

Äbel, E. F., 1954. Ein Beitrag zur Giftwirkung der Actinien und Function der Randsäckchen. *Zool. Anz.,* 153:259–268.

Bonnin, J.-P., 1964. Recherches sur la "reaction d'aggression" et sur le fonctionnement des acrorhages d'*Actinia equina. L. Bull. Biol. Fr. Belg.,* 1:225–250.

Carthy, J. D., and F. J. Ebling, Eds., 1964. *The Natural History of Aggression.* Institute of Biology Symposium No. 13, Academic Press, New York, 449 pp.

Francis, L., 1973. Clone specific segregation in the sea anemone *Anthopleura elegantissima. Biol. Bull.,* 144:64–72.

Hand, C., 1955. The sea anemones of central California. Part II. The Endomyarian and Mesomyarian anemones. *Wasman J. Biol.,* 13:37–97.

Roberts, B. J., 1941. A survey of the methods employed by intertidal organisms in resisting desiccation. *Masters thesis, Stanford University,* 68 pp.

AN INITIAL READING OF RESEARCH ON *ANTHOPLEURA ELEGANTISSIMA*

First, Professor Newberry looks through the entire research report, reviewing what he knew about the topic and thinking about how to read different parts of the report in different ways. Even though he is a marine biologist, he had not studied this sea anemone before. As he thumbs through the report, he tells us what he is looking for.

The first thing I do is look to see what the taxon is. (That is, what kind of animal this is. A taxonomy is a systematic classification of animals, and a taxon is one animal within that system.) Taxa [the plural of taxon] always appear in italics in biological papers. The title here tells me that this paper concerns one taxon in particular, Anthopleura elegantissima, *and then considers some others,—". . . Related Sea Anemones,"—but we're only going to be concerned with* Anthopleura elegantissima *today.*

As he finishes reading the title, Professor Newberry is pulling together what he knows about sea anemones in general and this kind in particular. He discovers that he is familiar with the place where Francis did her research.

I'm beginning to do a clearinghouse operation right away. I ask myself if I "know" any of these animals? Do I at least have a mental image of what they look like? This kind of biology is very visual. I work on sea squirts, which are quite different from Francis's anemones. When I see the name, Anthopleura elegantissima, *I know that I'm reading about an animal that forms clones. Cloning is a way of growing in which an organism, as it grows, divides into two genetically identical bodies. I know Liz and I know of her work.*

There's Pacific Grove; I've worked there. And she mentions Hopkins Marine Station: I can actually see those rocks she's been observing, I've spent so much time there.

Professor Newberry goes on to think about what the title, "Intraspecific Aggression and Its Effect on the Distribution of *Anthopleura elegantissima* and Some Related Sea Anemones," tells him about the paper.

I know the paper is about a specific taxon, but what's the topic? I see here it says, "intraspecific aggression." This tells me that the research is about the anemone's behavior, and, since intraspecific means within that species, that means that sea anemones aren't attacking other species, they are attacking members of their own species.

The word distribution *in the next phrase—"and Its Effect on the Distribution of* Anthopleura elegantissima*"—suggests that the research has something to do with the arrangement of groups of sea anemones. If she is talking about the distribution of groups of sea anemones, then I expect that she will talk about how this type of aggressive behavior arranges those groups. That's a guess. At any rate, I've already learned a lot about this research just from the title. It's a good title!*

Next, Professor Newberry thumbs through the rest of the paper. He notices the drawings on page 250. These prove very important as he plans for a close reading.

The drawings show some really thick tentacles coming out from beneath the oral disk (for instance, look at Figure 1g). Figure 1h zeros in on what appears to be very dramatic tenta-

cles. I might not have even noticed them before. Once you see them you can't miss them. So these drawings are going to be very important in understanding the text, as good graphics so often are.

WRITING AND LEARNING ACTIVITIES

1. **Journal Entry:** Look at the sequence of drawings on page 250. Describe in your own words what you see happening in that sequence of drawings before you read the captions.

2. **Journal Entry:** Write about what you expect to learn as you read about the sea anemone. From what Professor Newberry has said, what do you expect to learn about in this research report? What do you know already about biology or marine biology?

3. **Group Activity:** Look over the report with your group, and make a list of words you don't know. Jot down two or three questions that come to mind, and keep the list handy as you read the report more closely.

A CLOSE READING OF RESEARCH
ON *ANTHOPLEURA ELEGANTISSIMA*

In his second, more careful reading of the research report Professor Newberry reads to gather information. He describes his approach as follows:

I read research reports for information. I'm not trying to deconstruct this paper. I'm not reading it for style. I'm reading to find out what the investigator is reporting: observations and interpretations. Part of the idea of dividing a paper so conventionally—materials, methods, results, discussion (though this paper isn't divided exactly that way)—is to separate observations from interpretations.

WRITING AND LEARNING ACTIVITIES

1. **Reading:** Read Francis's research report.

2. **Journal Entry:** As you read, make notes about your reading process in your journal. Add any questions you have about the reading and any familiar or unfamiliar terms. Read the sentence you find the unfamiliar terms in and make an educated guess about each term's meaning. Also, note any places in the readings where you make connections to your own experience or to something you know about.

3. **Annotate the Text:** As you read, make notes in the margins of your textbook. Make brief notes about new terms, about the purpose for the study, and about questions you have.

The introduction to the research report identifies in a bit more detail the kinds of animals that Lisbeth Francis is studying and the behavior they engage in. As Professor Newberry reads along, he rephrases the introduction into his own words.

Anthopleura elegantissima is a species that clones, and the clones form tightly grouped bunches of bodies (contiguous aggregations). These groups stay apart from other clonal groups. So it would seem we have one group (or clone) over here, another group over there, and a space in between. During fieldwork, Professor Francis has also observed some very large, single Anthopleura elegantissima that remain isolated, each by itself.

She observed aggressive behavior (which she defines by quoting other researchers) between Anthopleura elegantissima of different clonal groups. Her purpose in this paper is to describe this behavior, which she says has never been reported before.

Read the section titled "Materials and Methods," paragraphs 2–7.

In the report's next major section, "Materials and Methods," Francis tells us about the area from which she collected the sea anemones, how she removed them from the rocks they cling to, and how she kept them alive in the laboratory. Most importantly, in a section subtitled, "Conditions Under Which Aggression Was Observed," Francis explains how she provoked the sea anemone's aggressive behavior. She explains that before this experiment she had moved entire anemones around so that they would be forced into contact with each other. But then she shifted to a simpler technique of touching one sea anemone from one group with just a tentacle she had cut off (excised) from another group's sea anemone (a non-clonemate). This was delicate and precise work; Francis had to monitor carefully how many tentacle touches produced the aggressive response.

Read the section called "Procedures, Observations, and Results," paragraphs 8–27 and follow the markings made by Professor New-berry as he read the text. The next few pages follow the research report quite closely, so you will want to keep that report open to the drawings on page 250.

A close reading of the next section of the text, "Procedures, Observations, and Results," should provide a detailed description of the sea anemone's aggressive behavior. Professor Newberry talks about his system for marking the text so that he can look back at it and find the important parts of the description.

When I read a paper, I use a pencil. I learned long ago not to carry pens into places that have valuable books. Ink stains forever. I am going to go through this paper and place stars where something is very important and question marks where I don't understand something. I'll use Xs and arrows when I want to go back, and so on.

As I read I try to clear up my questions or confusions. Sometimes what looked very important turns out not to be so important after all. Or I may have put a question mark next to something I don't understand. I can erase pencil marks or move them around. If you use a ballpoint pen you just make bigger and bigger marks. It's also important to have your own personal code, one that allows you to scan for information quickly and easily.

As Professor Newberry reads along he puts two stars next to the paragraph in which Francis begins her detailed description of the aggressive behavior of the sea anemone. She lists the behaviors by the five stages she has identified. Professor Newberry underlines those crucial items, so that he can go back later and find the definition that follows each one.

The First Stage of Aggressive Behavior: Stimulation

Professor Newberry begins reading the next paragraph aloud to himself to help him follow the description. He's looking for the description of the first portion of the aggressive behavior, "stimulation," and when he thinks he's found it, he puts a circled *1* next to the section. Let's follow along.

> When an expanded anemone is moved toward and first makes contact . . . (paragraph 12).

What their tentacles will do, first withdraw and then re-extend, like they are kind of feeling each other out on this. It may happen several times and I'm going to put a 1 there. This looks like she's talking about stimulation.

But then his eyes move down to the next paragraph and he reads,

> If anemones from different clones come within contact range of each other, the reaction is very different (paragraph 13).

Oops, I'm wrong. Here's where she begins talking about stimulation. I see now that she was just setting up a contrast. When anemones of the same clone make contact it's no big deal; the action occurs between anemones from different clones. So here's where I want the 1 to go. Where's my eraser? There—switched.

Professor Newberry reminds us how important it is to stay flexible during reading, always looking for the information you need and marking up the text as you read, but keeping the mark-up under control—like symbols on a map.

The less I underline the more I can let my eye roam. I read upwards as well as downwards. If I hadn't been reading ahead it would have taken me longer to discover where she actually starts talking about the first phase of aggressive behavior. I'm constantly scouting the whole page.

He continues reading, working to make sense of the description. He reads to understand some new terminology; he goes back and forth between the drawings and the text; and he repeatedly reads the captions under the drawings—aiming for a better sense of what happens as aggression really gets underway. One challenge is to figure out what Francis means by the term *acrorhagi*. Professor Newberry doesn't know what the word refers to, so he circles it. Francis notes that the acrorhagi can be seen "beneath the outer cycle of tentacles (Fig. 1c)" (paragraph 13). By looking at the caption to Figure 1c, he learns that Francis has already passed on to the second stage, called inflation.

The Second Stage of Aggressive Behavior: Inflation

Professor Newberry reads the caption under 1c and after going back and forth between the description in paragraph 13 and the drawings with their captions on page 250, he finally understands and "sees" what the acrorhagi are.

Now I look back at 1c and sure enough, there they are, hidden under the tentacles. At first, I thought maybe she was referring to those squiggly marks on the trunk of the anemone, but now I see that those little circles peeping out from under the tentacles are the acrorhagi. I've never seen them in the field. And now I look down further at the other drawings, and sure enough, I can see them in each one. Now I know what I'm looking at. It's only during the repeated tentacle contact that the acrorhagi become visible. There is a whole different set of structures down there underneath the outer circle of feeding tentacles. I put a star in the margin, because there's an important thing happening here: The anemone is putting out its guns, these acrorhagi.

The last sentence of the paragraph offers still another way to picture the relationship between tentacles and the acrorhagi. The writer reminds us that when the anemone is undisturbed the acrorhagi are almost invisible, hidden beneath the tentacles in a channel called the fosse. To help visualize this, Professor Newberry drew a quick sketch of that portion of the sea anemone in the margin of the paper.

In paragraph 14, Professor Newberry underlined *"The inflation stage"* and put a circled *2* in the margin. Francis is explaining that this second stage begins after the intruding anemone withdraws and re-extends its tentacles. The anemone originally being attacked "assumes a more upright posture (Fig. 1c, paragraph 14)." Now *it* becomes "the aggressor." He reads about the inflation stage and tries to explain the process in his own words,

Let's see . . . The next paragraphs (14–16) basically describe (or speculate, because Liz may be guessing here) how the acrorhagi become turgid, which means filled with water. The acrorhagi change from shriveled white balls to transparent rounded cones. We have several new terms here. She talks about the changes in the "gastrovascular cavity." I know that this cavity plays a lot of roles: it's a stomach and a kind of fluid skeleton. It looks like it takes in water and pushes it into the acrorhagi, filling them up, distending them. This involves muscular contractions. I'm putting an X next to what seems like an important fact: four to twelve acrorhagi become inflated during a single episode.

The next short paragraph (17), which concludes Francis's discussion, surprises Professor Newberry, so he marks it with a check and an exclamation point. Francis claims that this "acrorhagial inflation" has never been seen before and seems to be directly related to the aggressive behavior.

Professor Newberry remarked:

I'm going to put a check there because here is where the paper clearly says that it's bringing up absolutely new information. I may want to be able to refer back some time to remember just how novel this assertion is. I put an exclamation point here for a personal reason. I had been looking at these animals for twenty years before this paper was published and I never saw this happen. What an observation! I'm just kicking myself for never making it myself! Thanks to Liz's skill, we can all see it now.

The Third and Fourth Stages of Aggressive Behavior: Movement of Application and the Application of the Ectoderm

Francis identifies the "application" stage as a rapid movement requiring less than two minutes. Newberry turns back to paragraph 18, underlines the phrase "The movement of application," and places a circled 3 in the margin, and then tries to describe the movement in his own words.

Phew! Describing this movement pattern is like describing a dog walking. The words help, but a drawing helps a lot more. She's describing how the muscles of the sea anemone work (the process) to create this smooth downward motion (the product) that she has caught so clearly in Drawings 1e, 1f, and 1g. She says the anemone's ring of tentacles often leans over all the way down to the level of the pedal disc on the substratum. Pedal refers to "foot" in Latin and substratum means "ground." This downward motion can occur many times and even more acrorhagi continue to become inflated. And now I see that she's moving on to the next stage.

He underlines the phrase "application of the white tip" (paragraph 21) and places a circled 4 in the margin.

Professor Newberry returns to the drawings (Figure 1h) following paragraph 10, which now clearly illustrates this fourth stage, the application of the anemone's ectoderm, or its skin. This drawing focuses our attention on two things: first, the acrorhagi, after applying the ectoderm to the offending anemone, become transparent; second, we can see a bit of ectoderm left on the offending anemone. Professor Newberry studies all of this awhile and then places a star by the sentence explaining this process.

This anemone is applying something, and that's why Liz is using that word application. The clone-defending aggressor applies patches filled with destructive stinging cells. This is a pretty ferocious attack. That ectoderm is sticky, and the aggressive anemone is really zapping that little intruder, not just reaching out and biting it.

The Fifth Stage of Aggressive Behavior: Recovery

Francis describes the fifth stage of the attack as follows,

(5) recovery, during which the anemone returns to its normal posture (paragraph 11).

Professor Newberry puts a 5 next to the paragraph that describes the anemone's recovery, that is, its return to its original posture (paragraph 23). But then Francis turns to the fate of the "victim," the sea anemone that was attacked. Because the intruding victim, not the clone-defending aggressor, is now the subject of Francis's observations, he underlines the term *victim* twice,

The victim responds to the damage within a day; it's pulled back, withdrawn. Necrotic tissue (dead tissue that suggests lasting damage.): I'm going to underline that. We know the attack was not just a slap; it really did some serious harm. She mentions a specific kind of stinging cell that releases a protein-digesting enzyme, and the patch that got hit is actually being digested—eaten up. If you've ever been stung by a Portuguese man-o'-war— and I have—you know it's no laughing matter, even for animals as big as us.

Moving from Observations to Interpretations: Discussion Section

Read the discussion section in paragraphs 28–38.

The discussion section offers both the researcher and the reader an opportunity to think about the meaning of the reported observations. Professor Newberry read the earlier description of the sea anemone's behavior very carefully, working to get a picture in his mind's eye of the anemone's movements. Now he will read the discussion section, asking himself why this particular aggressive behavior might be important. In this section, the author, Lisbeth Francis, wants to say something about the big picture; that is, she places her observations in a larger context. She theorizes about how this particular aggressive behavior functions and how it evolved. But first, in paragraphs 28 and 29, she emphasizes what is special about this aggressive behavior.

What surprised me about the behavior Liz described is that the aggressive response can be set off just by the touch of a tentacle. How is it that the anemone can tell from just a brief touch of another tentacle that it comes from a non-clonemate? That's pretty perceptive behavior in such a simple animal. Also, this behavior apparently relies on body movements and equipment (the acrorhagi) that apparently have no other purpose. So, Francis is right to ask about the function of this behavior and its evolution.

Within the discussion section Francis finds it appropriate to compile a list (see paragraph 32) of the observational evidence for what she sees as the four functions of this aggressive behavior as kinds of sea anemones interact among themselves ("intraspecific interaction").

In paragraph 34, Francis summarizes what she has said so far and shifts the discussion to a far more speculative level. She asks, since the acrorhagi seem to have no other function than the one described in her four points above, why and how did this particular behavior evolve?

Finally, in paragraph 35, Francis speculates on why this response may have been important enough to have been selected and maintained through generations. Professor Newberry adds his thoughts on this topic:

Liz speculates that the aggressive response helps the clone survive when space is scarce or when food is scarce. In the next paragraph, she goes further and speculates that once an individual clone benefits from this aggressive response, the entire species has been nudged a little toward adopting aggressive behavior and weaponry such as the stinging cells on the acrorhagi, which make the aggressive behavior even more potent. Or, Liz suggests, the aggressive response may have developed to protect these anemones from other, larger animals. Before we can know for sure, we need to know more about the other anemones that have acrorhagi.

WRITING AND LEARNING ACTIVITIES

1. **Journal Entry:** Write in your journal about how this last section of Francis's research report is different from the previous sections. What new terms or ideas are introduced? What new problems does she try to solve? Which portion was easier for you to understand, the observations or the interpretations? Which was more interesting? Why?

2. **Journal Entry:** Write about the experience of following Professor Newberry reading this research report. Point out places in his reading where you saw or understood something you wouldn't have seen or understood by reading the research report alone. Point out places in his reading or in the text that still confuse you.

3. **Group Activity:** Meet with your group or in pairs and share your journal entries. What portions of the research report do you understand? What portions confuse you? Can you make better progress in understanding those portions by working together than you can on your own?

4. **Writing Activity:** Find a place to observe nature. Sit quietly in that one spot and take notes on what you see. Try to focus on one animal. Think about the language you use to observe and to report your observations. Use drawings to illustrate the observations.

MAKING MEANING IN BIOLOGY

Learning to participate in an academic discipline means several things. First, it means learning about the specialized texts that the specialists, biologists in this case, use to communicate the findings of their research. Second, it means developing your own interests in relation to the subject area. In other words, you must ask and answer the question, "What does this mean to me?" And, third, you must eventually be able to reflect on the practices of the discipline. What kinds of questions do researchers ask? How do they go about answering those questions? Would you ask different questions? Would you use different methods for answering them? What do *you* consider important research in this discipline?

Before you can evaluate research in any academic discipline, you must become familiar with the ways members of this discipline use language to make meaning. Professor Newberry's close reading of Lisbeth Francis's research helped us to see how to read a specialized text. In this section we go back and look more closely at how Professor Newberry used language to make meaning from Francis's research.

MAKING MEANING CAN MEAN TRIAL AND ERROR

It might have surprised you to see that Professor Newberry, a distinguished scholar in his field, relied on trial and error at times as he read Francis's research report. He found himself *misreading* part of the report the first time around and had to backtrack, going over the material a second time. After reading Francis's list in paragraph 11, he expected that the next paragraph would begin explaining the first stage, stimulation. So when he began to read the following paragraph, he began summarizing, in his own words, to formulate an understanding of this stage of the aggressive behavior.

> When an expanded anemone is moved toward and first makes contact . . . (paragraph 12).

What their tentacles will do, first withdraw and then re-extend, like they are kind of feeling each other out on this. It may happen several times and I'm going to put a 1 there. This looks like she's talking about stimulation.

That was the trial reading. His summary was an attempt at fixing the meaning in his own mind. It proved to be an error, however, as he found out when his eyes moved down to the next paragraph, where he read,

> If anemones from different clones come within contact range of each other, the reaction is very different (paragraph 13).

Immediately, he realized he was wrong and began reworking his mental summary and the mental picture he was creating of this five-step aggressive behavior.

WRITING AND LEARNING ACTIVITIES

1. **Journal Entry:** Review the notes you made in your journal while reading Lisbeth Francis's research report. Find places where you were wrong in your initial reading and had to revise your thinking.

2. **Group Activity:** Meet in pairs or in groups and share your "misreadings." Did many of you misread the same section? If so, talk about how the research report might have been clearer.

3. **Writing Activity:** Write a note to the next class who will read this research report. Offer them some suggestions on how to read it. Consider it a troubleshooting guide to reading this research report.

DEFINITIONS ALONE ARE NOT ENOUGH

Using a dictionary when you don't understand a word is often sufficient if you're reading about general information or studying an area that is familiar to you. As you enter a specialized field, such as marine biology or any of the other fields we cover in this textbook, you will need to do more than look up words in a general dictionary to understand the material you are covering. To understand specific words—often called terms or terminology—you must understand the words in their context and how they reflect concepts, observations, and ideas. Let's see how this works in Francis's research report.

Defining Aggressive Behavior

In Francis's introduction, she tells us that she has observed a specific type of behavior between non-clonemates, "an elaborate behavior pattern that usually results in damage to one or both animals" (paragraph 1). Francis defines this behavior pattern as aggressive behavior, using a definition from a natural history text on aggression, "An animal acts aggressively when it inflicts, attempts to inflict, or threatens to inflict damage on another animal. The act is accompanied by recognizable behavior symptoms and definable physiological changes" (quoted by Francis from Carthy and Ebling, 1964, p. 1).

If all that was needed was a definition, Francis could have ended her paper right there. But, in fact, the value of her work lies in her detailed observations and descriptions of behavior that, when shared with her readers—scholars and students such as yourself—convinces them that the behavior is, indeed, aggressive. She has gone beyond "defining" her observations to explain why it is important that we pay attention to this previously unobserved behavior of the anemone. In fact, she has added to our general knowledge of aggressive behavior as well as to its specific traits in the anemone.

Defining Acrorhagi

The term *acrorhagi* is never mentioned in Francis's introduction, yet because the acrorhagi turn out to be important to understanding this research, it is a word that needs to be clearly and fully defined. We really need to "see" in our mind's eye what Francis saw when she observed the anemones during their aggressive response. Next, we want to define how acrorhagi function during the aggressive response. Professor Newberry's first challenge was to identify the acrorhagi—to figure out what they look like. He explains how he finally came to "see" the acrorhagi:

Now I look back at 1c and sure enough, there they are, hidden under the tentacles. At first, I thought maybe she was referring to those squiggly marks on the trunk of the anemone, but now I see that those little circles peeping out from under the tentacles are the acrorhagi. I've never seen them in the field. And now I look down further at the other drawings, and sure enough, I can see them in each one. Now I know what I'm looking at.

Next Professor Newberry must explain to himself—define—how the acrorhagi *function* during the aggressive response.

It's only during the repeated tentacle contact that the acrorhagi become visible. There is a whole different set of structures down there underneath the outer circle of tentacles. I put a star in the margin, because there's an important thing happening here: The anemone is putting out its guns, these acrorhagi.

WRITING AND LEARNING ACTIVITY

---

1. Group Activity: Survey the research report and make a list of terms you don't understand fully. Gather three different types of materials: a standard dictionary, a specialized dictionary (pick one from the appendix, Directions for Further Research), and a textbook on marine biology. Look up the words in each of these sources and then reread the section from the research report where you found the term. In pairs or in small groups write your own explanation for these terms.

ASKING QUESTIONS TO FIND RELATIONSHIPS

A list of terms and their definitions, such as acrorhagi and aggressive behavior, only take us part of the way toward understanding a discipline's specialized language. To take the next step toward making meaning in biology, you'll need to think about the relationships among these terms and definitions. For example, how do the above terms you looked up relate to each other? One way to find out—and one that can be used in any discipline—is by asking questions and formulating answers to them. As Professor Newberry reads Francis's work, he does ask questions, the same thing he does when he observes nature. Earlier he told us:

I tell my students that the first thing they'll experience when they try to observe Nature is a standoff of sorts. Outdoors, you stare at Nature and Nature just stares back. The most important way to end the standoff is to ask questions. Questions are crucial; observations and measurements and the rest are merely ways of expressing them. Posing good questions is a remarkably difficult skill, just in itself.

Here are six questions some of my students wrote about particular sections of the research report:

Questions from the Introduction (paragraph 1)

1. *What does the term* contiguous aggregations *mean?*
2. *What happens when "genetically different individuals" get together?*
3. *What is aggressive behavior?*

Questions from Materials and Methods (paragraphs 2–7)

4. *What was the size of the anemones?*
5. *Where did she observe and collect the anemones?*
6. *How did she actually start the anemone's aggressive behavior?*

We see several types of questions here. Not all are ones that will help to illuminate the relationships among meanings. The first question, "What does contiguous aggregations mean?" can be answered by defining a term. It does not ask you to summarize the meaning of a larger section of text. The next question, however, "What happens when 'genetically different individuals' get together?" does just that. To answer that question, you have to think about what kind of behavior occurs between genetically different individuals and why it is important to this research. Your answer will have to build on terms you have already defined: *behavior* and *genetically different*. Look at the rest of the questions. Which ask you to think about the relationships between meanings and which ones ask only for a narrow, simple answer?

WRITING AND LEARNING ACTIVITIES

1. **Journal Entry:** Reread the subsequent sections of the research report, Procedures, Observations, and Results (paragraphs 8–27) and Discussion (paragraphs 28–38). Write questions that could be answered from the information in those sections.

2. **Group Activity:** In pairs or groups compare your questions. Decide which questions ask about important relationships and develop a list of them.

3. **Class Activity:** Practice asking and answering questions. Break into several groups. Each group should ask another group a question and the other group can confer and appoint one person to speak for the group.

DEVELOPING INTERESTS

You have read a great deal about the behavior of the sea anemone, its aggressive behavior toward non-clonemates, and its practice of separating clonal groups by creating anemone-free zones. Professor Newberry, both in his interview and in his close reading of one of the reports, helped us to see that the specialized academic discipline of marine biology values research that looks closely at natural phenomena and tries to explain the causes and significance of what is observed. We learned how it is possible to "see" what the researcher saw and how specific terminology helps to communicate the researcher's observations.

READING FOR THE BIG PICTURE

Much of the knowledge produced in marine biology appears in complex, specialized research reports such as the one you just read. There is also a need for writing aimed at a broader audience; it does not, perhaps, report the details of the research but offers an opportunity to learn about "the big picture." "The Anemone Below," a piece on marine life written in 1986 by Kenneth P. Sebens for a general audience, follows. It is much more readable than the research report. Published in *Natural History,* this article is aimed at a wider audience than the scholars and students who read from the *Biological Bulletin. Natural History,* published monthly by the American Museum of Natural History in New York City for museum members and other subscribers, typically includes articles on the biological sciences, ecology, anthropology, archaeology, geology, and astronomy. Written by scientists and scholars, the articles provide summaries and syntheses of work in particular areas for an intelligent and interested, but not necessarily scholarly, audience.

WRITING AND LEARNING ACTIVITIES

1. **Reading:** Read "The Anemone Below." Make notes in your journal about the process of reading this article. Write down any questions you have about the reading and any familiar or unfamiliar terms you encounter. Also, note any places in the readings where you make connections to your own experience or to something you know about.

2. **Journal Entry:** After the reading, write in your journal about what you now know about sea anemones. Also, write about how this article is different from the one you read by Lisbeth Francis.

3. **Developing Interests:** Look at the list of references offered in the appendix, Directions for Further Research. Find an additional source about some aspect of marine biology that interests you. Photocopy and bring to class enough copies of the report for members of a small group.

THE ANEMONE BELOW

COLORFUL CONTENDERS BATTLE FOR TERRITORY AMIDST TIDAL ROCK AND REEF

KENNETH P. SEBENS

■ ■ ■

A mile off the northwest tip of Washington State's Olympic Peninsula lies Tatoosh Island, a collection of small rocky islets separated by narrow draws that are protected from the ocean's thundering swells. Snorkeling here during high tide, swimming seaward through these draws, I saw giant green sea anemones, *Anthopleura xanthogrammica,* emerge from closed low-tide postures and unfurl sunbursts of brilliant blue-green tentacles.

With the first waves of the incoming tide, the anemones relax the muscles that cover their tentacles. Slowly, the tentacles unfold and inflate, more than doubling the animal's size. When fully expanded, water is pumped in through the mouth, filling the tentacles and body. This hydrostatic skeleton holds the tentacles erect even during the rush of water and foam from breaking waves. Once the tide rises a few feet, the anemones move only slightly with each wave surge. When I tossed a small mussel onto an anemone's tentacles, this normally slow-moving creature reacted instantly, wrapping around the mussel in a second or two. In less than a minute, the prey was swallowed and the tentacles were again at the ready.

Often compared to flowers, sea anemones are voracious carnivores that grasp, paralyze, and devour swimming prey, usually crustaceans and small fish, as well as mussels and barnacles dislodged by waves. They are also fierce defenders of their territories, using specialized tentaclelike organs to

The tentacle crowns of two *Anthopleura elegantissima* tangle. The anemone on the right has begun to inflate its acrorhagi—the white spheres between the pink-tipped tentacles. As the battle ensues, both anemones will retract their tentacles, fully extend the acrorhagi, and then bend to make contact.
Ann Wertheim

battle neighboring anemones on the rocky shores and crowded coral reefs they colonize. It was this agonistic behavior that I studied off Tatoosh Island's shores and which I then compared with the fighting practices of anemones on other rocky shores and reefs.

Anemones are members of the phylum Cnidaria, which also includes hydroids, jellyfish, sea pens, corals, gorgonians, and many other common forms in both temperate and tropical seas. Their closest relatives are the corals. A sea anemone is very similar in structure to a single polyp of a reef-building coral but lacks the coral's hard calcium carbonate skeleton. The evolutionary loss of the skeleton gave anemones the ability to move easily.

Cnidarian behavior is coordinated by simple nerve nets: one in the inner cell layer (endoderm, or gastrodermis); the other in the outer cell layer (ectoderm, or epidermis), with some cross-communication between. There is no central nervous system, no brain, not even a dense concentration of nerve cells that can be thought of as a center of coordination. Cnidarians, including sea anemones, are examples of animals with "simple" nervous systems, yet recent research continues to find them capable of increasingly complicated behaviors.

5   All cnidarians capture their prey by firing thousands of microscopic "harpoons" from structures called nematocysts. One type of nematocyst penetrates the prey's flesh and anchors itself with barbs; a similar capsule, the spirocyst, fires sticky threads that adhere to the hard outer skeletons of mollusks or crustaceans. Tentacles studded with these nematocyst and spirocyst capsules transfer captured prey to the anemone's mouth, where they are then ingested into the coelenteron, the central cavity that is the animal's equivalent of a gut. Certain anemone species are zooplankton feeders; others, especially the large anemones of temperate rocky shores, depend on wave action to dislodge mussels, snails, sea urchins, and other invertebrates, which then tumble into the grasp of their tentacles.

Marine animals and plants that live on rock surfaces grow and reproduce at a rate that rapidly fills the available space. Surfaces for attachment are a limited resource and competition for that resource is inevitable. A brief look at any tide pool or coral reef illustrates this fact. Every surface is filled with some sort of living creature, and many different species are present, each individual in contact with several others. It is at such contact points that aggression and defense of space occur, just as they do in territorial birds, mammals, or coral reef fish.

The simplest form of aggressive competition for space is overgrowth of one species by another. A successful defense is to build a wall of tissue or skeletal material that can stop the aggressor or to do something equally harmful in response. Judith Lang, working on reef corals in Jamaica, found that some coral species have just such a defense. If a coral of one species begins to grow over a neighbor's edge, the defending coral can throw its mesenterial filaments onto the intruder. These threadlike organs normally constitute the coral's digestive system within the coelenteron, but during aggressive encounters the filaments can be ejected out of the mouth and onto an adjacent coral. There, they begin to digest that coral's polyps, effectively stopping its growth. Some corals also develop sweeper tentacles, which, when developed and inflated in response to contact by a neighboring coral, can be more than ten times as long as the feeding tentacles. Sweeper tentacles contain dense fields of nematocysts that destroy coral tissue that they contact. Once defeated by the mesenterial filaments of a neighbor, certain corals can develop sweeper tentacles in response, then come back to win the long-term encounter.

Sea anemones, moving along the reefs or rock channels, commonly contact other anemones and corals. The giant green anemones of the North

American west coast move frequently when young. In a few weeks their movements, imperceptible to the human eye, can carry them across several yards of rock in search of currents and temperatures that will increase the likelihood of surviving and finding food. Larvae may settle far from their eventual adult home. Along the coast of Washington State, anemone larvae settle in intertidal beds of the large mussel *Mytilus californianus*—a safe haven with plentiful food in the crevices between mussels. There the small anemones grow and eventually migrate downward to the low intertidal pools and surge channels. This is a perfect position from which to capture mussels torn loose by wave action.

Lisbeth Francis, working on the California coast, and A. Bonnin, conducting research independently in France, noticed that certain anemones inflate saclike vesicles below the tentacles when they come into contact with other anemones. These vesicles, technically termed acrorhagi, lose their tips when they contact other anemones. These pieces of the vesicles stick to the body or tentacles of other anemones; large specialized "homotrichous" nematocysts in the tips inject chemical compounds that cause tissue death (necrosis). When the tentacles of two anemones come into contact there is an attack and counterattack. The tentacles are pulled back out of the way and the large white acrorhagi are raised and brought down in graceful arcs. The loser, usually the smaller individual, eventually ceases its counterattack, pulls in both tentacles and acrorhagi, and glides slowly away from the zone of contact.

10   Lisbeth Francis found that an anemone could discern whether it had just contacted an anemone of its own clone (identical genetic makeup, or genotype) or an anemone of another clone. The mechanism that makes anemones so discriminating is still unknown, but preliminary research indicates that any piece of intact tissue of a different genotype will stimulate the entire agonistic sequence. No chemical fraction of that tissue or surface mucus will do the same, however. This means that the recognition of self (identical genotype, whether connected or not) versus nonself (different genotype) may be similar to the immune reactions of humans and other mammals in which the body's defenses must recognize foreign, often dangerous, material. Recognition is accomplished by matching configurations of proteins on the cell membrane surfaces. Each individual has a slightly different pattern of those molecules just as each person's fingerprints are unique.

Many anemone species have the ability to divide in half or to pinch pieces off their base and thus form new anemones without sexual reproduction. All such species also reproduce sexually at the appropriate time of year. *Anthopleura elegantissima,* the west coast aggregating anemone, divides itself in half usually once a year, producing two individuals with each division. These "daughter" anemones remain close together and form aggregations of hundreds of individual polyps. Divided anemones are not attached and are thus physiologically independent, but genetically they are true clones of a single original individual.

Borders between aggregations of this small green anemone are battle zones, where genetically distinct clones contact one another. Lisbeth Francis found that anemones along these borders develop more and larger acrorhagi in response to frequent contact with anemones of other clones than do individuals at the center of the aggregation. Thus edge individuals become specialized as "soldiers," while individuals in the center never receive this stimulus and more of their available energy goes to growth and reproduction, instead of being used to build weapons. This division of labor is reminiscent of the differentiation of social insects into specialized castes.

Aggregating clonal anemones are not the only anemones that fight for space; solitary anemones also fight even when open space is apparently available nearby. This behavior may reduce crowding in the local population; fewer anemones increase the probability of each capturing prey.

Observing the giant green anemones as the tide was rising showed that they began their aggressive behavior when wave surge caused nearby anemones' tentacles to brush each other. The next fifteen to thirty minutes provided a spectacular display as a few large individuals inflated their acrorhagi and raised them high above nearby anemones. A slow contraction on one side of an anemone's body brought the acrorhagi down onto another's tentacles and body, causing that anemone to jerk away, then contract. During my research on Tatoosh Island I removed anemones and brought them into contact with their former neighbors or with anemones several yards away. Anemones battled all newcomers but tolerated their present neighbors even in a new position. Somehow, these anemones learn to recognize established bordering individuals and not waste time fighting them.

15   Acrorhagi are found in only one family of anemones. Some other anemones have tentacles, termed catch tentacles or fighting tentacles, similar to the sweeper tentacles of corals and use them in identical fashion. The fighting tentacles reach far beyond each anemone's own tentacle crown and seem to search out other clones in a radius around themselves. Once an anemone of another clone is touched, the tentacle tip is released and sticks to that anemone just as do the tips of acrorhagi. Nematocysts then inject toxins that destroy the tissues. Anemones thus damaged move away, relinquishing their space. Jennifer Purcell and Christopher Kitting found that some clones of *Metridium senile,* a common shallow water anemone throughout much of the Northern Hemisphere, tolerate each other but fight newly introduced clones and that, if forced into continuous contact, clones would habituate to each other and cease to inflate the fighting tentacles. Saul Kaplan, in a 1983 paper, presented the intriguing theory that *Metridium* fights only with clones of the same sex, never with those of the opposite sex. Laboratory experiments support the idea that sex recognition and segregation occur in this species. *Metridium* reproduces sexually by releasing eggs and sperm into seawater. Proximity to a clone of the opposite sex may increase the probability of eggs being fertilized.

Acrorhagi and sweeper tentacles are most often employed against other clones of the same anemone species. They are equally effective against anemones of other species and probably against corals as well. On coral reefs, anemones inhabit the interstices between living coral and often cover the surfaces of old coral rock. The large purple- or green-tipped Caribbean anemone *Condylactis gigantea* kills neighboring coral using its tentacle nematocysts, keeping the coral from growing over the anemone and interfering with its food capture. *Condylactis,* like the large anemones on temperate rocky shores (*Anthopleura xanthogrammica*), captures large mollusks and sea urchins that are rolled about by heavy wave action or that blunder into its tentacles.

If these agonistic behaviors were simply a matter of direct competition for space, the anemones might be expected to continue fighting until one clone won and could expand its area by asexual propagation. But there is always some space available on these rock surfaces. Although almost every square centimeter is covered by some plant or animal, many species can be overgrown or pushed aside by large anemones. Why, then, should a battle ensue? The message to newcomers from an established clonal group is, "This space is taken, go away." The response, with space available, may be, "I will do just that." But when space is scarce, and the newcomer settles down, a temporary battle will establish a border. Fighting tentacles or acrorhagi of adjacent anemones may then atrophy over time. If, however, individuals of one group wander too far over the border, the intruder's genotype will be recognized by anemones it has not contacted before and it will be attacked. On crowded reefs and rocky shores the anemone credo appears to be that good fences make good neighbors.

DEVELOPING QUESTIONS
TO EXTEND YOUR KNOWLEDGE

Below are questions generated by students working in small groups after reading Francis's research report and the Sebens article. The questions formulated by the group don't necessarily refer only to the most recent readings, although many of them reflect the general knowledge base that the students now have after reading a research report and a more general article on sea anemones. Other questions reflect their growing interest in research and in the sciences. Most of the questions reflect the personal interests of the persons who formulated them and could lead to further reading and research on this topic.

> *If anemones have no communication center, how do they carry out such complex behavior? How do the* Anthopleura xanthogrammica *that stay on the outside of the colony learn to tolerate their neighbors? How do sea anemones reproduce? Do they use both sexual and asexual reproduction?*

Do all the sea anemones possess the same defense mechanisms? Sea anemones don't have brains, so how are they capable of distinguishing their species from others? How are the acrorhagi developed as "soldiers" on the border? Are there different types of fighting appendages? Why doesn't the species dominate the area and kill off the other species? What can we learn about humans from studies of sea anemones? Are there ethical issues surrounding use of these animals for research? How do marine biologists get funding for research? When they work for a university, how do they spend their time? What do they do when they actually do research?

WRITING AND LEARNING ACTIVITIES

1. **Peer or Group Activity:** Working in pairs or in small groups, look over your readings, then put them aside. Formulate and jot down as many questions as you can about your readings. Don't worry about whether or not you know the answers or where they will come from.

2. **Peer or Group Activity:** Working in pairs or in small groups, exchange lists of questions and look them over. Identify which questions you would like to explore further, and keep them in mind as you choose questions to ask during the learning conversation that follows.

3. **Developing Interests:** Look through some of the popular science magazines listed in the Appendix. Bring to class an article that interested you. How does the information in the reading connect to what you have already learned? Does it suggest new areas to explore?

PARTICIPATING IN A LEARNING CONVERSATION

We now know a great deal about a sea animal that exhibits a curious aggressive behavior when its tentacles touch another animal from a different family. Formulating questions, as we did above, and responding to questions as we will do in this section offers one of the best ways to find out what we know, what we don't know, and what we would like to know more about.

Below is a learning conversation in which students question or interview each other to extend their learning process and to learn what interests them. They talk about the mechanism by which the anemone "knows" that the tentacle touching it is from another clonal group. They were interested in the new information provided by the *Natural History* article. Lisbeth Francis's paper (which had appeared in 1973) focused on the grouping of anemones and on the aggressive response but very little on the mechanism that caused that response. Let's follow the conversation:

BRIAN: I have a question. How is it that the acrorhagi become soldiers on the border and what about the anemones in the center? Do those anemones have acrorhagi or not and if they do, do they use them?

LAURA: Well, I know that the sea anemones around the border have larger acrorhagi because they are usually the defenders. The ones in the center usually have smaller acrorhagi, I think, because they come into contact with fewer anemones from different clones.

BRIAN: I think it's referred to as the division of labor. The outside of the anemone colony is protected from other anemones by the soldier anemones who have larger acrorhagi to defend the outside. The inner anemones concentrate on the reproduction because they aren't being bothered. That allows them to keep growing in size.

ILLYA: This makes me think about group behavior. In my sociology classes, we're always talking about group behavior and the different roles that people play. I wonder if members of other animal groups have distinct roles in their groups? I might try to find out something about this.

ROBERT: I was interested in the way they move around, so they can locate a better habitat, better places to find food, better drinking water, better schools for their children. (Laughter.) But seriously, I did want to learn more about how sea anemones can distinguish other species. After all, they don't have brains.

LAURA: Well, what I remember from the Sebens article is that it is similar to how our system recognizes enemies through chemical processes. When the tentacles come in contact, possibly there is an exchange of chemicals and the attacker knows if it is one of its own by reading the information on the cell.

PERWAIZ: Plus they have a fingerprint-type mechanism. They could recognize whether it had been contacted before or not. But still it is mind-boggling. I would buy the chemical thing. I'll bet that research on those chemicals might shed light on some human biochemical research.

ILLYA: I was wondering what kind of research has gone on since Francis did hers. When you think about it, it was in 1973; that was over twenty years ago. I guess those studies must be classics since Professor Newberry seemed to think that they showed something new about sea anemones. What has been going on in the last twenty years?

LAURA: I'll bet they're doing a lot of looking at that biochemical thing . . . about how the sea anemones recognize an enemy. I wonder where I could get more information. This is a very hot topic and I'm interested in it. I bet researchers are trying to simulate that chemical or find out how similar processes occur in other animals or even in humans.

WRITING AND LEARNING ACTIVITIES

1. **Learning Conversation:** Use the questions you developed in the previous set of activities to participate in a learning conversation with members of your class. Base your conversation on what you have read thus far, including the new readings you brought to class to share with your small groups.

2. **Journal Entry:** Following the learning conversation, write in your journal about what you know quite well, what you don't know or understand, and most importantly, what you are curious about. What would you like to learn more about?

◼▭ LINKED WRITING ASSIGNMENT

Writing a Summary of Work in Marine Biology (see Chapter 10, Summarizing Discipline-Specific Texts). In the previous section, Developing Interests, you began to identify issues and ideas that you might want to explore further. Finding personal connections to the material you are studying is one important way to participate more fully in an academic community. You will also need to learn how some everyday thinking strategies, such as summarizing, help you to participate in the disciplines you are studying here. Chapter 10 introduces you to the process of writing a summary and offers a reading from biology for you to practice summarizing.

CHAPTER

8

GEOLOGY

In "The Great Alaska Debate: Can Oil and Wilderness Mix?" Timothy Egan (1991) explores the complex set of decisions we face concerning one of our wilderness treasures, the Arctic National Wildlife Refuge (ANWR), a windswept coastal plain, home to caribou, musk oxen, polar bears, grizzly bears, and wolves. On the one hand, highly confidential tests by oil companies suggest that beneath this plain in northeastern Alaska lies what may be the last great untapped oil field on the continent, according to many geologists. This oil, whatever the quantity, however, lies under a highly vulnerable permafrost terrain: a layer of permanently frozen sand and rock beneath a thin surface that only thaws partially during the brief arctic summer. It is the geologist who studies the damage to this permafrost terrain by the heavy trains of trucks and equipment necessary for oil exploration and drilling.

In this chapter you will see how geological research sits at the crossroads of the debate between our need for oil and our desire to preserve wilderness areas. I interview Donna Jurdy, a geology professor, who will introduce you to her field and then offer a close reading of two research reports: an analysis of planned winter seismic disturbance; and an observation of the effects of off-road vehicle traffic on permafrost terrain. Following this, we will look closely at how researchers put what they have learned in the form of a conventional scientific research report. We will also focus on the relationship between research and the public debate on this issue (Egan's article). Finally, I ask you to consider what personal connections you might have with environmental issues.

AN INTERVIEW WITH A GEOPHYSICIST

Professor Donna M. Jurdy, a geophysicist, teaches a freshman seminar on "Death of the Dinosaurs" and other graduate courses on seismology and on the planet Venus at Northwestern University in Evanston, Illinois. She and co-author Michael Stefanick recently published an article in the *Philosophical Transactions of the Royal Society of London* titled, "The Forces Driving the Plates: Constraints from Kinematics and Stress Observations."

Tell us about how you became a geophysicist.

I grew up in the 1950s and had some interest in science, so I thought I'd become a science teacher. I didn't really think beyond that because I didn't know that anything more was possible. I don't think I knew of any women scientists or professionals while I was growing up. I certainly didn't know about careers in science. Sputnik changed all that. In 1957, the United States' pride took a fall when they learned that the Russians had the technology to actually launch and land a satellite on the moon. Suddenly, science became a national priority. In fact, anyone who had the ability should be doing science, even little girls.

The message was loud and clear; programs and scholarships to study science became available. I participated in a pre-college science center at the University of Bridgeport. It changed my life. The pre-college program focused on physics and astronomy, and students came from all over the country. By watching where students from the previous year's program went to college and seeing the kinds of things they studied I began to get ideas for how to shape my own education. I went to the University of Rochester for my undergraduate work and then to the State University of New York at Buffalo for my master's degree and the University of Michigan for my doctorate. I have never regretted my decision to do graduate studies in geophysics.

Much later, at a conference—the International Union of Geodesy and Geophysics—in Vancouver in 1987 commemorating the thirty-year anniversary of Sputnik, I met a Russian scholar named Dr. Gretchko, I think, who had actually worked on Sputnik. Through his translator, I thanked him for my career and my fulfilling life because if they hadn't launched Sputnik I wouldn't be doing what I'm doing today. He just chuckled.

How would you introduce geology to freshmen?

Geology is the study of the earth's history. In the first course, students might learn about minerals, the building blocks of the earth. So much is missing from the record that we have to guess about some things. I think the hardest thing for students to understand in a geology course is the time frame: thinking about the millions and millions of years it took to produce what we see. The study of geology helps us to interpret the rock record so that we can tell what has happened during that time. One might also learn about the history of life on earth, how life has modified the earth, and how the earth has controlled the kind of life that has developed. One might get into plate tectonics: how the surface of the earth has been changing over time and how it's moving at this very moment.

What kind of research do geologists do and what specializations exist within the field?

Research in this field varies tremendously because we study anything having to do with the earth. One researcher might study high-pressure minerals that form in meteorites.

Others might study the origins of life and what they find in the rock record. Another researcher might study the interior of the earth's core, what it's made of, and how seismic waves move through it. Someone else might do a laboratory study of groundwater, focusing on how it interacts with soils and rocks and what ions it has in it.

A geophysicist studies the physics of the earth—plate tectonics, the thermal field, or gravity—but a geohydrologist would study water on the earth. A cosmogeochemist might deal with meteorites and the formation of the elements. A seismologist might deal with the waves going through the earth and earthquakes. A volcanologist might study individual volcanoes. A geochemist might deal with the chemistry at the surface of the earth and deeper. A mineralologist might deal with specific mineral structures. A glacial geologist studies ash deposits to learn about the history of the earth, and a glaciologist studies the glaciers themselves.

What are some of the methods geologists use?

Seismologists use some detailed and sophisticated mathematical models to study how waves move through the earth. The geochemist who studies groundwater might use a chemical apparatus to tell about elements or impurities that might be in water. The mineralogist would study the detailed structure of the mineral. He or she might use all sorts of physical and chemical techniques to explore the structures. Scientists studying rocks might use many different techniques. They could go out into the field and collect them and then use all sorts of techniques to tell about their composition or their age. Radiometric dating could be done in the laboratory to tell how old the rocks are by the radioactive decay. So there are lots of ways of observing the environment and measuring its characteristics in order to understand what has happened over time.

What aspect of geophysics do you study?

When I arrived at graduate school, geophysicists were very excited about the theory of plate tectonics. The actual papers that put together this theory were very short but based on lots of data. Geophysical research relies on vast quantities of data. In fact, some of the earliest computers were developed specifically for geophysical research. Researchers travel the oceans and take magnetic and other readings of the ocean floor. I work with those data trying to explain how the current placement of plates has evolved from the last 100 million years of movement.

Scientists recognized that the shape and location of the continents and oceans that we see on the earth's surface did not always look the way they look now. Plate tectonic theory suggested that things had indeed moved. The outer portion of the earth, the lithosphere, which includes the earth's crust and extends inward for about 150 miles, is composed of a number of rigid plates or segments that constantly shift position. For instance, our North American continent moves along passively with the underlying North American plate. The Pacific plate, underneath the Pacific Ocean, is sliding along toward California. The pressures caused by this movement create the earthquakes we have witnessed recently in Santa Cruz and in Los Angeles. In other parts of the world the pressure of these moving plates causes volcanoes. Nothing is fixed; everything is moving. The ocean floor is being recycled.

I use data published by other people and develop mathematical models and theories to test hypotheses. We know the plates move. I am working to answer the question: What drives the plates? Or, in other words, how do they move? I think the plates drive themselves. The old dense plates are pulled along by the ocean floor. We don't need any other forces; the relative density of different plates moves them. The heavier plates are on the ocean floor and they sink. The continents, on the other hand are light and they don't sink. The heavier plates force themselves under the lighter plates causing a process called subduction.

Most recently, I have been looking at new data, not from Earth but from the planet Venus collected by the satellite Magellan. I've just received that data and am at the very beginnings of that project. We don't know much about the planet at all other than it has very intriguing features. Does it have hot spots like Hawaii? We don't know. The space satellite collected elevation data; later we'll get data on gravity. Lots of people are working on this project. The first thing I'll do is look at the pictures and see how things look to me. I'll ask myself, "Do I have any initial hypotheses?" Then I may begin a more detailed analysis of the computer data sets. I'll conduct this work as several projects with graduate students.

Have you gone on any interesting field trips?

Some geologists spend a great deal of time out in the field, actually observing aspects of the earth. I usually work with the data they bring back, but recently our whole geology department, graduate students and faculty, took a field trip north to Iceland. We started out in June but it was still so cold that there was plenty of snow left. We visited a volcano that had erupted a couple of years before; we saw the location of a phenomenon called "active separation," in which rocks and boulders are separating by about two centimeters every year. We saw the geyser after which all others are named. (Geyser is the Icelandic term for hot springs.) We also saw an energy plant that generates electricity from geothermal power, and a number of volcanic deposits that occurred when a volcano erupted underneath a glacier, leaving a strange sort of ash deposit. Most impressive was an old, active blue glacier that made loud rumbling noises.

How did you develop the ability to write technical papers?

Writing my first paper in graduate school turned out to be quite a challenge because up until that point I'd only read papers. Now I was trying to summarize one of my own research projects in a paper. I finally realized I was having so much difficulty because I hadn't separated the actual writing of the paper from the thinking part of producing the paper. The way I solved that problem was first to outline the paper completely. How was it going to go? What points should be raised in the introduction? How is each section going to be organized? What points are going to be in each section? I would try something and say, "Oh no, this isn't going to work." Only when I knew how every point was related to every other point, could I begin to draft the paper. By separating the job of thinking from the job of writing, things went a lot more smoothly. This kind of process worked for me and is especially important when writing scientific (or technical) papers because all the information has to fit into a highly structured format: introduction, method, results, and conclusion.

The first papers I wrote were the hardest. I wrote alone because they were graduate school projects. My advisor would revise them a bit and I would submit them for publication to the professional journals. It's a cruel world out there! When I submitted a paper to a professional journal they used the same professional standards for my first paper as for *everyone else's tenth or twentieth publication. I learned by trial and error, by constantly revising according to what the journal wanted so that the paper could be published. These days I write some papers alone but most are written with other colleagues and graduate students. Most of the writing I do is technical papers.*

Has the teaching of writing changed since you were an undergraduate?

Most definitely. Here at Northwestern University we have a program of Freshman Seminars in which the students take a seminar on a particular subject. I teach a course, "Death of the Dinosaurs," for instance. Or a student could take "Japanese Economics" or "Christ in Literature." In these courses the students do research and write papers. I don't remember having an experience like that when I was in college twenty years ago.

Do students do much work in the library for these courses?

Yes, absolutely—they spend a good deal of time in the library. In some cases they read the original sources. In others they read what people said about what other people said. For their final long research paper they explore a topic of their own choice; in that paper they will most likely be looking at some original research in the library.

During this process students come to see that so and so's ideas are this, whereas so and so over there said something else. They also learn that just because it's in a book doesn't make it true. It might simply be one scholar's idea. One very important purpose of the course is for students to learn to give proper credit to sources. I point out to students that sometimes the only difference between scholarship and academic dishonesty are those citations.

What do you tell students in that class about plagiarism?

I begin the class by telling the students two stories from my own family. My husband was reading a paper that a young relation had written for a high school class. The teacher wrote a note implying that this paper was unusually good, better than most of the papers in the class. As my husband read this paper on Lewis and Clark, the cadence, the content, the paragraphing told him that this was not the work of a high school student. He opened the only book in the house that had anything at all on Lewis and Clark in it, the Encyclopedia Britannica, and found that the whole paper had been copied paragraph by paragraph from the encyclopedia. So he said to his relative, "My goodness, you copied the whole thing!" The boy then turned to his mother and cried, "Mom, you copied the paper." The mother protested, "Well, I didn't have time to read the book either." The freshmen in my courses see that this is obviously plagiarism—blatant copying.

But the problem is not as simple as copying or not copying someone else's work. The other example concerns my sister. She once wrote a paper about eugenics (the science of improving the hereditary qualities of a race of people by controlling the mating process). My father seemed shocked that his daughter could really propose that two people should marry just to conceive children with a specific set of characteristics. It seemed like a horrifying idea. In fact, my sister was summarizing the ideas of someone else, but she had written the paper so that it sounded like her ideas. What she needed to do was give credit to those people who supported eugenics and separate out her own ideas on the topic. Learning to clarify your own ideas and to give credit to someone else's ideas is one of the goals in this freshman seminar.

Why is it important to study geology?

It is our environment; it is our resources; it is our energy. It deals with pollutants, mining, oil, energy, earthquakes, and volcanoes. Any undergraduate who hopes for a career that has an impact on the environment couldn't go wrong with a broad knowledge of geology.

WRITING AND LEARNING ACTIVITIES

1. **Journal Entry:** Look up a definition of geology in at least two of the reference sources listed in the appendix, Directions for Further Research. Consider the differences and similarities among the definitions. Report to the class on what you found.

2. **Question Posing:** Write three questions you would like to ask Professor Jurdy if you had the opportunity to speak with her.

3. **Peer Conversation:** With a partner, discuss your journal entries and questions for Professor Jurdy. Respond also to the following questions: Were you reminded by something she said of another experience you've had at home, school, or work? Have you had experiences like the fieldwork she discusses?

4. **Project:** Look up the description for the geology major in your college catalog. Respond to the following questions: How is the discipline of geology described? How does this description differ from Professor Jurdy's or from other definitions you've found? What are the required courses for the geology major? What are the possible areas of specialization? Next, interview someone who is a geology major. Why is he or she studying geology? What courses has this person taken? Is he or she specializing in any particular area? What does this person plan to do with a degree?

5. **Writing Activity:** Write a report about what it's like to major in geology and present it to the class.

6. **Developing Interests:** Go to your library's periodical section and browse through such magazines as *Earth, Discover, Nature, Geological Magazine,* or *Science News.* Look for articles on aspects of geology. Photocopy one that interests you, tell the class about it, and submit it in the class's "interest bank."

A GEOPHYSICIST READS ABOUT THE EFFECTS OF OIL EXPLORATION AND RELATED ACTIVITIES ON PERMAFROST TERRAIN IN NORTHERN ALASKA

Many of us have strong feelings and opinions about how best to sustain both our economy and our wilderness. Deciding what we should do often depends on conducting or evaluating research on this subject. Sometimes, though, research can be difficult to read because of the way the specialized knowledge of a discipline is communicated—a special type of writing called a research report. Professor Jurdy will be our guide to understanding how the "story" of the research—what actually happened—is written up in the genre of the formal research report.

Briefly look over the two research reports along with Professor Jurdy; see pp. 307–308.

AIRPHOTO ANALYSIS OF WINTER SEISMIC DISTURBANCE IN NORTHEASTERN ALASKA

MARTHA K. RAYNOLDS[1] AND NANCY A. FELIX[1]

■ ■ ■

ABSTRACT. Airphoto interpretation was used to quantify the extent of distur-bance caused by seismic exploration on the 60,000 [sic] ha coastal plain of the Arctic National Wildlife Refuge during the winters of 1984 and 1985. The rela-tionships of vegetation type, trail location and traffic pattern to the amount of disturbance were investigated. Approximately 20% of the seismic trails were photographed at 1:6000 scale, using color infrared film. Ground data collected at 194 sites were used to develop a photo interpretation key describing the photo signatures of seven vegetation types and four disturbance levels. Vegeta-tion types and disturbance levels were determined for 4914 circles of 3 mm di-ameter on the aerial photos (18 m ground distance). Fourteen percent of the points were interpreted as having no disturbance (level 0), 57% had level 1 dis-turbance (low), 27% had level 2 (medium) and 2% had level 3 (high). Wet or partially vegetated areas were the least susceptible to disturbance. Vegetation types with mounds, tussocks, hummocks or high-centered polygons and dryas terraces were more heavily disturbed. Camp move trails and overlapping seis-mic and camp move trails created in 1984 caused more disturbance than other trail types due to multiple passes of vehicles over narrow trails. U.S. Fish and Wildlife Service monitors were more successful at minimizing disturbance the second year by requesting that vehicle operators avoid multiple passes on the same trail, sensitive vegetation types, and areas of low snow cover.

Key words: airphoto analysis, winter seismic exploration, seismic trails, vege-tation disturbance, traffic patterns, Alaska, Arctic National Wildlife Refuge, arctic coastal plain

---

[1]Arctic National Wildlife Refuge, U.S. Fish and Wildlife Service, 101 12th Avenue, Box 20, Fair-banks, Alaska 99701, U.S.A. © The Arctic Institute of North America

(Received 25 November 1988; accepted in revised form 12 April 1989)

INTRODUCTION

The Arctic National Wildlife Refuge, located in the northeastern corner of Alaska, was established for the primary purpose of conserving wildlife habitat, including that of the Porcupine caribou herd, migratory birds, polar bears, grizzly bears, muskoxen, wolves and wolverines. The future of the arctic coastal plain of the Arctic Refuge is presently being debated by the U.S. Congress, with proposals ranging from designating the area as wilderness to leasing it for oil and gas development. The Alaska National Interest Lands Conservation Act of 1980 (U.S. Public Law 96–487) required baseline studies of the area's fish and wildlife resources (Garner and Reynolds, 1986) to provide Congress with information on the possible biological effects of oil and gas development. Limited geological studies, including seismic exploration, were authorized to assess the oil and gas potential of the arctic coastal plain.

Winter seismic exploration was conducted on the coastal plain of the Arctic Refuge in 1984 and 1985, as authorized by Congress. Approximately 2000 km of seismic lines, arranged in a 5 × 10 km grid pattern, were completed between January and May of both years. The drilled shothole technique, using buried dynamite to create seismic waves, was used in 1984. The vibrator technique, utilizing large trucks (vibrators) to provide an energy source, was used in 1985. Collection of data along each seismic line required multiple passes by tracked vehicles, including drills or vibrators, small personnel carriers (Bombardiers), geophone trucks and a recording vehicle. Ski-mounted camps pulled by D–7 Caterpillar tractors created a second series of trails, sometimes following separate routes through areas of deeper snow. U.S. Fish and Wildlife Service monitors accompanied the seismic crews to enforce regulations and permit stipulations developed to minimize impacts to wildlife and their habitats.

Vehicle trails from as long ago as the 1940s are still visible on the tundra west of the Arctic Refuge (Lawson et al., 1978; Walker et al., 1987). Vehicle disturbance decreases plant cover on trails and can cause short- and long-term species composition changes due to the relative resistance and resilience of different species (Bliss and Wein, 1972; Hernandez, 1973; Chapin and Chapin, 1980). Increased biomass or nutrient changes in some plant species have also been documented on vehicle trails (Challinor and Gersper, 1975; Chapin and Shaver, 1981). Subsidence of trails due to melting of permafrost occurs on more heavily disturbed trails (Haag and Bliss, 1974; Gersper and Challinor, 1975; Chapin and Shaver, 1981).

Many of the previous studies focused on trails that were severely disturbed due to summer travel over thawed ground or bulldozing of trails. Seismic trails created in the winter generally cause less damage but have been found to crush and break vegetation and disturb areas with higher microrelief, such as tussocks and hummocks, resulting in decreases in plant cover (Hernandez, 1973; Reynolds, 1982). The few studies that have focused on winter seismic trails were site-specific (Hernandez, 1973;

Reynolds, 1982; Densmore, 1985) and did not provide sufficient data to develop guidelines for seismic exploration on the coastal plain of the Arctic Refuge.

5   The use of airphoto interpretation allowed us to determine the effects of winter seismic exploration at a large number of sites throughout the Arctic Refuge coastal plain. Airphoto interpretation and other remote-sensing techniques have often been used in Alaska to investigate large areas that are otherwise inaccessible (Brooks and O'Brien, 1986). A number of researchers have interpreted tundra vegetation types from color infrared aerial photography (e.g., Swanson et al., 1983; Walker et al., 1983). Color infrared film was particularly appropriate for our purposes, as it discriminates between vegetative cover types and indicates the effects of stress or disturbance better than color or black-and-white film (Avery, 1977:11–12).

The objectives of this study were to determine the extent of disturbance caused by winter seismic exploration on the Arctic Refuge coastal plain and to investigate the major factors controlling the amount of disturbance occurring at a site, such as vegetation type and traffic pattern. The results provide information that will be valuable for monitoring or regulation of any future vehicle traffic in the arctic tundra.

STUDY AREA

The study area included over 600,000 ha of the coastal plain of the Arctic Refuge, between 142°W and 147°W and north of 69°34′N (Fig. 1). The area is in northeastern Alaska and is bordered by the Beaufort Sea on the north, the Brooks Range on the south, the Aichilik River on the east and the Canning River on the west. It is located in the Low Arctic Tundra (Murray, 1978) and is vegetated by low-growing plants, including dwarf shrubs, sedges, grasses, forbs, mosses and lichens. Shallow soils are underlain by permafrost, and the ground surface remains frozen from about

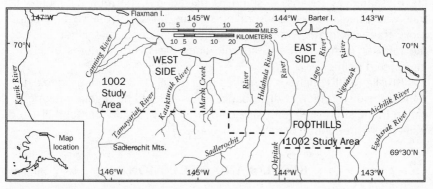

Figure 1.   Map of 60,000 [*sic*] ha study area on the coastal plain of the Arctic National Wildlife Refuge, Alaska. A 5 × 10 km grid of seismic lines (approx 2000 km total) was completed on this area during the winters of 1984 and 1985.

mid-September to mid-May. Snow is usually present by mid-September and remains until early June.

METHODS

Color infrared airphotos (1:6000 scale) were acquired in late July 1985 for approximately 20% of the 1984 and 1985 seismic trails. Line segments (16 km) were randomly selected within three strata: west of the Sadlerochit River, east of the Sadlerochit River and the eastern foothills (Fig. 1). Camp move routes associated with each line segment were also photographed.

A key describing the photo signatures of eight vegetation types (based on Walker et al., 1982) and four levels of surface disturbance was developed using ground data collected in 1984 and 1985 (Table 1). Ground data included point frame cover data by species for 24 sites (Felix and Raynolds, 1989a), line intercept cover data for 38 additional sites (Felix and Raynolds, 1989b) and qualitative vegetation community descriptions for another 132 sites. Three agreement tests were conducted as the key was being developed. Discrepancies between interpreters and between interpretations and ground data were examined, and the key was modified to maximize consistency and accuracy of interpretation.

10   Two interpreters used the key to analyze the airphotos, determining the dominant vegetation type and disturbance level in 49143 mm circles (18 m ground distance) located every 2.5 cm (150 m ground distance) along the trails. The traffic pattern was classified as seismic trail, camp move trail or overlapping trails, where both seismic lines and camp move trails overlapped. The year during which the disturbance occurred (1984 or 1985) was noted.

The proportion of trails in each disturbance level was calculated by tallying the interpreted points on each line segment, then determining the mean and standard deviation for all segments. The total distance of trail within each level of disturbance was estimated by multiplying the total kilometers of trail by the proportions in each disturbance level. Data are presented as means ± standard deviations. The total kilometers of trail was calculated as the sum of seismic lines (1910 km) and camp move trails (estimated by multiplying the total length of seismic lines by the ratio of camp moves to seismic lines based on numbers of photo-interpreted points).

Kruskal-Wallis analyses of ranked data (SPSS, 1986) were used to determine if the distribution of disturbance levels differed by vegetation type, location in the study area (east side compared to west side and foothills) and trail types (three traffic patterns, two years).

RESULTS AND DISCUSSION

Overall, 14% of the points examined were interpreted as having no disturbance (level 0), 57% as level 1 (low), 27% as level 2 (moderate), and 2% as level 3 (high) (Table 2). Extrapolating the proportions of disturbance levels

TABLE 1. Vegetation types and disturbance levels on winter seismic vehicle trails as recognized on color infrared aerial photographs (1:6000 scale), coastal plain, Arctic National Wildlife Refuge, Alaska

VEGETATION TYPE	DISTURBANCE LEVELS			
	0	1	2	3
Aquatic graminoid marsh— emergent communities on permanently flooded deep-water sites (more than 10 cm standing water). Ponds, lake margins and low-centered polygons with deep basins.	No impact.	Compression of standing dead emergent vegetation.		
Wet graminoid tundra— sedge- or grass-dominated communities on poorly drained, seasonally flooded sites. Low-centered polygons, strangmoor, tidal flats, lake and stream margins.	No impact.	Compression of standing dead to ground surface. May include slight scuffing of higher microsites.	Obvious compression of mosses and standing dead. Trail appears wetter than surrounding area. Common scuffing of micro-relief.	Obvious track depression. During wet years standing water apparent on trail that is not present in surrounding area.
Moist sedge-shrub tundra— sedge-willow meadows of upland slopes and flat or poorly developed high-centered polygons.	No impact. May have a few widely scattered scuffed microsites.	Compression of standing dead. Some scuffing of higher microsites or frost-boils if present. Less than 25% vegetation damage and broken shrubs.	Obvious compression of mosses and standing dead. Trail appears wetter than surrounding area. Scuffing of micro-relief common, small patches of soil may be exposed. Vegetation damage and broken shrubs 25–50%.	Obvious track depression, over 50% vegetation damage. Compression of mosses below water surface. During wet years standing water apparent in trail that is not present in adjacent area.

(continued)

TABLE 1 *(continued)*

VEGETATION TYPE	DISTURBANCE LEVELS			
	0	1	2	3
Moist graminoid/barren tundra complex—moist tundra communities with over 30% cover of hummocks or frost scars and less than 15% tussocks.	No impact to slight scuffing of micro-relief.	Compression of standing dead. May have up to 25% vegetation damage. Some scuffing of mound tops. 0–5% soil exposed.	Vegetation damage 25–50%. Exposed organic or mineral soil 5–15%. Scraping of mound tops common.	Nearly all mound tops scraped. Over 50% vegetation damage. Over 15% soil exposed.
Moist sedge tussock tundra—areas with more than 15% cover of cottongrass tussocks.	No impact to slight scuffing of tussocks and breakage of shrubs.	Scuffing of tussocks or mound tops. Vegetation damage 5–25%. Exposed organic or mineral soil less than 3%.	Mound top destruction of tussocks over 30%. Common mound top scuffing. Vegetation damage 25–50%. Exposed organic or mineral soil 3–15%.	Destruction of tussocks or mound tops nearly continuous. Ruts starting to form. Vegetation damage over 50%. Exposed soil over 15%.
Moist shrub tundra—shrub rich high-centered polygons and palsas.	No impact to occasional breakage of shrubs.	Vegetation damage 5–25%. Less than 25% shrub canopy decrease. Scuffing of tussocks and hummocks if present.	25–50% vegetation damage and shrub canopy decrease. Mound top destruction of some tussocks and hummocks.	Over 50% vegetation damage and over 50% broken shrubs.
Riparian shrubland—willow shrubland on gravel bars, floodplains and river banks.	No impact to slight breakage of shrubs.	Less than 50% shrubs broken, little impact to ground cover. Less than 25% decrease in total plant cover.	50–80% shrubs broken, sometimes to ground level. Some disturbance to ground cover. Total plant cover decrease 25–50%.	Over 80% removal of shrub canopy. Substantial disturbance to ground cover, over 50% decrease in total plant cover.
Dryas terrace—dry alkaline ridges, river terraces and bluffs.	No impact to few widely scattered scuffed microsites.	Less than 30% vegetation killed. Less than 5% soil exposed.	30–60% vegetation killed. Little disruption of vegetative mat. 5–15% soil exposed.	Over 60% vegetation killed, vegetative mat mostly disrupted. Over 15% soil exposed or over 50% increase in bare ground.

TABLE 2.   Percentage of disturbance levels within vegetation types from photo interpretation of vehicle trails resulting from winter seismic exploration on the coastal plain, Arctic National Wildlife Refuge, Alaska, 1985

| | DISTURBANCE LEVEL | | | | NUMBER OF | KRUSKAL-WALLIS |
VEGETATION TYPE	0	1	2	3	POINTS INTERPRETED	CATEGORY[a]
Water[b]	100				161	
Aquatic graminoid marsh[b]	91	9			11	
Wet graminoid tundra[c]	6	93		1	769	
Moist sedge-shrub tundra	10	62	26	2	1751	B
Moist graminoid/barren tundra complex	5	52	40	3	405	C
Moist sedge tussock tundra	1	52	44	3	1165	D
Moist shrub tundra	4	44	51	1	305	E
Riparian shrubland	41	37	22	1	74	A
Dryas terrace	9	27	36	27	11	E
Partially vegetated areas[b]	100				262	
Total					4914	
Percentage of all points	14	57	27[d]	2		

[a]Vegetation types with the same letter were not significantly different, $p < 0.05$.

[b]There was no level 1, 2 or 3 in water and partially vegetated areas and no level 2 or 3 in aquatic graminoid marsh.

[c]Level 2 was combined with level 1 in wet graminoid tundra.

[d]The overall percentage of level 2 disturbance may be underestimated, because levels 1 and 2 were combined for wet graminoid tundra.

in the sample to the total distance of seismic lines and camp move trails resulted in an estimate of 540 ± 424 km with no visible disturbance, 2050 ± 729 km with level 1 disturbance, 960 ± 605 km with level 2 disturbance, and 60 ± 172 km of trail with level 3 disturbance. This estimate is conservative because it includes seismic lines and the camp moves adjacent to seismic lines. It does not include the moves from one line to the next or other trails associated with exploration activities, such as supply routes and trails between camps and seismic lines, which were observed to have some of the highest levels of disturbance.

The distribution of disturbance levels varied by vegetation type (Table 2). Moist shrub tundra and dryas terrace had the highest levels of disturbance, followed by moist sedge tussock tundra, then moist graminoid/barren tundra complex (Kruskal-Wallis, $p < 0.05$). Shrub tundra, tussock tundra and barren complex have high micro-relief, such as hummocks, tussocks and high-centered polygons, which were easily scraped or crushed by vehicles. Wind redistribution of snow on the arctic coastal plain leaves these features with little protective snow cover (Felix et al., 1987). Other studies have also noted that tussocks and shrubs have low resistance to winter disturbance (Hernandez, 1973; Lawson et al., 1978; Reynolds, 1982). Dryas terraces have thin vegetative mats, consisting mostly of dwarf shrubs and mosses, which were easily disrupted and had little snow cover (Felix and Reynolds, 1989a). Barrett and Schulten (1975) also found *Dryas* to be especially sensitive to disturbance.

15   Moist sedge-shrub tundra had the next highest level of disturbance, which was close to the distribution of disturbance levels for all points. Riparian shrubland had the least amount of disturbance among those vegetation types with disturbance in all four levels (Kruskal-Wallis, $p < 0.05$). The high proportion of level 0 disturbance in riparian shrubland reflects the fact that vehicles were routed around this vegetation type unless deeper than average snow cover was present.

Most of the points in wet graminoid tundra were identified as level 1 disturbance (93%). Level 2 disturbance was not interpreted for this vegetation type, because it could not be differentiated on the photos. In subsequent field checking, 11% of the points in wet graminoid tundra were found to be level 2 on the ground (Raynolds and Felix, 1988). Based on this, wet graminoid tundra had less moderate and high level disturbance (levels 2 and 3) than the vegetation types discussed above. Only 1 out of 11 points in aquatic graminoid tundra had any visible disturbance (level 1). Other studies have also found that wet vegetation types had the highest resistance to disturbance by winter traffic (Hernandez, 1973; Lawson et al., 1978; Reynolds, 1982). Nine percent of all points were located in water or partially vegetated areas and therefore had no disturbance (level 0).

The western half of the coastal plain (west of the Sadlerochit River) had a significantly higher level of disturbance (Kruskal-Wallis, $p < 0.05$) than the east side and foothill areas (Table 3). Vegetation types and snow depths also differed between these areas. The trails on the west side crossed 8% more tussock tundra (an easily disturbed vegetation type) and 16% less wet graminoid tundra (a less sensitive vegetation type). Snow depth in 1985 on the west side was also lower (25 cm average) than the east side (32 cm) (Felix et al., 1987).

Camp moves in 1984 and overlapping camp moves and seismic lines in both years had significantly higher disturbance levels (Kruskal-Wallis, $p < 0.05$) than all other trail types (Table 4). The highest level of disturbance (level 3) was only found on trails where multiple passes of vehicles occurred over a narrow area.

Camp moves in 1984 caused more disturbance than 1984 seismic trails (Kruskal-Wallis, $p < 0.05$). Reynolds (1982), in a study of a western portion of the Alaskan arctic coastal plain, also found that camp move vehicles did more damage than seismic vehicles. Camp move vehicles were heavier than seismic vehicles.

20   Camp moves in 1985 resulted in significantly less disturbance than 1984 camp moves (Kruskal-Wallis, $p < 0.05$). Based on experience from the 1984 program, U.S. Fish and Wildlife Service monitors required that vehicles avoid narrow trails. As a result, the 1985 trails had almost no level 3 disturbance. Due to routing of camp moves through drainages with drifted snow, 1985 camp move trails also had more level 0 disturbance than other trail types. Camp moves were also routed to avoid sensitive vegetation types, and four times as much partially vegetated area was crossed by 1985

TABLE 3.   Percentage of disturbance levels for photo interpretation of winter seismic trails from two areas of the coastal plain, Arctic National Wildlife Refuge, Alaska, 1985

LOCATION	DISTURBANCE LEVEL				NUMBER OF POINTS INTERPRETED
	0	1	2	3	
East side and foothills	12	68	19	0	2945
West side	19	39	38	4	1969

Distribution of disturbance levels differs significantly (Kruskal-Wallis, $p < 0.05$).

TABLE 4.   Percentage of disturbance levels within trail types from photo interpretation of winter seismic trails on the coastal plain, Arctic National Wildlife Refuge, Alaska, 1985

TRAIL TYPE	DISTURBANCE LEVEL				NUMBER OF POINTS INTERPRETED	KRUSKAL-WALLIS[a]
	0	1	2	3		
1984 seismic	14	72	14	0[b]	957	B
1984 camp	17	48	30	5	1041	C
1984 overlapping	9	39	44	8	386	C
1985 seismic	5	70	25	0[b]	1265	B
1985 camp	28	43	29	0[b]	1217	A
1985 overlapping	0	60	40	0	48	C

[a]Trail types with the same letter were not significantly different, $p < 0.05$.
[b]These categories had 1–3 observations, much less than 1%.

camp moves than by the 1984 camp moves. Camp moves in 1984 and 1985 had similar proportions of level 1 and 2 disturbance.

Disturbance on the 1984 seismic lines was not significantly different from that on the 1985 seismic lines (Kruskal-Wallis, $p < 0.05$). However, the 1985 seismic lines did have 11% more level 2 disturbance and 9% less level 0 disturbance than the 1984 lines. The vibrator units used in 1985 were heavier (4.5 psi) and their tracks dug more deeply into the vegetative mat than the drills (2.8 psi) used in 1984. Level 3 disturbance rarely occurred on either 1984 or 1985 seismic lines.

CONCLUSION

Winter seismic trails through vegetation types with high micro-relief (tussock tundra, shrub tundra and barren complex) and dryas terraces had the highest levels of disturbance. Wet vegetation types (aquatic graminoid and wet graminoid) and partially vegetated areas were the most resistant to disturbance. Vehicle trails on the east side of the coastal plain had a lower level of disturbance than trails on the west side due to higher snow cover and a higher proportion of wet vegetation types.

Less disturbance occurred in 1985 than in 1984. This was partly due to greater snow depths in 1985. Another major difference between the two years was that in 1985 additional stipulations designed to minimize disturbance were enforced by the U.S. Fish and Wildlife Service. Disturbance was reduced on camp move trails by requesting that vehicle operators avoid overlapping or narrow trails, sensitive vegetation types and areas of low snow cover. Seismic lines were less affected by the stipulations, since their straight line routes were determined by seismic data-gathering parameters and were not often changed.

Airphoto analysis proved a useful tool for evaluating the extent of disturbance over a large area. Subsequent ground checks revealed that the proportions of points in each vegetation type and disturbance level were similar to the proportions determined by photo interpretation, although the interpretation of any particular point was not always correct (75% accuracy for vegetation types, 66% accuracy for disturbance levels) (Raynolds and Felix, 1988). Therefore, photo-interpreted disturbance levels were representative of the actual disturbance on the ground and provided a good relative measure in different vegetation types, areas and traffic patterns.

25   This study provides baseline data for determining the long-term effects of winter seismic exploration. Aerial photography of the same areas was taken in 1988, and photo interpretation is presently in progress using a detailed key based on current ground data. The results presented in this paper and the results of future studies can be used to develop regulations to minimize disturbance due to winter vehicle traffic on tundra vegetation.

ACKNOWLEDGEMENTS

We thank M. Torre Jorgenson and Robert Lipkin, who did the photo interpretation. The U.S. Fish and Wildlife Service provided funding for this study.

REFERENCES

Avery, T. E. 1977. Interpretation of Aerial Photographs. Minneapolis: Burgess Publishing Co. 392 p.

Barrett, P., and Schulten, R. 1975. Disturbance and the successional response of the arctic plants on polar desert habitats. Arctic 28(1):70–73.

Bliss, L. C., and Wein, R. W. 1972. Plant community responses to disturbance in the western Canadian Arctic. Canadian Journal of Botany 50:1097–1109.

Brooks, P. D., and O'Brien, T. J. 1986. The evolving Alaska mapping program. Photogrammetric Engineering and Remote Sensing 52(6):769–777.

Challinor, J. L., and Gersper, P. L. 1975. Vehicle perturbation effects upon a tundra soil-plant system: II. Effects on the chemical regime. Soil Science Society of America Proceedings 39:689–695.

Chapin, F. S., and Chapin, M. C. 1980. Revegetation of an arctic disturbed site by native tundra species. Journal of Applied Ecology 17:449–456.

Chapin, F. S., and Shaver, G. R. 1981. Changes in soil properties and vegetation following disturbance of Alaskan arctic tundra. Journal of Applied Ecology 18:605–617.

Densmore, R. 1985. Effects of dynamite and vibrator seismic exploration on visual quality, soils and vegetation of the Alaskan North Slope. Final report prepared for Geophysical Services, Inc., Anchorage, Alaska. 82 p.

Felix, N. A., and Raynolds, M. K. 1989a. The effects of winter seismic exploration on tundra vegetation in northeastern Alaska. Arctic and Alpine Research 21(2): 188–202.

_____. 1989b. The role of snow cover in limiting surface disturbance caused by winter seismic exploration. Arctic 42(1):62–68.

Felix, N. A., Jorgensen, M. T., Raynolds, M. K., Lipkin, R., Blank, D. L., and Lance, B. K. 1987. Snow distribution on the arctic coastal plain and its relationship to disturbance caused by winter seismic exploration, Arctic National Wildlife Refuge, Alaska, 1985. In: Garner, G. W., and Reynolds, P. E., eds. 1985 Update Report Baseline Study of the Fish, Wildlife and their Habitats. Anchorage: U.S. Fish and Wildlife Service. 1045–1080.

Garner, G. W., and Reynolds, P. E., eds. 1986. Final Report Baseline Study of the Fish, Wildlife and their Habitats. Anchorage: U.S. Fish and Wildlife Service. 695 p.

Gersper, P. L., and Challinor, J. L. 1975. Vehicle perturbation effects upon a tundra soil-plant system: I. Effects on morphological and physical environmental properties of soil. Soil Science Society of America Proceedings 39:737–744.

Haag, R. W., and Bliss, L. C. 1974. Energy budget changes following surface disturbance to upland tundra. Journal of Applied Ecology 11:355–374.

Hernandez, H. 1973. Natural plant recolonization of surficial disturbances, Tuktoyaktuk Peninsula Region, Northwest Territories. Canadian Journal of Botany 51:2177–2196.

Lawson, D. E., Brown, J., Everett, K. R., Johnson, A. W., Komarkova, V., Murray, B. M., Murray, D. F., and Webber, P. J. 1978. Tundra disturbances and recovery following the 1949 exploratory drilling, Fish Creek, northern Alaska. CRREL Report 82–27. Hanover, New Hampshire: Cold Regions Research and Engineering Laboratory. 59 p.

Murray, D. F. 1978. Vegetation, floristics, and phytogeography of northern Alaska. In: Tieszen, L. L., ed. Vegetation and Production Ecology of an Alaskan Arctic Tundra. New York: Springer-Verlag. 19–36.

Raynolds, M. K., and Felix, N. A. 1988. Accuracy assessment of airphoto interpretation of vegetation types and disturbance levels on winter seismic trails, Arctic National Wildlife Refuge, Alaska. ANWR Progress Report Number FY 86–2. Fairbanks: U.S. Fish and Wildlife Service. 17 p.

Reynolds, P. C. 1982. Some effects of oil and gas exploration activities on tundra vegetation in northern Alaska. In: Rand, P. J., ed. Land and Water Issues Related to Energy Development. Ann Arbor: Ann Arbor Science. 403–417.

SPSS INC. 1986. SPSSx User's Guide. New York: McGraw-Hill Book Company. 988 p.

Swanson, J. D., Kinney, M. P., and Scorup, P. C. 1983. Reindeer range vegetation inventory procedures. Acta Zoologica Fennica 175:39–41.

Walker, D. A., Everett, K. R., Acevedo, W., Gaydos, L., Brown, J., and Webber, P. J. 1982. Landsat-assisted environmental mapping in the Arctic National Wildlife Refuge, Alaska. CRREL Report 82–27. Hanover, New Hampshire: Cold Regions Research and Engineering Laboratory. 59 p.

Walker, D. A., Everett, K. R., and Webber, P. J. 1983. Chap. 2. Geobotany. In: Troy, D. M., ed. Prudhoe Bay Unit—Eileen West End Environmental Studies Program, Summer 1982. Prepared by LGL Alaska Research Associates, Inc., Fairbanks, Alaska, for Sohio Alaska Petroleum Company, Anchorage, Alaska. Available at

Alaska Resources Library, 222 W. 7th Avenue #36, Anchorage, Alaska 99513–7589, U.S.A.

Walker, D. A., Cate, D., Brown, J., and Racine, C. 1987. Disturbance and Recovery of Arctic Alaskan Tundra Terrain: A Review of Recent Investigations. CRREL Report 87–11. Hanover, New Hampshire: Cold Regions Research and Engineering Laboratory. 63 p.

LONG-TERM EFFECTS OF OFF-ROAD VEHICLE TRAFFIC ON TUNDRA TERRAIN

G. ABELE,* J. BROWN* AND M. C. BREWER†

■ ■ ■

Summary—Traffic tests were conducted at two sites in northern Alaska with an air cushion vehicle, two light tracked vehicles, and three types of wheeled Rolligon vehicles. The traffic impact (surface depression, effect on thaw depth, damage to vegetation, traffic signature visibility) was monitored for periods of up to 10 years. Data show the immediate and long-term effects from the various types of vehicles for up to 50 traffic passes and the rates of recovery of the active layer. The air cushion vehicle produced the least impact. Multiple passes with the Rolligons caused longer-lasting damage than the light tracked vehicles because of their higher ground contact pressure and wider area of disturbance. Recovery occurs even if the initial depression of the tundra surface by a track or a wheel is quite deep (15 cm), as long as the organic mat is not sheared or destroyed.

INTRODUCTION

The recent increase in petroleum exploration activities on the Arctic Coastal Plain of Alaska has resulted in a corresponding increase in surface transportation requirements. Not all traffic can be confined to the winter months when the ecological impact of vehicle operations is minimal [1]. Traffic across tundra during summer can produce effects that vary significantly in degree of severity, depending on the vehicle, traffic and terrain characteristics.

In 1971, a series of traffic tests was conducted near Barrow, Alaska, using an SK–5 air cushion vehicle (ACV) and a light tracked vehicle, an M–29 Weasel. The principal objective of the tests was to investigate the environmental impact of ACV operations on tundra and to compare the results with the impact caused by a well-known, standard tracked vehicle.

*U.S. Army Cold Regions Research and Engineering Laboratory, Hanover, NH 03755, U.S.A.

†U.S. Geological Survey, Anchorage, Alaska, U.S.A.

In 1974, additional traffic tests were conducted with a small Rolligon-type vehicle in the ACV test area to compare the impact of a wheeled vehicle with that of the ACV and of the tracked Weasel.

In 1976, traffic tests were conducted at Lonely, Alaska, 110 km southeast of Barrow, using two types of Rolligon vehicles and a small Nodwell tracked vehicle.

5   The main objectives of the study were to investigate the effects of different vehicle operations and traffic on tundra, specifically, the extent of surface depression, the degree of short-term and long-term damage to the vegetation, the subsequent effect on the soil thermal regime, and to determine the rate of recovery.

The impact of the various types of traffic on tundra was measured and observed, in most cases annually, to document the rate of recovery of the tundra active layer. The results of the study on the impact of ACV and Weasel traffic for the first 4 years after traffic have been reported previously [2, 3, 4]. The results of the Rolligon tests at Barrow (initial and after 1, 2 and 3 years) and those of the Rolligon and Nodwell tests at Lonely (initial and after 1 year) have also been reported [5], and experiences with other off-road vehicles have been discussed [6, 7, 8, 9, 10].

This paper describes the measurements and observations made through 1981 and, therefore, the data represent the impact conditions of the ACV and Weasel traffic 10 years after traffic, those of the Rolligon at Barrow 7 years after traffic, and those of the Rolligon and Nodwell traffic at Lonely 5 years after traffic.

DESCRIPTION OF STUDY

Test Sites

The site at Barrow, Alaska, was on a level, drained lake bottom with a relatively uniform and homogeneous saturated active layer and vegetation: the predominant vegetation was *Carex aquatilis* and *Eriophorum angustifolium* with a small percent of broadleaf species and a moss mat. The saturated moss mat had a soil moisture content of 1200%. The average depth of thaw was 20 cm.

The immediate test site at Lonely was a nearly homogeneous mesic coastal tundra, poorly drained, with weakly developed polygonal ground patterns. The organic layer was approximately 12 cm thick, with a mean soil moisture content of approximately 400% and thaw depths generally in the 20–30 cm range. The vegetation was similar to that occurring at Barrow.

Test Vehicles

10 The vehicles used are shown in Figs. 1–6, and their main characteristics are listed in Table 1. The wheeled and tracked vehicles carried no appreciable load (essentially empty).

Figure 1. Air Cushion Vehicle (Bell SK–5).

Figure 2. Weasel (M–29).

Figure 3.   Small Rolligon.

Figure 4.   CATCO Rolligon.

Figure 5.   Houston Rolligon.

Figure 6.   Nodwell (FN–10).

TABLE 1.   Test Vehicles

Vehicle	Weight (kg)	Ground pressure (kg cm² (psi))	Remarks
Air cushion (Bell SK–5)	6800	0.014 (0.2) (cushion pressure)	Air gap: 2 cm below front skirt, no gap between rear skirt
Weasel (M–29)	1200	0.07 (1.0)	Tracked
Rolligon (small)	4000	0.25 (3.5)	4 wheels, ribbed tires
Rolligon (CATCO)	11,700	0.35 (5.0)	8 wheels, smooth tires
Rolligon (Houston)	6800	0.25 (3.5)	6 wheels, ribbed tires
Nodwell (FN–10)	2250	0.1 (1.4)	Tracked

For wheeled vehicles, the mean ground contact pressure is approximately the same as the tire inflation pressure.

Test Layout

At Barrow, four traffic test lanes, approximately 30 m apart, were established for 1, 5, 25, and 50 passes with the ACV at a travel speed of 50–65 km/h. A corresponding number of Weasel passes were made adjacent to each ACV test lane. The Rolligon traffic tests, conducted 3 years later between the existing traffic lanes, included 1, 5, and 15 traffic passes.

A number of other ACV traffic tests (slow speed, hovering, travel over polygons, exit from a water body onto tundra) were also conducted nearby and at other locations to observe the impact of ACV operations on various terrain conditions [4]. No comparable tests were conducted with wheeled or tracked vehicles.

At Lonely, the test layout consisted of three traffic loops, one for each of three traffic conditions: 1, 5, and 10 passes. Each loop consisted of six parallel lanes, two for each test vehicle (CATCO and Houston Rolligons and the tracked Nodwell), for a total of 18 parallel test lanes, each approximately 100 m long.

The traffic tests with the various vehicles are summarized in Table 2.

Data Obtained

15   Immediately after the traffic tests, color photographs were taken of each test lane from the ground. Aerial photographs were also taken of each test area. Photographic documentation of all test lanes was continued annually to record the visual appearance of the traffic impact with time.

TABLE 2.   Summary of Tests and Observation Times

Year	Location	Vehicle	Traffic passes	Observations: years after traffic
1971	Barrow	ACV	1,5,25,50	0,1,2,3,4,5,6,10
		Weasel	1,5,25,50	0,1,2,3,4,5,6,10
1974	Barrow	Rolligon	1,5,15	0,1,2,3,7
1976	Lonely	CATCO	1,5,10	0,1,3,5
		Houston	1,5,10	0,1,3,5
		Nodwell	1,5,10	0,1,3,5

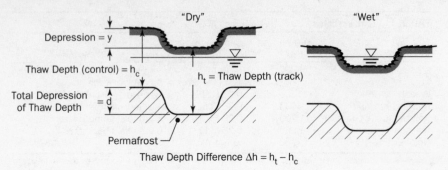

Figure 7. Nomenclature.

After each traffic test, the terrain surface depression in the vehicle tracks was measured. The specific locations of the measurements were marked to ensure that subsequent measurements were obtained at the same place.

Thaw depth measurements were started 1 year after the traffic tests and continued nearly annually (Table 2). The depth of thaw was measured at several marked locations in the vehicle tracks in each test lane and in the adjacent undisturbed area to determine the difference in the thaw depth between the trafficked and the undisturbed terrain (Fig. 7).

To minimize the effect of seasonal variations (the particular time of year) on the terrain conditions and the appearance of the traffic signatures, all measurements and observations were done at the same time each year, in this case the first week of August.

At the Lonely test site, soil moisture content, bulk dry density, and peat thickness data were obtained at various locations in the vehicle tracked and in the undisturbed areas after the traffic tests. One year later, the condition of the vegetation in each test lane was evaluated by using an impact rating scheme [10] to compare the damage caused by each vehicle/traffic condition in terms of vegetation compression, displacement, breakage, and deposition [5].

DISCUSSION OF RESULTS

Terrain Surface Depression

20 The ACV has no mechanical contact with the terrain surface, except for some skirt drag, and therefore produced no surface depression.

The depressed surface in the Weasel tracks has shown a remarkable ability to rebound to its normal level (Fig. 8). The original depression after 50 Weasel passes was 15 cm; after 5 years the depression surface had rebounded to within 1 cm of the adjacent undisturbed surface. After 10 years, there was no measurable depression. The 8-cm-deep depression caused by five Weasel passes had returned to its original level after 4 years.

Surface depression caused by the small four-wheel Rolligon also showed a strong tendency to rebound, but at a slower rate than that caused

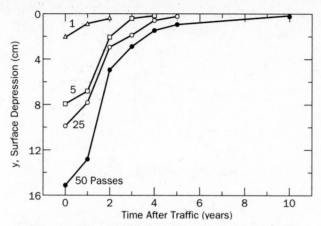

Figure 8. Surface depression vs time, Weasel traffic, Barrow.

by the tracked Weasel (Fig. 9). An initial depression of 10 cm, caused by 15 passes with the Rolligon, had returned to within 2–3 cm of its original level after 7 years. A 4-cm depression (five Rolligon passes) had rebounded completely after 7 years.

Rebound of the surface depression caused by 10 passes with the CATCO and Houston Rolligons and the tracked Nodwell in the Lonely tests is shown in Fig. 10. Here the rates of rebound for all three vehicles are noticeably slower than those observed in the tests at Barrow.

The difference between the surface depression rebound rates at Barrow and those at Lonely are most likely due to the differences in composition and characteristics of the active layers in these two locations.

From the initial Barrow test data, which indicated much higher rebound rates for the Weasel track depressions than those of the Rolligon wheel depressions (Figs. 8 and 9), it was speculated that a narrower depression rebounded more quickly than a wide one (the Rolligon wheel track being

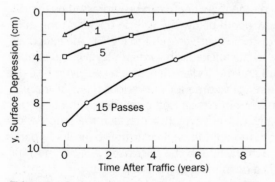

Figure 9. Surface depression vs time, small Rolligon traffic, Barrow.

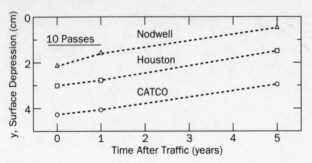

Figure 10. Surface depression vs time, large Rolligon and Nodwell traffic, Lonely.

approximately four times wider than that of the Weasel) because of the smaller area (or volume) per unit length of track depressed by the vehicle. Since the Weasel and Rolligon tests at Barrow were conducted in the same area (the Rolligon traffic lanes are between the Weasel traffic lanes), the active layer characteristics were generally the same. The thaw depth and surface water level conditions during both tests were approximately the same.

It is not clear if the cause of a surface depression has any effect on the subsequent rate of surface rebound. Nor has the mechanism that causes a depressed tundra surface to rebound been clearly identified. From the available data, a difference can be observed in the rebound rates of two depressions at the same site, equal in depth (10 cm) but produced by two different types of traffic: 25 passes with the Weasel and 15 passes with the Rolligon (refer to Figs. 8 and 9). The 10-cm depression in the Weasel track rebounded to its original level in 5 years. The 10-cm depression in the Rolligon track rebounded only approximately 6 cm during the first 5 years.

In the tests at Lonely, the rate of surface depression rebound during the first 5 years was approximately the same for the tracked Nodwell and the two wheeled Rolligon vehicles (Fig. 10).

Effect on Thaw Depth

The effect of vehicular traffic on the thaw depth can be expressed by the difference (Δh) between the thaw depth below the vehicle track and the thaw depth below the adjacent undisturbed surface (refer to Fig. 7). The total thaw depth depression (d) relative to the adjacent thaw depth level is the sum of the thaw depth difference (Δh) and the surface depression (y). Figures 11–14 illustrate the thaw depth difference vs time for the various types of traffic.

The impact on the thermal regime is caused primarily by the decrease in the insulating characteristics of the vegetative mat due to compression and damage to the vegetation. In addition, vehicular traffic results in darkening of the terrain surface, which, due to the decreased albedo and thus more heat absorption, causes a deepening of the active layer.

In the test area at Lonely, a rise in the surface water level was observed during the visits to the site 3 and again 5 years after the traffic tests. Some

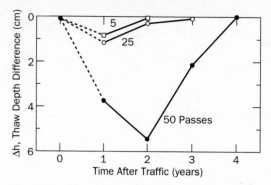

Figure 11. Thaw depth difference vs time, ACV traffic, Barrow.

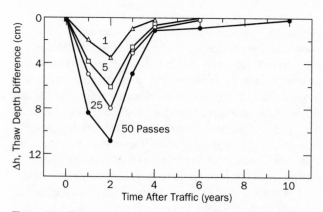

Figure 12. Thaw depth difference vs time, Weasel traffic, Barrow.

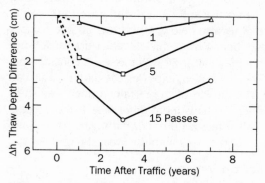

Figure 13. Thaw depth difference vs time, small Rolligon traffic, Barrow.

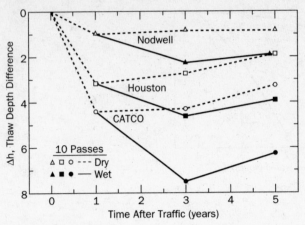

Figure 14. Thaw depth difference vs time, large Rolligon and Nodwell traffic, Lonely.

of the measurement locations, selected and marked 1 year after the tests, were in areas where the water level was now above the depressed surface in the vehicle tracks. Therefore, the thaw depth measurements obtained at these locations were designated as representing a 'wet' condition, and those obtained at locations where the water level was below the surface of the depressed vehicle track as representing a 'dry' condition (refer to Fig. 7). Data from both types of conditions are shown in Fig. 14. It is evident that the decrease in the active layer thickness in the 'dry' areas occurred sooner than that in the 'wet' areas. The observation that standing water in a vehicle track inhibits the recovery process is neither surprising nor new.

Although a rise in the surface water level during some years was also observed at the Barrow test area, the selected measurement locations happened to be where the water level remained below the depressed vehicle track surface. (The surface depression measurements, discussed previously, were made only in the 'dry' locations.)

An air-cushion vehicle does not cause a terrain surface depression; however, repeated ACV traffic can cause sufficient disturbance to the vegetation cover to affect the thermal regime below. At Barrow, surface contact with the rubber wearing strakes below the vehicle's rear skirt caused noticeable abrading of the terrain surface after 50 ACV passes. A considerable amount of the live vegetation was destroyed, exposing the dark organic soil below the vegetation canopy. The albedo of the terrain surface was sufficiently decreased to cause a 4–6 cm thaw-depth difference 1 and 2 years following the traffic (Fig. 11). This effect on the thermal regime was, however, significantly less than that of 50 passes with the Weasel (Fig. 12).

Impact on Vegetation

Because of the nature of its suspension system (a cushion of air), the ACV traffic produced the least impact on vegetation. Ordinarily, an ACV's effect on a tundra surface is limited to the removal of some or most of the loose, dead vegetation, depending on the number of traffic passes or the duration of hovering. In this case, due to the noticeable rear skirt drag, a more significant impact resulted: specifically, the matting of vegetation into the organic mat, removal of mosses, and general abrasion of the vegetative cover. The effect increased with the number of vehicle passes and was more pronounced on wet than on dry tundra.

The wheeled and tracked vehicles, because of their mechanical contact with the terrain surface, produced more significant impact than the ACV. The most obvious effect was compression of the vegetation carpet and flattening of the microrelief. The damage increased with the number of vehicle passes and with the increase in the tire or track's ground contact pressure.

35   Where vegetation was removed or otherwise disturbed by traffic, significant regrowth of some vascular species was evident during following seasons. In some cases, surface disturbances (scraping and depression of live and standing dead vegetation into the organic mat) actually stimulated growth of some types of vascular plants, aided by the increased decomposition of dead vegetation. The relative prominence of the green vegetation and the absence of standing dead vegetation resulted in the 'green belt' effect. Regrowth of mosses and lichens was considerably slower. A minimum of 3 years was required before any growth of new mosses or lichens could be noticed.

The extent of the surface depression after traffic is, for all practical purposes, an indicator of the degree of the initial impact on the vegetation. The damage to vegetation in a deep rut is ordinarily more serious than the damage where the tundra surface is only slightly depressed. However, it was observed that the regrowth of vascular species in a deep depression is almost as rapid as in a relatively shallow depression.

Visibility of Traffic Signatures

The most apparent effect of any vehicular traffic on tundra is the 'signature' left by the vehicle. The signature is the result of any disturbance to the natural condition of the terrain or vegetation; it can be caused by bending or removal of vegetation, matting of the vegetation into the organic layer, depression of the organic layer, and so forth. The type of disturbance and the characteristics of the terrain and vegetation influence the visual appearance of the signature and its change with time or rate of recovery. The presence of a traffic signature does not necessarily imply a serious ecological impact, but it may be objectionable for aesthetic reasons.

The visual appearance of the ACV traffic signatures was most pronounced immediately after the traffic. A decrease in the visible impact began during the next growing season and continued at a gradual rate during the following years. After 4 years, the 25- and 50-pass lanes were barely perceptible from the air, and after a few more years they were no longer visible at all.

The tracked and wheeled vehicle traffic signatures, especially those of multiple passes, were more visible after 1 year than immediately after traffic. The increased visibility of the traffic signatures can be attributed primarily to the 'green belt' effect. In the case of light traffic, such as some of the 1-pass lanes, or where very little disturbance of the vegetation had occurred, the signature visibility after 1 year was less than that immediately after the traffic.

40   It was also observed that the visibility of traffic signatures depends on the direction of travel relative to the viewer. Because the vegetation is bent in the direction of travel, exposing the lighter underside of the plants, when viewed in the direction of vehicle travel the traffic signatures appear lighter than the same signatures viewed against the direction of travel.

A numerical scheme, based on the relative visibility of the traffic signatures, has been used to describe the aesthetic impact for the first few years after traffic [5]. Since the traffic signature visibility can be realistically assessed only from color photographs, no illustrations of the traffic test lanes have been included here.

CONCLUSIONS

Recovery has occurred in all test lanes. Rebound of the depressed tundra surface is particularly noticeable. The deepest depression, 15 cm caused by 50 traffic passes with the Weasel, has rebounded to its original level after 10 years. The surface depressions caused by the large Rolligons are rebounding at a rate of approx. 0.25 cm/year.

The recovery of the soil thermal regime, or decrease in thaw depth below vehicle tracks, begins 2 or 3 years after the initial traffic impact. The most severe impact on the thermal regime was caused by 50 passes with the Weasel: the mean increase in thaw depth was 11 cm, resulting in a maximum depression of the permafrost table of over 20 cm. After 10 years, the depth of thaw was at the same level as that of the adjacent undisturbed terrain. Standing water in the vehicle tracks, which occurred in some locations in the Rolligon test lanes, inhibits the recovery of the thermal regime.

Significant regrowth of some vascular species is evident where the original vegetation was removed or depressed into the organic mat by traffic, resulting in the 'green belt' effect.

45   The aesthetic impact (traffic signature visibility) appears to be a more prominent and longer-lasting consequence than the surface depression or thermal impact (increase in thaw depth). That is, while a traffic signature may be visible because of the relative predominance of new green vegetation, it may not necessarily indicate a serious ecological impact.

In general, the ACV produced the least impact on the tundra surface. All three Rolligons caused longer-lasting damage than the light tracked vehicles, because of their higher tire-ground contact pressures and the width of the disturbed area.

From observations during the past 10 years of various vehicle tracks or traffic signatures on tundra near Barrow and Lonely, there appears to be sufficient evidence to form the following conclusion: the tundra vegetative mat will usually recover to nearly its original state within several years, as long as the disturbance from vehicular traffic is limited to depression of the surface, even though it may have involved serious damage to the growing vegetation, as long as it did not damage the root system below. If the disturbance due to traffic has resulted in shearing or separation of the organic mat due to excessive wheel or track depression, which is ordinarily accompanied by complete destruction of the mat, the result is a water-filled trough, and any recovery is very slow.

Acknowledgment.   This study was supported by several Corps of Engineers projects at the U.S. Army Cold Regions Research and Engineering Laboratory and by U.S. Geological Survey's projects in the National Petroleum Reserve, Alaska.

REFERENCES

1. P. C. Reynolds, Some effects of oil and gas exploration activities on tundra vegetation in northern Alaska, *Proceedings of the Fourth Annual Meeting of the International Society of Petroleum Industry Biologists, Denver, Colorado (1981).*
2. W. E. Rickard and J. Brown, Effects of vehicles on arctic tundra, *Environmental Conservation* 1 (1)(1974).
3. G. Abele, Effects of hovercraft, wheeled and tracked vehicle traffic on tundra, *Proceedings of the 16th Muskeg Research Conference, Canada* (1976).
4. G. Abele and J. Brown, Arctic transportation: operational and environmental evaluation of an Air Cushion Vehicle in Northern Alaska, *Journal of Pressure Vessel Technology* 99, ASME Paper No. 76-Pet–41 (1977).
5. G. Abele, D. A. Walker, J. Brown, M. C. Brewer and D. M. Atwood, Effects of low ground pressure vehicle traffic on tundra at Lonely, Alaska. Special Report 78–16: Hanover, N. H., U.S. Army Cold Regions Research and Engineering Laboratory (1978).
6. G. R. Burt, Summer travel on the tundra with low ground pressure vehicles. Institute of Arctic Environmental Engineering, University of Alaska, N7004 (1970).
7. J. R. Hok, *A Reconnaissance of Tractor Trails and Related Phenomena on the North Slope of Alaska.* U.S. Department of the Interior, Bureau of Land Management (1969).
8. P. G. Kevan, *Vehicle Tracks on High Arctic Tundra.* Defense Research Board, Ottawa, Canada, 'Hazen 41' (1971).
9. J. R. Radforth, Long term effects of summer traffic by tracked vehicles on tundra. Muskeg Research Institute, University of New Brunswick, ALUR 72–73–13.
10. D. A. Walker, P. J. Webber, K. R. Everett, and J. Brown, The effects of low-pressure wheeled vehicles on plant communities and soils at Prudhoe Bay, Alaska. Special Report 77–17: Hanover, N. H., U.S. Army Cold Regions Research and Engineering Laboratory.

PLANNING TO READ RESEARCH

Professor Jurdy places both reports down on the table in front of her and thumbs through them briefly. This first quick look allows her to think about how her own professional knowledge and experience will contribute to her reading.

I've never been to Alaska, or to any permafrost region for that matter, so I really have no expectations about these studies. I have had experience with the fieldwork associated with seismic exploration in very different terrains such as the swamps of Louisiana, the plains of Texas, and the mountains of Wyoming. Thus, I am appreciative of the possible danger to the environment, particularly to fragile areas.

Looking through these two research reports I see a map, tables, pictures of large trucks, and graphs among the usual divisions telling about the study, the methods, the results, and the discussion.

She picks up the one titled, "Airphoto Analysis of Winter Seismic Disturbance in Northeastern Alaska" (hereafter referred to as "Airphoto Analysis") by Martha K. Raynolds and Nancy A. Felix. Professor Jurdy notices the date of the article—1989—and that both authors are associated with the Arctic National Wildlife Refuge, which is maintained by the U.S. Fish and Wildlife Service in Alaska. The report was published in *Arctic,* an interdisciplinary journal read by a wide variety of individuals interested in the Arctic.

Professor Jurdy felt that the other report, titled, "Long-Term Effects of Off-Road Vehicle Traffic on Tundra Terrain" (hereafter referred to as "Long-Term Effects"), by G. Abele, J. Brown, and M. C. Brewer might be more technical than the first one (although probably covering a similar topic) because it was published in *Journal of Terramechanics.* She notices that of the three authors of this paper, one is associated with the U.S. Geological Survey in Anchorage, Alaska, the agency charged with geological research and mapping; and the other two are with the United States Army Cold Regions Laboratory in New Hampshire, a well-known research lab that works on "cold" problems.

READING "AIRPHOTO ANALYSIS"
A First Reading

WRITING AND LEARNING ACTIVITY

1. Reading: Read the text along with Professor Jurdy. Make notes in your journal about new ideas and new vocabulary. Continue to question yourself about ideas you don't understand or things you would like to know more about.

To begin, Professor Jurdy read the abstract, looked quickly through the research report itself, then read the section marked Conclusion. While reading the abstract, Professor Jurdy attempts to construct a picture of the study by summarizing.

So these people are going to look at the relationship between amount of disturbance and vegetation type, trail location, and traffic. What did they use? They used airphotos, photographed to a certain scale on color infrared film, and collected ground data to determine the disturbance to specific vegetation types.

While skimming through the report, Professor Jurdy paused at the technical measurement "60,000 ha coast plain" and wondered how much land that represented. Later, while reading the text more closely, Professor Jurdy discovers that the figure 60,000 ha in the abstract is an error. The correct figure is 600,000, but we will return to that problem later. She reaches for her specialized dictionary of geological terms and explains,

The term ha *is an abbreviation for the measurement term* hectare, *which in metric terms stands for 10,000 square meters or 2.471 acres. The section marked "Study Area" tells us that the coastal plain is about 600,000 hectares. That gives us some indication of the size of the area they're exploring. Looking at Figure 1, this is equivalent to about 45 × 60 miles or 2700 square miles. I can see already that because this area is so large there was no way they could examine it in vehicles; they had to use some sort of air surveillance.*

From the conclusion, Professor Jurdy tries to draw out the major results of the study. This will help her recognize what is important as she goes back and reads the study again more carefully.

A CLOSE READING

WRITING AND LEARNING ACTIVITIES

1. **Journal Entry:** As you read, make notes about your reading process in your journal. Write down any questions you have about the reading and any familiar or unfamiliar terms you encounter. Also, note anything you'd be interested in finding out more about.
2. **Annotate the Text:** As you read, make notes in the margins of your textbook. Make brief notes about new terms, about the purpose of your study, and questions that you have.

Read the Introduction, paragraphs 1–6.

Professor Jurdy reads these first six paragraphs aloud and then comments on what she has read as she works to identify the research problem that drives this study.

First, they offer the background for the study and then they go over the process of seismic exploration. In the third paragraph they cite other studies that have explored similar problems, such as Bliss and Wein's paper of 1972, or the 1973 paper of Hernandez. (Some of their own earlier work is cited in the Methods section.) There are fewer references in later sections because they are presenting a report of their own study. This distinction is important: the work, results, or ideas of others must be credited with a citation. We assume ideas or results that are not cited reflect the work of the authors.

The researchers tell us that previous research has mostly been concerned with summer exploration and when research was focused on damage during the winter, the studies had been limited to individual sites. So these researchers needed to figure out how to

*cover more land in order to study damage to the vegetation during winter seismic explo-
ration. Their method, using infrared airphotos, allows them to cover much more territory
and to identify the different types of vegetation.*

Read the section Study Area, paragraph 7.

This short section describes the geographic location of the study area
and points us to the map on page 285. The first line of this section may contain a typographical error. The abstract and the caption for Figure 1 tell us
the area covers 60,000 ha, yet the area in the Study Area section claims the
area covers 600,000 ha. To get to the bottom of the discrepancy, I wrote to
the authors of the article; they wrote back that the correct figure is 600,000.
Martha Raynolds also commented, "I expect this can serve as a good lesson
to your students as to what actually happens before things get into print.
Even if a paper is reviewed and edited many times (as this paper was), it
gets very difficult to find mistakes that may appear in later copies" (Correspondence, November 1, 1991). It's important to remember that errors can
be found in nearly any written document, so read critically. If something
strikes you as wrong, it just might be wrong.

Read the Methods section, paragraphs 8–12 and look at Table 1.

In this section Professor Jurdy reads to find out how Raynolds and Felix
actually went about answering their research question: what was the extent
of disturbance to vegetation type during winter seismic exploration in 1984
and 1985?

*Raynolds and Felix have color infrared photos of 20 percent of the seismic trails, and they
have divided their area of study into three sections. Next they need to tell us how they are
going to identify the various types of plants and the extent of the damage to them. Table 1
describes eight kinds of vegetation and four levels of disturbance. Apparently this vegetation classification comes from a work they had cited earlier (Walker et al., 1982).*

*All this talk about interpreters and agreement tells me that in order to finalize their
coding scheme (the chart we see in Table 1), two researchers (mentioned in a note at the
end of the report) sat down and looked at the pictures and the coding scheme and tried to
adjust the description to what they observed. Once they were reasonably confident about
their coding scheme they had to decide how to organize the next stage: seeing how the
vegetation looked in the infrared airphotos. They also wanted to look at three traffic patterns. The most important thing to remember is that they were looking for patterns of disturbance in the following variables (variables refer to the characteristics of the environment they wanted to measure):*

1. *Eight vegetation types (see Table 1; for example, marsh or tundra)*
2. *Three locations: one portion west of the Sadlerochit River, another portion east of the
   river, and a third in the eastern foothills*
3. *Three traffic patterns: the route of the seismic explorations, the route of the camp
   trails, and places where the routes overlapped*
4. *The years of the study: 1984 and 1985.*

Read the Results and Discussion section, paragraphs 13–21.

In this section the authors discuss the changes in vegetation, broken down by vegetation type, location, year, and the traffic pattern. They begin their explanation (in the first paragraph) of the results with the most general statement they can make about the disturbance. Looking at the bottom line in Table 2 we can see that most of the disturbance was at level 1 but a fair amount occurred at level 2 as well.

The next three paragraphs give a more detailed look at the results in Table 2. We learn specifically what types of vegetation sustained the most damage by seismic exploration. As Professor Jurdy reads this section she must think visually about the results. Where she doesn't recognize types of vegetation or other terms she reaches for a specialized dictionary.

If I look in the table under disturbance level 3 I see one high number—27. This is a percent. If I follow that line to the left I see more high numbers, all for the type of vegetation called dryas terrace. This type was heavily damaged at all levels. The next most serious disturbance appears in the disturbance level 2 column. These types of vegetation (in descending order of damage) are moist shrub tundra, moist sedge tussock tundra, and moist graminoid/barren tundra complex. Now that I feel like I know the table a bit, I'll go back to the text.

As Professor Jurdy returns to the text she has a better idea of the level of damage among specific types of vegetation, but new questions arise. She wants to develop a better picture of these types of vegetation.

If I had the Murray reference available right now I'd probably be able to go straight to pictures of specific kinds of plants. But Raynolds and Felix's explanation helps some. The plants with the most damage seem to be those that are more exposed: they stand up higher against the mostly flat terrain, being subjected to wind since they have little snow cover. I can imagine what the authors mean when they refer to the dryas terrace as a thin vegetative mat and easily disturbed.

I know that riparian means next to the river's edge. Here they explain that this type of vegetation didn't suffer because they avoided it. That's important to know because if vehicles had gone over it I'm sure it would have been demolished. I'm going to look up graminoid in my dictionary. I see that it means grass-like vegetation; now I can see how it would suffer less damage. It probably just lays flat while the snow rests on it and the vehicles travel over it. Hmmm . . . what an interesting view of the terrain I'm getting.

Raynolds and Felix move on to look at the other variables of their study: the location, traffic patterns, and years of the study.

Read Conclusion, paragraphs 22–25.

The conclusion of this paper summarizes the results and evaluates the usefulness of airphoto analysis. Professor Jurdy reads the conclusion as a way of fixing the study in her mind before going on to the next study.

I'm finally getting the picture here. Those types of vegetation that have some height are most vulnerable to damage while wet types suffer the least damage. Less damage occurred in 1985 than in 1984 due to protection provided by heavier snow and more cautious travel for camp moves. Raynolds and Felix support the method of airphoto analysis and tell us that they are currently analyzing new airphotos. But they also tell us that airphoto analysis only provides a relative guide; they agreed only 75 percent of the time for one measure and 66 percent of the time for another one.

I'm relieved to see that the authors present accurate appraisals of their method. On the whole it makes their work more convincing. I know that they work for the U.S. Fish and Wildlife Service. My guess is that they are very committed to preserving the environment. The oil companies on the other hand are committed to finding oil on the same plot of ground. When you have two such competing interests it's important to present your results as carefully and accurately as possible so that no one can accuse you of letting your personal interests influence your results. Of course, everyone has an interest or an agenda, but we try not to let it influence our presentation of results.

READING "LONG-TERM EFFECTS"
A First Reading

WRITING AND LEARNING ACTIVITY

1. Reading: Read the text along with Professor Jurdy. Make notes in your journal about new ideas and new vocabulary. Continue to question yourself about ideas you don't understand or things you would like to know more about. Also, try to anticipate what you might learn from this journal article.

As Professor Jurdy surveys the abstract (titled "Summary") for this study, she begins to notice similarities and differences with the "Airphoto Analysis" study.

This looks as if it addresses a similar topic: off-road vehicle traffic on tundra terrain. Here, though, we're looking at actual traffic tests. The abstract tells me they're looking at damage at two locations from three kinds of vehicles. They list the types of damage and tell us that they monitored the damage for up to ten years, which makes it a long-term study, thus the use of long-term *in the title.*

They don't have any maps, although I'm guessing that this study takes place in approximately the same area as the other study since they're both concerned about the Coastal Plain area. They have plenty of pictures of the different types of vehicles, none of which I've seen before. I'll have to figure this out later. They include two tables that describe the vehicles and the actual traffic tests.

Their Figure 7 is captioned "nomenclature," which means terminology. Here, I expect, they will define their key terms for describing the results of the traffic tests. Finally, I see plots or graphs, which are always helpful since they show me how the depressions changed with time for several different amounts of passage of these vehicles. I'm just flipping through looking at the plots at this point.

Professor Jurdy notices that the four subsections of the Discussion of Results section look at the results in terms of terrain surface depression, effect on thaw depth, impact on vegetation, and visibility of traffic signatures. Finally, Professor Jurdy glances at the reference list and wonders whether the authors of one report are aware of the work of the other researchers. Since scientists often consider themselves a community, she wondered if these researchers might be "talking" to each other by referencing each other's work.

This is a rather short reference list. I'm looking to see if one paper cites the other. No, this one was published in 1984 so it could not cite the other one published later, in 1989. So let's see if the 1989 ("Airphoto Analysis") paper cites the 1984 one. No cigar. So apparently these researchers consider themselves in different specialties. They're covering related topics but approaching them in different ways. One way is a traffic test with different types of trucks done in some sites in northern Alaska. The other one is a study of damage to specific types of vegetation.

A Close Reading

This study, like the previous one, looks at the effects of traffic on tundra terrain. Unlike the previous study, however, it conducts actual traffic tests with specific vehicles and then measures the results over a period as long as ten years. The abstract neatly summarizes the study and lists the specific ways that traffic impact is defined in this study: "surface depression, effect on thaw depth, damage to vegetation, traffic signature visibility." As we read along with Professor Jurdy, we certainly will want to learn what these four variables mean and how various traffic patterns influenced them.

WRITING AND LEARNING ACTIVITIES

1. **Journal Entry:** As you read, make notes about your reading process in your journal. Write down any questions you have about the reading and any familiar or unfamiliar terms you encounter. Also, note any places in the readings where you read about something you'd be interested in finding out more about.

2. **Annotate the Text:** As you read, make notes in the margins of your textbook. Make brief notes about new terms, about the purpose for the study, and questions you have.

Read the Introduction, paragraphs 1–7.

Professor Jurdy noticed that this study begins by explaining the reason for the study.

In the introduction the authors explain that there have been a lot of petroleum exploration activities in Alaska and trucks are needed to do the exploration. Since all the traffic can't be confined to the winter months, they want to find out what kind of damage occurs when they use trucks during the summer. They point out that this paper looks at the traffic patterns of specific vehicles, in specific locations, for a specific number of years.

Read the Description of the Study, paragraphs 8–19.

This section of the report describes the test sites, the test vehicles, the traffic test layout, and the data obtained. As is frequently the case in research that documents observations, the pictures and tables are as important as, if not more important than, the text. In this section, Professor Jurdy spends most of her time looking at the pictures of the vehicles (Figures 1–6), the two tables, and Figure 7.

The pictures help me to visualize the information in Table 1. The CATCO Rolligon seems like the heaviest vehicle with the most ground pressure. I would guess that they're most interested in how much damage it caused and how quickly the tundra could recover. The first vehicle listed must be the ACV or air-cushion vehicle, which doesn't weigh much and doesn't have much ground pressure. Now, I turn to Table 2, which tells me the location and number of passes for each vehicle.

In this study, like the last one, they took color and aerial photographs but the data they were most interested in was something they call "thaw depth," which they describe in Figure 7. In that figure, as far as I can tell, they have a drawing and an expression to describe what happens when a vehicle makes a track that, in turn, causes a depression. We know that permafrost terrain never thaws. Even though it is covered with a thin layer of soil and vegetation that thaws and freezes as the seasons change, the permafrost should stay frozen. When trucks roll over this terrain in the summer months they produce a rut that not only depresses the topsoil but also depresses the permafrost layer underneath. Once the topsoil is depressed it warms the permafrost beneath it, causing it to melt. What they call nomenclature, or terminology, is their definition of thaw depth.

Read the Discussion of Results section, paragraphs 20–41.

Professor Jurdy will examine each of the four subsections (which follow the same order listed in the abstract) in turn: terrain surface depression, effect on thaw depth, impact on vegetation, visibility of traffic signatures.

Terrain Surface Depression.   The most obvious result is that the air-cushion vehicle has almost no effect on the terrain, so its use is preferable. Now we need to look at the graphs to see what damage the other vehicles did. In Figures 8, 9, and 10 we want to see lines going up to the top of the graph at the right side. This means that over time, the original surface depression has, as they say, rebounded. Then we can think about which vehicle caused how much damage. For instance, in Figure 10 we can see that the largest vehicle, the CATCO Rolligon caused surface depressions that were still 3 cm deep after five years, whereas Figure 8 shows that after ten years the depression made by 50 passes of the much lighter Weasel is almost gone. What's especially interesting about this is that these tests were made at different locations; so, as readers we have to ask ourselves whether we think that the different locations make any difference in the results. That's part of reading critically.

Effect on Thaw Depth.   In this section of the results, things get just a bit more complicated. We still have graphs but they are showing thaw depth—remember that expression?—rather than a simple depth measurement. And we have two very difficult sentences in paragraph 29.

> The impact on the thermal regime is caused primarily by the decrease in the insulating characteristics of the vegetative mat due to compression and damage to the vegetation. In addition, vehicular traffic results in darkening of the terrain surface, which, due to the decreased albedo and thus more heat absorption, causes a deepening of the active layer.

The term thermal regime *simply means the temperature of the land they're studying. As the trucks move over the terrain they crush the topsoil or "active layer" and the vegetation above the permafrost. Once the vegetation is crushed, the active layer has less "albedo" or reflective power and the darker soil then absorbs more heat. This layer can no longer insulate the permafrost, causing the permafrost to melt, which, in turn, is measured by the researchers as an increase in the thaw depth.*

Interestingly, what the researchers are saying here is that even though the air-cushion vehicle does not create a surface depression, by scraping the vegetation away it caused the thaw depth to increase (see Figure 11).

Impact on Vegetation; Visibility of Traffic Signatures.   These two sections remind me of the research in the airphoto analysis report. They are also concerned with damage to vegetation and note that the air-cushion vehicle did damage the vegetation, mostly due to the drag caused by the rear skirt of the vehicle. This particular vehicle caused more damage to the wet terrain than to the dry, and when new vegetation grew back it was prominently seen as a "green belt." Any changes to the terrain by wheeled vehicles causes a "traffic signature," which may not harm the tundra but does change the aesthetics or beauty of it.

Read the Conclusions, paragraphs 42–47.

Since the results of this study will have an environmental impact, the most important results concern how long it takes for the terrain to recover from vehicular traffic during the summer. Professor Jurdy summarizes what she sees as the most important conclusions.

Recovery can take as long as ten years, but quick recovery of surface depression seems to depend on the weight of the vehicle. What you can't see by looking at the terrain is the change in thaw depth, so that seems like an important addition to the research in this area. In the other study ("Airphoto Analysis") we learned about damage to vegetation only during the winter. In "Long-Term Effects" we're told that traffic during the summer, when snow doesn't cover and insulate the ground, damages the permafrost layer. What's particularly interesting is that this damage didn't even begin until two or three years after the initial tracks were made. In general, we would want to use the ACV as often as possible, and we would want to stay away from wet terrain.

WRITING AND LEARNING ACTIVITIES

1. Writing Activity: Reread the first paragraph of either the "Airphoto Analysis" or the "Long-Term Effects" report. Notice how the authors of both reports use an authoritative, unbiased, informative voice to present the circumstances of their research. Imagine you are one of the researchers and compose a fictional personal letter to a friend expressing how you feel about oil and gas exploration in the arctic wilderness. How might your personal feelings influence what you write in the letter?

2. Developing Interests: Go to the library's current periodical room and browse through several popular science journals that contain studies of the arctic or various topics in geology. See what other topics are discussed in *Arctic,* for example. Write in your journal about the range of topics you noticed and which ones interested you.

3. Peer or Group Activity: Working in groups, pairs, or on your own write up an introductory guide to the terminology used in arctic research based on the two articles you've read. List each new term and in your own words describe what it means, how it is used, and why it is important.

MAKING MEANING IN GEOLOGY
THE SCIENTIFIC RESEARCH REPORT

What did Abele, Brown, and Brewer actually do when they conducted their research? What they did most simply, was look at tire tracks. What did Raynolds and Felix do? They looked at plants. Is doing science just that simple? In some ways it is and in some ways it isn't. In this section we want to examine how science can be "simply looking" but at the same time be much more than that.

Doing science is a process of asking questions and developing answers for those questions. This process has been formalized into a method—the scientific method—with particular steps, beginning when someone makes an observation and asks a question. The scientist then formulates an explanation, called the hypothesis, which answers the question. The next step is to test the hypothesis by closer observation or by conducting an experiment. At the conclusion of the experiment the scientists determine whether their answer to the question is the one they expected. They then evaluate the answer and propose a theory or a general statement for how other, similar, questions would be answered. When the research has been completed, the results are written up in a highly formalized genre called the research report.

The research report reflects the scientific method. First the problem and the question are presented in a section called Introduction. Next, they explain how they observed or conducted an experiment, the Methods section. In the Results section, they offer an answer to their question, which they examine further in the Discussion section. Here they might also conclude by talking about how this particular study fits in with other studies or about what type of research should be conducted to answer the next question. Science is built upon the many attempts to ask and answer narrow questions. The body of knowledge, then, builds as more contributions are made through the scientific method.

A CLOSER LOOK AT THE RESEARCH REPORT

Let's follow this process in one of the research reports we just read. In "Airphoto Analysis of Winter Seismic Disturbance in Northeastern Alaska," Martha Raynolds and Nancy Felix explain that Congress had authorized some limited exploration on the arctic coastal plain in 1984 and 1985. Some individuals from the U.S. Fish and Wildlife Service accompanied the crews to monitor damage to the area.

Let's look closely at the language used in this report. The introduction to the report offers as background the "observations" of other geologists, for instance, the following sentence "Subsidence of trails due to melting of permafrost occurs on more heavily disturbed trails (Haag and Bliss, 1974; Gersper and Challinor, 1975; Chapin and Shaver, 1981)." The technical term *subsidence*—which comes from the Latin, to sink or settle—helps us to "see" that the more heavily traveled trails had obvious depressions. We assume that the researchers listed in the citations at the end of the sentence actually saw these depressions, but in a research report we are typically referred to other reports.

Even when Raynolds and Felix do their own observing to answer their questions about damage to the vegetation from vehicle traffic, they can't go out and "simply look." The area they need to observe is huge, around 900 square miles. To do this, they developed a technique—airphoto analysis—to observe specific portions of the area. Then they put their data together to develop a picture of the entire area. This is where you, the reader, must determine if the way they "observed" makes sense to you.

WRITING AND LEARNING ACTIVITIES

1. **Rereading:** Reread one of research reports and make notes on the way it followed the scientific method. What question were the researchers trying to answer? What did they hypothesize, or what did they guess the answer would be? What did they conclude? What do you think will be the impact of their research for oil exploration?

2. **Group Activity:** Meet in small groups with others who looked over the same article. Develop a presentation to the class on your findings. As a class, discuss how the two research reports are similar or different.

THE LANGUAGE OF SCIENCE
IS NOT ALWAYS NEUTRAL

The scientific method is designed in part to help us "see" the same thing the researchers did. In this way it has a persuasive function. When researchers describe how they observed and when they explain the meaning of what they saw, they are influenced by all the research that has gone before and by what they are looking for. Research is never conducted in a vacuum—it always reflects the discipline the researchers belong to.

When you read research in the natural sciences, the key ideas are usually tied to the special vocabulary used among scholars in that field. To make meaning from this vocabulary we construct a set of relationships among these words. Many of the words used in this statement have special meanings. But you'll need to read critically, asking yourself whether the specialized terms mean the same thing in both research reports. For instance, in each report, the researchers tell us that they are observing damage to the terrain. Their observations help them to document this damage. Yet one study speaks about their objective in terms of "damage" and the other in terms of "recovery." Does it make a difference which term the researchers choose?

In paragraph 6 of "Airphoto Analysis" Felix and Raynolds tell us the objective of their study. They are measuring the extent of disturbance.

> The objectives of this study were to determine the extent of disturbance caused by winter seismic exploration on the Arctic Refuge coastal plain and to investigate the major factors controlling the amount of disturbance occurring at a site, such as vegetation type and traffic pattern.

While Felix and Raynolds want to learn about how badly the coastal plain was damaged, notice that Abele, Brown, and Brewer, in "Long-Term Effects," have focused, in paragraph 5, on the rate of recovery, that is, how many years it will take for the damage to be erased,

> The main objectives of the study were to investigate the effects of different vehicle operations and traffic on tundra, specifically, the extent of surface depression, the degree of short-term and long-term damage to the vegetation, the subsequent effect on the soil thermal regime, and to determine the rate of recovery.

It is important to ask how a particular word or term is used in any study. We can ask about the context of a word in a sentence; we can ask what other words might fit in its place; and we can ask if others might understand this word differently. If you were arguing for or against further oil development, which language would you want to use? In an article you will read below, Egan defines permafrost. You might also find a definition in a textbook, but here he also explains how such a definition can become controversial. Egan says, "The coastal plain is underlaid by up to 1,500 feet of permanently frozen water, rock, sand and loose soil. . . . The thin layer atop this, which thaws to a depth of several feet, is considered extremely vulnerable to environmental damage" (paragraph 19). How will researchers, environmentalists, and oil companies define "vulnerable"? How will they define "damage" and, conversely, "recovery"? These questions extend far beyond what we would like to think of as "objective" science, for they depend on the context in which the science is conducted.

WRITING AND LEARNING ACTIVITIES

1. **Class Activity:** List terms from the research reports and explain them in your own words. Who might agree or disagree with your explanations? Here's a sample list. Place a star next to any word whose definition might cause disagreement between environmentalists and proponents of oil development: damage, signature, impact, wilderness, vegetation, tundra, permafrost, ecology, thaw depth, coastal plain, recovery, infrared, traffic, vehicle, seismic, exploration, surface depression, oil development, camp site, green belt, tractor, bare ground, undisturbed area, ground pressure.

2. **Journal Entry:** Choose five terms that might not be easily defined. Write what they mean in your own words. How might someone else define them differently?

3. **Writing Activity:** Write a summary in your own words of one of the research reports.

4. **Peer or Group Activity:** Meet as a group with those who wrote about the same research report. Compare your summaries. Look closely at how each of you defined the important terms used in that study.

PARTICIPATING IN A LEARNING DEBATE

Professor Bonnie B. Spanier, who was trained in microbiology and molecular genetics at Harvard and who now directs the Women's Studies Department at the State University of New York at Albany, has thought long and hard about how to get students to see that science is more than just a set of facts. She'd like to see students understand the key concepts of science, but also to see that science is a human endeavor that exists in a social context. If you have been taught that science is simply a set of facts, then you are likely to feel unmotivated to discover when and in what circumstances those facts might be true or not true. Spanier asks students to think from a personal perspective about what they know, what they read, and what they experience. She want students to take a position on whether or not the research makes sense to them (1992).

Think about the knowledge that the research discussed in this chapter contributes to the current debate on the relative value of oil and wilderness. To extend your knowledge and to highlight some of the issues, we have an additional essay, by Timothy Egan, "The Great Alaska Debate: Can Oil and Wilderness Mix?" which appeared in the *New York Times Magazine* of August 4, 1991.

THE GREAT ALASKA DEBATE
CAN OIL AND WILDERNESS MIX?
TIMOTHY EGAN

■ ■ ■

The best-kept secret in the oil industry lies under a steel pipe, six inches in diameter, that pokes out of the tundra inside one of the world's last truly wild places. Eight months of the year, the pipe is surrounded by the frozen chop of snow and blue ice that covers the coastal plain of the Arctic National Wildlife Refuge in northeast Alaska. A desert, with less than 10 inches of annual precipitation, the flat land bordering the Beaufort Sea holds the imprint of a savage wind for most of the year: snowdrifts contorted and hardened, a landscape like paste from a blender.

In the summer, when the sun circles the horizon but never sets, the snow melts, wildflowers rise in the plain and great masses of caribou arrive to give birth to their young, seeking the coastal wind as refuge from swarms of mosquitoes. Driven by biological imperative, the animal herds gorge themselves on grass and flowers, storing fuel for the long migration through the Brooks Range in mid-summer.

In September, the tundra freezes again, the sea hardens, grizzly bears hibernate in pockets of warmer air near the mountains, daylight is squeezed from the sky. Through the seasons, the pipe remains—a totem of the great mystery whose resolution may determine the future of American energy policy. The five-foot shank of steel marks an exploratory oil well, called KIC–1, that was drilled by a partnership led by Chevron U.S.A. in 1985 and 1986 at a cost of more than $40 million. The oil companies drilled to a depth of 15,200 feet on land owned by an Eskimo regional corporation in order to peek beneath the permafrost. They may have discovered the largest recoverable oil field in North America, or they may have struck out, reaching only natural gas or water in a reservoir mapped out by geologists.

Fewer than 10 people know what was found beneath the pipe, says Tom Cook, a geologist who is Chevron's exploration representative in Alaska. The oil company considers the information obtained from its exploratory well proprietary and will not share its findings. Test drilling for oil, like trying to forecast the weather, is risky, an inexact science. Nobody, not even the Chevron geologists, knows for sure how much oil there may be under the refuge, or how much of it is recoverable. But the test results must have been tantalizing enough, prompting the intense lobbying now underway in Congress by the major oil companies.

5   "What you get from that kind of well is a better understanding of the geology," Cook says, poker-faced. He lights a cigar inside one of the drab huts latched to the tundra in the oil town of Deadhorse, at Prudhoe Bay, 65 miles west of the refuge. "Hopefully that puts us at a competitive advantage when—if—we start production," he says.

The question of whether the nation's second-largest wildlife refuge (the biggest is the Yukon Delta Refuge in western Alaska) will be opened to roads, drilling pads and the clank of industry pursuing another jackpot is up to Congress. In May, the Senate Energy Committee passed legislation that would allow drilling in the refuge, and the full Senate is expected to take up the matter in the fall. For the time being, by law, the 19-million-acre refuge is for the predominant use of wildlife so abundant inside the Arctic Circle that the area is often called the American Serengeti. (*Map on page 325.*) In a symmetry so perfect it suggests a modern parable, the refuge also happens to contain what many geologists consider the last great untapped oil field on the continent—with a potential for yielding up to nine billion barrels, nearly matching that of Prudhoe Bay, America's biggest. More than 180,000 caribou, a herd that is to the native Gwich'in people what the Great Plains bison were to the Lakota Sioux, migrate annually to calving grounds in the same general area where the oil is supposed to be. Chief among the questions now before Congress is whether oil production and caribou can share the same patch of cold ground.

Beyond that, the fight over the Arctic refuge has once again raised the question of just how far Americans are willing to go for more domestic oil—how many more wilderness areas, pristine beaches and wildlife refuges will be violated as the oil runs out. Eighteen years have passed since the oil crisis of 1973, but American energy policy has barely changed. More than 100 years ago, when oil production began in earnest in this country, the wells were located on industrial land, close to cities. Now drillers are knocking at the door of an Arctic wilderness in the most remote corner of the continent. For conservationists who would draw the line around this vast home for caribou and musk oxen, all other environmental battles are dwarfed by this epic struggle over the Arctic refuge. It may be the last big land fight of its kind.

President Bush has made drilling in the refuge the centerpiece of his national energy policy; Democrats, joined by many Republicans, are pushing fuel efficiency as an alternative. Increasing the average fuel-economy standard for new cars from 27.5 to 34 miles a gallon by the year 2001, the argument for conservation goes, would save more oil than could ever be pumped from the refuge. But the President will veto any energy bill, according to Energy Secretary James D. Watkins, that does not include lifting the restrictions on Arctic oil development.

For those who want cheap Alaskan crude to keep flowing into the next century, the argument is simple. As Tom Cook says, "Do you want your energy policy always to be, 'Shoot the guy who's got the oil,' or should we develop our own resources?"

10   Sixty-five percent of the world's known oil reserves are in the Middle East; the United States has only about 4 percent. Conservationists point out that even if the Arctic refuge proved to be a bonanza as big as Prudhoe Bay, which produces about 1.5 million barrels a day but is declining at a rate of roughly 10 percent a year, the United States will continue to have to import

up to half its oil. "We simply cannot drill ourselves to energy independence," says George T. Frampton Jr., president of the Wilderness Society.

The Arctic refuge—with its prehistoric-looking musk oxen, millions of migratory birds, Dall sheep, wolf packs, moose, majestic caribou herds and fearsome polar bears—has taken on an importance well beyond its potential ability to keep gas prices down and soldiers out of foreign lands. The ancient human cultures of Inupiat Eskimos on the one side and Gwich'in Indians on the other are also part of the refuge's ecology. As metaphor, the refuge is a sort of frozen Eden, the last paradise at the far northern edge of the Final Frontier. Larger than 10 of the states, it is without the industrial footprints that cover the rest of the globe—the "geography of hope," as the writer Wallace Stegner defined wilderness.

Even the most poetic of nature writers find themselves straining to describe the coastal plain—8 percent of the total refuge—which is where oil drilling would take place if Congress gives its approval. Few would call it majestic. "Grave, austere and beautiful" is how Peter Matthiessen described it recently. Unlike the rest of the refuge, which enjoys the more moderate climate of the south and abounds with spruce trees, flowering heathers and alpine crags, the 1.5 million acres of the coastal plain are flat and harsh. For most of the year, the area lacks color and the untidy edges of life. "A barren desert," in the words of Alaska Senator Ted Stevens, perhaps the most vocal proponent in the Senate of opening the refuge to drilling. But its emptiness is what some people find so redeeming. They see value in what the plain does not have—the heavy metal and caterwauling tools of the oil industry. Of the 1,100 miles of northern Alaska coast along the Arctic Ocean, only the 125-mile stretch inside the refuge is off limits to development.

"Oil and gas development would destroy this area, with all its wild and spectacular diversity, forever," Sydney J. Butler, a vice president of the Wilderness Society, wrote in a letter to United States Senators in May. At the same time, three major environmental groups—the National Wildlife Federation, the Natural Resources Defense Council and Trustees for Alaska—released a report in which they pleaded with Congress to keep the refuge inviolate. At stake, the report said, is "the biological integrity of America's only Arctic sanctuary and the future of the wildlife it protects."

Flying low over the snow on a day when the surface is crackling under 24-hour sun, we leave the intersecting roads around Prudhoe Bay and enter a white wilderness. The landscape seems to be in a hurry to make the elemental transformation from ice to water—alive with "breakup," a word used by Alaskans to describe late spring. The snow pack is surprisingly low, less than a foot on average. Bits of grass show here and there. The Beaufort Sea is just starting to reveal itself through broken ice; offshore, Eskimos have begun their annual hunt for seals. Inland, about 25 miles from the coast, grizzly bears are rousing themselves from a winter slumber in the foothills of the Brooks Range. And all through the low draws and passes of the range, caribou, led by pregnant cows, are heading north.

15   A large, picked-over piece of whalebone, a remnant of a spine bigger than most living rooms, is perched on the beach outside the town of Kaktovik, the only human community inside the refuge. Entering the village of 200 people, you can see the two worlds, past and future, of the Inupiat, a name that means "the Real People." They still hunt bowhead whales, their centuries-old source of subsistence. But the town has satellite dishes, off-road vehicles, new housing—all spoils of oil money. Chevron's exploratory well was drilled just a few miles from this village, on lands for which the mineral rights are owned by the Arctic Slope Regional Corporation, whose shareholders are Eskimos. Any further drilling would require Congressional approval.

"We don't want to return to the past," says Archie Brower, a Kaktovik resident, toothless and chain-smoking. "Oil is the future."

In 1980, 20 years after the refuge was set aside, Congress designated the northernmost 1.5 million acres as a "special study area" for its oil and gas potential. In 1987, the Interior Department estimated there was about a 20 percent chance of recovering large quantities of oil in the Arctic refuge. This year, citing more accurate geologic studies and recent wells drilled on the periphery of the refuge, the department upped the odds to 46 percent—a move environmentalists label political, timed to influence the legislation now making its way through Congress.

The Government places the amount of recoverable oil in the refuge at between 600 million and 9.2 billion barrels. The mean, estimated at 3.57 billion barrels, would be enough to meet the United States' total oil demand for 200 days. But if that oil were pumped at a rate of only 1 million barrels a day, it would keep the Trans-Alaska Pipeline—the vital artery on which Alaskans depend for everything from an annual check to performing-arts subsidies—busy for another decade or two. For the companies that run the pipeline, timing is crucial; the vast oil complex inside the Arctic Circle must be fed a steady diet of North Slope crude. If the refuge were opened to drilling today, it would take 8 to 12 years in exploration and construction time before oil could flow from the coastal plane to the pipeline.

In one report, the Interior Department drew a picture of what oil development in the refuge would be like. The handful of oil companies expected to be involved would need about 100 miles of pipeline, 120 miles of main roads and 160 miles of less-developed spur roads, two airfields, some 60 drilling pads and up to 50 million cubic yards of gravel, used to make hard surfaces over the tundra. The coastal plain is underlaid by up to 1,500 feet of permanently frozen water, rock, sand and loose soil—called permafrost. The thin layer atop this, which thaws to a depth of several feet, is considered extremely vulnerable to environmental damage. To minimize the industrial footprint, the oil companies have said they would try to do much of the construction work in winter, using ice roads instead of those made of gravel. They say new technological advances make it possible to put all the drill pads and service centers closer together and to use about half the space required for the construction at Prudhoe Bay in the early 70's.

20   The oil would be sent to the lower 48 states through the Trans-Alaska Pipeline, which dissects the state and runs 800 miles from its origin in Prudhoe to the ice-free port of Valdez. What happens after the oil leaves the frozen north, of course, has as much to do with the politics of opening the refuge as what may happen near the drill sites. Legislation to allow drilling cleared the Senate Energy Committee once before, in 1989—eight days before the Exxon Valdez struck a reef and ruptured, spilling nearly 11 million gallons into Prince William Sound. The nation's worst oil spill, killing more than 260,000 birds, at least 3,500 sea otters, 200 harbor seals and staining a marine wilderness with blankets of crude, caused many in Congress—and in Alaska—to think twice about the pursuit of black gold inside the Arctic Circle. The measure to open the refuge died in the 1989 Congressional session.

"After the spill, when I went to give talks about oil development in the refuge, I had some people spit on me, call me every name in the book," Cook, the Chevron geologist, says. "It was rough."

One who did not change his mind about Alaska's relationship with oil was Walter J. Hickel, the state's new Governor. He dismisses the Exxon spill as a "mechanical thing" that would never have happened if there had been tugs escorting oil tankers all the way through the sound. Running on the platform of Alaska's Independence Party—which advocated secession from the Union, an idea he later disavowed—the 71-year-old Hickel was returned to the Governor's mansion last fall, more than 20 years after an earlier term in the Statehouse. Elected with less than 40 percent of the vote in a three-way election, Hickel's vision for Alaska includes opening up the refuge, laying railroad tracks to the far north and constructing a pipeline to deliver fresh water from his state to the parched metropolises of Southern California.

The state controls less than one-third of Alaska's 370 million acres. The rest is tied up in national parks, wilderness preserves, wildlife refuges, military fields and land owned by native corporations, the 13 regional groups that represent 70,000 Aleuts, Eskimos and Athabascan Indians. In his inaugural address this year, Governor Hickel described Alaska as "a state on the brink of colony status once again—because we have let our rights be taken away by the Federal Government."

The Governor's plan for Alaska has been dubbed "Wally World" by the Anchorage press. He has just limped through a legislative session in which few of his initiatives were passed into law, and his deal to settle all legal claims against Exxon in return for a payment of $1.1 billion fell apart under a shower of criticism. Nonetheless, in his disdain for official wilderness areas, he speaks for a large segment of Alaskans. Wild areas, off limits to motorized vehicles and resource extraction, are, he says, "places where people have to break laws in order to see them."

25   Certainly, few people have ever tried to see the Arctic refuge. Last year, only about 15,000 visitors were recorded, an amount equal to, say, the number of people who might cross the street in Times Square on a given morning. Hiking the coastal plain, in summer, has been compared to walking on a water bed. Those who do visit come to raft under the midnight

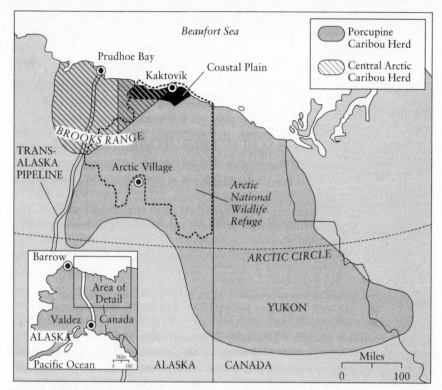

Showdown
For conservationists who draw the line around this vast home for caribou and musk oxen, other environmental battles are dwarfed by the struggle over the Arctic refuge.

sun, to camp in the foothills of the Brooks Range, to take pictures of the big animals or to exalt in the feeling of being an inconsequential part of nature.

Even if a million visitors a year came to the Arctic refuge, it would not change the core argument against oil development. For ANWR (pronounced an-whar), as it is called, is not primarily for people, but for animals.

In arguing that industry and wild animals can share the same land, the oil companies that want to drill in the refuge—Chevron, ARCO, British Petroleum, among the major ones—cite the experience of the Central Arctic caribou herd, just to the west of the refuge. The fear expressed during the last great Alaska lands debate, over the pipeline, was that North Slope production would harm this herd. But in the last 18 years, following large-scale development at Prudhoe Bay, the herd has grown from 3,000 to nearly 20,000. Pictures of caribou crossing under elevated pipelines and over gravel roads are regularly trotted out to show that oil drilling has had no discernable effect on the animals. During the 1988 Presidential campaign, George Bush proclaimed that caribou like to "snuggle up next to the pipeline."

The animals are a common sight at Prudhoe during the summer. "They cross pipelines and roads with very few problems," says G. Scott Ronzio, manager of environmental sciences for ARCO Alaska. While conceding that there is "a lot of mystery to these animals," Ronzio says, "I'm fairly confident that oil development can continue on the North Slope with no harm to caribou."

The expansion of the Central Arctic herd has been attributed by biologists to a retreat of predators, mainly wolves and grizzly bears, which keep their distance from humans, to a series of mild winters and to normal ups and downs of animal population cycles. Caribou have increased throughout Alaska. Most biologists, Ronzio among them, think the Central Arctic herd will eventually decline, and there is evidence that their growth rate is already shrinking.

30   The animals that migrate to the refuge, known as the Porcupine caribou herd (named for the Porcupine River, which flows through the southern edge of the refuge), are a different story. For one thing, the Porcupine herd is nearly 10 times larger than the Central Arctic herd. For another, the bigger herd does its calving in an area where oil development would take place; about half of the Central Arctic calving takes place away from oil facilities. Few biologists know exactly what would happen if pregnant caribou cows, given their limited time to give birth, tried to calve within sight and sound of an industrial complex.

"Among the Central herd, females have never adjusted to oil development," says Dr. David R. Klein, a biologist considered one of the nation's foremost experts on caribou. A frequent witness before Congressional hearings, Klein has been studying Arctic caribou for nearly 30 years. "What oil could mean to the Porcupine herd is that the females and their young would be deprived of their best feeding grounds," he says.

Caribou eat grasses and flower buds, at a rather intense rate, during the short Arctic summer. The swarms of mosquitoes that rise from the sponge-like tundra have driven them to the coast for the relief of ocean breezes. If the animals were forced to scatter inland, says Klein, insects would likely harass them to a point where they would be unable to eat enough food for their return migration, a march of nearly 1,000 miles.

Of equal concern to Klein are the musk oxen, which look like creatures out of the "Star Wars" movies. The musk oxen are native to Alaska, but were hunted to extinction. Since their reintroduction 20 years ago, they have thrived in the refuge, where they live year round, eating shrubs and willows in the valleys of the Brooks Range. Now numbering about 500, the musk oxen in the refuge make up one of the largest populations in North America. Klein worries that gouging streams in the refuge to build new roads would displace the shaggy, lumbering oxen from their prime habitat, a concern that the oil companies say is ill-founded. According to Ronald W. Chappell, a spokesman for ARCO Alaska, gravel would most likely be taken from one or two central pits.

Klein speaks in the cautious language of science. Both sides of the refuge debate have tried to use his conclusions to bolster their arguments. When asked for his opinion on whether the Porcupine herd could survive oil drilling in the refuge, he says: "These animals are extremely complex, but I believe it would be very difficult for oil development to take place in the coastal plain without having a detrimental effect on them. How great that would be, no one knows."

35   For the Gwich'in Indians, who live in 15 tiny communities just south of Alaska's Brooks Range and the Canadian Yukon, the caribou are a matter of survival. Most Gwich'ins, who number about 7,000, live a subsistence life, depending on the Porcupine caribou herd as their primary food source, much the way some coastal Alaskan communities still survive on seasonal salmon runs. The Gwich'ins are the northernmost Indian tribe in North America, perhaps the last big aboriginal group to resist assimilation and modern ways.

"For too long this has been an issue about environment versus energy, and no one wanted to hear about the Gwich'in," says Sarah James, a native leader who lives in Arctic Village, just south of the refuge. In a statement before the Senate Energy Committee in April, James compared the Gwich'in to the buffalo-hunting Sioux of the Great Plains: "The Gwich'in are caribou people. For thousands of years we have lived with caribou right where we are today. We're talking about an Indian nation that still lives on the land and depends on this herd. In my village, about 75 percent of our protein comes from caribou."

In Arctic Village, heat from the summer sun is used to dry caribou meat. Unlike other native people, the Gwich'ins do not own any mineral rights in the refuge and have not organized into a regional corporation. Caribou is the center of their lives. The Gwich'ins consider themselves part of the natural ecology of the Arctic refuge. "We think of it as a biocultural reserve, not just a wildlife refuge," James says.

The Gwich'ins, who have barely been heard from during the decade-long debate, came together for a meeting in the summer of 1988, the first time all the tribal communities had gathered in one place in more than 100 years. They signed a proclamation, agreeing to "speak as a single voice" against oil development in the refuge.

The other native people near the refuge, Eskimos on the northern border, take the opposite stand. Whale hunters represented by a powerful regional corporation, the Inupiat say oil has changed their lives for the better. They receive millions of dollars in royalties from drilling on the North Slope, and stand to gain additional millions if the refuge is opened. About 6,000 Inupiat live in eight villages inside the Arctic Circle, most of them in the town of Barrow.

40   "We used to be afraid of what the oil industry would do, but we saw that it has not harmed fish or wildlife," says Warren Matumeak, an Inupiat elder who lives in Barrow. "Things have changed for the better. We have schools, roads, firefighting equipment. Our houses have kitchens and flush toilets and TV's. It's sad that some people think we should have to go back to the old ways."

Matumeak was with his grandson, fishing for char, a type of Arctic trout, four summers ago, when he suffered a heart attack. "I said, 'Grandson, I'm going to where Jesus is.'" His cholesterol built up, he said, because he was spending too much time in front of the television, dipping caribou fat in whale blubber—a tasty snack. He survived the heart attack, thanks to a helicopter from Barrow that airlifted him to a hospital—a search-and-rescue made possible by oil money. Matumeak still remembers when some Eskimos lived in igloos; now his grandchildren wear Los Angeles Raiders caps and the family takes occasional vacations to Disney World.

Some Inupiat are angry that they cannot lease their own land, inside the refuge, to oil companies. "We've lived here thousands of years," says Matumeak. "We should be able to do what we want with our own land. And what we want is to allow drilling. Oil is the best thing that ever happened to us."

Despite such statements, the Eskimos take a somewhat contradictory approach to oil drilling in the far north. While they advocate opening the refuge, which would benefit them economically, they are among the strongest opponents of an Interior Department plan to allow offshore drilling in the Arctic Ocean, which poses a potential threat to their whale hunting.

For most Americans, it would be easier if all the remaining oil fields were in West Texas or Oklahoma. But the search for petroleum has now gone to the far edges, near pleasure beaches in Florida and California, off the wilderness coast of the Olympic Peninsula in Washington State and inside an Arctic preserve that was supposed to belong to wild animals. These potential drill sites, on or near national treasures, force the question of just how far the nation will go to satisfy its oil habit.

45   Those who want to open the Arctic to development see a peculiar form of American naïveté in the arguments for preservation. The idea of all that oil just sitting there, untapped, while the United States ups its trade imbalance with Middle Eastern countries is ludicrous, they say. But by keeping the refuge inviolate, the counter argument goes, Americans can take the first steps toward independence from a substance that, once pulled from the ground, inevitably spawns trouble—wars, foul air and dirty water. The debate, in itself, is familiar. What has changed is that we are running out of places over which to have the argument.

Activity 3 below takes you through the process of preparing for a learning debate. This type of debate offers the opportunity to explain your position on an issue, respond to questions or objections, critique what you have read, and, finally, reaffirm or reconsider your position. It allows for lively back-and-forth exchanges that take into account the reading you have done thus far. This type of dialogue also allows you to synthesize what you know from many sources, combining the language of science with your personal knowledge on the issue. Here are some questions to ask as you prepare for your learning debate.

Who does Egan see as the key participants in this debate? What positions do they take? What is their interest in this issue? How has the current situation changed from earlier discussions of the same issue? Does Egan take sides? How would you characterize his position? Do you feel his comments are reliable? If he had actually cited the two research reports you had read, where do you suppose he would have referenced them in his article? What information do Raynold and Felix contribute to this debate? Abele, Brown, and Brewer? Does one report offer more support for one side or another of this issue?

Most importantly, where do you stand on this issue? Do you support oil development or maintaining the wilderness? Is the debate that simple? How did you decide on your position and what evidence can you offer for it? What personal experiences contributed to your decision? Ask others about how their personal experiences influenced their position. How does the research support your position? Do you have questions about any of the research you read that would cause you to question the results? How could you convince others to consider your position? What would it take for you to change your position?

WRITING AND LEARNING ACTIVITIES

1. **Reading:** Read Egan's essay, "The Great Alaska Debate." Make notes on all the questions asked about it above. In which cases do you agree with the positions Egan presents and in which do you disagree? Write about your position. What do *you* think should occur in the Arctic National Wildlife Refuge?

2. **Group Activity:** Meet in a small group with others who hold a similar position and develop yours. How can you support your position? How can you question the position of those who take a different one?

3. **Conducting a Learning Debate:** As a class, talk about the guidelines you would need for a productive discussion and not a knock-down-drag-out free-for-all. What rules should the class establish for conducting the debate? How long will people speak? Who will moderate the debate? Divide the class into two teams and have each team present their case. A third group should be the audience for the debate; they would determine, through a judging procedure, which team argued most effectively for their position.

DEVELOPING INTERESTS

Where do you go from here? My students were asked what, if any, personal connections they have to the field of geology that might help them search for a topic or develop an interest in this area. Have you, for instance, ever worked on an environmental project at home or in your community? Have you traveled to any area with different terrain and wondered about its geological make-up? Have you any connection personally, through hobbies, work, or past schooling with geological issues, concerns, or individuals in the field? Here are some journal entries students wrote in response to these questions:

This might sound strange, but the state of Michigan has a state stone—believe it or not! It is a fossil mostly found along the northeastern part of Lake Michigan, including the upper peninsula. This stone (or fossil) is called the Petoski stone. I collect those fossils. Some vendors cut them and sell them in the shape of the state. Another strange hobby is that I like to collect samples of dirt from different parts of the world—although it is only a small collection. The variety of colors is quite astonishing. It makes me wonder why or what formed those particular colors.

ROSE HANBURY

I have an interest in the field of geology, especially earthquakes because I have relatives who live in Los Angeles who encounter this problem. I am also curious about them because a long time ago I did research on earthquakes. I want to know how much advancement we have made in this field in the past five to ten years. Besides all these factors I am also curious about earthquakes because I experienced them during my childhood in India.

AMIT GARG

WRITING AND LEARNING ACTIVITIES

1. **Journal Entry:** Write about the questions above. What personal connections, interests, or questions do you have about this field?

2. **Class Activity:** List on the board the connections and interests of the members of the class. Notice the range of interests. How could people learn more about more of these areas of interest?

▣ LINKED WRITING ASSIGNMENT

Writing a Synthesis of Work in Geology (see Chapter 11, Synthesizing Discipline-Specific Texts). In the previous section, Developing Interests, you began to identify issues and ideas that you might want to explore further. Finding personal connections to the material you are studying is one important way to participate more fully in an academic community. You will also need to learn how some everyday thinking strategies, such as synthesizing, help you to participate in the disciplines you are studying here. Chapter 11 introduces you to the activity of synthesizing and offers readings from geology for you to practice synthesizing material from several sources.

9

NUTRITION

D o you have a grandmother who has fallen and broken a leg or an arm? She may suffer from osteoporosis—literally, "porous bone"—a disease that affects or will affect one out of every four American women. It has been called a silent disease because it develops over many years before any physical signs—such as hips and wrists that break easily—appear. We have always thought that eating more dairy products or taking calcium supplements would prevent osteoporosis, but research in nutrition now suggests that we rethink the relationship between calcium intake and osteoporosis.

Nutrition, a specialty in the biomedical sciences, examines the role of diet in health and disease as well as the social, psychological, and economic factors that influence eating patterns and food choices. Researchers might observe or interview groups in various communities, study individuals in experimentally controlled settings, examine biochemical processes in laboratories, or investigate the behavioral aspects of food and food choices.

In this chapter, I interview a professor of nutrition, Dr. Elaine Prewitt, who will tell you something about her field and then do a close reading of a research report examining the relationship between protein intake and osteoporosis in a particular group, North Alaskan Eskimos. Then some ideas about how scientific arguments are constructed and how you can analyze them are introduced. Most importantly, I invite you to think about how your own personal connections to this material can help you to understand research in nutrition.

INTERVIEWING A NUTRITIONIST

Dr. Elaine Prewitt, who has a doctorate in public health nutrition, teaches and conducts research in the Department of Preventative Medicine and Epidemiology at the Loyola University Medical Center. In the following interview, Dr. Prewitt talks about her education, her research, and tells us what recent research in the field suggests about nutrition.

Tell us about your education. How did you become a nutrition researcher?

Before I went to college my grandfather wanted me to be a nurse; I wanted to be a pharmacist; and my father wanted me to be a dentist. So nutrition, which was my final choice, combined some of the best things of each profession. The school where I went for my undergraduate work didn't have a school of pharmacy. In an introductory nutrition course, though, I began to see the link between diet and health. At that time, the interest in diet as a major factor in preventing or lowering the risk of certain diseases had not yet captured national attention. However, I had heard about public health programs that targeted high-risk populations and utilized multidisciplinary approaches to health care. I started looking for master's programs in public health nutrition in my senior year of college.

I went to graduate school in nutrition and took an emphasis in maternal and child health. After getting my degree I worked as a nutritionist within a public health department. I was a member of a multidisciplinary health team that consisted of a physician, nurse, social worker, and nutritionist who provided a range of prenatal care services to high-risk mothers in order to reduce the rate of low-birth-weight babies.

How did your schooling prepare you for helping people who didn't know much about nutrition?

I was excited about working with the health department because I thought I could really make a difference, especially with pregnant women. In that setting, though, I was reminded that my knowledge was useful only if it could be explained and applied in practical ways. Let's face it, the patients wanted to know basically "Can I eat this or can I eat that for a healthy baby?" They were not interested in protein metabolism during pregnancy.

I remember one woman in particular who had a history of pica, which means the consumption of nonfood items like ice, starch, or clay. This woman had a history of eating starch. Since this practice obviously can reduce the nutritional quality of the diet, I had to address the issue with her during a counseling session and encourage her not to eat clay or starch at all, particularly not while she was pregnant. She surprised me at one of her clinic visits by announcing to me that she had decided not to eat starch anymore. I asked her why. She explained that when her last baby was born it was covered all over with a starch-like material. She did not realize that this substance is present on all newborns. I told her she had made a good decision and encouraged her to stick to it. In my next job, I taught nutrition at a college and became more and more interested in nutrition research. As a result, I decided to go back to school for my doctorate.

Did you have a hard time deciding on a topic for your doctoral research?

Maternal and child health still fascinated me. My experiences in public health and teaching nutrition at the college level made me keenly aware of the limitations of the methods used in determining a person's nutritional status. Basically, the existing measures were only useful in diagnosing relatively severe malnutrition. I wanted to identify a measure that correlated closely with dietary intake—specifically protein and energy intake during pregnancy and/or growth. This measure—what I called a dietary status indicator or bio-chemical marker—should tell whether nutritional status was normal or not. I had been interested in this area for a long time and in graduate school I learned how to describe more precisely the research project I wanted to conduct.

What steps did you have to take to prepare for actually doing your dissertation research?

I took advanced nutrition courses, biostatistics, basic science, epidemiology, maternal and child health, research methods, and laboratory methods courses. During my course work, I began talking to researchers on the faculty, trying to narrow down the topic and identify a person to guide me in carrying out a project. I spent almost a year reading the literature and talking to faculty members trying to figure out how to approach my research project.

The first two projects I proposed fell through. As I recall, I had read about a certain hormone produced during pregnancy that responded to nutritional status. This looked promising but after following up on the topic, I ran into a dead end. I was at probably one of my lowest points. Shortly afterwards, a faculty member told me about a "growth factor" that might relate to my interest and recommended that I read the literature on it. As I began to do so, I found that in malnutrition the growth factor was reduced, but after refeeding, it returned to normal levels. I was excited about this; it was just the sort of observation I had been looking for—a biochemical indicator that responded to dietary status. As it turned out, a group of pediatric endocrinologists on campus were actively involved in research on this particular growth factor. I was able to learn techniques in their laboratory for measuring the growth factor. Since I completed my research, the growth factor has been intensively studied by other investigators under various nutritional conditions in humans and in experimental animals.

Tell us something about the process of writing your dissertation.

I learned a lot writing my doctoral dissertation, which was the largest writing project I had done up to that point. Once I finished collecting my data, completed the analyses, and found that I had positive results, I had something to write about. I was relieved that I could explain that I had in fact observed what I had expected to observe. After my dissertation was completed, the findings were published in a scientific journal.

The writing itself was somewhat difficult. I kept writing and getting feedback from the members of my committee. I would write a draft and give it to the committee members; they would make comments and give it back to me. Their comments would include things like, "Why would you say this happened, based on what's in the literature? Why did your results turn out this way?" Writing the literature review was not a big problem since I had spent so much time reading and collecting journal articles. The methods section was not very difficult either, since I only had to explain step by step what I did.

The difficult part for me was the discussion section because, among other things, I had to explain clearly what contribution my project made to the field of nutrition. What new knowledge resulted? What were the implications of the knowledge? I had to present the new information and be persuasive about its value. Had I found a biochemical indicator of dietary intake or not? My results told me the answer was "yes." I had to communicate this so my readers would understand the significance of my study.

*I couldn't write the discussion section for a long time. I just couldn't get it down on paper. Looking back, it seems as though I was too involved in the project to see the forest for the trees. I remember very clearly when the breakthrough came. I was working in an office, starting to write a page. I ripped it up and threw it in the trash can. I got up and walked to the door, put my hand on the handle, and suddenly had a flash of insight. I had the idea I needed to make the whole discussion come together and make sense. Generally speaking, I needed to make the point that the indicator I had measured was sensitive enough to respond to suboptimal dietary intake before clinical signs of deficiency were evident. In other words, the **early** signs of malnutrition—such as biochemical changes in the blood—could be detected before the obvious signs of malnutrition—such as weight loss. This point provided the underlying argument that helped me to pull things together. I remember thinking about this earlier in the study and that this was the bottom line of the whole thing.*

What kind of research are you doing now?

I am currently involved in a dietary intervention study with the goal of reducing the risk of heart disease through decreasing the amount of fat in the diet. While we hear a lot about how to eat to stay healthy, the real issue is how to apply what we've heard to our everyday eating patterns. The study I am currently conducting will teach participants how to incorporate recommendations for healthy eating into their usual food patterns.

Do you teach undergraduate courses in nutrition?

Yes, I have taught several undergraduate nutrition courses. It is important for students to understand that when you study nutrition you're looking at the cumulative effect of what you eat on health, well-being, and risk for various diseases. These classes cover a range of topics, including the basics of nutrition, nutrition in the life cycle, diet and exercise, weight control, and the relation of diet to various chronic diseases such as heart disease, diabetes, and hypertension.

What kinds of problems do researchers in nutrition try to solve?

Nutrition researchers address a range of problems: nutrition at the molecular and cellular levels, biochemical and physiological aspects of nutrition, clinical nutrition, nutrition education, sociocultural aspects of diet and food behavior, nutrition and disease in populations, and food and nutrition policy, to name a few. For example, in nutrition education research, one area focuses on nutrition knowledge, attitudes, and practices, and factors related to changing dietary behavior. For example, one might conduct a nutrition education program aimed at increasing fiber in the diet, since this is an important dietary constituent for reducing the risk of certain diseases. Participants' knowledge and attitudes about dietary fiber as well as some idea of the amount of fiber in the diet could be measured before the program starts and at the end of it. By looking at knowledge, attitudes, and dietary practices before and after the program, we can get some idea of the impact of the program on these variables.

What is the field of nutrition discovering that people on the street don't know?

One message that is getting out to the public is the relationship between diet and chronic disease. There is strong evidence that several things in the diet, particularly high intakes of fat and sodium and low intakes of fruits, vegetables, and dietary fiber are risk factors for heart disease, hypertension, cancer, and other diseases. The solution is to change to a healthy eating pattern. Although changing one's diet can be difficult sometimes, it is possible to do it with practice and commitment. One thing we have learned is that heart disease risk can be reduced by decreasing saturated fat in the diet and by decreasing total fat in the diet to less than 30% of total calories.

WRITING AND LEARNING ACTIVITIES

1. Journal Entry: Look up a definition of nutrition or dietetics in two of the specialized sources listed in the appendix. Consider the differences and similarities among these definitions. Report to the class on what you found.

2. Question Posing: Write three questions you would like to ask Professor Prewitt if you had the opportunity to talk with her.

3. Peer Conversation: With a partner, discuss your journal entries and questions for Professor Prewitt. Respond also to the following questions: Were you reminded by something she said of an experience you've had at home, school, or work? Have you thought about nutrition at all? Have you had to make any choices in your life regarding your nutrition?

4. Research Project: Look up the description for the nutrition or dietetics major in your college catalog. Respond to the following questions: How is the discipline of nutrition or dietetics described? How does this description differ from Professor Prewitt's description or from other definitions you've found? What are the required courses for the major? What are the areas of specialization? Next, interview someone who is a nutrition major. Why is he or she studying this? What courses has this person taken to prepare for this major? What does he or she plan to do with a degree in nutrition?

5. Writing Activity: Write a report about what it's like to major in nutrition or dietetics and present your report to the class.

6. Journal Entry: Write a description of your family or your culture's eating patterns. What foods are eaten daily and on special occasions? If your family emigrated recently from another country, have your eating habits changed? Bring to class the name and description of a food or dish you think few others will be familiar with.

7. Developing Interests: Go to the library and browse through popular newsletters on nutrition and health, such as the *Tufts University Diet and Nutrition Newsletter, Food and Nutrition,* the *University of California Wellness Letter,* and *Women's Sports and Fitness.* Make a list of interesting topics that you would like to know more about.

A NUTRITIONIST READS RESEARCH ON BONE LOSS

In the interview above, Professor Prewitt tells us that the study of nutrition focuses on the relationship between what you eat, that is, the basic nutrients you ingest, and its effect on your health. The report below, "Bone

Mineral Content of North Alaskan Eskimos," published in 1974 in the *American Journal of Clinical Nutrition*, focuses on the relationship between the eating of a high quantity of protein and the presence of a disease called osteoporosis, which largely affects the elderly, causing bones to break easily.

PLANNING TO READ RESEARCH IN NUTRITION

I asked Professor Prewitt to tell us about situations in which she might be called upon to present what she had learned from reading this research.

I might very well have to make a presentation at a conference or scientific meeting, for instance at a roundtable discussion devoted to calcium metabolism. At a scientific meeting, my audience would be researchers working in similar areas; they want to network, to find out what's going on, to share results. For this audience, I would analyze and evaluate the research and suggest other studies that need to be done. Or I might give a presentation in a continuing education setting for practitioners who don't conduct research but who work directly with clients, as I did when I worked in public health. These folks often attend a professional meeting or regional conference to get an update on research in the field.

Look over the text along with Professor Prewitt. Notice what type of information is included in each section of the research report; see pp. 350–352.

BONE MINERAL CONTENT OF NORTH ALASKAN ESKIMOS[1, 2, 3]

RICHARD B. MAZESS, PH.D., AND WARREN MATHER, B.S.

■ ■ ■

ABSTRACT   Direct photon absorptiometry was used to measure the bone mineral content of forearm bones in Eskimo natives of the north coast of Alaska. The sample consisted of 217 children, 89 adults, and 107 elderly (over 50 years). Eskimo children had a lower bone mineral content than United States whites by 5 to 10% but this was consistent with their smaller body and bone size. Young Eskimo adults (20 to 39 years) of both sexes were similar to whites, but after age 40 the Eskimos of both sexes had a deficit of from 10 to 15% relative to

[1] From the Bone Mineral Laboratory, Department of Radiology (Medical Physics), University of Wisconsin Hospital, Madison, Wisconsin 53706.

[2] Supported by Grants Y-NGR–50–002–051 from the National Aeronautics and Space Administration and (11–1)–1422 from the Atomic Energy Commission, Washington, D.C.

[3] This study was part of the investigation of circumpolar populations, Human Adaptability Section of the International Biological Program.

white standards. Aging bone loss, which occurs in many populations, has an earlier onset and greater intensity in the Eskimos. Nutritional factors of high protein, high nitrogen, high phosphorus, and low calcium intakes may be implicated.   Am. J. Clin. Nutr. *27:916–925, 1974.*

Eskimos throughout the circumpolar regions have a diet highly dependent on animal foods, and the Eskimos of the north coast of Alaska in the past and even today have among the highest meat intakes. Caribou, sea mammals, fish, and birds constitute staple foods, and the supply is generally adequate, though seasonal variation does exist. This dependence on meats provides high intakes of protein and fat (and of course nitrogen, phosphorus, sulfur, and acid); there was a low intake of carbohydrates until the current importation of manufactured foods. Recent nutritional investigations of Alaskan Eskimo populations have generally shown adequate intakes of all major nutrients and little biochemical evidence of poor nutritional status (1–5), except for some anemia and marginal vitamin B_6 excretion in younger subjects. Growth and development from early infancy on appears normal for a group with small adult stature. Eskimos seem to tolerate their dietary fat (6, 7) but have difficulties in handling carbohydrates to which they are relatively unaccustomed; both sucrose and lactose intolerance have been demonstrated in Alaskan and Greenland Eskimos (8–10), and impairment of glucose tolerance exists in Canadian Eskimos (11). Eskimos, and even whites in the Arctic, seem to tolerate the high meat diets well, but the long-term effect of this diet in particular on mineral metabolism has not been studied, although it is well-known that a meat diet, or high intakes of phosphorus or acid, will cause calcium loss. Meat diets have been shown to cause bone rarefaction (12), and among humans, vegetarians have less aging bone loss than omnivores (13). It was therefore of interest to examine the skeletal status of Eskimo natives of the Alaskan north slope.

MATERIALS AND METHODS

Direct photon absorptiometry as developed at the University of Wisconsin was used to determine the bone mineral content (14–17). This method uses an external radionuclide for transmission scanning and has been shown to provide precise and accurate (approximately 2% error) measurements of the local mineral content (18–20). Moreover, an absorptiometric scan at a site on a long bone is highly correlated ($r > 0.9$) to the total weight of that bone, to the total skeletal weight (21, 22), and to total body calcium (23, 24). We used a portable system allowing immediate digital readout of bone mineral content and bone width for the Eskimo measurements (25). The absorptiometric scans were done with ^{125}I (28 kev), and calibration was done against ashed bone sections and various standards including the widely used three-chamber bone phantom of saturated dipotassium hydrogen phosphate (26).

Measurements were made on Eskimos of Wainwright in 1968 and 1969 using standard sites on the humerus, radius, and ulna shafts. A preliminary report of the 1969 data has been published (27). In 1970, additional subjects were measured in Pt. Hope and Pt. Barrow; measurements were made on the radius and ulna shaft and also on the distal radius and ulna (2 cm from the ulnar styloid). In each subject, an average of approximately four determinations was taken at each of the scan sites. The coefficient of variation (CV) for bone mineral content (BMC) in each set of determinations was approximately 2 to 4%; the variation decreased in larger bones and was smaller in adults than children. This was somewhat greater variability than encountered in surveys in Wisconsin and apparently was due to variable local generators. The ratio of the mineral to width (BMC/W) was calculated and used as an index of mineral content adjusted for bone and body size.

In all, 413 subjects were measured, of which 217 were children (ages 5 to 19 years), 89 were adults (ages 20 to 49 years), and 107 were elderly (over 50 years). Sixty-three of the Wainwright subjects were measured in successive years, and average values were taken in these cases. For the 20 adults who had measurements in both years, the correlations between the measurements were 0.94 to 0.98 for bone mineral, and 0.90 to 0.93 for bone width. Student's t tests were done to examine differences in each age-sex group among the three villages surveyed, but nearly all of the few significant differences were due to highly variable measurements of the bone width at the distal ulna site. Consequently the data were merged.

RESULTS

5   The heights and weights of the Alaskan Eskimos are given in Table 1. Eskimos of both sexes and all ages were significantly ($P < 0.01$) smaller than our white population (28, 29) by a fairly uniform 6%. Despite this, Eskimo females at all ages were of almost identical weight as Caucasians. Eskimo males were approximately 5% lighter in body weight than whites in preadolescent years, but as in females, the differences were not significant. During and after adolescence, the Eskimo males were almost 10% lighter than whites, and significant differences were observed. These differences merely confirm the known fact that Eskimos are smaller and stockier in body build than whites, and that there is less sexual dimorphism in body build among Eskimos.

Tables 2 to 6 outline the bone mineral measurements of the Eskimos, and give their values as a percentage of available standards for the white population (28) where sufficient data are available on the latter. The significance of t tests for Eskimo–white differences are also given. Coefficients of variation in each age-sex group were similar to those observed in whites.

Eskimo bone widths were generally similar (within ± 5%) to those of whites for most sex-age combinations except for the distal radius site, for which the adult Eskimos had a markedly larger (25%) bone width. On the shaft of the radius and ulna, the widths were nearly 2% lower than those in whites and in the humerus the widths were 5% lower in Eskimos, but these

TABLE 1   Morphology of Alaskan Eskimo children and adults; Eskimo values as a percent of white values are given[a]

Sex	Age, years	No.	Height, cm				Weight, kg			
			X̄	SD	CV	Per-cent	X̄	SD	CV	Per-cent
Males	5–7	23	116.9	5.3	4.6	93.2[b]	23.3	2.8	12.1	94.0
	8–9	19	129.8	7.5	5.8	94.1[b]	30.4	5.1	16.8	97.4
	10–11	22	140.1	7.4	5.3	95.6[b]	35.2	5.4	15.4	95.4
	12–14	20	151.0	8.9	5.9	94.0[b]	47.5	10.8	22.7	94.8
	15–16	9	162.9	5.6	3.5	92.6[b]	55.1	6.5	11.8	81.6[b]
	17–19	15	171.0	8.5	5.0	94.9[b]	69.7	7.0	10.0	91.3[c]
	20–29	16	168.6	4.7	2.8	94.2[b]	70.0	6.5	9.3	91.7[c]
	30–39	17	167.7	7.1	4.2	93.4[b]	67.4	10.1	15.0	84.5[c]
	40–49	7	166.9	6.8	4.1	94.3[b]	67.9	8.9	13.0	86.2[b]
	50–59	13	166.1	4.0	2.4	93.6[b]	74.5	11.6	15.5	93.7
	60–69	27	163.2	4.8	2.9	93.2[b]	67.7	12.9	19.0	89.2[c]
	70–82	13	163.0	4.8	2.9	93.2[b]	69.8	12.6	18.1	94.2
Females	5–7	26	119.5	7.5	6.3	94.4[b]	24.8	5.8	23.4	102.5
	8–9	22	123.0	5.9	4.6	90.2[b]	28.9	3.9	13.7	97.6
	10–11	17	139.7	7.7	5.5	95.5[b]	37.3	8.2	21.9	100.3
	12–14	22	151.8	6.5	4.3	93.3[b]	53.1	11.1	21.6	107.9
	15–16	10	157.4	3.8	2.4	94.6[b]	58.7	6.6	11.3	104.6
	17–19	12	157.6	4.6	2.9	95.3[b]	59.8	5.3	8.8	102.4
	20–29	14	157.1	5.6	3.5	96.0[b]	60.8	12.7	20.9	104.6
	30–39	19	155.1	6.0	3.9	94.1[b]	63.6	14.2	22.3	97.5
	40–49	16	152.3	7.6	5.0	95.0[b]	65.5	15.9	24.2	102.7
	50–59	23	153.3	7.7	5.0	95.2[b]	62.4	11.5	18.5	97.8
	60–69	20	152.8	5.6	3.7	96.0[b]	65.5	15.4	23.6	104.3
	70–81	11	141.3	10.2	7.2	89.3[b]	48.6	10.7	22.0	77.6[b]

[a]Significance of difference by t test: [b]$P < 0.01$; [c]$P < 0.05$.

differences were generally not significant. The BMC was approximately 5 to 10% lower in Eskimo children than in whites, but this was in part a reflection of their smaller body and bone size; the Eskimo children were lower in BMC/W by less than 5%. In occasional cases, there were differences of 8 to 10% which were significant. In young adults (20 to 39 years), the BMC and BMC/W for all sites except the distal radius were almost the same as in whites; the Eskimos had approximately a 4% lower BMC and a 2% lower BMC/W than whites. By age 40 to 50 significant differences became apparent, with the Eskimos being close to 5% lower on the average than whites; by age 60 to 69, the difference on the average was nearly 10%.

Probably the best comparison can be made at the midshaft radius site. This is the most anatomically uniform of the measuring sites, and in our experience, it has been the most valuable for both clinical and survey evaluations. It is the site for which the greatest amount of data has been collected. Here as elsewhere the Eskimo deficit of bone with respect to white values appeared to increase with age. During the decade from 40 to 49, the Eskimos had 10% lower values than U.S. whites and the deficit increased to 14% in the succeeding two decades. During the seventies, the Eskimo males were 15% below comparable whites, but Eskimo females were almost 30% below.

TABLE 2   Bone mineral measurements of the shaft of the radius of Alaskan Eskimo children and adults; Eskimo values as a percent of white values are given[a]

Sex	Age, years	No.	Mineral, mg/cm				Width, m × 10⁻⁵				BMC/W			
			X̄	SD	CV	Per-cent	X̄	SD	CV	Per-cent	X̄	SD	CD	Per-cent
Males	5–7	23	462	73	15.9	93.3	1,006	203	20.2	102.3	0.466	0.061	13.0	92.6[b]
	8–9	19	536	71	13.3	92.6[c]	1,005	117	11.6	96.0	0.533	0.045	8.6	96.4
	10–11	22	626	90	14.4	93.7	1,086	93	8.5	96.4	0.574	0.060	10.5	96.8
	12–14	20	760	138	18.1	92.9	1,189	137	11.5	94.7[c]	0.636	0.060	9.4	98.0
	15–16	9	926	87	9.4	84.5[b]	1,293	87	6.7	89.7[b]	0.715	0.050	7.0	94.1
	17–19	15	1,163	130	11.8	94.2	1,411	95	6.7	95.4	0.823	0.059	7.1	98.4
	20–29	16	1,273	155	12.2	97.4	1,497	157	10.5	101.4	0.852	0.088	10.4	96.3
	30–39	17	1,200	117	9.7	90.8[b]	1,458	110	7.6	98.6	0.823	0.066	8.0	92.0[b]
	40–49	7	1,171	91	7.8	89.8[b]	1,514	128	8.4	102.0	0.774	0.061	7.8	88.0[b]
	50–59	13	1,125	96	8.5	85.7[b]	1,508	119	7.9	101.3	0.748	0.072	9.6	85.0[b]
	60–69	27	1,017	160	15.7	83.0[b]	1,499	160	10.6	95.5	0.680	0.100	14.7	86.1[b]
	70–82	13	1,058	103	9.7	84.2[b]	1,530	148	9.6	98.5	0.693	0.063	9.1	85.5[b]
Females	5–7	26	437	72	16.4	98.2	922	151	16.4	101.2	0.475	0.056	11.9	97.3
	8–9	22	483	53	11.0	92.4[c]	929	121	12.4	97.3	0.497	0.054	11.0	90.7[b]
	10–11	17	558	70	12.6	91.9	958	104	10.9	92.6[b]	0.582	0.040	6.9	99.7
	12–14	22	762	129	16.9	96.7	1,115	135	12.1	95.9	0.681	0.078	11.4	100.6
	15–16	10	848	50	5.8	97.0	1,184	103	8.7	98.7	0.718	0.045	6.3	98.5
	17–19	12	878	100	11.4	95.7	1,192	154	12.9	97.5	0.738	0.049	6.6	98.4
	20–29	14	889	108	12.1	93.4[c]	1,166	144	12.3	94.8[c]	0.764	0.055	7.2	98.7
	30–39	19	928	127	13.7	92.8	1,262	168	13.3	96.8	0.736	0.059	8.0	95.7
	40–49	16	883	124	14.1	90.4[b]	1,273	125	10.0	98.1	0.693	0.066	9.5	90.8[b]
	50–59	23	782	140	17.8	88.4[b]	1,282	118	9.2	102.4	0.609	0.081	13.4	86.3[b]
	60–69	20	685	112	16.4	89.1[c]	1,278	144	11.3	101.5	0.536	0.072	13.5	87.9[b]
	70–81	11	507	131	25.9	70.2[b]	1,264	78	6.2	100.7	0.399	0.090	22.5	69.4[b]

[a]Significance of difference by t test: [b]$P < 0.01$. [c]$P < 0.05$.

TABLE 3 Bone mineral measurements of the shaft of the ulna of Alaskan Eskimo children and adults; Eskimo values as a percent of white values are given[a]

Sex	Age, Years	No.	Mineral, mg/cm				Width, m × 10⁻⁵				BMC/W			
			X̄	SD	CV	Per-cent	X̄	SD	CV	Per-cent	X̄	SD	CV	Per-cent
Males	5–7	23	402	71	17.5	99.5	906	129	14.3	105.8	0.443	0.041	9.4	93.7[c]
	8–9	19	456	84	18.4	95.6	928	149	16.1	99.8	0.490	0.050	10.2	95.5
	10–11	22	543	94	17.3	98.0	1,012	107	10.6	105.2[c]	0.535	0.064	12.0	92.7[b]
	12–14	20	661	111	16.7	100.5	1,062	114	10.7	102.7	0.618	0.058	9.3	97.3
	15–16	9	817	62	7.6	89.0[c]	1,162	95	8.2	96.8	0.706	0.073	10.4	92.4
	17–19	15	1,005	126	12.6	97.2	1,167	70	6.0	92.6[c]	0.859	0.085	9.8	103.9
	20–29	16	1,060	119	11.3		1,205	90	7.4		0.877	0.069	7.8	
	30–39	17	1,067	135	12.7		1,189	81	6.8		0.895	0.083	9.3	
	40–49	7	1,032	85	8.2		1,223	84	6.9		0.844	0.053	6.3	
	50–59	13	1,066	132	12.4		1,308	102	7.8		0.815	0.072	8.8	
	60–69	27	930	181	19.5		1,235	136	11.0		0.751	0.111	14.7	
	70–82	13	946	125	13.2		1,251	82	6.6		0.755	0.075	9.9	
Females	5–7	26	371	63	16.7	100.8	826	80	9.7	103.1	0.455	0.055	12.0	98.9
	8–9	22	412	58	14.0	92.0	865	94	10.9	100.6	0.477	0.053	11.2	90.9[c]
	10–11	17	480	60	12.6	95.4	862	117	13.6	94.8	0.558	0.046	8.2	101.5
	12–14	22	642	117	18.2		958	107	11.1		0.669	0.093	13.9	
	15–16	10	752	45	6.0		1,043	69	6.6		0.721	0.045	6.3	
	17–19	12	767	98	12.8		1,011	95	9.4		0.759	0.070	9.2	
	20–29	14	793	65	8.2	94.1	980	87	8.9	91.2	0.810	0.057	7.1	102.4
	30–39	19	815	88	10.7	93.7	1,024	102	9.9	95.8	0.797	0.076	9.5	96.7
	40–49	16	811	90	11.2		1,106	118	10.6		0.734	0.058	8.0	
	50–59	23	712	148	20.8	88.6[c]	1,096	112	10.2	99.2	0.646	0.093	14.4	88.7[b]
	60–69	20	647	105	16.3	92.2	1,110	129	11.6	100.1	0.585	0.093	15.9	93.6
	70–81	11	462	133	28.9	75.1[b]	1,037	109	16.5	94.0	0.442	0.106	23.9	78.6[b]

[a]See Tables 1 or 2 for explanation of [b] and [c].

TABLE 4 Bone mineral measurements of the midshaft of the humerus of Alaskan Eskimo children and adults; Eskimo values as a percent of white values are given[a]

Sex	Age, Years	No.	Mineral, MG/CM				Width, M × 10⁻⁵				M/W			
			X̄	SD	CV	Per-cent	X̄	SD	CV	Per-cent	X̄	SD	CV	Per-cent
Males	5–7	9	974	147	15.1	90.4	1,384	115	8.3	95.2	0.701	0.082	11.8	94.6
	8–9	10	1,138	153	13.4	89.7[b]	1,535	125	8.1	97.0	0.737	0.056	7.6	91.8[b]
	10–11	8	1,432	168	11.7	97.6	1,699	117	6.9	98.1	0.840	0.059	7.0	99.2
	12–14	7	1,773	256	14.4	101.5	1,883	90	4.8	98.5	0.937	0.116	12.4	102.6
	15–16	3	1,982	276	13.9	84.4	1,987	46	2.3	91.2[c]	0.995	0.122	12.3	92.5
	17–19	8	2,518	316	12.5	91.4[c]	2,110	81	3.8	93.2[c]	1.191	0.133	11.1	97.7
	20–29	12	2,760	327	11.8	99.8	2,157	160	7.4	93.6[c]	1.279	0.122	9.5	106.6[b]
	30–39	10	2,840	393	13.8	103.9	2,256	140	6.2	98.1	1.254	0.125	10.0	105.6
	40–49	4	2,748	349	12.7	104.0	2,145	126	5.9	92.7	1.279	0.143	11.1	108.3
	50–59	3	2,763	233	8.4	99.4	2,213	193	8.7	94.5	1.259	0.196	15.6	105.9
	60–69	9	2,336	472	20.2	90.6	2,228	92	4.1	96.9	1.047	0.201	19.2	93.3
	70–82													
Females	5–7	12	917	146	16.0	93.4	1,309	112	8.5	92.4[c]	0.696	0.069	10.0	100.3
	8–9	9	1,015	137	13.5	86.6[b]	1,433	92	6.4	93.1[c]	0.706	0.090	12.8	92.9[c]
	10–11	9	1,106	154	13.9	87.5	1,519	63	4.2	95.1	0.727	0.099	13.6	92.5
	12–14	14	1,635	278	17.0	97.2	1,771	169	9.6	97.0	0.920	0.116	12.6	100.1
	15–16	5	1,898	167	8.8	100.1	1,812	151	8.3	96.6	1.045	0.054	5.2	103.2
	17–19	4	1,724	226	13.1	86.5	1,852	123	6.6	98.3	0.929	0.099	10.7	87.9[c]
	20–29	6	1,820	215	11.8	86.7[c]	1,817	93	5.1	91.4[c]	0.988	0.067	6.8	93.6
	30–39	9	2,001	257	12.9	94.5	1,902	191	10.0	96.6	1.052	0.104	9.8	98.0
	40–49	4	1,911	206	10.8	91.8	1,917	67	3.5	95.2	0.993	0.075	7.6	96.1
	50–59	4	1,570	184	11.7	86.7	1,845	130	7.1	95.1	0.855	0.137	16.1	90.7
	60–69													
	70–81													

[a] See Tables 1 or 2 for explanation of [b] and [c].

TABLE 5 Bone mineral measurements of the distal radius of Alaskan Eskimo children and adults; Eskimo values as a percent of white values are given[a]

Sex	Age, years	No.	Mineral, mg/cm				Width, m × 10^{-5}				BMC/W			
			$\bar{X}$	SD	CV	Per-cent	$\bar{X}$	SD	CV	Per-cent	$\bar{X}$	SD	CV	Per-cent
Males	5–7	14	478	86	18.0		1,464	194	13.2		0.326	0.043	13.1	
	8–9	9	554	80	14.5		1,592	269	16.9		0.349	0.019	15.4	
	10–11	14	608	80	13.2		1,740	164	9.4		0.349	0.039	11.1	
	12–14	13	769	207	26.9		1,917	489	25.5		0.407	0.072	17.6	
	15–16	6	1,007	225	22.3		2,459	501	20.4		0.409	0.033	8.0	
	17–19	7	1,397	248	17.7		2,701	391	14.5		0.517	0.068	13.1	
	20–29	4	1,568	179	11.4	113.1	3,020	391	13.0	128.9[b]	0.523	0.069	13.2	87.2
	30–39	7	1,433	185	12.9	108.8	2,702	221	8.2	118.4[b]	0.530	0.058	11.0	90.1
	40–49	3	1,308	238	18.2	100.8	3,300	171	5.2	152.6[b]	0.395	0.062	15.7	65.0[b]
	50–59	19	1,213	255	21.0	91.2	2,847	348	12.2	129.3[b]	0.428	0.090	21.0	69.7[b]
	60–69	18	1,052	209	19.9	88.3	2,712	335	12.3	114.8[c]	0.394	0.098	24.8	76.4[b]
	70–82	10	1,029	190	18.4	86.7	2,535	396	15.6	108.8	0.410	0.075	18.2	76.5[c]
Females	5–7	14	423	67	15.8		1,305	180	13.8		0.326	0.048	14.8	
	8–9	13	438	80	18.2		1,442	271	18.8		0.307	0.044	14.5	
	10–11	8	539	83	15.4		1,561	297	19.1		0.357	0.087	24.3	
	12–14	8	712	185	25.9		2,014	346	17.2		0.352	0.058	16.5	
	15–16	5	881	182	20.6		2,352	90	3.8		0.373	0.066	17.7	
	17–19	8	969	153	15.8		2,121	513	24.2		0.473	0.092	19.5	
	20–29	8	1,080	191	17.7	109.8	2,435	480	19.7	131.1[b]	0.449	0.060	13.4	83.3[b]
	30–39	10	964	163	16.9	100.9	2,404	423	17.6	147.0[b]	0.468	0.079	16.9	83.0[c]
	40–49	12	1,042	162	15.6	111.7	2,364	256	10.8	121.0[c]	0.444	0.069	15.6	89.9
	50–59	10	935	218	23.3	105.4	2,382	362	15.2	128.3[b]	0.397	0.097	24.4	82.4[b]
	60–69	18	696	161	23.2	93.8	2,256	368	16.3	118.6[b]	0.315	0.088	27.9	78.4[b]
	70–81	11	472	146	30.9	65.7[b]	1,830	457	24.9	100.5[b]	0.263	0.084	31.9	65.9[b]

[a]See Tables 1 or 2 for explanation of [b] and [c].

TABLE 6 Bone mineral measurements of the distal ulna of Eskimo children and adults; Eskimo values as a percent of white values are given[a]

Sex	Age, years	No.	Mineral, MG/CM				Width, M × 10⁻⁵				BMC/W			
			X̄	SD	CV	Per-cent	X̄	SD	CV	Per-cent	X̄	SD	CV	Per-cent
Males	5–7	14	271	54	19.9		876	103	11.8		0.311	0.055	17.6	
	8–9	9	305	57	18.7		915	181	19.7		0.336	0.033	9.9	
	10–11	14	330	49	14.9		945	108	11.5		0.351	0.050	14.5	
	12–14	13	415	87	21.1		1,045	220	21.1		0.400	0.066	16.6	
	15–16	6	520	82	15.8		1,191	147	12.3		0.436	0.044	10.2	
	17–19	7	712	142	20.0		1,319	273	20.7		0.544	0.078	14.3	
	20–29	4	847	103	12.1		1,423	241	17.0		0.598	0.034	5.7	
	30–39	7	721	103	14.3		1,140	116	10.2		0.630	0.046	7.3	
	40–49	4	699	54	7.7		1,285	110	8.5		0.545	0.038	6.9	
	50–59	10	656	125	19.1		1,242	126	10.2		0.532	0.110	20.6	
	60–69	18	563	118	20.9		1,196	136	11.4		0.472	0.086	18.3	
	70–82	10	514	81	15.7		1,133	159	14.1		0.455	0.053	11.6	
Females	5–7	14	234	35	15.0		776	88	11.4		0.303	0.048	15.8	
	8–9	13	236	35	14.7		831	114	13.7		0.287	0.046	16.2	
	10–11	8	307	64	20.9		876	87	10.0		0.355	0.092	26.1	
	12–14	8	368	71	19.4		1,057	149	14.1		0.348	0.052	14.9	
	15–16	5	465	91	19.6		1,171	211	18.1		0.406	0.098	24.2	
	17–19	8	503	76	15.1		1,091	251	23.0		0.476	0.095	20.0	
	20–29	8	528	98	18.7	103.3	1,089	207	19.0	109.0	0.494	0.099	20.0	96.7
	30–39	10	483	70	14.6	96.9	1,042	125	12.0	103.4	0.468	0.079	16.9	92.4
	40–49	12	503	118	23.4		1,052	118	11.2		0.479	0.099	20.6	
	50–59	19	470	102	21.7	104.0	1,098	129	11.8	113.1[b]	0.427	0.071	16.6	91.0
	60–69	18	333	75	22.6	91.5	1,012	130	12.9	101.2	0.332	0.079	23.9	90.7
	70–81	11	220	74	33.8	66.7[b]	889	259	29.1	85.6[c]	0.254	0.066	26.3	79.9[c]

[a]See Tables 1 or 2 for explanation of [b] and [c].

344

DISCUSSION

North Alaskan Eskimos appeared to have relatively normal bone mineral status compared with whites during the periods of growth and early adulthood. However, in both sexes there was an early and large loss of bone with aging so that Eskimos over age 40 had an average of 10 to 15% less bone than comparable whites. I. G. Pawson (personal communication) has measured the radiographic compact bone thickness of the metacarpal in a subsample, from Wainwright, of the groups reported here and found essentially similar results. The finding of an essentially normal bone mineral content during growth and early adulthood is not surprising in view of previous studies indicating normal growth in Eskimos (3–5), and lack of apparent nutritional deficiency (1–3). The bone loss in older Eskimos, however, was quite unusual. The aging bone loss was not a function of smaller body size or bone size in the over–40 age groups; use of the BMC/W to compensate for size minimizes any such differences to the extent that they exist.

10   In the Eskimos, the onset of bone loss appears to be in the late thirties in both sexes, whereas in white females, it is in the forties and in white males in the fifties (28). Apparently, some continuous process accompanies aging in Eskimos that accelerates and exacerbates the aging bone loss evident in so many other populations (20, 28, 30–33). In white females, the rate of bone loss between ages 45 and 74 is approximately 9.5% per decade, and there is a change to almost 4.5% per decade thereafter (28). In white males, the onset of loss is later, and the rate of loss after age 55 is nearly 4.5% per decade. The present results indicate that Eskimo males lost almost 6 to 7% per decade, and Eskimo females close to 10 to 12% per decade after the late thirties and early forties. The rate of loss in Eskimos appeared to approximate 2 to 3% per decade greater than that of corresponding whites. As the onset of loss was earlier than in whites by age 50, the Eskimos had substantially lower bone mineral than whites. This may be medically significant for, invariably, lower bone mineral content indicates lower bone strength, and in whites at least, bone loss seems to dispose the individual to fractures (15, 20, 24).

There is always the possibility that these cross-sectional data do not represent actual longitudinal bone loss, or that there may be a nonuniform distribution of aging bone loss. However, in Eskimos as in whites (28), the variances of BMC and BMC/W do not increase with age, suggesting that there were no subpopulations with differing rates of loss.

In whites, it has been shown that a radius shaft bone mineral value of 680 mg/cm discriminates between normals and osteoporotic females (Smith and Cameron, personal communication). Interestingly, white females tend to have a plateau in their bone loss at approximately this value during their seventies (28). Eskimo women reached this state of demineralization during their sixties, a full decade earlier than white females, and the Eskimos showed no evidence of a plateau in bone loss, so that in the seventies, demineralization continued to even greater levels. Sixty percent of

Eskimo women over age 60 would be classified in the population at risk of fracture by the above criterion, and by age 70, virtually all Eskimo women were in this class.

These findings amplify and substantiate our preliminary report on Alaskan Eskimo bone mineral (27). We have made similar observations on living Canadian Eskimos and also on skeletons. Studies on the bones of a modern Eskimo archaeological population, the Sadlermiut Eskimo from Southampton Island at the northern border of Hudson Bay, have indicated that the Sadlermiut had normal bone composition, and that the densities of bone sections and of whole bones were comparable to those of our white population. However, the older group of Sadlermiut (over 35 years), both male and female, had almost 10 to 15% lower bone weights and densities than the young adults (34, 35). This is a striking concordance with present results on living Eskimos. Interestingly the studies of Merbs (36, 37) on Sadlermiut skeletal pathology have indicated that there was a high incidence of vertebral compression fractures. Recent investigations (Merbs and Mazess, unpublished observations) have indicated that density of long bones was correlated with number and severity of compression fractures in the Sadlermiut. The extensive aging bone loss in contemporary Eskimos may also be correlated with bone pathology, including fractures and tooth loss. As Eskimo longevity increases, it is possible that skeletal pathology as a result of demineralization could present public health problems.

The explanation of the early and large aging decline of bone in Eskimos may involve the numerous factors implicated in the aging bone loss of other populations (38–40). Lack of physical activity in the elderly is one mechanism that probably can be excluded for the Eskimos because this population, especially the male, tends to remain quite active. The northern Eskimos do face a long sunless winter, which might suggest a vitamin D deficiency. There have been suggestions that the elderly are vitamin D-deficient (41), especially in northern climates (42), and it has been recognized that Ca absorption may be decreased in the elderly as a result of this and other factors (43, 44). The Eskimos, however, are exposed to sunlight dur-ing the summer, and their own storage, supplemented by animal fats, probably accounts for the lack of evidence of any vitamin D deficiency even in children. Calcium intake (1, 2) appears sufficiently high (500 to 2,500 mg daily) to preclude a deficiency of this mineral even in the presence of poor absorption.

15   The most obvious factor in the 2 to 3% higher rate of bone loss in middle-aged Eskimos would be their meat diet. Several studies (11, 45, 46) have indicated that young animals develop bone demineralization on meat diets. Ellis et al. (13) have also demonstrated that elderly vegetarians have less aging bone loss than do omnivores. There is considerable controversy over the mechanisms responsible for bone and calcium loss with meat diets. The effects of the high phosphorus and acid production are most obvious, but calcium, copper, and manganese deficiencies have also been implicated. High P intakes, with high P/Ca ratios, can increase Ca-excretion through the

obvious mechanisms of secondary hyperparathyroidism, and also, as shown by Draper (47–49), in aging rats by other mechanisms as yet unclear. It has not been shown, even in the latter studies, that moderate phosphorus intakes would affect animals with intact calcitonin secretion. In normal humans, high phosphate intakes produce hypocalcemia but there is little corresponding increase of Ca excretion or bone loss (50–52) even though parathyroid hormone is stimulated (53). It appears unlikely that the moderate phosphorus intake of 1,000 to 2,000 mg daily (1, 2) would account for the excess Eskimo bone loss.

In contrast, the acidic effect of a meat diet, presumably as related to oxidation of sulfur rather than handling of organic phosphates (54), appears a more likely factor. It has long been known that acidosis increases Ca excretion and causes bone dissolution (55–57), and it has been supposed that bone serves as a homeostatic buffer (58, 59). In humans, a high protein diet (142 g daily), even with controlled intakes of Ca and P, greatly increases urinary Ca and causes negative balance (60–62). This hypercalciuria is not due to increased Ca absorption (63). At Eskimo levels of protein intake (approximating 200 to 400 g daily in times of availability), the net deficit of Ca based on the above balance studies in whites would be over 100 mg daily or 365 g per decade of life. In addition, occasional periods of starvation or ketoacidosis from a total meat diet might also produce high Ca losses, as much as several hundred milligrams daily (64, 65). This clearly is too great a loss to be sustained and is of far greater magnitude than the excess loss, or even the total loss, in older Eskimos. It does indicate, however, that the high protein intake from the meat diet has sufficient potential effect to account for the observed bone loss even should there be long-term adjustment to the hypercalciuric effect of high protein.

The exact mechanisms responsible for the aging bone loss in Alaskan Eskimos, and the health consequences of this loss, warrant further examination. Consideration of the possible nutritional influences also suggests the merit of examining the mechanism whereby Eskimo children maintain normal bone growth despite the potentially harmful effect of a high meat diet.

REFERENCES

1. Heller, C. A. The diet of some Alaskan Eskimos and Indians. J. Am. Dietet. Assoc. 45:425, 1965.
2. Mann, G. V., E. M. Scott, L. M. Hursh, C. A. Heller, J. B. Youmans, C. F. Consolazio, E. B. Bridgforth, A. L. Russell and M. Silverman. The health and nutritional status of Alaskan Eskimos. A survey of the Interdepartmental Committee on Nutrition for National Defense–1958. Am. J. Clin. Nutr. 11:31, 1962.
3. Heller, C. A., E. M. Scott and L. M. Hammes. Height, weight and growth of Alaskan Eskimos. Am. J. Diseases Children 113:338, 1967.
4. Baker, G. L. Nutritional survey of northern Eskimo infants and children. Am. J. Clin. Nutr. 22: 612, 1969.
5. Sauberlich H. E., W. Goad, Y. F. Herman, F. Milan and P. Jamison. Biochemical assessment of the nutritional status of the Eskimos of Wainwright, Alaska. Am. J. Clin. Nutr. 25:437, 1972.

6. Ho, K-J., B. Mikkelson, L. A. Lewis, S. A. Feldman and C. B. Taylor. Alaskan Arctic Eskimo: responses to a customary high fat diet. Am. J. Clin. Nutr. 25:737, 1972.

7. Feldman, S. A., K-J. Ho, L. A. Lewis, B. Mikkelson and C. B. Taylor. Lipid and cholesterol metabolism in Alaskan Arctic Eskimos. Arch. Pathol. 94:42, 1972.

8. McNair, A., E. Gudmand-Hoyer, S. Jarnum, and L. Orrild. Sucrose malabsorption in Greenland. Brit. Med. J. 2:19, 1972.

9. Bell, R. R., H. H. Draper and J. C. Bergan. Sucrose, lactose and glucose tolerance in northern Alaskan Eskimos. Am. J. Clin. Nutr. 26:1185, 1973.

10. Duncan, I. W., and E. M. Scott. Lactose intolerance in Alaskan Indians and Eskimos. Am. J. Clin. Nutr. 25:867, 1972.

11. Schaefer, O., P. M. Crockford and B. Romanowski. Normalization effect of preceding protein meals on "diabetic" oral glucose tolerance in Eskimos. Can. Med. Assoc. J. 21:733, 1972.

12. Hammond, R. H., and E. Storey. Measurement of growth and resorption of bone in rats fed meat diet. Calcified Tissue Res. 4:291, 1970.

13. Ellis, F. R., S. Holesh and J. W. Ellis. Incidence of osteoporosis in vegetarians and omnivores. Am. J. Clin. Nutr. 25:555, 1972.

14. Cameron, J. R., and J. A. Sorenson. Measurement of bone mineral in vivo: an improved method. Science 143:230, 1963.

15. Cameron, J. R. (editor). Proc. of the Bone Measurement Conference. U.S. AEC Conf. 700515. Springfield, Virginia: Clearinghouse for Federal Scientific and Technical Information, 1970.

16. Sorenson, J. A., and J. R. Cameron. A reliable in vivo measurement of bone mineral content. J. Bone Joint Surg. 49-A:481, 1967.

17. Sorenson, J. A., J. R. Cameron and R. B. Mazess. Measurement of bone mineral by the direct photon absorption method: experimental results. In: Progress in Methods of Bone Mineral Measurement, edited by G. D. Whedon and J. R. Cameron. Washington, D. C.: U.S. Govt. Printing Office, 1970, p. 269.

18. Mazess, R. B., J. R. Cameron, R. O'Connor and D. Knutzen. Accuracy of bone mineral measurement. Science 145:388, 1964.

19. Cameron, J. R., R. B. Mazess and J. A. Sorenson. Precision and accuracy of bone mineral determination by the direct photon absorptiometric method. Invest. Radiol. 3:141, 1968.

20. Smith, D. M., C. Johnston, Jr. and P-L. Yu. In vivo measurement of bone mass. J. Am. Med. Assoc. 219:325, 1972.

21. Mazess, R. B. Estimation of bone and skeletal weight by direct photon absorptiometry. Invest. Radiol. 6:52, 1971.

22. Horsman, A., L. Bulusu, H. B. Bentley and B. E. C. Nordin. Internal relationships between skeletal parameters in twenty-three male skeletons. In: Proc. of the Bone Measurement Conference, U.S. Atomic Energy Conference, edited by J. R. Cameron, Springfield, Virginia: Clearinghouse for Federal Scientific and Technical Information, 1970, p. 365.

23. Chestnut, C. B., E. Manske, D. Baylink and W. B. Nelp. Correlation of total body calcium (bone mass) and regional bone mass. Clin. Res. 21:200, 1973 (abstr.).

24. Cohn, S. H., K. J. Ellis, I. Zanzi, J. M. Letteri and J. Aloia. Correlation of radial bone mineral content with total-body calcium in various metabolic disorders. In: Proc. Intern. Conf. Bone Mineral Measurement, edited by R. B. Mazess. Washington, D.C.: U.S. Govt. Printing Office, 1974. In press.

25. Mazess, R. B., J. R. Cameron and H. Miller. Direct readout of bone mineral content using radionuclide absorptiometry. Intern. J. Appl. Radiation Isotopes 23:471, 1972.

26. Witt, R. M., R. B. Mazess and J. R. Cameron. Standardization of bone mineral measurements. In: Proc. of the Bone Measurement Conference, U.S. Atomic Energy Conference, edited by J. R. Cameron. Springfield, Virginia: Clearinghouse for Federal Scientific and Technical Information, 1970, p. 303.

27. Mazess, R. B. Bone mineral content in Wainwright Eskimo: preliminary report. Arctic Anthropol. 7:114, 1970.

28. Mazess, R. B., and J. R. Cameron. Bone mineral content in normal U.S. Whites. In: Proc. Intern. Conf. Bone Mineral Measurement, edited by R. B. Mazess, Washington, D.C.: U.S. Govt. Printing Office, 1974. In Press.

29. McGammon, R. W. Human Growth and Development. Springfield, Illinois: Thomas, 1970.

30. Garn, S. M. The Earlier Gain and Later Loss of Cortical Bone. Springfield, Illinois: Thomas, 1970.

31. Dequeker, J. Bone Loss in Normal and Pathological Conditions. Leuven: Leuven Univ. Press, 1972.

32. Johnston, C. C., D. M. Smith, P-L. Yu, and W. P. Deiss, Jr. In vivo measurement of the bone mass in the radius. Metab. Clin. Exptl. 17:1140, 1968.

33. Garn, S. M., C. G. Rohmann and B. Wagner. Bone loss as a general phenomenon in man. Federation Proc. 26:1729, 1967.

34. Mazess, R. B. Bone density in Sadlermiut Eskimo. Human Biol. 38:42, 1966.

35. Mazess, R. B., and R. Jones. Weight and density of Sadlermiut Eskimo long bones. Human Biol. 44:537, 1972.

36. Merbs, C. F. Patterns of Activity-Induced Pathology in a Canadian Eskimo Isolate, Ph.D. Thesis in Anthropology. Univ. of Wisconsin (Univ. Microfilms 70–3624). Madison, Wisconsin, 1969.

37. Merbs, C. F., and W. H. Wilson. Anomalies and pathologies of the Sadlermiut Eskimo vertebral column. Natl. Museum Canada Bull. 180. Contrib. Anthrop. Part 1:54, 1960.

38. Barzel, U.S. (editor). Osteoporosis. New York: Grune & Stratton, 1970.

39. Harris, W. H., and R. P. Heaney. Skeletal renewal and metabolic bone disease. New Engl. J. Med. 280:193, 253, and 303.

40. Frame, B., A. M. Parfitt and H. Duncan. Clinical Aspects of Metabolic Bone Disease. Amsterdam: Excerpta Medica, 1973.

41. Exton-Smith, A. M., H. M. Hodkinson and B. R. Stanton. Nutrition and metabolic bone disease in old age. Lancet 2:999, 1966.

42. Smith, R. W., J. Rizek and B. Frame. Determinants of serum antirachitic activity. Am. J. Clin. Nutr. 14:98, 1964.

43. Bullamore, J. R., R. Wilkinson, J. C. Gallaher, B. E. C. Nordin and D. H. Marshall. Effect of age on calcium absorption. Lancet 2:535, 1970.

44. Spencer, H., J. Menczel, I. Lewin and J. Samachson. Absorption of calcium in osteoporosis. Am. J. Med. 37:223, 1964.

45. Tal, E., and K. Guggenheim. Effect of copper and manganese on calcification of bones of rats fed on meat. Nutr. Dieta 7:62, 1965.

46. Gaster, D., E. Havivi and K. Guggenheim. Differential effects of low calcium diets on the bones of mice and rats. Nutr. Dieta 9:200, 1967.

47. Draper, H. H., T. L. Sie and J. G. Bergan. Osteoporosis in aging rats induced by high phosphorus diets. J. Nutr. 102:1133, 1972.

48. Anderson, G. H., and H. H. Draper. Effect of dietary phosphorus on calcium metabolism in intact and parathyroidectomized adult rats. J. Nutr. 102:1123, 1972.

49. Krishnarao, G. V. G., and H. H. Draper. Influence of dietary phosphate on bone resorption in senescent mice. J. Nutr. 102:1143, 1972.

50. Herbert, L. A., J. Lemann Jr., J. R. Peterson and E. J. Lennon. Studies of the mechanism by which phosphate infusion lowers serum calcium concentration. J. Clin. Invest. 45:1886, 1966.

51. Farquharson, R. F., W. T. Salter and J. C. Aub. Studies of calcium and phosphorus metabolism. XIII. The effect of ingestion of phosphates on the excretion of calcium. J. Clin. Invest. 10:251, 1931.

52. Goldsmith, R. S., C. F. Woodhouse, S. H. Ingbar and D. Segal. Effect of phosphate supplements in patients with fractures. Lancet 1:687, 1967.

53. Reiss, E., J. M. Canterbury, M. A. Bercovitz and L. Kaplan. The role of phosphate in the secretion of parathyroid hormone in man. J. Clin. Invest. 49:2146, 1970.

54. Lennon, E. J., J. Lemann, Jr., A. S. Relman and H. P. Connors. The effects of phosphoproteins on acid balance in normal subjects. J. Clin. Invest. 41:637, 1962.

55. Barzel, U. S. The effect of excessive acid feeding on bone. Calcified Tissue Res. 4:94, 1969.

56. Farquharson, R. F., W. T. Salter, D. M. Tibbetts and J. C. Aub. Studies of calcium and phosphorus metabolism. XII. The effect of the ingestion of acid-producing substances. J. Clin. Invest. 10:221, 1931.

57. Barzel, U.S., and J. Jowsey. The effects of chronic acid and alkali administration on bone turnover in adult rats. Clin. Sci. 36:517, 1969.

58. Lemann, J., Jr., J. R. Litzow and E. J. Lennon. The effects of chronic acid loads in normal man: further evidence for the participation of bone mineral in the defense against chronic metabolic acidosis. J. Clin. Invest. 45:1608, 1966.

59. Litzow, J. R., J. Lemann, Jr. and E. J. Lennon. The effect of treatment of acidosis on calcium balance in patients with chronic azotemic renal disease. J. Clin. Invest. 46:280, 1967.

60. Johnson, N. E., E. N. Alcantara and H. Linkswiler. Effect of level of protein intake on urinary and fecal calcium and calcium retention of young adult males. J. Nutr. 100:1425, 1970.

61. Walker, R. M., and H. M. Linkswiler. Calcium retention in the adult human male as affected by protein intake. J. Nutr. 102:1297, 1972.

62. Margen, S., N. A. Kaufman, F. Costa and D. H. Calloway. Studies in the mechanisms of calciuria induced by protein feeding. Federation Proc. 29:566, 1970 (abstr.).

63. Spencer, H., L. Kramer, C. Norris and J. Samachson. Effect of protein intake on calcium absorption and calcium balance in man. Federation Proc. 31:708, 1972 (abstr.).

64. Reidenberg, M. M., B. L. Haag, B. J. Channick, C. R. Shuman and T. G. G. Wilson. The response of bone to metabolic acidosis in man. Metab. Clin. Exptl. 15:236, 1966.

65. Garnett, J., E. S. Garnett, R. J. Mardell and D. L. Barnard. Urinary calcium excretion during ketoacidosis of prolonged total starvation. Metab. Clin. Exptl. 19:502, 1970.

Professor Prewitt noted the title of the article and explained some important terminology in it.

The phrase "bone mineral content" in the title stands out because of its relationship to the disease osteoporosis. Osteoporosis is the age-related loss of bone mass. In young adulthood, bones are in a dynamic state of equilibrium, which means that calcium deposition (bone buildup) and calcium loss are equal, occurring simultaneously. The problem comes when the amount of calcium lost from bone is greater than the amount deposited. As one ages, this loss becomes cumulative and bones become more fragile.

Here's what Professor Prewitt told us about the journal the article appeared in:

The American Journal of Clinical Nutrition is a well-known, highly regarded journal that screens what it publishes carefully. The fact that this paper appears here makes me think that it will be a reasonably good study. However, methods, techniques, and other factors have changed in the field of osteoporosis research since the article was published in 1974. This journal, as its title suggests, usually publishes clinical research, such as biochemical laboratory research in which samples are taken and analyzed.

This article reports an epidemiological study not a clinical one, however. Epidemiology is the study of the frequency and distribution of disease in populations or large groups of people. Nutritional epidemiology is the study of nutrition in large groups. By looking quickly at the title and the first part of the introduction I can see that this study focuses on the nutritional patterns of Alaskan Eskimos and the relationship of those patterns to osteoporosis.

Professor Prewitt looks quickly through the report, focusing briefly on each of the sections typically found in a research report. She reads the abstract to determine the major findings of the study and then looks at the introduction to find out what the research problem is and what research has previously been done on this problem. She skims the materials and method section to see how the researchers measured bone mineral content and to see how well the subjects, the people being studied, were described. She explains:

The group of people in the study is called the "sample." The investigators chose a smaller number from a larger population to learn about that larger population. When we make assumptions about the larger population from the smaller one, we are generalizing. To learn about the study, I ask such questions as, "How many people were included in the sample? Who was included and excluded and why?" Sometimes a group or people with certain characteristics might be excluded from the study and that can change the results quite radically. How widely we can generalize the results often depends on the choice of the sample.

Next, Professor Prewitt looks over the tables that display the results. She reads the discussion section more carefully to learn how the researchers qualify and explain their results. She wants to be persuaded by their results and keep their arguments in mind as she goes back and reads the report again more carefully.

The researchers make this claim, "The present results indicate that Eskimo males lost almost 6 to 7% [bone mass] per decade, and Eskimo females close to 10 to 12% [bone mass] per decade after the late thirties and early forties"(paragraph 10). They then qualify their results by reminding us that these data are cross-sectional. That is, they come from observing groups of 40-year-olds, 50-year-olds, 60-year-olds, and so on. We don't know if the result would be the same if the study was conducted for 60 years following the same person and measuring his or her bone density. This study looks at one point in time and doesn't follow people over time.

In paragraph 13, the authors express a concern that: "As Eskimo longevity increases, it is possible that skeletal pathology as a result of demineralization could present public health problems." Here they're suggesting the significance of this research. They indicate that osteoporosis in this culture will have important public health consequences. When older adults sustain fractures, they experience a tremendous economic burden and loss of personal independence. The family and health care system have to assume responsibility for taking care of victims of the disease.

WRITING AND LEARNING ACTIVITY

1. **Journal Entry:** Why did Professor Prewitt notice these particular portions of the text? What have you learned so far about nutrition? Any new terms? What do you expect to learn as Professor Prewitt reads the text more thoroughly?

READING RESEARCH IN NUTRITION

Now Professor Prewitt begins a careful, detailed reading. She comments and elaborates on each section, summarizing points, defining concepts, raising questions, and analyzing ideas.

WRITING AND LEARNING ACTIVITIES

1. **Reading:** Read the research report, "Bone Mineral Content of North Alaskan Eskimos," along with Professor Prewitt.
2. **Journal Entry:** As you read make notes about your reading process in your journal. Write down any questions you have about the reading and any familiar or unfamiliar terms you encounter. Also, note any places in the readings where you make connections to your own experience or to something you know about.
3. **Annotate the Reading:** As you read make brief notes in the margins. Underline or highlight key ideas. Place question marks next to passages that you don't understand. Note areas of personal interest. Ask questions about areas you'd like to know more about.

Read the Introduction, paragraph 1.

This is an observational study that examines the effects of the Eskimo's dietary pattern, one that is high in protein. In the introduction the researchers tell us they are particularly interested in animal protein in the diet and its effect on bone mineral content.

They're saying that Eskimos consume the highest quantity of meat—when compared to most other populations, past and present—since meat is a staple in their food supply; and that there's something about this particular nutrient that may have some implications for bone mineral content.

When people eat a diet high in meat, they get other units along with the meat, such as nitrogen, phosphorus, and sulfur, all minerals, and acid. If people are eating a lot of meat, proportionately they're getting fewer carbohydrates in their diet. A person can only eat so many calories in a day so we look to see what proportion of total calories are taken up by meat, carbohydrates, and so on. The long-term diet for these people has been high protein/low carbohydrate, even if that has shifted a bit recently.

On the whole, this population enjoys adequate nutrition. In some individuals, however, there may be some risk of low intake of certain essential nutrients. For example, lactose, commonly called "milk sugar," is the carbohydrate found in milk. Some people do not produce the enzyme to utilize lactose, so they are called "lactose intolerant." If they eliminate milk from the diet entirely, they are also eliminating the major dietary source of calcium, as well as other essential nutrients. The "intolerance" problem can be avoided by adding lactose enzyme pills to milk or by drinking low lactose milk, which can be purchased at the grocery store.

At the end of the introduction, the authors pose the problem that is the subject of their research: what are the long-term effects of a high-meat diet on this particular population. They know from short-term clinical feeding studies in which subjects ate a lot of meat that calcium is lost through the urine; there is a relationship between high-protein intake and calcium excretion. But we don't know what happens in the long term, perhaps the body finds ways to adjust to the calcium loss. One of the advantages of an observational study like this is that you're not changing the way the Eskimos eat—you are just reporting what you observe. It's a good check against the short-term clinical study.

Read Materials and Methods, paragraphs 2–4.

In this section the researchers tell us how they measured bone mineral content. The procedure, photon absorptiometry, scans the bone based on the mineral content and reads the bone density. It measures the degree to which light does not go through the bone.

Next, the researchers need to convince us of the effectiveness of their measurement procedure, so they tell us they have found only 2% error in measurement comparisons, suggesting that we can trust their measurements to be accurate. The measurement technique has been worked out and reported in other articles. In this report, all that's necessary is to name the technique and to tell the reader where to go for more information. In the second paragraph of the methods section, the researchers tell us that once they had the measurements they adjusted them (by using a statistical measure) to take into account the size of the bone and the size of the subject's body. They came up with a single figure called a "ratio of mineral to width" or BMC/W (Bone Mineral Content divided by Width). The numbers that represent this ratio will turn up later in tables in the Results section. The researchers made the bone content measurements on three places on the arm: the ulna (elbow), the humerus (the long bone of the upper arm from shoulder to elbow, and the radius (the thicker and shorter bone of the forearm).

The researchers decided that since their measurement procedure was reliable they could combine data from three different communities: Wainright, Point Barrow, and Point Hope. Altogether they looked at measurements from 413 individuals at a variety of ages.

Read the Results section, paragraphs 5–8.

The results section answers the question, "Do Alaskan Eskimos suffer more age-related bone loss than does the white population?" Professor Prewitt takes us through the steps necessary to determine the answer, which is yes. The first step is to describe the Alaskan Eskimo's body type in relation to Caucasian body type so that comparisons of bone mineral content at various ages can be made.

Table 1 lists heights and weights of Alaskan Eskimo participants in the study by age. Their height and weight are listed as percentages of the values for the white population. From this information the authors can say that Eskimos are typically smaller and stockier in body build than whites. They also say there is less sexual dimorphism, which I take to mean less difference in body type between the Eskimo male and female than between white males and females.

The second paragraph in the results section introduces the five tables that report the measurements taken on the Eskimos' bones. Table 2 measured the shaft of the radius, Table 3 the shaft of the ulna, Table 4 the midshaft of the humerus, Table 5 the distal radius, and Table 6 the distal ulna. Professor Prewitt explains how the researchers actually determined a measurement that could be compared with the white population.

The references tell us that these researchers had available to them complete figures on the bone mineral content for all these bone locations in a white population. They're using a reference—an established yardstick—against which to compare differences in the Eskimos. For instance, if an Eskimo is listed as having 100 percent bone mineral content, then he or she has exactly the same as whites. If an Eskimo has 93.3% then he or she has less than the standard. Eskimos and whites have about the same bone mineral content until they are 39 years old. After that, during their forties, fifties, and sixties, the Eskimos experience much greater bone loss than the comparable white population.

Table 2 contains data from the largest number of subjects at the most reliable measurement site, the shaft of the radius. To understand the pattern of increasing loss of bone mineral content in Eskimos, especially in Eskimo women, Professor Prewitt focuses our attention on Table 2.

What I like to do at this point is something called "scanning the data." I look at the way the data is presented in the table and try to find the pattern that is reported in the results section. It might even be a good idea to get a pencil and paper out and graph the results so that we can see the changes visually.

First, as an orientation to the table we can see that the data for males and females are listed separately, with males on the top half. We get three types of percents: percent of mineral content; percent of bone width; and the ratio of bone mineral content divided by

*width. This last column is the one we should look at; the ratio adjusted for the Eskimo
body type gives us a number we can compare with the standard bone mineral content for
men and women various ages.*

The results cited at the end of the results section state,

During the decade from 40 to 49, the Eskimos had 10% lower values than U.S.
whites and the deficit increased to 14% in the succeeding two decades (paragraph 8).

*I'm checking this with my pencil. It looks like the male bone mineral content in the
forties was 88 percent and the female was 90.8 percent. I'd guess that they averaged
those figures to come up with the 10 percent result. Likewise with the 14-percent figures:
they averaged the results from males and females during the fifties and sixties.*

*As the researchers point out, the most startling loss of bone mineral content occurs
in the seventies. Eskimo men are 15 percent below the standard in that age group, but Eskimo women are almost 30 percent below.*

*If you look down the column and read the numbers, the males don't start losing bone
mineral content until their forties. For women, it's not until their fifties. But, then, it drops
to 86 or 87 percent and then down to 69 percent. I'll be looking for the reasons for this in
the discussion section. We know they are going to connect it to the high-meat diet, but I'll
be interested to see how they eliminate other possibilities that might cause that rapid
bone loss.*

Read the Discussion section, paragraphs 9–17.

Professor Prewitt begins to think about the discussion section by asking
herself, "What is the larger meaning of bone loss for Alaskan Eskimos?" As
she reads, she looks for the answer to that question.

*In the first paragraph of the discussion section they talk about differences in bone loss
with aging: there's a greater bone loss in Eskimos than in whites. The terms that might be
used in this discussion—bone mineral content, bone mass, fractures, and bone loss—are
all key words that you might use to find more information by medical search procedures, in
Index Medicus, or on Med-line, for instance. All these terms mean "osteoporosis" to me.
In this particular study the authors are trying to explain bone loss by differences in cultural
eating habits.*

*When you compare Eskimos with whites in terms of bone mineral content during
growth and early adulthood the measures are essentially the same. The feature that
stands out is the degree to which bone is lost in older Eskimos. The report points out that
bone loss occurs earlier in Eskimos, "in the late thirties in both sexes, whereas in white
females, it is in the forties and in white males in the fifties" (paragraph 10). That point is
referenced to another study for its data on whites since Mazess and Mather did not do any
measurements on whites.*

The authors' first strategy in the discussion section, Professor Prewitt
explains, is to summarize their results by comparing them to results in the
standard white population. The authors continue to amplify or explain the
findings of their particular study by bringing in additional findings. First,

however, they must concern themselves with a possible criticism of their study.

In the third paragraph of the discussion section they find it necessary to admit that their cross-sectional data might not represent their data fairly. Since the main force of their results rests on what happens to Eskimos throughout their life, that is, longitudinally, the authors must be sure that their cross-sectional data, which examines groups of people in specific decades of their lives, reflects the lifelong pattern. The authors insist that it does, citing statistical results concerning the ratio they used.

The authors focus on women because among whites osteoporosis is more prevalent in females. So here they're talking about the fact that bone mineral content loss occurs even earlier in Eskimo women than in white women. In fact 60 percent of Eskimo women would be classified as at risk for fracture, an incredibly high number. This information didn't come directly from the tables in this study. At the beginning of paragraph 12 they offer a figure that tells them at what rate of bone loss you can actually say that someone has osteoporosis. The citation which says, "personal communication" tells me that they had a telephone conversation (or correspondence) with colleagues about this topic; this is fine—that's the way you give credit for this information.

In paragraph 13 they're still citing evidence that older Eskimos have lower bone mineral content. They even find evidence of this trend in an archaeological study of Eskimo skeletons: the bones of older Eskimos had 10 to 15 percent less mineral content than those of younger Eskimos. Here again is that age-related loss of bone, which, in turn, points to osteoporosis. All of these data, the authors suggest, create a convincing picture that complements their own data.

Professor Prewitt points out to us that paragraph 14 in the discussion section signals a shift. Until now the authors have been detailing in a variety of ways what happened to the Eskimos. Now they will answer the question "Why is it happening?" and explain why this shift in bone mineral content comes about. But first, they offer two possible explanations for the loss in bone content and discount both of them.

The two possible explanations for loss of bone mineral content are lack of physical activity and a vitamin-D deficiency. The authors claim that Eskimos, especially the males, maintain an active lifestyle. I have to wonder on what basis they make that claim. While one might assume this, none of the references listed support the claim. In addition, they say males are active but the problem is more severe for females. Did they observe the population for this factor? I don't have enough information here to satisfy me that that's not a factor in the bone loss.

As for a vitamin-D deficiency, they seem to have documented their argument satisfactorily. Eskimos store enough vitamin D over the summer months, even if they didn't they take in enough calcium to prevent a deficiency.

At this point, Professor Prewitt explains that part of the process of developing a convincing claim involves eliminating alternate explanations, which the authors did above. The next step is giving the explanation they feel best explains the bone loss experienced by older Eskimo women and men: the high-meat diet.

It's important to remember, though, that they didn't measure meat intake. They're depending on the description of the cultural practice of eating meat, and proposing that meat is the cause of the bone loss. Animal studies have suggested that meat diets cause bone loss; studies of vegetarians versus meat eaters also suggest that a high-meat diet causes mineral bone loss. But because they didn't actually measure meat intake, they probably couldn't title the report something like "The Relationship of a High-Meat Diet to Bone Mineral Loss in Alaskan Eskimos."

At this point we get into some technical material. Meat is high in the mineral phosphorus, and there's a balance between the calcium and phosphorus that must be maintained. When the ratio between the two minerals is stable, the appropriate amount of calcium will be excreted. Here's a difficult sentence:

High P [phosphorus] intakes, with high P/Ca can increase Ca excretion . . . (paragraph 15).

In other words, taking in a lot of phosphorus can cause one to excrete more calcium. A root dictionary or medical dictionary would help with the forms hypocalcemia and hypercalciuria. Here are some definitions: hypo means low; calc means calcium; emia means blood; hyper means high; uria means urine. So, hypocalcemia means low calcium in the blood; hypercalciuria [discussed in paragraph 16] means high calcium in the urine. What they're saying is that they don't think the phosphorus intake is so high that it's going to shift the calcium balance and cause calcium excretion. They're still looking at the meat diet but excluding phosphorus as the cause of the bone loss.

In paragraph 16, Professor Prewitt tells us, the authors consider the possibility that the bone loss is related to the oxidation of sulfur found in the meat. Some amino acids are more acidic than others, those containing sulfur (such as cystine) increase calcium excretion. Professor Prewitt reads aloud:

In humans, a high protein diet (142 g daily), even with controlled intakes of Ca and P, greatly increases urinary Ca and causes negative balance (60–62). This hypercalciuria [high calcium in the urine] is not due to increased Ca absorption (63) (paragraph 16).

These results come from clinical feeding studies. Eskimos are eating about 200 to 400 grams of protein a day. At 4 calories per gram that's between 800 and 1600 calories from protein a day. If whites were eating this much protein, the net calcium deficit based on the cited balance studies would be 100 mg daily or 365 g per decade. A high-protein diet of even 142 grams for whites greatly increases a negative calcium balance.

So what Mazess and Mather are saying is that Eskimos may have adapted to a high-protein intake. They do lose bone mass, but it's not as rapid or as complete as you'd think it would be based on these studies. Even so, the high, protein diet still provides the explanation for the bone loss.

The authors conclude with two suggestions for further research: on the mechanisms responsible for bone loss in Alaskan Eskimos, and normal bone growth in Eskimo children. Suggestions for future research is a fairly standard way to conclude research reports.

WRITING AND LEARNING ACTIVITIES

---

1. **Journal Entry:** In your journal write what you have learned from this article about the relationship between calcium and loss of bone mineral content. You might want to consider these questions: What role do a high-meat diet, physical activity, and vitamin D play in the relationship? What is your opinion about the importance of these factors?

2. **Group Activity:** In a group or in pairs, compare journal entries from the activity above.

3. **Writing Activity:** Write a letter to a real or imagined friend whose mother or grandmother suffers from osteoporosis in which you pass on whatever information you've gathered thus far. Summarize the main points of the research report we just read and combine them with information you learned in the group activity above.

MAKING MEANING IN NUTRITION

To analyze a text, a research report, or even our personal circumstances means to ask questions about the object of our concern and to explain our concern to others. When you question whether or not a parking ticket was fairly given, you are engaging in analysis. When you wonder why your favorite sports team cannot seem to win a game, you are engaging in analysis. This sort of analysis relies on common sense: your ability to reach intelligent conclusions based on your life experiences. Getting to know a specific academic discipline, in this case nutrition, also depends on the personal knowledge and experience that you bring to the task, as well as on how this particular discipline makes knowledge.

Such detailed and complex research reports as the one we just read on the cause of bone loss in North Alaskan Eskimos may make you wonder how you can bring your own common sense to bear on the analysis of scientific research. The next sections will talk first about the language of science and how it aims at certainty; then we will discuss a process for understanding the steps in the sorts of arguments commonly used in the sciences that contribute to this language of certainty. Finally, and most importantly, we show you how to apply your own experiences to this analysis in order to question the research report in ways that you will find meaningful.

SCIENCE AND THE LANGUAGE OF CERTAINTY

Scientific research reports are written to convince you that they are reporting the true and objective results of research. This view of science makes us feel as though we are outsiders, that science is a domain for experts. This has been referred to as the mystique of science (Lemke, 129). In recent years sociologists and rhetoricians have begun to examine more closely how this mystique developed. Sociologists, for instance, observed scientists at work doing experiments and writing up their results, watched their process and listened as they discussed the reports they were writing. They began to see how much the scientists were influenced by political, economic, and social issues. They began to see, too, that scientists were *constructing* knowledge, not simply observing a phenomenon and writing about what they saw.

This language of certainty is adopted in the genre of the research report. Rarely do you hear a scientist speaking in the first person. First, the researchers tell us that this particular study follows from many other studies by directing us to the long list of references at the end of the study. Next, they tell us in great detail about their methods. Mazess and Mather, for instance, used a sophisticated measurement tool called photon absorptiometry to determine their subjects' bone mineral content. Finally, in the discussion section, the researchers tell us why their results are important and how they fit in to other research being conducted on the same problem. All of this combined can indeed make it seem as though we have no place questioning the results of such rigorous scientific endeavors.

SCIENCE AND PRACTICAL REASONING

Even though scientific research reports appear to report "the truth," we can in fact question or analyze the claims they make. Here is a method developed by Stephen Toulmin in a 1958 book called *The Uses of Argument*, and later developed further (in 1984) in *An Introduction to Reasoning*. (This material is also discussed in the "Making Meaning" section of Chapter 1.) In Toulmin's view, the research report is a rhetorical argument that leads us through a process of asking questions about a claim, that is, a dialogue among researchers. The author of a report is making a claim. She imagines the questions the reader will ask and answers them as she writes, although, admittedly, this is particularly difficult to imagine for the reasons I gave above—the research report is written to be the answer to a research question and not to be a conversation about it. However, we can imagine it more easily if we remember how Professor Prewitt read the research report. She was essentially engaging in a dialogue with the authors, asking questions of the authors and looking for their answers in the report. For instance, in the discussion section she wonders about the authors' assertion that lack of physical activity could not have caused the bone loss (paragraph 14).

The authors claim that Eskimos, especially the males, maintain an active lifestyle. I have to wonder on what basis they make that claim. While one might assume this, none of the references listed support the claim. In addition, they say males are active but the problem is more severe for females. Did they observe the population for this factor? I don't have enough information here to satisfy me that that's not a factor in the bone loss.

Let's work our way through this report as an argument, looking at its parts and how they function. The parts, listed below, are the tools we use to question the strength and appropriateness of any claim.

Claim

The claim is the result of the research. It is the statement that says: "The following is acceptable or true . . ." and the entire research works to support it. The researchers tell you in the literature review why the claim was reasonable to test, the results section explains how their methods yielded the support for the claim, and the discussion indicates how they might eliminate competing claims. What claim do Mazess and Mather make about the bone mineral content of North Alaskan Eskimos?

Data (Also Referred to as Grounds, Evidence, and Reasons)

You are probably most familiar with this part of the argument. Since grade school you have been asked to give reasons for your claims. We have many synonyms for *reasons,* since different discourse communities rely on slightly different terms. Any of the terms listed above—*grounds, data, evidence,* and *reasons*—may be used to refer to this part of an argument. Suppose you do not accept a claim or would like to know how the speaker established it. Your first step would be to inquire about the data: "What have you got to go on?" In Toulmin's scheme the data are the specific facts that the speaker uses to support a claim. What data does Mazess and Mather's study depend on?

The Warrant

This aspect of an argument may be new to you, but it is very important for developing an argument in an academic discipline. If you are not satisfied by the facts provided by the data, you can ask more probing questions, such as "How did you get from your data to your claim?" This question asks the speaker to build a bridge—a warrant—from the data to the claim. This is a more difficult concept to understand since warrants are frequently unspoken. You could think of a warrant as a license or permit that authorizes you to say that the data provide the necessary facts for the claim.

Specialized discourse communities frequently use warrants connected to the methods used in specific disciplines. For instance, Mazess and Mather would tell us that their claim is warranted by this data because it is appropriate in epidemiological research to compare specific features, such as bone density, of one population with those of another population. Thus, the warrant tells us that the researchers proceeded in a methodologically sound manner, convincing us that the data does indeed support the claim.

The Qualifier

To consider the strength of the link between the data and the claim, you may want to add a qualifier: "Is the claim completely true in all situations or do we need to limit it in some way?" Qualifying a claim allows us to insert language such as "apparently, evidently, possibly, presumably, in some cases, or, it is expected that."

The Rebuttal

If you cannot accept a claim completely, without a shred of doubt, you will explain the specific circumstances that tell you that the claim is not as strong as originally proposed. This explanation is called the rebuttal, and it is one of the most difficult aspects of an argument for students. If you are writing a paper in support of a claim, then you must become a questioner and imagine what challenges this person would make to the strength or appropriateness of your claim. Ask yourself: "What is the other side to this argument?" or "What problems might someone else have with this argument?" If you are questioning someone else's claim, your challenge is to articulate how the claim must be qualified. Below we work on developing questions about this research report. The questions might well form the basis for a rebuttal and qualifications to the claim.

WRITING AND LEARNING ACTIVITIES

1. **Journal Entry:** Think of an issue currently being debated on the news, in the newspaper, or on your campus. Write a dialogue between yourself and another person in which one of you states a claim and the other questions the data and warrant.
2. **Group Activity:** Review each group member's dialogue written for the activity above. Choose one dialogue for the group to work with; identify the parts of the argument. Revise the dialogue if necessary to make the argument clearer.
3. **Class Presentation:** Two people from each group should act out the dialogue for the class. The audience should respond by making notes about which parts of the argument seemed most convicing.
4. **Group Activity:** Reread Mazess and Mather's report and look over Professor Prewitt's comments. Identify the parts of the argument in the research report and present them to the class.

DEVELOPING INTERESTS

In discussing the mystique of science, Jay Lemke offers this definition of a fact: "A fact is an assertion that is not currently being challenged" (143). When we analyze a research report and ask questions about it, we are challenging assertions. Often, the best places to come up with these challenges is our own common sense, our own experiences, and what we know about the world, in other words, common sense personal connections. Students in my classes were asked to develop challenges from personal connections, hunches, and just plain common sense. Students worked alone and in small groups thinking and rethinking how they might connect to this research report in order to develop questions. Here are a few of the connections they uncovered:

I work out as often as I can and I read popular magazines on health and fitness and weightlifting, so my eye caught that statement about physical activity. I also have seen movies like "Shadow of the Wolf," which show the lifestyle of native Alaskans from many years ago, and that life was tough, to say the least. I can't believe they could pass over this fact so lightly. I think things must have changed over the past fifty years. Didn't I read something in the last chapter about a native Alaskan who had to get helicoptered to a hospital for a heart attack caused because he ate too much high-fat food and got no exercise? With the discovery of oil in Alaska things have changed a lot. When did that happen? Was it after this research was done?

JOE VERBURG

I kept saying to myself, how could I have anything in common with these people. I'm blown away by how much meat they eat in a day. I like my hamburgers as well as the next guy and I could never imagine being a vegetarian. But still. . . . Then I realized that the article was about cultural eating patterns and how different my culture was from theirs. I grew up in Vietnam where everyone was a farmer and meat was the scarcity. I still think that's why I like burgers so much.

DENNIS HUANG

I took a women's studies course last semester, and now anytime I see the word "standard" I look more closely. I just wonder what exactly the standard is that they're comparing them [the Eskimos] to. Our country is a salad bowl, even our class is, so how do we know who they are comparing the Eskimos to? I also wondered about the reasons for the women having so much more bone loss than the men. I mean I know that osteoporosis is a woman's disease but still that result was huge. I wanted to hear more about the difference between men and women.

SALLY SINGER

Each of these journal entries holds the germ of a more thorough analysis. Each questions some aspect of the researcher's argument. If physical activity has been undervalued in this report, for example as Joe Verburg thinks, then perhaps the researchers have not gathered enough data. Or they may have ignored a change in important cultural practices. Research in nutrition is conducted according to the expectations of that discipline, and reports of research in it follow the conventions of science. To university students it might seem difficult to participate in this research community. If, however, you can understand the way arguments function, you can analyze the arguments in research reports by bringing your personal experience and common sense into the picture.

WRITING AND LEARNING ACTIVITIES

1. Group Activity: Expand the list of personal connections above. Read and reread the research report to find a fact or an issue that you have even the slightest question about. Where does that question come from? From what personal experience? From a class you have taken? From experiences at work or another location?

2. **Class Presentation:** Choose one person from your group to report on the range of personal connections or questions about the research report.

▣ LINKED WRITING ASSIGNMENT

Writing an Analysis of Work in Nutrition (see Chapter 12, Analyzing Discipline-Specific Texts). In the previous section, Developing Interests, you began to identify issues and ideas that you might want to explore further. Finding personal connections to the material you are studying is one important way to participate more fully in an academic community. You will also need to learn how some everyday thinking strategies, such as analyzing, help you to participate in the disciplines you are studying here. Chapter 12 introduces you to the activity of analyzing and offers readings from nutrition for you to practice developing an analysis.

P A R T

II

STRATEGIES FOR WRITING AND LEARNING

10

SUMMARIZING DISCIPLINE-SPECIFIC TEXTS

To treat a "big" subject in the intensely summarized fashion demanded by an evening's traffic of the stage when the evening, freely clipped at each end is reduced to two hours and a half, is a feat of which the difficulty looms large.

HENRY JAMES

WHAT DOES IT MEAN TO SUMMARIZE?

A friend asks you what's the best movie you've seen lately and you tell her about *Jurassic Park*. You tell her just what you think is essential: a bit about the story and a lot about the special effects, which you found to be stunning. Summarizing what someone else has said or written is one of the most frequent activities we engage in, yet summarizing in academic disciplines is neither simple nor easy. Whenever you summarize, you are putting the source in your own words and in a more concise form than the original.

You must consider several important issues. For instance, when you summarize a piece of philosophical writing, you need to know something about making meaning in that particular discipline: How are claims supported? What kind of evidence is acceptable for claims? What kinds of issues are discussed? What sort of method is used to develop the argument?

One of the most challenging aspects of writing a summary is "putting it in your own words" to represent the ideas of the author. At first you may feel that you are only mimicking the language of the text, but as you continue to learn by participating in the intellectual work of the discipline, it will be easier to use your own words.

Summaries may be used by a writer to tell you about important background information she feels you should know. For instance, Chapter 1 offered an excerpt from the work of Philippe Ariès who had done ground-breaking research on the history of the family in the middle ages. The publication of Ariès's study encouraged other historians to continue research that looked at the nature of the family. As they do so, they rely heavily on the work done up to that point. That work is improved on by asking a question in a new way, or looking for new answers, or using new methods. One part of this process is to summarize the previous work. The summary is then often followed by some questions raised by the previous work, which, in turn, gives rise to a new research project.

Let's take a look at how this works. Ariès's work is now considered a classic. In 1987 the *Journal of Family History* devoted an entire issue of the journal to research that was inspired by the publication of Ariès's work nearly twenty-five years earlier. One writer decided to test some of Ariès's claims, the one's he had drawn from paintings, books, and letters, by using quantitative data such as numbers of births and deaths. S. Ryan Johansson began her journal article by summarizing the portion of Ariès's work that helped her to design her study. Here's a portion of that summary:

> To Ariès childhood was one of the most interesting and significant entry points into the historical study of the evolution of ordinary life—not ordinary life as led by ordinary people, but ordinary life as lived by elite families in a specific time and place. In *Centuries of Childhood* (1962), Ariès focused almost exclusively on the experience of materially and socially privileged families from the late Middle Ages to the nineteenth century (343–344).

Professor Todd Newberry, a marine biologist, told us that if he were to summarize Professor Lisbeth Francis's research report (see Chapter 7) in one of his own papers, it might only be one sentence of text. Here's an example of Professor Francis summarizing someone else's work in paragraph 30 of her report.

> The acrorhagi are specialized "organs" which have been observed to function only during aggression (Abel, 1954; Bonnin, 1964) and apparently the acrorhagial atrich nematocysts are also used only during aggression.

What this means is that two researchers—Abel, in a report published in 1954, and Bonnin, in a report published in 1964—wrote about acrorhagi. Professor Francis read their reports, found the information valuable to her study, summarized the pertinent information in the first part of the sentence, and gave them credit for their ideas by citing their names and the dates of their research.

As you thumb through academic journals you will often see a short paragraph (usually under 150 words) in small type at the beginning of a report called an Abstract. This special summary is often written after the study is complete and summarizes the purpose of the study, the methods, and the results. Abstracts are often included in bibliographies so that a researcher can determine whether or not the entire report is something he or she will find useful.

WRITING AND LEARNING ACTIVITIES

1. **Journal Entry:** Summary is an everyday activity of making meaning both in and out of the classroom. Summarize a conversation you participated in or overheard, a class lecture, religious sermon, or sporting event.

2. **Group Activity:** As a group choose a specific topic, such as a particular song, book, television show, or event, but work separately to summarize this topic in a word, sentence, and paragraph. How do your summaries compare? What points are similar and what are different?

3. **Peer Activity:** With a friend, agree to take notes on the same class. Each write a brief summary of the material covered during that class. Compare your notes and report back to the class on the similarities and differences in your summaries.

4. **Journal Entry:** Look over several of the readings contained in this textbook. Find at least two examples of summarizing. Write in your journal about the writer's purpose for summarizing.

THE PROCESS OF SUMMARIZING A SPECIALIZED TEXT

In this section, I demonstrate a useful and flexible process for developing a summary of a discipline-specific text. The source for this summary, an excerpt from *Centuries of Childhood: A Social History of Family Life* by Philippe Ariès, can be found in Chapter 1. (You may want to reread this selection before we proceed.) This process offers ways of thinking about how a text reflects the concerns of its academic discipline. It also offers a method by which you can begin to write about the text using your own language. Some situations in which you might need to write a summary for a specific purpose, for example, a historical text are:

1. You are studying for a history essay test and making notes from your textbook and from articles you've had to read.
2. You are summarizing what you have learned from a book on social history to support an argument you are making in a paper.
3. You have been asked to present to your history class the summary of a particular article or book.

In the next section are some additional discipline-specific readings so that you can follow the process of writing a summary that I demonstrate below.

THINKING ABOUT THE DISCIPLINE

The kinds of texts read in upper-level history classes are called specialized academic texts or discipline-specific texts. Unlike regular textbooks, which organize and summarize general knowledge for you, discipline-specific texts are made up of the same readings that historians read and which make up an important part of their discipline. We need to ask ourselves: How does what I know about the discipline of social history affect my process of summarizing its specialized texts?

We learned in the first part of this textbook that historians, like scholars in other disciplines, tackle certain types of problems in certain ways. In Chapter 1, Social History, as Professor Lynn Weiner read an excerpt from Ariès's book, *Centuries of Childhood,* she demonstrated how this particular reading contributed to the field by giving us an idea about what led to the development of the modern family. She pointed out that although Ariès's piece occasionally sounded like a story, we needed to pay close attention to his argument. She asked herself how this text fit into the kind of thinking that social historians typically engage in.

In preparing to summarize any specialized text, it's a good idea to ask the following questions:

> What field is this text from? What do I know about the discourse community of this field? What was the author's purpose in writing the text? How did he or she present knowledge to persuade me of his or her main point? What specialized words does the author use in the text? What methods are used in this discipline?

IDENTIFYING GROUPS OF RELATED IDEAS

Once you have done some of the discipline-centered work by answering the questions above, you are ready to begin thinking about the ideas in the text itself. The first step is to identify groups of related ideas that might focus on different parts of the argument or different claims. Sometimes specialized texts have subtitles that give you an idea of how the author has grouped related ideas. In other specialized texts, of which the Ariès excerpt is an example, the text has very few divisions and the ideas flow one after another. The challenge for you in planning to write a summary of such a text is to identify a group of related ideas, a portion of the argument that you could report on in your own words. Here's what to do:

> Read quickly through the text. Your purpose is to identify groups of ideas that you are sure you want to include in your summary. When you see such a grouping draw a line down the side of a photocopy of the text and number each group consecutively. Do not feel that you have to include the entire text.

Professor Weiner demonstrated this part of the process by identifying five groups of related ideas in the Ariès excerpt (see pages 17–24). For a student writer, identifying groups of related ideas is the first step toward developing authority for what you say about the text. Even though the author may have divided the text in a certain way, identifying a group of ideas is something you do in your head or in your notes in preparation for the summary you will write. Identifying the parts of the text that you find most important for your summary may seem a little confusing or daunting at first, but the act of identifying is the first step toward making the specialized language and methods of a discipline your own. There is no right or wrong size of a group of ideas—only what you decide should be in relationship to the summary you are going to write. Here are some questions to ask yourself as you identify groups of related ideas:

 Have I marked a section of the text that contains an idea I could summarize in a sentence or two? Have I identified a group of ideas in which the author introduces an important definition? In which the author states a claim or subclaim? In which the author offers grounds for a claim? In which the author explains something about his or her method?

DRAFTING SENTENCES FROM GROUPS OF IDEAS

It is at this point in the process of writing a summary that you turn the source text into *your* words and *your* summary. This crucial moment depends on how well you understand the text and the discipline it comes from. There's an old expression that says you really don't know something until you can teach it. Can you explain the text you're summarizing to someone else and do it in your own words? If you can't, you might end up plagiarizing the source, because you have used the author's words to summarize the text. Here's what to do:

 A. Reread the group of ideas. B. Put the reading somewhere else so you're not looking at it. Perhaps take a short break from studying to clear your head. The purpose here is to free yourself from the text as the author has written it and to think about it in your own words. C. Write out a sentence or two in your own words. Don't worry about how rough the sentence is. The object is to tell about the ideas contained in the group in your own words.

Once you have done this ask yourself the following questions:

 Have I identified the most crucial ideas in the report and eliminated unnecessary details? Have I expressed the meaning of the group of ideas in my own words, using only key terms that are important to the understanding of the text?

Here's how this might be done with the Ariès reading. Professor Weiner writes a sentence or two for each group of ideas. (Also included are any notes she made to herself.)

Idea Group #1: In middle ages in West family was charact. by placing children out (apprenticeship) (paragraphs 1–3).

Idea Group #2: Apprenticeship was the major means of education; domestic service was thus performed by children of all classes (paragraphs 4–7).

[Notes] apprenticeship = education.
skip the stuff about the hunting school—not important enough

Idea Group #3: Therefore, education ~~between the generations~~ *of the young* "en-sured by the everyday partic. of children in adult life." "art of living" #3a. The family was thus not sentimental, but moral and social (paragraphs 8–9).

> *[Notes] He says that children and adults are all mixed up together in this Group. I would want to quote the phrase he uses. I would also include the page number. And I'll also include the phrase, "art of living."*

Idea Group #4: ?Begin, in 15th cent., according to Ariès, the extension of formal schooling ~~leads to~~ *was related to* a change in family life (paragraphs 10–14).

> *[Notes] key paragraph about the extension of schooling. Ariès claims that the extension of formal schooling caused (leads to) the change but I would summarize by saying that the rise in formal schooling is related to the change in the family. Ariès says one "caused" the other but I don't completely buy it, so I'll back off and say, "was related to."*

Idea Group #5: The school becomes the normal path for social initiation. There is now more intimacy between parent and child. And, the sentimental climate of the family becomes more modern (paragraphs 15–19).

> *[Notes] Family now seen differently as reflected in changing attitudes to primogeniture, i.e. new love and affection for each child, leading to concept of equality among children.*

WRITING THE SUMMARY
DRAFTING THE INTRODUCTION
Formulating the Essential Idea

Introducing your summary can be the most difficult part of the process be-cause you now are creating the link between the specialized text you have studied and the reader you are summarizing it for. The first task is to com-pose a sentence or two that offers the reader the essential idea of the read-ing. Ask yourself: What is the author trying to say?

 Reread your sentences. Underline the parts that you think contribute to the main point the author is trying to make.

Here's the sentence that Professor Weiner wrote to express the essen-tial or main idea of Ariès's piece:

> *The transition of the education of children from apprenticeship to for-mal schooling is one measure, according to Ariès, of a changing family life and a new view towards sentimentality in the 15th century and later in the West.*

Notice that Professor Weiner used the term *one measure* in her state-ment. Even though a summary primarily reflects the author's ideas, we can-not help but form an opinion about the persuasiveness of his or her presen-tation when we read. Where we strongly disagree, we can find a way to insert our own understanding of his or her work into the summary. Still, the main purpose of a summary is to accurately represent another author's work.

Filling Out the Introduction

A successful summary of a specialized text in social history (or in any academic discipline), lets readers know how this piece fits into the field. They need to know more than what the essential idea is; they also need to know how the writer achieved that idea. What method was used? You can answer this by talking about what this particular reading contributes to social history or by telling the reader about the type of data or the method that was used. (In the summary included below, for example, Professor Weiner tells us that Ariès used letters, paintings, and advice books as his sources.)

In addition, you should decide how much bibliographic information (that is, when and where the reading was published) you need in the body of your introduction. For this summary, which might be a class assignment, we have included all the bibliographic information in the introduction. It could also be placed in the works cited or reference list at the end of your paper. The purpose is to make your source available to the reader.

DRAFTING THE SUMMARY

Thus far in the process you have done enough thinking and preparation to now begin to develop a rough draft of the summary. Take a break and think broadly about the task as a whole. How do you want to organize the sentences you have developed from groups of ideas? How will you shape your summary? Here is Professor Weiner's draft.[1]

From Apprenticeship to School:

The Beginnings of the Modern Family

    The transition of the education of children
from apprenticeship to formal schooling is one
measure, according to Ariès, of a changing family life
and a new view towards sentimentality beginning in the
fifteenth century in the West. Philippe Ariès, in an
excerpt from Chapter 2 of Centuries of Childhood: A
Social History of the Family (trans. from the French
by Robert Baldick, New York: Alfred A. Knopf, 1962)
uses letters, paintings, and advice books to document
what he sees as "a slow and profound revolution" (369;

---

[1]References include both the original page number and the paragraph number used in this textbook.

paragraph 10) in family life. Family life in the middle ages was characterized by the placing out of children into other families' homes to work as apprentices. This apprenticeship was the major means of education; domestic service was thus performed by children of all classes. Education of the young was "ensured by the everyday participation of children in adult life," thus teaching the youth of the community the "art of living" (368; paragaph 8). As such during medieval times, the family was not a sentimental unit, but a moral and social one.

Beginning in the fifteenth century, according to Ariès, the extension of formal schooling can be related to a change in family life creating a closer, more sentimental relationship between parent and child and at the same time allowing the school to handle some of the moral and social teachings that had previously been learned through apprenticeship. For example, with this new view of the family, all children could be treated equally instead of reserving the inheritance for the oldest son.

REVISING THE SUMMARY

Once you have drafted the summary you will want to go over it and revise your writing. We suggest you give it several readings, focusing on one aspect at a time. Here's a guide for revision.

An Overall Reading

Read the summary over once all the way through. Ask yourself the following questions:

Have I thought about why I am writing this summary? Have I included the appropriate bibliographic material in the introduction? Does my introduction explain the author's essential idea? Have I discussed how this reading fits into a specialized discipline by using specific types of data? Have I focused on the author's work and downplayed my own opinions and interpretaions? Have I included only the most important information and left out unnecessary details? Have I used and discussed the most important key terms in the reading?

A Sentence-by-Sentence Reading

In this reading focus on the relationships between sentences. Ask yourself:

> Have I used paragraphs to show shifts among the ideas in my summary?
> Does each sentence connect to the next one appropriately? Have I used
> words like the following to create relationships between sentences: further-
> more, likewise, and, yet, however, on the other hand, but, then, with this in
> mind, because, first, next, and to sum up? Should I use a particular noun and
> when can I use a pronoun to refer to it? Should I be using a synonym for the
> noun? Is the pattern of my sentence structure monotonous? Is the same
> subject and verb pattern used in each? Have I used forms of the verb "to be"
> too often? Does it create the emphasis I intended?

Reading for Editing and Proofreading

In this last close reading of the draft you need to look for errors of mechanics, style, usage, or punctuation. Use an English handbook to be sure your
draft follows the rules for correctness.

WRITING AND LEARNING ACTIVITIES

1. **Journal Entry:** Consider these questions: Is the process of writing a summary as we have outlined it here different from the way you usually write
academic papers? In what way? Does anything about the process confuse
you? Seem clearer now? What aspects of this process do you predict will
be particularly difficult or easy?

2. **Group Activity:** Think about classes you have taken in different disciplines.
As a group, brainstorm about how the disciplines differ. Appoint a scribe and
make lists for each one discussed. How do you think summarizing will differ
among these disciplines? What similarities and differences among the
sources used in these disciplines will you find? Can you predict how your
own personal experience might be important to developing a summary in
these disciplines?

SOURCES FOR SUMMARIZING

To give you practice in the process of reading specialized texts and writing
summaries, I have included in this section a source to summarize from
three of the disciplines covered in this book: social history, philosophy, and
marine biology. Before each reading is a set of questions to guide you in
thinking about the summary. At the end of the chapter is a set of activities
that will guide you through the process of writing a summary for each of the
source materials, or for any other sources—from other chapters or provided
by you or your instructor—you may wish to summarize.

A SOURCE FROM SOCIAL HISTORY

Social historians study the everyday lives of people who lived in the past. Below is a source from social history for you to practice the process of reading a specialized text and writing a summary about it. "Images of the Family, Then and Now," is the second chapter in a book by John Demos titled *Past, Present, and Personal: The Family and the Life Course in American History*. In this excerpt Demos examines the "image" of the family through three periods of American history. Much that you learned in reading the work of Phillipe Ariès will apply here even though the two authors are writing about very different time periods.

Here are some questions that will help you to plan a summary of the Demos chapter. Think about these first, then follow the guide for summarizing included at the end of the chapter.

ASK YOURSELF

Keep in mind that Demos is a historian and as such has special ways of constructing arguments. Have I identified Demos's arguments and his evidence? Demos traces images of the family through three historical periods. What image does he offer for each of the three periods? How does the image of the home change? Of the woman and the mother? What does Demos say about our current time period? How sure is he of his claims? Do I agree with him? Why or why not?

CHAPTER II
IMAGES OF THE FAMILY, THEN AND NOW
JOHN DEMOS

■ ■ ■

My apprenticeship in family history was strictly pre-professional. Efforts to uncover and organize source materials, to pose questions and frame arguments, to develop a suitable expository style: such were its leading elements. I aimed to add my piece to historical knowledge, to gratify my fellow-historians (teachers and peers), and, not least, to find a niche for myself in one or another college-level History Department.

Family history proved, however, to have an unusually wide orbit of concern. My research drew me repeatedly toward the "social sciences"—toward demography, psychology, anthropology, and sociology. And scholars from those disciplines reciprocated my interest. More and more I found myself operating in an explicitly inter-disciplinary mode.

A little later the orbit swung out in a different direction—toward literature, philosophy, and the "humanities" in general. And from there it was only a short

---

This essay was first published in Virginia Tufte and Barbara Myerhoff, eds., *Changing Images of the Family* (New Haven: Yale University Press, 1979), 43–60.

distance further to "policy"—and broadly "public" concerns. Lecture-invitations, conferences, and commission-memberships posed a challenge to the academic historian in me: how to make what I knew meaningful for an audience beyond the bounds of my discipline, indeed of the Academy itself.

The second essay in this volume was one of my first attempts to respond to the challenge. Initially prepared for a conference on family "images," and subsequently presented in a variety of public settings, it offers a quick sketch of American family history at large. It invites (at least obliquely) a reader-listener to contrast our contemporary notions of family life with those of our historical predecessors.

5 *In fact, the "images" theme offers an especially good opening to historical contrast. Much early research in family history was directed to demographic questions; and the results landed more on the side of continuity than change. (Thus, for example, "average household size" shows remarkable stability over long periods of time, and even the composition of families has altered less than one might think.) However, the expectations people bring to family life, the rewards they seek from it, the costs they are willing to pay: this is another, far more fluid and variable, story. And "images" cut right to its heart.*

Within the past twenty years professional historians in several countries have directed special attention and energy to the study of family life. "Family history" has become for the first time a legitimate branch of scholarly research. The entering wedge of this research was, and remains, demographic; by now we know more about the history of such circumstances as mean household size and median age of marriage than reasonable people may want to know. But investigation has also been moving ahead on other, more "qualitative," tracks: one thinks immediately of recent and challenging studies of the history of childhood, of women, of sexual mores and behavior, and even of domestic architecture.[1]

Meanwhile, the contemporary experience of families has also come under increasingly intense scrutiny. There is a diffuse sense of "crisis" about our domestic arrangements generally—a feeling that the family as we have traditionally known it is under siege, and may even give way entirely. The manifestations of this concern are many and varied—and by now have high visibility. Presidents, legislators, and other government officials regularly invoke the needs of families—and weigh public policy against such needs. One sees as well a new flowering of commissions, task forces, and conferences on this or that aspect of family life—on income supports, on child abuse, on family law, on "parenting."[2]

These two streams of interest have run a similar, but not an intersecting, course. It is arguable that either one might have developed—just about as it actually has developed—had the other never taken life at all. Still, we should perhaps consider the bridges that might usefully be built between them. To put the matter quite simply: what light can a historian throw on the current predicament in family life? For one thing he is tempted right away to strike a soothing note of reassurance. The core structure of the family has evolved and endured over a very long period of Western history, and it is extremely hard to imagine a sudden reversal of so much weighty tradition. Moreover, for at least a century now the American family in particular has been seen as beleaguered, endangered, and possibly on the verge of extinction. The sense of crisis is hardly new; with some allowance for periodic ebb and flow, it seems an inescapable undercurrent of our modern life and consciousness.

Is this, in fact, reassuring? And does such reassurance help, in any substantial way? Somehow, historians must try to do better.

10   These considerations will serve to frame (and perhaps to excuse) certain features of the present essay. The scale of discussion will be very large indeed—nothing less than the entire sweep of American history. The substance will be somewhat more modest, with the focus held for the most part on "images" of the family (not behavior); but even this encompasses a broad, and highly variable, territory. The tone will be, at least occasionally, judgmental and partisan; even the most "objective" scholar need not wholly suppress his own sense of gains derived, and prices paid, from the central perceptions of domestic life in the past.

More specifically, the essay proposes a three-part model of family history as a way of periodizing the field. In doing so it necessarily lumps together many highly variegated bits of research; and obviously, other histories—other historians—might fashion quite a different set of lumps. In emphasizing images of family life, it accepts an implicit social and economical bias, for such images have been created largely by people of Anglo-Saxon origin in the more comfortable layers of our social system—in short, by middle-class WASPs. Nonetheless this same middle class has, in our country, traditionally played a style-setting role—even for those who might seem to espouse alternative ways and traditions. Immigrants, blacks, workers of all sorts, are thus profoundly implicated here. The nature of these connections is highly complex—one might well say, ambivalent. But the larger point is that Americans of every color, every creed, and every economic position have been drawn toward the cultural middle. And embedded just there are the very images that form the subject of this discussion.

I

Consider, as the first part of our sequential model, the "colonial" and "early national" phases of American history—a period of time lasting into the nineteenth century. It should be recognized, incidentally, that this inquiry does not lend itself to precise chronological markings; the end of one stage and the start of the next are so fully merged that one might well think in terms of a transitional process. And if, for the first stage, one assigns a terminal date of 1820, this is only to indicate a midpoint in the transition. The precursors of change were visible in some quarters as early as the Revolutionary era, and the process was still working itself out during the time of the Civil War.

Now comes a rather perverse twist. When a scholar seeks to approach the colonial American family, one thing he notices immediately is that the "image" itself seems rather thinly sketched. In short, people of that rather distant time and culture did not have a particularly self-conscious orientation to family life; their ideas, their attitudes in this connection, were far simpler than would ever be the case for later generations of Americans. Family life was something they took largely for granted. It was no doubt a central part of their experience, but not in such a way as to require special attention. This does not mean that they lacked ideas of what a "good family" should be and do—or, for that matter, a "bad" one—just that such notions carried a rather low charge in comparison with other forms of social concern.[3]

In any event, there are some points that one can deduce about their orientation to family life, and a few that can be pulled directly out of the documentary record they have left to us. Here is a particularly resonant statement, taken from an essay by a "Puritan" preacher in the early seventeenth century:

> A family is a little church, and a little commonwealth, at least a lively representation thereof, whereby trial may be made of such as are fit for any place of authority, or of subjection, in church or commonwealth. Or rather, it is as a school wherein the first principles and grounds of government are learned; whereby men are fitted to greater matters in church and commonwealth.[4]

Two aspects of this description seem especially important. First, the family and the wider community are joined in a relation of profound reciprocity; one might almost say they are continuous with one another. (This is, incidentally, a general premodern pattern—in no sense specific to American life and conditions—which was analyzed first and most incisively by Philippe Ariès, in his path-breaking study of twenty years ago published in English under the title *Centuries of Childhood.*[5]) To put the matter in another way: individual families are the building blocks out of which the larger units of social organization are fashioned. Families and churches, families and governments, belong to the same world of experience. Individual people move back and forth between these settings with little effort or sense of difficulty.

15   The membership of these families was not fundamentally different from the pattern of our own day: a man and a woman joined in marriage, and their natural-born children. The basic unit was therefore a "nuclear" one, contrary to a good deal of sociological theory about premodern times. However, non-kin could, and did, join this unit—orphans, apprentices, hired laborers, and a variety of children "bound out" for a time in conditions of fosterage. Usually designated by the general term "servants," such persons lived as regular members of many colonial households; and if they were young, the "master" and "mistress" served *in loco parentis*. Occasionally, convicts and indigent people were directed by local authorities to reside in particular families. Here the master's role was to provide care, restraint, and even a measure of rehabilitation for those involved; they, in turn, gave him their service. Thus did the needs of the individual householders intersect the requirements of the larger community.[6]

But it was not simply that the family and the community ran together at so many points; the one was, in the words of the preacher, "a lively representation" of the other. Their structure, their guiding values, their inner purposes, were essentially the same. Indeed the family was a community in its own right, a unit of shared experience for all its individual members. It was, first and foremost, a community of work—in ways hard for us even to imagine today. Young and old, male and female, labored together to produce the subsistence on which the whole group depended. For long periods they worked literally in each other's presence—if not necessarily at the same tasks. In other ways as well the family lived and functioned as a unit. Most leisure-time activities (which consisted largely of visiting with friends, relatives, and neighbors) were framed in a family context, as were education, health care, and some elements of religious worship.

Religion, however, brings new considerations into view; in effect, it conjures up another, quite different community. Clarity on this point requires a brief detour into the esoteric particulars of church organization. Consider the typical seating plan of colonial churches (at least in New England).[7] (1) Men and women were separated on opposite sides of a central aisle. (2) Within these sex-typed enclaves individual communicants were assigned places in accordance with certain "status" criteria. (In general, the oldest, wealthiest, and most prominent citizens sat at the front.) (3) Children were relegated to still another section of the church (usually in the back, sometimes in an upstairs gallery). Now these arrangements have an important bearing on the present inquiry. Presumably, the members of a typical family started out for church together, but upon reaching their destination they broke apart and went off in different directions. The church had its own mode of organization, vividly reflected in its spatial aspect; preacher in the pulpit, elders sitting just below, regular parishioners carefully distributed on the basis of sex, age, and social position. Family relationships were effectively discounted, or at very least submerged, in this particular context. In sum, the family community and the religious community were fundamentally distinct—though formed from the same pool of individuals. Much later (in most cases, the early nineteenth century), Protestant congregations went over to the pattern that still prevails today, with seating inside the church arranged on a family basis. And the change had a profound symbolic significance. No longer was the family simply one form of community among others; from thenceforth it constituted a special group, whose boundaries would be firmly declared in all imaginable circumstances.

There is one more vital aspect of colonial family life which deserves at least to be mentioned. Since the functions of the household and the wider society were so substantially interconnected, the latter might reasonably intervene when the former experienced difficulty. Magistrates and local officials would thus compel a married couple "to live more peaceably together" or to alter and upgrade the "governance" of their children. This, too, is the context of the famous "stubborn child" laws of early New England, which prescribed the death penalty for persistent disobedience to parents. Such extreme sanctions were never actually invoked, but the statutes remained on the books as a mark of society's interest in orderly domestic relations.[8]

II

As noted earlier, it is hard to say just how and when this colonial pattern began to break down; but by the early decades of the nineteenth century at least some American families were launched on a new course, within a very different framework of experience. For the most part these were urban families, and distinctly middle-class; and while they did not yet constitute anything like a majority position in the country at large, they pointed the way to the future.[9]

20   Here, for the first time, American family life acquired an extremely sharp "image"—in the sense of becoming something thought about in highly self-conscious ways, written about at great length and by many hands, and worried about in relation to a host of internal and external stress-points. Among other things, there was a new sense that the family had a history of its own—that it was not fixed and unchanging for all time. And when some observers, especially "conservative" ones, pondered the direction of this history, they reached an unsettling conclusion: the family, they believed, was set on a course of decline and decay. From a stable and virtuous condition in former times, it had gradually passed into a "crisis" phase. After mid-century, popular literature on domestic life poured out a long litany of complaints: divorce and desertion were increasing; child-rearing had become too casual and permissive; authority was generally disrupted; the family no longer did things together; women were more and more restless in their role as homemakers.[10] Do these complaints have a somewhat familiar ring even now? In fact, it is from this period, more than one hundred years ago, that one of our most enduring images of the family derives—what might be called the image, or the myth, of the family's golden past. Many around us appear still to believe that there is some ideal state of domestic life which we have tragically lost. The consequences of such belief are profound—since it implies that our individual efforts and our public policies in regard to family life should have a "restorative" character. But this is another topic, best left to a different setting.

How, then, shall we further characterize the nineteenth-century image of family-life? One point is immediately striking. The family—far from joining and complementing other social networks, as in the earlier period—seemed to stand increasingly apart. Indeed its position vis-à-vis society at large had been very nearly reversed, so as to become a kind of adversary relation.

The brave new world of nineteenth-century America was, in some respects, a dangerous world—or so many people felt. The new egalitarian spirit, the sense of openness, the opportunities for material gain, the cult of the "self-made man": all this was new, invigorating, and liberating at one level—but it also conveyed a deep threat to traditional values and precepts. In order to seize the main chance and get ahead in the ongoing struggle for "success," a man had to summon energies and take initiatives that would at the very least exhaust him and might involve him in terrible compromises. At the same time he would need to retain some place of rest and refreshment—some emblem of the personal and moral regime that he was otherwise leaving behind.[11]

Within this matrix of ideas the family was sharply redefined. Henceforth the life of the individual home, on the one hand, and the wider society, on the other, represented for many Americans entirely different spheres. ("Spheres" was indeed the term they most frequently used in conceptualizing their varied experiences.) The two were separated by a sharply delineated frontier; different strategies and values were looked for on either side.

Some of the new "home" values have been mentioned already, but it is necessary to investigate them more fully. Home—and the word itself became highly sentimentalized—was pictured as a bastion of peace, of orderliness, of unwavering devotion to people and principles beyond the self. Here the woman of the family, and the children, would pass most of their hours and days—safe from the grinding pressures and dark temptations of the world at large; here, too, the man of the family would retreat periodically for repose, renewal, and inner fortification against the dangers he encountered elsewhere.[12]

25   Pulling these various themes together, one can reasonably conclude that the crucial function of the family had now become a protective one. And two kinds of protection were implied here: protection of the ways and values of an older America that was fast disappearing, and protection also for the individual people who were caught up in the middle of unprecedented change. If the notion of "the family as community" serves to summarize the colonial part of this story, perhaps for the nineteenth century, the appropriate image is "the family as refuge." Two short passages, chosen from the voluminous domestic literature of the period, will convey the underlying melody:

• From the corroding cares of business, from the hard toil and frequent disappointments of the day, men retreat to the bosoms of their families, and there, in the midst of that sweet society of wife and children and friends, receive a rich reward for their industry. . . . The feeling that here, in one little spot, his best enjoyments are concentrated . . . gives a wholesome tendency to [a man's] thoughts, and is like the healing oil poured upon the wounds and bruises of the spirit.

   We go forth into the world, amidst the scenes of business and of pleasure; we mix with the gay and the thoughtless, we join the busy crowd, and the heart is sensible to a desolation of feeling; we behold every principle of justice and of honor, disregarded, and the delicacy of our moral sense is wounded; we see the general good sacrificed to the advancement of personal interest; and we turn from such scenes with a painful sensation, almost believing that virtue has deserted the abodes of men; again, we look to the sanctuary of home; there sympathy, honor, virtue are assembled; there the eye may kindle with intelligence, and receive an answering glance; there disinterested love is ready to sacrifice everything at the altar of affection.[13]

This imagery had, in fact, particular features which deserve careful notice. For one thing, it embraced the idea of highly differentiated roles and statuses within the family—for the various individual family members. The husband-father undertook an exclusive responsibility for productive labor. He did this in one or another setting well removed from the home-hearth, in offices, factories, shops, or wherever. So it was that family life was wrenched apart from the world of work—a veritable sea-change in social history. Meanwhile, the wife-mother was expected to confine herself to domestic activities; increasingly idealized in the figure of the "True Woman," she became the centerpiece in the developing cult of Home. Intrinsically superior (from a moral standpoint) to her male partner, the True Woman preserved Home as a safe, secure, and altogether "pure" environment.[14] The children of this marital pair were set off as distinctive creatures in their own right. Home life, from their point of view, was a sequence of preparation in which they armored themselves for the challenges and difficulties of the years ahead.[15] The children, after all, carried the hopes of the family into the future; their lives later on would reward, or betray, the sacrifices of their parents. Taken altogether, and compared with the earlier period, these notions conveyed the sense of a family carefully differentiated as to individual task and function, but unalterably united as to overall goals and morale. Like other institutions in the "Machine Age," the family was now seen as a system of highly calibrated, interlocking parts.

It is clear enough that such a system conformed to various practical needs and circumstances in the lives of many Americans—the adaptation to urban life, the changing requirements of the workplace, the gathering momentum of technology. But it must have answered to certain emotional needs as well. In particular, the cult of Home helped people to release the full range of aggressive energies so essential to the growth and development of the country—helped them, that is, to still anxiety and to ward off guilt about their own contributions to change. At the same time there were costs and difficulties that one cannot fail to see. The demands inherent in each of the freshly articulated family roles were sometimes literally overwhelming.

The husband-father, for example, was not just the breadwinner for the entire family; he was also its sole representative in the world at large. His "success" or "failure"—terms which had now obtained a highly personal significance—would reflect directly on the other members of the household. And this was a grievously heavy burden to carry. For anyone who found it too heavy, for anyone who stumbled and fell while striving to scale the heights of success, there was a bitter legacy of self-reproach—not to mention the implicit or explicit reproaches of other family members whose fate was tied to his own.

Meanwhile, the lady of the house experienced another set of pressures—different, but no less taxing. The conventions of domestic life had thrown up a model of the "perfect home"—so tranquil, so cheerful, so pure, as to constitute an almost impossible standard. And it was the exclusive responsibility of the wife to try to meet this standard. Moreover, her behavior must in all circumstances exemplify the selflessness of the True Woman. Her function was effectively defined as one of service and giving to others; she could not express needs or interests of her own. This suppression of self exacted a crushing toll from many nineteenth-century women. Few complained outright, though modern feminism dates directly from this era. But there were other, less direct forms of complaint—the neurasthenias, the hysterias, indeed a legion of "women's diseases," which allowed their victims to opt out of the prescribed system.[16]

30   The system also imposed new difficulties on the younger members of the household. In the traditional culture of colonial America the process of growth from child to adult had been relatively smooth and seamless. The young were gradually raised, by a sequence of short steps, from subordinate positions within their families of origin to independent status in the community at large.[17] In the nineteenth century, by contrast, maturation became disjunctive and problematic. As the condition of childhood was ever more sharply articulated, so the transition to adulthood became longer, lonelier, more painful.[18] And there was also another kind of transition to negotiate. For those who absorbed the imagery of Home the moment of leaving was charged with extraordinary tension. To cross the sacred threshold from inside to outside was to risk unspeakable dangers. The nostalgia, the worries, the guilt which attended such crossings are threaded through an enormous mass of domestic fiction from the period. Marriage itself was experienced as the sudden exchange of one family for another—with a little of the flavor of a blind leap.[19]

In sum, the "ideal family" of the nineteenth century comprised a tightly closed circle of reciprocal obligations. And the entire system was infused with a strain of dire urgency. If the family did not function in the expected ways, there were no other institutions to back it up. If one family member fell short of prescribed ways and standards, all the others were placed in jeopardy. There is a short story by T. S. Arthur—an immensely popular author during the middle of the century—which makes this point very clearly.[20] A young couple marry and set up housekeeping. The husband is an aspiring businessman, with every prospect of "success." His wife shares his ambitions and means to become an effective "helpmeet"; however, her management of the household is marred by a certain inefficiency. The husband regularly returns from his office for lunch (an interesting vestige of premodern work rhythms), but soon a problem develops. The wife cannot hold to a firm schedule in preparing these meals, and often her husband is kept waiting. Earnest conversations and repeated vows of improvement bring no real change. Finally, one particular delay causes the husband to miss a crucial appointment—and the consequences for his business are devastating.

Domestic fiction played out similar themes in the relation of parents and children. Only the most careful and moral "rearing" would bring the young out safe in later life; anything less might imperil their destiny irrevocably. Conversely, the well-being of parents depended in large measure on their offspring. If the latter, having grown to adulthood, were to stray from the paths of virtue, the old folks might feel so "heartbroken" that they would sicken and die.[21] Here the stakes of domestic bonding attained an aspect of life-threatening finality.

III

To some degree the image of "the family as refuge" remains with us today. Many people still look to home life for buffering, or at least for relief, against the demands and pressures of society at large. There is a continuing sense of inside-outside, and an idea of domestic inviolacy well expressed by the cliche that "each man's home is his castle."

And yet for some time the tide has been running in another direction. It seems reasonable, therefore, to posit a third stage in family history, while acknowledging that the second has not yet exhausted itself. To identify the new trend precisely is no easy task, and the argument of the following pages must be regarded as provisional at best. A scholar is *perforce* reduced to the role of an everyday observer—indeed a participant-observer (!)—of contemporary family life.

35   Domestic imagery can be expected to reflect changes in the social context of experience, and for millions of Americans that context is now a different one. The twentieth century has gathered up a host of "modernizing" forces; one overused but still helpful phrase for describing the process is "the rise of mass society." Truly, we do take significant parts of life in the mass—as workers (mostly for large organizations), as consumers (mostly of highly standardized services and products), as citizens (mostly under a "big government"). For many Americans this situation has brought a measure of security and comfort unprecedented in previous generations. Jobs are less liable to disruption, income is steadier, health care is somewhat more regular, and so on. And yet these gains have been purchased at a cost. Comfortable as many of us are, we have a sense of flatness, even of emptiness, about large sectors of our experience. Increasingly we feel that we are not masters of our own fate, that our individual goals and deeds count for nothing when weighed in such a large aggregate. We cannot, in short, make much of a difference in our own lives. Thus ever larger numbers of us do not bother to vote (what difference is made by one ballot more or less?), and we are disinclined to protest inferior products, inefficient services, or even blatant injustice when such things directly touch our lives. "Apathy" is the currently fashionable word to describe our social climate—and it does seem to hit the mark.

For a shorthand contrast between this situation and the social climate of a century ago one need only consult the favorite period metaphors. History has moved, it seems, from the "jungle" of the nineteenth century to the "rat race" (or the "grind") of our own day. This progression expresses clearly a lessened sense of threat—and also a growing feeling of monotony and meaninglessness."

The implications for family life—specifically, for images and expectations of family life—are profound. As the threat is tempered, the wish for protection, for armoring, wanes. Or rather it shades gradually into something else. Home is less a bunker amidst the battle than a place of "rest and recuperation" (pursuing the military analogy). According to this standard, families should provide the interest, the excitement, the stimulation missing from other sectors of our experience. If we feel that "we aren't going anywhere" in our work, we may load our personal lives—especially our family lives—with powerful compensatory needs. We wish to "grow" in special ways through our relations with family partners; a familiar complaint in counseling centers nowadays is the sense of blocked opportunities for growth. We want our spouses, our lovers, even our children, to help us feel alive and invigorated—to brighten a social landscape that otherwise seems unrelievedly gray. Again, some contrasts with the earlier setting may be helpful. Then Home was to be a place of quiet, of repose. Now it must generate some excitement. Then the True Woman served as the appointed guardian of domestic values; as such she was "pure," steady, in all ways self-effacing. Now there is the figure of the "Total Woman"—who, to be sure, keeps an orderly house and seeks consistently to help her man, but who is also sensual and assertive within limits.[22]

Indeed an entire spectrum of roles and responsibilities within the family is increasingly in question. No longer can we automatically accept that principle of differentiation which, in the nineteenth century, assigned to each household member a "sphere" deemed appropriate to his or her age and gender. Some families now advocate an opposite principle, which exalts the diffusion and mixing of roles. Mother must do her share of the "breadwinning," Father must do his share of the household chores, and so on. Much of this, of course, comes directly from the "women's movement," and involves a long-overdue effort to right the balance of opportunity between the sexes. However, that is not the whole story. If Father is urged nowadays to help with the children or wash the dishes or take care of the laundry, this is not just in order to lighten the burdens that have traditionally fallen on Mother. There is also a feeling that such activities are good for him. Somehow his sensibilities will be expanded and his personal growth advanced—just as Mother expands and grows through her work outside the home. As a further benefit of these rearrangments the couple discovers new byways of marital communication. Since they share so much more, they understand each other better; and their relation to one another is "deepened" accordingly. Even children are invited to join in this celebration of openness and reciprocity. The parents believe that they must listen carefully and at all times to their children, even that they can learn from their children—ideas which would have seemed quite preposterous just a few generations ago.

If all goes well—if reality meets expectation and conforms to image—Home becomes a bubbling kettle of lively, and mutually enhancing, activity. But, alas, all does not invariably go well; so we also have, for the first time in American history, a negative image—an "anti-image"—of the family. Seen from this viewpoint, domestic relationships look dangerously like an encumbrance, if not a form of bondage, inhibiting the quest for a full experience of self. Monogamous marriage is liable to become boring and stultifying; in other things, after all, variety is "the spice of life." Moreover, responsibility for children only compounds the problem. The needs and requirements of the young are so pressing, so constant, as to leave little space for adults who must attend to them. "Spice" and "space": these are, in fact, the qualities for which we yearn most especially. And the family severely limits our access to either one.

40   These contrasting notions of family-life—image and anti-image—appear at some level to converge. In fact, they are opposite faces of the same coin. Each affirms the primacy of family experience in relation to larger goals of personal growth and self-fulfillment. The difference lies in the effects imputed to such experience—in the first case, a beneficial effect, in the second, an adverse one. Both images assume a deep threat of inward stagnation, implicit in the "rat race" which surrounds us all.

There are, of course, other ways to fight the rat race. Encounter groups, assertiveness-training, consciousness-raising of all kinds should certainly be mentioned here—as well as the vicarious excitements that come, for example, from celebrity-watching. Presumably these activities are not antithetical to good, growing family life; on the contrary, their effects should be complementary and enhancing. Indeed the most suitable caption for this third (current) stage of family history is: "the family as encounter group." For the central values attaching to domestic experience nowadays—at least by the reading presented here—are those which underscore significant personal encounters.

IV

In closing, it seems necessary to reemphasize the distortion introduced by any discrete model of family history. The problem is not simply one of arbitrary chronological boundaries; there is also a risk of failing to see the cumulative element in all historical process. "Stage three," as previously noted, retains a good part of "stage two"—and even some traces of "stage one." (We continue, after all, to see individual families as the "building blocks" of the nation as a whole.) Thus our present arrangements are best construed as a complex and heavily layered precipitate of our entire social history.

Two points about this history deserve some final underscoring. In both the second and the third of our major stages the family has been loaded with the most urgent of human needs and responsibilities. Indeed one might well say overloaded. In each case the prevalent imagery conjures up a compensatory function: the family must supply what is vitally needed, but missing, in social arrangements generally. It must protect its individual constituents against imminent and mortal danger, or it must fill a void of meaninglessness. To put the matter in another way: the family is not experienced in its own right and on its own terms, but in relation to outside circumstances and pressures. It is for this reason, presumably, that we have become so extraordinarily self-conscious about family-life—and, more, have broached it for so long from an attitude of crisis.

There is a concomitant of this attitude which also has deep historical roots. Briefly, we have isolated family life as the primary setting—if not, in fact, the only one—for caring relations between people. The nineteenth-century images made an especially powerful contribution here: each family would look after its own—and, for the rest, may the best man win. Relationships formed within the world of work—which meant, for a long time, relationships between men—would not have an emotional dimension. Nineteenth-century women seem, on the evidence of very recent scholarship, to have maintained "networks" of affection which did cross family boundaries, but even this pattern recedes as we follow the trail toward the present.

45   Much of the same viewpoint has survived into our own time, and it underlies certain continuing tensions in our national experience. The United States stands almost alone among Western industrialized countries in having no coherent "family policy." More particularly, our inherited habits and values—our constricted capacity for extra-familial caring—partly explain public indifference to the blighted conditions in which many families even now are obliged to live. The results are especially tragic as they affect children, and they leave us with a terrible paradox. In this allegedly most child-centered of nations, we find it hard to care very much or very consistently about *other people's children*. A historian may think that he understands such a predicament; he does not, however, know how to change it.

·   ·   ·

NOTES

1. See the discussion (and references) in Chapter One, above.
2. Several recent publications exemplify the trend: e.g. Kenneth Keniston and the Carnegie Council on Children, *All Our Children: The American Family Under Pressure* (New York, 1977); Assembly of Behavioral and Social Sciences, National Research Council, *Toward a National Policy for Children and Families* (Washington, D.C.: National Academy of Sciences, 1976). See also the various publications of the Family Impact Seminar Series (Temple University Press) and the Committee on Child Development Research and Public Policy (National Research Council, Washington, D.C.)
3. On the colonial family, see, for example, John Demos, *A Little Commonwealth: Family Life in Plymouth Colony* (New York, 1970), Edmund S. Morgan, *The Puritan Family,* rev. ed. (New York, 1966), and Daniel Blake Smith, *Inside the Great House: Planter Family-Life in Eighteenth-Century Chesapeake Society* (Ithaca, N.Y., 1980).
4. William Gouge, *Of Domesticall Duties* (London, 1622).
5. See Philippe Ariès, *Centuries of Childhood: A Social History of Family Life,* trans. Robert Baldick (New York, 1962).
6. See Morgan, *Puritan Family,* ch. 4.
7. On the practice of "seating the meetinghouse," see Robert J. Dinkin. "Provincial Massachusetts: A Deferential or a Democratic Society" (Ph.D. diss., Columbia University, 1968), and Ola Winslow, *Meetinghouse Hill,* 1630–1783 (New York, 1952).
8. See Edwin Powers, *Crime and Punishment in Early Massachusetts, 1620–1692: A Documentary History* (Boston, 1966), 268, 283ff.

9. See Kirk Jeffrey, "The Family as Utopian Retreat from the City," *Soundings* 55 (1972):21–41; and Barbara Laslett, "The Family as a Public and Private Institution: An Historical Perspective." *Journal of Marriage and the Family,* 35 (1973):480–92.

10. Examples of this viewpoint may be found in William A. Alcott, *The Young Wife* (Boston, 1837), William Thayer, *Hints for the Household* (Boston, 1853), and Artemas B. Muzzey, *The Fireside* (Boston, 1854).

11. See Jeffrey, "Family as Utopian Retreat." Also Barbara Welter, "The Cult of True Womanhood: 1820–1860," *American Quarterly* 18 (1966):151–74.

12. An immensely popular expression of this viewpoint was the novel by Catharine Maria Sedgwick, *Home* (Boston, 1854).

13. Quoted in Jeffrey, "Family as Utopian Retreat."

14. See Welter, "Cult of True Womanhood."

15. See Bernard Wishy, *The Child and the Republic: The Dawn of Modern American Child Nurture* (Philadelphia, 1972).

16. See Ann Douglas Wood, "'The Fashionable Diseases': Women's Complaints and Their Treatment in Nineteenth-Century America," *Journal of Interdisciplinary History* 4 (1973):25–52; and Carroll Smith-Rosenberg, "The Hysterical Woman: Some Reflections on Sex-Roles and Role Conflict in Nineteenth-Century America," in *Social Research,* 39 (1972), 652–78.

17. Demos, *A Little Commonwealth,* ch. 10.

18. Joseph Kett, *Rites of Passage: Adolescence in America, 1790 to the Present* (New York, 1977).

19. See, for example, the marriages described in Sedgwick, *Home.* This theme is explored in Ellen K. Rothman, *Hands and Hearts: A History of Courtship in America* (New York, 1984).

20. T. S. Arthur, "Sweethearts and Wives," in *The Root of Bitterness,* ed. Nancy F. Cott (New York, 1972).

21. The plot line in Sedgwick's novel is a case in point.

22. Marabel Morgan, *The Total Woman* (Old Tappan, N.J., 1975).

A SOURCE FROM PHILOSOPHY

In Chapter 4 we learned that philosophers sometimes use a method called thought experiments to analyze important problems on the topic of personal identity. And we read an important essay by John Locke on this topic. Our interest in personal identity did not end in the 1600s with John Locke; it is still an important concern for philosophers and others. "What We Believe Ourselves to Be," an excerpt from Chapter 10 of Derek Parfit's book *Reasons and Persons,* which was published in 1984, is our next reading. He opens the chapter with a fascinating thought experiment about sending a replica of one's body to Mars via a teletransporter; he then uses that thought experiment to question notions of personal identity.

Before you begin your summary, think about the questions below, then use the guide at the end of this chapter to develop your summary:

ASK YOURSELF

What have I learned thus far about philosophical issues of personal identity? What claims does Parfit make and how does he support them? Does he use thought experiments as Locke did? How else does he support his claims? How can I share with my reader something about the meaning-making processes of that community? How did the philosopher achieve his or her claim? What method did he use? How does this particular reading contribute to problems or methods in philosophy? How would I introduce this text to someone who knows very little about philosophy?

10

WHAT WE BELIEVE OURSELVES TO BE
DEREK PARFIT

■ ■ ■

I enter the Teletransporter. I have been to Mars before, but only by the old method, a space-ship journey taking several weeks. This machine will send me at the speed of light. I merely have to press the green button. Like others, I am nervous. Will it work? I remind myself what I have been told to expect. When I press the button, I shall lose consciousness, and then wake up at what seems a moment later. In fact I shall have been unconscious for about an hour. The Scanner here on Earth will destroy my brain and body, while recording the exact states of all of my cells. It will then transmit this information by radio. Travelling at the speed of light, the message will take three minutes to reach the Replicator on Mars. This will then create, out of new matter, a brain and body exactly like mine. It will be in this body that I shall wake up.

Though I believe that this is what will happen, I still hesitate. But then I remember seeing my wife grin when, at breakfast today, I revealed my nervousness. As she reminded me, she has been often teletransported, and there is nothing wrong with *her*. I press the button. As predicted, I lose and seem at once to regain consciousness, but in a different cubicle. Examining my new body, I find no change at all. Even the cut on my upper lip, from this morning's shave, is still there.

Several years pass, during which I am often Teletransported. I am now back in the cubicle, ready for another trip to Mars. But this time, when I press the green button, I do not lose consciousness. There is a whirring sound, then silence. I leave the cubicle, and say to the attendant: 'It's not working. What did I do wrong?'

'It's working', he replies, handing me a printed card. This reads: 'The New Scanner records your blueprint without destroying your brain and body. We hope that you will welcome the opportunities which this technical advance offers.'

5   The attendant tells me that I am one of the first people to use the New Scanner. He adds that, if I stay for an hour, I can use the Intercom to see and talk to myself on Mars.

'Wait a minute', I reply, 'If I'm here I can't *also* be on Mars'.

Someone politely coughs, a white-coated man who asks to speak to me in private. We go into his office, where he tells me to sit down, and pauses. Then he says: 'I'm afraid that we're having problems with the New Scanner. It records your blueprint just as accurately, as you will see when you talk to yourself on Mars. But it seems to be damaging the cardiac systems which it scans. Judging from the results so far, though you will be quite healthy on Mars, here on Earth you must expect cardiac failure within the next few days.'

The attendant later calls me to the Intercom. On the screen I see myself just as I do in the mirror every morning. But there are two differences. On the screen I am not left-right reversed. And, while I stand here speechless, I can see and hear myself, in the studio on Mars, starting to speak.

What can we learn from this imaginary story? Some believe that we learn little. This would have been Wittgenstein's view.[1] And Quine writes: 'The method of science fiction has its uses in philosophy, but . . . I wonder whether the limits of the method are properly heeded. To seek what is 'logically required' for sameness of person under unprecedented circumstances is to suggest that words have some logical force beyond what our past needs have invested them with.'[2]

10   This criticism might be justified if, when considering such imagined cases, we had no reactions. But these cases arouse in most of us strong beliefs. And these are beliefs, not about our words, but about ourselves. By considering these cases, we discover what we believe to be involved in our own existence, or what it is that makes us now and ourselves next year the same people. We discover our beliefs about the nature of personal identity over time. Though our beliefs are revealed most clearly when we consider imaginary cases, these beliefs also cover actual cases, and our own lives. In Part Three of this book I shall argue that some of these beliefs are false, then suggest how and why this matters.

75. SIMPLE TELETRANSPORTATION AND THE BRANCH-LINE CASE

At the beginning of my story, the Scanner destroys my brain and body. My blueprint is beamed to Mars, where another machine makes an organic *Replica* of me. My Replica thinks that he is me, and he seems to remember living my life up to the moment when I pressed the green button. In every other way, both physically and psychologically, my Replica is just like me. If he returned to Earth, everyone would think that he was me.

Simple Teletransportation, as just described, is a common feature in science fiction. And it is believed, by some readers of this fiction, merely to be the fastest way of travelling. They believe that my Replica *would* be me. Other science fiction readers, and some of the characters in this fiction, take a different view. They believe that, when I press the green button, I die. My Replica is *someone else,* who has been made to be exactly like me.

This second view seems to be supported by the end of my story. The New Scanner does not destroy my brain and body. Besides gathering the information, it merely damages my heart. While I am in the cubicle, with the green button pressed, nothing seems to happen. I walk out, and learn that in a few days I shall die. I later talk, by two-way television, to my Replica on Mars. Let us continue the story. Since my Replica knows that I am about to die, he tries to console me with the same thoughts with which I recently tried to console a dying friend. It is sad to learn, on the receiving end, how unconsoling these thoughts are. My Replica then assures me that he will take up my life where I leave off. He loves my wife, and together they will care for my children. And he will finish the book that I am writing. Besides having all of my drafts, he has all of my intentions. I must admit that he can finish my book as well as I could. All these facts console me a little. Dying when I know that I shall have a Replica is not quite as bad as, simply, dying. Even so, I shall soon lose consciousness, forever.

In Simple Teletransportation, I am destroyed before I am Replicated. This makes it easier to believe that this *is* a way of travelling—that my Replica *is* me. At the end of my story, my life and that of my Replica overlap. Call this the *Branch-Line Case.* In this case, I cannot hope to travel on the *Main Line,* waking up on Mars with forty years of life ahead. I shall stay on the Branch-Line, here on Earth, which ends a few days later. Since I can talk to my Replica, it seems clear that he is *not* me. Though he is exactly like me, he is one person, and I am another. When I pinch myself, he feels nothing. When I have my heart attack, he will again feel nothing. And when I am dead he will live for another forty years.

15   If we believe that my Replica is not me, it is natural to assume that my prospect, on the Branch Line, is almost as bad as ordinary death. I shall deny this assumption. As I shall argue later, being destroyed and Replicated is about as good as ordinary survival. I can best defend this claim, and the wider view of which it is part, after discussing the past debate about personal identity.

76. QUALITATIVE AND NUMERICAL IDENTITY

There are two kinds of sameness, or identity. I and my Replica are *qualitatively identical,* or exactly alike. But we may not be *numerically identical,* or one and the same person. Similarly, two white billiard balls are not numerically but may be qualitatively identical. If I paint one of these balls red, it will cease to be qualitatively identical with itself as it was. But the red ball that I later see and the white ball that I painted red are numerically identical. They are one and the same ball.

We might say, of someone, 'After his accident, he is no longer the same person.' This is a claim about both kinds of identity. We claim that *he,* the same person, is *not* now the same person. This is not a contradiction. We merely mean that this person's character has changed. This numerically identical person is now qualitatively different.

When we are concerned about our future, it is our numerical identity that we are concerned about. I may believe that, after my marriage, I shall not be the same person. But this does not make marriage death. However much I change, I shall still be alive if there will be some person living who will *be* me.

Though our chief concern is our numerical identity, psychological changes matter. Indeed, on one view, certain kinds of qualitative change destroy numerical identity. If certain things happen to me, the truth might not be that I become a very different person. The truth might be that I cease to exist—that the resulting person is someone else.

77. THE PHYSICAL CRITERION OF PERSONAL IDENTITY

20   There has been much debate about the nature both of persons and of personal identity over time. It will help to distinguish these questions:

(1) What is the nature of a person?
(2) What makes a person at two different times one and the same person? What is necessarily involved in the continued existence of each person over time?

The answer to (2) can take this form: 'X today is one and the same person as Y at some past time *if and only if. . .* ' Such an answer states the *necessary and sufficient conditions* for personal identity over time.

In answering (2) we shall also partly answer (1). The necessary features of our continued existence depend upon our nature. And the simplest answer to (1) is that, to be a person, a being must be self-conscious, aware of its identity and its continued existence over time.

We can also ask

(3) What is in fact involved in the continued existence of each person over time?

Since our continued existence has features that are not necessary, the answer to (2) is only part of the answer to (3). For example, having the same heart and the same character are not necessary to our continued existence, but they are usually part of what this existence involves.

Many writers use the ambiguous phrase 'the criterion of identity over time'. Some mean by this 'our way of telling whether some present object is identical with some past object.' But I shall mean *what this identity necessarily involves, or consists in.*

In the case of most physical objects, on what I call the *standard view,* the criterion of identity over time is the spatio-temporal physical continuity of this object. This is something that we all understand, even if we fail to understand the description I shall now give. In the simplest case of physical continuity, like that of the Pyramids, an apparently static object continues to exist. In another simple case, like that of the Moon, an object moves in a regular way. Many objects move in less regular ways, but they still trace physically continuous spatio-temporal paths. Suppose that the billiard ball that I painted red is the same as the white ball with which last year I made a winning shot. On the standard view, this is true only if this ball traced such a continuous path. It must be true (1) that there is a line through space and time, starting where the white ball rested before I made my winning shot, and ending where the red ball now is, (2) that at every point on this line there was a billiard ball, and (3) that the existence of a ball at each point on this line was in part caused by the existence of a ball at the immediately preceding point.[3]

25   Some kinds of thing continue to exist even though their physical continuity involves great changes. A Camberwell Beauty is first an egg, then a caterpillar, then a chrysalis, then a butterfly. These are four stages in the physically continuous existence of a single organism. Other kinds of thing cannot survive such great changes. Suppose that an artist paints a self-portrait and then, by repainting, turns this into a portrait of his father. Even though these portraits are more similar than a caterpillar and a butterfly, they are not stages in the continued existence of a single painting. The self-portrait is a painting that the artist destroyed. In a general discussion of identity, we would need to explain why the requirement of physical continuity differs in such ways for different kinds of thing. But we can ignore this here.

Can there be gaps in the continued existence of a physical object? Suppose that I have the same gold watch that I was given as a boy even though, for a month, it lay disassembled on a watch-repairer's shelf. On one view, in the spatio-temporal path traced by this watch there was not at every point a watch, so my watch does not have a history of full physical continuity. But during the month when my watch was disassembled, and did not exist, all of its parts had histories of full continuity. On another view, even when it was disassembled, my watch existed.

Another complication again concerns the relation between a complex thing and the various parts of which it is composed. It is true of some of these things, though not true of all, that their continued existence need not involve the continued existence of their components. Suppose that a wooden ship is repaired from time to time while it is floating in harbour, and that after fifty years it contains none of the bits of wood out of which it was first built. It is still one and the same ship, because, as a ship, it has displayed throughout these fifty years full physical continuity. This is so despite the fact that it is now composed of quite different bits of wood. These bits of wood might be qualitatively identical to the original bits, but they are not one and the same bits. Something similar is partly true of a human body. With the exception of some brain cells, the cells in our bodies are replaced with new cells several times in our lives.

I have now described the physical continuity which, on the standard view, makes a physical object one and the same after many days or years. This enables me to state one of the rival views about personal identity. On this view, what makes me the same person over time is that I have the same brain and body. The criterion of my identity over time—or what this identity involves—is the physical continuity, over time, of my brain and body. I shall continue to exist if and only if this particular brain and body continue both to exist and to be the brain and body of a living person.

This is the simplest version of this view. There is a better version. This is

The Physical Criterion: (1) What is necessary is not the continued existence of the whole body, but the continued existence of *enough* of the brain to be the brain of a living person. *X* today is one and the same person as *Y* at some past time if and only if (2) enough of Y's brain continued to exist, and is now X's brain, and (3) this physical continuity has not taken a 'branching' form. (4) Personal identity over time just consists in the holding of facts like (2) and (3).

(1) is clearly true in certain actual cases. Some people continue to exist even though they lose, or lose the use of, much of their bodies. (3) will be explained later.

30   Those who believe in the Physical Criterion would reject Teletransportation. They would believe this to be a way, not of travelling, but of dying. They would also reject, as inconceivable, reincarnation. They believe that someone cannot have a life after death, unless he lives this life in a resurrection of the very same, physically continuous body. This is why some Christians insist that they be buried. They believe that if, like Greek and Trojan heroes, they were burnt on funeral pyres, and their ashes scattered, not even God could bring them to life again. God could create only a Replica, someone else who was exactly like them. Other Christians believe that God could resurrect *them* if He reassembled their bodies out of the bits of matter that, when they were last alive, made up their bodies. This would be like the reassembly of my gold watch.[4]

78. THE PSYCHOLOGICAL CRITERION

Some people believe in a kind of psychological continuity that resembles physical continuity. This involves the continued existence of a purely mental *entity,* or thing—a soul, or spiritual substance. I shall return to this view. But I shall first explain another kind of psychological continuity. This is less like physical continuity, since it does not consist in the continued existence of some entity. But this other kind of psychological continuity involves only facts with which we are familiar.

What has been most discussed is the continuity of memory. This is because it is memory that makes most of us aware of our own continued existence over time. The exceptions are the people who are suffering from amnesia. Most amnesiacs lose only two sets of memories. They lose all of their memories of having particular past experiences—or, for short, their *experience memories.* They also lose some of their memories about facts, those that are about their own past lives. But they remember other facts, and they remember how to do different things, such as how to speak, or swim.

Locke suggested that experience-memory provides the criterion of personal identity.[5] Though this is not, on its own, a plausible view, I believe that it can be part of such a view. I shall therefore try to answer some of Locke's critics.

Locke claimed that someone cannot have committed some crime unless he now remembers doing so. We can understand a reluctance to punish people for crimes that they cannot remember. But, taken as a view about what is involved in a person's continued existence, Locke's claim is clearly false. If it was true, it would not be possible for someone to forget any of the things that he once did, or any of the experiences that he once had. But this *is* possible. I cannot now remember putting on my shirt this morning.

35   There are several ways to extend the experience-memory criterion so as to cover such cases. I shall appeal to the concept of an overlapping chain of experience-memories. Let us say that, between X today and Y twenty years ago, there are *direct memory connections* if X can now remember having some of the experiences that Y had twenty years ago. On Locke's view, only this makes X and Y one and the same person. But even if there are *no* such direct memory connections, there may be *continuity of memory* between X now and Y twenty years ago. This would be so if between X now and Y at that time there has been an overlapping chain of direct memories. In the case of most adults, there would be such a chain. In each day within the last twenty years, most of these people remembered some of their experiences on the previous day. On the revised version of Locke's view, some present person X is the same as some past person Y if there is between them continuity of memory.

This revision meets one objection to Locke's view. We should also revise the view so that it appeals to other facts. Besides direct memories, there are several other kinds of direct psychological connection. One such connection is that which holds between an intention and the later act in which this intention is carried out. Other such direct connections are those which hold when a belief, or a desire, or any other psychological feature, continues to be had.

I can now define two general relations:

Psychological connectedness is the holding of particular direct psychological connections.

Psychological continuity is the holding of overlapping chains of *strong* connectedness.

Of these two general relations, connectedness is more important both in theory and in practice. Connectedness can hold to any degree. Between X today and Y yesterday there might be several thousand direct psychological connections, or only a single connection. If there was only a single connection, X and Y would not be, on the revised Lockean View, the same person. For X and Y to be the same person, there must be over every day *enough* direct psychological connections. Since connectedness is a matter of degree, we cannot plausibly define precisely what counts as enough. But we can claim that there is enough connectedness if the number of direct connections, over any day, is *at least half* the number that hold, over every day, in the lives of nearly every actual person.[6] When there are enough direct connections, there is what I call *strong* connectedness.

Could this relation be the criterion of personal identity? A relation *F* is *transitive* if it is true that, if *X* is F-related to *Y,* and Y is F-related to *Z,* X and Z *must* be F-related. Personal identity is a transitive relation. If Bertie was one and the same person as the philosopher Russell, and Russell was one and the same person as the author of *Why I Am Not a Christian,* this author and Bertie must be one and the same person.

Strong connectedness is *not* a transitive relation. I am now strongly connected to myself yesterday, when I was strongly connected to myself two days ago, when I was strongly connected to myself three days ago, and so on. It does not follow that I am now strongly connected to myself twenty years ago. And this is not true. Between me now and myself twenty years ago there are many fewer than the number of direct psychological connections that hold over any day in the lives of nearly all adults. For example, while most adults have many memories of experiences that they had in the previous day, I have few memories of experiences that I had on any day twenty years ago.

40 By 'the criterion of personal identity over time' I mean what this identity *necessarily involves or consists in.* Because identity is a transitive relation, the criterion of identity must also be a transitive relation. Since strong connectedness is not transitive, it cannot be the criterion of identity. And I have just described a case in which this is clear. I am the same person as myself twenty years ago, though I am not now strongly connected to myself then.

Though a defender of Locke's view cannot appeal to psychological connectedness, he can appeal to psychological continuity, which *is* transitive. He can appeal to

> *The Psychological Criterion:* (1) There is *psychological continuity* if and only if there are overlapping chains of strong connectedness. X today is one and the same person as Y at some past time if and only if (2) X is psychologically continuous with Y, (3) this continuity has the right kind of cause, and (4) it has not taken a 'branching' form. (5) Personal identity over time just consists in the holding of facts like (2) to (4).

As with the Physical Criterion, (4) will be explained later.

There are three versions of the Psychological Criterion. These differ over the question of what is the *right* kind of cause. On the *Narrow* version, this must be the *normal* cause. On the *Wide* version, this could be *any reliable* cause. On the *Widest* version, the cause could be *any* cause.

The Narrow Psychological Criterion uses words in their ordinary sense. Thus I remember having an experience only if

(1) I seem to remember having an experience,
(2) I did have this experience,

and

(3) my apparent memory is causally dependent, in the normal way, on this past experience.

That we need condition (3) can be suggested with an example. Suppose that I am knocked unconscious in a climbing accident. After I recover, my fellow-climber tells me what he shouted just before I fell. In some later year, when my memories are less clear, I might seem to remember the experience of hearing my companion shout just before I fell. And it might be true that I did have just such an experience. But though conditions (1) and (2) are met, we should not believe that I am remembering that past experience. It is a well-established fact that people can never remember their last few experiences before they were knocked unconscious. We should therefore claim that my apparent memory of hearing my companion shout is not a real memory of that past experience. This apparent memory is not causally dependent in the right way on that past experience. I have this apparent memory only because my companion later told me what he shouted.[7]

Similar remarks apply to the other kinds of continuity, such as continuity of character. On the Narrow Psychological Criterion, even if someone's character radically changes, there is continuity of character if these changes have one of several normal causes. Some changes of character are deliberately brought about; others are the natural consequence of growing older, others are the natural response to certain kinds of experience. But there would not be continuity of character if radical and unwanted changes were produced by abnormal interference, such as direct tampering with the brain.

45   Though it is memory that makes us aware of our own continued existence over time, the various other continuities have great importance. We may believe that they have enough importance to provide personal identity even in the absence of memory. We shall then claim, what Locke denied, that a person continues to exist even if he suffers from complete amnesia.

Besides the Narrow version, I described the two Wide versions of the Psychological Criterion. These versions extend the senses of several words. On the ordinary sense of 'memory', a memory must have its normal cause. The two Wide Psychological Criteria appeal to a wider sense of 'memory,' which allows either any reliable cause, or any cause. Similar claims apply to the other kinds of direct psychological connection. To simplify my discussion of these three Criteria, I shall use 'psychological continuity' in its widest sense, that allows this continuity to have *any* cause.

If we appeal to the Narrow Version, which insists on the normal cause, the Psychological Criterion coincides in most cases with the Physical Criterion. The normal causes of memory involve the continued existence of the brain. And some or all of our psychological features depend upon states or events in our brains. The continued existence of a person's brain is at least part of the normal cause of psychological continuity. On the Physical Criterion, a person continues to exist if and only if *(a)* there continues to exist *enough* of this person's brain so that it remains the brain of a living person, and *(b)* there has been no branching in this physical continuity. *(a)* and *(b)* are claimed to be the necessary and sufficient conditions for this person's identity, or continued existence, over time. On the Narrow Psychological Criterion, *(a)* is necessary, but not sufficient. A person continues to exist if and only if *(c)* there is psychological continuity, *(d)* this continuity has its normal cause, and *(e)* it has not taken a branching form. *(a)* is required as part of the normal cause of psychological continuity.

Reconsider the start of my imagined story, where my brain and body are destroyed. The Scanner and the Replicator produce a person who has a new but exactly similar brain and body, and who is psychologically continuous with me as I was when I pressed the green button. The cause of this continuity is, though unusual, reliable. On both the Physical Criterion and the Narrow Psychological Criterion, my Replica would *not* be me. On the two Wide Criteria, he *would* be me.

I shall argue that we need not decide between these three versions of the Psychological Criterion. A partial analogy may suggest why. Some people go blind because of damage to their eyes. Scientists are now developing artificial eyes. These involve a glass or plastic lens, and a microcomputer which sends through the optic nerve electrical patterns like those that are sent through this nerve by a natural eye. When such artificial eyes are more advanced, they might give to someone who has gone blind visual experiences just like those that he used to have. What he seems to see would correspond to what is in fact before him. And his visual experiences would be causally dependent, in this new but reliable way, on the lightwaves coming from the objects that are before him.

50   Would this person be *seeing* these objects? If we insist that seeing must involve the normal cause, we would answer No. But even if this person cannot see, what he has is *just as good as* seeing, both as a way of knowing what is within sight, and as a source of visual pleasure. If we accept the Psychological Criterion, we could make a similar claim. If psychological continuity does not have its normal cause, it may not provide personal identity. But we can claim that, even if this is so, what it provides is *as good as* personal identity.

·   ·   ·

NOTES

1. See, for example, *Zettel,* ed. by G. Anscombe and G. von Wright, and translated by G. Anscombe, Blackwell, 1967, Proposition 350: 'It is as if our concepts involve a scaffolding of facts. . . . If you imagine certain facts otherwise . . . then you can no longer imagine the application of certain concepts.'
2. Quine (1), p. 490.
3. This states a necessary condition for the continued existence of a physical object. Saul Kripke has argued, in lectures, that this condition is not sufficient. Since I missed these lectures, I cannot discuss this argument.

4. On this view, it could be fatal to live in what has long been a densely populated area, such as London. It may here be true of many bits of matter that they were part of the bodies of many different people, when they were last alive. These people could not all be resurrected, since there would not be enough such matter to be reassembled. Some hold a version of this view which avoids this problem. They believe that a resurrected body needs to contain only one particle from the original body.

5. Locke, Chapter 27, Section 16.

6. This suggestion would need expanding, since there are many ways to count the number of direct connections. And some kinds of connection should be given more importance than others. As I suggest later, more weight should be given to those connections which are distinctive, or different in different people. All English-speakers share a vast number of undistinctive memories of how to speak English.

7. I follow Martin and Deutscher.

BIBLIOGRAPHY

Locke: J., *Essay Concerning Human Understanding,* partly reprinted in Perry.

Martin and Deutscher: 'Remembering,' *Philosophical Review,* 1966.

Perry: J., ed., *Personal Identity,* Berkeley, University of California Press, 1975.

Quine: W. V., reviewing Milton K. Munitz., ed., *Identity and Individuation,* in *The Journal of Philosophy,* 1972.

A SOURCE FROM MARINE BIOLOGY

The reading in Chapter 7, Marine Biology, in which you learned about research on the sea anemone *Anthopleura elegantissima,* documented an aggressive behavior that had never been seen before. You also learned something about how important observation is to marine biology. To further practice summarizing, I have included another report by Lisbeth Francis. In fact, both research reports were published one after the other in *Biological Bulletin.* In this research report, "Clone Specific Segregation in the Sea Anemone *Anthopleura elegantissima,*" Francis studies why some groups of sea anemones crowd together, leaving spaces between the groups. Below is a list of questions to guide you as you develop your summary.

ASK YOURSELF

How do I read a research report in the sciences differently now than I did before learning something about the discipline? What do I see differently now? What role do definitions play in my understanding of the research report? What does the researcher claim that she has learned about the sea anemones? How does she support her claim? What methods does she use?

CLONE SPECIFIC SEGREGATION IN THE SEA ANEMONE *ANTHOPLEURA ELEGANTISSIMA*

LISBETH FRANCIS

■ ■ ■

The west coast sea anemone *Anthopleura elegantissima* commonly lives inter-tidally in dense beds. These beds are frequently divided into two or more separate aggregations by anemone-free zones. These zones may be irregular and rather unremarkable areas occupied by limpets, chitons, snails, barnacles and algae. However, under crowded conditions on inclined surfaces that face toward the sea, these zones are often conspicuous, long, narrow, relatively bare strips anywhere from a fraction of a centimeter to about 5 cm wide. I have also observed that the position of these zones is relatively constant over periods of up to four years. Whether they are wide or narrow, regular or irregular, these zones separating adjacent aggregations of anemones are apparent to the careful observer because the distance across the zones is obviously greater than the distance between anemones in the midst of the aggregations.

There are also short anemone-free pockets penetrating single aggregations of the anemones. Some of these clearings may be made by the chiton *Mopalia muscosa,* which Field has found to be capable of maintaining and extending artificially created clearings within aggregations of the anemones (Field, Department of Biology, University of California, Santa Barbara, personal communication in 1969), or by the turban snail *Tegula funebralis* which I have observed living in such pockets.

The subject of this paper and associated work (Francis, 1973) is the nature of the relatively permanent anemone-free zones separating adjacent aggregations of the sea anemone *Anthopleura elegantissima* and the relation of these zones to the distribution and behavior of the anemone.

MATERIALS AND METHODS

Animals and Collecting Methods

The anemones used in the experiments were all individuals of the aggregating form of *Anthopleura elegantissima* collected intertidally within ten miles of the Hopkins Marine Station at Pacific Grove, California. I removed them from the very large rocks on which they were found by gently working a thin spatula under the edges of the pedal discs.

Laboratory Holding Conditions

5   At Hopkins Marine Station the anemones were kept in glass finger-bowls supplied with flowing sea water at about 13° C. The anemones were fed intermittently except during experiments, when food was withheld.

Biology Department, University of California, Santa Barbara, California, 93106

Anemones to be used in behavioral experiments were always kept in the laboratory for a few weeks to allow them time to recover from minor damage inflicted during collecting, and to shed the debris that was usually pulled loose from the rocks by the clinging pedal discs.

Only animals that appeared healthy and that attached to the holding bowls by their pedal discs were subsequently used in behavioral experiments. To remove anemones from a holding bowl, I hit the bowl firmly and repeatedly against a hard surface until the anemones released their footholds. Anemones treated in this way appeared to suffer no damage, and they settled in the experimental chambers much more quickly than did anemones that had been forcefully pried loose.

Sex Determination

The freshly collected anemones were cut in half lengthwise or in the case of larger specimens, in quarters; and the mesenteries were examined for the presence of gonads. During the summer months when the gonads are ripe (Ford, 1964), female gonads are obvious as brownish-pink bodies. Because the yellowish-white male gonads are less easily identifiable, several mesenteries from each nonfemale anemone were examined microscopically for the presence of spermatocytes. Occasional checks were also made for the presence of oocytes in the smaller female gonads. Anemones having at least one identifiable gonad containing oocytes or spermatocytes were scored as reproductively mature.

Dry Weight Determination

After sex determination was accomplished, the anemones were blotted using a piece of tissue paper and weighed to ± 0.01 g. The animals were then individually dried to constant weight in a drying oven at between 75° and 91° C (18 to 24 hours were usually required).

PROCEDURES AND RESULTS

Clonal Nature of the Aggregations

The anemones living in aggregations separated by anemone-free strips were examined closely in order to determine whether those living on opposite sides of the strips differed from each other in any discernible way.

10   *Anthopleura elegantissima* shows a variety of color patterning which allows for considerable variation among individuals. For example, a pink pigment is present in the tentacle tips of some but not nearly all individuals. Further, the mesenterial insertion line on the oral disc may be marked with pigment ranging from red-brown to purple in color, and the oral disc may or may not be marked with a radiating white or gold pattern. All of the anemones belonging to a continuous aggregation were observed to have the same color patterning. If more than one color pattern was observed in a bed of anemones on a single rock, the bed was always found to be divided by anemone-free spaces into aggregations of anemones that were segregated by color pattern.

TABLE I.   Distribution of males and females on rocks bearing adjacent aggregations of anemones separated by anemone-free zones

IDENTIFYING NO. FOR EACH AGGREGATION	NO. OF DEVELOPED MALES	NO. WITH SEX UNDEVELOPED	NO. OF DEVELOPED FEMALES	COMPARISON OF SEX BETWEEN ADJACENT AGGREGATIONS
⎰ 100	—	8	2 ⎱	♀/♀
⎱ 101	—	8	2 ⎰	
⎰ 102	—	6	4 ⎱	♀/♀
⎱ 103	—	9	1 ⎰	
⎰ 104	—	6	3 ⎱	♀/♀
⎪ 105	—	8	2 ⎪	♀/♀
⎪ 106	—	2	8 ⎪	♀/♂
⎱ 107	7	2	— ⎰	
⎰ 108	10	8	— ⎱	♂/♂
⎱ 109	8	2	— ⎰	

The sexes are separate in this anemone, and samples were taken July 13, 1968 to determine the distribution of the sexes with respect to the anemone-free zones. Samples of at least nine anemones were collected from each of ten contiguous aggregations, each of which was separated from at least one adjacent aggregation by an anemone-free zone. Care was taken in collecting the anemones to select animals from widely separated parts of each aggregation and to include animals from the edges as well as animals from the middle of each aggregation. The results (Table I) show no mixing of the sexes within a single contiguous aggregation. In the single case in which male and female anemones were found living on the same rock, they were found in two unisexual groups separated by an anemone-free strip. In the experiment described below, 99 anemones (a significant fraction of the aggregation) from a single aggregation were collected and examined for the presence of gonads. Of these, 21 had female gonads and 78 had no gonads. There were none with male gonads.

Since it is known that these anemones reproduce asexually by longitudinal fission (Hand, 1955), it is apparent that each contiguous aggregation of the sea anemone *Anthopleura elegantissima* is a single clone and that the anemone-free zones described above separate adjacent clones of the anemones. No other hypothesis can simply explain the observed segregation into unisexual groups in which all the group members have the same color patterning.

Size and Sexual Maturity

It may be noted that some anemones from each clonal group lacked gonads at what is usually the peak period for the gonad index (Ford, 1964).

Both Ford's work and my own casual observation suggested a correlation with the size of the animals. To test this idea, I collected all the anemones (99 anemones) from one section of a female clone on July 29, 1968, and after assaying the reproductive state, I determined the dry weights for each anemone. The results (Table II) show that within this clone, animals smaller than 0.6 g dry weight were not reproductive. The pooled

TABLE II. Gonad maturity and dry body weight

WHOLE BODY DRY WEIGHT (G)	99 ANEMONES FROM A SINGLE FEMALE CLONE		94 ANEMONES FROM 12 SEPARATE CLONES BOTH MALE AND FEMALE	
	No. OF INDIVIDUALS WITH DEVELOPED GONADS	No. OF INDIVIDUALS WITHOUT DEVELOPED GONADS	No. OF INDIVIDUALS WITH DEVELOPED GONADS	No. OF INDIVIDUALS WITHOUT DEVELOPED GONADS
0.0–0.2	0	16	0	10
0.2–0.4	0	18	4	19
0.4–0.6	0	20	3	10
0.6–0.8	3	10	12	7
0.8–1.0	2	7	4	0
1.0–1.2	8	1	8	2
1.2–1.4	2	2	5	0
1.4–1.6	1	2	5	0
1.6–1.8	1	1	0	0
1.8+	4	1	5	0

data from smaller samples from 12 different clones, both male and female, collected between July 13 and August 18, 1968, show that none of the individuals below 0.2 g dry weight were reproductive (Table II).

15   From this it would appear that reproductive state is related to size in these anemones, even among genetically identical individuals, the smallest individuals being nonreproductive while some proportion of those over 0.2 g dry weight are reproductively mature.

Clonal Segregation and Separation in the Laboratory

Reaggregation into Uniclonal Groups.   An experiment was conducted in order to determine whether or not the observed segregation into clonal groups is a result of an active process carried on by the anemones.

Anemones from two clones (Clone 1 and Clone 2) living adjacent to each other in the field were collected and brought into the laboratory where they were kept with their clonemates in bowls supplied with running sea water.

Ten small to medium sized anemones (from about 0.5 to about 2.3 cm across the expanded oral disc) from each of the two clones were pinned with insect pins to a foam plastic ball about 5 cm in diameter. They were crowded together as closely as possible in five rows of four animals, the individuals from the two clones being arranged alternately in both the horizontal and vertical rows to cover more than half the surface of the ball. This arrangement maximized contact between anemones and allowed contact between both clonemates and non-clonemates. The buoyant ball was fastened to a lead weight using a piece of monofilament line and placed in an aquarium where the ball was held below the surface of the water by the weight. Running sea water at 13° C was continuously supplied to the aquarium. In three days when all the anemones seemed to be adhering to the ball, the pins were removed to allow the anemones to move freely.

After 13 days of free movement, four anemones had fallen off the ball and the remaining 16 anemones had rearranged themselves into two segregated clonal groups. There was at that time no contact between the tentacles of non-clonemates. The anemones continued to move about after 13 days and some further reassortment occurred, but it remained apparent that contact was maintained only between clonemates.

20   It is apparent from this that clonal segregation within aggregations can be actively accomplished by the anemones.

Formation of an Anemone-Free Trail in the Laboratory.   The following experiment was designed to determine whether or not the anemones will form anemone-free zones between adjacent clonal groups in the absence of naturally associated species and various environmental factors such as tidal cycle.

The anemones used in the experiment were collected from two different but not adjacent clones (Clone 3 and Clone 4). These animals were maintained in the laboratory for periods varying from several months to a year prior to this experiment. A pyrex baking dish approximately 36 cm by 18 cm and 5 cm deep was lined with a sheet of foam plastic glued to the bottom. One end of the sheet was entirely covered by Clone 3 anemones pinned side by side with insect pins, and the other end was covered with Clone 4 anemones. Where the two clones met at an uneven interface, a barrier of microscope slides fastened together with tape was set on edge between the two clones. The unevenness of the interface served to maximize the area of contact between the clones. Running sea water was introduced

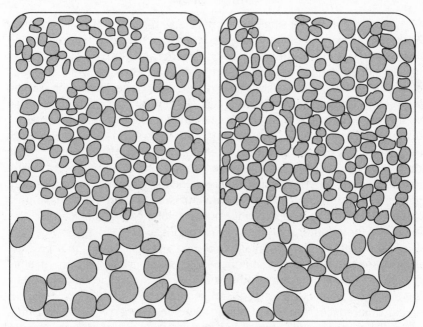

Figure 1. The position of anemones from Clone 3 and Clone 4 just after the barrier between the two groups was removed (right) and 14 days after the barrier was removed (left) (see text for details).

into the dish at one end; and because the anemones tend to move upstream (Buchsbaum, 1968), the position of the water inlet was changed periodically to prevent a consistent unidirectional migration in response to current. After a few days when the pedal discs of the anemones had become attached to the substratum, the pins attaching the anemones to the foam plastic sheet were removed as was the barrier between the clones. The animals that released their footholds on the substratum during the rest of the experiment were removed from the dish on the assumption that such animals would have been removed by wave action under field conditions.

Photographs were taken from a fixed position above the dish once a day. The position of the anemones at the beginning of the experiment just after the barrier was removed and their position 16 days later are shown in Figure 1. The outlines of the oral discs exclusive of tentacles are shown here, and the outlines of the anemones from Clone 3 are shown stippled.

Under these conditions an anemone-free zone was formed between the two clonal groups within three weeks (Fig. 1, left). During this time numerous aggressive episodes (Francis, 1973) were observed at the border between the two groups. (This was not observed during the previous experiment, which was conducted before I discovered the aggressive behavior of this animal.) Apparently then, clonal isolation as well as clonal segregation can be actively accomplished by the anemones.

DISCUSSION

25   The anemones in a single continuous aggregation of the sea anemone *Anthopleura elegantissima* are observed to resemble each other in two obvious ways: (1) all have the same color pattern, and (2) all individuals having developed gonads are of the same sex. Furthermore, while sustained contact between individuals within an aggregation is very common, contact between individuals from different aggregations has been found to initiate an instraspecific aggressive response resulting in the separation of these individuals (Francis, 1973). These animals are known to reproduce asexually by longitudinal fission, and it is therefore concluded that the aggregations must each be comprised of anemones from a single clone. It seems to me improbable that anything other than genetic identity could account for aggregations of up to thousands of individuals of the same sex, having the same color patterns and showing mutual tolerance for contact with each other and for no other members of the species.

What might be the advantage to the anemones of living in segregated aggregations? There are a number of possible advantages to a small anemone in living adjacent to other members of the species rather than living alone. (1) Contact between anemones decreases their effective surface areas. This reduces water loss during low tides (Roberts, 1941) and minimizes the area exposed to the pulling and battering effects of the waves and the abrasive effects of suspended matter. (2) An area of rock closely covered by a sheet of anemones provides no place for the settlement of other sessile organisms (such as the larger algae) which may compete with the anemones for space. (3) A single small anemone would have little chance of catching and holding large organisms against the force of the waves; however, I have often seen several anemones in an aggregation together holding and ingesting a large jellyfish or squid.

Anemones of the solitary form of this species are usually larger than individuals of the clonal form. These animals live in more protected circumstances than individuals of the clonal form, usually in nooks and crevices, and often with their bases attached to rocks below the sand level (Hand, 1955). That these larger animals should be found in a more protected habitat than their smaller conspecifics fits well with the preceding analysis. Increased size would make these anemones more vulnerable to the pulling and battering of the waves and therefore less able to occupy flat exposed rock surfaces. At the same time, decrease in the surface to volume ratio of the solitary as compared with the clonal form decreases water loss by evaporation, thus reducing this problem of the solitary living habit. I have observed (as the name of the form itself suggests) that individuals of the solitary form of *Anthopleura elegantissima* also remain isolated from adjacent members of the species.

The advantage to the anemones of segregation into strictly uniclonal groups and separation from adjacent clonal groups is not immediately apparent (see Francis, 1973). However, segregation among genetically different animals of the same species is not peculiar to the species or to the phylum. The growth patterns reported for some colonial coelenterates, tunicates and bryozoans seem to be of the same type.

Schijfsma (1939) reports that young colonies of the hydroid *Hydractinia echinata* seem to fuse completely but that, "When they meet at an older (perhaps different) age a remarkable zone of demarcation is formed," (p. 102). He also notes that when the borders of the same colony meet, for example in growing around a shell, no such line of demarcation is formed.

30   Theodor (1966) reports a similar phenomenon for the gorgonian *Eunicella stricta*. Two specimens were found growing very close together; and although the bases of the animals were in close contact, the tissues remained unfused. In the laboratory he found that homografts (grafts between genetically different individuals of the same species) always failed to show tissue fusion. Autografts (grafts involving tissue from only one individual) were always successful; and the fused tissues in the graft area appeared normal histologically.

Workers have also observed complete fusion at the interface between separate growing edges of the same colony both in the encrusting ascidian *Botrylus* and in a variety of bryozoa. Knight-Jones and Moyse (1961), referring to these observations, report that, "if two colonies of the same species (of encrusting ascidian or bryozoan) meet, each seems to respect the other's well-marked frontier and spreads only in other directions," (page 88).

What ties these phenomena together with the clone specific segregation and separation reported here for *Anthopleura elegantissima* is the contrast between the intimacy of association among genetically identical "individuals" in colonies or clonal groups, and the relative isolation between genetically different individuals of the same species. All of these animals apparently respond differently to contact with a genetically identical conspecific than to contact with other conspecifics.

I thank Dr. James J. Childress, Dr. Joseph Connell, and Dr. Demorest Davenport for reading this manuscript; the staff and students of the Hopkins Marine Station for help and encouragement during the research; and the NIH (predoctoral fellowship to the author) for its financial support.

SUMMARY

The anemones in a single continuous aggregation of the sea anemone *Anthopleura elegantissima* are observed to resemble each other in two obvious ways: (1) all have the same color pattern, and (2) all individuals having developed gonads are of the same sex. Futhermore, while sustained contact between individuals within an aggregation is very common, contact between individuals from different aggregations has been found to initiate an intraspecific aggressive response resulting in the separation of these individuals (Francis, 1973). These animals are known to reproduce asexually by longitudinal fission, and it is therefore concluded that the aggregations must each be comprised of anemones from a single clone. It seems to me improbable that anything other than genetic identity could account for aggregations of up to thousands of individuals of the same sex, having the same color patterns and showing mutual tolerance for contact with each other and for no other members of the species.

35   Even among anemones within a single clone, the presence of gonads containing gametes is shown to be related to size. Anemones smaller than 0.2 g dry wt consistently lack developed gonads, while some proportion of those over 0.2 g have gonads with gametes.

In the field, adjacent clonal groups are observed to remain separated from each other. In the laboratory a mixed group of anemones will reaggregate into isolated uniclonal groups, implying that clone specific segregation is actively accomplished by the anemones.

Living in aggregations has a number of potential advantages for the anemones such as reducing their effective surface area and thereby reducing water loss and the battering effects of wave action, excluding interspecific competition for space by promoting effective blanketing of an area, and allowing for cooperation in the capture and holding of larger prey. The function for the anemones of clone specific segregation and separation is not yet clear (see Francis, 1973); however, the phenomenon is not without parallel since some other coelenterates as well as some bryozoans have also been observed to respond differently to contact with a genetically identical conspecific than to contact with other conspecifics.

LITERATURE CITED

Buchsbaum, V., 1968. Behavioral and physiological responses to light by the sea anemone *Anthopleura elegantissima* as related to its algal symbionts. *Ph.D. thesis, Stanford University,* 123 pp.

Ford, C. E., 1964. Reproduction in the aggregating sea anemone *Anthopleura elegantissima*. *Pac. Sci.,* 18: 138–145.

Francis, L., 1973. Intraspecific aggression and its effect on the distribution of *Anthopleura elegantissima* and some related sea anemones. *Biol. Bull.,* 144: 73–92.

Hand, C., 1955. The sea anemones of central California, Part II. The Endomyarian and Mesomyarian anemones. *Wasman J. Biol.,* 13: 37–99.

Knight-Jones, E., and J. Moyse, 1961. Intraspecific competition in marine animals. Pages 73–95 in F. L. Milthorpe, Ed., *Mechanisms in Biological Competition.* Symposia of the Society for Experimental Biology No. XV.

Roberts, B. J., 1941. A survey of the methods employed by intertidal organisms in resisting desiccation. *Master's thesis, Stanford University,* 68 pp.

Schijfsma, K., 1939. Preliminary notes on early stages in the growth of colonies of *Hydractinia echinata* (Flem.). *Arch. Necrl.,* 4: 93–102.

Theodor, J., 1966. Contribution à l'étude des gorgones (V); Les greffes chez les gorgones: étude d'un systéme de reconnaisance de tissus. *Bull. Inst. Oceanogr. Monaco,* 66 (1374): 1–7.

WRITING AND LEARNING ACTIVITIES: A GUIDE TO SUMMARIZING

The activities below will guide you through the process of writing a summary of the source materials included here, in other chapters, or provided by you or your instructor.

READING THE TEXT

1. **Reading:** Read the source you plan to summarize. As you survey the reading, think first about what you already know. Next, read the report closely, noting the claims the author makes and how he or she supports those claims with data.

2. **Journal Entry:** Write in your journal as you read, jotting down questions you have about the reading, familiar and unfamiliar terms, and notes about how this chapter is different from other work you have read in this and other disciplines. As you read, consider what you have learned about the discipline this research comes from.

3. **Annotate the Text:** As you read mark the text to help you follow the argument. Use a highlighter to identify key claims and maybe use another color to identify data or evidence. Place question marks next to places that confuse you and restate main points in your own words in the margins.

THINKING ABOUT THE DISCIPLINE

1. **Journal Entry:** What discipline does this text represent and what have you learned about it? What was the author's purpose in writing this text? How did she present knowledge to persuade me of his or her main point? What specialized words does the author use?

2. **Group Activity:** Compare your journal entries and talk about the similarities and differences in your understanding of the text.

IDENTIFYING GROUPS OF RELATED IDEAS

1. Journal Entry: Review the text again and draw a line in the left margin of the text for each group of related ideas that could be summarized into one or two sentences, using your own words. How do those groups of ideas reflect the author's claims and grounds? Write questions you had about this process in your journal. Use two different color highlighters, one to mark the claims and another to identify the examples or support.

2. Peer or Group Activity: Compare your groups of ideas with those found by others in class. Talk about why you may have marked different sections as groups of related ideas. Report back to this class.

DRAFTING SENTENCES FROM GROUPS OF IDEAS

1. Journal Entry: Summarize each idea group into one or two sentences using your own words. Have you included the main ideas you searched for in your close reading?

2. Peer Activity: Read your sentences to a partner and ask whether or not your sentences sound as if they are in your own words. Ask your partner if you have covered all the essential information from the source text. Repeat the process for him or her.

DRAFTING THE INTRODUCTION

1. Writing Activity: Make notes on what you will include in the introduction. Think about how to express the essential idea and about how the author supports his or her claim. What is the significance of this work—why is it important? How might you introduce this text to someone who knows little about this discipline? What bibliographic information will your reader need?

DRAFTING THE SUMMARY

1. Peer Activity: With a partner, look at how Professor Weiner put her summary together. How does she use idea groups to support her main idea in the opening paragraph? How does she link similar idea groups? Report to the class.

2. Writing Activity: Working from the sentences you wrote for each group of ideas in the text, draft your summary. Keep in mind also that your introduction should tell the reader what he or she needs to know to understand the summary.

REVISING THE SUMMARY

1. Peer Critique: Exchange papers with a partner and give his or her paper the three separate readings described under "Revising the Summary," pages 374–375: first, an overall reading; second, a sentence-by-sentence reading; and third, a reading for editing or proofreading errors. Write a response to the questions for the first two readings and return the paper to your partner.

2. Journal Activity: Respond to the experience of being critiqued as well as doing a critique. Consider the benefits and the difficulties. Were you able to predict the problems identified by your partner?

SYNTHESIZING DISCIPLINE-SPECIFIC TEXTS

The new shopping malls make possible the synthesis of all consumer activities, not least of which are shopping, flirting with objects, idle wandering, and all the permutations of these.

JEAN BAUDRILLARD

WHAT DOES IT MEAN TO SYNTHESIZE?

Synthesizing means to combine different ideas, images, materials, or data into a new whole. The strategy used to do this is looking for patterns or connections among the different sources. You do this every day when, for instance, you detect a pattern in the weather, in the crime rate around your campus, in traffic at certain times of the day, or as Jean Baudrillard suggests above, in consumer activities. The challenge of this type of thinking is to use your own knowledge and experience to guide you in identifying the patterns and connections and then to create a new understanding.

Writing a synthesis essay poses different challenges than writing a summary. The summary requires you to accurately and clearly represent the author's work in a condensed form. The synthesis essay allows you much more authority. It is you who identifies common patterns of information, issues, and ideas from many sources. It is you who explains to the reader why these particular patterns are important. What you choose to identify as a pattern inevitably grows out of who you are, your experiences, your knowledge, and your understanding of the world around you. This writing and thinking strategy is not very different from analysis, discussed in the next chapter. In analysis, the focus shifts away from identifying connections to developing a position. These three strategies—summary, synthesis, and analysis—form the cornerstone of the intellectual work you do in college. They are presented in separate chapters here, but in your reading and writing you will be moving from one to another in a seamless way.

To build knowledge in any academic discipline, students and faculty alike must synthesize what is known in the field, along with their personal understanding of it, to develop a new understanding of how it all fits together. For instance, to do the ethnographic research on Chicano families in Chicago that was reported in "The Expanded Family and Family Honor" (discussed in Chapter 2, Cultural Anthropology), Ruth Horowitz relied on several sources. Her field notes from her observations of the Chicano families on 32nd Street were her major source of information. She also relied on previous research she had read by other scholars on Chicano families, gender, gangs, and other related topics. Another source that may not have appeared prominently in the chapter, but was still very important, was Ruth Horowitz's personal experience and how it informed her understanding of her work. To do this research and write about it, Ruth Horowitz had to find patterns among these diverse sources and combine them into a new whole that would help her readers to better understand the Chicano families she was studying.

Sometimes a writer may synthesize information from diverse sources to include in a larger article or project. In a 1991 feature-length article, "The Great Alaska Debate: Can Oil and Wilderness Mix?" published in the Sunday *New York Times Magazine* (see Chapter 8, Geology), Timothy Egan uses a variety of strategies to explore the question of whether the Arctic National Wildlife Refuge (ANWR) should be opened for oil development. The entire article is a synthesis in which Egan considers diverse ideas he has brought together by reading and thinking about information from a variety of sources. He quotes experts and politicians, he summarizes research, and he analyzes the positions taken by politicians, scientists, and native inhabitants, questioning each individual's self-interest or perspective.

Here's an example of how Egan synthesizes information within the article. He reminds us that ANWR is intended as a refuge for animals and as such we must pay close attention to the fate of the caribou, although, he says, the oil companies argue that the caribou not only survived, but thrived, during oil development at Prudhoe Bay. Egan synthesizes the results of research that support this assertion. He has not just reported information; he has gathered ideas from a number of sources and put together a picture for us that helps us to see the complexity of this situation.

> The expansion of the Central Arctic herd has been attributed by biologists to a retreat of predators, mainly wolves and grizzly bears, which keep their distance from humans, to a series of mild winters and to normal ups and downs of animal population cycles. Caribou have increased throughout Alaska. Most biologists, Ronzio among them, think the Central Arctic herd will eventually decline, and there is evidence that their growth rate is already shrinking (paragraph 29).

In the more formal genre of the scientific research report, we often see syntheses in the review of literature section or the introduction, in which the researcher introduces the problem for the current study by documenting and synthesizing past work. Here is a section from another research report written by Nancy Felix and Martha K. Raynolds, titled "The Role of Snow Cover in Limiting Surface Disturbance Caused by Winter Seismic Exploration," published in *Arctic* in 1989 in which they synthesize previous research to identify the problem for their research.

> Most studies of winter vehicle traffic on tundra have focused on the construction of snow- or ice-capped roads to protect vegetation (Abele, 1963; Adam and Hernandez, 1977; Keyes, 1977; Johnson and Collins, 1980). Studies of seismic traffic have found that winter exploration caused less surface disturbance than summer operations (Bliss and Wein, 1972; Hernandez, 1973). Although the protective nature of snow cover has long been recognized, the amount of snow cover needed to protect the tundra from disturbance due to off-road vehicle traffic has not been well-defined (63).

In a scientific research report, the researchers must document others' research; Egan, on the other hand, writing a feature article for a popular magazine, does not need to follow such rigorous conventions for documentation. In the first two sentences of Felix and Raynolds' report, they summarize the research of several other writers. These sentences offer a synthesis as well since the researchers identified this common research interest among many sources. The researchers have pulled together diverse sources to identify a question about how much snow is needed to protect the tundra from vehicle damage. In doing so, they have created a synthesis—a new picture of the problem for us.

Whether you are synthesizing research results on traffic across the tundra, on the fate of the caribou, on the nature of the expanded family in a Chicano community, or on the activities possible in our shopping malls, you are creating a new whole from the ideas, images, and data you have gathered. The remainder of this chapter illustrates a process for developing an essay based on synthesis and offers you several opportunities to try your hand at this intellectual strategy using sources from anthropology, literary studies, and geology.

WRITING AND LEARNING ACTIVITIES

1. **Journal Entry:** Synthesizing is an everyday activity of making meaning both in and out of the classroom. Synthesize information from the local news section of your newspaper. What overall picture do these different stories give of your town or city? Find news stories that connect to your personal experience in some way and write about the connection.

2. **Group Activity:** In your group, choose something you have been learning about in other classes. Tell what each of you knows about that topic and how you know it. Pool your knowledge by brainstorming and then look for patterns among the ideas you have identified. Report your synthesis to the class.

3. **Group Activity:** Syntheses can be found in a variety of types of texts: encyclopedias, research reports, reviews of the literature, feature articles in the news, textbooks, and popular magazine articles. Assign each member of the group a type of text. Decide, as well, on a general topic to explore. Browse through a variety of sources at the library, looking for syntheses. Photocopy samples and ask your group to report back to the class about the syntheses you found and what you have learned about the topic you explored.

THE PROCESS OF SYNTHESIZING A SPECIALIZED TEXT

This section of the chapter demonstrates the process of writing an essay based on information you have synthesized from a variety of sources. You will learn how to find patterns among issues, ideas, and information and to develop an essay in which you help your readers to see those connections.

The example given below follows the work of a student, Nada Markelis, as she plans, drafts, and revises an essay that synthesizes two short stories by Elizabeth Bishop, "The Baptism" and "In the Village," along with an excerpt from a critical text by David Kalstone.[1] These stories were discussed in Chapter 5, Literary Studies. You may want to go back and read or reread the two stories before you go on.

THINKING ABOUT THE DISCIPLINE

Although we all engage in synthesizing daily, when we synthesize information or ideas from a specific academic discipline, we rely heavily on the approaches and methods of that discipline. In planning her synthesis essay Nada must consider the special concerns of literary scholars. How do they make meaning from literary works? What has she learned thus far about the field? Although the background information gained by answering the following questions may or may not be included in the essay, thinking about them will involve you in the work of literary scholars.

 How do literary scholars make meaning from texts? What sorts of textual conventions do they pay attention to when they read? How is a literary interpretation like building an argument? What sorts of issues does literary criticism focus on? What is appropriate evidence for a literary interpretation? How is reading criticism different from reading literary works? What do we mean when we speak of the "interestedness" of a writer, reader, or literary scholar? How is the meaning-making process of literary scholars different from that of members of other specialized disciplines?

---

[1]The student essay included here reflects work done in class, it may include errors or stylistic problems. It is included here so that you can follow the writer's progress.

GETTING STARTED

Nada had already read the two short stories by Elizabeth Bishop and a portion of David Kalstone's critical text before beginning this synthesis essay. Now, she needed to go back through them again, thinking not only about the special concerns of literary scholars, but about the process of synthesizing. Nada's first step was to reread the stories (actually several times in all), take notes, write in the margins, use a highlighter to mark sections that seemed significant, and brainstorm about similarities and differences between the two stories. Her next step was to reread the excerpts from the critical text, highlighting the sections that related to any of the patterns she had uncovered when she reread the stories. Knowing that you are reading to find patterns between the two stories changes your reading process. You focus on different ideas and images than when you read the story for the first time. In addition, knowing that you are working in a particular scholarly discipline helps to focus the kinds of questions you need to ask.

 Consider the sources you have available for interpreting literary works: yourself, the text, and critical readings of the literary work. What can you draw from each? Have you considered how your knowledge and experiences contribute to an "interested" reading? What features of the text need to be considered carefully? What arguments can you identify in the criticism you have read? What is David Kalstone saying about Elizabeth Bishop and her work? How does this agree with your understanding of her short stories and how is it different from your interpretation?

MAKING CONNECTIONS

The central activity of synthesizing is finding a pattern among ideas. Finding this pattern involves both what you know about the specialized discipline and the personal knowledge and experiences you bring to the reading. As Nada read and reread "The Baptism," "In the Village," and Kalstone's criticism of Bishop's work, she made notes in her journal about the process. Eventually she began to notice a pattern of connections that interested her. She identified a pattern in the text that concerned the issue of escape because escape had been a concern in her own day-to-day life. Here's a portion of one of Nada's journal entries:

> *The idea of escape keeps popping up for me. When I get really frustrated with personal relationships or with work I get in my car and I drive for hours. I remember when I was young and my mother used to yell at me for any number of things. I would listen silently but repeat a little poem I had memorized in school again and again. I can relate to those kinds of things going on in the story.*

The patterns you identify may reflect aspects of the text or ideas that come from a critical treatment of the text, or they may reflect your personal response to the story. The challenge at this point is to sift through the jumble of associations and ideas being generated as you read to find the one idea that you can develop into a synthesis. One way to find it is to develop a list of similarities and differences; this may help you to focus on how you will write about aspects of both stories in a way that will help your reader see them in a new way. Here are some questions to help you focus on this part of the process.

 Have I identified the similarities and differences among the sources I am using? What specific elements of the texts contribute to them? Is there one similarity or difference among the sources that really stands out to me? Can I write a sentence or two characterizing one or the other? Could I build a synthesis around that similarity or difference?

BECOMING AN AUTHORITY

If you can identify what the issues you are writing about mean to you personally, you'll develop a sense of personal authority in your academic work. Even though you may have a personal stake in what you are writing you still need to decide whether or not you want to include this material in it. Just knowing that you are writing about meaningful issues has a way of strengthening your voice and supporting your writing process. If you look at Nada's essay below, you'll see that she included an example from her personal life. In addition, she identified strongly with the need to escape, since, as we just read in her journal, when she herself needs to escape she gets into her car and drives for hours. To plan for your synthesis essay ask yourself the following questions:

 How do my personal knowledge and experiences contribute to what I know about these similarities and differences? What do I think is most important or meaningful about the patterns I see in these short stories?

DEVELOPING AN ORGANIZING IDEA

After reviewing all your notes about personal connections and the similarities and differences among your sources, you'll need to identify a single issue, connection, or idea that you would like to write about. This organizing idea will become the focus of your synthesis essay. Ask yourself:

 How do I see these sources differently now that I've started to find patterns and synthesize them? What is the single most important idea that helps me synthesize these sources?

Nada wrote in the following journal entry what she first identified as the key organizing idea that would direct her synthesis. She focused on the notion of escape and connected that notion to the stories as well as to her personal life. The underscored section suggested to Nada a working claim that will guide the development of her essay.

". . . she seems to be in her own world lately" or "why did she run away like that?" Does this sound familiar? People (especially children) try to escape from uncomfortable situations. Some run away, but some withdraw into themselves. This is what I see happening in both of Bishop's stories. I want to focus on the methods of their escape: psychological and physical. Kalstone seems to be talking about the same kind of thing, he almost suggests that Bishop was trying to escape from the memories of her early childhood. It's interesting to see how knowing about someone's life can help you understand their writing.

WRITING THE ESSAY
DRAFTING THE INTRODUCTION

Most of the above planning activities were aimed at helping you to sort out your ideas about what you want to include in your synthesis essay. In your introduction you have the opportunity to draw the reader into your essay and share with him or her an approach to reading short stories and literary criticism. You will want the introduction to: (1) tell the reader a bit about the stories and perhaps something about the author; (2) introduce the reader to the critical material you have read; and most importantly, explain your special approach to synthesizing these stories by talking about your organizing idea. Some writers find it easier to draft their essay first and then write the introduction; others use the introduction to guide them through the draft. Which do you think will work better for you? Here are some things to do.

 Look back over your notes about your organizing idea, the Bishop stories, and the critical material. Draft an introduction to your synthesis essay and share it with a partner. Ask yourself as you read how helpful the introduction is in getting you started as a reader. Does it catch your interest? Do you get a sense of where the writer is going? Look at Nada Markelis's introduction (pp. 421–422). What revisions did she make? How did the revisions improve Nada's introduction?

DRAFTING THE ESSAY

Your central task in drafting an essay is to build, for your reader, a case or argument that demonstrates that your way of seeing things—your synthesis—is appropriate and convincing. Your preparatory work—reading, rereading, looking for patterns, and identifying similarities and differences—is done. Now you must organize this information in such a way that the reader will see how the new picture you have put together is a convincing one.

In writing a synthesis, you are arguing that your claim, or organizing idea, is supported by evidence from your sources. Since we are in the field of literary studies, Nada Markelis looked in the stories and a piece of literary criticism for passages that supported her claim. (In other disciplines, the evidence you use to support your claim depends on what is valued as evidence in that academic context; for example, a geologist might value observations made about physical landforms, while a cultural anthropologist might value what informants say about their community.)

Nada decided to argue in support of her claim that: "People, especially children, tend to escape from situations which they find uncomfortable, unfamiliar, or simply frightening." She argued that people escape both physically and psychologically. Let's take a look at Nada's first draft of the paragraph that appears at the end of the essay just before the conclusion and see how she later revised it to strengthen her argument.[1]

> Escapism can also include a "physical method," which
> means physically removing one's self from an
> uncomfortable situation. In In the Village Bishop
> shows how the young girl's mother is attempting to
> talk to her about how much she has grown, "Hands are
> on my head, pushing me down; I slide out from under
> them" (261; paragraph 97). Here, escape is shown
> through the child "sliding" out of an uncomfortable
> situation. Consider this moment in The Baptism: "Lucy
> went under without a movement . . . " (169; paragraph
> 82). This description of Lucy's baptism through total
> immersion (a form of baptism in which the entire body
> is completely placed under water) represents her
> escape through a physical act. An intriguing point in
> The Baptism is that Bishop takes first the physical
> method and places it within the psychological method,
> in Lucy's attempt to escape reality. This point may be
> understood by comprehending the fact that Lucy's
> physical method of escape was the total immersion,
> which was the direct result of the developments
> through her psychological method of escape, which
> was accomplished through religious obsession.

Let's look at the paragraph as it appears in the final essay. The underscored material was added and the material that is crossed out was deleted.

> Escapism can also include a "physical method," which
> means physically removing one's self from an
> uncomfortable situation. In "In the Village" Bishop

---

[1]References include both the original page number and the paragraph number used in this textbook.

shows how the young girl's mother is attempting to talk to her about how much she has grown. "Hands are on my head, pushing me down; I slide out from under them" (261; paragraph 97). Here, escape is shown through the child "sliding" out of an uncomfortable situation. <u>The child also finds comfort through an escape to a nearby pasture: "For a while I entertain the idea of not going home today at all, of staying safely here in the pasture all day, playing in the brook. . . "</u> (265; paragraph 135). Consider this moment in "The Baptism": "Lucy went under without a movement. . . " (169; paragraph 82). This description of Lucy's baptism through total immersion (a form of baptism in which the entire body is completely placed under water) represents her escape through a physical act. ~~An intriguing point in "The Baptism" is that Bishop takes first the physical method and places it within the psychological method, in Lucy's attempt to escape reality. This point may be understood by comprehending the fact that Lucy's physical method of escape was the total immersion, which was the direct result of the developments through her psychological method of escape, was accomplished through religious obsession.~~ <u>First, Lucy's religious obsession led her to psychological escape, but later through the baptism she found escape through a physical method. In the end, Lucy's death brings her an ultimate form of escape.</u>

Nada makes two very significant changes to this paragraph that strengthen her argument. She adds another example of physical escape from "In the Village"—the child "escapes" to the pasture. In the second change Nada deleted two sentences and added another. This helped to clarify a complicated point which she felt was important to her argument, but which was difficult for her readers to understand.

REVISING THE ESSAY

Once you have drafted the essay you will want to go over it, rethinking and revising the material. Give it several readings, focusing on one problem at a time. Once Nada had produced a rough draft she went to the Writing Center to work with a tutor; and she exchanged papers with another student during a class focused on peer critique. Her teacher also commented on the rough draft. Give your essay at least three readings following the guidelines below. Nada's responses to the revision process following each reading are included below.

An Overall Reading

Read your synthesis essay all the way through. Ask yourself the following questions:

 Does my introduction explain how I am approaching this essay? Will it appeal to readers? Do I sound like a writer with authority, or do I sound like I am mimicking someone else? Have I considered what I have learned about literary criticism? Have I introduced the Bishop stories to the reader, stating generally what they are about? Have I found some specific point of connection between the two stories and explored how the stories are similar and different? Have I cited specific passages from the text and explained how they support the connection I am writing about?

A Sentence-by-Sentence Reading

In this reading focus on the relationships between sentences. Consider these questions:

 Is each paragraph focused on a specific idea and does each help to develop my main argument? Does each sentence connect to the next one appropriately? Have I used words like the following to create relationships between sentences: furthermore, likewise, and, yet, however, on the other hand, but, then, with this in mind, because, first, next, and to sum up? When should I use a particular noun and when should I use a pronoun to refer to it? Should I be using a synonym for the noun? Is the pattern of my sentence structure monotonous? Is the same subject and verb pattern used in each? If so does it create the emphasis I intended?

Reading for Editing and Proofreading

In this last close reading of the draft you need to look for errors of mechanics, style, usage, and punctuation. Ask yourself questions like:

 Have I used paraphrasing and quotation correctly? Have I cited bibliographic sources correctly and included a Works Cited list? Use an English handbook to be sure your draft follows the rules for correctness.

Nada's Comments

Here are a few comments Nada made in her journal as she reflected on the process of revising.

I sometimes feel like I'm mimicking a professor when I use terms like "the psychological and physical methods of escape," but, on the other

*hand, it seemed important to give them names. In several places I had to
add sections to help my reader understand me. At first I was writing to explain it to myself and gradually as my teacher or someone else didn't understand, I had to clarify it. I had to connect my personal experience to the
stories and to my main point. I, of course, understood, but some of my
readers didn't.*

*I had to break a section up into two paragraphs. I thought I was talking
about the same thing, but people kept telling me it was too long. I made the
mistake of underlining the titles of both stories all the way through the essay, but it wasn't too hard to fix with the search and replace option on my
word processor. My spellchecker has just about done away with spelling errors. I had to fix some little things like between and among and I got some
practice using content verbs and getting rid of the "to be" verb by rewriting
the sentence, "The child enters. . . ."*

THE REVISED DRAFT

Here are the final revisions Nada Markelis made to her draft. Additions to
her original draft are underscored, and deleted material is crossed out.

In Her Own World

People, especially children, tend to escape from
situations which they find uncomfortable, unfamiliar
or simply frightening. But how do they escape? What
are their methods of escape? What events lead up to
their escape? ~~These questions are commonly asked when
reading the short stories of Elizabeth Bishop.~~ "The
Baptism" and "In the Village," both depict the theme
of escapism, ~~(definition:~~ defined in Webster's Tenth
Collegiate Dictionary as, "habitual diversion of the
mind to purely imaginative activity or entertainment
as an escape from reality or routine" (395). In the
first story, "The Baptism," a young girl named Lucy is
tormented with the fear that she would die before she
could be baptized. It was this fear which led her to
escape into the world of religion. Bishop's other
story, "In the Village," is about a young girl who had
to deal with not only her mother's mental illness, but
with the embarrassment she felt regarding the illness.
It was the child's embarrassment and fear of the
illness which led her to escape into a "world" of
imaginative dreams. ~~When compiling these two stories~~

~~we develop an understanding of why and how Bishop's characters escape. Our primary focus will be on their methods of escape.~~ In reading these two stories, we begin to develop an understanding of how these two girls escape, one through the physical escape of death and the other through psychological escape.

Children tend to escape reality by creating and/or retreating to a "world of their own," a world in which they feel safe, one that accepts and comforts them. The methods used and type of "world" they escape to differs ~~between~~ among children and their situations. Some use the psychological method of daydreams and/or fantasy, to escape their uncomfortable situation. Others simply remove themselves physically from the uncomfortable situation. It is not uncommon within the two stories for Bishop's characters to apply both methods of escape. In addition, both stories show that it was a negative occurrence which led to both characters' need to escape, consequently retreating to their own "worlds." Again, escapism offers two different methods which sometimes coincide, one psychological, the other physical.

In Bishop's "The Baptism," Lucy escapes the issue of death through religious obsession. The direct entrance she uses to her comforting "religious world" is shown through prayer and hallucinations. For example, Lucy writes in her journal:

> The house shook, and I thought about the House founded on the Rock. I was terribly frightened . . . Then there was a lull. It was very black and my heart pounded so I thought I was dying. I couldn't think of a prayer. Then suddenly a low voice began to talk over the head of the bed. I couldn't make out the words, they weren't exactly the words I knew, but I seemed to understand them. What a load dropped from my mind! . . . I was so happy . . . (165; paragraph 49).

In this example Bishop shows how Lucy escapes her frightening experience through prayer and through imaginative voices coming from her "religious world." I consider this a psychological method of escape.

In "In the Village" Bishop depicts a child's attempt to escape the haunting memory of her mentally ill mother's screams. The ~~direct entrance the~~ child enters ~~uses to~~ the comforting "world of daydreams" ~~is through~~ her wandering and vivid imagination. This example shows the child viewing the material from her mother's dress, which is still in the making:

> The purple stuff lies on the table; long white threads hang all about it. Oh, look away before it moves by itself, or makes a sound; before it echoes, echoes, what it has heard!" (258–259; paragraph 79).

This child's dream world shows how ~~is an example of~~ psychological escapism can help her to leave an uncomfortable reality behind. Professor John Huntington points out how the child has "made animate what would be inanimate as if the cloth has absorbed" the scream (184). The child is afraid of the scream but it's all she has left of her mother.

Sometimes it is not the dream world but the real world that allows the child to psychologically escape. In Becoming a Poet: Elizabeth Bishop with Marianne Moore and Robert Lowell, David Kalstone suggests that the child's observations and hyperattention to details help her to avoid confronting pain head-on. Instead of thinking about her mother's scream, she describes the blacksmith's shop. Kalstone explains that "Feeling is deflected, refigured as the child becomes absorbed in the outside world, her Nate's blacksmith shop" (164). Again, instead of dwelling on her feelings, the child sends them out into the world--into the blacksmith shop, into a meadow, or even in shoes in a shoe store.

Psychological escapes are not uncommon; in fact almost every person at one point in their lifetime has

experienced or observed this form of escape. I
observed an escape within my own family. My young
cousin (age 6) dealt with a frightening situation when
his parents had to put his very ill dog to sleep.
Every time the topic came up my cousin began singing a
song. Then, the day the dog was taken away he began to
sing this same song. Finally, when he was told the dog
was dead, he sang the song all day until he fell
asleep. Singing that song was my cousin's escape,
first from his fears, then from his sadness or denial
about the dog's death. Eventually, when this topic no
longer upset him, we no longer heard that song,
meaning that he no longer needed to escape. My
cousin's escape parallels that of the child in "In the
Village." Both were trying to escape an uncomfortable
situation, my cousin in dealing with his dog's death
and the child in dealing with her mother's illness.
Kalstone goes even further, suggesting that Elizabeth
Bishop may have decided to write about early deaths in
her stories as a way to search "the horizon for her
own childhood" (35; paragraph 9). By showing us how her
characters escaped, she was finding a way to escape
from memories that she didn't know how to deal with.

Escapism can also include a "physical method,"
which means physically removing one's self from an
uncomfortable situation. In "In the Village" Bishop
shows how the young girl's mother is attempting to
talk to her about how much she has grown, "Hands are
on my head, pushing me down; I slide out from under
them" (261; paragraph 97). Here, escape is shown
through the child "sliding" out of an uncomfortable
situation. The child also finds comfort through an
escape to a nearby pasture, "For a while I entertain
the idea of not going home today at all, of staying
safely here in the pasture all day, playing in the
brook. . ." (265; paragraph 135). Consider this moment
in "The Baptism": "Lucy went under without a

movement. . . " (169; paragraph 82). This description of Lucy's baptism through total immersion (a form of baptism in which the entire body is completely placed under water) represents her escape through a physical act. ~~An intriguing point in "The Baptism" is that Bishop takes first the physical method and places it within the psychological method, in Lucy's attempt to escape reality. This point may be understood by comprehending the fact that Lucy's physical method of escape was the total immersion, which was the direct result of the developments through her psychological method of escape, was accomplished through religious obsession.~~ First, Lucy's religious obsession lead her to psychological escape, but later through the baptism she found escape through a physical method. In the end, Lucy's death brings her an ultimate form of escape.

While the characters in her stories may have been practicing escape, Elizabeth Bishop may have been doing just the opposite: trying to recover her past. Kalstone suggests that both of these stories, "The Baptism" and "In the Village," might have provided a way to steer her way through a very foggy past (Kalstone 33; paragraphs 5-6). During the year her mother died, Elizabeth Bishop did not write about her childhood in the journals which literary scholars have been able to see (Kalstone 32; paragraph 2). Yet in these stories, she shows us children and adults may escape from uncomfortable situations.

WORKS CITED

Bishop, Elizabeth. "The Baptism." Elizabeth Bishop: The Collected Prose. Ed. Robert Giroux. New York: Farrar, Straus, Giroux, 1984. 159-170.

—. "In the Village." Elizabeth Bishop: The Collected Prose. Ed. Robert Giroux. New York: Farrar, Straus, Giroux, 1984. 252-274.

Feldman, Ann Merle. "Literary Studies." Writing and
Learning in the Disciplines. New York:
HarperCollins, 1996.

Kalstone, David. Becoming a Poet: Elizabeth Bishop
with Marianne Moore and Robert Lowell. Ed. Robert
Hemenway. New York: Farrar Straus Giroux, 1989.

Webster's Tenth New Collegiate Dictionary. Springfield,
Mass.: G. & C. Merriam Co., 1993. 395.

WRITING AND LEARNING ACTIVITIES

1. **Journal Entry:** Consider these questions: Is the process demonstrated here different from the way you usually write academic papers? In what way? Does anything about the process confuse you? Seem clearer now? What aspects of this process do you predict will be particularly difficult or easy?

2. **Group Activity:** By this point you may have been introduced to other disciplines. Or think about the other classes you are taking and the disciplines they reflect. In your group, brainstorm about how the disciplines differ. Appoint a scribe and make lists for each discipline. How do you think synthesizing will differ among these disciplines? On what basis will you find similarities and differences among the sources from these disciplines? Can you predict how your own personal experience might be important to developing a synthesis in these disciplines?

SOURCES FOR SYNTHESIZING

This section includes several sources to synthesize from three of the disciplines covered in this book: cultural anthropology, literary studies, and geology. Working with these sources will give you practice developing synthesis essays. I introduce each reading with a set of questions to think about. At the end of the chapter, I have included a set of activities that will guide you through the process of developing a synthesis essay from the sources provided here or from other sources provided by you or your instructor.

SOURCES FROM CULTURAL ANTHROPOLOGY

Cultural anthropology is a discipline that relies on extensive participant observation; that is, an anthropologist lives in a community in order to study it. Anthropologists typically work from notes and audiorecordings to write an ethnography, which is a detailed and rich description of a community. In this textbook, you can read two anthropological reports of fieldwork in Chapter 2, one about kinship in an urban, African-American community and one about the extended family in a Chicano community (if you have not already done so).

For you to practice synthesis on your own, we offer two additional readings from cultural anthropology, both by Oscar Lewis, from his *Five Families: Mexican Case Studies in the Culture of Poverty.* Lewis wrote this book to provide a rich and realistic picture of five Mexican families. Two of the five case studies—the Gomez family and the Gutierrez family—have been excerpted here. Lewis reminds us that when an anthropologist shifts from studying tribal people in distant places to studying the poor in urban settings, possibly quite close to home, he or she has to rethink his or her relationship with the people being studied, and in Lewis's case, to rethink the way we view poverty. While anthropologists may have assumed poverty was an essential part of tribal life in preindustrialized societies, poverty in the midst of modern nations "suggests class antagonism, social problems, and the need for change; and it often is so interpreted by the subjects of the study" (2).

Lewis tells us that he—"a foreigner and 'norte-Americano'—lived with the families he studied, spoke their language, and participated in their celebrations and in their sadness. He chose to study the family unit rather than the community or the individual (5), focusing on issues such as their "material culture, economic life, social relations, religious life, and interpersonal relations" (4). Further, he made the decision to select a single day—and an ordinary day rather than the day of a special celebration—during which he and a trained assistant stenographer who had lived in the *vecindad* transcribed the conversations word for word. During this day he would try to see life in the *vecindad* through the eyes of the family he was studying.

THINKING ABOUT THE DISCIPLINE

As you read each of the readings excerpted from Lewis's *Five Families,* make notes about connections you notice between what you have learned about the discipline and what you are now reading. How are these readings similar or different from your previous readings in this area or other readings you have done? Also write about connections you see between these families, your own families, the families of other students in your class, and families portrayed in books you have read or movies you have seen.

ASK YOURSELF

What have I learned about anthropology? How do anthropologists conduct their research? How do they write about what they have learned? How is their writing different from or similar to the writing of members of other disciplines? What types of issues would you expect to see in the writing of anthropologists?

THE GOMEZ FAMILY
OSCAR LEWIS

■ ■ ■

Between the Street of the Barbers and the Street of the Tinsmiths, only a short distance from the Thieves' Market, stands the Casa Grande. This is a giant *vecindad* or one-story tenement which houses over seven hundred people. Spread out over an entire square block, the Casa Grande is a little world of its own, enclosed by high cement walls on the north and south, and by rows of shops which face the streets on the other two sides. These shops—food stores, a dry cleaner, a glazier, a carpenter, a beauty parlor, together with the neighborhood market and public baths—supply the basic needs of the *vecindad* so that many of the tenants, particularly those who come from rural areas, seldom leave the immediate neighborhood and are almost strangers to the rest of Mexico City. This section of the city was once the home of the underworld, and even today people fear to walk in it late at night. But most of the criminal element has moved away and the majority of the residents are poor tradesmen, artisans, and workers.

Two narrow, inconspicuous entrances, each with a high gate, open during the day but locked every night at ten o'clock, lead into the *vecindad* on the east and west sides. Anyone coming or going after hours must ring for the janitor and pay to have the gate opened. The *vecindad* is also protected by its two patron saints, the Virgin of Guadalupe and the Virgin of Zapopan, whose statues stand in glass cases, one at each entrance. Offerings of flowers and candles surround the images and on their skirts are fastened small shiny medals, each a testimonial of a miracle performed for someone in the *vecindad*. Few residents pass the Virgins without some gesture of recognition, be it only a glance or a hurried sign of the Cross.

Within the *vecindad* stretch four long, cement-paved patios, or courtyards, about fifteen feet wide. These are formed by wide rectangular cement buildings divided into 157 one-room apartments, each with a barn-red door which opens onto the patios at regular intervals of about twelve feet. In the daytime, rough wooden ladders stand beside most of the doors, leading to low flat roofs over the kitchen portion of each apartment. These roofs serve many uses and are crowded with lines of laundry, chicken coops, dovecotes, pots of flowers or medicinal herbs, tanks of gas for cooking, and an occasional TV antenna. A few feet back, a higher roof that is less accessible and usually bare rises over the main room.

In the daytime the patios are crowded with people and animals, dogs, turkeys, chickens, and an occasional pig. Children play here because it is safer than the streets. Women queue up for water or shout to each other as they hang up clothes and street-vendors come in to sell their wares. Every morning a garbageman wheels a large can through the patios to collect each family's refuse. In the afternoons gangs of older boys often take over a patio to play a rough game of soccer. On Sunday nights there is usually an outdoor dance. Within the west entrance is the public bathhouse and a small garden whose few trees and patch of grass serve as a meeting place for young people and a relatively quiet spot where the older men sit and talk or read newspapers. Here also is a one room shack marked "administration office" where a bulletin lists the names of families who are delinquent in paying their rent.

5   The tenants of the Casa Grande come from twenty-four of the thirty-two states of the Mexican nation. Some come from as far south as Oaxaca and Yucatan and some from the northern states of Chihuahua and Sinaloa. Most of the families have lived in the *vecindad* for from fifteen to twenty years, some as long as thirty years. Over a third of the households have blood relatives within the *vecindad* and about a fourth are related by marriage and *compadrazgo*. These ties, plus the low, fixed rental and the housing shortage in the city, make for stability. Some families with higher incomes, their small apartments jammed with good furniture and electrical equipment, are waiting for a chance to move to better quarters, but the majority are contented with, indeed proud of living in the Casa Grande. The sense of community is strong, particularly among the young people who belong to the same gangs, form lifelong friendships, attend the same schools, meet at the same dances held in the patios and frequently marry within the *vecindad*. Adults also have friends whom they visit, go out with, and borrow from. Groups of neighbors organize raffles and *tandas* (informal mutual savings and credit plans), participate in religious pilgrimages together, and together celebrate the festivals of the *vecindad* patron saints, the Christmas *Posadas,* and other holidays.

But these group efforts are occasional; for the most part adults "mind their own business" and try to maintain family privacy. Most doors are kept shut and it is customary to knock and wait for permission to enter when visiting. Some people visit only relatives or *compadres* and actually have entered very few of the apartments. It is not common to invite friends or neighbors in to eat except on formal occasions such as birthday or religious celebrations. Although some neighborly help occurs, especially during emergencies, it is kept at a minimum. Quarrels between families over the mischief of children, street fights between gangs, and personal feuds between boys are not uncommon in the Casa Grande.

The people of the Casa Grande earn their living in a large miscellany of occupations, some of which are carried on within the *vecindad*. Women take in washing or sewing, men are shoemakers, hat cleaners, or vendors of fruit and candy. Others go outside to work in factories or shops or as chauffeurs and small tradesmen. Living standards are low but by no means the lowest in Mexico City, and the people of the neighborhood look upon the Casa Grande as an elegant place.

Number 60, the one-room home of the Gómez family, was the last in the long row in the third courtyard. The latch on the battered door was broken, and the door was held shut at night by placing the ladder against it on the inside. During the day, when the ladder was kept in the patio, the door was usually half-open; Rosa didn't believe in locks because they were "an invitation to thieves."

Inside the dark, windowless room, crowded with furniture, the Gómez family slept huddled under thin covers on a cold January morning. The smells of unwashed feet, sweat, shoe leather, and fried food pervaded the room. Agustín Gómez and his wife Rosa slept on a narrow cot against the right wall, she at the head and he at the foot. Alberto, the eldest son, aged twenty, Ester, the daughter, aged fourteen, and Juanito, the youngest son, aged six, all slept in the big bed which jutted out from the left wall across half the small room. When Agustín and Rosa quarreled, he would leave the narrow cot and exchange places with little Juanito, so that sometimes Ester would awaken in the morning to find that she had been sleeping between her father and her older brother. Rosa was the only one who lamented the crowded sleeping arrangements. She frequently scolded her husband for not building a *tapanco* or balcony, as some of the neighbors had done, so that the boys could sleep "upstairs."

10   The kitchen, just inside the front door, formed a passageway to the bedroom. This area had not been roofed when the *vecindad* was built and each tenant had to provide his own roof. Agustín had solved the problem by attaching two sheets of corrugated tar paper to a stick laid across the center, forming a low peak. The front portion was left open to allow smoke from the stove to escape. But it also permitted rain to enter, and during the rainy season the kitchen floor was often wet and sometimes the table had to be moved into the bedroom to keep the food dry. Hanging from the roof as a good luck charm was an infant's shoe that Alberto had found in his bus. On the wall was a calendar with a picture of Marilyn Monroe.

The other side of the kitchen contained the family's most valuable possessions, a new American-made gas range, a white metal cabinet, and a breakfast set consisting of a table and four chairs. Hector and Alberto had presented Rosa with the stove and cabinet on the last Mother's Day, promising to pay monthly installments of one hundred and twenty-nine pesos for two years. Alberto also undertook to pay for the breakfast set at sixty-four pesos a month. The new furnishings created no small problem in the tiny kitchen. Rosa could not open the oven door without moving the table, which then blocked the front door. But since she used the oven only to store pots and pans and empty soda bottles, it was not too inconvenient. However, there was not enough room to permit the family to eat together.

At four in the morning the alarm clock rang noisily. It was Agustín's turn for the early morning shift on the bus line. He had been a bus driver since he and Rosa had come to the city seventeen years before. They both had been born and raised in the little village of Azteca and Agustín had farmed his widowed mother's land, working occasionally on a nearby sugar plantation. Rosa had hated her mother-in-law, however, and Agustín had found the work of a peasant difficult and unrewarding. Both of them believed that life would be easier in the city and that their children would get a better education. So they had moved to the Casa Grande and Agustín had found a job with one of the private bus lines that serviced the city. Now Alberto too was a driver on the same route.

Agustín let the clock ring itself out, hoping it would wake Rosa. He wanted her to get up and make some hot coffee to wash away the taste of the bitter herb mixture he drank each morning for his diabetes. Rosa did not move. He sat up, roughly pulling the cotton bedspread which covered them. She muttered something angrily, covered herself, and went back to sleep. He sighed. It had been different in Azteca; there a wife knew how to care for her husband.

Agustín's poor health had begun five years before when he had been severely burned in a bus accident. His recovery was slow and he had never regained his former strength. His stammer had become worse and he had developed diabetes. But the worst blow, one which often made him want to die, was his sexual impotence. Since the accident Agustín had not once been able to satisfy his wife and she had become ill-tempered and aggressive toward him, accusing him of rejecting her for another woman and tormenting him daily for one thing or another. Agustín believed that low blood pressure, caused by a loss of blood in the accident, had brought about his impotence. Rosa was convinced that another woman had bewitched him.

15　　As a matter of fact, Agustín *had* found another woman, a young girl named Alicia, whose gentle patience and affection were a great comfort to him. He usually visited her twice a week but came home to sleep. Two years before he had managed to impregnate her and he was very pleased with their little son. He had been with Alicia last evening and wondered anxiously if she were satisfied with him. He would try to give her more money for expenses, come what may at home.

Religious pictures of various sizes were tacked to the pink plaster wall above the altar. A large glass-framed image of the Virgin of Guadalupe hanging in the center was the most imposing. On a shelf beneath it a small red electric light bulb, intended to illuminate the holy pictures, had long since burned out. A short, thick votive candle in a glass jar stood beside it and Agustín noted with annoyance that Rosa had forgotten to light it the night before. She tended to be careless about Catholic ritual, particularly if it involved spending centavos. Agustín was of the opinion that Rosa was more backward and "Indian" than he in religious matters. Like the women in her village she rarely went to confession or took communion. She grumbled about the time her daughter "wasted" attending Mass every Sunday and confessing once a month, and she laughed at little Juanito for kissing the hand of the priest as he had learned in catechism class.

Agustín criticized his wife for not encouraging the children to respect the priest. "That is why our children do not respect us," he told her. "How can they respect their father if they do not even respect the priest?" Rosa disagreed. Besides, she considered herself the more religious of the two for *he* was "the bigger sinner." She too was devoted to the Virgin of Guadalupe and had twice gone barefoot to her shrine. But Rosa's particular devotion was to the Sacred Heart. She kept a picture postcard of the Sacred Heart in her purse and had presented several silver medals to its image in thanks for help in overcoming her terrible jealousy at the infidelities of her husband.

Wearily, Agustín put on his necktie, wiped the corners of his eyes with his handkerchief, and picked up his leather windbreaker from the kitchen chair. Moving the ladder to one side, he turned out the light, opened the door, and stepped into the patio. He fumbled in his pocket for a twenty-centavo piece as he rang the bell to summon the gatekeeper. While waiting he dropped a centavo piece in the alms box next to the Virgin of Zapopan and crossed himself. The doorkeeper's old wife came to unlock the gate to the street, and with scarcely a greeting Agustín gave her the coin and went out.

Agustín hated his job. The hours were irregular, and the bus he drove was a battered one that frequently needed repairs and caused him to lose many work days every month. Also, the hectic traffic of the capital had begun to frighten him. He didn't react as quickly as he once had and he lived in dread of another accident. He had looked for a different job and was wait-ing now to hear about getting a position driving a CEIMSA truck. CEIMSA was the government food distribution system and Agustín was confident he would be accepted because he had had a letter of recommendation from a senator who happened to be Rosa's cousin and a native of Azteca.

20   At seven the crowing of the roosters and a blast of the bathhouse whistle awakened Ester. She was in the sixth and last grade of the neighborhood public primary school and had to be there by seven-thirty. She slipped out of the big bed, leaving only Juanito lost among the blankets. Ester was look-ing forward to her graduation and the long lazy days when she could sleep late. She also hoped to go to commercial school and learn to be a stenogra-pher so that she could wear silk stockings and pretty dresses, but her father made no promises. It would cost fifteen pesos a month, plus uniforms, books, and bus fare, and where would the money come from? Her brothers would not help her for they both had many other uses for their money. Rosa had declared she would go back to work in order to give her daughter two years of "Commercial" but Ester did not place much hope in that. She was afraid her father would never let Rosa do it.

Ester put on her school uniform, a blue cotton skirt and a white blouse, washed her hands and face at the kitchen sink, combed her hair, and put on a sweater. She had already worn the uniform three days, but she had no other and her mother washed only once a week. The sweater was quite new; her mother had bought it on time, paying ten pesos a week. Ester, too, examined her face in the mirror. She resembled her brother Alberto, even to the acne. Were it not for her skin condition she would have been quite pretty; her complexion was not too dark, her hair was wavy, and she had a nice easy smile. She was fourteen and found it an exciting age.

Her mother had promised her a pink dress of transparent cloth for her graduation and had even hinted at a fifteenth birthday party, with cham-berlains and a birthday cake—the dream of all young girls in the *vecindad*. Ester knew it would be too much to expect a dance band or *mariachi* singers; she would be content with a rented record player. She imagined for the twentieth time how she would look dancing the first dance with her father. Her fifteenth birthday would be a turning point in her life for after that she would be a "señorita."

It was not until eight-thirty that Rosa sat up and swung her feet to the cold cement floor, feeling for her old black shoes under the bed.

Rosa was a sturdy woman with strong features and a deep, hearty laugh, who moved and spoke with energy and directness. She looked older than her thirty-nine years. Fat shoulders and arms, a short neck, and heavy bulging breasts made her look powerful. She was dark-skinned, with dark brown hair and almost black circles under her eyes. The rest of her face was covered with freckles and pockmarks. She was usually very talkative and she dominated her whole family even though she claimed that she could no longer control her sons and was afraid of her husband's temper. Her main complaint was that the men of the family gave her too little money to run the house and gave it irregularly. As a result she often threatened to go back to work. She had worked as a waitress for two years when Agustín was burned and knew that she could get her old job back.

Rosa decided to comb her hair before going for the milk. "If I don't comb my hair now I have no time later."

25   The patio had become more lively. Doors were open, bird cages had been hung outside on nails, and women could be seen here and there combing their hair or shaking a blanket. Rosa could hear the slapping of *tortillas* into shape, for some women still made them at home. For her part she was "through with slavery" and bought ready-made ones despite the protests of her husband and sons. On the two-block walk to the store she met and greeted several neighbors out on similar errands. The women walked unhurriedly, some dragging a sleepy child by the arm, others carrying infants under their shawls. Rosa did not pause to chat for unlike many women in the *vecindad* she kept to herself. She liked sociability and gossip as much as anyone but she was convinced that it always led to trouble. In Azteca village, she had learned to mind her own business and keep her affairs within the family. For this reason she did not have many friends, and in all the time they had lived in the Casa Grande not one of the tenants had invited her and Agustín to become their *compadres*.

But in spite of herself Rosa got into quarrels with neighbors because of her children whom she always defended whether they were at fault or not. Just last week she had had trouble with the "butcher women." Eutikia, one of the butchers' wives, had started the trouble because her daughter had allowed Ester to hold her gold chain and Ester had lost it. Rosa could not see why she should pay for the chain. Was it not Eutikia's daughter's mistake to have entrusted such a valuable thing to Ester? But Eutikia and her two sisters, who were also married to butchers, were dangerous to tangle with.

At the store Rosa bought a liter of milk which the storekeeper poured into her jar. She then moved on to a stand near the entrance of the Casa

Grande where she bought a quarter pound of freshly ground coffee. The family preferred coffee from their village but she had used up her supply and would not get more until the end of the month when they went to Azteca for the carnival. She was about to leave when a woman seated on the sidewalk near the coffee stand called, "Don't you want *tortillas?*" "Ah, yes, I almost forgot." Rosa asked for two dozen and both women counted carefully as the vendor picked up the *tortillas* from the large basket beside her on the walk.

Hurrying back to the *vecindad,* Rosa pushed open her door to find Juanito sitting on the floor putting on his shoes. He had already pulled on his worn cotton pants and buttoned his blue shirt. Rosa put her purchases on the table and Juanito came running, a shoe in one hand and a sock in the other, to see what she had bought. Ignoring him, she lit the stove, set the jar of milk to boil, and began to heat the coffee again. Juanito lost interest and sat down on a chair to get into his sock and shoe, then wandered out to the patio, untied shoelaces dangling. Rosa added a spoonful of fresh coffee to the pot and began to grind some leftover chile. In the midst of her grinding she left the stone mortar to go to the sink and wash the rag she used to clean the stove. Meanwhile Juanito had found the patio empty of friends and had returned to sit down at the table. Resting his chin on his hands, he watched his mother.

Rosa bit into a strong, green chile and helped herself to rice. She ate unhurriedly, half-listening to what Juanito was saying about the film he had seen on television the week before. Every Friday evening and sometimes on Saturday and Sunday he and Ester went to one of the neighbors to watch television. They paid from twenty to fifty centavos for this privilege and stayed until the stations stopped broadcasting at about midnight. Competition for customers was keen among owners of TV sets. At one time there had been only a few sets in the *vecindad;* people had flocked to watch them and the owners sometimes earned enough to meet their monthly payment on the set or to pay the electric light bill. Now that there were many sets, some owners offered customers free potato chips or candy and let them remain as long as they liked. Rosa always sent her children to the house that offered the most.

30 Rosa was aware of the way life in the *vecindad* had changed in recent years. Since the coming of television people stayed up later. Previously, children and young girls had not been allowed out after dark and most families went to bed at about ten o'clock. Now people no longer listened to their radios as much or went to the movies as often; children spent more time indoors. Girls dressed more in style and more things were bought on the installment plan as a result of television advertising. People also had new ideas—a neighbor's daughter wanted to become a ballet dancer after she had seen a dance group on TV.

The electric record player too had brought changes. Now every Sunday night and also on special occasions dances were held in the *vecindad* courtyards, and boys and girls danced to American, Cuban, and Mexican records until one or two in the morning! Hector liked to organize dances and as a result many of them were held outside the Gómez house where Rosa could sit and watch. Agustín did not permit her to dance. Ester was allowed to dance only with other girls but lately Rosa had caught her dancing with boys. Ester was growing up and Rosa would have to keep a sharper eye on her. She did not want her daughter to have a sweetheart like the other shameless girls of the *vecindad,* many of whom became pregnant and never married.

Rosa began to collect dirty clothes to be washed. She took three pairs of pants from a box at the foot of the bed. "This white one is very dirty. I'll soap it and put it in the sun today and wash it tomorrow. These others I'll wash once and for all." On her way to the sink she saw Beto's dirty shirt on the toilet door and threw it into the tub along with the tablecloth. Just then the landlord, Señor Gallardo, greeted her from the open doorway. She dried her hands and stood still in the middle of the kitchen without inviting him in.

"Señora, isn't Señor Gómez at home?"

"No, sir, he isn't." Rosa's voice was not friendly.

35   "Well, you know why I've come. Tell me if I should send your contract to you because the rent is going up to fifty pesos. There will be an increase of twenty pesos."

"Well, we'll see once my husband gets here. We'll see what he says."

"Please tell him, Señora, that I have a hundred and twenty contracts signed, so you can see that the majority have accepted. There are only a few who are unwilling and they will just have to take up the matter with my lawyers. You understand that I can't continue to support myself with the same income I had twenty or thirty years ago." Señor Gallardo was becoming excited. "Prices have gone up, you know that, and besides I'm not being unfair. I only want to balance the expenses I've had here—fixing the floors, painting the doors, changing the beams on the roof, whitewashing and, well, small expenses that I haven't been able to cover. I'm trying to speak as a friend because this house is supposed to be torn down and I'm trying to negotiate an agreement with the government so that it won't happen." He paused a moment. "If you all help me I will be very glad to try to keep this house standing. As you see, even though the *vecindad* is poor it isn't like others that make one ashamed to live in them. You are witnesses that I am trying to keep it decent. This house is unprofitable for me now so, as I say, I don't think it's too much to raise only twenty pesos."

Rosa had stood listening to all this with her arms crossed. Now she blurted out, "Another raise? Five years ago we had one and I suppose in five more there will be another."

Señor Gallardo protested, "No. Five years ago it was done by mutual agreement also. But I don't know why they are so unwilling. I tell you the majority have accepted with the exception of eight who have treated me with insults. But I'm ready to turn their cases over to my lawyers. And another thing. I am coming in person so that you will be able to say, 'Señor Gallardo in person came to the house,' so that you will have a pleasant memory of the matter, isn't that so? Because I haven't sent out only a notice or told you all to come to my offices. I come personally, knocking on all the doors and trying to make arrangements with all of you. It's impossible for me to continue this way. Things aren't eternal, Señora!"

40   Rosa laughed, "That should prove to you, Señor Gallardo, that if you who has money can't make ends meet, now tell me if we can!"

"That's just why, Señora. You know yourself, when I ordered a new floor laid down for you, you saw how you didn't give me one cent for it even though you had agreed to pay a certain amount."

"Yes," Rosa challenged him, "we didn't give you anything because we didn't have anything and it's the same way now. If you who have so much can't make out we can do even less, isn't that true? The more you have the more you spend, so since we have little we spend little and even then we can't make out. Now the beams you ordered put in, well, I don't know why, the old ones were better than these filthy dry sticks they came to put in."

"That's right, Señora. Up to now not one person has said, 'Señor Gallardo, thank you very much for this thing or the other.' That's what one gets. I tell you up to this minute I haven't met a single person who has thanked me. On the contrary, many have gotten angry."

She hurriedly wrung out the white pants and climbed to the roof to hang them out. A red cloth was on the line; she folded it on her way back to the kitchen and put it away before returning to her washing. A little after three Alberto walked in.

45   With a smile for his mother, he said, "Mamá, I'm very hungry, get going. I'm in a hurry."

Rosa did not stop what she was doing. "Oh, you always have very important things to do. Come on, give me the money. I didn't have enough. Come on. I don't know and I don't care."

Alberto had washed his hands at the sink. He held out some money. "Take this. That's all I have until borrow day." Four days before payday the bus drivers were permitted to borrow an advance on their wages.

Rosa did not want to wait. "This is all? You've only given me twenty pesos in the last ten days. I'm missing forty pesos. This is not enough!" She did not take the money.

"You don't want it? Then I'm going to a movie or I'll get drunk and that will be the end of it," Alberto laughed.

50   "No, no. What an idea! Come on, give me the money."

Alberto explained that he was short of money because the company was discounting more than usual from his pay.

"That's why sometimes there isn't any food," his mother retorted, "because I have to beg you for money."

Alberto shrugged his shoulders and stood looking out of the door. Ester had finished her work and was sitting in the sun crocheting. "Lazy girl, come and wash the dishes," Alberto said. His sister did not answer. Rosa called to her, "Come and beat the egg for me," and without a word she went inside. Alberto turned to his mother, "Come on. Give me my dinner. I have to leave."

Rosa looked annoyed. "What? What? You know, Señor Gallardo came to waste my time."

55 "What does he want? What did he say?" Alberto was interested.

"He wants to raise the rent, what do you think of that? He reminded me of the hundred pesos for the floor."

"What did you say to him?"

"I said to him, 'Ah! And why do you think we don't give it? Because we have the money or because we don't have it?' The old goat made fun of me."

"Well, am I going to get something to eat?" he added impatiently.

60 "Well, there's only beans. I didn't get dinner because I didn't have any money."

"All right. Heat them up for me then."

Alberto was annoyed with his mother. He finished his meal and went out to the patio. It was quite dark. There was to be a dance the next night in honor of the Virgin of Guadalupe and the committee was putting up extra lights. Alberto intended to take Susana to the dance and wondered if he had clean pants to wear. He saw his father talking to someone at the *vecindad* entrance and ducked around a corner to avoid him.

Rosa had just sat down to drink her coffee when her husband walked in. He had been gone from the house eighteen hours; the time between shifts he had spent at Alicia's. He was grimy and spotted with grease and he sagged with weariness. He had drunk a bottle of soda at the terminal and now he was worried that the sugar might make him ill. Without greeting anyone he went to the stove, looking for his herb medicine. Silently Rosa pointed to it and he poured out a glassful and drank it down. Then he went into the bedroom and sat down on the cot. Juanito joined him and snuggled up to him, lifting his father's inert arm and putting it around his shoulders. His father smiled down at him and patted him on the head. "W-w-what's new? What d-d-did you do in school?" Juanito told him some of the things he had done during the day. Agustín listened with interest until he saw the child was yawning. At his father's suggestion Juanito went to the toilet and then to bed.

Rosa looked at her husband. "Why so late? Did you meet one of your lady friends?"

65 Agustín ignored the insinuation. "My crate broke down again and I spent hours looking for a Stillson wrench. I finally fixed it and it didn't cost me anything."

"That damned bus! How much time did you lose?"

"Almost all afternoon. I tell you I must get that government job. This job is killing me and I don't earn enough with this old bus."

"My cousin, the senator, will get it for you," Rosa said. "He is an important man. They say he will be the future governor of Morelos."

Agustín smiled. "Then," he said, "I will ask him for the job of assistant."

70 "Assistant! In what would you assist him? You cannot even carry a pistol!" his wife snapped back.

Agustín was quiet. "Is there a bit of coffee for me?" he asked almost timidly. He added, "I can give you the rest of the money on borrow day . . .

on Monday." To his surprise his wife stood up and poured a cup of coffee and milk for him. She also poured one for Ester who was almost asleep, her crocheting in her hand. "Come, daughter, have your coffee and then you can go to sleep." Juanito was lying on top of the blanket, fast asleep. His mother took off his trousers, placed him in the center of the bed to separate Ester and Alberto, covered him up, and turned out the light.

The three of them sat drinking coffee crowded around the table that stood half in the bedroom, half in the kitchen. They heard firecrackers go off somewhere. "It is for our Virgin of Guadalupe. It is her Saint's day today," Ester explained. "There was a procession and music today, papá, and they sang *mañanitas*." Ester wondered if this were a good time to ask for permission to go to the dance. She decided it would be better to wait until her father was not at home. "I'm going to bed," she said with a yawn and went into the bedroom.

Agustín, too, rose and went to bed, first removing his soiled shirt and trousers. He turned to the wall, covered his face, and was soon asleep. Rosa ate the food remaining in the pot, stacked the dirty dishes and jars, but left them on the kitchen table. Almost always she left the dishes for the next morning so as not to disturb the sleepers. She washed her face and hands, undressed, and lay down at the opposite end of the cot next to her husband. She got up again to light the votive candle to the Virgin of Guadalupe and to turn out the kitchen light. The door was left slightly ajar for Alberto, who was still out. A few minutes later, at a quarter past eleven, she heard him come in. When he had slipped out of his clothes and had arranged himself under the covers, Rosa closed her eyes and fell asleep.

THE GUTIÉRREZ FAMILY
OSCAR LEWIS

On a bare lot between two brick buildings at No. 33, Street of the Bakers, the Panaderos *vecindad* lay exposed to the full view of passers-by. It was a small *vecindad* and one of the poorest in Mexico City—only a row of twelve small, windowless one-room apartments that housed fifty-four people. The apartments, built of adobe brick, were joined by a common cement roof and extended as a single, narrow structure down the left side of the lot. Each apartment had a small, low-ceilinged entranceway which also served as a kitchen. The kitchen roofs were flimsily put together of scraps of tar paper, tin, and corrugated metal, and were held in place by heavy stones. Firewood heaped in piles and covered with old gunny sacks and pieces of cardboard were stored on the roofs. The doors to the apartments were so low that one had to stoop to enter. In front of some of them the artisan-tenants had built makeshift sheds or lean-tos to provide themselves a dry, shady place to work.

On the sixteenth day of July, at five-forty in the morning, the little *vecindad* was quiet and all the doors were shut tight. The saloon where the men drank pulque and where the children were sent to buy the even cheaper *chinchol* was still closed. The bathhouse across the street had not yet opened for early customers. Now and then the silence was broken by a rickety bus or by a dog barking at a passing stranger. The first door to open was that of Señora Guadalupe, the wife of Ignacio the news-vendor. A rag wrapped about her neck and a twig broom in her hand, she came out to sweep the walk and the yard or patio. She was paid ten pesos a month by Ana, the janitress, to do this chore every morning. Before she began to sweep, the old woman paused for a moment, bending her gray head, to murmur her simple, daily prayer, "Oh, Lord, help me, help me!"

The door of No. 5, the "Casa Gutiérrez," as Guillermo had it printed on his business cards, opened noisily and his wife, Señora Julia Rojas, a short, stocky woman of forty-six, stepped out over the high ledge. She adjusted her wool shawl over her shoulders and smoothed her wrinkled black cotton dress. Seeing Guadalupe, she said, "Good morning, *comadrita*. At it already?" Guadalupe was Julia's sister-in-law by her second husband and godmother of "the blessed ribbons of Chalma" to each of Guillermo's children.

"Yes, yes. Going for the milk now?"

5   "Yes. Let's see if they'll give me enough. Having a ticket doesn't mean a thing. They are a bunch of mules!"

Every morning before six Julia went to the nearby government CEIMSA store to queue up for the milk sold there at half-price. Rumor said it was diluted with water and vegetable fat, but Julia paid no attention to that for she needed four quarts a day to feed the many people who depended upon her. She went early to be sure the milk would not be sold out and to queue up twice, since she could obtain only two quarts at a time. She was late this morning and hurried, clutching her shawl around her against the cold. She had bronchitis and her chest hurt, but if she did not go for the milk no one else would and her stepchildren and grandchildren would have to go without.

Julia felt put upon: she thought her married daughter, Yolanda, or her stepdaughter, Lola, should properly go for the milk when she herself was ill. But Yolanda, who lived two doors down in No. 7, was lazy and besides had recently given birth to her fifth child. Lola was only fourteen and was not permitted by her father to go out so early. Panchita, the wife of Julia's son, Maclovio, who lived in No. 9, could not be expected to go because she worked and her husband paid Julia fifty pesos a month to cook for them and their two children. The only other woman available was Julia's mother, Rufelia, who lived in a tiny room in a nearby *vecindad,* but she was old and no longer in her right mind. No matter how Julia fumed and complained about her heavy responsibilities, she continued to provide food for these people, sixteen in all, because she knew that they depended upon her. Julia had been the eldest of twelve children and was accustomed to assuming the burdens of others.

It was six-thirty when Julia returned to the *vecindad*. Guadalupe was still sweeping.

"You back already? Did they sell you all you wanted?"

10   "Same as always, little sister. My ticket wasn't worth a damn."

Ana, the stout janitress, carrying a pile of dirty clothes, joined the two women at the washing place. "If I don't do it now I won't get it done. When those old women start washing there is no room for anyone!" During the rainy season the women competed with each other to wash and dry their clothes while the sun was shining. Some had to finish their scrubbing out in the rain and hang the wet things in their crowded rooms. Ana knelt at the water trough and poured water over her clothes. Guadalupe went over to her, dragging her broom, and said, "Do you love me a lot, *comadre?*" This was the way the *vecindad* people asked to borrow money. Ana shook her head regretfully. "No, I don't love you today, *comadrita.*" Without another word Guadalupe went on sweeping.

Inside the "Casa Gutiérrez" the family still slept. The small windowless room had a foul smell. The bedclothes, the torn blankets, and the lumpy mattresses were damp and musty from lack of sun. The bedroom and the kitchen passageway were so cluttered that even after Julia "cleaned" they looked messy. The passageway, six feet wide and three feet long, was just inside the front door. The right-hand side, a space of only two by three feet, was used by Guillermo as an indoor workshop. Here on a high worktable were his precious tools: a screw driver, a hammer, a file, scissors, pincers, and a vise. "These are like my eyes," Guillermo said of his tools, "for without them I am blind." The top of the worktable was gouged from blows of his hammer, spattered with paint, and strewn with screws, rivets, empty soda bottles, an oilcan, boxes, and jars. Above the table, on a shelf supported by two wires, was a battered radio which Guillermo kept tuned to its one station while he worked. The shelf also held a small rusty scale, a light socket, some nails, and pieces of metal. On top of the radio was a bottle of aluminum paint and Guillermo's dirty blue apron. On the wall under the shelf two large calendars had been nailed up: one was a portrait of the boxer, Ratón Macias, the other of the Virgin of Fátima. Two installment tickets and a rent receipt were impaled on another nail.

Underneath the worktable there were more soda bottles, a twenty-liter tin can holding old iron bars, a jug of gasoline, a pair of old shoes, and a caved-in rubber ball. Every inch of the remaining space, from the floor to the ceiling, was filled with a large pile of scrap metal strip, new, but showing signs of rust and hopelessly tangled. A piece of limp red garden hose draped over this pile, like a decoration, and a pair of child's yellow sandals hung from a protruding strip. On a wide board supported by a chair, one hundred and twenty-four newly painted metal frames for the toy bottles had been set to dry.

The kitchen side of the passage was more orderly. The earth floor was swept, clay and enamel pots and two frying pans hung on nails hammered into the adobe brick wall, and a few chipped plates and mugs stood on shelves over the stove. The rest of the dishes and mugs and three glasses, still dirty from last night's supper, were stacked on the little table beside the three-burner stove. The stove rested on a cement charcoal brazier, now unused.

15   At the back of the brazier, leaning against the wall, were a stained tray and a huge clay casserole that Julia used when she prepared *mole* or other food to sell in the street. On the floor were a pail of charcoal and a portable brazier with a clay griddle on which Julia made *tortillas*. On the lowest shelf over the stove Julia kept foodstuffs—salt in a glass shaker, powdered chile in a broken cup, a paper package of flour in the bowl of a soup ladle, a piece of bread in a covered pot, an empty oil bottle. A clay jar held four or five bent spoons, two kitchen knives, and a wire egg beater in the shape of a flower. On a stool near the door a glass-covered tray held chocolates, marshmallows, and other cheap candies which Guillermo sold to the people of the *vecindad*. This "candy store" was one of his more recent business enterprises.

The inner room was reached by stepping down one step through a second doorway. A votive light burning on a shelf in the rear lighted up twelve pictures, large and small, of various virgins and saints. The two largest pictures, and the only ones in frames and covered with glass, were of the Virgin of Guadalupe and San Martín Caballero, the patron saint of merchants. The shelf, draped with an orange-colored cloth, held a bunch of paper flowers in a jar and a wooden box with a glass door through which could be seen the Sacred Heart of Jesus and a tiny wooden crucifix. Streamers of colored crepe paper hung from the ceiling beams above the holy pictures.

The eight-foot square room was almost completely filled with furniture; only a narrow aisle, about a foot wide, had been left free for walking. On the left was a narrow blue metal bedstead which Guillermo and Julia, his common-law wife, shared. A small table and a wooden wardrobe, both cluttered with boxes and other objects, took up the rest of this side of the room. On the right a high shelf or half-balcony, about four and a half feet from the floor and four feet wide, jutted out from the wall. On this an old bedspring and a cotton mattress provided a sleeping place for Guillermo's three children—Lola, age fourteen, Maria, age eleven, and Herminio, age nine. The unused metal headboard and foot of the bed were stored on the shelf along with twelve bicycle rims, twelve used tires, and a pailful of scrap iron. Several enamelware pots, the largest of which contained ground chile, sesame seeds, and peanuts for *mole,* also were piled up on the shelf.

The rear wall from the parents' bed to well under the sleeping platform was occupied by a large, new, combination radio, record-player, and television set. It was shiny and truly resplendent in the midst of all the junk around it, the one unscratched, unmarred piece of furniture in the house. Still protected on the top and sides by its original paper carton, only the family photos and the alarm clock were allowed to be placed on it. Guillermo had warned his family, when the set had been delivered, that they had to take good care of it, "better than we do of ourselves."

He had bought it on the installment plan, using his first set as down payment and paying one hundred pesos a month. The total cost was seventy-five hundred pesos or six hundred dollars, but to Guillermo it was an investment, even a form of savings, for he calculated that while he was making the payments it would bring in one or two pesos a day from the children who came to see the programs and when the last installment was paid he would re-crate it "as good as new" and sell it. He was counting on the possibility that prices would continue to rise, as they had for the past several years, and on finding a customer whom he could convince that the machine was factory-new. With the money he would make he planned to buy a plot of land in an undeveloped area where land was still cheap. Later it would be worth a great deal more, for the city was growing and land values were going up. This was Guillermo's scheme for starting up the ladder to success. "That's why I take more care of the TV set than of my children," he said. "I'm even buying records for it so I can sell it for more."

20   The day the set had arrived had been memorable for everyone in the *vecindad* but especially for Guillermo. He had stood there among his neighbors and listened elatedly to their exclamations of wonder at the size and quality of the machine. His brother-in-law had said, "Huuuy, you will soon be a rich man, Guillermo." He had answered calmly, "Yes, one must hustle. One must *do* something to *be* something." He had been happy that day, feeling that he was making progress in the world. He did not expect to run into difficulties, and he had paid no attention to the *indirectas* and criticisms made by some of the women.

Ana had said, "A washing machine would bring in more money." Señora Chole of No. 3 had said, "What do bean-eaters living like that want with it? Better wait until they have a parlor with armchairs to watch in comfort from." Old Guadalupe had said, "It is just pure ambition! He won't part with five centavos for a piece of garlic and Julia has to come borrowing from me!" Still another neighbor remarked, "They are so presumptuous that they will lose everything. It would be better to buy a piece of land. If someone digs a hole in that, you can fill it up with a little earth, but if someone puts a hole in this machine what will they do?" Guillermo dismissed it all as natural envy and was pleased when his neighbors came every evening to watch the programs for twenty centavos apiece.

At seven-thirty Julia yawned, stretched her arms, and pushed aside the dirty quilt for the second time that day. Guillermo, plump, light-skinned, twelve years her junior, slept on. Julia made the sign of the cross, said a brief prayer, and got out of bed to look for her cloth, hemp-soled slippers. She was mumbling to herself, ". . . one hour in line to get milk." She noticed that Lola, her light brown hair in curlers, was awake and watching her from the shelf. The girl smiled at her stepmother, who said, "Didn't you say you were going to get up early? Just look at what time it is."

Lola placed one foot on the table for support, jumped down from the shelf, smoothed the ragged brown silk dress she had slept in, and bent down to pull out her shoes from under her father's bed. Lola had finished the third grade in school and now worked in a little shoeshop in the *Lagunilla* market. Every ten days she gave her father fifty pesos out of which he allowed her money for bus fare, lunches, and baths. Lola claimed the fifty pesos were all she earned but Guillermo was not convinced. "I don't know," he would say, "what child tells the truth about that! None! Who is going to say, 'Well, I earn so much.' I believe they pay her more."

Guillermo sat up to dress. He was wearing a soiled T shirt and shorts made of coarse sacking. Over these he pulled on a pair of thoroughly dirty cotton trousers and then pushed his feet into his old shoes. He never tied his shoelaces, even when he wore his better pair downtown, because he believed his shoes lasted longer this way. "If I tie them they get tight and then when I sit down the shoes bust on me." Sometimes Julia complained of his unshaven, disheveled appearance and ragged clothing, but he would answer that it was better to go about looking poor so that people would repay what they owed him.

25 Without washing or combing, Guillermo went to his worktable in the passageway, turned on the radio, and sat down to work. A ranchero song was being sung. "When we were sweethearts there were kisses and gifts. Now that we're married there are punches and kicks." Guillermo smiled at his wife. "It's true, isn't it? When we were courting I used to hug and kiss you."

Julia nodded and laughed, "You were a skinny bastard then. I could surround you with one arm."

"Really? Don't be a liar."

"Do you remember when you used to take me on the bike I'd hang on with twenty nails? With my teeth and nails and everything! I was afraid because I didn't know you. I thought you were trying to get rid of me."

"Honestly, old girl, I planned to throw you into the canal." They both laughed again.

30 Lola came in carrying an electric iron and her wet apron. She arranged a towel on a chair, unscrewed the light bulb, plugged the iron into a socket hanging from the electric cord, and stood waiting for the iron to get hot. The apron was too wet to iron so she hung it from the shed roof to dry. Kneeling before the chair, she began to press a blue dress she intended to wear to work. Lola had five dresses, all bought second-hand by Julia, and she always seemed to be washing or ironing one of them just before going out. Julia had often scolded her for leaving such things to the last minute and now, irritation with her stepdaughter mounting, Julia rummaged through the wardrobe pulling out one wrinkled dress after another.

"You're going to have to spend a little time ironing these," she said.

"Sure I will, Julia, but not now. I've got to go to work."

"And why did you leave those rags behind the door? They belong in the box. You don't like to do anything! You're as lazy as they make them. Just because your father never tells you anything you take advantage. I started to work when I was a tiny kid. You sly brat! You'll see how you make out when you get married. You are just like your mother! You can't do a thing. I'm going to bit you even though your father makes me pay for it!"

Guillermo and Lola were silent at Julia's outburst. In the past Guillermo had attempted to defend his favorite daughter's distaste for housework, but Julia had always argued him down. When he said that Lola worked in a shop all day and had a right to rest when she was at home, Julia retorted, with justice, that she too peddled towels all day and then came home to cook and clean for everyone. When Guillermo protested that Lola was still young, Julia pointed to the many fifteen-year-old girls in the neighborhood who already had babies. "She will be hitching up with a man soon and she still doesn't know how to work properly." Guillermo had no answers; all he could do was slip his daughter money once in a while. He had to keep peace with Julia, for without her he would be lost.

35   Guillermo had prospered in the seven years he had been with Julia, and he was still grateful to his friend Canuto for advising him to join up with a woman much older than himself. That was after his first wife, Esmeralda, had deserted him for a jewelry-worker. Penniless because he had spent all his money getting his three children back from their mother, he began looking for someone who could take care of them. He had seen Julia selling *enchiladas* outside the bathhouse where he went every Saturday and recognized her as a neighbor whose son he had played with when he was a child. Since Julia did not remember him, he never mentioned this to her or to Maclovio, her son. She had seemed to him a likely candidate for marriage and he made a point of buying something from her and talking with her every time he saw her.

Julia, too, had been willing to talk and she told him all about herself. Her father had been a miner in Guanajuato but had abandoned his wife and children. He came to Mexico City where he fell in love with Rufelia, Julia's mother, who was many years his junior, and lived with her in free union for thirty-five contented years. In this marriage he was kind and good but always very poor.

On her part Julia was pleased with Guillermo's youth, fair skin, and mild manner and impressed by the fact that he neither smoked nor drank. When he invited her to go bicycle riding she accepted, and after one or two walks together in the Villa they agreed to join in free union. Guillermo and his three children, the youngest then aged two, thereupon moved into Julia's room. She had hoped to be able to stay home and keep house, but she soon found that she would have to hustle if the children were not to go hungry. She also learned that her husband's placid nature had a drawback; at night he slept peacefully by her side and only rarely showed sexual interest in her. He said that he was afraid the children would notice and that this inhibited him. But he never lost his temper or beat her and she enjoyed his good-humored joking. She became fond of him and the children, even though she realized that in this relationship she would have to give more than she received.

One day Guillermo saw miniature water bottles in metal stands on sale at a toy market. He figured out how to produce them inexpensively and went into business again. He bought the bottles at a glass factory, trading in broken glass to bring down the price. The other necessary equipment—the metal strips, rivets, chains, corks, labels, wax paper, wire, and aluminum paint—he bought in quantity at a cost of about twenty-three centavos a toy.

He kept no record of how many bottles he produced and sold but he had the impression that at the beginning he made from one hundred and fifty to two hundred a day. "I worked without stopping from morning till night. I was working like an animal. You know, I was sort of going crazy. People talked to me and suddenly I answered with something else, like that, without noticing it. I was losing my reason from all the work. I tell you, I never left this table, just worked and worked."

Another of Guillermo's money-making schemes had been to supply electric current to four of his closest neighbors by running extension cords from his light socket to theirs through the walls. His neighbors paid him a fixed monthly sum well under the minimum of the electric company, and he made a profit because of the reduced rates on higher consumption of power. That is, it worked out for Guillermo so long as the neighbors used one weak light bulb and were sparing in their use of electrical appliances. To protect his interests Guillermo had to become overseer; this led to quarrels and finally to the discontinuance of the scheme.

40   In his spare time Guillermo worked on various inventions. He was most hopeful about a hand-operated apparatus he had made out of various pieces of scrap (a typewriter roller, a crank, a corset stay) to speed up pasting labels on a child's lottery game. Above the roller Guillermo fixed a perforated tin can containing glue. The glue dripped onto the roller, making it possible for him to paste labels rapidly and to produce the games in some quantity at his workshop. But he did not have the money to go into business nor had he yet looked for an outlet to market the product.

Guillermo was aware that his neighbors and in-laws criticized him. "I know what they say, that I'm a fool, that I'm sick in the head. But I know I'm not so why should I worry? I know what I want. I think I'm smarter than anyone else here because they are worse fools. No one else here has television or bicycles or a bottle refrigerator. And you know, it makes them mad that I'm getting along better. As if it was hurting them! That's why at times I would rather not do anything so that they would leave me alone. But I do my little inventions because I have to. Not everyone can do them."

Guillermo had continued making water bottles but his business began to fall off when a *compadre* in the *vecindad* copied his product and undersold him. Now he made only two hundred a week, selling them at a profit of about seventy-five pesos. He began to invest his money in unclaimed articles from pawnshops as well as in stolen goods, reselling them at a profit. At one time he had in his home three radios, a gold wristwatch, gold cuff links, and a ring with a precious stone. His chief handicap was lack of capital; he often had to beg loans from his wife or borrow from a moneylender at the exorbitant interest of twenty per cent every twenty-four days.

To remedy this situation, Guillermo organized a sort of mutual credit society that he called, simply, the "savings box." Members bought one or more tickets or shares at five pesos a week and were thereby entitled to borrow up to one hundred pesos on each share at an interest charge of three per cent a week. At the end of a year the fund was to be divided up among the shareholders. Guillermo, who kept the savings box in his home, dipped into it in small emergencies, repaying his loans without interest. He considered this his privilege since he was the administrator of the fund. He kept notebooks full of names, addresses, and figures, he gave receipts, he went personally to collect the weekly contributions from forgetful members, and he had the responsibility of guarding the money. He kept it in a cigar box—on his worktable during the day and under his bed at night. "It's just like a bank, see? I'm like a bank manager and take the deposits. It's like a cooperative society. It's like the Russians do, you see, when they build a house. It doesn't belong to one person but to many. That's what I'd like to do with this money, see if we can build us a little house. I mean all of us together and then we divide it up. This is a good thing, for instead of wasting their money on movies, they save it. That's how it grows big. Later we'll lend on things, instead of them going to the pawnshops where they give anything they feel like. God willing it will keep on growing!"

Guillermo stopped hammering and opened the savings box to count the money. After that he looked in a notebook to see who still owed money and calculated how much he would have in the box by the end of the day. He did this several times a day to relax and also because he felt the responsibility of his position.

45   Lola was still ironing, kneeling on the floor, Julia stood at the front door looking at the sky.

"Ay, what a hard rain we had last night!" she said to her husband. "It's a good thing you fixed the floor or we would have had water up to the mattress like that other time."

Guillermo nodded. "Yes, old girl, they say it rained hard but I didn't even know it for I was at the movies."

Going to the movies was Guillermo's one passion. Before he bought the TV set he had gone almost every night. Now he went two or three times a week because, he said, he did his best thinking there and got new ideas, especially from the American films. He often prayed for luck in the movies, reciting the same prayer over and over. Even when he fell asleep Guillermo did not consider it time wasted because he prayed in his dreams. Julia had been annoyed at first—he never took her with him and it cost money—but she later realized that somehow it helped him and she stopped complaining.

When Julia again complimented her husband on keeping their little house from being flooded, Guillermo smiled but said nothing. He had been especially pleased with this scheme for he had earned money with it. He had placed a high slab of stone on the doorsill to keep out the water and then he had raised the floor of the kitchen by covering it with three truckloads of gravel that he had obtained free from the overseer of a construction project. When the neighbors in the *vecindad* saw the improvement, they wanted to do the same. He had told them, "Good, if you want to fill in like I'm doing, I'll sell you gravel at ten pesos a load." He then arranged to give the overseer three pesos for each free load of gravel and made a profit of seven pesos a load. He was proud of his shrewdness. "It was good business, no? You have to be smart to make money here and there. I made more than one hundred pesos just from that. They benefited because if they had had to hire a truck it would have cost them more. Well, that's how we defend ourselves."

SOURCES FROM LITERARY STUDIES

Literary studies offers a number of methods for reading and interpreting texts. In Chapter 5, Literary Studies, Professor John Huntington, in his discussion of two of Elizabeth Bishop's short stories, illustrated a process of "reading in slow motion." This process allows the reader to recognize when something in the text is not as clear as it should be. Next we read a piece of criticism that looked at her work from a biographical perspective, from David Kalstone's literary biography, *Becoming a Poet: Elizabeth Bishop with Marianne Moore and Robert Lowell.* Literary biography is only one of many approaches that might be taken in studying literary texts. Professor Huntington listed several others: the psychoanalytic, reader response, feminist/ cultural studies, Marxist, new-historicism, and deconstruction.

Earlier in this chapter we followed Nada Markelis as she synthesized patterns she found in the earlier Bishop stories and Kalstone excerpt. For practice in developing a synthesis essay on your own, I have included here another short story by Bishop and another excerpt from the Kalstone book. "Gwendolyn," first published in *The New Yorker* in 1953, is the story of the friendship between an eight-year-old girl (the narrator) and Gwendolyn Appletree, who comes to visit her over the course of a summer. The Kalstone excerpt recounts what was happening in Bishop's life around the time she wrote "Gwendolyn" and then discusses the story itself. You might also want to consider what you've learned from reading Bishop's other stories or other excerpts from Kalstone's work.

In developing an interpretation that synthesizes material from several sources, you will probably focus on one or two elements of the stories that you see as significant, whether characters, mood, or images of various kinds. The following questions will help you get started.

THINKING ABOUT THE DISCIPLINE

Read each of the selections included here. Read the story and critical piece again, in "slow motion," taking note of confusions that persist as you read and reread. As you read, make notes in your journal about the textual conventions you notice, such as character, plot, images, and language in the story. In addition, notice how you respond personally to the confusions that do not clear up after the first reading. To what extent do these confusions reflect your sense of "interestedness"? As you read and reread the critical text, think about how it opens up the story for you. Does it clarify some of your confusion? Does it raise a new confusion that you find intriguing?

ASK YOURSELF

What are the special concerns of literary scholars? What have I learned thus far about the field? How do literary scholars make meaning from literary works and texts? What sorts of textual conventions do they pay attention to when they read? How do they write about literature? What is appropriate evidence for a literary interpretation? How is reading criticism different from reading literary works? What do we mean when we speak of the "interestedness" of a writer, reader, or literary scholar? How is the meaning-making process used by literary scholars different from that used by members of other disciplines?

GWENDOLYN
ELIZABETH BISHOP

■ ■ ■

My Aunt Mary was eighteen years old and away in "the States," in Boston, training to be a nurse. In the bottom bureau drawer in her room, well wrapped in soft pink tissue paper, lay her best doll. That winter, I had been sick with bronchitis for a long time, and my grandmother finally produced it for me to play with, to my amazement and delight, because I had never even known of its existence before. It was a girl doll, but my grandmother had forgotten her name.

She had a large wardrobe, which my Aunt Mary had made, packed in a toy steamer trunk of green tin embossed with all the proper boards, locks, and nailheads. The clothes were wonderful garments, beautifully sewn, looking old-fashioned even to me. There were long drawers trimmed with tiny lace, and a corset cover, and a corset with little bones. These were exciting, but best of all was the skating costume. There was a red velvet coat, and a turban and muff of some sort of moth-eaten brown fur, and, to make it almost unbearably thrilling, there was a pair of laced white glacé-kid boots, which had scalloped tops and a pair of too small, dull-edged, but very shiny skates loosely attached to their soles by my Aunt Mary with stitches of coarse white thread.

The looseness of the skates didn't bother me. It went very well with the doll's personality, which in turn was well suited to the role of companion to an invalid. She had lain in her drawer so long that the elastic in her joints had become weakened; when you held her up, her head fell gently to one side, and her outstretched hand would rest on yours for a moment and then slip wearily off. She made the family of dolls I usually played with seem rugged and childish: the Campbell Kid doll, with a childlike scar on her fore-head where she had fallen against the fender; the two crudely felt-dressed Indians, Hiawatha and Nokomis; and the stocky "baby doll," always holding out his arms to be picked up.

My grandmother was very nice to me when I was sick. During this same illness, she had already given me her button basket to play with, and her scrap bag, and the crazy quilt was put over my bed in the afternoons. The button basket was large and squashed and must have weighed ten pounds, filled with everything from the metal snaps for men's overalls to a set of large cut-steel buttons with deer heads with green glass eyes on them. The scrap bag was interesting because in it I could find pieces of my grandmother's house dresses that she was wearing right then, and pieces of my grandfather's Sunday shirts. But the crazy quilt was the best entertainment. My grand-mother had made it long before, when such quilts had been a fad in the little Nova Scotian village where we lived. She had collected small, irregularly shaped pieces of silk or velvet of all colors and got all her lady and gentleman friends to write their names on them in pencil–their names, and sometimes a date or word or two as well. Then she had gone over the writing in chain stitch with silks of different colors, and then put the whole thing together on maroon flannel, with feather-stitching joining the pieces. I could read well enough to make out the names of people I knew, and then my grandmother would sometimes tell me that that particular piece of silk came from Mrs. So-and-So's "going-away" dress, forty years ago, or that that was from a necktie of one of her brothers, since dead and buried in London, or that that was from India, brought back by another brother, who was a missionary.

5   When it grew dark—and this, of course, was very early—she would take me out of bed, wrap me in a blanket, and, holding me on her knees, rock me vigorously in the rocking chair. I think she enjoyed this exercise as much as I did, because she would sing me hymns, in her rather affectedly lugubri-ous voice, which suddenly thinned out to half its ordinary volume on the higher notes. She sang me "There is a green hill far away," "Will there be any stars in my crown?" and "In the sweet bye-and-bye." Then there were more specifically children's hymns, such as:

> Little children, little children,
> Who love their Redeemer,
> Are the jewels, precious jewels,
> Bright gems for his crown . . .

And then, perhaps because we were Baptists—nice watery ones—all the saints casting down their crowns (in what kind of a tantrum?) "around the glassy sea"; "Shall we gather at the river?"; and her favorite, "Happy day, happy day, when Jesus washed my sins away."

This is preliminary. The story of Gwendolyn did not begin until the fol-lowing summer, when I was in my usual summer state of good health and had forgotten about the bronchitis, the realistic cat-and-kitten family in my chest, and the doctor's cold stethoscope.

Gwendolyn Appletree was the youngest child and only daughter of a large, widely spaced family that lived away out, four or five miles, on a lonely farm among the fir trees. She was a year or so older than I—that is, about eight—and her five or six brothers, I suppose in their teens, seemed like grown men to me. But Gwendolyn and I, although we didn't see each other very often, were friends, and to me she stood for everything that the slightly repellent but fascinating words "little girl" should mean. In the first place, her beautiful name. Its dactyl trisyllables could have gone on forever as far as I was concerned. And then, although older, she was as small as I was, and blond, and pink and white, exactly like a blossoming apple tree. And she was "delicate," which, in spite of the bronchitis, I was not. She had diabetes. I had been told this much and had some vague idea that it was because of "too much sugar," and that in itself made Gwendolyn even more attractive, as if she would prove to be solid candy if you bit her, and her pure-tinted complexion would taste exactly like the icing-sugar Easter eggs or birthday-candle holders, held to be inedible, except that I knew better.

I don't know what the treatment for diabetes was at that time—whether, for example, Gwendolyn was given insulin or not, but I rather think not. My grandparents, however, often spoke disapprovingly of the way her parents would not obey the doctor's orders and gave her whatever she wanted to eat, including two pieces of cake for tea, and of how, if they weren't more sensible, they would never keep her. Every once in a while, she would have a mysterious attack of some sort, "convulsions" or a "coma," but a day or two later I would see her driving with her father to the store right next door to our house, looking the same as ever and waving to me. Occasionally, she would be brought to spend the day or afternoon with me while her parents drove down the shore to visit relatives.

These were wonderful occasions. She would arrive carrying a doll or some other toy; her mother would bring a cake or a jar of preserves for my grandmother. Then I would have the opportunity of showing her all my possessions all over again. Quite often, what she brought was a set of small blocks that exactly fitted in a shallow cardboard box. These blocks were squares cut diagonally across, in clear reds, yellows, and blues, and we arranged them snugly together in geometric designs. Then, if we were careful, the whole thing could be lifted up and turned over, revealing a similar brilliant design in different colors on the other side. These designs were completely satisfying in their forthrightness, like the Union Jack. We played quietly together and did not quarrel.

10 Before her mother and father drove off in their buggy, Gwendolyn was embraced over and over, her face was washed one last time, her stockings were pulled up, her nose was wiped, she was hoisted up and down and swung around and around by her father and given some white pills by her mother. This sometimes went on so long that my grandfather would leave abruptly for the barn and my grandmother would busy herself at the sink and start singing a hymn under her breath, but it was nothing to the scenes of tenderness when they returned a few hours later. Then her parents al-

most ate her up, alternately, as if she really were made of sugar, as I half suspected. I watched these exciting scenes with envy until Mr. and Mrs. Appletree drove away, with Gwendolyn standing between them in her white dress, her pale-gold hair blowing, still being kissed from either side. Although I received many demonstrations of affection from my grandparents, they were nothing like this. My grandmother was disgusted. "They'll kiss that child to death if they're not careful," she said. "Oh, lallygagging, lally-gagging!" said my grandfather, going on about his business.

I remember clearly three episodes of that summer in which Gwendolyn played the role of beautiful heroine—the role that grew and grew until finally it had grown far beyond the slight but convincing talents she had for acting it.

Once, my grandparents and I went to a church picnic. As I said, we were Baptists, but most of the village, including the Appletrees, were Presbyterians. However, on social occasions I think the two sects sometimes joined forces, or else we were broad-minded enough to go to a Presbyterian picnic—I'm not sure. Anyway, the three of us, dressed in our second-best, took a huge picnic supper and drove behind Nimble II to the picnic grounds beside the river. It was a beautiful spot; there were large spruce and pine trees right to the edge of the clear brown water and mossy terra-cotta-colored rocks; the ground was slippery with brown pine needles. Pans of beans and biscuits and scalloped potatoes were set out on long tables, and all our varieties of pickles and relishes (chowchows and piccalillis), conserves and preserves, cakes and pies, parkins and hermits—all glistening and gleaming in the late sunshine—and water for tea was being brought to the boil over two fires. My grandmother settled herself on a log to talk to her friends, and I went wading in the river with mine. My cousin Billy was there, and Seth Hill, and the little McNeil twins, but Gwendolyn was missing. Later, I joined my family for supper, or as all Nova Scotians call their suppers, "tea." My grandmother spoke to one of the Appletree boys, filling his plate beside us, and asked him where his father and mother were, and how Gwendolyn was.

"Pretty poorly," he answered, with an imitative elderly-man shake of his head. "Ma thought we'd lost her yesterday morning. I drove down and got the doctor. She's resting better today, though."

We went on drinking our tea and eating in silence, and after a while my grandfather started talking about something else. But just before we finished, when it was beginning to get gray, and a sweet, dank, fresh-water smell had suddenly started to come up off the river, a horse and buggy turned rapidly in to the picnic grounds and pulled up beside us. In it were Mr. and Mrs. Appletree, and Gwendolyn—standing between them, as usual—wearing one of her white dresses, with a little black-and-white-checked coat over it. A great fuss was made over them and her, and my grandfather lifted her down and held her on his knee, sitting on one of the rough benches beside the picnic tables. I leaned against him, but Gwendolyn wouldn't speak to me; she just smiled as if very pleased with everything. She looked prettier and more delicate than ever, and her cheeks were bright pink. Her mother made her a cup of weak tea, and I could see my grandmother's look as the sugar went into it. Gwendolyn had wanted to come so badly, her mother said, so they thought they'd bring her just for a little while.

15   Some time after this, Gwendolyn was brought to visit me again, but this time she was to spend the whole day and night and part of the next day. I was very excited, and consulted with my grandmother endlessly as to how we should pass the time—if I could jump with her in the barn or take her swimming in the river. No, both those sports were too strenuous for Gwendolyn, but we could play at filling bottles with colored water (made from the paints in my paintbox), my favorite game at the moment, and in the afternoon we could have a dolls' tea party.

Everything went off very well. After dinner, Gwendolyn went and lay on the sofa in the parlor, and my grandmother put a shawl over her. I wanted to pretend to play the piano to her, but I was made to stop and go outside by myself. After a while, Gwendolyn joined me in the flower garden and we had the tea party. After that, I showed her how to trap bumblebees in the foxgloves, but that was also put a stop to by my grandmother as too strenuous and dangerous. Our play was not without a touch of rustic corruption, either. I can't remember what happened, if anything, but I do remember being ordered out of the whitewashed privy in the barn after we had locked ourselves in and climbed on the seats and hung out the little window, with its beautiful view of the elm-studded "interval" in back of us. It was just getting dark; my grandmother was very stern with me and said we must never lock ourselves in there, but she was objectionably kind to Gwendolyn, who looked more angelic than ever.

After tea, we sat at the table with the oil lamp hanging over it for a while, playing with the wonderful blocks, and then it was bedtime. Gwendolyn was going to sleep in my bed with me. I was so overwrought with the novelty of this that it took me a long time to get ready for bed, but Gwendolyn was ready in a jiffy and lay on the far side of the bed with her eyes shut, trying to make me think she was asleep, with the lamplight shining on her blond, blond hair. I asked her if she didn't say her prayers before she got into bed and she said no, her mother let her say them in bed, "because I'm going to die."

At least, that was what I thought she said. I couldn't quite believe I had really heard her say it and I certainly couldn't ask her if she had said it. My heart pounding, I brushed my teeth with the icy well water, and spat in the china pot. Then I got down on my knees and said my own prayers, half aloud, completely mechanically, while the pounding went on and on. I couldn't seem to make myself get into my side of the bed, so I went around and picked up Gwendolyn's clothes. She had thrown them on the floor. I put them over the back of a chair—the blue-and-white-striped dress, the waist, the long brown stockings. Her drawers had lace around the legs, but they were very dirty. This fact shocked me so deeply that I recovered my voice and started asking her more questions.

"I'm asleep," said Gwendolyn, without opening her eyes.

20   But after my grandmother had turned out the lamp, Gwendolyn began to talk to me again. We told each other which colors we liked best together, and I remember the feeling of profound originality I experienced when I insisted, although it had just occurred to me, that I had always liked black and brown together best. I saw them floating in little patches of velvet, like the crazy quilt, or smooth little rectangles of enamel, like the paint-sample cards I was always begging for at the general store.

Two days after this visit, Gwendolyn did die. One of her brothers came in to tell my grandmother—and I was there in the kitchen when he told her—with more of the elderly-man headshakes and some sad and ancient phrases. My grandmother wept and wiped her eyes with her apron, answering him with phrases equally sad and ancient. The funeral was to be two days later, but I was not going to be allowed to go.

My grandfather went, but not my grandmother. I wasn't even supposed to know what was taking place, but since the Presbyterian church was right across the village green from our house, and I could hear the buggies driving up over the gravel, and then the bell beginning to ring, I knew quite well, and my heart began to pound again, apparently as loudly as the bell was ringing. I was sent out to play in the yard at the far side of the house, away from the church. But through one of the kitchen windows—the kitchen was an ell that had windows on both sides—I could see my curious grandmother drawing up her rocking chair, as she did every Sunday morning, just behind a window on the other side of the ell, to watch the Presbyterians going to church. This was the unacknowledged practice of the Baptists who lived within sight of the church, and later, when they met at their own afternoon service, they would innocently say to each other things like "They had a good turnout this morning" and "Is Mrs. Peppard still laid up? I missed her this morning."

But today it was quite different, and when I peeked in at my grandmother at one side of the ell, she was crying and crying between her own peeks at the mourners out the other side. She had a handkerchief already very wet, and was rocking gently.

It was too much for me. I sneaked back into the house by the side door and into the shut-up parlor, where I could look across at the church, too. There were long lace curtains at the window and the foxgloves and bees were just outside, but I had a perfectly clear, although lace-patterned, view of everything. The church was quite large—a Gothic structure made of white clap-boards, with non-flying buttresses, and a tall wooden steeple—and I was as familiar with it as I was with my grandmother. I used to play hide-and-seek among the buttresses with my friends. The buggy sheds, now all filled, were at the back, and around the large grass plot were white wooden pillars with double chains slung slackly between them, on which my cousin Billy, who lived right next door to the church, and I liked to clamber and swing.

25   At last, everyone seemed to have gone inside, and an inner door shut. No, two men in black stood talking together in the open outside doorway. The bell suddenly stopped ringing and the two men vanished, and I was afraid of being in the parlor alone, but couldn't leave now. Hours seemed to go by. There was some singing, but I didn't recognize the hymns, either because I was too nervous or because, as they sometimes did, the Presbyterians sang hymns unfamiliar to me.

I had seen many funerals like this before, of course, and I loved to go with my grandfather when he went to the graveyard with a scythe and a sickle to cut the grass on our family's graves. The graveyard belonging to the village was surely one of the prettiest in the world. It was on the bank of the river, two miles below us, but where the bank was high. It lay small and green and white, with its firs and cedars and gravestones balancing against the dreaming lavender-red Bay of Fundy. The headstones were mostly rather thin, coarse white marble slabs, frequently leaning slightly, but there was a scattering of small urns and obelisks and broken columns. A few plots were lightly chained in, like the Presbyterian church, or fenced in with wood or iron, like little gardens, and wild rosebushes grew in the grass. Blueberries grew there, too, but I didn't eat them, because I felt I "never knew," as people said, but once when I went there, my grandmother had given me a teacup without a handle and requested me to bring her back some teaberries, which "grew good" on the graves, and I had.

And so I used to play while my grandfather, wearing a straw hat, scythed away, and talked to me haphazardly about the people lying there. I was, of course, particularly interested in the children's graves, their names, what ages they had died at—whether they were older than I or younger. The favorite memorial for small children was a low rectangle of the same coarse white marble as the larger stones, but with a little lamb recumbent on top. I adored these lambs, and counted them and caressed them and sat on them. Some were almost covered by dry, bright-gold lichen, some with green and gold and gray mixed together, some were almost lost among the long grass and roses and blueberries and teaberries.

But now, suddenly, as I watched through the window, something happened at the church across the way. Something that could not possibly have happened, so that I must, in reality, have seen something like it and imagined the rest; or my concentration on the one thing was so intense that I could see nothing else.

The two men in black appeared again, carrying Gwendolyn's small white coffin between them. Then—this was the impossibility—they put it down just outside the church door, one end on the grass and the other lifted up a little, to lean at a slight angle against the wall. Then they disappeared inside again. For a minute, I stared straight through my lace curtain at

Gwendolyn's coffin, with Gwendolyn shut invisibly inside it forever, there, completely alone on the grass by the church door.

30   Then I ran howling to the back door, out among the startled white hens, with my grandmother, still weeping, after me.

If I care to, I can bring back the exact sensation of that moment today, but then, it is also one of those that from time to time are terrifyingly thrust upon us. I was familiar with it and recognized it; I had already experienced it once, shortly before the bronchitis attack of the previous winter. One evening, we were all sitting around the table with the lamp hanging above it; my grandfather was dozing in the Morris chair, my grandmother was crocheting, and my Aunt Mary, who had not yet gone away to Boston, was reading *Maclean's Magazine*. I was drawing pictures when suddenly I remembered something, a present that had been given to me months before and that I had forgotten all about. It was a strawberry basket half filled with new marbles—clay ones, in the usual mottled shades of red, brown, purple, and green. However, in among them were several of a sort I had never seen before: fine, unglazed, cream-colored clay, with purple and pink lines around them. One or two of the larger ones of this sort even had little sprigs of flowers on them. But the most beautiful of all, I thought, was a really big one, probably an inch and a half in diameter, of a roughly shiny glazed pink, like crockery. It moved me almost to tears to look at it; it "went right through me."

Anyway, I started thinking about these marbles—wondering where they had been all this time, where I had put them, if they had got lost—until at last it became unbearable and I had to go and find them. I went out to the kitchen in the dark and groped around on the floor of a cupboard where I kept some of my belongings. I felt the edges of riffled old books and sharp mechanical toys, and then, at the back, I did feel the strawberry basket. I dragged it out and carried it into the sitting room.

My relatives paid no attention. I stared into the basket and took out a few of the marbles. But what could have happened? They were covered with dirt and dust, nails were lying mixed in with them, bits of string, cobwebs, old horse chestnuts blue with mildew, their polish gone. The big pink marble was there, but I hardly recognized it, all covered with dirt. (Later, when my grandmother washed it off, it was as good as new, of course.) The broad lamp flame started to blur; my aunt's fair hair started to blur; I put my head down on top of the marbles and cried aloud. My grandfather woke up with a jerk and said, "Heavens, what ails the child now?" Everyone tried to comfort me—for what, they had no idea.

A month or so after the funeral—it was still summer—my grandparents went away for the day to visit Cousin Sophy, "over the mountain." I was supposed to stay with another aunt, the mother of my cousin Billy, and to play with him while they were gone. But we soon left his yard and wandered back to mine, which was larger and more interesting, and where we felt the additional charm of being all alone and unwatched. Various diversions, quarrels, and reconciliations made up the long, sunny afternoon. We sucked water from jelly glasses through chive straws until we reeked of them, and fought for the possession of insects in matchboxes. To tease me, Billy deliberately stepped on one of the boxes and crushed its inhabitant flat. When we had made up after this violence, we sat and talked for a while, desultorily, about death in general, and going to heaven, but we were growing a little bored and reckless, and finally I did something really bad: I went in the house and upstairs to my Aunt Mary's bedroom and brought down the tissue-paper-wrapped, retired doll. Billy had never seen her before and was as impressed with her as I had been.

35   We handled her carefully. We took off her hat and shoes and stockings, and examined every stitch of her underclothes. Then we played vaguely at "operating" on her stomach, but we were rather too much in awe of her for that to be a success. Then we had the idea of adorning her with flowers. There was a clump of Johnny-jump-ups that I thought belonged to me; we picked them and made a wreath for the nameless doll. We laid her out in the garden path and outlined her body with Johnny-jump-ups and babies'-breath and put a pink cosmos in one limp hand. She looked perfectly beautiful. The game was more exciting than "operation." I don't know which one of us said it first, but one of us did, with wild joy—that it was Gwendolyn's funeral, and that the doll's real name, all this time, was Gwendolyn.

But then my grandparents drove into the yard and found us, and my grandmother was furious that I had dared to touch Aunt Mary's doll. Billy was sent straight home and I don't remember now what awful thing happened to me.

ABOUT "GWENDOLYN"
DAVID KALSTONE

■ ■ ■

In November 1951 Bishop set out on a trip that would change the course of her life. She had won the first Lucy Martin Donnelly Fellowship from Bryn Mawr and sailed from New York on a Norwegian freighter (nine passengers) bound for the Straits of Magellan. Bishop had read a great deal about South America, and especially admired E. Lucas Bridges's *Uttermost Part of the Earth,* a book which, "although it is factual and not a fact of the imagination, should be classed with *Robinson Crusoe* for a suspense of strangeness and ingenuity and courage and loneliness." She envisioned herself as "a sleeping mouse dreaming of nibbling away to measure the circumference of a

From *Becoming a Poet.*

vast dream cheese." Loneliness, measurement, and dream—these were in-separable promptings which made her interest in travel seem, as her metaphor suggests, more like an appetite, a wary curiosity which guesses at, yearns for the interior from a tour of its circumference.

In Rio de Janeiro, Bishop stopped over to visit Brazilian friends. There, she had a violent allergic reaction to the fruit of the cashew and had to give up her dream trip to the Straits of Magellan. After she recovered, finding herself "enthralled by the Brazilian geography and landscape, by the para-doxical, affectionate, spontaneous Brazilian people, and the complications of a world at once feudal, 19th century, and contemporary," she decided to stay on and started building a country home (near Petrópolis, a mountain resort about forty miles from Rio) with Lota de Macedo Soares, an old friend whom she had first met in New York in 1942. For some fifteen years, with occasional visits to New York, Bishop shared with Lota their house in the mountains and an apartment in Rio de Janeiro. What began by accident, al-most as a whim, soon became, thanks to Lota, a deep attachment. It was Lota who mediated Brazil for her, whose understanding and whose way of life made Bishop almost instantly a part of the world that so attracted her. Elizabeth Hardwick, who saw them often while she and Lowell were in Brazil in 1962, describes Lota as

> witty indeed, civilized—and yet different from the women I had known. She had wonderful, glistening, dark eyes and wore glistening dark-rimmed glasses. You felt, or I felt, in her the legacy or curse of the Spanish-Portuguese women of the upper classes. Some of the privileges and many of the restraining expecta-tions were there, and they were not altogether in balance because she was not smug and not naturally tropical and indolent. She spoke French and had lived in France, I think. Her English was fluent, fractured, and utterly compelling.

However talkative and sophisticated, Lota was also, in Hardwick's eyes,

> somehow melancholy too, the Iberian strain. I think there was great shyness also, and the rather unbalancing combination of the proper and the misfit . . . It did not appear that Lota got on well with most of her family, her sister or sis-ters. Brazil pioneered in the face-lift and that gives you some idea of the occu-pation of the well-to-do Brazilian woman.
>
> L. was very intense indeed, emotional, also a bit insecure as we say, and loyal, devoted and smart and lesbian and Brazilian and shy, masterful in some ways, but helpless also. She adored Elizabeth and in the most attractive way, in this case somewhat fearfully, possessively, and yet modestly and without any tendency to oppress.
>
> The two were a *combinazione* very striking. Lota would drive a car with great zest and speed and Elizabeth couldn't or didn't drive. Lota was helpless in the kitchen and about the household, which Elizabeth indeed was not. Lota was watchful in the matter of Elizabeth's drinking and the sober period had lasted many years and did not last out the summer, when at the end there was a brief, I think, regression or defiance or just plain inclination.

But on the whole Bishop thrived in what she herself felt was "an atmosphere of uncritical affection."

She would write to Lowell in the second year of her stay: "I am extremely happy, for the first time in my life." The change was especially striking after her "dismal" year in Washington as Consultant in Poetry at the Library of Congress and after an equally depressing stay at Yaddo in the fall and winter of 1950–51. As she put it to Lowell, "I certainly didn't really want to wander around the world in a drunken daze for the rest of my life—so it's all fine and dandy."

Alcohol and asthma continued to rob Bishop of rest and her work time, as they had for years. We know more about her afflictions in the late 1940s and the 1950s because Bishop had begun to report them in detail in her letters to a New York doctor, Anny Baumann, who served Bishop all her later life not just as a physician but as conscience and even psychiatric adviser. The connection was important enough for Baumann to become the dedicatee of her next book, *A Cold Spring*. Bishop explains to Dr. Baumann that she has had asthma from childhood on but that in the 1940s she has had it almost every day and night, has never been able to lie down in bed. Her letters record a constant struggle to find an effective drug, especially in Brazil—mostly falling back on adrenaline and cortisone and packages of monosodium sulfate sent with some difficulty from a New York pharmacy. Her alcoholism was equally troubling: the usual—but no less painful for its familiarity—roller coaster of depression, drinking bouts, guilty recovery, and resolutions to stop drinking. Her father, grandfather, and three uncles had to give up alcohol—and Bishop is acutely conscious in 1951 that she has reached the age at which her father died. Her drinking seems to have dwindled in Brazil—to one or two evenings a month—thanks to Lota's influence and a life that seemed less exhausting, less upsetting than in her habitats to the north, Key West and New York.

5   Lota's family had been prominent in Brazilian society and in diplomatic circles for generations, and through her Bishop met most of the country's writers, artists, and intellectuals, though her version for Lowell was that she knew about ten people, two of them " 'literary'—and I go to Rio once in three or four months." Nor did she feel out of touch with American literary life. "I was always too shy to have much 'intercommunication' in New York, anyway, and I was miserably lonely there most of the time . . . "

Brazil placed Bishop at an enabling distance from America. She had all the "news" she needed through correspondence and periodicals. (They subscribed to *Partisan Review, The Hudson Review* and *Kenyon Review, Botteghe Oscure, Poetry,* the airmail *New York Times Book Review,* and so on.) But more important, she began to write letters, fiction, and poems which were to allow her to be both "in the world" and (to use the title of her story) "in the village." She led a life, in its intimacies and domesticities, curiously reminiscent of her happiest years—the early ones in Nova Scotia. In its strangeness there was an odd streak of familiarity: "What I'm really up to," she was to say much later, "is recreating a sort of deluxe Nova Scotia all over again in Brazil. And now I'm my own grandmother." She found herself trying to write a poem about salt codfish, "having come from the land where it's prepared to the lands where it's a weekly institution."

By the middle of 1952 it was clear that Bishop planned to stay in Brazil. On a brief trip to the United States, she packed up all her books, which were to be in the studio that Lota was having built especially for her. Though she and Lota kept an apartment in Rio "on that famous carte postale beach," Bishop always preferred the house in Petrópolis, where the country was "magnificent and wild." It wasn't just the setting which drew her, but also the fact that for years the house wasn't finished, that there was a Crusoe-like element of improvisation and planning in their lives. The house, "ultra-modern," was on the side of a black granite mountain "with a waterfall at one end, clouds coming into the living room in the middle of the conversation, etc." At first they had to use oil lamps; the floors weren't yet laid, just cement "covered with dogs' footprints." But there were all the Key West flowers she knew, plus orchids, Northern apples, and pears.

By the time Elizabeth Hardwick visited in 1962, the house was

> filled with beautiful old furniture of polished Brazilian woods; a large old painted mermaid ship's prow stood in the hall and all about there were brilliant little treasures collected by Elizabeth—crèches made by nuns, necklaces of feathers made by Indians, shells, boxes, paintings. And they had their Manuel-zinhos (or one such) and a few not very handy half-breeds padding around barefoot. It was a setting, not elaborate, but personal, charming and done with careful, anxious expressiveness.

Bishop's studio, up behind the house and overlooking the waterfall, was built of gray-blue rock with mica in it—one large whitewashed room with a fireplace and a herringbone brick floor, a place where she could gather all her books and papers together after years of dispersal.

Sometimes life there reminded her of her daydream of being a lighthouse keeper "absolutely alone, with no one to interrupt my reading or just sitting—and although such dreams are usually dismissed at 16 or so they always haunt one a bit, I suppose—I now see a wonderful cold rocky shore in the Falklands, or a house in Nova Scotia on the bay, *exactly* like my grandmother's—idiotic as it is, and unbearable as the reality would be."

10   Once after three days alone in the Petrópolis house—alone except for the cat being dewormed and the toucan, which had a sore foot, Bishop wrote:

> The most terrific storm in my experience here raged all those days. (A family of seven were wiped out in a landslide in Petrópolis—the road was impassable, etc.—although I knew none of this until later.) And I read Coleridge, and read him, & read him—just couldn't stop—until he and the waterfall *roaring* under the windows, and ten times its usual size, were indistinguishable to my ears. By the time he'd had "flying irregular gout," got himself drenched once more, was in debt, hating his wife, etc.—I couldn't believe that I really existed, or not what you'd call *life,* compared to that—dry, no symptoms of any sort, fairly solvent, on good terms with all my friends (as far as I know).

Not that Brazil, at other moments, did not interfere with such absorption. There were the natural accidents, revolutions, even the steady procession of other people's babies through the house. Nearby—two minutes away— lived a Polish zoo man whose collection included a black jaguar, a camel, beautiful birds—and, a gift to her, the toucan. This of course provided material for many letters to Moore. The bird was called Uncle Sam. It was black with "electric blue eyes, a blue and yellow marked beak, blue feet, and red feathers here & there—a bunch under his tail like a sunset when he goes to sleep." Toucans sleep tails up over their backs and heads under their wings, "like large inverted commas." The blue skin glimpsed underneath when it bathed was "just the color of blueberries—or as if he had blue jeans on under the feathers." One night during the rainy season she forgets to put the cover on his cage. "It started pouring and when I rushed out he was standing stretched straight up with his beak in the air and his eyes shut, the water pouring down him—like Brancusi's 'Bird in Flight'—I didn't know he could make himself so long."

The joy in shaping such day-to-day encounters for her American correspondents—not only, but especially, Lowell and Moore—is apparent in her letters. More so than ever, they are full of poems in the making—sometimes, as with the toucan, entering into drafts but not finished. Through her letters Bishop made Brazil a place where she could lead congenially double lives. In one sense the letters were the shuttle between her art and her life, a new loom. Coleridge and the toucan, North and South—she could take the present in its confused and exotic and absorbing randomness and also, in correspondence, bring into play the distanced eye of friends. More important, her new home allowed her to heal the deepest breaches in her life—to strike a balance between village and city and to give voice to both the child and the adult, once sundered, in her experience. It is rare that the imaginative possibilities of a life find so real a base. But, as Auden said of Henry James—a passage Bishop was fond of quoting: "It is sometimes necessary for sons to leave the family hearth; it may well be necessary at least for intellectuals to leave their country as it is for children to leave their homes, not to get away from them, but to re-create them."

Not long after she settled in Brazil, and partly as a way of exercising her Portuguese, Bishop began translating what was to appear in 1957 as *The Diary of "Helena Morley."* Her original and more accurate title for it was *My Life as a Girl (Minha vida de menina)*; it was a well-known Brazilian book first published in 1942, the diary of a young girl between the ages of twelve and fifteen reared in the remote mining town of Diamantina, in the interior state of Minas Gerais, in the 1890s. "There's a huge family of aunts and uncles and ex-slaves, ruled by a grandmother, all very poor and religious and superstitious, and the girl really wrote extremely well. She is funny and hardheaded and the anecdotes are very full of detail about the life, food, clothes, priests, etc." What engaged Bishop's interest was the authenticity and mystery of youthful energies revealed in the child's *own* words: "This was a real, day-by-day diary, kept by a real girl, and anything resembling it that I could think of had been observed or made up, and written down, by adults."

Bishop's attention to childhood during these first years in Brazil, though it may have had its source in the losses and displacements she herself had experienced, went boldly beyond them. *"Helena Morley"* struck a vein she was to explore in fiction written at the same time that she was engaged in the translation. What gave her fiction its haunting and unfamiliar force was Bishop's reawakened sense of the recuperative powers of childhood, the secrets of survival—her own and those of the young "Helena Morley."

Robert Lowell, back in America after three years in Europe, wrote playfully and grumpily about Bishop's absence: "Like a rheumatic old aunt, I would gladly spoil all your fun just to have you back." In fact, the separation—and the correspondence it entailed—proved fruitful for both of them. Neither was able to write much poetry at the time. Both of them turned, under quite different pressures, to autobiographical prose; and each profited from the competitive scrutiny of their exchanges. Lowell had written her from Amsterdam of himself and Hardwick and Bishop: "You know we are a unique class, the only three American writers of our generation who don't have to work. Usury has made us; I can hear Karl Marx muttering out a review to prove that our biases are identical." Despite the proprietary tone and the glibness of the statement, Lowell was suggesting something important about his own work and Bishop's in the 1950s. Leisure allowed each of them to consolidate and assimilate the landscapes of their pasts. Even in Europe, Lowell was tempted in that direction. Choosing Amsterdam for his second winter in Europe—he and Hardwick had spent their first winter abroad in Italy—Lowell explained that the Dutch city had been "a baroque, worldly, presbyterian, canal-and-brick, glorious Boston." By the summer of 1955 he had decided, not without trepidation, to return to the Boston he had left so angrily twenty years before. He and Hardwick bought a house at 239 Marlborough Street, not far from where his parents once lived, but the thought of going back to Boston "sometimes makes me feel like a flayed man, who stands quivering and shivering in his flesh, while holding out a hand for his old sheet of skin." It was in the 1950s that both his parents died and that he began to suffer regular and severe psychotic episodes. The pressures were partly relieved or faced down in the move to Boston, in attempts at autobiographical prose, and eventually in the poems which would appear as *Life Studies* in 1959.

15   For Bishop, on the other hand, it was only in the protection of and prompted by a life both exotic and domestic that she began to write directly about the losses of her own childhood years: two remarkable stories, "In the Village," which tells of her mother's insanity and early disappearance from her life, and "Gwendolyn," the story of the death of a young playmate. Both were published in *The New Yorker* in 1953. She wrote "In the Village" in a single stretch, straight off the typewriter—the first time she'd ever done

such a thing. She had made notes for various bits of the story but no more, and then was given too much cortisone for her asthma—occasionally, still, it was very bad—and couldn't sleep. "I sat up all night in the tropical heat," she told Elizabeth Spires years later. "The story came from a combination of cortisone, I think, and the gin and tonic I drank in the middle of the night. I wrote it in two nights."

She told Lowell—encouraging him to write *his* autobiography—that writing the two stories had given her a great deal of satisfaction: "that desire to get things straight and tell the truth—it's almost impossible not to tell the truth in poetry, I think, but in prose it keeps eluding me in the funniest way." Lowell, too, found prose a recalcitrant medium: "a hell of a job," he wrote her, "it starts naked, ends as fake velvet." The point for each of them was not simply a deflection into prose. They were exploring the *limits* of prose as a vehicle for autobiography—just the reverse of what these efforts appeared to be. They were sharpening and altering their notions of what it meant to tell the truth in verse.

"In the Village" is the less oblique of Bishop's two autobiographical stories. But both of them bear out her remarks about the indirection of prose, as does the order in which they were written. "Gwendolyn," written first, recounts events which occurred two years or so after the crucial last breakdown and disappearance of Bishop's mother. Indeed, "Gwendolyn" elides those painful memories, with no explicit acknowledgment that it is odd for a young girl to be living with her aunts and grandparents. It recalls the mode of "The Baptism," that other story in which the suspension of family ties and the isolation of children are taken for granted. Such fore-shortened views of childhood—were these the necessary preludes to the writing of "In the Village," whose action underlies and precedes the earlier stories and more openly embraces the links between personal present and past? Lowell advised her to put the three "girls' stories" together as a "grown-up novel." They would indeed have made an arresting collection—not just for what they reveal about Bishop's early years, but for what they reveal of the strategies she needed in approaching the center of her youthful experience. "Gwendolyn" and "In the Village" are an especially striking diptych. Bishop tells both stories through the eyes of the young girl she was. The adult can be seen trying to recapture the waywardness and unpredictability of childhood vision, to which her translation of *"Helena Morley"* had helped attune her. Morley, "funny and hardheaded," had the toughness Bishop associated, often guiltily, with her own powers to survive a blasted childhood.

Both stories try to sort out loss, guilt, and strength—to find a style for survival and memory. "Gwendolyn" is the more schematic of the two; it insists, perhaps too rigorously, on causation and explanation. It recounts the death of a playmate, pampered and delicate in ways the narrator feels she herself as a child was not. The fact that Gwendolyn was diabetic only heightens her young friend's sense of her as a foil, the perfect little girl, all sugar and spice, carefully tended and dressed by doting parents.

("Patriquin," the surname of the "real" Gwendolyn, becomes "Appletree" in the story, a stylized reminder that the fictional Gwendolyn is "pink and white, exactly like a blossoming apple tree.") The figure of the doomed child is a magnet for a number of conflicting feelings. Her early death is one of Bishop's inexplicable childhood losses, like that of her own mother, or her cousin Arthur, near her own age, about whom she would write in "First Death in Nova Scotia" (1962). At the same time, she feels envy and even some revulsion for Gwendolyn as "beautiful heroine," a role that "grew and grew until finally it had grown far beyond the slight but convincing talents she had for acting it." Both she and her grandmother feel distaste for the saccharine demonstrativeness of Gwendolyn's parents, who almost "eat her up" and "kiss her to death." She finally comes to identify Gwendolyn with a doll of her Aunt Mary's, preciously hidden away in pink paper, and only once, when the young narrator has bronchitis, brought out for her to play with. The doll has lace drawers like Gwendolyn's, a contrast to her own ragged dolls. At the end of the story she and her cousin Billy do something "really bad" by ferreting out the doll, wreathing it in flowers, and then realizing "with wild joy" that the nameless doll should be called Gwendolyn and that they were performing her funeral.

The act serves as a kind of atonement, but is even more resonant because, along with envy, the child has at another level experienced a cautious identification with Gwendolyn. The shock of Gwendolyn's death is crystallized by a hallucination in which she sees the child's closed coffin standing outside the church and then imagines the dead girl "shut invisibly inside it forever, there, completely alone." She screams involuntarily; then she remembers howling with just such inexplicable pain a few years before when she discovered some prized marbles, especially a favorite pink one, encrusted with dirt. The horror of finding them soiled, buried in their strawberry basket, prompts a reaction like the one she was to have to Gwendolyn in her coffin, one of those sensations visited upon us without warning. Disorder, the loss of purity—these are particularly painful to the young girl. The specter of Gwendolyn in her coffin is very different from the children's graves with their toylike lambs which she admired in the village cemetery. The death of Gwendolyn confirms the burial of any sense of purity or immunity or pampering she might have associated with her own childhood, and the doll Gwendolyn's funeral, which closes the story, is inextricably bound to her own sense of being "bad," unworthy. The figure of Gwendolyn draws to it, then, a cluster of irreconcilable feelings: inexplicable loss of childhood figures, envy, identification with the death of the young. Through Gwendolyn's death the bristling contradictions can be both experienced and kept at a safe symbolic distance. The fiction has performed its function neatly. Too neatly, perhaps. Over and over Bishop consigns these children who die young—Gwendolyn, her cousin Arthur, Lucy in "The Baptism"—not to extinction so much as to a tortured perpetual innocence, "forever, alone" like the doll-like whitened figure of Cousin Arthur:

> But how could Arthur go,
> clutching his tiny lily,
> with his eyes shut up so tight
> and the roads deep in snow?

20   The image of youth "buried alive" was one she would counter in her next story, "In the Village." She seems now more at home with the lessons of *"Helena Morley,"* "the book that has kept her childhood for us, as fresh as paint."

●   ●   ●

NOTES[1]

1. "although it is factual": EB, draft of introduction to the unfinished *Brazil-Brasil* (V). See E. Lucas Bridges, *Uttermost Part of the Earth* (New York: E. P. Dutton, 1950).
1. "a sleeping mouse": Ibid.
2. a violent allergic reaction: EB to Anne Stevenson, August 15, 1965 (W).
2. "enthralled by the Brazilian geography": Ibid.
2. "witty indeed": Elizabeth Hardwick, in correspondence with the author.
2. "uncritical affection": EB to U. T. and Joe Summers, April 21, 1953.
3. "I am extremely happy": EB to RL, July 28, 1953 (H).
3. "all fine and dandy": Ibid.
3. explains to Dr. Baumann: EB to Dr. Anny Baumann, August 5, 1948.
4. the age at which her father died: EB to Dr. Anny Baumann, January 17, 1951.
5. "I go to Rio": EB to RL, May 20, 1955 (H).
5. "I was always too shy": EB to RL, July 28, 1953 (H).
6. "a weekly institution": EB to MM, June 5, 1956 (R).
7. "carte postale beach": EB to RL, March 21, 1952 (H).
7. "magnificent and wild": Ibid.
7. "with a waterfall": Ibid.
7. all the Key West flowers: EB to MM, February 14, 1952 (R).
8. "filled with beautiful old furniture": Elizabeth Hardwick, in correspondence with the author.
9. "absolutely alone": EB to RL, July 27, 1960 (H).
10. "The most terrific storm": EB to RL, December 2, 1956 (H).
10. "electric blue eyes": EB to MM, February 14, 1952 (R).
10. "color of blueberries": EB to Dr. Anny Baumann, July 28, 1952.
10. "It started pouring": EB to RL, December 5, 1953 (H).
11. "It is sometimes necessary": W. H. Auden, speaking of Henry James at the Grolier Club, New York, October 24, 1946, as quoted by Moore in her commentary on Auden in *Predilections,* reprinted in Moore, *Complete Prose,* p. 465.
12. "There's a huge family": EB to RL, November 30, 1954 (H).
12. "a real, day-by-day diary": Introduction to *The Diary of "Helena Morley"* (New York: Farrar, Straus and Giroux, 1957), p. x; Bishop, *Collected Prose,* p. 82.
14. "Like a rheumatic old aunt": RL to EB, November 29, 1953 (V).
14. "a unique class": RL to EB, February 1952 (V).
14. "baroque, worldly, presbyterian": RL to EB, November 1951 (V).
14. "like a flayed man": RL to EB, July 18, 1955 (V).

---

[1]For an explanation of the abbreviations see p. 196.

15. "in two nights": EB, interview with Elizabeth Spires, *Paris Review* 80 (Summer 1981), p. 73.
16. "that desire to get things straight": EB to RL, May 20, 1955 (H).
16. "it starts naked": RL to EB, November 15, 1954 (V).
17. "girls' stories": RL to EB, January 1, 1954 (V).
18. "Patriquin": EB to Anne Stevenson, March 23, 1964 (W).
18. a role that "grew and grew": Bishop, "Gwendolyn," *Collected Prose,* p. 218.
19. "shut invisibly inside it": Ibid, p. 224.
20. "as fresh as paint": Introduction to *"Helena Morley,"* p. xxxiv; Bishop, *Collected Prose,* p. 108.

SOURCES FROM GEOLOGY

Research in geology contributes greatly to our understanding of our environment. In Chapter 8, Geology, Professor Donna Jurdy guided us through a reading of two scientific reports on the effects of oil exploration on the land in the Arctic National Wildlife Refuge (ANWR). You also read "The Great Alaskan Debate: Can Oil and Wilderness Mix?" by Timothy Egan. Included here are three additional sources related to geological research. The first, an article that appeared in *Science* magazine in November, 1987, looks at the long-term damage caused by oil exploration in Prudhoe Bay. The report covers a wide range of environmental issues but adds to our knowledge base in particular by focusing on the long-term, unanticipated impact of oil exploration on the northern Alaskan landscape.

The other two readings respond more directly to the political situation that existed at the time oil exploration seemed imminent in the Arctic National Wildlife Refuge, and will further expand your thinking about the impact of oil exploration on the environment. The first is a very brief insert from the *Congressional Quarterly Abstract* about the status of a bill to allow exploratory drilling. Then a short article from the "Washington Watch" section of the journal *BioScience* reports on the status of this same bill.

THINKING ABOUT THE DISCIPLINE

Read the three additional sources included here. As you read, make notes about your reading. Write about connections you notice between what you have learned from other readings about geology and the environment. How are these readings similar or different from your previous readings? How do these readings support or negate your personal views about the environment?

ASK YOURSELF

What have I learned thus far about geology? How do geologists observe the natural environment? What sorts of questions do they ask? How do they measure their observations? When do the "facts" they determine come into question? How does the knowledge generated by geologists contribute to debates in other areas of our society?

CUMULATIVE IMPACTS OF OIL FIELDS ON NORTHERN ALASKAN LANDSCAPES

D. A. WALKER, P. J. WEBBER, E. F. BINNIAN,
K. R. EVERETT, N. D. LEDERER,
E. A. NORDSTRAND, M. D. WALKER

■ ■ ■

Proposed further developments on Alaska's Arctic Coastal Plain raise questions about cumulative effects on arctic tundra ecosystems of development of multiple large oil fields. Maps of historical changes to the Prudhoe Bay Oil Field show indirect impacts can lag behind planned developments by many years and the total area eventually disturbed can greatly exceed the planned area of construction. For example, in the wettest parts of the oil field (flat thaw-lake plains), flooding and thermokarst covered more than twice the area directly affected by roads and other construction activities. Protecting critical wildlife habitat is the central issue for cumulative impact analysis in northern Alaska. Comprehensive landscape planning with the use of geographic information system technology and detailed geobotanical maps can help identify and protect areas of high wildlife use.

The Department of Interior has recommended leasing 1.5 million acres of the coastal plain portion of the Arctic National Wildlife Refuge (ANWR) for oil exploration (1–3). The recommendation was based on the nation's need for new energy resources and a perception that major ecological impacts could be avoided because of knowledge gained from experience in the Prudhoe Bay Oil Field. Although many lessons were learned at Prudhoe Bay about avoidance of problems related to construction in permafrost regions and conflicts with wildlife, there are still difficult issues regarding cumulative effects of the existing and proposed oil fields.

The regulatory definition of cumulative impacts is (4)

> . . . The impact on the environment which results from the incremental impact of the action when added to other past, present, and reasonably foreseeable future actions regardless of what agency (Federal or non-Federal) or person undertakes such actions. Cumulative impacts can result from individually minor but collectively significant actions taking place over a period of time.

Cumulative impacts are of particular concern in the ANWR because several oil fields may affect the wilderness and wildlife resources. A vast

D. A. Walker, P. J. Webber, M. D. Walker, Plant Ecology Laboratory, Institute of Arctic and Alpine Research, and Department of Environmental, Population, and Organismic Biology, University of Colorado, Boulder, CO 80309. E. F. Binnian and E. A. Nordstrand, North Slope Borough GIS, Anchorage, AK 99501. K. R. Everett, Byrd Polar Research Center and Department of Agronomy, Ohio State University, Columbus, OH 43210. N. D. Lederer, Plant Ecology Laboratory, Institute of Arctic and Alpine Research, University of Colorado, Boulder, CO 80309.

Source: From *Science*, Vol. 238, Nov. 6, 1987.

complex of roads, pipelines, and service centers stretching across the Arctic Coastal Plain could have unpredictable long-term impacts on the total function of the coastal plain ecosystem. The environmental impact statement process must, by law, examine cumulative impacts, but there currently are no standardized methods for doing this.

CUMULATIVE IMPACTS IN ARCTIC WETLANDS

Flooding and thermokarst are important aspects of cumulative impacts in arctic wetlands. Permafrost is largely responsible for poor drainage and for thaw lakes that cover the Arctic Coastal Plain. Many of the most valuable wetlands form in drained thaw-lake basins that represent one phase in the thaw-lake cycle (5). These low areas are particularly susceptible to flooding caused by road and gravel-pad construction. Most buildings, oil wells, and roads in the region are constructed on thick gravel pads that rise 1.5 to 2 m above the flat tundra. This design helps prevent melting of the underlying permafrost and subsequent subsidence of the roads or buildings, but it also causes roads and gravel pads to act as dams, intercepting the natural flow of water. Where roads traverse drained thaw-lake basins, flooding is a predictable result. Natural water levels, including their seasonal and year-to-year variability, are critical to maintaining the wetland diversity and function. A flooded wetland can have as large an impact on wildlife as a drained wetland because flooding alters the heterogeneous mosaic of water and terrestrial microsites essential for waterfowl and shorebird feeding, breeding, and nesting (6).

5   Thermokarst is a localized thawing of ground ice resulting in a surficial depression and eventual erosion (7). Thermokarst is involved with thaw-lake formation as a natural process (5), but it can also be initiated and accelerated by man's activities, and when in close proximity to buildings and roads, has the potential for destructive consequences. Such depressions often fill with water, and water's low albedo usually results in heat absorption at the site and further growth of the thermokarst feature. Thus, the process of thermokarst is difficult to stop once it has been initiated (8), and often it must run its course until a state of equilibrium is reestablished (9). Thick road berms, pilings for buildings, and elevated oil pipelines are examples of engineering designs that are used to prevent melting of ground ice. There are, however, numerous situations where it is difficult to prevent thermokarst. One example is in roadside areas where the combination of road dust, flooding, and warming effects of the road can result in thermokarst (10, 11). This is a common phenomenon along the older heavily traveled roads in the Prudhoe Bay Oil Field.

THE PRUDHOE BAY OIL FIELD:
EXPERIMENT IN ARCTIC ECOSYSTEM MANAGEMENT

Other published analyses of cumulative impacts have stressed the importance of examining large landscapes (12–18) and of using long-term historical case studies (1, 12, 16, 17). At Prudhoe Bay, we focused on three large

1. Geologists, enviromental, Biologists.

2. Impact on a wetland.

3.

22 km² areas where there have been major impacts. We mapped the original landscape from aerial photographs taken by the U.S. Navy in 1949, and then mapped sequential years of development from 1968 to 1983 using a series of aerial photographs taken by the oil industry. This information was entered into a geographic information system (GIS) data base consisting of layers of geobotanical information, natural disturbance, and anthropogenic disturbances (*19, 20*). The basic geobotany of the region was previously described and mapped (*21–25*).

We asked a series of specific questions regarding the history of development. What were the spatial arrangement and relative cover of natural geobotanical features (vegetation, water cover, landforms, surface forms, soils, and landscape units) before development? What were the rates of growth of the major disturbance types (for example, roads, gravel pads, and flooding)? Were the patterns of anthropogenic disturbances related to broad landscape units (flat thaw-lake plains as opposed to floodplains and terraces)? How do areas covered by direct, planned development (for example, roads and gravel pads) compare with areas covered by indirect, unplanned impacts (for example, flooding and thermokarst)? Are certain geobotanical features more frequently used than others for construction sites? Is there any evidence of synergistic impacts? [Synergistic impacts are those that have interactive reinforcement over time and are distinguished from cumulative impacts which represent a simple aggregation of impacts (*17*).] Here, we focus on the differences in impacts on the two major landscape units, (i) flat thaw-lake plains and (ii) floodplains and terraces. These units are areas of distinct similar geobotanical character and, to a large extent, define regional distribution patterns for plant and wildlife species. Flat thaw-lake plains are covered by oriented thaw lakes and drained thaw-lake basins. The areas between lakes are flat and generally wet with expanses of pond complexes and low-centered ice-wedge polygons. This unit contains drained thaw-lake wetland habitat and pingos (ice-cored hills), both of which are sites of high biotic diversity (*26–28*). The floodplains and terraces unit is associated with streams and rivers. It includes young terrace surfaces that have channel patterns and other topography typically associated with fluvial systems, and no oriented thaw lakes. This unit is particularly important in the total function of the landscape because the river systems have high floristic diversity and are movement corridors for numerous large animals such as caribou, musk-ox, grizzly bear, and wolf.

PATTERNS OF DEVELOPMENT

The Entire Oil Field. The Prudhoe Bay Oil Field presently occupies about 500 km² between the Kuparuk and Sagavanirktok rivers. In the final year of our study (1983), there were more than 350 km of roads, 21 km² of tundra covered by gravel, and another 14 km² that had been flooded because of road and gravel-pad construction. The pace of development proceeded at a nearly constant rate throughout the first 15 years since discovery of the

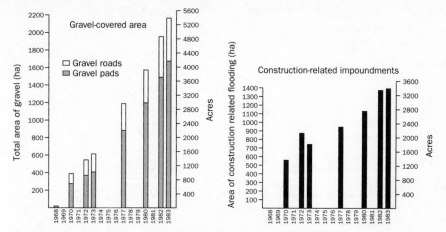

Figure 1. Historical progression of gravel placement and flooding in the Prudhoe Bay Oil Field. Bars are shown only for years of available photography. The more irregular growth of flooding reflects yearly differences in timing of aerial photographs (early summer photos generally have more flooding), varying amounts of summer precipitation, and new culverts which drain old impoundments (19).

field in 1968 (*19*) (Fig. 1). In 1983, the growth of the road network within the relatively new Kuparuk Oil Field just west of the Prudhoe Bay field was simultaneously proceeding at a rate similar to that at Prudhoe Bay, thus doubling the total rate of new development on the North Slope (*19*).

Comparison of Landscape Units. Approximately 1730 hectares had some form of disturbance by 1983. The area covered by gravel pads showed a steady increase throughout the 15-year period. New pads were built and others were enlarged to accommodate expanded camp facilities. In one instance, a pingo was removed to level the site for a gravel pad.

The patterns of disturbance within the two landscape units are distinctly different (Fig. 2). Within the flat thaw-lake plains, the rate of growth of the road network began leveling off after about 5 years. This pattern was noted previously for densely developed portions of the field (*19*).

Flooding was the most extensive impact on the flat thaw-lake plains, where over 22% of the area in the map was flooded. The most severe flooding occurred in drained lake basins, particularly where roads and gravel pads blocked the natural drainage patterns.

Excavations were essentially absent on the flat thaw-lake plains but were a dominant component of anthropogenic disturbance within the floodplains and terraces landscape unit. When Prudhoe Bay was first being developed, the obvious gravel resources in the braided rivers were heavily exploited. Gravel mining destroyed a portion of the narrow floodplain of the Putuligayuk River. In comparison, the extensive excavations on the broad, braided Sagavanirktok River floodplain had relatively minor effects on habitat along the river's margins. There was also a noticeable decline of the total

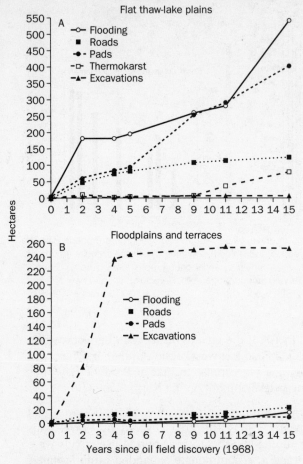

Figure 2. Historical progression of common anthropogenic disturbances on the principal two landscape units. (A) The pattern for roads follows a saturation curve for the total study area and for densely developed areas, but in less developed areas road growth continued at a steady pace throughout the period of the study. The inflection point at 5 years on the "Pads" curve reflects an oil-industry decision to increase oil-well density from one well per square mile to four wells per square mile. Flooding follows a fluctuating but steady growth and exceeds the area of any other single impact. Thermokarst shows a notable increase after 1977. (B) On the floodplains and terraces, excavations (gravel mines) are the primary disturbance. However, the study area did not include any drill pads on floodplains but these do occur in other parts of the oil field. Direct impacts are roads, pads, and excavations; indirect impacts include flooding and thermokarst. On the flat thaw-lake plains, indirect impacts exceed the direct impacts, whereas on the floodplains and terraces, direct impacts were dominant.

area affected in the Sagavanirktok River because annual flooding helped restore natural channel patterns. The implication is that narrow floodplains are poor sites for gravel mines, and broader braided rivers may offer some sites that could be naturally restored, providing precautions were taken not to block fish or wildlife corridors. There are still major gravel mines on the rivers, but most new mines are open-pit operations on old alluvial deposits away from rivers. Such mines are a good alternative because they completely avoid conflicts with extant riparian ecosystems.

Thermokarst—A Synergistic Impact.   Thermokarst occurs primarily on the flat thaw-lake plains. Its virtual absence on floodplains and terraces is due to low ground-ice content in these areas. The amount of thermokarst just exceeds the area covered by roads on the flat thaw-lake plains. There is generally a delay between the construction of a road or pad and the onset of thermokarst around the feature. The thermal effects are most noticeable where there is a combination of disturbance factors such as stripping the tundra vegetation mat, accumulation of large amounts of road dust, flooding, or heating of the tundra caused by flaring operations. Thermokarst associated with construction is thus an example of a synergistic effect. Figure 2 shows low levels of thermokarst before 1977, but increasing thereafter. At present, it is unlikely that the existence of the oil field alone would lead to widespread thermal disintegration of the landscape; however, the possibility that heat generated by the field operations combined with climatic warming (*28*) could lead to more extensive thawing of ground ice cannot be ruled out.

Direct Impacts Compared to Indirect Impacts.   If impacts are examined in terms of direct (roads, gravel pads, excavations) and indirect (flooding, thermokarst, construction debris, road dust) effects, there is considerable difference between landscape units. On the flat thaw-lake plains, indirect impacts exceeded direct impacts (844 compared to 560 ha). This was due largely to flooding, especially in the wettest portions of the flat thaw-lake plain. For example, in the region of the wettest terrain mapped, indirect impacts were more than double those of direct impacts (522 compared to 223 ha); in the floodplains and terraces, direct impacts (mostly excavations) were dominant.

15 *Selection of Well-drained Terrain in Wet Landscapes.*   It is of interest to know if certain vegetation types were preferentially (perhaps unintentionally) affected by disturbance. We found that there was a selection for well-drained sites where roads and pads are often routed around wet terrain (Fig. 3). Dry and moist sites are disproportionately selected as construction sites in wet landscapes, where they are less common and are also most valuable for waterfowl and shorebirds. They are well-drained components in mosaics of wetland habitat. Such sites are usually heterogeneous with high biotic diversity, as is the case in most complex landscapes with abundant habitat edge (*29*).

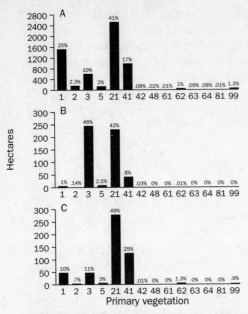

Figure 3. Areal analysis of the three 1:6000-scale maps as of 1983. (A) Percentage distribution of potential natural vegetation; (B) percentage of each vegetation type disturbed by flooding; (C) percentage of each vegetation type disturbed by gravel placement. For the entire data set there was no statistically significant difference between the gravel-covered vegetation and the natural distribution of vegetation types, but on wetter portions of the field there was a significant difference. The analysis excluded lakes because roads are normally routed around these. The total impact on vegetation type 3 (aquatic sedge marsh) covers over 53% of the total available area of this stand type and suggests that this unit is particularly susceptible to indirect impacts. Vegetation legend: 1, water; 2, aquatic grass marsh; 3, aquatic sedge marsh; 5, aquatic moss marsh; 21, wet sedge tundra; 41, moist, nontussock-sedge, dwarf-shrub tundra; 42, moist, tussock-sedge, dwarf-shrub tundra; 48, moist low shrubland; 61, dry, dwarf-shrub, fruticose-lichen tundra; 62, dry, dwarf-shrub, crustose-lichen tundra; 63, dry, dwarf-shrub, forb, lichen tundra; 64, dry, dwarf-shrub, forb, grass tundra; 81, dry forb tundra; and 99, barren.

CUMULATIVE IMPACT ANALYSIS AND FUTURE DEVELOPMENT IN NORTHERN ALASKA

Before judging the effectiveness of the designs used to prevent environmental damage on the North Slope, one must consider the information that was available at the time of development. For example, how well could potential impacts from flooding or thermokarst have been predicted and avoided 15 years ago? Undoubtedly, some areas should have been avoided altogether, but damage was less predictable in other areas. We now have the benefit of the Prudhoe Bay experience, but the lessons learned in the wet landscape at Prudhoe Bay may be less relevant in better drained areas such as the Arctic National Wildlife Refuge. For example, flooding would be less of a problem in the ANWR, but other unforeseen problems could develop. More extensive thermokarst could occur in acidic tundra areas, which are susceptible to damage from alkaline road dust (*11*). [The Prudhoe Bay Oil Field is in an area of alkaline tundra, which is highly buffered against the effects of dust (*11, 23, 25*).] The highly ice-rich permafrost terrain of the hilly landscapes combined with greater topographic relief could cause additional thermokarst problems (*9*). Long-term monitoring of the Kuparuk Oil Field with the same techniques used in this study could provide useful insights for proposed development in ANWR. The more hilly terrain in the Kuparuk field is similar to that in much of the ANWR, and recent construction practices have incorporated many of the lessons learned at Prudhoe Bay.

The major points to consider from this study are the following: (i) there have been major landscape impacts caused by the Prudhoe Bay Oil Field, (ii) indirect impacts, such as thermokarst, may not develop until many years after the initial planned developments, and (iii) the total area covered by direct and indirect impacts can greatly exceed the area of the planned development. We have discussed only the impacts to the geobotanical landscape. The implications of a gradually expanding oil-field network for wetland values, wildlife corridors, calving grounds, and regional aesthetics also need to be addressed; however, the lack of baseline wildlife information at Prudhoe Bay prior to development hampers such studies. There is a need to develop methods to assess cumulative impact and to foster comprehensive regional planning to anticipate the large impacts that are likely to occur on the coastal plain in the next few years.

REFERENCES AND NOTES

1. Fish and Wildlife Service, *Arctic National Wildlife Refuge Coastal Plain Resource Assessment* (U.S. Department of Interior, Washington, DC, 1986).
2. M. Crawford, *Science* 234, 1317 (1986).
3. *Anchorage Daily News,* 21 November 1986, p. B7.
4. 40 Code, *Fed. Reg.* 1508.7 (30 July 1979).
5. M. E. Britton, in *Arctic Biology,* P. Hansen, Ed. (Oregon State Univ. Press, Corvallis, 1967), pp 67–130.
6. D. M. Troy *et al.*, in *Prudhoe Bay Waterfowl Environmental Monitoring Program 1982* (report prepared for U.S. Army Corps of Engineers, Alaska District, Anchorage, AK, 1983).
7. A. L. Washburn, *Geocryology, a Survey of Periglacial Processes and Environments* (Wiley, New York, 1980).
8. P. J. Webber and J. D. Ives, *Environ. Conserv.* 5, 171 (1978).
9. D. E. Lawson, *Arct. Alp. Res.* 18, 1 (1986).
10. L. F. Klinger *et al.*, in *Proceedings of the Fourth International Permafrost Conference,* Fairbanks, AK, 1983, pp. 628–633.

11. D. A. Walker and K. R. Everett. *Arct. Alp. Res.*, in press.

12. D. Strayer *et al.*, "Long-term ecological studies: An illustrated account of their design, operation, and importance to ecology." *Occas. Publ. Inst. Ecosystem Stud. 2* (1986).

13. J. G. Gosselink and L. C. Lee, "Cumulative impact assessment in bottomland hardwood forests" (LSU-CEI-86-09, Center for Wetland Resources, Louisiana State University, Baton Rouge, 1987).

14. R. F. Noss and L. D. Harris, *Environ. Manage.* 10, 299 (1986).

15. G. E. Beanlands *et al.*, "Cumulative environmental effects: A binational perspective" (Canadian Environmental Assessment Research Council, Ottawa, Ontario, and National Research Council, Washington, DC, 1987).

16. L. D. Harris. *The Fragmented Forest* (Univ. of Chicago Press, Chicago, 1984).

17. G. C. Horak *et al.*, "Methodological guidance for assessing cumulative impacts on fish and wildlife" (U.S. Fish and Wildlife, Eastern Energy and Land Use Team, Kearneysville, WV, 1983).

18. P. Adamus and L. R. Stockwell, "A method for wetland functional assessment" (Federal Highway Administration, Washington, DC, 1983), vol. 1, FHWA-IP-82-23; vol. 2, FHWA-IP-82-24.

19. D. A. Walker *et al.*, *Environ. Conserv.* 13, 149 (1986). Geobotanical and anthropogenic disturbance maps were produced at 1:6000 scale from the Prudhoe Bay Oil Field GIS database which consists of 19 components: 10 geobotanical variables, 3 years of natural disturbance information, and 6 years of anthropogenic disturbance. This information has been integrated into a single composite map called an Integrated Geobotanical and Historical Disturbance Map. Maps of any single variable or maps based on models involving numerous variables are produced from the database using the ARC/INFO GIS software. The database is useful for testing hypotheses involving landscape-anthropogenic disturbance interactions. The maps were used to examine the details of disturbance within three intensive study areas in the most heavily disturbed portions of the oil field. A 1:24,000 scale map was made to determine the full extent of roads, gravel-covered tundra, and large impoundments (Fig. 1).

20. D. A. Walker *et al.*, "Cumulative landscape impacts in the Prudhose Bay Oil Field 1949-1983" (report prepared for U.S. Fish and Wildlife Service, Habitat Resources Section, Anchorage, AK, 1986).

21. K. R. Everett *et al.*, in *Proceedings of the Third International Conference on Permafrost* (National Research Council of Canada, Ottawa, 1978), pp. 359-365.

22. D. A. Walker *et al.*, *Geobotanical Atlas of the Prudhoe Bay Region, Alaska* (Report 80-14, U.S. Army Cold Regions Research and Engineering Laboratory, Hanover, NH, 1985).

23. D. A. Walker, *Vegetation and Environmental Gradients of the Prudhoe Bay Region, Alaska* (Report 85-14. U.S. Army Cold Regions Research and Engineering Laboratory, Hanover, NH, 1985).

24. ——— and W. Acevedo, *Vegetation and a Landsat-Derived Land Cover Map of the Beechey Point Quadrangle, Arctic Coastal Plain, Alaska* (Report 87-5, U.S. Army Cold Regions Research and Engineering Laboratory, Hanover, NH, 1987).

25. D. A. Walker, *et al.*, *Landsat-Assisted Environmental Mapping in the Arctic National Wildlife Refuge, Alaska* (Report 82-87, U.S. Army Cold Regions Research and Engineering Laboratory, Hanover, NH, 1982).

26. D. A. Walker *et al.*, *Arct, Alp. Res.* 17, 321 (1985).

27. M. D. Walker, thesis, University of Colorado, Boulder, CO (1987).

28. A. Lachenbruch and B. V. Marshall, *Science* 234, 689 (1986).
29. R. T. T. Forman and M. Godron, *Landscape Ecology* (Wiley, New York, 1986).
30. Funded by the U.S. Environmental Protection Agency and the Cold Climate Environmental Research Program under U.S. Department of Energy Interagency Agreement DE-A–106–84RL10584 with the U.S. Fish and Wildlife Service, Habitat Resources Section, Anchorage, AK. Support for manuscript preparation came from the DOE Response, Resistance, Resilience and Recovery from Disturbance to Arctic Ecosystems (R4D) program. We thank the North Slope Borough, the Environmental Systems Research Institute, Inc., Sohio Alaska Petroleum Co., and Arco Oil and Gas Co. for logistical support, funding, and help during these mapping programs. We thank R. Meehan for help in obtaining data and for providing helpful suggestions; J. Nickles, K. Bayha, T. Rockwell, R. Sumner, J. McCarty, J. States, and J. Brown for sponsoring and encouraging this work.

ARCTIC REFUGE BILL STALLS ONCE AGAIN

The Senate Energy Committee on Oct. 11 decided against an end-of-the-session bid to persuade Congress to open Alaska's Arctic National Wildlife Refuge (ANWR) to oil drilling. The issue received a boost after Iraq's invasion of Kuwait reopened the issue of energy dependency.

Frank H. Murkowski, R-Alaska, wanted the committee to include the panel's ANWR-drilling bill (S 684) in the budget-reconciliation bill. But he backed off after hearing that the move was opposed by Senate and House Democratic leaders. "It seems to me you would be doing damage to your cause by bringing it up and losing," committee Chairman J. Bennett Johnston, D-La., warned Murkowski.

Debate over drilling within the refuge's 1.5 million-acre coastal plain (about half the size of Connecticut) had raged since before 1980, when Congress abandoned efforts to settle the issue by ordering the administration to study the question for a while. *(1980 Almanac, p. 575)*

In response to a 1987 report by the Reagan administration, committees dominated by pro-industry members—House Merchant Marine and Senate Energy—reported out bills during the 100th Congress to open the ANWR to oil exploration. Both bills sought to safeguard against environmental damage.

Nevertheless, attempts to appease drilling opponents failed, and the legislation went nowhere. The high hopes oil-drilling proponents held going into the 101st Congress were dashed when the *Exxon Valdez* spilled 11 million barrels of crude oil in Alaska's Prince William Sound on March 24, 1989—just eight days after Senate Energy approved S 684. *(1989 Almanac, p. 678)*

Source: From *Congressional Quarterly Almanac,* 1990, p. 315.

The issue was sidelined indefinitely. But Iraq's invasion of Kuwait in August 1990 shifted the political landscape. *(Persian Gulf crisis, p. 717)*

The Bush administration estimated that there could be enough recoverable crude beneath the plain to produce 600,000 barrels a day over 15 years—roughly what the United States was importing from Iraq and Kuwait before the invasion.

Environmentalists who wanted to preserve the virtually untouched landscape were suddenly on the defensive as both sides girded for a renewed confrontation in the decadelong struggle.

"The Middle East crisis wiped the *Exxon Valdez* off the ANWR map as quickly as the *Exxon Valdez* wiped ANWR off the legislative map," said one House aide.

But even some who favored drilling said the long stalemate very well would continue into the 102nd Congress, leaving the wilderness off-limits at least through the next two years. That was because drilling advocates faced tough foes with a formidable advantage—stubborn environmentalists who could prevent drilling merely by obstructing any effort to change the status quo.

Environmentalists had "the home-field advantage because all they have to do is block us," said Jim Hughes, a deputy assistant secretary of the Interior. "Blocking something is always easier than doing something affirmative, so in a 50–50 battle, that certainly could tip the scales in their favor."

ARCTIC NATIONAL WILDLIFE REFUGE: OIL FIELD OR WILDERNESS?

AMANDA SPITLER

■ ■ ■

The second session of the 100th Congress will see continued debate over the prospect of oil and gas drilling on a 19-million-acre expanse of mountains and tundra known as the Arctic National Wildlife Refuge (ANWR). Three congressional committees have already held hearings: the House Interior Committee, the House Merchant Marine Committee, and the Senate Energy Committee. During the summer recess, members of these committees visited the refuge. On his return, energy committee chair Senator J. Bennett Johnston (D–LA) vowed to make his committee face the "bare bones" issue: "oil field or wilderness?"

The arctic refuge, most of which lies above the Arctic Circle, is larger than any refuge in the lower 48 states. Because of its size, the area supports a broad range of linked ecosystems. Of particular concern is the 1.5-million-acre coastal plain, which may be targeted for development. The coastal

Source: From Washington Watch in *BioScience*, B Vol. 37, No. 10 1987, p. 714.

plain provides a home, at least part of the year, to Alaska's porcupine caribou. Now numbering about 18,000, the herd migrates each summer to the coastal plain to calve. The area offers an advantageous climate and the predator protection required to replenish the herd. The coastal plain also supports many other forms of wildlife—including the wolf, arctic fox, brown bear, polar bear, and arctic peregrine falcon, which is listed as a threatened species.

Although few members of Congress deny the value of protecting the amazing variety of life on the coastal plain, some insist that limited drilling could be conducted without destroying crucial habitat. This is also the position of Interior Secretary Donald Hodel, despite a finding by the department's biologists that perhaps 20%–40% of the caribou population might be lost or displaced if development proceeds.

Last July, the department tentatively divided some of the targeted lands among native corporations in preparation for leasing to oil companies. In response to what was felt to be an attempt to overstep congressional authority, the House passed HR 2629, banning this kind of land deal without congressional approval. In essense, the measure reiterated congressional authority provided by the Alaska National Interest Lands Conservation Act (ANILCA) of 1980. This act mandated the study of environmental threats and oil potential by the Department of Interior, while putting the ANWR coastal plain off-limits to development without an explicit congressional directive.

Two other measures now exemplify the dichotomy of congressional opinion. HR 1082, which opens ANWR to drilling, is supported by 145 members (32 Democrats and 113 Republicans). HR 39, which closes the refuge to drilling, is the legislative effort of interior committee chair, Representative Morris Udall (D–AZ) and has 88 cosponsors (80 Democrats and 8 Republicans). Biologists have been working through the AIBS Public Responsibilities Program to provide scientific information supporting the ban. AIBS Public Responsibilities Committee Chair, Neal M. Barnett of the University of Maryland in College Park, has contacted Udall and the other HR 39 cosponsors to reiterate the support of professional biologists for this measure, which is intended to protect species indigenous to the Alaska coastal plain.

Barnett stressed that although much publicity has focused on the spectacular caribou, the musk oxen native to the Arctic range have been little emphasized. During the 19th century, the native arctic musk oxen were completely wiped out by hunters. Today's musk ox population of about 500 is descended from approximately 40 musk oxen transplanted from Greenland. Drilling operations could have a drastic impact on the musk ox population, reducing it by as much as half.

Although dramatic, the fate of a single species or population should not be taken to represent the total problem. The potential effects of drilling projects extend beyond loss of wildlife; they include desecration of the land itself. An extensive drilling option could require perhaps 100 miles of pipeline, 400 miles of road, and, most importantly, processing facilities whose construction would involve substantial excavation. Destruction of the thin topsoil and exposure of the permafrost layer below inevitably would ensue.

Can limited drilling proceed in harmony with preservation of a wilderness and its indigenous species? Most life scientists are skeptical. Although a compromise measure—penned by Representative Walter Jones (D–NC) and not yet introduced to Congress—will be of great interest, it is unlikely to circumvent the need for an "either-or" choice. Just as Johnston vowed to confront his committee, will the refuge, in fact, be an "oil field or wilderness?" Through AIBS, biologists are committed to ensuring that, if a choice must be made, it will be the sound one.

WRITING AND LEARNING ACTIVITIES: A GUIDE TO SYNTHESIZING

The activities below will guide you through the process of writing a synthesis essay of the source materials included here, in other chapters, or provided by you or your instructor.

READING THE TEXTS

1. **Reading:** Survey the sources you plan to synthesize. As you read, think about what you already know. Next, read the text closely, noting the claims the author makes and how he or she supports those claims with evidence.

2. **Journal Entry:** Write in your journal as you read, jotting down questions you have about the reading, familiar and unfamiliar terms, and notes about how this source is different from other works you have read in this and other disciplines. Also, consider what you have learned about the discipline this research comes from.

3. **Annotate the Text:** As you read, mark the text to help you follow the argument. Use one color highlighter to identify key claims, and another color to identify data or evidence. Place question marks next to statements you have questions about.

THINKING ABOUT THE DISCIPLINE

1. **Journal Entry:** What have you learned thus far about the disciplines these sources come from? What was the author's purpose in writing this text? How did the author present material to persuade you of his or her main point? What specialized terms does the author use?

2. **Group Activity:** Meet in groups and compare your journal entries. Talk about the similarities and differences in your understanding of the sources.

MAKING CONNECTIONS

1. **Journal Entry:** Think about what might connect your personal and community experiences with the reading you have been doing. How might some personal experience help you to identify a pattern among ideas in the read-

ing? Does your experience match those described in the reading? How are they similar? How different? What problem could you solve by writing this synthesis essay?

2. **Journal Entry:** Think about connections to your audience. Who are they? What are their primary interests? How might they use my essay? What terms might you and your audience disagree on? Could you each have a different perspective on the problem?

3. **Journal Entry:** Think about connections among your sources. What similarities and differences can you identify among my sources? How does each writer present information?

4. **Group Activity:** Meet in groups and exchange the connections you came up with. Make a presentation to the class.

BECOMING AN AUTHORITY

1. **Journal Entry:** One of the most difficult things for students to do is see themselves as having enough knowledge to synthesize the work of scholars already in the field. Indeed it is a daunting task and one which you will be asked to do often in other college activities. One of the most important things you can do to move you toward a position of authority is to ask yourself: "What does this research mean to me?" Write a response to this question in your journal.

2. **Writing Activity:** Write a letter to one of the authors whose work you have read. Keep in mind that writing a letter, like having a conversation, can help you develop authority as you respond to the writer's work and offer your own experiences as a way of understanding it. Ask the author questions about his or her study. Tell the writer about your own family background and how it differs from or is similar to the groups he or she was studying.

DEVELOPING AN ORGANIZING IDEA

1. **Journal Entry:** Look over all the notes and annotations you have made as you read and reread your sources. Choose a point of similarity or difference that you would like to build your essay around. Write a few sentences characterizing an organizing idea that you'd like to explore further in your synthesis essay; this idea will become the focus of your essay.

2. **Group Activity:** Meet in small groups and share your organizing ideas. Ask each other how you plan to develop your essay out of your organizing idea.

DRAFTING THE INTRODUCTION

1. **Writing Activity:** Write a draft of the introduction.

2. **Peer Exchange:** After drafting the introduction, exchange it with a partner and ask the following questions about his or her introduction. Has the writer indicated the importance of the issue? Included enough information about the sources? Explained something about the academic discipline and offered some indication of the method of research? Explained to the reader the perspective the essay takes or the problem it considers?

DRAFTING YOUR SYNTHESIS ESSAY

1. **Writing Activity:** Look over all of your notes on these sources and develop a draft that synthesizes some aspect of the information you find important. You should think of your audience as an interested group of students or faculty who have not been studying these particular issues. If you use any special terms that you think your readers won't know, be sure to define them. Also quote and paraphrase material from your sources to support your organizing idea.

REVISING YOUR SYNTHESIS ESSAY

1. **Peer Critique:** Exchange papers with a partner and give his or her paper the three separate readings described under "Revising the Essay," pp. 419–421. Write a response for each reading and return it to your partner.

2. **Revising:** Evaluate your partner's critique, do your own critique, and make the appropriate revisions to your draft.

12

ANALYZING DISCIPLINE-SPECIFIC TEXTS

The comic spirit is given to us in order that we may analyze, weigh, and clarify things in us which nettle us, or which we are outgrowing, or trying to reshape.

THORNTON WILDER

WHAT DOES IT MEAN TO ANALYZE?

When you look up the word *analyze* in the *American Heritage Dictionary of the English Language,* you find this definition: "To separate into parts or basic principles so as to determine the nature of the whole; examine methodically." The entry then refers more specifically to chemical analyses or to mathematical analyses. You engage in more informal, less scientific kinds of analysis every day; for example, if your car doesn't start, you sort out the various reasons, decide which seems most likely to be the case, and then do what you can to remedy the situation.

In this textbook analysis is viewed as a strategy for helping you take a position or make claim for what *you* think about a particular topic or issue, a view that may surprise you. For instance, you might decide to study the changing role of women in the Mexican-American family. As a result of your analysis you will develop a position about this subject. One of my students, Bruce Earl Williams, whose research essay is featured in Chapter 16, said about writing an analysis, "I thought you were supposed to pick away at the report and find everything that's wrong with it." This is a common understanding of analysis. I told him that analysis is not just, as the dictionary put it, examining something methodically. Whenever you examine or analyze something, you are doing it through your eyes, informed by your particular experience and resources. So, actually, at the core of every good analysis is someone's perspective. Bruce's response: "Oh, you mean I can use what I know from my personal experience? Wow! So those are my chits in this situation."

All three intellectual strategies—summary, synthesis, and analysis—work together seamlessly as you read the work of others and as you write. They are separated in this text only to point out and practice important features of each. As discussed earlier, in writing a summary, you attempt to recreate the writer's argument in a more concise form than the original. In synthesizing, the emphasis is on finding patterns among sources—aided, of course, by your own personal experiences. When you analyze, you examine your sources methodically, again taking into account your personal experiences, to develop a position or claim that you believe to be true.

Synthesis and analysis are more alike than they are different. Both involve looking at multiple sources to identify patterns. Both ask you to consider how your personal and cultural experience and knowledge contribute to what you see in the sources. Synthesis stresses pattern-finding activity; analysis, on the other hand, stresses the importance of taking a position. What does this research mean to *you*—based on your unique experience and your knowledge of a specialized discipline and its methods of research and writing—and how does your perspective affect your understanding of it?

This can be a real challenge. As students, you are frequently asked to read and write about material from specialized academic discourse communities. In the humanities, for example, you may be asked to develop an analysis of a work of art or a piece of literature. You will probably rely on the critical tradition—what other scholars have said about the art object or the piece of fiction—but it is also important to examine your expectations for how you will "see" or "read" the object. If you were looking at Matisse's painting *Conversation*, as we did in Chapter 6, it would be necessary to find out what art historians (for example, Jack Flam) think of the painting. But also think about how your own personal or family experiences might influence your analysis. When we write any kind of analysis, we are offering an expanded reading. The reader learns more than he or she would have by simply reading the report or story or only viewing the work of art. In your analysis your personal connections are integrated with the criticism you have read, resulting in new understanding for your readers.

To illustrate how summary, synthesis, and analysis work together, we have included here selected quotes from an article titled "Calcium and Osteoporosis," which appeared in a public health bulletin published by the Physicians Committee for Responsible Medicine (Messina, 7–8). Written by doctors for those interested in developing a healthy eating lifestyle, this information is closely related in content to the report found in Chapter 9 on the bone mineral content of Alaskan Eskimos. The newsletter writers summarize, synthesize, and analyze a great deal of research on nutrition and offer their position on how certain eating habits can promote health.

This article began by posing a problem. Why, the author asked, if Americans, and especially women, are told to take calcium supplements to prevent osteoporosis, do we have such a high incidence of osteoporosis? The article offered an analysis of this problem in which the author reexamined the assumption that additional calcium is the answer to osteoporosis. She does this by summarizing and synthesizing research on this topic. At the end of the article she restates in very concise terms the position that drives her analysis. Again, it's important to remember that summary, synthesis, and analysis are usually woven together, they are separated here for you to see how they work.

- POSITION STATEMENT (ANALYSIS)   *Intro*

A healthy diet that is moderate in protein can provide sufficient calcium without the use of supplements. (Messina, 8)

Below, the author summarizes the results of a single study [found in Chapter 9] that suggests that it is actually the high protein content in the Alaskan Eskimo's diet that contributes to bone loss, or osteoporosis.

SUMMARY

A study of Alaskan Eskimos revealed that even with calcium intakes as high as 2,500 milligrams a day, bone loss was greater in this group than in Caucasian Americans. One important aspect of the Eskimo's diet is that they consume as much as 400 grams of protein per day, or seven times the RDA.[5,6] (Messina, 7)

In the next quote the author synthesizes research that demonstrates that eating large amounts of protein can cause a loss of calcium through the urine.

SYNTHESIS

It has been known since the 1920's that protein causes calcium loss through urine. Laboratory studies have shown this repeatedly. When calcium intake is held constant, the greater the intake of protein, the greater the loss of calcium.[7,8,9] A comparison of the number of hip fractures among countries shows that as protein intake increases, so do the number of hip fractures. In affluent western countries, protein intake is high—generally twice the recommended dietary allowance. (Messina, 7)

WRITING AND LEARNING ACTIVITIES

1. **Writing Activity:** Over a few days, jot down any instances in which you hear, read, or observe someone analyzing a situation and taking a position. Was it in one of your college classes, in the media, or during a conversation with your friends? Were you convinced by the analysis?

2. **Group Activity:** Choose an issue that most participants in your group know something about. Develop a presentation in which you summarize some information, synthesize other information, and present an analysis. Write your position on the board or on the overhead projector and discuss with the class how you arrived at it.

THE PROCESS OF ANALYZING SPECIALIZED TEXTS

Whether you are studying a discipline in the humanities, sciences, or social sciences, you will be called upon frequently to take a position on some research you have read. Following are the steps of a process that can guide you in producing an analysis, using an example from the social sciences—a research report by Susan De Vos (found in Chapter 3), titled "Leaving the Parental Home: Patterns in Six Latin American Countries," You may want to read it and Professor Michael Maltz's discussion of it. The first step in the process is to know something about the methods used in this discipline. This particular study is based on a large-scale survey collected for another purpose from which the author pulled information about nest-leaving. The second step is to identify what you bring to the report—your own personal experiences with nest-leaving. Later in the chapter I invite you to try this process with one source each from the social sciences, humanities, and sciences.

THINKING ABOUT THE DISCIPLINE

Information about the special language and perspective of the discipline is particularly important as you consider your audience. If the analysis is to appear in a campus newspaper in a section on students moving into dorms, you can be sure your audience won't know much about the specialized language of social researchers, you would thus probably want to simplify this information a great deal. Assuming, however, that your audience will be your classmates and professors you will want to explain whose research you are reading and something about their disciplines. Answering the following questions will help you focus on what you know as background information.

 What have I learned thus far about quantitative social research? How do social researchers conduct their research? How do they write about what they have learned? How is their writing and research different from that of other disciplines? What types of issues do I expect to see in their writing?

GETTING STARTED

Writing an analysis means both reading closely and thinking broadly. Even if you've read a source once already for class, you need to read it again (and perhaps several times) to prepare to analyze it. It's not even too early to begin asking yourself if you see things differently than the author. Perhaps you are not persuaded by some aspect of the author's argument. Here are some questions to ask yourself.

 Am I thoroughly familiar with this material? Have I read it closely enough so that I understand the author's claims and evidence? Have I highlighted portions that illustrate claims and evidence? Do I understand the terms used in the reading? Most importantly, have I placed a question mark where I am confused about some aspect of the reading or where I disagree?

MAKING PERSONAL CONNECTIONS

Analysis often begins with making a link between your experience and some aspect of the research you are reading. Expand on this initial connection. You establish your position in an analysis when you can say what *you* think a particular research report means and what it means to you. Ask yourself the following questions:

 What personal experiences do I or others I know have with this social situation? Is the community being described very different from my own? In what ways? Are my experiences similar or different? Did a portion of the research report confuse me, or seem silly or just plain wrong? Is that because the experience being described was different from mine?

SUMMARIZING THE RESEARCH

An analysis of a research report must contain at least a brief summary of its essential features, one of which will probably lead you to make a personal connection, and then, in turn, to establish your position. To summarize these essential features, reread the report and mark the sections that you think are important. Try to summarize the point of the entire report by asking yourself: "What general behavior, situation, or idea is the researcher exploring?" Use these questions as a guide:

 What specific question is the researcher asking? How does she answer it? What method does she use? What variables? How does she break down her specific question into actual behaviors or situations? What are her results? Does she demonstrate her results convincingly? Why does she think the study is significant?

Here are some of one student's journal notes summarizing the De Vos research:

Main purpose of De Vos's research: gather baseline data on nest-leaving patterns. De Vos wants to know what affects nest-leaving, so she looks at these variables (behaviors/characteristics): marital status, age, sex, residence, education, work status. Data comes from World Fertility Survey, so it wasn't collected for her study. She says nest-leaving is often considered to be going from a "family of orientation to a family of procreation" (paragraph 1). She finds this is true for the countries she's observing, because most people leave home for marriage. She also finds that education is not an important reason to leave home. Sometimes young women are sent out to work but young men stay home in rural settings to manage the family farm or land.

Brian Boll

ESTABLISHING A POSITION

The central activity in writing an analysis essay is establishing a position or claim. Your position states what you believe to be true, based on what you have learned through reading and experience. It may be as a claim that you develop and support as you draft your essay. Frequently, your analysis may question or reconsider key terms and definitions that are used in the text. Or you may decide to question some underlying assumptions in the text. You might even question whether this is, indeed, the best way to answer the question being asked. Your position, offers your readers a broader view of the topic and invites them to consider accepting your position on the subject.

Your experiences and observations about nest-leaving are very important in relation to this report. Each person, family, culture has different ways of working out this important transition in family life. Look back over your notes about this specialized discipline, your summary of the research, and your notes on personal connections to the research.

Your position will undoubtedly be based on *your* personal experiences. Student Manuel Aceves for example, was most interested in De Vos's suggestion that males are most valuable to the economy of the family, and he questioned whether this was still true. Aware from his own Mexican background of the important economic role of women to the family, he wrote about factories established in Mexico during the 1960s that utilized mostly young women. He took the position that De Vos should have considered gender as the most important variable in the study. Natalie Acevedo, on the other hand, saw a strong connection between the traditional culture of Latin America and the closeness of her Ukrainian community in that marriage was considered to be the chief nest-leaving event. These cultural similarities formed the basis of Natalie's analysis below.

DEVELOPING THE INTRODUCTION

Some writers prefer to work out the introduction before they actually draft the essay, using the introduction as a way of figuring out what they want to say in the remaining portion of the essay. Other writers wait until they have drafted their essay; then they reread the essay and focus on the introduction, thinking primarily about what the reader will need to know. You need to decide which of the two methods is most productive for you. Here are some questions to consider:

 What is the specialized area of academic work that this research belongs to? What kinds of research typically go on in this area? How does this research fit into the specialized discipline? What is the specific question the researcher is asking? What other aspects of the research report will I be concerned with? Is the question it asks significant? Why or why not?

Read the introduction in Natalie Acevedo's[1] essay below. Notice that she draws the reader into the analysis by connecting something her mother always told her with the issue discussed in the research. There are many options for introducing research and you might not choose so personal an opening. An alternative is to talk about the kinds of research that sociologists do and how this study fits into this specialized discipline. Notice, too, that Natalie has included all the bibliographic information on the De Vos article so that the reader can find the source in the library if necessary.

DRAFTING THE ESSAY

Once you have summarized the research, considered how your personal experience relates to it, and established a position, you are ready to begin drafting the body of your analysis. Your task is to present your position as a claim you are making and then to support that claim by developing evidence for it. This might involve a redefinition of key terms or a questioning of the assumptions of the work. You can draw on your reading, but your observations, experiences, and personal connections are valuable sources for working out your analysis. Natalie Acevedo, for example, shared her own experiences about the relation of culture to marriage and nest-leaving.

Some professors may not request or accept personal stories in your work. Even if your personal connections remain in your notes and do not make it into your draft, they are still a crucial part of the planning and writing process. As you work back and forth between your planning notes, notes on your personal connections, your position statement, and notes that summarize the report, ask yourself the following questions:

Have I explained fully the position I am taking with respect to this research? Whether I am exploring a point offered by the researcher or making a personal connection, does my explanation unfold so that a reader can follow it? Do I offer specific support for the analysis I am making? Does the material I quote or paraphrase from my source support my analysis? Do I define or explain key terms? What single aspect of the research report do I plan to spend much of my analysis on?

Here is Natalie Acevedo's essay.

        Leaving the Parental Home: What Does It Mean?
        Many times my mother has said that she started to
    let me go the minute I was born. Let me go? I never
    fully understood what she meant but now as I grow
    older I realize what she was saying. There comes a

---

[1]This essay reflects work done in class. As such, it may include errors or stylistic problems. It is included here so that students can follow the writer's progress.

time in everyone's life when leaving home becomes a
reality. What does this reality mean? How does one's
cultural background influence that reality? In
"Leaving the Parental Home: Patterns in Six Latin
American Countries" (Journal of Marriage and the
Family, 51, August, 1989, 615-626), Susan De Vos
describes nest-leaving patterns for young people in
six Latin American countries. De Vos shows us how
important the cultural context can be on the decision
to leave home. This mirrors my experience in my
Ukrainian community. The decision to leave home is one
of the most important decisions a young person can
make and it is important to think about how culture
influences that decision.

De Vos's study makes use of cross-sectional data
collected from the World Fertility Survey in 1979.
This type of data is based on current information
about who has left home and who is still living at
home, rather than longitudinal data which would follow
young people from a young age through the home-leaving
experience. Her purpose is to gather some baseline
information on variables such as marital status, age,
sex, residence (rural or urban), education, and work
status. De Vos admits that the cross-sectional data
could present problems; it would have been better, if
possible, to study nest-leaving as it occurred over
the long term. In addition, she tells us that she left
out the data for divorced and separated couples. In
spite of these problems, her research touches on an
important issue.

De Vos found that in Latin America most young
people leave home only when they marry. What happens
when one gets married? How does life change? Does one
become more independent or less? How does your culture
influence your decision to marry or to leave your
home? De Vos says that marriage brings "added

responsibility and independence" (p. 615; paragraph 4). In my Ukrainian community marriage is the primary and almost the only reason for anyone to leave home. Leaving sooner would be looked down upon and seen as a rejection of the culture.

In De Vos's study most people were not educated past the eighth grade. This is a major difference with my community because some sort of education beyond high school is available for nearly everyone. Leaving home to go to school is not frowned upon, but it is not widely accepted among the Ukrainian community either. The traditional Ukrainian family sees no need for a child to go away to school—there is always a good college or university in the area. If it is absolutely necessary to leave home, it is usually the Ukrainian males that are the first to leave. Parents feel that the daughters may not be ready for the real world and still need protection. This plays into the typical male stereotype that plagues most cultures. Ironically, De Vos tells us that the Latin American sons are more likely to remain in the family as economic assets while the girls are working as maids or already married (p. 616; paragraph 6).

The Ukrainian culture, like the Hispanic one, is very traditional, and staying home until marriage is considered normal. Many of my friends who do not come from such a close community do go away to school. I'm not sure how much independence they gain, since their parents usually help with their finances and they move back home for the summer. One girlfriend who had a good job got an apartment with other friends and she did seem really independent.

Cultural norms play a big role in an individual's decision about when is the appropriate time to leave home. Even with marriage being the most appropriate time in the Latin American countries De Vos studied

```
and in my own culture, I see some important
differences. The level of education might offer
choices to me and my friends—economic and career
choices—that simply are not available to the people De
Vos studied. For me staying with my family until I
marry is a pleasure and but not a necessity.
```

REVISING THE ESSAY

Revising an essay takes place continuously: as you plan the essay, as you draft it sentence by sentence, and then again as you review it to see if it says what you want it to say. During the process of revision you are stepping back and looking at your writing again—"re" and "vision" are literally a "seeing again."

Revision is not an easy task. When we write we become very involved with our work. We often need specific strategies for stepping outside and seeing our work as others will see it. Up to this point we have encouraged you to become deeply involved with your essay, looking for personal connections, making claims that are important to *you*, developing *your* position with respect to the sources you read. You have been asked to develop authorship and ownership of your essay. In the revision process, you are being asked to shift your perspective again. You have to review your work as though it is not yours. Below are strategies for doing this on your own and with the help of other readers, in essence by reading the text through several times and looking at it from a different perspective each time.

An Overall Reading

Read the essay all the way through and then ask yourself the following questions:

 Have I stated my position in this analysis clearly? Have I included the appropriate bibliographic material in the introduction or at the end of the essay in a works cited list? Does my introduction explain the main point of the research? Have I considered how this report fits into a specialized discipline? Have I included the most important information, left out unnecessary details, and made clear the importance of this research? Have I defined the most important key terms used in the reading? Do I maintain my own voice or do I begin to sound too much like my sources?

Rereading Paragraph by Paragraph

With this next reading shift your focus to individual paragraphs. Look primarily at how you support your claims and subclaims, your major and minor points. The most important thing you can do is read each paragraph and ask yourself:

What does this paragraph say? Can I write a single sentence stating what this paragraph is about? Have I indicated paragraphs where I shift to a new topic in my analysis?

Rereading Sentence by Sentence

In this reading the focus is even tighter, more concentrated—like shining a penlight on each sentence. Ask yourself the following questions:

 Does each sentence connect to the next one appropriately? Do I use the same terms across sentences or do I switch terms? Have I indicated the appropriate logical relationships between sentences with words such as furthermore, likewise, and, yet, however, on the other hand, but then, with this in mind, because, first, next, and to sum up. Have I used the best word and avoided clichés and casual language? Do I use the same subject and verb pattern in each sentence? Is my sentence structure monotonous? Should I rearrange the parts of any sentence? Do I use active verbs and avoid excessive use of the verb *to be?*

Rereading for Editing and Proofreading

You are now within sight of the finish line, but if this last reading is not done carefully and completely you risk not getting as much credit for your essay as it deserves. Go through the essay looking for errors of mechanics, style, usage, or punctuation. Check that you have quoted material accurately and paraphrased appropriately. In addition you should check that you have placed all your sources correctly in the text and that you have matching references in the final reference list. It is an unfortunate fact that errors of this type—while not crucial to the meaning of your essay—can cause a reader to discount all the hard work you have put in up to this point.

WRITING AND LEARNING ACTIVITIES

1. **Journal Entry:** Reexamine the analyzing process suggested above. How is this different from other academic writing you have been asked to do? From writing that asks you to summarize or synthesize? Is there anything about this process that surprises you or confuses you?

2. **Group Activity:** Look through the readings in this textbook, noticing places where analysis takes place. Think about the discipline that the reading is drawn from. How do you suppose the discipline influences the writer's approach to analyzing the problem? Look for personal connections. You will probably find very few. Why do you suppose they are absent? Do you think there should be more personal connections in academic writing or are you satisfied with what you have found?

3. **Peer Activity:** Find a newspaper editorial that takes a strong position on a topic. Discuss how you might apply the process described above in analyzing this short editorial. What position would you take and how would you develop your analysis?

SOURCES FOR ANALYZING

A SOURCE FROM QUANTITATIVE SOCIAL RESEARCH

Social science researchers are interested in learning how the social world shapes an individual's behavior. In Chapter 3 and in this chapter (Natalie Acevedo's report) we have explored the behavior called nest-leaving, young people leaving home. When you connect your personal experiences with what is known from research on this topic, you are using what sociologist C. Wright Mills calls the "sociological imagination."

The following source for your analysis essay, "Family Structure and Conflict: Nest-leaving Expectations of Young Adults and Their Parents," was published in 1989 in the *Journal of Marriage and the Family.* The authors, Frances and Calvin Goldscheider, from the Department of Sociology at Brown University, are well-known experts on the topic of nest-leaving. In this social research report they use a survey of high-school students and their parents to learn about both groups' expectations for when and under what circumstances the young people will leave home.

The research report is segmented in a way similar to the one in Chapter 3 (which was the basis for Natalie Acevedo's analysis). An abstract gives you an overview of the study and also introduces a new term for nest-leaving: *PRI, premarital residential independence,* used to refer to nest-leaving that occurs prior to marriage. The next section, although unlabeled, offers a literature review, followed by a statement of the hypotheses, or research questions. In the section titled Data and Measures, the researchers list their variables. In the last two sections they report on their results and discuss what they think the results mean.

It might be useful to reread the process that Professor Mike Maltz demonstrated earlier (Chapter 3, Quantitative Social Research). Survey the text to become familiar with the sections of the text, graphs and tables, and new terminology. Even during your surveying process, pay special attention to the statement of the hypotheses (or claims) and to the discussion section. Reading research reports such as these usually means paying closer attention to some sections than to others. Give yourself time to reflect on what the research means to you personally. Then, read it all the way through once more, paying closer attention to some sections than to others. Remember, your purpose for reading is to understand the research and your connection to it, and to establish a position that explains what it means to you. Think about the issues presented below and then go through the process of writing an analysis, using the guide at the end of the chapter.

ASK YOURSELF

As I read the research report called "Family Structure and Conflict: Nest-leaving Expectations of Young Adults and Their Parents," consider how this research builds on what I already have learned about research in the discipline of social research. Also write about connections between my personal experiences and the research reported here. Do the results strike me as reasonable? Do they match my experiences or are they different? What are my expectations about establishing Premarital Residential Independence for myself if I have not already done so? How does my home-leaving story differ from others in my class or from the research report? What influence does culture, employment, personal finances, marriage, or education have on the pattern?

FAMILY STRUCTURE AND CONFLICT: NEST-LEAVING EXPECTATIONS OF YOUNG ADULTS AND THEIR PARENTS

FRANCES K. GOLDSCHEIDER AND CALVIN GOLDSCHEIDER
Brown University

■ ■ ■

Whether unmarried children should continue to live with their parents until marriage or should move out and establish an independent residence beforehand is a family decision that involves both the child and the parents, reflecting and affecting the relationships between the generations. In this article, we explore the expectations of parents about the sequence of marriage and nest-leaving for their children and consider how the factors influencing parents' expectations resemble those that shape their children's. We examine intergenerational differences in expectations and ask: How does variation in family structure, particularly membership in one-parent and stepparent families, influence the expectations of parents and children about premarital residential independence (PRI)? Using data from students in the High School and Beyond (HSB) senior cohort, together with their parents, we show that young adults are more likely than their parents to expect PRI, in two-parent as well as in one-parent and stepparent families. The effects of family structure operate through different pathways, however. Stepparent families lead to greater expectation of PRI because children are expected to establish an independent residence at an early age and to marry at a normal age, a pattern reflecting the low intergenerational closeness experienced in families in which stepparents and

---

Department of Sociology, Brown University, Providence, RI 02912.

Journal of Marriage and the Family 51 (February 1989): 87–97.

stepchildren must relate to each other in the same household. In contrast, young people from mother-only families expect PRI only because they expect to delay marriage.

One of the most common forms of family fission takes place when young adults leave the parental household to establish an independent residence. Until this point, those involved have typically shared a family structure with a nuclear core of parents and children for approximately two decades. With nest-leaving, each enters a new stage in a more separate life course. Children continue their transition to adulthood and parents have a more child-free lifestyle and an emptier nest as they continue through middle age.

Both parties, of course, share the expectation that this residential split is normal and appropriate. Family extension has generally been rare in the United States (Laslett, 1973; Pryor, 1972); remaining in the parental home after marriage has normally been reserved for short-term and emergency situations. On the other hand, it was also the case until recently that few children left home before marriage, except for temporary sojourns in college dormitories, military barracks, or other semiautonomous living arrangements that normally ended with a return to the parental home (Goldscheider and DaVanzo, 1986; Kett, 1977; Kobrin, 1976). In short, marriage marked the "normative" occasion for moving out of the parental home.

Since World War II, a new pattern of leaving home before marriage has emerged and, during the 1960s, accelerated (Goldscheider and LeBourdais, 1986; Kobrin, 1976). By the 1980s, this new life course pattern had become normative for young adults, largely displacing the more traditional pattern of nest-leaving. According to one recent national survey, fully three-fourths of high school seniors in 1980 expected to reside in their own home or apartment before marriage (Goldscheider and Goldscheider, 1987). This new pattern is likely to change the relationships between parents and children, since premarital residential independence reduces parental influence over the daily lives of their children. It also may have implications for future family structure and relationships, since young adults who have experienced premarital residential independence become less traditional in their adult family orientations (Waite, Goldscheider, and Witsberger, 1986).

Children's leaving home, like other forms of household fission, is usually a mutual decision, and it is not clear to what extent the parents of young adults share their children's expectations. These parents reached adulthood in the years before the greatest period of change in premarital residential independence; thus, they were less likely to have observed or followed such a pattern themselves. They might discourage it on the grounds that separate living is more expensive and requires parental subsidies they might rather avoid (Goldscheider and DaVanzo, in press). Parents who are members of more traditional religious and ethnic groups might be even more reluctant to see their children live independently before marriage. For all these reasons, parents and children may disagree on whether it is appropriate for children to move out of the parental home before marriage.

5   It is also possible, however, to argue the opposite for some contemporary parents. A select number may welcome this new life course for their children, since in many ways their lives have changed as much or more than have their children's. This possibility is based on several premises. First, they bore their children before fertility commenced its sharpest declines in the late 1960s, but raised them in its midst, subject to all the pressures that led their younger peers to delay or forgo parenthood. Thus, by the 1980s, they may view early nest-leaving less as a departure from norms than as an opportunity to reduce parental responsibility in favor of a more adult-oriented lifestyle.

Moreover, they have gone through the divorce revolution, and many have experienced remarriage and stepparenthood. It has been argued that blended families have weak institutional and normative supports for step relationships, thereby leading to strain (Cherlin, 1978). Research has shown that the presence of stepchildren often leads to family conflict and that stepchildren may therefore leave home earlier than others (White and Booth, 1985). Parents raising children alone, typically in female-headed families, might also look forward to reducing their disproportionate parental responsibilities. Hence, changing family structures may make contemporary parents more likely to expect their children to leave home before marriage than are the children themselves. From both sides of the parent-child relationship, then, we may discover a generation gap over the timing of children's residential independence, one that should crystallize toward the end of adolescence when the issue of residential independence begins to surface as a realistic concern and possibility. Nevertheless, on average, children are more likely than parents to expect to establish an independent residence before marriage.

In this article we explore the expectations of parents about the sequence of marriage and nest-leaving for their children and consider how these expectations accord with their children's. What factors promote parental expectations of premarital residential independence, and do they resemble those that affect the expectations of children? How does variation in family structure, particularly membership in one-parent and stepparent families, influence the expectations about premarital residential independence? Are there systematic areas of difference between the expectations of parents and children that might lead to intrafamily conflict, and what are the factors affecting the likelihood of a generation gap over this issue?

CONCEPTUAL FRAMEWORK AND HYPOTHESES

Our analysis of parents' and children's expectations about premarital residential independence (PRI) in young adulthood rests on the following premises: Setting up an independent residence before marriage is more expensive than remaining in the parental home. Privacy and autonomy compete for available family resources and are more likely among those with access to higher incomes. However, not all those with adequate resources will choose PRI over other options; some will prefer to maintain closer family ties. Since PRI is a relatively new phenomenon, such differences will be characteristic of traditional ethnic and religious communities, particularly those that maintain a foreign language.

We view PRI as a life course phenomenon that is much more likely among those who marry relatively late and who are at longer risk for other changes in early adulthood, such as job shifts, that would make residential mobility necessary. Those who expect PRI at younger ages, consistent with early or normal marriage ages, are indicating a much stronger preference for residential independence prior to marriage. Thus we see PRI as arising through two routes: through factors that act on expected marriage timing and through those that increase the likelihood of expecting PRI independent of expected age at marriage.

10   The family environment where children are raised is also likely to influence choices about living arrangements in early adulthood. Disrupted and newly blended families may foster preferences for children's earlier residential independence, compared with persons living in more stable, nuclear families. Further, parents and children may have different expectations about premarital residential independence, because of differences in generational viewpoint, interests, and access to family resources.

Previous analyses restricted to high school seniors have shown that males and those with higher socioeconomic status are more likely to expect PRI, as are those who expect to marry at later ages. Those who used a foreign language in the home and those associated with more traditional ethnic or religious groups are less likely to expect PRI (Goldscheider and Goldscheider, 1987; 1988). We expect the same patterns for their parents, but frequently with differing strengths. Specifically, we hypothesize:

1. Parents with sons and those with higher socioeconomic status are more likely to expect PRI for their child, with these factors having more influence for parents than for children.
2. Parents affiliated with more traditional ethnic or religious groups or families reporting greater use of a foreign language are less likely to expect PRI for their child, with these factors having more influence for parents than for children.
3. Parents who expect their child to marry at a later age are more likely to expect PRI for their child, with similar effects for both.

Going beyond previous research, we expect that the structure of families will have a similar impact on the PRI expectations of parents and children:

4. Persons in one-parent households or those in families with a stepparent should have higher expectations for PRI than those in other families.

However, we hypothesize that parents will differ from their children in significant ways in their likelihood of expecting PRI for their child:

5. Parents in general will be less likely to expect PRI for their children than their children expect for themselves.

The above hypotheses pertain to general similarities and differences in the factors influencing whether parents and children expect PRI for the child. However, our argument also suggests that there would be circumstances under which one might expect differing attitudes that lead to intrafamily conflict. For example, to the extent that parents and children differ in their expectations in response to resource constraints, intrafamily conflict over PRI should be less at higher levels of SES. Further, if parents make stronger gender distinctions than children, because children have absorbed more of the sex role revolution, there should be more agreement with sons than with daughters. Similarly, rapid generational change normally occurs in acculturating immigrant groups and should result in more intrafamily conflict. Finally, given the relationship between expecting PRI and expected marriage age, it seems likely that parents and children with different views about the child's likely marriage age will differ, as well, over the issue of PRI. Thus, we hypothesize:

6. Families with higher socioeconomic status are less likely to experience intergenerational conflict over PRI.
7. Families with daughters are more likely to experience intergenerational conflict over PRI.
8. Families in which parents speak to their children in a language other than English are more likely to experience intergenerational conflict over PRI.
9. Families where children expect to marry at a different age than their parents expect for them are more likely to experience conflict over the child's PRI.

DATA AND MEASURES

15 We use data from the High School and Beyond (HSB) senior cohort, a nationally representative panel study of seniors in American high schools in 1980. HSB is uniquely suited to our study: it furnishes data on expectations for PRI for the entire sample of seniors as well as for a subsample of parents who, along with their children, were asked questions about the expected timing of leaving home and marriage for their child.[1] The parents surveyed included mothers and fathers, and extensive sociodemographic data were collected. The availability of selected family structural variables enables us to examine the factors associated with variation in the nest-leaving expectations of parents and children. The major limitation of HSB is that it excludes previous high school dropouts.[2]

The following describes how we constructed certain key variables and operationalized marriage and independent residence expectations. Table 1 presents means and standard deviations of the variables tested.

Dependent Variables

Our first dependent variable indicates expecting PRI. It was constructed from two questions, asked of both parents and children: *(a)* At what age do you expect (your child) to get married? and *(b)* At what age do you expect

TABLE 1.   Description of Variables Used in the Analysis

Variable	Definition	Mean[a](SD)
Dependent variables		
PRI	Independent residence expected before marriage by parent or child	59.1
Conflict	Parent-child disagreement over PRI	34.0
Independent variables		
Male	Gender	42.6
SES	Scale combining parental income, education, occupational prestige, and ownership of household items	−.067 (.76)
Black	Self-reported race = black	10.7
Hispanic	Self-reported origin = Hispanic	6.6
Jewish	Self-reported religion = Jewish	2.1
Protestant 1	Self-reported denomination = Baptist or "other Protestant"	22.8
Other religion	Self-reported denomination = other Christian or "other religion"	10.1
No religion	Self-reported denomination = none or missing	7.6
Nonfundamentalist Christian (reference category)	Self-reported denomination = Catholic, Lutheran, Presbyterian, Episcopalian, or Methodist	56.8
Southern European	Self-reported origin = Portugal, Italy, or Greece, and religion = Catholic	5.9
Female-headed family	Mother or female guardian present; father absent or not reported	14.3
Stepparent family	One natural parent and a guardian of the opposite sex	7.0
Language use	Average extent a foreign language used in home, school, and neighborhood	.27 (.732)
Expected marriage age	Age parent or child expects child to marry	23.1
Marriage are gap	Age child expects to marry less age parent expects child to marry	−.16 (2.55)

[a]Pooled sample, unweighted. Means for dummy variables given as percentages.

(your child) to live in your/his own home or apartment?[3] Respondents who specified an expected age at independent residence younger than their expected age at marriage were classified as expecting PRI. Those who gave the same age for marriage and independent residence, as well as those few who expected to marry before establishing an independent residence, were classified as offering a "traditional" normative response, that is, not expecting to move out before marriage. (For more detail on these measures, see Goldscheider and Goldscheider, 1987.)[4]

The relationship between expectations for PRI and actual patterns of premarital residential independence remains unexplored in this research. Our focus here is on the plans of young adults and their parents. We note that there is a substantial body of evidence showing that expectations about the timing of other life course events, such as marriage and childbearing, are useful indicators both of individual and aggregate behavior (Hendershot and Placek, 1981; Modell, 1980). The data from the HSB will allow us to pursue the relationship between expectations and actual behavior on this aspect of young adulthood for subsequent panels.

Our second dependent variable, derived from the first, indicates agreement or disagreement between parents and children. We distinguish cases in which the expectations of parents and children are similar, with both expecting residential independence for the child before marriage or at marriage, from cases where parents and children have differing expectations, which generally means that parents are less likely and children more likely to expect PRI. At a stage in the family cycle in which it is likely that children will leave home, differences between parents and children in expectations about this issue imply intergenerational conflict. While we do not measure the extent of conflict directly, we take differences in expectations (attitudinal conflict) to indicate this dimension. We coded attitudinal conflict when either the parent did not expect the child to establish a separate home before marriage and the child expected PRI, or when the parents expected PRI for the child while the child expected to remain at home until marriage.[5]

Measures of Family Structure

20   Two family structure variables were constructed from questions asked of the seniors. They indicated whether the respondent's family was (*a*) female-headed or (*b*) stepparent. These two variables were based on responses to questions asked about the presence or absence in the household of mother, father, male guardian, or female guardian, as well as other potential household members. A *mother-headed family* was defined as one in which no father or male guardian was present (or where information on these variables was missing) and the student's household included a mother or female guardian. A *stepparent family* was defined as one that included a parent of one sex and a guardian of the other. The third category comprised all *other families*. Most of these (93 %) were characterized by seniors as having both a mother and a father (but not a male or female guardian) present.

Race, Ethnic, and Religious Variables

To define *foreign language use,* we drew on 10 separate questions tapping frequency of foreign language use in specific contexts, including family, school, peer groups, and stores. The scale we constructed indicates average level of language use across these contexts.

Racial and ethnic groups were delineated on the basis of responses to questions about race and national origin.[6] Blacks were categorized on the basis of the race question and Hispanic group membership was based on the origin question. Hispanics share similar family patterns, although there is considerable variation within the Hispanic group (Goldscheider and Goldscheider, 1988). However, the use of the subsample including parents limits our ability to make more refined distinctions among Hispanics.

Measures of *religious denomination* were derived from the question, "What is your religion?" We distinguished Jews and Catholics, and subdivided Protestants according to their relatively less and more fundamentalist denominations. Thus Methodists, Presbyterians, Lutherans, and Episcopalians were separated from Baptists and other Protestants (referred to below as

Protestant 1). We combined "other Christian" and "other religion" to indicate a religious affiliation other than Protestant, Catholic, or Jew, and distinguished those with no religious affiliation (none) from the others.

Other explanatory variables included are gender and a measure of socioeconomic status constructed by the survey group on the basis of a combination of parental education, occupation, and income. In some models, we include the parent's and the child's expected age for the child to marry.

ANALYSIS

25 To examine the determinants of expecting PRI for parents and children as well as the sources of conflicting expectations, we have performed two separate analyses using multivariate logistic regression. In the first, we predict the log odds of the likelihood of expecting PRI, pooling the records of parents and children and including measures that indicate whether the respondent was a child or a parent. (There are 5,062 cases where information was available for child and/or parent.) In the first model we include variables important in previous research on high school seniors, most of whose parents were not surveyed (Goldscheider and Goldscheider, 1987, 1988); we include as well our measures of family structure. In our second model we introduce the measures of differential perspective (parent versus child) and variables constructed to test interactions that may result from the different points of view (e.g., how parents and children might use additional parental resources). Finally, we test whether differences in the likelihood of expecting PRI result from differences in expected age at marriage (since PRI expectations are much more likely among those who expect to marry later), or whether the effects are directly on the likelihood of expecting PRI, net of expected age at marriage.

In the analysis of attitudinal conflict, the parent's and child's responses for a given parent-child pair were combined on a single record, and the dependent variable was measured from combinations of their responses. (There are 2,078 cases where information was available for both the child and parent.) In the first model, we include all variables except expected marriage age; in the second model, we include both measures of the marriage age expected and differences in marriage age expected between the parent and the child.

Premarital Residential Independence

The data in Table 2 model the factors affecting the likelihood that parents and children expect the child to experience PRI. Model 1 (presented in col. 1) indicates that patterns observed for young adults in previous analyses (Goldscheider and Goldscheider, 1987, 1988) also characterize the full population of parents and children. Persons in families with higher socioeconomic status and those in families with male students are more likely to expect PRI. Hispanics, those from southern Europe, those affiliated with more traditional religious denominations (fundamentalist Protestants and

TABLE 2.   Models Predicting Premarital Residential Independence Among Parents and Children (Logistic Regression Coefficients)

VARIABLE	MODEL 1	MODEL 2	MODEL 3
Intercept	.344*	.679*	−8.781*
Male	.348*	.302*	−.118
SES	.310*	.250*	−.034
Black	.091	.073	−.608*
Black • SES	−.357*	−.384*	−.272**
Hispanic	−.453*	−.485*	−.454*
Hispanic • Male	.446**	.517**	.732*
Jews	.290	.293	−.324
Protestant 1	−.239*	−.235*	−.030
Other religion	−.308*	−.303*	−.125
No religion	.214	.235	.323**
Southern Catholic	−.240**	−.236**	−.412*
Foreign language use	−.161*	−.029	−.228*
Female-headed family	.203*	.209*	.122
Stepparent family	.188**	.202**	.367*
Parent	—	−.728*	−.881*
Parent • male	—	.122	.045
Parent • SES	—	.172*	.199*
Parent • language use	—	−.423	−.556*
Expected marriage age	—	—	.430*
Chi-square	213.05	423.11	1365.32
(df)	(18)	(22)	(23)
N	5,062	5,062	5,062

*$p < .05$; **$p < .10$ (two-tailed test).

those of "other" religions), and those using a foreign language are less likely to expect PRI for the child. Greater gender differentiation characterizes Hispanics.[7] Most important, living in a female-headed family and having a stepparent in the household, as hypothesized above, significantly increase the likelihood of expecting PRI, with effects of nearly equal size.

The second model tests for differences in the factors influencing the expectations of parents compared with children (col. 2).[8] As hypothesized, parents are significantly less likely to expect PRI for their children than their children do for themselves. The data also show that socioeconomic status has a more powerful effect on the expectations of parents than on those of their children, as we expected. However, there is no confirmation of our hypothesis that parents make greater distinctions between their expectations for their sons and daughters than their children make for themselves. The effect is in the hypothesized direction, suggesting that parents are more likely to expect PRI for their sons than their daughters when compared to the expectations of the sons and daughters about themselves, but the coefficient is not significant in this model.

In column 3, expected age at marriage is added to the model. As hypothesized, this has an extremely powerful effect, with those expecting later marriage far more likely to expect PRI. Adding this variable also has strong effects on many of the other coefficients in the model. The positive coefficients for males become negative, and the positive effect of socioeconomic status is eliminated for children, although it remains significantly positive for parents. Hence, much of the effect of these variables on PRI was through their impact on expected age at marriage. In contrast, when expected age at marriage is controlled, blacks have a lower likelihood of expecting PRI, which indicates that their high expected marriage age was obscuring their relatively low likelihood of expecting PRI, given their expected age at marriage. There are also continuing effects of religious group membership on PRI (traditional Protestants and other Christians are less likely to expect PRI), and those claiming no religious affiliation are now significantly more likely to expect PRI.

30   Family structure also continues to influence PRI when expected age at marriage is controlled. However, the data reveal strongly contrasting pathways to PRI for those experiencing living in a female-headed household compared with living in a stepfamily. Living in a female-headed family increases the likelihood of PRI only through the later age at marriage expected of children in these households; hence, the effect becomes insignificant when expected marriage age is controlled. In contrast, having a stepparent in the household increases the likelihood of expecting PRI overall, independent of when the children expected to marry. This suggests that the response of stepparent family members is to plan earlier residential autonomy for young adults.

Finally, the distinctively lower likelihood of expecting PRI among parents is greatly strengthened when expected marriage age is introduced, and this effect is particularly powerful among those using a foreign language. This occurs because parents, particularly those who are foreign-born, expect their children to marry at somewhat later ages than the children themselves expect, and this difference obscures part of the generational difference in orientation toward PRI per se. Thus, parents are envisioning rather different life course sequences for their children than their children are: parents are likely to be surprised both by their children moving away from home to PRI earlier than they expect, and by having their children marry earlier as well.

The Generation Gap

Clearly, parents and children can differ on the timing of leaving home relative to the timing of marriage. However, the analysis so far has not considered differences in expectations between parents and children *in the same household*. Since parents overall are less likely to expect their children to leave home before marriage, some disagreement is inevitable. Further, since several factors systematically affect children's expectations differently from those of their parents, these results suggest the contexts that are likely to lead to the greatest parent-child conflict. Table 2 shows that the expectations of parents as a group more closely resemble those of children as a group in high- than in low-SES families; similarly, average levels of parental expectations for their child's PRI are particularly lower than average levels expressed by the students themselves among families with high levels of usage of a non-English language. Other factors may systematically increase

TABLE 3. Models Predicting Parent-Child Conflict Over Premarital Residential Independence (Logistic Regression Coefficients)

Variable	Model 1	Model 2
Intercept	−.854*	.467
Male	.274*	.375*
SES	−.072	−.021
Black	.631*	.830*
Black • SES	.303	.294
Hispanic	.404	.363
Hispanic • Male	.002	−.059
Jews	.260	.357
Protestant 1	.091	.009
Other religions	.221	.165
No religion	.219	.288
Southern Catholic	.091	.097
Foreign language	.013	.046
Female-headed family	−.328*	−.298*
Stepparent family	−.088	−.139
Expected marriage age	—	−.059*
Parent-child marriage age difference	—	.134*
Chi-square	39.8	73.53
(df)	(18)	(20)
N	2,078	1,959

*$p < .05$.

consensus (even in the face of overall bases of disagreement) or foster conflict, and disagreement on other unrelated grounds. Thus, we focus on the dyad of parent and child, investigating circumstances under which they are more or less likely to be in agreement on this household issue that for many needs to be resolved in the near future.

The data in Table 3 test how much the parent-child differences that can be inferred from the aggregate analysis actually predict household-level parent-child disagreement over whether the child should experience PRI. The results indicate that the relatively high level of intergenerational conflict on this issue (35% of all families, as indicated in Table 1) is not strongly influenced by the factors studied here. Moreover, the results often are opposite the direction predicted. In the first model, only families with sons, black families, and female-headed families have levels of agreement significantly different from other families.

The results for sons, however, are the reverse of the direction hypothesized. The earlier analysis, which treated parents and children in the aggregate, suggested that there was greater *potential* for intergenerational conflict over PRI for daughters than sons, since parents are somewhat more likely (although not significantly so) to make gender distinctions favoring sons on this issue than are the children themselves. On average, then, parents should be more likely to disagree with their daughters. But in actual parent-child pairings, families with sons show higher levels of disagreement. More detailed examination of the data shows that more parent-son pairs jointly expect the child to leave home before marriage than do parent-daughter pairs.

However, parents who expect to have their child remain at home until marriage are much less likely to have sons agree with them than daughters. Similarly, among parents who expect PRI for their children, their sons are much more likely than daughters to disagree, and expect to remain at home until they marry. Thus, an objective basis for parent-child agreement does not translate into actual accord in families with sons. In contrast, despite a good basis for disagreement over PRI, parents and their daughters seem to be able to minimize its effects.

35   Black families also tend toward conflicting expectations on this issue, and their pattern resembles that of families with sons. Further, these risks appear to increase for black families at higher levels of SES (although the difference is not significant). Black families have displayed distinctive patterns in all our analyses of these data; they present a substantial research challenge for a closer, more systematic analysis of the interactive effects of socioeconomic status and marriage expectations.

The only other significant effect in this model is for female-headed households, and the direction again is not as predicted. Children and parents living together in female-headed households are significantly *less* likely to be in conflict in their expectations about the child's PRI.[9] This result contrasts sharply with the lack of effect for stepparent families; whatever their other sources of conflict, they seem to be no more likely than other families to have disagreement over PRI.

In addition to these puzzling findings, we also have negative results (i.e., no effect on the likelihood of parent-child attitudinal conflict) for factors that differentially affect parents' and children's likelihood of expecting PRI for the child. Most, however, are in the predicted direction. Socioeconomic status, for example, may slightly reduce the likelihood of conflict; however, it is evident that having enough resources to subsidize PRI does not reduce conflict over the issue very much. Similarly, Hispanic families and those of "other" religions are slightly more likely to be in conflict, as are Jews and those with no religious affiliation. However, no effects can be discerned at all for families in which a foreign language is spoken.

Examining these patterns with controls for the expected marriage age of children and the difference in the expected marriage age between parents and children shows that the generational conflict in PRI expectations is related to conflict between parents and children in expected marriage age: the greater the difference between parents and children in their expectations about marriage age, the greater the likelihood of conflict over PRI. However, parents and children who expect a later age at marriage for the child show significantly less likelihood of conflict over PRI.

DISCUSSION

Whether unmarried children should continue to live with their parents until marriage or should move out and establish an independent residence beforehand is a family decision that involves both the child and the parents, reflecting and affecting the relationships between the generations. It involves the views of each on the role of the child in the family, including the sharing of space, responsibilities, and rights reflected in the nature and extent of parental control over children. PRI is an emerging family phenomenon associated with less intergenerational sharing and greater independence from the kind of face-to-face monitoring that continued coresidence into adulthood implies for both generations.

40   We examined a series of hypotheses about this new form of intergenerational autonomy. Our findings show that parents and children differ in their expectations, which suggests that point of view within the family has an effect on a critical household event in the family life course. Further, family structure shapes differences in points of view, with female-headed households exhibiting unusually low intergenerational conflict and step-parent families tending toward expectations for early nest-leaving.

Examined in more detail, our results suggest that families opt for greater intergenerational separation for their sons than their daughters and for children of both sexes when they have more resources. Families that are more traditional on other grounds (e.g., Hispanics, southern Europeans, fundamentalist Protestants, and those using a foreign language) are more likely to associate leaving home with marriage.

A second set of hypotheses that we tested focuses on the differences between parents and children in PRI expectations. Consistent with our argument, our findings indicate that parents are significantly less likely to expect PRI for their children than are the children themselves, with socioeconomic status and recency of immigration, as indexed by language use, affecting parental expectations more than the expectations of their children.

Many of the findings reflect differences between groups and between the generations in definitions about the normal pathways young people should take out of the parental home. Some factors have effects on the likelihood of PRI, per se, and thus on whether it should be viewed as a normal, albeit new, stage in the early adult life course, independent of marriage age. Other factors primarily influence PRI through their effects on the expected timing of marriage.

Most of those that operate primarily through their direct effects on PRI—Hispanic or southern European origin, foreign language usage, and generation (parent vs. child)—imply rapid normative change in intergenerational relationships and in the control of parents over their children's lives, of which PRI is only a part. Although the data do not confirm significant levels of current intrafamily conflict, it seems likely that the children's greater exposure to modern lifestyles after high school will increase their expectations for PRI and place them in greater conflict with their parents.

45   The results for stepparent families reinforce the portrait of low intergenerational closeness experienced in families in which stepparents and stepchildren must relate to each other in the same household. Only the finding that young people reporting no religion are more likely to expect PRI, independent of marriage age, does not fit the overall pattern. The high

levels of autonomy among young adults who are not religiously affiliated may reflect rebellion on the part of children, since the parents were not asked religious affiliation, and the levels of nonaffiliation reported by these high school seniors are considerably higher than those for national samples.

In contrast, those factors that primarily operated through expected marriage age—gender, SES, and traditional religious affiliation—seem to represent more fundamental axes of life course structure and marriage timing. The continued preference for an age gap between spouses means that men will have more time for such experiences as PRI in early adulthood than will women. The SES results point to the continued role of higher education in the postponement of marriage, and to the likelihood that for some, this period of postponement will include PRI. Similarly, it is reasonable to argue that young people who currently identify themselves with relatively fundamentalist religious groups avoid PRI primarily because they are aiming for earlier marriage, since the greatly reduced approval of sex outside of marriage (Studer and Thornton, 1987) gives them less option to delay marriage, compared to those with a less restrictive sexual code.

It is less clear that the result showing that young people from mother-only families are delaying marriage represents such a fundamental life course axis. Nevertheless, the pattern is expressed clearly and strongly by both generations, since there is significantly less likelihood of intergenerational conflict over PRI expectations in such families.

Much more research needs to be directed to uncovering the basis of generational consensus and conflict over the patterns of PRI. Such an effort is particularly important given the family nature of the decision to leave home and establish an independent household. As new data from the longitudinal survey of these young adults are analyzed, we should be able to re-examine these generational differences and establish empirically "who wins" when disagreement characterizes the generations, and see whose expectations for the timing of nest-leaving are more predictive of the actual patterns of leaving home before marriage. Parents and children are likely to surprise each other, as each proceeds along their joint and separate life courses. Yet, the majority of these families appear to share expectations about residential independence for young adults before marriage; the emerging patterns seem to be having an increased impact on the parental generation as well as on young adults.

NOTES

The research reported here is part of a project, Premarital Residential Independence among American Ethnic Communities, supported by NICHD Center Grant P-50-HD12639 to the Rand Corporation. Joan W. Keesey helped in organizing the data; Peter Morrison and Linda J. Waite provided constructive comments.

1. Only 10% of students had a parent surveyed as well, but the sample size is so large (30,000 cases) that the resulting subsample yields 3,000 parents for analysis.
2. The sophomore cohort was also asked these questions but had greater difficulty responding to questions on events so much further in the future, with non-

response rates greater than 20%. (For further information, see Jones, Sebring, Crawford, and Spencer, 1986.)

3. The options included single years of age between 18 and 29, less than 18, 30 or more, have already done so, and do not expect to do so.

4. To investigate the possibility that semiautonomous living arrangements such as college dorms and military barracks might have been included by parents or children as an "own home," we tabulated a separate question answered by children on expected living arrangements "next year," which included as options "dorms" and "barracks," by the sequence of residence-marriage expectations (by age). The vast majority of respondents planning to be in dorms or barracks (93%) did not treat them, nor in most cases were they treated by their parents, as residential independence.

5. Most of the cases of attitudinal conflict involved the first pattern. We performed separate analyses of cases in which parents expected PRI but children did not, seeking to identify any systematic pattern associated with families in which parents are disappointed in their children's delayed progress toward independence (Schnaiburg and Goldenberg, 1986). However, the factors predicting this type of conflict did not differ from those we discuss below, so we merged the two categories.

6. There were direct questions asking "What is your race?" and "What is your national origin?"

7. Unlike in earlier analyses, Jews and those with no religious affiliation were not significantly more likely to expect PRI; this appears to reflect the effect of the 90% case loss required by moving to the subsample including parents, since these are very small groups.

8. The coefficients not tested for parent-child differences were essentially the same in all three specifications: the sample of parents only, the sample of children only, and the pooled sample of parents and children.

9. This result is not due to collinearity between black and female-headed families and, in fact, does not characterize black families when black and white families are considered separately.

REFERENCES

Cherlin, Andrew. 1978. "Remarriage as an incomplete institution." *American Journal of Sociology* 84: 634–650.

Goldscheider, Calvin, and Frances Goldscheider. 1987. "Moving out and marriage: What do young adults expect?" *American Sociological Review* 52: 278–285.

Goldscheider, Calvin, and Frances Goldscheider. 1988. "Ethnic continuity and leaving home: The structural and cultural bases of traditional family values." *Sociological Forum* 3: 525–547.

Goldscheider, Frances, and Julie Da Vanzo. 1986. "Semiautonomy and the transition to adulthood." *Social Forces* 65: 187–201.

Goldscheider, Frances, and Julie Da Vanzo. In press. Pathways to independent living in early adulthood: Marriage, semiautonomy, and premarital residential independence." *Demography* 26.

Goldscheider, Frances, and Celine LeBourdais. 1986. "The falling age at leaving home, 1920–1979." *Sociology and Social Research* 70: 99–102.

Hendershot, Gerry, and Paul Placek (eds.). 1981. *Predicting Fertility: Demographic Studies of Birth Expectations,* Lexington, MA: Lexington Books.

Jones, Calvin, Penny Sebring, Joanna Crawford, Brenda Spencer, and Marjorie Butz. 1986. High School and Beyond: 1980 Senior Cohort, Second Follow-up (1984). Data File Users Manual. Washington, DC: National Center for Education Statistics.

Kett, Joseph F. 1977. *Rites of Passage: Adolescence in America, 1790 to the Present.* New York: Basic Books.

Kobrin, Frances E. 1976. "The primary individual and the family: Changes in living arrangements since 1940." *Journal of Marriage and the Family* 38: 233–239.

Laslett, Barbara. 1973. "The family as a public and private institution: An historical perspective." *Journal of Marriage and the Family* 35: 480–494.

Modell, John. 1980. "Normative aspects of American marriage timing since World War II." *Journal of Family History* 5: 210–234.

Pryor, Edward T., Jr. 1972. "Rhode Island family structure: 1875 and 1960." In Peter Laslett and R. Wall (eds.), *Household and Family in Past Time.* Cambridge: Cambridge University Press.

Schnaiberg, Allan, and Shelly Goldenberg. 1986. "From empty nest to crowded nest: Some contradictions in the returning-young-adult syndrome." Paper presented at the annual meeting of the American Sociological Association, New York.

Studer, Marlena, and Arland Thornton. 1987. "Adolescent religiosity and contraceptive usage." *Journal of Marriage and the Family* 49: 117–128.

Waite, Linda, Frances Goldscheider, and Christine Witsberger. 1986. "The development of individualism: Nonfamily living and the plans of young men and women." *American Sociological Review* 51: 541–554.

White, Lynn, and Alan Booth. 1985. "The quality and stability of remarriages. The role of stepchildren." *American Sociological Review* 50: 689–698.

A SOURCE FROM ART HISTORY

In the humanities, an analysis frequently depends on both the subject of the analysis, such as a painting or a short story, and the critical tradition, that is, what others have written about it. Both of these sources will be considered as you develop your analytic perspective. In this section we will look at a painting by Henri Matisse and what one critic, Jack Flam, who writes frequently about Matisse's work, says about it. (Chapter 6 includes an excerpt from his book on Matisse.) This piece by Flam, about the painting called *Bathers with a Turtle*, appeared in *ARTnews* in December, 1990. As you read Flam's discussion, you will see similarities to his discussion of *Conversation* (Chapter 6). He tells us something about the painting's creation and describes the actual work of art. And he suggests again that Matisse's work is hardly as simple as it seems.

In analyzing a work of art you must take time to study the work itself in addition to reading what critics have to say about it. Spend some time answering the questions below and then follow the guide for analyzing at the end of this chapter.

VIEWING THE WORK OF ART

Look at the reproduction of *Bathers with a Turtle*. Write in your journal about what you see, describing it in your own words. What do you think is happening? Why do you think it is called *Bathers with a Turtle?* Could you be a figure or character in this painting? Why or why not? What story does this painting tell? How does it tell it? What do you think Matisse was trying to communicate with this picture? How does the picture make you feel? What is there about it that makes you feel this way? How is it alike or different from other artwork you have seen? If you had a poster of this piece of art, where would you hang it and why would you choose that particular location? Be sure to include a description of the work in your analysis.

ASK YOURSELF

As I read the essay closely, how does Flam explains the painting? What claims does he make about the painting? How does he support them? Does he tell a story as he did about *Conversation?* What questions do I have about the reading; note terms that are unfamiliar and those that have now become familiar. What personal experiences have I or others had that would cause me to look at this piece of art in a special way? Are my experiences similar or different from those of others? Does what Flam say about the painting make sense to me? If something doesn't make sense to me, could it be because my personal experiences were different from those described in the article?

HENRI MATISSE
BATHERS WITH A TURTLE
JACK FLAM

■ ■ ■

Bathers with a Turtle, by Henri Matisse (1869–1954), was painted at the beginning of 1908 and is one of the artist's most concentrated and severe early paintings. Its sober color and austerely simplified composition mark a departure from the bright hues and flamboyant brushwork that characterized so many of the paintings he had done over the previous three years, during his Fauve period. In the summer of 1907, Matisse had gone to Italy, where he studied early Renaissance frescoes. The legibility, emotional gravity, and simple color harmony of *Bathers with a Turtle* seem to reflect his deep admiration for the work of Giotto.

[handwritten margin note: different style—influenced by Renaissance frescoes]

Jack Flam is professor of art history at Brooklyn College and the graduate center of CUNY and art critic of the *Wall Street Journal*.

Matisse painted *Bathers with a Turtle,* 1908, after a trip to Italy, where he had studied early Renaissance frescoes.

(margin note: evokes over confusion)

Because of its visual clarity, *Bathers with a Turtle* reproduces quite well. But no reproduction of it prepares you for the shock you experience when you stand before the actual painting, which is in the St. Louis Art Museum. This is one of those rare pictures that somehow seem to affect your central nervous system. In part this reaction is a response to the vivid presence of the life-size figures and to the intense way that the paint has been applied. Your feelings of unease are quickened by the disturbing counterpoint that the painting sets up between the outward calm of its subject and the roughness, even the ferocity, of its inner tensions. The more you look, the less certain you are about what is going on, and the more you become aware of a kind of metaphysical void that seems to exist just below its surface.

(margin note: each figure is different —isolated)

The painting represents three nude figures on the shore of what appears to be a sea or lake. Although the figures are set quite close to one another and share a common interest in the turtle that one of them is enticing with a bit of food, none of them communicates with either of the others. This underlying sense of mutual isolation is underscored by the way that the figures are arranged. Nowhere do their forms overlap or touch. Only in the areas around the knees and head of the woman on the right does human contact seem to be even a possibility.

The picture's language of representation is more complex and ambiguous than is apparent. All of the figures are more three-dimensionally rendered than the flattened space of the landscape allows for, and the woman on the right—who appears to be seated—has an especially contradictory relationship to the space around her. Logically, there should be some incline or bump on the ground below her. But the landscape is treated so abstractly—as a flat color field severely arranged in three horizontal bands— that there is hardly space for her body to occupy.

lack of landscape
drab color
primitive

The other figures are also puzzling. It is impossible to tell for certain whether the figure at the left is supposed to be male or female, and it seems equally impossible to tell what the woman in the center is doing with her mouth. Is she supposed to be whistling, moaning, or silently grasping herself in a fit of agitation? And why does her face have such a strongly simian aspect? As you study this enigmatic painting, such questions multiply.

the more you stare, the more you wonder

5   Measuring approximately six by seven feet, *Bathers with a Turtle* is one of Matisse's largest paintings; at the time he executed it only *Le bonheur de vivre* (1905–06) had been painted on a (slightly) bigger canvas. Like *Le bonheur de vivre,* this was one of the relatively few paintings that Matisse had done from imagination rather than directly from nature, even though by 1908 the theme of nude figures in a landscape had already preoccupied him for a few years. In fact, the general theme of three nudes in a landscape, and even the poses of the figures in *Bathers with a Turtle,* are clearly related to the *Three Bathers* of 1907, painted just a few months earlier. The considerable differences between the styles of the two paintings evoke divergent meanings despite their similar subjects.

lifesize

Although the earlier painting also involved an extreme simplification of the figures, its subject was made more topical by a more detailed and specific kind of landscape, and by the fairly specific activities of the figures, who seem to be drying themselves with towels. The setting of *Bathers with a Turtle,* by contrast, is much less specific. Here, in fact, the designation *bathers* seems to be merely a nod to the conventional name for nudes in a landscape, rather than a literal description of the figures represented. In *Bathers with a Turtle,* the figures seem more like primeval creatures set in some indefinite place at the very ends of the earth than like traditional bathers.

simple landscape + lack of activity add to primitive setting

The poses of the three figures, moreover, suggest a progression in states of being. The closed position of the figure at the left is almost fetal, the one on the right is more open, while the center figure is nearly vertical, though still related to the coiled poses of the others by the exaggerated bend of her neck. These poses imply a strong sense of unfolding or evolution. Combined with the roughness of the rendering and the primordial visage of the central figure, they evoke a primitive or primeval state of being—a feeling that is intensified by the presence of the turtle. Itself a primordial creature, the turtle here seems to symbolize the earth, as it does in primitive cultures, where it is also associated with the life force, fecundity, and transformation. The intensity with which the three figures attend to the turtle, coupled with the energetic and atypical liveliness of the turtle, focuses our own attention on the primeval aspects of the painting.

Such primitivizing themes were not uncommon at the time that Matisse painted *Bathers with a Turtle*. A similar theme can also be discerned in Picasso's *Three Women,* painted that same year, which also suggests evolving states of being. Although these two paintings—which are almost exactly the same size—are stylistically very different, they seem to share this concern with primitivism and notions of becoming. They also both occupy prominent places within the oeuvres of their creators. Picasso's *Three Women* marked an important phase in the development of the style that would later be called Cubism. Matisse's *Bathers with a Turtle* was an important step in the development of the flat, decorative pictorial language that would lead to the large *Dance and Music* panels of 1909–10, and that eventually would culminate in his spectacular late cutouts.

A SOURCE FROM NUTRITION

Analyzing scientific research reports can be rather daunting, since the language of science aims at certainty and truth. The conventional scientific research report—the review of the literature, the question for research, the results, and the discussion—seems formatted to report to us about new knowledge about the natural world contained in the report. If you are not familiar with research practices in the sciences, the process of analysis might seem even more difficult than in other disciplines. Nevertheless, in studies of nutrition—and especially in reports of cultural eating patterns— you indeed have a lens through which to read this research. Your own personal and cultural eating patterns offer you a perspective from which to analyze research on nutrition.

The source for your analysis essay, "Incidence of osteoporosis in vegetarians and omnivores" was published in 1972 in the *Journal of Clinical Nutrition*. In Chapter 9 the reading was a study that looked at how the cultural eating habits of meat-eating Alaskan Eskimos affected their bone mineral content. In contrast, this study examines the bone content of vegetarians. The research report is segmented similarly to the previous one. An introduction gives you the background for the study. In the Materials and Methods section, the researchers describe how they measured bone content. In the last two sections they report on their results and discuss what they think the results mean.

As you engage in the activities suggested below, survey the text to become familiar with its sections and the new terminology. Even during this initial reading, pay special attention to the statement of the hypothesis (or claim) and to the discussion section. Reading this kind of research report usually means paying closer attention to some sections rather than others.

Give yourself time to reflect on what this research means to you personally and try to make personal connections between your experiences and the research you've read on calcium and osteoporosis. As you write your analysis you can take into account these other readings. Remember, your purpose for reading is to understand the research and your connection to it, and to establish a position that explains what it means to you.

ASK YOURSELF

As I read "Incidence of osteoporosis in vegetarians and omnivores," consider how this research builds on what I already have learned about research in the discipline called nutrition. Are there any about connections between my personal experiences and the research reported here? Do the results strike me as reasonable? Do they match my experiences or are they different? What are my expectations about the bone content of vegetarians? Do I know anyone with osteoporosis? Am I or any of my relatives at risk for osteoporosis? Do I know any vegetarians? What have I learned recently about nutrition and health?

INCIDENCE OF OSTEOPOROSIS IN VEGETARIANS AND OMNIVORES[1,2]

FREY R. ELLIS,[3] M.D., F.R.C. PATHOL., SCHURA HOLESH,[4] M.B.CH.B., F.F.R., D.M.R.D., AND JOHN W. ELLIS,[5] B.SC.

■ ■ ■

This investigation was initiated by the hypothesis proposed by Wachman and Bernstein (1) that "bone dissolution is considered as a possible mechanism to buffer the fixed acid load imposed by the ingestion of an 'acid ash' diet in man." If this hypothesis is feasible, one would expect to observe a greater degree of bone dissolution in a diet that contains meat (a primary source of acid ash) than in a vegetarian diet.

Various studies (2, 3) have shown that there is an increased bone loss with age; this loss begins at approximately age 35 to 45 in women and approximately 45 to 65 in men. The rate of loss is also greater in females than in males.

---

[1]From the Kingston Hospital, Kingston-upon-Thames, Surrey, England.

[2]Supported by a grant from the South West Metropolitan Regional Hospital Board.

[3]Consultant Haematologist.

[4]Consultant radiologist.

[5]Research Assistant.

Source: From *The American Journal of Clinical Nutrition,* 25: June 1972, pp. 555–558.

The diagnosis of osteoporosis by subjective study of X-rays is inaccurate unless the changes are gross. As a result, various quantitive methods have been devised for the measurement of bone density, e.g., X-ray and gamma-ray densitometry. The hands are usually examined, as this is more convenient for the subject and there is less soft tissue to affect density readings. West and Reed (4), however, have found the best results by examination of the femur. Another method of assessing bone density is by measuring the cortical thickness and the total diameter of the 2nd metacarpal. The result is expressed as cortical thickness to total thickness ratio because this value is a function of bone density rather than bone mass and has a much smaller standard deviation (5, 6).

MATERIALS AND METHODS

A group of twenty-five British vegetarians (ovolacto vegetarians), consisting of eight males and seventeen females with an age range of 53 to 79 years, was studied. A blood sample was taken for laboratory investigation.

5   In this short preliminary investigation, it was decided to use a simple method of testing bone density, particularly as the more complicated apparatus was not available and patients came intermittently from various parts of the country.

The right hand was examined in all instances except in two patients who were left-handed. Kodak cassettes with high resolution screens and rapid process films were used. The X-ray factors were 45 kv, 50 to 70 ma, at 58 inches tube-focus distance to avoid as much magnification as possible. A graduated aluminum step-wedge (1 to 8 mm) was placed on each film to ensure uniformity of density. The processing of all X-rays was by a 90-sec automatic apparatus.

As the 3rd finger was in the center of the X-ray film, it was decided to determine the density of the center of the third metacarpal medulla and the proximal phalanx using a Baldwin Radiological Densitometer. The centers of these bones were accurately measured and great care was taken to place this area in the center of the densitometer aperture. Because of the age of some of the patients, there was not a sufficiently clear distinction between the medulla and cortex and it was felt that cortical measurements would be inaccurate. All the densitometer readings were determined on the same day to ensure uniformity and accuracy.

The hemoglobin and white cell count were determined on a Coulter Model S, the sedimentation rate by the method of Westergren, and the serum concentrations of urea, cholesterol, calcium, phosphate, and proteins were determined by standard automated laboratory techniques. The serum B_{12} was determined by the *Lactobacillus leichmannii* method (7) and the serum folate by the method of Chanarin (8).

A control group of 25 omnivores, matched for age (± 3 years) and sex, were also studied (Table 1).

TABLE 1

| Controls | | | | Vegetarians | | | |
Weight, KG	Height, CM	Age, YEARS	Sex	Age, YEARS	Height, CM	Weight, KG	Years as Vegetarian
73.2	175	53	M	55	170	76.1	35
59.8		57	M	56	165	57.3	42
63.9	179	58	M	59	180	70.0	35
75.4	176	61	M	64	168	65.2	30
83.0		65	M	65	175	69.1	20
71.4		67	M	65	172.5	53.7	52
97.3		68	M	71	174	61.9	59
		81	M	83	176	73.3	30+
66.4	167	55	F	53	140.5	60.6	53
66.2	159	56	F	54	172	76.0	30
64.7	166	57	F	55	153	63.5	35
51.2	156	58	F	57	148.5	51.2	12
60.0	156	58	F	57	153.5	65.9	39
65.2	161.5	61	F	58	150.5	70.8	20
64.9	155	61	F	61	150.5	47.8	13
63.0	162	63	F	62	163	45.0	10
63.5	162.5	64	F	63	142.5	41.9	35
		65	F	68	169.5	56.0	68
68.0		68	F	69	162	49.6	17
53.5	149	73	F	71	147	55.8	33
73.0	160	73	F	72	152	54.0	12
70.6		75	F	74	160	48.5	21
67.5	154	78	F	77	150.5	52.0	77
73.2	163	78	F	77	161	44.8	54
61.5		79	F	79	154	62.9	64

RESULTS

10 In Table 2, the results of the radiological and laboratory investigations are given as the mean ($\pm$ SD) of the two separate groups. The mean of the serum folate and proteins in the control group were determined on groups of 21 and 24, respectively; in all other cases, the means are for groups of 25.

The significance was determined by applying a t test on the paired observations and the level of significance was taken as $P < 0.05$.

Table 2 shows that the density of the bones that were measured was significantly greater in the vegetarians than in the omnivores, whereas the hemoglobin, urea, calcium, vitamin B_{12}, and total proteins were significantly lower. In all the other findings there was no significant difference.

Table 3 shows the relationship between bone density and age. The density of the bone is shown as a mean ($\pm$ SD) for each of the three age groups: 50 to 59, 60 to 69, and 70 to 79 years. The results are given for the density of both the proximal phalanx of the 3rd finger and for the 3rd metacarpal. In all age groups, the bone density of the vegetarians was greater than that of the controls. The mean bone densities of the 70- to 79-year age groups of the vegetarians was greater than the densities of the 50- to 59-year age group of the omnivores.

TABLE 2

Investigation	Vegetarians Mean	SD	Controls Mean	SD	Significance
Density of proximal phalanx of 3rd finger	1.37	0.31	0.88	0.24	$P < 0.001$
Density of 3rd metacarpal	1.06	0.25	0.64	0.17	$P < 0.001$
Hb, g/100 ml	13.1	1.0	14.5	1.3	$P < 0.001$
WBC,/mm^2	6,300	1,800	7,300	3,100	$0.1 < P < 0.2$
ESR (Westergren), mm/1 hr	20	18	15	16	$0.2 < P < 0.3$
Urea, mg/100 ml	32	7	37	10	$P < 0.05$
Cholesterol, mg/100 ml	245	64	246	57	$0.95 < P < 0.975$
Calcium, mg/100 ml	9.4	0.7	10.0	0.4	$P < 0.005$
Phosphate (as P), mg/100 ml	3.5	0.5	3.6	0.6	$0.5 < P < 0.6$
Vitamin B$_{12}$, pg/ml	261	112	411	207	$P < 0.01$
Folate, ng/ml	11.8	6.6	7.9 (21)	4.7	$0.05 < P < 0.1$
Total proteins, g/100 ml	7.3	0.4	7.5 (24)	0.5	$P < 0.05$

Except where figures are shown in parentheses, all sample sizes are 25.

TABLE 3

Age groups, years	Density of proximal phalanx of 3rd finger Vegetarians Mean ± SD	Controls Mean ± SD	Density of 3rd metacarpal Vegetarians Mean ± SD	Controls Mean ± SD
50–59	1.50 ± 0.22 (9)	1.02 ± 0.19 (7)	1.14 ± 0.18 (9)	0.71 ± 0.17 (7)
60–69	1.27 ± 0.27 (8)	0.88 ± 0.27 (10)	1.01 ± 0.19 (8)	0.68 ± 0.19 (10)
70–79	1.32 ± 0.40 (8)	0.73 ± 0.17 (7)	1.03 ± 0.36 (7)	0.55 ± 0.14 (7)

Figures in parentheses denote the number of subjects in that group.

DISCUSSION

The vegetarians included in this study had bone densities significantly greater than those of individually matched omnivores. Because the vegetarians were matched for age and sex with the omnivores, any variation due to these two criteria would tend to be removed. These results support the hypothesis of Wachman and Bernstein (1) that bone dissolution is greater in individuals who utilize a diet high in acid ash, i.e., omnivores, whether in fact this difference is due to acid ash or any other dietary differences, e.g., calcium intake, has yet to be determined. The results also suggest that vegetarians are less prone to osteoporosis than omnivores.

15   When bone density was related to age, both sets of measurements showed that the bone density of the omnivores decreased with age; this was also seen in the vegetarian group but to a lesser degree. No further decrease in bone density appeared to take place in the vegetarians who were approximately 69 years old, whereas it continued to decrease in the omnivore group. These results suggest that there is less likelihood of vegetarians developing osteoporosis in old age.

The serum calcium in vegetarians was significantly lower than it was in the controls, but both mean values were within the normal range (8.5 to 10.5 mg/

100 ml). There was, however, no significant difference in serum phosphate concentrations (normal range 2.5 to 4.8 mg P/100 ml). The dietary intake of calcium has been shown to be greater in vegetarians than in omnivores (9); therefore, the lower serum level in vegetarians is unlikely to be due to a dietary inadequacy. If the hypothesis of Wachman and Bernstein is true, then there will be greater dissolution of bones in omnivores, and this may give rise to a higher serum calcium level. The serum phosphate was no higher in the omnivores, as might have been expected if a greater degree of bone dissolution was occurring. This may be accounted for, however, by the phosphate being removed during its buffering action of the acid ash.

The serum concentration of vitamin B_{12} was significantly lower in vegetarians than in the controls; this has been shown in other studies on vegetarians and vegans (10, 11). The reason for this low level is the low dietary intake in these minority groups. There was no significant difference in the serum folate, which has been found to be higher in vegans (9, 12) due to their high dietary intake of green vegetables. Nine omnivores had folate concentrations below the normal values (6 to 20 ng/ml), whereas only two vegetarians had values below normal. The results of the vitamin B_{12} concentrations showed that only one omnivore had a serum vitamin B_{12} value below 150 pg/ml, whereas three vegetarians had concentrations below this level (normal range 150 to 900 pg/ml).

The serum urea levels in vegetarians were significantly lower than those of the omnivores, but both mean values were within the normal range (13 to 44 mg/100 ml). A similar finding has been demonstrated in vegans (12). This lower blood urea may be a reflection on the lower dietary intake of protein in vegetarians (9) and may also account for the significantly lower serum total protein levels.

SUMMARY

A study of the bone density of vegetarians compared with age- and sex-matched omnivore controls was carried out. A significant difference was noted in vegetarians, which suggests that they are less prone to osteoporosis than omnivores. Other biochemical differences were also found.

We are grateful to Dr. B. W. Meade for the biochemical investigations, Dr. L. Bernstock for the serum folate estimations, and Dr. J. W. T. Dickerson for his kind advice. Thanks are also due to Mr. Greenslade for the loan of the densitometer, Miss M. Bean for taking the radiographs, and Mrs. A. Harper for her help with the measurements of the hands. We are also indebted to Mrs. J. Stopford for secretarial assistance.

REFERENCES

1. Wachman, A., and D. S. Bernstein. Diet and osteoporosis. *Lancet* 1:958, 1968.
2. Newton-John, H. F., and D. B. Morgan. Osteoporosis: disease or senescence? *Lancet* 1:232, 1968.
3. Adams, P., G. T. Davies and P. Sweetman. Osteoporosis and the effects of ageing on bone mass in elderly men and women. *Quart. J. Med.* 39:361, 1970.

4. West, R. R., and G. W. Reed. The measurement of bone mineral in vivo by photon beam scanning. *Brit. J. Radiol.* 43:886, 1970.
5. Barnett, E. E. C., and B. E. C. Nordin. The radiological diagnosis of osteoporosis:
   a new approach. *Clin. Radiol.* 11:166, 1960.
6. Nordin, B. E. C. Clinical significance and pathogenesis of osteoporosis. *Brit. Med.
   J.* 1:571, 1971.
7. Chanarin, I., and V. Berry. Estimation of serum *L. casei* activity. *J. Clin. Pathol.*
   17:111, 1964.
8. Spray, G. H. An improved method for the rapid estimation of vitamin B_{12} in
   serum. *Clin. Sci.* 14:661, 1955.
9. Ellis, F. R., and P. Mumford. The nutritional status of vegans and vegetarians.
   Proc. Nutr. Soc. 26:205, 1967.
10. Ellis, F. R., and F. Wokes. The treatment of dietary deficiency of vitamin B_{12} with
    vegetable protein foods. *Nutr. Dieta* 9:81, 1967.
11. West, E. D., and F. R. Ellis. The electroencephalogram in veganism, vegetarian-
    ism, vitamin B_{12} deficiency and in controls. *J. Neurol. Neurosurg. Psychiat.*
    29:391, 1966.
12. Ellis, F. R., and V. M. E. Montegriffo. Veganism, clinical findings and investiga-
    tions. *Am. J. Clin. Nutr.* 23:249, 1970.

WRITING AND LEARNING ACTIVITIES:
A GUIDE TO ANALYZING

The activities below will guide you through the process of writing an analysis
of the source materials included here. You may work on source materials
from other chapters or provided by your instructor, or identify materials connected with your research interests.

READING THE TEXT

1. **Reading:** Read the text you plan to analyze.

2. **Journal Entry:** Write in your journal as you read. Consider how this research
   builds on what you already have learned about research in the discipline of
   social research. Also write about connections between your personal experiences and the research reported here. Do the results strike you as reasonable? Match your experiences or are different? What are your expectations
   about establishing Premarital Residential Independence for yourself if you
   have not already done so?

3. **Annotate the Text:** As you read, mark the report to help you follow the research. Use highlighters to mark key points. Restate the researchers' claim in
   the margins. Put question marks where you don't understand something or
   where it contradicts your personal experience.

THINKING ABOUT THE DISCIPLINE

1. **Journal Entry:** What have you learned thus far about the disciplines these
   sources come from? What was the author's purpose in writing this report or
   piece? How did the author present knowledge to persuade you of his or her
   main point? What specialized terms does he or she use?

2. **Group Activity:** Compare your journal entries. Talk about the similarities and differences in your understanding of the sources and of the disciplines they are part of.

SUMMARIZING THE RESEARCH

1. **Writing Activity:** Write a summary of the source you are analyzing. How much information should be included? Include those aspects of your source that you respond to in your analysis. If you are analyzing an artwork, be sure to describe both the piece of art as well as summarize what a critic said about it.

MAKING PERSONAL CONNECTIONS

1. **Journal Entry:** What personal experiences have you or others had with issues described in your reading? Are your experiences similar or different? If you did not understand a portion of the research report, could it be because your personal experiences were different from those described in the research?

2. **Group Activity:** Compare how your personal connections differ from or are similar to each other. Did your experiences match or differ from those presented in the reading? Report to the class on the relationship of your experiences to those described in your reading.

ESTABLISHING YOUR POSITION

1. **Journal Entry:** Write about what position you will take in response to the research report you just read. Write about what evidence from your readings and what personal experience you will use to support your position.

2. **Writing Activity:** Reread your notes on the discipline, your personal connections, and your summary of the research. Draft a position statement that gives your perspective on this research.

3. **Group Activity:** Share your position statements in small groups. Tell the group how you arrived at that position and how you will support it. Others should ask questions about aspects of your position that are unclear.

DEVELOPING YOUR INTRODUCTION

1. **Writing Activity:** Reread your notes and draft an introduction that will help the reader understand your analysis of this specialized research.

2. **Peer Exchange:** Exchange your introductions and ask your partner how well yours introduces the analysis.

DRAFTING THE ESSAY

1. **Group Activity:** Look over Natalie Acevedo's draft. How well do you feel she explained and supported her position? What would you have done differently? Did she help you to understand the research from her perspective? Did she help you to see the significance of the research? Did she alert you to any pitfalls in the research?

2. **Writing Activity:** Look over the notes you've accumulated throughout this process. Draft an essay in which you establish a position with respect to the reading you have done, supporting your claim with evidence from your reading and your personal experience.

REVISING THE ESSAY

1. Rereading: Give your essay three separate readings, focusing on one problem at a time. Follow the guide for revision presented under "Revising the Essay," pages 490–491.

2. Peer Review: Exchange papers with a partner and give his or her paper the same three separate readings.

3. Journal Entry: Respond to the experience of peer review, considering the benefits and difficulties. Were you able to predict the problems identified by your partner?

ACADEMIC SKILLS FOR WRITING AND LEARNING

13

READING AND ANNOTATING DISCIPLINE-SPECIFIC TEXTS

I always begin at the left with the opening word of the sentence and read toward the right and I recommend this method.

JAMES THURBER

Readers are less and less seen as mere non-writers, the subhuman "other" or flawed derivative of the author; the lack of a pen is no longer a shameful mark of secondary status but a positively enabling space, just as within every writer can be seen to lurk, as a repressed but contaminating antithesis, a reader.

TERRY EAGLETON

READING

What do you think of James Thurber's advice? If you've skimmed some of the very specialized readings included in this textbook or begun to work with them, you may find Thurber's tongue-in-cheek comment less than helpful. Reading is sometimes more complicated than a left-to-right, top-to-bottom march down the page.

It may be obvious that participating in an academic community means going to classes, talking to teachers and students, and writing papers, but the role that reading plays is sometimes not so clear. Becoming a better reader *will* help you become a better writer. Terry Eagleton, quoted above, claims that, as a reader, you are not simply a receptacle into which written material is poured. Rather, through reading, you can become an active participant. Up to this point I have emphasized how important it is to understand the methods and special approaches of the disciplines you study. Reading specialized texts requires strategies for reading that reflect the way knowledge is made in each of these disciplines; for example, you may have

523

to read a text more than once or read specific parts several times. But this chapter offers some general reading strategies, focusing on reading for understanding, reading critically, and reading for personal connections.

READING FOR UNDERSTANDING

This is the most basic, preliminary type of reading. For relatively familiar material this is the only reading you need to do. In academic work, this kind of reading is the groundwork for the later readings that help you to read critically and to evaluate the work.

1. What is your purpose for reading? Are you skimming to find out if the text contains information you need for a paper, or are you looking for evidence in support of a claim? Or are you reading for pleasure on a topic that interests you?
2. Look over the entire text before reading it. Look at the title and any introductory material. Who is the author? Do you know anything about the author or his or her work? Is the text segmented into sections? What is emphasized in each section? When was the text written? What kinds of other works does it cite? What kind of information is included in the notes at the end? Do you need to look up some key terms or topics in a specialized dictionary or encyclopedia? What ideas do you think the author will discuss? What is one question you think the author will answer?
3. What is the text about? What issue is the author concerned about? What do you know about this topic? What point is the author trying to make? Who is the intended audience? What was the author's purpose in writing this piece?

READING CRITICALLY

Reading critically asks you to think more carefully, more deeply, and in more sophisticated ways about the text. It asks you to question the author(s) and to consider the discipline the work is conducted in. You will often have to read a text two or more times in order to approach it critically. In Chapters 1 through 9, specialists in various academic disciplines provided excellent examples of how to read critically.

1. What academic discipline is this work being done in? Have you taken any courses in this field? What do you know about the field's typical kinds of research or inquiry? How does this reading contribute to ongoing work in this discipline? What assumptions seem to guide the research? Why is the text organized the way it is?
2. Most academic texts make an argument. What does the author(s) argue here? Does the text make a claim that something is true and support that claim with evidence? Evaluate the argument. Does it seem reasonable, based on what you know about various academic disciplines? What key terms are the author(s) using? How are they defined within the context of the reading and how do they contribute to the argument? How do scholars in other disciplines discuss this topic? Evaluate the methods

used to make the argument and the evidence used to support the claim. Do you still have a clear idea of what the text is about? Reflect on how your ideas about the text have changed during your reading process.

READING FOR PERSONAL CONNECTIONS

Reading for personal connections can be done at any time or you can give the text a special reading for that purpose alone. Sometimes personal connections pop up without being invited, especially if you are open to them. Personal responses, which can be positive or negative, occur any time a voice in your head comments on what you are reading or some aspect of the reading recalls one of your life experiences. Being aware of these connections will help you to establish your own position with respect to the work you are reading.

1. Notice what makes you react to the text. Does something ring true or strike you as obviously false? How does your personal experience fit with what the text says is true? If you have no common experience with the text, why do you suppose that is?
2. Think of your response as "talking back" to the text. What makes you trust or distrust it? Explain why you react the way you do. What is your current position on the issues raised in the reading? What could cause you to change your position? What questions do you think the author should discuss but has not?

WRITING AND LEARNING ACTIVITIES

1. **Journal Entry:** Make an informal inventory of all the different kinds of reading you have done over the past month: from reading a subway map, to setting up a computer, to reading a novel for pleasure, and doing your homework. List the various purposes for each type. Who is your favorite author? What kind of reading do you most like to do when you have a choice?

2. **Group Activity:** Meet in small groups and share your lists. How are they different from or similar to each other. Can you make any general statement about your group's reading activity? Report back to class.

3. **Writing and Learning Activity:** Look at the first two pages of the reading excerpt from Philippe Ariès's book *Centuries of Childhood: A History of Family Life* featured in Chapter 1, Social History (pages 11–36). Try out the reading strategies listed above. Which is most effective for you? Have these strategies changed your response to the material?

ANNOTATING

Participating in an academic community means that you should always be thinking of yourself as an *active* participant, as entering into the conversation of that academic discipline. Being an active reader means reading critically to evaluate and make sense of what you read. It also means read-ing with a pen, pencil, and highlighter in your hand to encode—that is, to annotate—your thoughts on the page of your text, on Post-It notes, or on a photocopy. Annotating includes making note of questions, defining terms in your own words, illustrating patterns of ideas, evaluating claims and evi-dence, clarifying points, and interpreting the text. You may not want to an-notate everything you read, but the strategies presented here will be very helpful in working through a difficult text and learning the ways people make meaning in various disciplines.

Annotating texts is not something only students do. It's a skill that guides nearly everyone's reading process at some time or another. In Chap-ter 7, Marine Biology, Professor Todd Newberry told how he annotated a text:

When I read a paper, I use a pencil. I learned long ago not to carry pens into places that have valuable books. Ink stains forever. I am going to go through this paper and place stars where something is very important and question marks where I don't understand some-thing. I'll use X's and arrows when I want to go back, and so on. As I read I try to clear up my questions or confusions. Sometimes what looked very important turns out not to be so important after all. Or I may have put a question mark next to something I understand now. . . . It's important to have your own personal code, one that allows you to scan for in-formation quickly and easily.

You will want to develop your own annotating code. As you mark a text, remember that you are trying to identify what it is you will need to come back to in the text. Keep the marks to a minimum so that when you revisit the text, the most important points will stand out for you. Here are some options for annotating texts:

Underline the author's main point.

Bracket examples.

Use wavy lines under new terms.

Use question marks to indicate uncertainly.

Use exclamation points to illustrate surprise.

Highlight important explanations.

Use different-colored highlighters to emphasize different topics.

Use a slash to indicate a transition to a new idea.

Number lists or related points.

Use arrows and lines to refer back or ahead to related points.

Circle something you might want to quote.

Place a star next to a personal connection and jot down a note in the margin.

Make marginal notes to restate a main point.

In the margins, write down questions you need answered.

After reading, jot down a very brief summary of the reading.

Below is a passage that was annotated during a critical reading. It is the first three paragraphs of Chapter 2 of Philippe Ariès's *Centuries of Childhood: A History of Family Life* (365–366) (see Chapter 1, Social History). It was annotated as the writer read the text and Professor Weiner's commentary on it.

Title suggests a change over time

II

FROM THE MEDIEVAL FAMILY TO THE MODERN FAMILY

■ ■ ■

Ariès claims change in attitude made family change.

= visual art

The preceding analysis of iconography has shown us the new importance assumed by the family in the sixteenth and seventeenth centuries. It is significant that in the same period important changes can be noted in the family's attitude to the child; as the attitude towards the child changed, so did the family itself.

claim

Italian says English aren't affectionate toward kids— evidence = apprenticeships = work in other people's houses at chores

An Italian text of the late fifteenth century gives us an extremely thought-provoking impression of the medieval family, at least in England. It is taken from an account of England by an Italian:[1] 'The want of affection in the English is strongly manifested towards their children; for after having kept them at home till they arrive at the age of seven or nine years at the utmost [in the old French authors, seven is given as the age when the boys leave the care of the womenfolk to go to school or to enter the adult world], they put them out, both males and females, to hard service in the houses of other people, binding them generally for another seven or nine years [i.e. until they are between fourteen and eighteen]. And these are called apprentices, and during that time they perform all the most menial offices; and few are born who are exempted from this fate, for everyone, however rich he may be, sends away his children into the houses of others, whilst he, in return, receives those of strangers into his own.' The Italian considers this custom cruel, which suggests that it was unknown or had been forgotten in his country. He insinuates that the English took in other people's children because they thought that in that way they would obtain better service than they would from their own offspring. In fact the explanation which the English themselves gave to the Italian observer was probably the real one: 'In order that their children might learn better manners.'

cruel? like domestic work or extensive babysitting? get paid?

why? really!

evidence from will — This way of life was probably common in the West during the Middle Ages. Thus a twelfth-century Mâcon knight called Guigonet, whose family Georges Duby was able to describe from a study of his will, entrusted his two young sons to the eldest of his *from articles?* — three brothers.[2] At a later date, numerous articles of apprenticeship hiring children to masters prove how widespread was the custom of placing children in other families. It is sometimes specifically stated that the master must 'teach' the child and 'show him the details of his merchandise' or that he must 'send him to school'.[3] But these are exceptional cases. As a general rule, the principal duty of a child entrusted to a master is to 'serve him well and truly'. Looking at these contracts without first of all ridding ourselves of our modern habits of thought, we find it difficult to decide whether the child has been placed as an apprentice (in the modern meaning of the word), or as a boarder, or as a servant. We should be foolish to *different times / different views* — press the point: our distinctions are anachronistic, and a man of the Middle Ages would see nothing in them but slight variations on a basic idea—that of service.

☆ *apprentice purpose Couldn't be done today*

=

not looked down on — The only type of service which people could think of for a long time, domestic service, brought no degradation and aroused no repugnance. In the fifteenth century there was an entire literature in the vernacular French or English, listing in a mnemonic verse form the rules for a good servant. One of these poems is entitled in French: 'Régime pour tous serviteurs'.[4] The English equivalent is 'wayting servant'— which has remained in modern English with the word 'waiter'. True, this servant must know how to wait at table, make beds, accompany his master, and so on. But this domestic service goes with what we would nowadays call a secretary's duties: and it is not a permanent condition, but a period of apprentice-*temporary lifestyle* — ship, an intermediary stage.

evidence from poem

WRITING AND LEARNING ACTIVITIES

1. **Writing and Learning Activity:** Your instructor will choose a passage from a text in this book that you have not read yet. Use the three types of reading discussed above and practice annotating the chosen text.

2. **Group Activity:** Discuss your reading process in your groups and compare your annotations. Report to the class on the similarities and differences in your annotations and in your understanding of the readings.

WRITING IN JOURNALS

Along with reading and annotating texts, one of the most productive activities you can do is to write informally in journal entries about what you are learning. These entries serve a number of purposes: to help you participate in ongoing activities in class, to learn, and to reflect on all that is occurring on a day-to-day basis. Journal entries can also help you keep track of ideas for essays and longer research papers. Other uses are listed below. Use your journal:

To *talk back,* to respond to things that occurred in class that you may not have been ready to comment on.

As an informal means of participating by *working out something that puzzles you.*

As a *reading log,* noting the successes and difficulties you have with a specific reading.

To *write about personal connections,* about how your own experiences shape what you know and believe. How these connections shape the way you respond to the reading or to class discussion.

To *write about critical issues.* Try to look for patterns across readings or take apart a particular reading to see how the argument works.

To *take notes on your readings.*

As a commonplace book, *jotting down everyday thoughts and experiences* beyond the scope of this class.

To write about what is happening in other classes or at home. Events have the most curious way of connecting to each other, especially if you've been writing about them and looking for connections.

To *compose letters* to an author whose work you've been reading or a close friend. You may or may not send the letter, but directing a letter to someone helps to focus our thoughts.

HOW STUDENTS HAVE USED JOURNALS

Included below are examples of how some of my students have used journals. Journal entries are especially useful for developing personal connections. Here Gina Marie Rossi writes about her personal response to a specific aspect of Elizabeth Bishop's short story "In the Village," included in Chapter 5, Literary Studies.

In "In the Village," the child's mother comes back from Boston to stay with her as she continues to mourn the death of her husband. The mother has suffered a severe mental collapse and the child was confused, uncomfortable, and "unaccustomed to having her back" (paragraph 8). The child has a distinct outlet in her visits to the town's blacksmith, Nate. When the child hears him working, Bishop writes, the noises he makes produce a bursting sound which fill the child's world. "Clang. Clang. Oh, beautiful sounds, from the blacksmith's shop at the end of the garden!" (paragraphs 9–11) Visiting Nate offers her a break from her reality, giving her somewhere to go to forget about life for a little while. I think everyone has to have an outlet. When my aunt gets angry at my cousins or my uncle she goes into their living room and plays the piano. People in the house could be screaming and fighting, but she just remains at the piano like nothing else matters. The child in the story needs an outlet because she doesn't understand the situation she is in.

In this brief portion of a journal entry, also included in the introduction, Liza Beier "talks back" about classroom life.

There is sort of a game we play when we enter a classroom. We listen to the teacher. We wait to hear his views. We notice the words he uses and then we incorporate them into our writing.

After reading Ruth Horowitz's description of a Hispanic community in Chapter 2, Cultural Anthropology, Fernando Escobar was able to compare his own community with the one in the reading and to make sense of the term *reciprocal relationships*.

For me, 32nd Street is a reality. I was born in Mexico. Half of my family is here and half is there. I'm part of a society in transition and there can be many levels of transition even within the same family. My mother-in-law is very traditional; the man should be strong and free and the woman should take care of the family. My wife, on the other hand, is more educated and no longer accepts those traditions. I also can identify with Stack when she describes how members of a very poor community depend on each other economically as a network. In my block there is a mechanic who does electrical work and we often trade off. My father-in-law lets me have an apartment very cheap and in exchange I work on his car. So, to use the same word, we have a reciprocal relationship.

After reading the two short stories by Elizabeth Bishop in Chapter 5, Literary Studies, Salvador Gonzalez characterized the difference between the stories as follows:

"The Baptism" seemed to be written from a distance, with a colder kind of writing. Bishop seemed to write with more emotion in "In the Village," as though she was willing to expose more of herself and her past experiences.

Journals can also be used simply to summarize your reading. Brian Boll writes about a research report on the causes of leaving home in Latin American countries (found in Chapter 3, Quantitative Social Research).

Main purpose of De Vos's research: gather baseline data on nest-leaving patterns. De Vos wants to know what affects nest-leaving so she looks at these variables (behaviors/characteristics): marital status, age, sex, residence, education, work status. Data comes from World Fertility Survey, so it wasn't collected for her study. She says nest-leaving is often considered to be going from a "family of orientation to a family of procreation" (p. 615) She finds this is true for the countries she's observing, because most people leave home for marriage. She also finds that education is not an important reason to leave home. Sometimes young women are sent out to work but young men stay home in rural settings to manage the family farm or land.

Sally Singer used her journal to work toward an analysis of a research report exploring the cause of osteoporosis among North Alaskan Eskimos. She read critically, questioning the material in the report based on something she had learned in another class.

I took a women's studies course last semester and now anytime I see the word "standard" I look more closely. I just wonder what exactly the standard is that they're comparing them to. Our country is a salad bowl, even our class is, so how do we know who they are comparing the Eskimos to? I also wondered about the reasons for the women having so much more bone loss than the men. I mean I know that osteoporosis is a woman's disease but still that result was huge. I wanted to hear more about the difference between men and women.

For all these students, their journals and conversations offered essential tools for participating in academic communities. Unless you can be clear on how what you learn connects to your current experience and knowledge, you'll feel as though you are memorizing material without making real sense of it. Reading actively, annotating texts, writing in journals, and talking to others about what you are learning will help make you a part of a community of learners that will make your writing and learning worthwhile.

WRITING AND LEARNING ACTIVITIES

1. **Journal Entry:** Have you ever used a journal before this class? If you have, write about your experience; if you haven't, write about how you think you might best use a journal in this class or in other situations.

2. **Journal Entry:** Write about the process of reading and annotating texts you've recently read. Reflect on the process you went through. Were parts of the process difficult or confusing? Helpful? How will it change the way you read and annotate texts?

3. **Group Activity:** Decide together on a reading from this textbook that your group will work with. Individually, read a portion of the text, focusing on (1) reading for understanding, (2) reading critically, and (3) reading for personal connections. Annotate a portion of the text. Write a brief journal entry. As a group, compare your approaches to this specialized text. What approaches do you predict will be most effective for you? How do you think your reading and annotating practices will change?

_____

14

PARAPHRASING AND QUOTING

It is long ere we discover how rich we are. Our history, we are sure, is quite tame: we have nothing to write, nothing to infer. But our wiser years still run back to the despised recollections of childhood, and always we are fishing up some wonderful article out of that pond; until, by and by, we begin to suspect that the biography of the one foolish person we know is, in reality, nothing less than the miniature paraphrase of the hundred volumes of Universal History.

RALPH WALDO EMERSON

By necessity, by proclivity, and by delight, we all quote.

RALPH WALDO EMERSON

Imagine sitting down to lunch with three of the authors you've been reading. You are able to ask them questions about the reading you have been doing and they tell you all about their ideas on the topic you're writing about. You'd like to use some of these ideas in your paper. When you repeat, in your own words what one of the writers says, however, you must give credit for his or her ideas through the proper citation. When you draw on any outside sources of information and ideas, whether books or people, you need to share with your readers where those ideas came from and whose research and scholarship you are building on.

PLAGIARISM

One way to lose authority and find yourself in academic hot water is to quote and paraphrase incorrectly—to copy the work of another writer without acknowledging his or her contribution. This is called plagiarism and the consequences can be serious, maybe even requiring you to withdraw from the university. But, if you have not done much academic reading or research you may find yourself plagiarizing sources without realizing it. For instance, in writing a summary you may use the author's words as your own or may even carry the same grammatical pattern over into your own writing. One way to avoid this is to put the source text away while you compose sentences in your own words. After writing, go back to the source text and check your words against the author's to be sure you have not plagiarized. Being able to use other writers' words in appropriate ways expands your options as you develop your writing and research abilities. The following sections show you how to do this.

PARAPHRASING

Paraphrasing is putting a portion of someone else's text in your own words. Suppose your source is written in dense academic jargon. Instead of quoting the passage you want to use, you restate it in your own words. Students, however, frequently find this activity more difficult than they think it should be. If it were simple it would be more like translating (which is not as simple as it seems, either)—simply look up each word in a thesaurus and substitute the new words. Voila—a new bit of text in your own words! But, if you've ever tried this, you know it doesn't usually work. Instructors frequently comment that it doesn't "sound" like you. Writing something in your own words is a meaning-making activity that depends on your understanding of the work of the academic discipline, the context of the writing to be paraphrased, and your purpose for including that information in your paper.

You might be wondering about the difference between paraphrasing and summarizing since you often hear the words used interchangeably. There are some important similarities and some important differences. In both you demonstrate your learning and authority by putting someone else's ideas and research into your own words, and both require some kind of citation. The goal of a *summary* is to tell about a source in your own words in a more concise form than the original. (Look at the sample summary illustrated in Chapter 10 on pages 373–374; Professor Lynn Weiner briefly summarized an excerpt of Philippe Ariès's research on the family life of everyday people in the middle ages.) In *paraphrasing*, on the other hand, you do not necessarily reduce the original source; rather, you reproduce it, point by point, in your own words.

Paraphrasing offers some important options. First, it provides a test of your learning. If you can paraphrase a source, chances are that you understand it. Second, you can help others to understand material that might be heavily laden with special, difficult-to-understand terms and concepts.

Let's use a portion of paragraph 10 from the Ariès's reading in Chapter 1 to illustrate paraphrasing. You have decided to write a paper tracing the roots of the modern family and want to use Ariès as a source. In particular, you have found a portion of Ariès's work that you could paraphrase to explain his central idea. Below are the original source, a summary, and incorrect and correct paraphrasing of the source.

ORIGINAL SOURCE

Starting in the fifteenth century, the reality and the idea of the family were to change: a slow and profound revolution, scarcely distinguished by either contemporary observers or later historians, and difficult to recognize. And yet the essential event is quite obvious: the extension of school education. We have seen how in the Middle Ages children's education was ensured by apprenticeship to adults, and that after the age of seven, children lived in families other than their own. Henceforth, on the contrary, education became increasingly a matter for the school. The school ceased to be confined to clerics and became the normal instrument of social initiation, of progress from childhood to manhood. (369)

SUMMARY

Ariès traces a major turning point in the history of
the family to the time after the fifteenth century
when children were no longer educated through
apprenticeship and the school became the place where
children joined society. (Ariès 369)

Notice that in this summary the writer accurately restated the gist of the passage in her own words. More importantly, she integrated the summary into the body of her paper by saying, "Ariès traces a major turning point in the history of the family. . . ." She also indicated the author and the page of the source, which is the Modern Language Association (MLA) style of in-text citation. This style is used throughout this section because the work being cited would be cited in this discipline's journal articles or books. Professor Weiner explained that although history is seen as a discipline in both the humanities and the social sciences, most historians use the MLA style of documentation. (How to document sources in the humanities and sciences, as well as social sciences is discussed in the next chapter.)

INACCURATE PARAPHRASE

Ariès tells us that the nature of the family changed
beginning in the fifteenth century. Apprenticeship,
which had been the way children were educated, slipped
in popularity. Children were no longer being placed
out in other people's homes. Instead they were now
going to schools to learn about religion and how to
become adults. My feeling is that we should not have
let apprenticeship go so easily. There is a lot we can
learn from it. (Ariès 369)

In this paraphrase the writer does restate the first sentence accurately. However, the next two sentences are a combination of opinion and misreading. To say apprenticeship "slipped in popularity" is going beyond what Ariès said; to say that children now learned "about religion and how to become adult" is a misreading of what Ariès said. Finally, the last two sentences offer the writer's opinion, which is inappropriate in a paraphrase. The writer will want to evaluate and critique all of his or her sources, but this should be done during the course of the paper and not before the reference citation that tells us we are reading a paraphrase of Ariès's work.

PLAGIARIZED PARAPHRASE

Ariès tells us that beginning in the 1400's <u>the reality and the idea of the family</u> changed. However, the change was such a <u>slow and profound revolution</u> that people at that time and, later, historians did not see it. But the event itself, <u>the extension of school education</u>, was quite striking. Prior to that time children were educated <u>by apprenticeship to adults</u> from the age of seven. Once schools were no longer limited to religious study they replaced apprenticeship as society's means of educating the young and initiating them into society. (Ariès 369)

The underscored segments in the paraphrase above are plagiarized. They are taken from the text, in Ariès's language, but are displayed as the language of the writer. Quotes should have been put around those phrases or sentences taken directly from Ariès. You can avoid plagiarism by quoting appropriately from your sources (see following section entitled "Quotations").

ACCURATE PARAPHRASE

Ariès tells us that beginning in the 1400s the way we viewed the family and the actual reality of the family changed. However, the change was so slow and subtle that people at that time and, later, historians did not see it. But the event itself, the growing importance of school, was quite striking. Prior to that time children were educated from the age of seven by being placed out or apprenticed to other families. Once schools were no longer limited to religious study

```
they replaced apprenticeship as society's means of
educating the young and initiating them into society.
(Ariès 369)
```

In this paraphrase the writer restates, point by point, the content of Ariès's passage, a difficult one with some unusual stylistic features. The writer had to make decisions about the appropriate tense and the order of information, but she did maintain the content of the original passage. One last tip: because it is easy to remember words exactly as they were written, do not spend too much time looking at the text—write from the ideas in your head. When you are done, however, check your work against the source to be sure that you have set off language from the original text with quotation marks.

WRITING AND LEARNING ACTIVITIES

1. **Writing Activity:** Identify from this textbook two portions of a reading that you might want to paraphrase in a paper. Write a note explaining why you chose each portion and what each might contribute to a paper, then write the paraphrases.

2. **Peer Critique:** Exchange your paraphrases and explanation with a partner. Check each other's paraphrases for accuracy. Do they restate the passage point by point in your peer's words without plagiarizing?

3. **Writing Activity:** Write a summary of the "accurate paraphrase" paragraph above. Tell what it is saying in a sentence or two.

QUOTATIONS

Why quote? In Professor Weiner's summary example in Chapter 10, she used three quotes from Ariès. She used two of Ariès's phrases—"slow and profound revolution" (369; paragraph 10) and "art of living" (368; paragraph 8)—for their striking language, language that she felt did the best possible job of expressing the essential meaning of the piece. In other situations you might use quoted material to support a point you are making, or you might quote something in order to comment on it. The most important thing to remember is you are using quotation as support. You will lose authority as a writer if you use so many quotations that the reader hears others' voices and not yours. The following examples show some of the patterns available for blending other writers' words with your own.

DIRECT QUOTATION

This type incorporates in your work an entire sentence by another author. In the direct quotation below the sentence is reproduced exactly, including capitalizing the first letter. Notice also that a comma separates the introductory phrase from the quotation. The quotation is contained by quotation marks, and the page number citation fits in between the final quotation mark and the period.

> Ariès tells us, "There was no room for the school in this transmission by direct apprenticeship from one generation to another" (367).

If you want to use only a portion of another author's sentence in your work, paraphrase another portion of the quote so it is integrated into the grammatical structure of the sentence. This approach is preferable since it allows you to quote just the material you want to quote while maintaining control of the grammatical structure of the sentence. Also, for this sort of integrated quotation a separating comma may not be needed. Again, the page number citation follows the final quotation mark but precedes the period.

> Ariès's argument that apprenticeship was the major form of education is supported by books from the fifteenth century, which provided "an entire literature in the vernacular, French or English, listing in a mnemonic verse form the rules for a good servant" (366).

LONG QUOTATIONS

A long quotation, also called a block quotation, is one that is longer than four typed lines. You would not use a long quotation in a short summary but you might in a long paper. Long quotations should be used only occasionally, when you feel the exact wording is too important to paraphrase. Begin the quotation on a new line and indent it ten spaces. Do not use quotation marks—you have indicated that it is a quote by indenting it. If you are quoting two or more paragraphs, the first line of each paragraph should be indented an additional three or four spaces. The page number citation follows the final period. Double space the quotation.

> The child learnt by practice, and this practice did not stop at the frontiers of a profession, all the more so in that at that time and for a long time afterwards there were no frontiers between professional and private life; sharing professional life—an anachronistic expression in any case—meant sharing the private life with which it was confused. It was by means of domestic service that the master transmitted to a child, and not his child but another man's, the

```
knowledge, practical experience, and human worth
which he was supposed to possess. (366)
```

ELLIPSES

An ellipsis—three spaced dots—allows you to make a long quotation shorter by deleting words, which, in turn, can emphasize what is especially important in that quotation. Remember, though, that even after portions of a quotation have been deleted, what is left should still reflect a complete thought and be able to be read as a complete sentence. Let's see how we might shorten the long quotation we used above.

```
The child learnt by practice, and this practice did
not stop at the frontiers of a profession . . .
[S]haring professional life . . . meant sharing
the private life with which it was confused. It
was by means of domestic service that the master
transmitted to a child . . . the knowledge, practical
experience, and human worth which he was supposed to
possess. (366)
```

INTERPOLATION

Interpolation is a technique used to alter a quotation. We know that a quotation must be reproduced exactly, but what if it contains an error? What if you want to emphasize one word? When you change any part of a quotation, call attention to an error, or note a special emphasis, you must indicate the change to the reader. If the change immediately follows the closing quotation marks, it appears in parentheses. If it goes inside the quotation, it must appear in square brackets. For example, you may have seen "[sic]" in a published text; *sic,* Latin for "thus," indicates that an error existing in the original is being reproduced. When you see such an error, reproduce the quotation exactly as it was printed but insert [*sic*] after the error to indicate that you noticed it. The following mistake received a lot of attention from the media:

> When Dan Quayle revised the spelling of the word potatoe [sic], the entire nation knew about it.

You can also use brackets to indicate that you have changed a quotation. In the shortened Ariès quotation above, the deletion of some material resulted in a sentence that began with a small letter *s*. To correct this, the letter was changed to a capital *S* but it was placed in brackets to indicate the change. If you underline (or make italic) a word or words or emphasize them in some other way, you should add, after the quotation, brackets that say "[emphasis added]." If, for instance you were quoting this statement of Ariès's and you wanted to emphasize that he did not think families were sentimental you could underline his words:

> The family <u>scarcely had a sentimental existence at all among the poor;</u> and where there was wealth and ambition, the sentimental concept of the family was inspired by that which the old lineal relationships had produced [emphasis added] (369).

WRITING AND LEARNING ACTIVITIES

1. **Journal Entry:** Have you ever had a friend or family member take your words out of context? When this happens, what you said is usually not represented in this new context in the way you intended it. Describe such a situation. What did you say? How was it misrepresented later? What was the outcome?

2. **Writing Activity:** Choose from a reading a sentence or two that you might want to quote in a paper. Write a note explaining why you would quote from that portion and what it might contribute to a paper. Write an introductory sentence for the quotation and then use it.

3. **Peer Critique:** Exchange your quotations and explanations with a partner. Check each other's work for accurate punctuation and to see that the quotation could be integrated into the paper smoothly.

15

DOCUMENTING SOURCES

Increasingly I have felt that the art of writing is itself translating, or more like translating than it is like anything else. What is the other text, the original? I have no answer. I suppose it is the source, the deep sea where ideas swim, and one catches them in nets of words and swings them shining into the boat . . . where in this metaphor they die and get canned and eaten in sandwiches.

URSULA K. LE GUIN

Each time you refer to the work of another writer or use data or material provided by another writer you must identify the source through documentation. Each time you summarize, synthesize, or analyze you are dipping into LeGuin's "deep sea where ideas swim," and catching a source. Each time you make a personal connection between your experience and the work of another writer you will want to document that material. While much of the textbook emphasizes the fishing aspect of LeGuin's metaphor for writing, this chapter focuses on her tongue-in-cheek reference to the "canning" aspect of the process. The process of documentation—rule-laden and technical—is an important part of participating in the work of specific academic disciplines.

DOCUMENTATION

A source is first documented in your essay—called the in-text citation—and second, it is documented in a works cited or reference list at the end of the text. Whether you paraphrase or quote a source directly, you will want to provide an in-text citation for it. This citation gives the reader enough information to find the full bibliographic reference in the list at the end of the text. You do not need to document ideas that are considered "general knowledge," common sayings, or obvious conclusions. For example, if you were to comment that Elizabeth Bishop is a well-known twentieth-century American poet, you are simply stating something that is considered general knowledge, and therefore you do not need to provide a specific citation. You also do not need to document your personal opinions and conclusions.

All three forms of documentation—the APA style, used in the social sciences; the MLA style, used in the humanities; and the CBE style, used in the sciences—have the same goal: to provide readers the information they need about your sources. Professors may ask you to use one form or another, but you should have a familiarity with all three. The procedures involved in each developed over time into systems of rules. Some rules may seem arbitrary to you; you will notice when you browse through different journals that the documentation system used may vary slightly among journals in a related field. For instance, even though we place history in the social sciences, historians frequently use the MLA documentation style.

At first, these systems may seem confusing. You do not need to memorize them, though. Keep a handbook with a fuller description of the form (or this textbook) nearby when you are documenting sources. Simply looking at examples and using them to form documentation is helpful. Also, some word-processing programs help you create the reference list at the end of your research essay, and separate programs especially for creating bibliographies are available.

IN-TEXT CITATIONS
Options for In-Text Citation

Whatever documentation system you use, choose the most productive way to place your citations in the text. Where you place your citations shows the reader what you think is most important in your essay. Here are three options using the APA style from the social sciences.

Example A. In the Flats, the African-American families define members of their "essential kin" as, "those people who actively accept responsibility toward them" (Stack, 1974, p. 10).

Example B. Stack (1974) illustrated how African-American families in the Flats define members of their "essential kin" as, "those people who actively accept responsibility toward them" (p. 10).

Example C. In 1974, Carol Stack's ethnography, All Our Kin, illustrated how African-American families in the Flats define members of their "essential kin" as, "those people who actively accept responsibility toward them" (p. 10).

As the writer, you want to make it easy for the reader to follow your writing. Which approach you choose depends on how much you rely on one or more sources and how often you cite them in the text. For instance, if you were introducing Carol Stack's work and wanted to emphasize when it was written, you might choose Example C above. If, however, you had already written an entire paragraph describing Stack's ethnography and were continuing your discussion of it, you do not need to call attention to the author's name. In this case you would choose Example A. If you were comparing the work of three ethnographers in the same paragraph, you might use their names in the text followed by the dates of each one's source in parentheses like Example B. This allows the reader to follow the comparisons you are making. You could also use any of these options as the paragraph below from a paper by Steven Kim indicates.

> Another cultural difference which results in different kinship networks is the value placed on virginity and childbearing. In Ruth Horowitz's ethnography, Honor and the American Dream (1983), virginity is one of the basic canons of their religion and is highly valued. Bearing children before marriage is shameful as could be seen in the case of Alicia, who had to hide under the sink to conceal her pregnancy. The opposite is true in Carol Stack's All Our Kin (1974), where no emphasis is placed on virginity and childbearing is honored. This can also be inferred from Oscar Lewis's (1959) description of the Gutierrez family, since Julia and Yolanda had their first children at the ages of 15 and 16, respectively. Without the religious values placed on virginity, the poverty-stricken families see more children as a means of extending the network.

DOCUMENTING SOURCES IN THE SOCIAL SCIENCES (APA STYLE)

Many social scientists rely on a system developed by the American Psychological Association and published in a lengthy handbook for teachers and researchers in the fields of anthropology, history, and the quantitative social sciences. Originally developed for use in the sciences in which research projects usually take up a question or problem left unanswered in a previous study, the date of the research is thus very important. Below is an abbreviated version of the APA system. If you are not sure how to handle an unusual situation, make a decision that will help your reader to follow your documentation process, or consult the latest edition (1994), if available, of the *Publication Manual of the American Psychological Association,* in the library's reference section.

IN-TEXT CITATION
Citation for a Single-Author Source

This style uses an author-date method of citation. The author, date, and page number of the source are inserted in parentheses at the end of the sentence, as shown below. You may also choose to incorporate some of this citation information in your sentence (see Examples B and C on page 542).

```
In the Flats, the African-American families define
members of their "essential kin" as, "those people who
actively accept responsibility toward them" (Stack,
1974, p. 10).
```

Citation for Sources with Two or More Authors

Much of the writing and research in the social sciences and sciences is done by collaborative teams, books, articles, and reports often having two or more authors. If you are referring to a two-author source, use the word *and* to connect them, but if you refer to them parenthetically in a citation, for example "(Horowitz & Schwarz, 1974)," use the ampersand (&).

First and Subsequent Citations

If there are more than two authors, name all the authors at the first citation; for subsequent citations use only the last name of the first author followed by "et al." (not underlined and with no period after the "et") and the year. "Et al." is an abbrevation of the Latin phrase *et alia,* which means "and others."

```
Wright, Salinas, and Peluso (1967) describe how street
gangs gain in status. . . . Wright, et al. (1967) go on
to describe . . .
```

Same Author with Two or More Works Having Same Publication Date

If you are citing several works by the same author that were published in the same year, assign a small letter of the alphabet as a suffix to the date. Mark it the same way in the reference list.

```
Horowitz has written several chapters on the subject
of family reciprocity (1982a, 1982b).
```

Personal Communications

Sometimes you will want to include in your paper information that comes from an interview, telephone conversation, or letter. Since this information is considered unrecoverable, it does not appear in your reference list. When citing, give the initials as well as the last name of the person and as exact a date as possible.

> Professor Marcia Farr (personal communication, March 2, 1993) explained how the role of humor among Mexican women . . .

REFERENCE LIST

This list offers examples of the most common types of references. Normally, references are organized in alphabetical order. The order is changed here to present the most basic types of arrangements first. The reference list should be double-spaced, and should be formatted with a hanging indent, where the first line of each entry extends to the left margin and the subsequent lines are indented five spaces.

REFERENCE LIST

> Stack, C. B.(1974). All our kin: Strategies for survival in a black community. New York: Harper & Row.

Single-author book: Author's last name is followed by initials. Year of publication is in parentheses followed by a period. Title of the book is underlined; only the first word is capitalized, except for proper nouns. Place of publication is followed by a colon; publisher's name is followed by a period.

> Firth, R., Hubert, J. & Forge, A. (1970). Families and their relatives: Kinship in a middle-class sector of London. New York: Humanities Press.

Book with two or more authors: Use ampersand (&) instead of "and" to separate last two authors' names. Only the first word in the title and the first word after the colon are capitalized; proper nouns are also capitalized.

> Park, R. & Burgess, E. (Eds.). (1967). The growth of the city. Chicago: University of Chicago Press.

Edited book: Use the last names and initials of all editors. Put "Ed." or "Eds." in parentheses followed by a period.

> Keesing, R. M. (1970). Toward a model of role analysis. In R. Cohen & R. Naroll (Ed.), A handbook of methods in cultural anthopology (pp. 330–351). New York: Natural History Press.

Chapter in an edited book: List author of chapter and chapter title first. Next use editors' initials first and then last name. Only capitalize first word in title. Give page numbers.

> Tran, H. (1992). Kinship based on social and economic values. Unpublished manuscript.

Unpublished manuscript: If the cited source has not been published, simply write "Unpublished manuscript" after the title, as was done with this student paper. If you have the information, put the address to which a reader can write for the manuscript.

> Baca Zinn, M. (1976). Political familism: Toward
>
> sex role equality in Chicano families. Aztlan:
>
> Chicano journal of the social sciences and the
>
> arts, 6, 13-26.

Journal article: Include the author or authors' last name(s) followed by initials and the date of publication in parentheses followed by a period. Include the title of the journal article, capitalizing only first letter and letter following colon. Underline the journal name and capitalize the first word in the name and the first word after a colon, if applicable (see above). Underline the volume number followed by a comma. The page numbers, followed by a period, are last.

DOCUMENTING SOURCES IN THE HUMANITIES (MLA STYLE)

Many scholars in fields such as philosophy, literary studies, and art history rely on the system outlined in the *MLA Handbook for Writers of Research Papers* (4th ed., MLA, 1995). The guidelines for this style of documentation have been developed by the members of the Modern Language Association of America, an organization of teachers and scholars working in languages and literature. I include here a brief version of the MLA system. If you are not sure how to cite a particular item, make a decision that will help your reader follow your documentation process, or consult the *MLA Handbook,* in your library's reference section.

IN-TEXT CITATIONS
Citation for a Single-Author Source

The standard in-text citation includes putting the source author and the page number of the information in parentheses. If a work you are citing has no author, include an abbreviated version of the work's title in the in-text citation where the author's name would go. Another way of citing a work is to include the author's name in the text and include only the appropriate page numbers within the parentheses. Having the author's name in the text emphasizes the author and helps clarify whose ideas you are using, which is especially helpful if you are comparing many authors in your essay.

> "In the Village" opens with the description of the
>
> mother's scream, which seems to hover in our ears as

we read the story, much as it hangs in the memory of
her child (Bishop 251).

Elizabeth Bishop opens "In the Village" with the
description of the mother's scream, which seems to
hover in our ears as we read the story, much as it
hangs in the memory of her child (251).

Citing More Than One Work by the Same Author

Because more than one Elizabeth Bishop story is listed in the sample Works
Cited list below, the in-text citation must distinguish between the stories.
The first example emphasizes the content of your statement by placing the
work's title within the parenthetical citation. The second example, however,
emphasizes the title of the work, which may be helpful if you are writing
about several works by the same author.

The funeral exemplifies Emma and Flora's deeper
concern for appearances than for Lucy's problems
(Bishop, "The Baptism" 170).

In "The Baptism," the funeral exemplifies Emma and
Flora's deeper concern for appearances than for Lucy's
problems (Bishop 170).

Citation for Sources with Two or More Authors

If there are two authors, use "and" between the authors' names. If there are
more than two, use "et al." after the first author's name, in place of the
other authors' names. You may also list all the authors' names, separating
the last two with "and." You may place the names in the text or the citation.

Constance Rooke and Bruce Wallis offer a critical
analysis of Katherine Anne Porter's "The Grave" . . .
(61–68).

Interview

Interviews are a good way to gather first-hand information. For example, if
you are doing a paper on Lucy's religious preferences, you may want to interview someone about the differences between Baptists and Presbyterians. If you quote this source to support your ideas, you would use the following type of documentation:

As Reverend Simon points out, . . . (interview).

Work of Art

Generally you will be citing only one version of a particular work of art, either
the original work (as you would find it in a museum) or a reproduction of

the work in an article or book. In this case, you would not need to include any parenthetical citation in the body of your paper, only a citation in your Works Cited list. However, if you are comparing two different versions of the same work (the original in Chicago's Art Institute and a reproduction in an art history text, for example), then you would need a parenthetical citation to indicate which work you are discussing.

```
I was surprised to see that the colors of the scenery
outside the window in Matisse's Conversation
(Hermitage) are fairly subdued, even washed
out looking.
```

WORKS CITED LIST

All bibliographic citations must include the author(s)' names, the title, and publication information. A period separates each of these sections. Entries in the Works Cited list should be arranged alphabetically by the first word in the entry, whether it is the author's last name or the title of a work. In each entry the first line should be flush with the left margin and each line after that should be indented five spaces. Also, the list should be double-spaced, both within and between the individual citations.

```
                    WORKS CITED
    Millier, Brett C. Elizabeth Bishop: Life and the
        Memory of It. Los Angeles: U of California
        Press, 1993.
```

Single-author book: Author's last name is followed by first name. Title is underlined, and the first word, last word, and all principal words are capitalized. The city of publication is followed by a colon, then the name of the publisher, a comma, and the date of publication.

```
    Bloom, Harold, ed. Katherine Anne Porter. Modern
        Critical Views Series. New York: Chelsea
        House, 1986.
```

Edited book: When citing an entire edited book or collection, give the last name of the editor, followed by the first name, followed by "ed." or "eds." Note that if the book belongs to a series, the name of the series and the series number (if applicable) should be included before the publication information.

```
    Bishop, Elizabeth. "In the Village." The Collected
        Prose. Ed. Robert Giroux. New York: Farrar,
        Straus and Giroux, 1984. 251-278.
```

```
---."The Baptism." The Collected Prose. Ed. Robert
    Giroux. New York: Farrar, Straus and Giroux,
    1984. 159-170.
```

Two or more works by the same author: In the second citation, the author's name is replaced by three hyphens (—-), followed by a period. The works should be listed in alphabetical order according to the titles.

```
Schwartz, Lloyd, and Sybil P. Estess, eds. Elizabeth
    Bishop and Her Art. Ann Arbor: U of Michigan
    Press, 1983.
```

Book by two or more persons: The first author/editor is listed in the usual inverted way (last name first), followed by a comma. All others are listed with their first names followed by their last names. Use "and" to separate the last two authors' names.

```
Rooke, Constance, and Bruce Wallis. "Myth and Epiphany
    in Porter's 'The Grave.'" Ed. Harold Bloom.
    Katherine Anne Porter. Modern Critical Views
    Series. New York: Chelsea House Publishers,
    1986. 61-68.
```

Chapter in an edited volume: List the author(s) of the chapter first, followed by the title of the chapter in quotation marks. Next include the editor's first and last name, preceded by "Ed." or "Eds." Then give the title of and publication information for the book. Last, give the inclusive page numbers for the chapter being cited.

```
Dickie, Margaret. "Seeing is Re-seeing: Sylvia Plath
    and Elizabeth Bishop." American Literature 65
    March 1993: 131-146.
```

Journal article: List the author's last name, followed by first name and a period. Give the title of the article in quotation marks, with a period before the concluding quotation mark. Next list and underline the title of the journal and give the volume number of that issue of the journal. The year of publication is followed by a colon, a space, and the page numbers for the article, followed by a period.

```
Matisse, Henri. Conversation. Hermitage, St.
    Petersburg. Illus. 246 in Matisse: The Man and
    His Art 1869-1918. By Jack Flam. Ithaca, NY:
    Cornell University Press, 1986.
```

Work of art: State the artist's name and underline the title of the work. Give the name of the institution housing the work (e.g., a museum), and the city where the institution is located. If you are using a photograph of a work, include the publication information for the work that contains the photo, as in the example above.

Simon, Samuel. Personal interview. 28 June 1993.

Interview: Give the name of the person being interviewed, state the type of interview, whether personal or telephone. Give the date on which the interview was conducted.

DOCUMENTING SOURCES IN THE SCIENCES (CBE STYLE)

Students, professors, and researchers in scientific fields frequently use a style manual called *Scientific Style and Format: The CBE Manual for Authors, Editors, and Publishers* (6th ed., Cambridge University Press, 1994). This edition was written by the Style Manual Committee of the Council of Biology Editors. Two brief versions of the CBE system are described: the name-year system and the number (or citation-sequence) system. Both were used in the articles you have read in this textbook.

NAME-YEAR SYSTEM FOR IN-TEXT CITATION

For the name-year system, the name(s) of the author(s) and the year of publication are cited in the text. This system was used by Raynolds and Felix in their research report titled "Airphoto Analysis of Winter Seismic Disturbance in Northeastern Alaska," included in Chapter 8, Geology. The examples used to illustrate this system are taken from that article, although they have been updated to reflect the most recent edition of the Council of Biology Editors' Manual.

Citation for a Source with Single or Multiple Authors

To cite articles with one or more authors, place the author's or authors' last name(s) and date of publication in parentheses at the end of the sentence or within the sentence near the idea you are citing. For stylistic variety, you may want to use the name(s) of the authors in the sentence, in which case, only the date is placed in parentheses after the name(s).

Barrett and Schultern (1975) also found Dryas to be
especially sensitive to disturbance.

It is located in Low Arctic Tundra (Murray 1978) and
is vegetated by low-growing plants,. . .

Airphoto interpretation and other remote-sensing
techniques have often been used in Alaska to
investigate large areas that are otherwise
inaccessible (Brooks and O'Brien, 1986).

Wind redistribution of snow on the arctic coastal
plain leaves these features with little protective
snow cover (Felix and others 1987).

Citations for Several Sources

When citing several articles together, list the names and dates in chronological order, beginning with the oldest one, in parentheses and separated by a
semicolon.

Vehicle trails from as long ago as the 1940s are still
visible on the tundra west of the Arctic Refuge
(Lawson and others 1978; Walker and others 1987).

Vehicle disturbance decreases plant cover on trails
and can cause short- and long-term species composition
changes due to the relative resistance and resilience
of different species (Bliss and Wein 1972; Hernandez
1973; Chapin and Chapin 1980).

Citations for Articles by the Same Author(s) in Same Year(s) of Publication

When the author(s) and year(s) are the same for more than one reference,
insert lower-case letters after the dates in alphabetical order after the year.
Mark the same way in the reference list.

Ground data included point frame cover data by species
for 24 sites (Felix and Raynolds 1989a), line
intercept cover data for 38 additional sites (Felix
and Raynolds 1989b)...

Page Numbers

Although the CBE Manual does not require that page numbers be included
with in-text citations, your instructor may want you to do so.

The Gwich'in Indians depend on the caribou to supply
them with food. One native woman explains that her
people get 75% of their protein from caribou (Egan,
1991 p 49).

NUMBER SYSTEM FOR IN-TEXT CITATION

The number system is very easy to use. In this system, references are numbered in the order in which they appear in the text. In other words, the first
in-text citation you use is given the number 1 in parentheses at the end of
the sentence—(1). The numbers of the in-text citations match the numbers

in the list of references. The main advantage of this system is that numbered citations do not interrupt the reading activity with long strings of names and dates. Citation numbers can also be inserted in the text as a superscript separated by commas with no spaces. The superscript's typeface should be smaller than that of the text. You may also see other variations in which the numbers are included in brackets or parentheses.

Sample In-Text Citations Using the Number System

Not all traffic can be confined to the winter months[1] when the ecology impact of vehicle operations is minimal.

The results of the study on the impact of the ACV and Weasel traffic[2,3,4] for the first 4 years after traffic have been previously reported.

LIST OF REFERENCES

The arrangement in the list of references depends on how references are cited in the article. For the name-year system, the entries are arranged alphabetically by author (and chronologically if the authors of two or more entries are the same). In the number system, each entry in the list of references appears in the order of its first mention in the text. The reference list should be double-spaced and formatted with a hanging indent. The first line of each entry should be at the left margin with all subsequent lines indented five spaces. You will notice some differences between this list and the list in some of the articles you read. This occurs because individual journals sometimes have their own stylistic conventions. This reference list follows the name-year style.

REFERENCES

Hernandez H. 1973. Natural plant recolonization of
    surficial disturbances, Tuktoyaktuk Peninsula
    Region, Northwest Territories. Canadian Journal of
    Botany 51:2177-2196.

Journal article with one author: Includes author's name, last name and first initial or name. Next include the year, and the month if you know it. List the title of the article and journal; the latter may be abbreviated. Do not capitalize the words in the title of the article, except for the first word, and do not underline the title of the journal. The volume number is separated from the page numbers with a colon. Page numbers follow.

Raynolds MK, Felix NA. 1982. Airphoto analysis of
    winter seismic disturbance in northeastern Alaska.
    Arctic 42 (4):78-83.

Journal article with more than one author: Separate the names of the authors with a comma. If there is an issue number, enclose it in parentheses and place it after the volume number.

> Avery TE. 1977. Interpretation of aerial photographs.
>
> Minneapolis: Burgess Publishing Co. p. 392.

Book with author: Include author or authors' last name(s) followed by the year. Do not underline or capitalize title of book and subtitle, except for first word. Include the number of the edition, last name and initials of editor or translator, if applicable. Put a colon after the city of publication, followed by the name of the publisher. The current edition (6th) of the manual now recommends that you add the total number of pages in the book.

> Tieszen L, editor. 1978. Vegetation and production
>
>   ecology of an Alaskan arctic tundra. New York:
>
>   Springer-Verlag 686 p.

Book with editor as author: Identify the editor by placing a comma and the word "editor" after the name, followed by the year. Include the title of the book followed by the publication information.

> Reynolds PC. 1982. Some effects of oil and gas
>
>   exploration activities on tundra vegetation in
>
>   northern Alaska. In: Rand PJ, editor. Land and
>
>   water issues related to energy development.
>
>   Proceedings of the fourth annual meeting of the
>
>   International Society of Petroleum Industry
>
>   Biologists; 1981 September 22-25; Denver,
>
>   Colorado. Ann Arbor, MI: Ann Arbor Science
>
>   Publishers; p. 403-416.

Conference proceedings: Conference proceedings are often published as books with editors. You may cite an entire proceedings, but it is far more common to cite one of the papers given at the conference. Include the author's last name and initials, the year of publication, followed by the title of the paper, capitalizing only the first word. Indicate the source by using the word "In" followed by a colon. Next, include the editor's name or names, last name first followed by initials and "ed." or "eds." The title of the conference proceeding follows, then a semicolon, and the year, month, and days that the conference took place. Next include the publisher and the pages of the chapter you are citing.

> Brown J, Grave, NA. 1979. Physical and thermal
>
>   disturbance and protection of permafrost. 42 p.

```
        Special report 79-5. Available from: U.S. Army
        Corps of Engineers, CRREL, Hanover, NH.
```

Technical reports: Many scientific studies are published as technical reports. Authors of these reports are frequently affiliated with university or private research laboratories or governmental agencies. If you do not have the author's name, use the name of the agency responsible for the report. Include the author's or authors' last name(s) and initials followed by the date. The title of the report ends with a period. Next, include the number of pages followed by "p" and the number of the report. Include where the technical report is available from.

WRITING THE RESEARCH ESSAY

16

WRITING THE
RESEARCH ESSAY

Just as the largest library, badly arranged, is not so useful as a very moderate one that is well-arranged, so the greatest amount of knowledge, if not elaborated by our own thoughts, is worth much less than a far smaller volume that has been abundantly and repeatedly thought over.

ARTHUR SCHOPENHAUER

CONNECTING PERSONAL INTERESTS
WITH ACADEMIC ISSUES

When do you know that you have begun participating meaningfully in the work of an academic discipline? The answer: when you discover that you have something to say to others about a topic or issue that is important to you.

Dead tired and in need of a cup of coffee, Andrea Filipiak was leafing through a recent issue of Science News *when she came across a short report of research on caffeine withdrawal. A committed coffee drinker, she decided to learn more about the topic. What she discovered was that her dependence on caffeine was now considered an addiction. She had to decide the position she would take in an essay on the topic of caffeine addiction.*

Kris Arthur had always been intrigued by multiple personality disorder, in which a person exhibits more than one personality. His reading of the portion of John Locke's essay (see Chapter 4) provided two important tools:

First, the idea of personal identity helped him define what a person was. Second, the idea of a thought experiment helped him see how you can ask questions about the nature of humanity even though you can't "prove" your answers in the same way you can prove that water is composed of hydrogen and oxygen, for example. Using Locke's definition of personal identity, Kris would argue for a novel explanation of the cause of multiple personality disorder.

Bruce Earl Williams was struck by Carol Stack's portrayal of kinship in a poor, urban African-American community. He felt that Stack did a good job of painting the relationships among women in her ethnographic study of the Flats. His own experience as a young African-American father, however, challenged him to question the stereotypical view of the absent African-American father. In his research essay, he took the position that the role of such a father needs to be redefined to emphasize parenting more than financial support.

Writing a research essay puts you in the center of work being done on an issue or problem and allows you to participate in that work by adding your perspective to the ongoing conversation. This type of project is often open-ended, allowing you to identify some aspect of a topic that has significance for you and to make a claim about it. Often this project, which can cross boundaries of various academic disciplines, will involve you in a variety of activities over a period of weeks or months.

You develop your essay by: defining a problem, seeing how it has been studied, identifying the underlying issues, and developing your own position. Throughout the writing process you will ask questions and answer them; you will learn about the positions of key scholars in particular disciplines; and you will summarize, synthesize, and analyze their work as you develop your essay.

You need to rely on just about everything we have talked about to this point. You have already practiced summary, synthesis, and analysis. You also learned how to quote and paraphrase sources and how to search for them and then document them. All of these activities become part of the process of developing your research essay. But your greatest challenge in writing the essay may be to establish your position and explain to your reader how all of your sources fit together to support your position.

WRITING AND LEARNING ACTIVITIES

1. Journal Entry: Brainstorm about topics that interest you. Survey all the reading you have done thus far for this course; consider topics you would like to read more about; or consider issues you have recently seen handled in the movies or discussed in the news. Browse through popular journals in the fields you are exploring. Look through the appendix, Directions for Further Research, for sources to get started. What do you know and what would you like to know about this topic? Is there debate on it that you have an opinion on?

2. **Group Activity:** Talk about your topic ideas by first letting each person tell about the topics he or she has been considering, then taking a bit more time with each person. Each person should ask the others questions about their topics in order to help move them toward a clearer understanding of the topic. Ask questions such as the following: How do you define your topic and how has it changed or been redefined over time? What disciplines might focus on this topic? What methods do particular disciplines use to study it? How do various cultures view your topic? Why are you interested in this topic? What are you hoping to learn about it?

CONNECTING KNOWLEDGE AND DEVELOPING CLAIMS
SEARCHING FOR PERSONAL CONNECTIONS

In this section, I ask you to maintain a dual focus: on *your* interests and on problems or issues that emerge from the reading you've been doing. The key question is "What does this mean to me?" You often have to make the connections between your personal experiences and your learning experiences on your own, but when you do you benefit from a greater understanding of yourself and the material you are studying and writing about.

How do you identify personal connections with academic issues? We can illustrate the process by listening in on two students who are using their previous reading—a chapter by John Demos titled, "Images of the Family, Then and Now" (included in Chapter 10)—as a point of departure. Demos traces the history of the American family and changes in it through three periods, which he characterized by "images." Of most interest to Laura was the middle period, in which the family is seen as a place of refuge and the mother is seen as the "True Woman," selfless and all-giving. The present image of the family is more difficult to assess and the role of the mother has both changed and remained the same. It is this issue that Laura finds interesting.

LAURA: Even as a little kid I knew that each person in the family had a role to play to keep it going. I didn't feel like the family was much of a "refuge," as Demos says it is, at least in part. It's supposed to buffer or at least provide relief from the demands and pressures of everyday life.

RICK: So where does that take you?

LAURA: Nowhere in particular. I'm still just thinking. Why is the divorce rate so high? I mean, back in the nineteenth century, how many times did you hear of divorce, as opposed to now? I'm just trying to figure out what the reasons are for that. Now you hear of the father deserting the mother and the whole family. Demos also mentioned that the woman in the family has become more restless and is looking for a career.

RICK: Well, what reasons will you give to prove that the family is changing? Are you going to do it like from colonial times . . . ?

LAURA: No, that's too big a problem and that's just what Demos did. I guess I'm more interested in the role of the mother. Demos talks about how the image changes from "True Woman" to "Total Woman." Maybe I'll look at "images" of the mother.

WRITING AND LEARNING ACTIVITIES

1. **Peer Dialogue:** Choose a specific reading that interests you. Explain to your partner the personal connection you find in that reading. The two of you should explore the relationship between the connection and the academic issues the reading discusses.

2. **Class or Group Activity:** Assemble your class into "special interest" groups by listing the issues or problems students are interested in—environmental issues, historical topics, research on divorce and the family—and grouping students through some common link. Members with connected interests should meet and explore their interests, each member writing a list of four questions he or she is interested in exploring through a research essay.

DEVELOPING CLAIMS

Having identified a problem or topic is not enough. To begin your research essay you must establish a position on the topic, expressing it as a specific statement you believe to be true. This statement is your working claim. You can modify and elaborate it later if the need arises, but this first effort will help you get started. The following steps will help you "focus" your claim so that you can go to the library and conduct research.

1. *State a claim that you believe to be true or accepted.*

   The mother's role has changed since the 1800s as the family has changed.

   [Stated as true, but too large a claim for an 8 to 10 page research essay since you would have to study the role of the family as carefully as the role of the mother.]

2. *Refine your claim so that it suggests how your research is explored through specific disciplines.*

   The change in image from Demos's "True Woman" to the "Total Woman" over the last 150 years has influenced the role of motherhood.

[Much more specific. Good idea to use John Demos's idea of an "image." This will be helpful in choosing appropriate evidence from your reading. Predict what the change has been and state it in your claim. You can revise your claim as you learn more about your topic.]

3. *Make your revised claim so specific that it will allow you to identify support for your claim.*

   Final claim: The change in image from Demos's "True Woman" to the "Total Woman" over the last 150 years has expanded the role of motherhood; now women must balance their responsibilities inside the home with those in the workplace, creating additional stress and difficulty.

   [Now you can begin researching your claim. What evidence will you use? What disciplines and what research methods will you draw on? Will you look at studies of time spent at home and at work, for example? Will you look at historical changes in childcare? How will you gather material that will help you look at these changing images over time?]

WRITING AND LEARNING ACTIVITIES

1. **Peer Activity:** Write an initial working claim and exchange it with your partner. Ask your partner questions that help him or her refine and revise the claim: What evidence would support your claim? How might you need to qualify this claim? What is the other side to the argument?

2. **Question Posing:** Based on your working claim and the possible evidence you have identified in group work, where would you begin to research your claim? What disciplines might be exploring this problem? What different kinds of research or scholarship exist on this question?

THE PROCESS OF WRITING A RESEARCH ESSAY

This section takes you through the actual writing process. Sometimes the best way to learn about how to undertake a project as complex as this is to follow others as they carry out their work. Bruce Earl Williams, the student whose work we follow in this chapter, connected with Carol Stack's portrayal of kinship in a poor, urban African-American community. This initial connection helped him to formulate a working claim, search for sources, and develop his essay. Bruce's claim was that the role of the young African-American father needs to be redefined to emphasize parenting more than financial support. The following sections offer some advice and illustrates Bruce's process.

MONITORING THE RESEARCH PROCESS

Plan Ahead

To work toward your goals, design a calendar just for this project. Work backwards from the date the essay is due. Include in the calendar other deadlines and important dates to be considered during your research process. Consider the tasks involved in the project and determine when you will begin and complete each task. Be sure to schedule in appointments with your professor or teaching assistant and people you want to interview, leaving enough time to write about the latter. Be sure to also leave time for revision and to have someone else read it over.

Learn About Your Library

Your professor may arrange a library tour to help get you started, or you can visit on your own. Steve Nash's experience below (typical of many students) illustrates that you need to give yourself enough time and not be afraid to ask for help from your professor or the librarians.

> *About mid-semester, after I had a tour of the university library as part of my writing course, I went to the library to look for sources for my research essay. I brought my friend along because I thought it would be a quick trip. I had, after all, already had a tour of the library and I knew where everything was (or so I thought). When we got into the library, it seemed like a totally different place than I remembered. I didn't know where to start, where to go for anything. After several false starts I asked the librarian for help and she helped me with the computerized searches for sources that had looked so simple during the tour. Needless to say, my friend left. I had arrived at 5:00 expecting to be gone by 7:00; at 10:30 I was still there. It sure took longer than I expected.*

Keeping Records

Whether you use a computer or a pen, develop a system of note taking that helps move your research process along. Record the bibliographic information on any related source, even if you are not sure you will use it or are not quite sure of its value—it may turn out to add strength to a point you are making. Also, record the library call numbers of all items so you can find them again if you need to. You may want to give each source a code name. For instance, Bruce Williams kept bibliographic information on a journal article titled "Parental Responsibility and Self-Image of African-American Fathers" by Kenneth Christmon (published in the journal *Families in Society* in 1990). He coded it "Self-image" and whenever he worked on his paper he wrote "Self-image" in his notes to refer to that source.

CASTING THE SEARCH NET WIDE: AN OVERVIEW

You have now identified a topic you would like to develop and stated a claim you think you can support. The next step is to see what is written in general on the topic, what issues are being discussed in particular disciplines, and what scholars' names appear again and again. This overview helps you to see whether your claim can be researched or whether it covers too much material for the scope of your paper.

Specialized Guides, Dictionaries, Bibliographies, and Encyclopedias

The encyclopedias in your library's reference section provide the most general information about any topic. However, your specific claim may best be explored by looking through some specialized guides. (The appendix, Directions for Further Research, includes many general reference works, professional journals, and indexes.) Bruce Williams already knew something about his topic from personal experience and from reading Carol Stack's ethnography, so he was ready to dive into a search for specific sources. Yet later in his research process Bruce returned to a general reference, the *Statistical Record of Black America,* from which he gathered some data that would support his description of African-American male adolescents.

The Anchor Source

Often one source—an important book, a review article, an edited collection—will offer you an anchor for your project. From this single source you can learn what the major issues are, what topics are controversial, what questions remain unanswered. Bruce Williams, for instance, found a journal article called "Black Adolescent Fathers: Issues for Service Provision," in which the author reviewed the problem of adolescent parenthood for African-American males in order to suggest solutions for social workers. From this review Bruce determined that his claim was a reasonable one to pursue. And, through the article's reference list, he was able to identify some of the key authorities in this area.

LOCATING RELEVANT SOURCES

The library provides you with a massive amount of information. Finding the specific sources for the information you need, however, requires detective work. The link between your claim and the library information often lies in finding key words or subject headings. These words—which frequently reflect the specialized language of the discipline you are studying—along with subject headings, also tell you how others are referring to your topic in books and articles. Without this information you may think there are no sources on the subject you are interested in.

Library of Congress Subject Headings

The Library of Congress Subject Headings (LCSH), a list of standardized terms for topics that scholars and students frequently need to look up, is one way to search computer databases or through indexes. You must first, however, use the LCSH reference manual (available in your library) to find what these terms are. Bruce Williams looks up *African American* (all listings are in alphabetical order), but he does not find anything. Why? The term used by the LCSH is *Afro-American*. To use this resource you need to determine the appropriate terms that will open the door to the sources you need, trying one term after another if need be.

Key Words

Another way to search is to use key words. The computer will look anywhere in the online database for the word you choose. If Bruce were to use the word *African-American* in a key word search, the computer would list any sources that used that term in the title of an article, book, or journal, or in the description of the item. Key-word searching is very flexible and productive. The description that comes up can also include the LCSH headings for a reference. This allows you to move back and forth between the two search methods, thus increasing your opportunities to find the sources you need.

Online Databases

Computerized search programs are one of the most exciting additions to many libraries. Most card catalogs are being entered into computer databases. Now you can do more than look up books by author, title, and subject; you can search for books or articles by subject or keywords as discussed above.

The reference librarian can provide information about how to conduct these online searches since details of the process may differ from place to place. First, find the terms that the database "understands," and then combine or arrange those terms so that they will not be too general or too narrow. Let's follow Bruce Williams as he identified a range of sources—books and journal articles—that he could evaluate as to their usefulness.

Bruce did two series of searches for his essay; one through an online database for books and another on a computerized version of the *Wilson Social Sciences Index* to search for journal articles. He had identified four key terms: *adolescents, males, fathers,* and *African American.*

Searching for Books.   Bruce began by entering a command to search for all books on African Americans. Since he knew that the LCSH used the term *Afro-American* he entered that command and learned that there were 5000 books on the subject! Far too many to even browse through the titles. He then tried the subject heading *teenage pregnancy* and found a list of 51 books. He scanned through the titles and year of publication, making note of any that seemed interesting. By typing a book's line number, Bruce could get more information about the book and then decide whether he wanted to take the next step: finding the book on the shelves and evaluating its usefulness for his project. Skimming through the book descriptions, he found that the books were primarily about teenage mothers. His interest was in teenage fathers so he continued his search.

Bruce tried using a combination of terms: *Afro-American teenage boys.* His search found only one source, but it was an important one for his paper. Here is the description of the book that he pulled up on the computer screen. Notice that in the book's table of contents there is a chapter on teenage fathers, just what Bruce had been looking for.

```
      Title: Black male adolescents : parenting and education in
             community context / edited by Benjamin P. Bowser.
  Published: Lanham : University Press of America, c1991.
Description: 352 p. : ill. ; 24 cm.
      Notes: Includes bibliographical references and indexes.
   Contents: Black male genocide : a final solution to the race
             problem in America / Robert Staples -- Pushed out
             of the dream : sorting-out Black males for
             limited economic mobility / Walter Stafford --
             Changing the inner city : Black urban
             reorganization / Hardy T. Frye -- "Betcha cain't
             reason with' em": bad Black boys in America /
             Anthony J. Lemelle, Jr. -- The flip side of teen
             mothers : a look at teen fathers / Grace Massey
             -- Black mothers to sons : juxtaposing African-
             American literature with social practice / Joyce
             King and Carolyn Mitchell -- We are the children
             of everybody : community co-parenting, a
             biographic note / Loften Mitchell -- Success
             against the odds : young Black men tell what it
             takes / Benjamin P. Bowser and Herbert Perkins.
          You can teach wisdom : ways to motivate Black male
             adolescents / Lawford L. Goddard -- Black men,
             Black sexuality and AIDS / Robert Fullilove and
             Mindy Fullilove -- Returning formal education to
             the family : experiencing the alternative /
             Omonike Weusi-Puryear and Muata Weusi-Puryear --
             Tapping into teen talk : parenting strategies for
             bridging the intergenerational communication gap
             / Faye C. McNair-Knox -- Black male adolescent
             development deviating from the past : challenges
             for the future / Ronald J. Hudson -- Hurling
             oppression : overcoming anomie and self hatred /
             James Moss -- The literary empowerment of Black
             male youth / Daphne Muse.
          Encouraging constructive parenting through humane
             portrayals of Black fathers (or rock steady,
             let's call this song exactly what it is) / Peter
             Harris -- Conclusion / Benjamin P. Bowser.
       ISBN: 0819179752 (alk. paper)
For other items by author(s), type A=
             Bowser, Benjamin P.
```

```
For other items on LC subject(s), type S=
                Afro-American teenage boys.
                Parent and teenager--United States.
                Afro-American teenage boys--Education.
LOCATION:       CALL NUMBER              STATUS:
Main            E185.86 .B5256 1991      Check IO/LCS for circ info
```

Searching for Journal Articles.   To locate research on a specific topic in the social sciences you would go to the *Wilson Social Sciences Index*, which covers articles written in fields such as psychology, sociology, anthropology, economics, environmental psychology, ethnic studies, ethnography, feminist studies, geography, law and criminology, policy science, social work, urban studies, and the social aspects of medicine. To use the book version, you find a particular year and look up your subject heading, author, or title alphabetically.

You have more flexibility using the online database; you can combine subject headings to find the articles that are cross-referenced. One caution, however: database searching gives you much greater access to information, but the process can be tricky and frustrating. You must find the right subject headings or key words. After trying many different subject headings and combinations, Bruce met with success when he searched for articles cross-referenced under "teenage with father." The database listed entries for 23 academic journal articles, including the name of the article, where it was published and, perhaps most important for further searching, other, related subject headings. Bruce sifted through the whole list and identified the ones he thought he could use. Below is a copy of the printout for two articles he used in his paper.

```
      4 OF 23
AN BSSI91003748 9100.
AU Christmon-Kenneth.
TI Parental responsibility and self-image of African American
   fathers.
SO Families in Society. v. 71, Nov. '90, p. 563-7.
IS 1044-3894.
LG English (EN).
DE Unmarried-fathers: Attitudes. Teenage-fathers: Attitudes.
   Blacks: Attitudes. Self-perception.
PT Article.
AC Feature-article.
YR 1990.
CP United-States.

      14 OF 23
AN BSSI88026487 9100.
AU Smith-Linda-Anderson.
TI Black adolescent fathers: issues for service provision.
SO Social Work. v. 33, May/June '88, p. 269-71.
IS 0037-8046.
LG English (EN).
```

DE Social-work-with-blacks. Black-youth. Teenage-fathers.
PT Article.
AC Feature-article.
YR 1988.
CP United-States.

EVALUATING SOURCES

Once you have a list of possible books and journal articles, find them on the shelves and evaluate whether they will be of use to you. The most important advice here is to keep your claim in mind. Bruce was able to eliminate many sources during his online database search, but to decide about others he had to actually look at the book or article. Another thing to remember is that the research process can expand. You may discover new sources by browsing the shelves near a book you have already found. Also, the works cited and reference lists in useful books and articles can identify still other important sources for your paper. So always remember that the detective work does not stop after an initial search for sources.

How do you evaluate the sources you are considering for use in your paper? First, be sure that you have tapped into the best scholarly work being done in the academic area you are exploring. Skimming the table of contents and the reference list gives a broad view of the contents of the item. Reading the introductory and concluding paragraphs of chapters and books, and the discussion section of journal articles, helps determine whether the item responds specifically to your claim. Do the same names, articles, and books keep coming up again and again? Have you identified the key people in the field? Bruce Williams found that several researchers' names were in many of the reference lists. These scholars are known for their work with African-American teenage fathers. Ask about each source:

 How will this help me develop my claim? Does it provide valuable background information? What academic discipline does this source represent? Does it articulate one or more points of view in the field? Does it pose questions I need to answer? Does it review the thinking that has gone on recently about my topic? Is the source a report of original research or is it a summary of others' research? Does it offer a case study or narrative that helps illustrate my claim? Or does it present quantitative or experimental research?

What you have learned so far about academic disciplines will help you evaluate the usefulness of a source. How timely is the source; does the date of its publication make any difference in the usefulness of its claims? Historical scholarship that depends on first-person reports can be very useful, but a psychological report based on outmoded ideas about memory could damage the strength of your essay. In evaluating your sources, consider also the range of academic disciplines you have drawn from. If you rely on articles from one journal only, you have probably considered the problem from too narrow a perspective. To help you explore the problem fully, use books and articles from a range of disciplines using a variety of methods and perspectives.

WRITING AND LEARNING ACTIVITIES

1. **Question Posing:** Either on your own or in a group, make up a list of questions to ask the research librarian.

2. **Research Activity:** If you have developed a topic and identified a claim, check the LCSH manual to find out what subject headings or keywords are appropriate for your claim. (It's always easier and more productive to have a topic and a specific claim when you go to the library.)

3. **Journal Entry:** Write a short paragraph about your initial experience searching for sources in the library. What surprised you? What difficulties did you encounter, if any? Write down any questions that arose during your search, either about finding sources or evaluating them. Make notes on each of the sources you found and whether or not you think they'll be useful.

4. **Group Activity:** Bring four books or articles to class. In small groups tell each other how you evaluated each source and how you think it will be useful for your essay.

MAKING THE MATERIAL YOUR OWN: TAKING NOTES

Bruce now had his sources. His next task was to organize his research project. He wanted to allow enough time for all aspects of the project, including getting personal interviews with friends and acquaintances who could offer a first-hand dimension to his project. The most challenging part of the project, he told us, was reading and rereading his source materials to see how each contributed to the big picture, that is, his claim that fatherhood should be redefined among African-American teenage fathers to focus on parenting. This, he said, caused him more anxiety and took more time than actually writing the report. Once he had a complete set of notes and had generated a source focus chart (see pages 571–572) and focus outline (see page 573), the actual drafting of the essay seemed much less difficult than he had originally anticipated.

When you were identifying your sources you probably skimmed them quickly to determine whether they were appropriate. The next step is to read each one carefully. The challenge here is to begin to make the material your own. Taking notes on your sources can be extremely time consuming, so be strategic: do not summarize everything that might be important in the article or chapter. Instead, try to think how each source will contribute to your essay. Only summarize what you think will support your claim. In addition, ask yourself these questions:

 How does this source fit in with other sources? What aspects of it seem to support my position? What aspects cast doubt on my claim?

The strategy that I have found works best for note taking relies on a double-entry note format. (You can also do this on your computer using hypercard stacks or Windows notecards.) Fold a notebook page in half or draw a line down the middle. Across the top of the page give your code name for the source. On the left side summarize, paraphrase, or quote whatever material you think is appropriate. On the right side of the page, make notes on how this material fits into your paper. Here are some questions to ask about the source:

What discipline is this source from? What type of research method is used? How does this support my claim? Does the information here add to other information I've found? Does it present a different point of view? How can I use it in my research essay?

If you're beginning to think about the organization of your paper, you might even suggest what section of the paper this source would contribute to. Below are Bruce Williams's notes on one of his sources.

Example: Page from a double-entry notebook

Massey: "Flip Side"

Data about adolescent male fathers from the point of view of teenage mothers. Teenage pregnancy is epidemic, especially among African-American youth. For example, in Oakland, California . . . "of the city's adolescent births, approximately 73% are to young Black teenagers" (p. 117).

Describes issues about the plight of the African-American male. Describes the racism present in everyday life, ". . . an extreme, exotic environment. . . . mundane, extreme environment; that is an environment where racism and subtle oppression are ubiquitous, constant, continuing, and mundane" (p. 118).

Data Collection
50 teen mothers filled out survey; most 15–17 years old and lived with their mothers. Their partners (fathers of their children) could not support them financially.

Interesting research; good idea to get the views of the mothers. Haven't seen anything like this before. You get more of a feeling of what the mothers were thinking because the researcher includes a lot of quotes from the mothers. This seems more like ethnography because I'm getting a feel for the people. Most of the sources I'm looking at are very quantitative.

I'll certainly want to use this to show that the fathers are willing but probably unable to be financially responsible. How else could they participate?

Results of the surveys showed that over 50% of the young mothers thought that their partners were good or excellent partners and friends.

Massey says fathers are not denying paternity even when they cannot fulfill financial responsibility.

WRITING AND LEARNING ACTIVITY

1. Notetaking: Keeping your claim in mind, begin taking notes by annotating your photocopies of articles, chapters, and portions of books. Take notes in the double-entry format for the sources you think will be most important. On the right side of the page note how you think that source will help you support your claim and how it might fit into your essay's organization.

DEVELOPING A SOURCE FOCUS CHART: READING AND REREADING

Bruce now faced the complex task of reading and rereading his source materials, looking for ways to develop his claim. As he read, he had to continually ask whether or not his claim was reasonable. Did some material present opposing points of view or differences that related to a particular discipline, and how did those scholars think about this particular problem? Bruce had to ask himself again and again about personal connections and their relation to his sources. He said it was like swimming in a sea with all the chapters and articles swirling around him just out of reach. He had to find a way to get control of the process and figure out how this material could contribute to his ideas on the topic and his paper.

To help make sense of his hundreds of pages of source materials, Bruce developed a "source focus chart," in which he sorted his materials into three categories that allowed him to highlight useful information:

USE: How do I plan to use this source in my essay? Write a single focus statement about the contribution of that source to the essay and most importantly to the claim.

CONNECTIONS: How does it connect with my other sources? How does it confirm or elaborate information I already have from other sources? Write a sentence or two describing the connections.

DISAGREEMENTS: How does this source contradict my other sources or offer a different perspective? Write a sentence or two describing the disagreements among sources.

Notice that in the example below Bruce listed each source by the author's last name and date—just as he will cite them in the body of his essay.

In addition he identifies the source by an abbreviated title that helps him focus on that source's contribution to his essay. Notice, too, that as he rereads looking for connections and disagreements, he has begun to see his paper in "chunks" or sections, that he will use to develop the course of his argument. He has already determined that there will be a "first part," in which he introduces the problem, and another major "chunk" in which he redefines fatherhood.

Source Focus Chart

Claim: Fatherhood for teenage African-American males needs to be redefined to emphasize parenting over financial support.

Christmon (1990a) "Self-image"
<u>***Use:</u> 2nd half of paper to redefine fatherhood. Claims the self-image of an African-American teenager is the strongest influence on whether or not he is able to take responsibility for parenting.
<u>Connections:</u> talks about defining fathering as other than financial contribution. Makes suggestions to reach these teens. Quantitative social research on African-American teen fathers (like Furstenberg) describes results in more detail than other Christmon report. Defines terms well. Connects to Massey & Hendricks.
<u>Disagreements:</u> Christmon seems to think the problem can be solved by helping the teen to work on his self-image. Smith sees the problem more socially/outside oriented. See Smith.

Christmon (1990b) "Parental Responsibility"
<u>***Use:</u> Do not use. Not very helpful. Reports on same study as 1990a. Focuses on defining variables for the study not on the results or what to do about the problem.

Massey (1991) "Flip Side"
<u>***Use:</u> Very important. Shows how teen mothers view teen fathers. Use in 2nd half of paper to redefine fatherhood. Shows what teen mothers think is important and how they see the fathers of their children. Good place to start from.
<u>Connections:</u> Introduction connects with Smith in showing how these African-American teens are in a high-risk population. Uses a lot of direct information from the mothers, so it sounds more like an ethnography than a quantitative report.
<u>Disagreements:</u> sees things differently than Christmon. When seen through the eyes of teen fathers' partners, the fathers seem to be more like fathers and less like pictures of one kind of self-image or another. Seems a more real picture than the one social researchers give.

Smith (1988) "Service Provision"
<u>***Use:</u> Very important overview article. Gave me idea for redefining fatherhood.

Connections: She's a social worker. Service Provision means outreach. So she's aiming to offer practical suggestions like Hendricks. She emphasized "historical restriction of opportunity" like Massey does in her introduction. Disagreement: She sees the problem bigger than Christmon. She is concerned with the high-risk population and the historical reasons for it while Christmon is in the here and now with self-image.

As you look over Bruce's entries you see that he has sorted out how his sources contribute to the argument he is building in his research essay. Two papers by one author, Christmon, reported on the same study, but Bruce will only use the "Self-image" article because it offers very specific support for his claim.

Three sources seemed to provide a web of connections and disagreements that helped Bruce think about how to define fatherhood. The information presented in "Self-Image," "Flip Side," and "Service Provision" offered Bruce an opportunity to consider how young fathers see themselves, how they are a part of a social system, and how they are seen by others. By categorizing the disagreements among these three sources, he learned how each author saw the issue differently and why some may disagree with his position. The connections helped Bruce synthesize the work of several scholars in different disciplines.

WRITING AND LEARNING ACTIVITIES

1. **Group Activity:** Choose one source and explain to the group how you found it, and why you think it will be useful. Tell how something you learned from that source will support the claim you are developing in your essay.

2. **Journal Entry:** Develop a source focus chart following Bruce Williams's method.

3. **Group Activity:** Explain your chart to each other; you will get a clearer idea of how you can synthesize this information to support your claim. Tell the group about the connections and disagreements you found among three or four of your sources.

DEVELOPING A FOCUS OUTLINE

As you continue to read your sources, you move back and forth between your ideas for your essay and the support for those ideas found in your sources. At some point, however, you need some distance from your sources. Bruce Williams found this to be true. He knew that he needed to think about the problem from his own perspective; he did not want to follow the reasoning or format of any one article. So he tried to put the sources away at this time and not think about them directly. Instead, he formulated focus statements that would guide the development of his essay. A focus statement tells, in your own words, the main point you want to develop in a particular portion of the essay—in effect a road sign that tells you where you are going. You might type it or print it in bold type at the begin-ning of a section or paragraph you plan to write. After the essay is drafted you can remove these road signs. In the focus outline below Bruce has pushed his plans for his essay further ahead. He now has identified sections for the paper and written focus statements for the topics he will cover in each section.

Focus Outline

Claim: Fatherhood for teenage African-American males needs to be rede-fined to emphasize parenting over financial support.

I. Background to the problem
✓ Most research on teen parenting focuses on young women.
✓ Young African-American men are viewed as the problem and only seen as the solution if they can contribute financially.

II. Exploring the problem
✓ The African-American teen is first a man in the society and as such a member of a high-risk group.
✓ Personal interviews show the difficulties of combining parenting and employment.

III. Redefining fatherhood
✓ Fatherhood can be defined as biological, legal, or, as in the focus for this paper, willing parent. Being a willing parent means taking respon-sibility for parenting your child ("Self-image").
✓ Summarize Smith's ("Service Provision") three-part cycle: historical restriction of opportunity, constricted view of self in the environment, and limited life plans.
✓ Show how Christmon ("Self-image") adds to our understanding of Smith's "view of self."
✓ Show how Massey ("Flip Side") makes us think twice about what re-search tells us about male adolescent fathers.

IV. Outreach to African-American teen fathers
✓ Social workers need to change their view of the teen father as a fi-nancial resource for the mother and child.
✓ Social workers should focus on understanding the teen father as a possible willing parent.
✓ We need this not just for this particular group of teen fathers but for us all.

This outline illustrates one of many kinds of activities that can help you think through the way you will present your argument in a research essay. At an earlier stage of the research process you might do some list-making or free association or just write in your journal on the topic to see what ideas emerge. At a later stage you might construct a more detailed outline in which you specify what is contained in each paragraph. Some professors even ask that you produce a formal outline of your paper—as a guide for the reader—after you have completed the essay.

WRITING AND LEARNING ACTIVITIES

1. **Journal Entry:** Make a list of focus statements—statements that name a point you want to develop in your essay. Don't worry about their order or whether they are the same length; just work to write a statement for each point you want to make in your essay. Next, look over your list. Do some focus statements seem broader than others? Do some seem narrower? Which ones should you place earlier in your essay and which ones later?

2. **Group Activity:** Report to your group on the current state of your focus outline. Tell what statements you plan to develop first, second, and third. Ask for their response. Do they follow your plan? Can they see how you plan to develop your essay? What portions of your plan confuse them and what portions seem particularly clear?

3. **Peer Exchange:** After you have drafted the focus outline, exchange it with your partner. Tell your partner whether or not you can follow his or her argument. Does the outline clearly suggest how the writer will support the claim? Where do you suspect there may be problems?

USING SUMMARY, SYNTHESIS, AND ANALYSIS IN WRITING

At this point in planning your essay you are probably still mulling over the ideas presented by the various sources and thinking about how you can present them to a reader so that your claim will be convincing. Your next task is to find just the right words to communicate your argument to your audience. Your thinking will be refined even further as you try out sentences and develop paragraphs that keep the ideas flowing one after another. Drafting the research essay is the point at which you take full responsibility and authority for your work. You have finished the preliminary work of building on personal connections, you have identified your topic, and developed an initial claim and searched for sources that would allow you to explore and support that claim. Your challenge now is to find an organizational approach that lets your reader see what you think about your sources.

Here is the final version of Bruce Williams's research essay.[1] Note how he used summary, synthesis, and analysis to present and argue his claim. In addition, he used all of the other textual practices we have discussed, such as quoting and paraphrasing. He used the APA style of referencing his work, which requires that the name and date be included in the in-text citation.

---

[1]This student essay reflects work done in class. As such, it may include errors or sylistic problems. It is included here so that students can follow the writer's progress.

Fatterhood and the Unmarried Adolescent
African-American Male

Bruce Earl Williams

Just about a quarter of all
children are now born out of
wedlock. . . . Add to that the
substantial fraction of children
born into marriages that will not
survive. . . . What do these high
rates of marital instability imply
for patterns of childbearing, and
especially for fathers' involvement
with their children? (Furstenberg &
Harris, 1992, p. 199)

The vast amount of research on the topic
of adolescent pregnancies has historically
focused on the female (such as Furstenberg,
1976 and Stack, 1974). Social scientists have
tried to understand the problem and also help
the adolescent mother following her decision
to give birth to a child. In some places,
such as Oakland, California, 73% of
adolescents giving birth are African American
(Smith, 1988, p.269; Massey, 1991, p. 117).
With this in mind, social workers have spent
most of their efforts helping adolescent
African-American women. The Department of
Children and Family Services (DCFS) and Aid
to Families of Dependent Children (AFDC)
offer help for many women and their children.
Unfortunately, the social workers usually
"viewed Black adolescent fathers either as
a cause of the problem of adolescent
parenthood or as a partial solution in
their assigned role of financial provider"
(Smith, 1988, p. 269).

Introductory quote focuses on the general problem of fathers' involvement with their children. Furstenberg is considered an expert in the topic of pregnancy among adolescents and the changing American family.

Introductory paragraph identifies the context for the research as the social sciences, and suggests how this research has influenced social workers. Sources provide general background information, specific statistics, and a strong quote by Smith.

Society and economic factors have played a damaging role within the African-American home and continue to deal a damaging blow to the African-American male. Social workers historically have viewed an unmarried mother as having a life ahead of continued financial dependence because of the African-American male's lack in this area. If a male is not supporting the mother financially, the social workers write off the male. As opposed to writing them off, social workers should reach out to adolescent fathers. This essay will try to redefine fatherhood for adolescent African-American fathers with more attention to becoming a willing parent and less attention to the father's ability to provide financial support. As I proceed I will also try to explain why the young fathers may not be present and explain some of their feelings. I will conclude by offering some ways to reach out to these young fathers.

This paragraph focuses on the aims of the essay. The key elements of the argument are included here: adolescent African-American fathers, social and economic factors, redefining fatherhood, and willing parenting.

The African-American Male in Society

Before an African-American father becomes a parent, he is first a male in society. To reach the age of twenty in urban American neighborhoods is a feat in itself. Most studies begin with a description of the population they are studying. In this case, the description is uniformly dismal. Smith (1988), relying on information from the census bureau, lists a depressing series of statistics: young African-American males who occupy low-wage and low-status jobs have a shorter life expectancy and increasingly are diagnosed with mental illness. Homicide is the leading cause of death, and the suicide

This paragraph synthesizes information from several sources to provide a picture of the social and economic context these young fathers live in. Uses a quote to highlight a particularly hard-hitting statement.

rate for young African-American men has risen sharply in recent years. The <u>Statistical Record of Black America</u> (1990) confirms this picture. In a study I will discuss below, Grace Massey describes the context of the male African-American adolescent as a "uniquely oppressive environment" where "racism and subtle oppression are ubiquitous, constant, continuing and mundane" (1991, p. 118).

With shorter life expectancy, higher homicide rate, high suicide rates, and fewer job offerings, the adolescent male must now confront the issue of fatherhood. Adolescent parenthood interrupts the schooling of both mother and father. Interrupted schooling means a lower hourly wage in the work force and little chance of improving the quality of life. A young man named Charles, age 20, talked to me about his situation as an adolescent parent. He adores his son, Charles III, who just turned two. He related how the system leaves him with few resources. "I can't get a job, because everybody wants a degree. Even the jobs that don't need degrees want experience. Two and three years of experience at that" (personal communication, April 2, 1993). I knew of his desire to go to school at night to get the necessary hands-on experience. He told me how the financial aid at his school was "dried up" and no banks would offer him a loan. He had had a good job with the railroad but had gotten laid off and was trying to support himself and his family while going to school.

A woman named Jean, age 24, explained to me that although she and "husband" Edward,

These two paragraph sharpen the focus by including information obtained through personal interviews, which illustrate in a more human way the problems established in the previous paragraph. Note that interviews are cited as personal communications and, as such, do not appear in the reference or works cited list.

age 27, are not legally married, she has lived with this man and their eight-year-old child for six years. They met when she was 16 and he was 19. She and her child stayed at her mother's home until Edward was able to move the two into an apartment. "Marriage is nothing but a state of mind. Just because that woman on the street has a piece of paper does not mean that she is any more married than I am" (personal communication, March 22, 1993). I realized that she had a valid point. She gets more money on the AFDC program by being single than by being married. Legally married couples can receive federal assistance in the form of money and food stamp coupons, but a comparatively lower amount than a single woman because the program assumes that the husband has some income. However, if there is no job for the father, there is no subsidized income. Edward's lack of a job necessitates that Jean remain "married" by her own definition.

Fatherhood and Parenting

We can think about fatherhood in three ways: biological father, legal father, and willing parent. Studies of the family from the early 1900s on have stressed the weakness of the male's biological link to the child as opposed to the universally accepted maternal bond (Furstenberg & Harris, 1992, p. 197). In any marital union (legal, or personal, as in Jean's above) or even after the union has ended—the father is expected to "bring home the bacon." When African-American fathers cannot provide this economic support, they find themselves in a double-bind. Grace

This paragraph includes important introductory material that prepares the reader for Bruce's redefinition of fatherhood. It offers three ways to define fatherhood and later eliminates the first two by referring to specific sources.

Massey explains that they are. . . "expected to 'prove' their manhood through providing the primary economic support of their families and the lack of means to play this role puts 'manhood' for Black men at risk" (1991, p. 118).

The final role and the one which I think can best redefine fatherhood is the "willing" parent. Carol Stack described how kinship depends on who you accept as kin, not who is biologically your kin, or who is legally your kin (Stack, 1974). It is not enough to say, as Christmon does, that fatherhood can be redefined as "willingness to be involved in the parenting of his child" (1990, p. 563). The situation is much more complex than that: 'willingness' develops or does not develop in a complex social and economic situation.

Here "willingness" is identified as a key ingredient in redefining fatherhood. Begins the process of identifying connections and disagreements in his sources on this issue.

Linda Anderson Smith (1988) identifies three factors that relate to fatherhood among adolescent males: (1) historical restriction of opportunity; (2) constricted view of self in the environment; and (3) subsequent development of limited life plans. She stresses that the three factors work in a cyclical manner, being set into motion by historical restriction of opportunity. With a constricted view of self in the environment, the adolescent male may develop limited life plans, perhaps resulting in adolescent fatherhood which, in turn, further drives the cycle.

These two paragraphs summarize Smith's work, which presents the broadest view of the problem.

Historical restrictions of opportunity in American institutions leave the African-American male searching for alternative ways to enter adulthood that are sought after but are usually nonexistent or never found. The adolescent male, according to Smith, then "perceives self as unable to manipulate the environment by traditional means" (Smith, 1988, p. 270). This constricted view of self in the environment is where the male begins to feel "as if on a leash." Hope begins to fade and anxiety begins to rise. The male begins to look upon goals as if they were out of reach. This may happen when the adolescent male is in high school, doing well, but suddenly drops out. Smith emphatically points out that this should not be confused with low self-esteem, because the self feels capable, only constricted by the environment.

The opposite of Smith's "manipulate the environment by traditional means," can be seen in drug dealing. The male feels the constraining forces of his environment through a lack of employment and may find solutions in dealing drugs. The "traditional means" of punching the clock for an eight-hour day and forty-hour week is no longer an option for some adolescent African-American males. Selling dope, making easy money, and living a life of luxury is the way that some males choose to "manipulate the environment." What can keep a sixteen-year-old male in school when his eighteen-year-old friend drives a Mercedes-Benz?

Theorists have shown that human behavior is affected by the anticipation of future events. If we feel today will be a good day, it probably will be. Adolescent African-American males, in the third part of Smith's cycle, develop limited life plans. It is seen in the thinking of living for the present. A childhood friend of mine named Marlon

In this paragraph, Bruce offers an analysis, an expanded reading, of Smith's concept of "manipulating the environment." This analysis relies on his own observations.

This paragraph extends the analysis through personal connections. Given the cycle that Smith describes, Bruce concludes that fatherhood could offer a way out of the cycle.

explained that he knows that drugs destroy
homes and people; but he has to "get paid"
(personal communication, March 14, 1993). I
tried to understand how he could live each
day with the fear of being shot by a rival
drug dealer, and he replied: "Hey, if they
get me, they get me." With limited life
plans, African-American males might view
fatherhood as one of the few ways to attain
adulthood.

Smith's three-part cycle illustrates how
historical circumstances and the young
father's view of himself work together to
create a situation where fatherhood can be
seen as a positive outcome of very difficult
circumstances. Christmon largely ignores the
historical circumstances but gives us a
detailed look at how the young father's self-
image might influence his willingness to
become involved in caring for his child.
Three aspects of self emerge as important to
the father's willingness to parent
(Christmon, 1990). Most important was the
familial self: how the young father related
to his family of origin. In another study,
Hendricks (1988) found that young fathers in
three ethnic groups reported being close to
their mothers, offering an opportunity for
support (1988).

The second most important aspect of the
young African-American father's self-image
was his sexual self. If a father is
uncomfortable with his own sexuality, it
becomes very hard for him to overcome any
specific sex-type roles for men. The
adolescent male may believe that there are
certain things that a mother must do and

Here, Bruce shows through both analysis and synthesis how Smith's work relates to others' work in the same area. Smith takes the broad view and Christmon focuses narrowly, perhaps too narrowly, on only self-image. Work by another source contributes to our understanding of the importance of the family of origin.

fathers must not. He may see nurturing (i.e., feedings, changing diapers) as a threat to his manhood and look upon stereotypical feminine roles as taboo. Social providers can help the adolescent male feel comfortable with duties that he feels should be exclusively for mothers.

These two paragraphs continue the summary of Christmon that was begun above.

The third most important aspect of the young father's self-image is his ability to cope. Here is where we see another way of talking about the father's ability, in Smith's terms, to "manipulate the environment." This is where social workers can assist the adolescent male in developing positive skills to cope with his environment.

These researchers and social workers look at the young African-American father from the outside, describing a group of people different from themselves. In "The flip side of teen mothers: A look at teen fathers," Grace Massey (1991) gives us some feedback from the partners of these young men. The results of Massey's survey are quite startling. Instead of seeing the cup as half empty, these young mothers see the cup as half-full. On the one hand, the young fathers fit the description above of members of this high-risk population: they dropped out of school, they're unemployed, and they may be taking drugs. Yet when asked about their partner's participation, more than half of these young women rated their partners as good or excellent fathers and friends. How should we think about these two different pictures presented by different researchers? Massey reminds us that the young women's responses may be "relative" to how they see

To conclude this section and push the essay toward considering solutions, Bruce uses information gained from Massey's research to offer an analysis of the research reported above. Massey offers a different perspective, that of the young female partners. Bruce uses this new perspective to question the findings of the other researchers and to offer a transition to his next section.

things in their community. Yet there is still something positive here to work with; perhaps the picture from the inside offers a place for social workers begin.

Reaching Out to Help Young Fathers
Traditionally, social workers have viewed these young men quite differently from the young mothers in Massey's study. From the outside they are seen as "deviants in need of rehabilitation" (Smith, 1988, p. 270). High homicide rates, high suicide rates, few job options, lack of schooling, and limited life plan foster within the adolescent male the belief that he must survive. Fathering a child may make the young man feel that he is an adult but he still does not see the emotional and financial needs of the mother. He may be oblivious to the needs his child, who can greatly benefit from his presence. The adolescent father, because of his constricted view of self, created by society, looks out for only himself. But in light of this redefinition of fatherhood as willing parenting, social workers should have an outstretched hand for adolescent males instead of a hardened heart. With such mountains of obstacles, is there any hope for the African-American male and his family?

Social workers must understand that to attain adulthood, fathering a child is the adolescent male's choice to achieve an important goal. The counselors must also understand that the familial self, sexual self, and adjustment factors greatly affect the willingness to fulfill parental responsibility. These young fathers are not

Here, we are reminded that the prevailing view among social workers is that the father is the problem. Bruce synthesizes his own argument up to this point and extends it by analyzing the feelings of the young men.

The essay concludes with not only some specific suggestions for social workers to consider, but more importantly with a plea to consider the issue one that involves our whole society, not just one group within that society.

apathetic to their parental responsibility, and need vocational and educational courses so that they might manipulate the environment in a positive manner. A positive male in society greatly benefits us all.

REFERENCE LIST

Christmon, K. (1990). Parental responsibility and self-image of African-American fathers. Families in Society: The Journal of Contemporary Human Services, 71, 563–567.

Furstenberg, F. & Harris, K. (1992). The disappearing American father? Divorce and the waning significance of biological parenthood. In S. J. South & S. E. Tolnay (Eds.), The changing American family: Sociological and demographic perspectives (pp. 197–223). Boulder, Colorado: Westview Press.

Furstenberg, F. (1976). Unplanned parenthood: The social consequences of teenage childbearing. New York: Free Press.

Hendricks, L. E. (1988). A preliminary report on three ethnic groups. Adolescence, 91, 711–720.

Horton, C. P. & Smith, J. C. (Eds.) (1990). Statistical record of Black America. Detroit: Gale Research, Inc.

Massey, G. (1991). The flip side of teen mothers: A look at teen fathers. In B. P. Bowser. (Ed.), Black male adolescents: Parenting and education in community context (pp. 117–128). New York: University Press of America.

Smith, L. A. (1988). Black adolescent fathers: Issues for service provision. Social Work, 33. 269–272.

Stack, C. B. (1974). <u>All our kin: Strategies for survival in a black community</u>. New York: Harper & Row.

REVISING YOUR ESSAY

You have now completed a draft of your essay. On the next page is a sample peer review worksheet that you can use with a partner. Getting someone else's feedback—another student or your instructor—can make a great difference in how you shape the final version of your essay.

WRITING AND LEARNING ACTIVITIES

1. **Journal Entry:** Write about your response to Bruce Williams's essay. How do your personal experiences connect to the material presented? What questions are still unanswered for you? Does this essay raise any questions that you would like to explore in an essay of your own?

2. **Group Activity:** Discuss Bruce Williams's essay in your group. What is his claim? How does he establish his own authority as the writer of the essay? How does he use his sources to provide support for his claim? Identify places where his essay is particularly convincing or where your group thinks the essay needs work.

3. **Writing Activity:** Write Bruce Williams a letter responding to his essay.

PEER REVIEW WORKSHEET

Writer's Name _____

Writer's Comments: In the space below state what you think works best in your essay and what needs more work. Write down a few questions about any aspect of your essay that you would like the reviewer to consider.

Reviewer's Name _____

1. Review the essay's introduction.

   Does the writer state his or her claim clearly? Do you get a sense of why the topic is important? Does the writer include enough background information? Do you feel as though you are being invited into the subject matter of the essay and the questions it asks?

2. Read through the entire essay and respond to these questions about its effectiveness as a whole.

   As you read through the essay as a whole, do you feel as though the writer is speaking with authority, having made sense of a body of material and applied it to his or her particular claim? Do you believe what the writer is telling you? Does the writer stay focused?

3. Read the entire essay through again and respond to these questions about the relationship of the evidence to the writer's claim.

   Does the writer use sources effectively as support for the claim? Does he or she suggest alternative interpretations or examine both sides of an issue? Does the writer define key terms? Are there places in the essay where you would like to see summary, synthesis, and analysis used differently?

4. Examine the essay for correctness.

   Examine the essay for problems with sentence structure, style, quoting and paraphrasing, in-text citations, diction, grammar, and spelling. Does the reference list follow the appropriate format?

5. State at least one strength that you see in the essay.

6. Make at least one concrete suggestion for improving the essay.

DIRECTIONS FOR FURTHER RESEARCH IN THE SOCIAL SCIENCES, HUMANITIES, AND SCIENCES

This section offers you resources for following up on a particular interest as you plan and develop your research essay. Each of the following three resource sections—social sciences, humanities, and sciences—offers a list of journals, encyclopedias, general references, and indexes in that field. If you have only a very broad idea of what you would like to write about, you can browse through the academic journals to see what topics are covered. Or you could look through some of the general references, which would give you an idea of the specialized language used to discuss your topic. Once you have identified a topic and developed a working claim, you will want to use the indexes to identify specific sources for your research essay.

RESOURCES IN THE SOCIAL SCIENCES

American Anthropologist. Washington, DC: American Anthropological Association, 1988 and yearly.

Each issue offers five to ten major articles, several condensed research reports, book and film reviews, responses to previous articles, and occasionally obituaries. This journal is sponsored by the American Anthropological Society and American Ethnological Society.

American History and Life. Santa Barbara, CA: ABC-CLIO.

Bibliography of historical literature covering the U.S. and Canada. Indexes article abstracts, citations of reviews, and doctoral dissertations. Includes four indexes: subject, author, title, and reviewer indexes. Published in four quarterly issues per year, plus the annual index.

American Sociological Review. Washington, DC: American Sociological Association. Published bimonthly.

Each issue contains approximately six feature articles, along with a comments section. The articles focus primarily on quantitative research in the different subfields of sociology, although some feature other methodologies as well.

Atlas of Mankind. Chicago: Rand McNally, 1982.

Designed for novices in the field, this atlas provides easy-to-understand descriptions. The first section focuses on topical issues. The longer second section focuses on cultural specifications of eleven groups of peoples throughout the world.

Cayton M. K., E. J. Gorn, and P. W. Williams. *Encyclopedia of American Social History.* Vols. I–III. New York: Charles Scribner's Sons, 1993.

Includes short articles on topics in the field of social history. See Volume III, Part XI, in particular, for information and a bibliography of works in the area of family history.

Current Anthropology. Chicago: University of Chicago Press, 1960 and continuing.

This journal includes articles with commentaries following each article, research and conference reports, and shorter news items and letters. The format of this journal provides a discussion-like atmosphere where many sides to an issue are debated as people respond to the article or the commentaries.

Ethnology. Pittsburgh: University of Pittsburgh, 1962.

Covering international issues of cultural anthropology, this journal also cites previous studies, which allows readers interested in the field to find other resources. It is one of the few journals dedicated to publishing ethnographies.

Historical Abstracts. Santa Barbara, CA: ABC-CLIO.

Part A: Modern History Abstracts 1450–1914, and Part B: Twentieth Century Abstracts 1914–present. Bibliography of historical literature about the world, exclusive of the U.S. and Canada. Indexes article abstracts and annotations, recently published books, and doctoral dissertations. Includes a subject and an author index; three quarterly issues plus the annual index are published.

Illustrated Encyclopedia of Mankind. New York: Marshall Cavendish. 22, 1989.

This resource targets a general audience, including undergraduates new to the field. The encyclopedia contains color photos and descriptive essays. The last five volumes compare many cultures.

Journal of Family History. Greenwich, CT: JAI Press. Published quarterly.

This interdisciplinary journal features articles on the history of the family, kinship, and population. Each issue contains approximately five feature articles and one or two review or debate essays. Articles show a range of disciplinary approaches, including historical, anthropological, and sociological.

Journal of Marriage and the Family. St. Paul, MN.: National Council on Family Relations. Published quarterly.

Approximately 20 feature articles and 20 book reviews are included in each issue. The articles are grouped according to specific topics and tend to be heavily empirical, although some are theoretical. Each issue also includes research notes, commentaries on articles, and book reviews.

Journal of Social History. Pittsburgh, PA: Carnegie Mellon University. Published quarterly.

Each issue contains approximately six to seven feature articles (the abstracts for which are included at the end of the issue) and 30 book reviews. The feature articles address American and European social history, prior to 1945 for the most part. The extensive bibliographies of these articles provide a good source for further research information.

Kibbee, J. Z. *Cultural anthropology: A guide to reference and information sources.* Englewood, CO: Libraries Unlimited, 1991.

This easy-to-use reference book is divided into nine chapters and offers material on general reference sources, bibliographies, subfields of anthropology, area studies, and periodicals.

Seymour-Smith, C. *Dictionary of anthropology.* Boston: G. K. Hall, 1986.

This dictionary focuses on cultural/social anthropology and includes current cultural anthropological thought, such as feminist theory. This dictionary has more than 1,000 entries and a useful bibliography that can point the way to further reading.

Social History. London: Routledge. Published three times a year.

Each issue contains approximately three feature articles (the abstracts for which are included at the beginning of the issue), approximately twelve book reviews, as well as a few comment articles and review essays. The articles present a broad, international coverage of social historical issues, with greater emphasis on Europe than on the U.S.

Social Sciences Citation Index. Philadelphia, PA: Institute for Scientific Information, Inc.

This citation index is useful if you want to find out what others have written about a particular author or a particular work. Journals from virtually every discipline in the social sciences are indexed here. Entries are listed by authors' names first, followed by their specific works.

Social Sciences Index. New York: H. W. Wilson.

This index is helpful if you are searching for current articles on a particular topic. It provides an author and subject index to articles in social science journals, including major sociological, anthropological, and historical journals. An online version of this index is also available at many university libraries.

Sociological Abstracts. San Diego, CA: Sociological Abstracts, Inc.

Indexes journals published by sociological institutes and associations, as well as journals in the related fields of anthropology, economics, political science, and so on. Includes book reviews and abstracts for journal articles, books, conference papers. Entries are organized by main subject areas and are indexed according to author, source, and reviewers.

Sociology and Social Research. Los Angeles, CA: University of Southern California. Published quarterly.

Each issue includes four or five feature articles, as well as a few articles addressing recent social trends or current issues. The articles are arranged according to specific topics and tend to be fairly brief and readable, although many include detailed quantitative data analysis. The articles addressing current issues in particular might provide you with some ideas for topics for your papers.

RESOURCES IN THE HUMANITIES

American Literature. Durham, NC: Duke University Press. Published quarterly.

Each issue contains approximately seven articles, and numerous book reviews of critical works in American literary studies. Articles are longer, fairly academic and in-depth, with useful bibliographies.

Arntzen, Etta Mae and Robert Rainwater. *Guide to the Literature of Art History.* London: Art Book Company, 1980.

This work includes over 4,000 references and research tools, major exhibition catalogs, and author/title and subject indexes. There are four major divisions: general reference sources; general primary and secondary sources; specific arts such as painting, architecture, sculpture, prints, and photography; and serials.

Art Index. New York: H. W. Wilson, 1930–v. 1 and continuing.

This quarterly journal is both an author and a subject index. The entries, from over 190 American and foreign periodicals, include articles, book reviews, exhibition information, and illustrations.

Bertman, Martin A. *Research Guide in Philosophy.* Morristown, NJ: General Learning Press, 1974.

This 252-page guide is geared for undergraduates. Information includes philosophical methods, library usage, a selective bibliography, and a glossary of terms.

Contemporary Authors. Detroit: Gale Research, Inc.

A bio-bibliographic guide to writers in fiction, poetry, nonfiction, journalism, drama, movies, television, and other fields. Each author entry includes personal information, a career summary, awards and honors, writings, work in progress, as well as biographical and critical sources that you can check for further information.

De George, Richard T. *The Philosopher's Guide to Sources, Research Tools, Professional Life, and Related Fields.* Lawrence: Regents Press of Kansas, 1980.

> This comprehensive guide provides short annotations that may be used as starting points for finding additional sources. The chapters are divided into philosophy, general research tools, and related fields, and there is a general introduction to each chapter. The author, title and subject index helps you locate specific information. This resource would be best used after you have narrowed down your topic and are ready to start researching.

Edwards, Paul (editor-in-chief). *Encyclopedia of Philosophy.* New York: Macmillian Publishing Company, 1972.

> This eight-volume encyclopedia includes almost 1,500 articles, 900 of which focus on specific scholars. The topics include eastern and western philosophers and ancient, medieval, and modern time periods. In addition, the articles explain philosophy's points of contact with other disciplines. The last volume is an index.

Encyclopedia of World Art. New York: McGraw-Hill, 1959–83

> Articles describing architecture, sculpture, painting, and a variety of man-made objects fill half of each volume. The plates that these articles describe comprise the rest of each volume. The articles cover all countries and time periods, and there are extensive bibliographies.

Gardner, Helen. *Art Through the Ages.* 7th edition. New York: Harcourt, 1980.

> This two-volume illustrated resource provides general information for the art history novice. It is a standard work and is often used as a textbook for introductory art history courses.

Humanities Index. New York: H. W. Wilson

> Cumulative index to English-language periodicals in the fields of archaeology and classical studies, area studies, folklore, history, language and literature, performing arts, philosophy, religion and theology, and related subjects. Lists author and subject entries to periodicals, arranged alphabetically. Published four times a year, with an annual cumulative index. It is available online at many libraries.

Jones, Lois Swan. *Art Research Methods and Resources: A Guide to Finding Art Information.* 2d ed. Dubuque, IA: Kendall/Hunt, 1984.

> This resource is easily accessible to students. Four sections help a student move through the art history research process. There are indexes and an appendix of art terms in the back.

Lacy, Alan Robert. *A Dictionary of Philosophy.* New York: Routledge, 1986.

> Students are this work's target audience since the author defines the "commonest of terms" and explains how philosophers view them. The end of each section cites sources for further research.

Meyers, Bernard S. (ed.). *McGraw-Hill Dictionary of Art.* New York: McGraw-Hill, 1969.

> This five-volume illustrated dictionary provides long articles on topics ranging from artists' lives and careers and artistic terms and periods,

to museums and monuments of major cities. The emphasis of this work is on primitive, near East, and Far East art.

MLA International Bibliography of Books and Articles on the Modern Languages and Literatures. New York: Modern Language Association of America.

Includes citations for articles from published journals and series. The four main subject areas covered are: national literatures, linguistics, literary theory and criticism, and folklore.

Studies in Short Fiction. Newberry, SC: Newberry College. Issued quarterly.

Issues have approximately ten articles and 15 reviews per issue. Articles are short and readable, covering major and less well known authors from many countries.

Twentieth-Century Literary Criticism. Detroit: Gale Research, Inc.

Includes excerpts from the criticism of the works of novelists, poets, playwrights, and other creative writers who lived between 1900 and 1960. Each volume includes entries for approximately 10 to 15 authors, or for four to six general topics. Each entry begins with a brief outline of the author's life and career, list of principal works, annotated excerpts of criticism, and concludes with a further reading list. Other series published by Gale Research may be helpful—*Contemporary Literary Criticism* (1960 to present), *Nineteenth-Century Literature Criticism* (1800–1899), *Black Literature Criticism, Short Story Criticism,* and a number of other volumes.

RESOURCES IN THE SCIENCES

Abbott, D. (gen. ed.) *The Biographical Dictionary of Scientists, Biologists.* New York: Peter Bedrick Books, 1983

Offers biographies of significant biologists from ancient times through present day.

Anglemeye, Mary. *A Search for Environmental Ethics: An Initial Bibliography.* Washington, DC: Smithsonian Institute, 1980.

An annotated bibliography of works from a variety of fields such as science, philosophy, religion, education, politics, and others that concern the natural environment.

Current Contents. Philadelphia: Institute for Scientific Information. Weekly.

Reproduces the tables of contents from the most recent journals in a variety of fields.

Durbin, Paul T. (gen. ed.) *A Guide to the Culture of Science, Technology, and Medicine.* New York: Free Press, 1980.

Includes recent survey articles that explore the problems of values in contemporary culture and their relationship to science, technology, and medicine. There is not much coverage of environmental issues. Each entry offers suggestions for further reading.

Environment Abstracts. New York: Environment Information Center, Inc. Monthly.

This index includes radio and television programming, newspaper articles, significant books, as well as journals.

Environment Index. New York: Environment Information Center, Inc. Annual.

This reference tool offers an index for *Environment Abstracts* (above). The subject index can be used independently and offers an annual listing of environmental books and films and summarizes the year's events in the field.

Environmental Health-Related Information. Washington, DC: National Technical Information Service, 1984.

A source intended for health professionals to identify materials for educating their clients, including students and patients. Subjects such as air pollution or asbestos are arranged alphabetically.

General Science Index. New York: H. W. Wilson. Monthly.

Offers a subject index to general science periodicals.

Gornick, V. *Women in Science.* New York: Simon & Schuster, 1990.

Interviews with women scientists in which the author asks: "What has a career in science been like for you?"

Gray, P. (ed.). *The Encyclopedia of the Biological Sciences.* 2d ed. New York: Van Nostrand Reinhold, 1970.

This encyclopedia offers the nonspecialist articles on subject matter in biology, including biographies and bibliographies for further work.

Hammond, K. A., Macinko, G. and Fairchild, W. *Sourcebook on the Environment: A Guide to the Literature.* Chicago: University of Chicago Press, 1978.

Provides a broad guide to the environmental literature through introductions to various areas by specialists.

Index Medicus. Washington, DC: National Library of Medicine. Monthly.

Offers a comprehensive index to the world's medical literature from reputable journals.

Last, J. (ed.). *A Dictionary of Epidemiology.* New York: Oxford University Press, 1983.

Contains short and essay-length definitions of topics such as community and public health, demography, and biostatistics.

McGraw-Hill Encyclopedia of Science and Technology. 5th ed. New York: McGraw-Hill, 1882.

This 15-volume, illustrated encyclopedia covers all branches of science and technology. Introductory articles cover broad topics; separate, shorter articles cover the subdivisions. Bibliographies are included.

O'Brien, R. and Cohen, S. *The Encyclopedia of Drug Abuse.* New York: Facts on File, 1984.

Comprehensive coverage of all aspects of drug abuse.

Parker, Sybil P. (ed.). *McGraw-Hill Dictionary of Scientific and Technical Terms.* New York: McGraw-Hill, 1984.

This dictionary is considered the standard for science and technology. Offers brief definitions according to the field.

Primack, Alice Lefler. *Finding Answers in Science and Technology.* New York: Van Nostrand Reinhold, 1984.

A guide geared to the interests of hobby scientists, arranged by subject with sections that explain how to find further resources.

Rees, A. M. and Judith, J. *The Consumer Health Information Sourcebook.* New York: Bowker, 1984.

An up-to-date, complete guide to health information for the layperson, identifying essential materials and information sources: books, pamphlets, periodicals, newsletters, and professional literature.

Smith, D. ed. *The Cambridge Encyclopedia of Earth Sciences.* Cambridge: Cambridge University Press, 1982.

This collection of long articles written by well-known scholars is designed as a book to be read as well as a reference.

Steen, Edwin B. *Dictionary of Biology.* New York: Barnes & Noble, 1971.

Brief definitions for the most commonly used terms in the study of biology.

Stiegeler, Stella E. *A Dictionary of the Earth Sciences.* New York: Universe Books, 1977.

A handy, easy-to-use concise dictionary for the earth sciences.

POPULAR JOURNALS IN THE SCIENCES

Academic journals in the sciences are very specialized, which makes it difficult for students to browse through them looking for ideas for research. For this reason, I have also included a list of popular science journals, dealing with a variety of topics, that offer an introduction to some issues currently under study in biology, geology, nutrition, and generally in studies about the environment.

Audubon: Covers environment, wildlife, and preservation of wildlife habitat.

BioScience: Contains articles from all areas of biological sciences, including animals, humans, plants, and the environment.

Discover: Science newsmagazine providing extensive coverage of science and technology in nontechnical language.

Geological Magazine: Covers a range of geological topics.

Geology: Topical scientific papers on all earth science disciplines worldwide.

Geotimes: News of the earth sciences.

Natural History: Includes articles on the biological sciences, ecology, anthropology, archaeology, geology, and astronomy.

Nature: Scholarly publication. Publishes original scientific research reports, review articles, and other commentary.

New Scientist: Offers comprehensive coverage of a wide range of science-related fields and topics. Subjects of articles include botany, physics, evolution, nuclear power, mathematics, and environmental studies.

Science News: Publishes reports on new research findings and developments and issues in all disciplines of science, for a nonspecialist audience. Includes short reports from major conferences and congresses, reviews of results published in scientific journals, and coverage of legislative and political events related to scientific policy.

Sciences: Contains a wide selection of articles on scientific subjects. Topics covered include space technology, environmental science, agriculture, electronics, and computer sciences.

Scientific American: Original articles on a variety of scientific topics: current research trends, historical issues, and a "how-to" section for amateur scientists.

Smithsonian: Disseminates all aspects of the sciences as well as history and the arts.

Wildlife Conservation: Popular articles for the general public about wildlife conservation worldwide.

WORKS CITED

"Analyze." *American Heritage Dictionary of the English Language*, 3rd ed. 1992.

Abele, G., J. Brown, and M. C. Brewer, "Long-term Effects of Off-Road Vehicle Traffic on Tundra Terrain." *Journal of Terramechanics* 21.3 (1984): 283–94.

Ariès, Philippe. *Centuries of Childhood: A Social History of Family Life*. New York: Alfred A. Knopf, 1962.

Berger, John. *Ways of Seeing*. New York: Penguin Press, 1972.

Bishop, Elizabeth. "The Baptism" *Elizabeth Bishop: The Collected Prose*. Ed. Robert Giroux. New York: Farrar, Straus and Giroux, 1984. 159–70.

———. "In the Village." *Elizabeth Bishop: The Collected Prose*. Ed. Robert Giroux. New York: Farrar, Straus and Giroux, 1984. 252–74.

———. "Gwendolyn." *Elizabeth Bishop: The Collected Prose*. Ed. Robert Giroux. New York: Farrar, Straus and Giroux, 1984. 213–26.

Brower, Reuben, and Richard Poirier. *In Defense of Reading: A Reader's Approach to Literary Criticism*. New York: Dutton, 1962.

Bryson, Norman. *Vision and Painting: The Logic of the Gaze*. New Haven: Yale UP, 1983.

Congressional Quarterly Almanac. "Arctic Refuge Bill Stalls Once Again," xlvi: (1990) 315.

Cuddon, J. A. *The Penguin Dictionary of Literary Terms and Literary Theory*. 3rd ed. New York: Penguin Books, 1992.

De Vos, Susan. "Leaving the Parental Home: Patterns in Six Latin American Countries." *Journal of Marriage and the Family* 51 (1989): 615–26.

Demos, John. *Past, Present, and Personal: The Family and the Life Course in American History*. New York: Oxford UP, 1986.

Eagleton, Terry. *Criticism and Ideology: A Study in Marxist Literary Theory*. London: Verso, 1978.

Egan, Timothy. "The Great Alaska Debate." *New York Times Magazine*. 4 Aug. 1991: 21–26, 49.

Ellis, Frey R., Schura Holesh, and John Ellis. "Incidence of Osteoporosis in Vegetarians and Omnivores." *The American Journal of Clinical Nutrition* 25 (1972): 555–58.

Felix, Nancy, and Martha K. Raynolds. "The Role of Snow Cover in Limiting Surface Disturbance Caused by Winter Seismic Exploration." *Arctic* 42.1 (1989): 62–68.

Fish, Stanley. *Is There a Text in This Class? The Authority of Interpretive Communities*. Cambridge, Massachusetts: Harvard UP, 1980.

Flam, Jack. "Henri Matisse: *Bathers with a Turtle*," *ARTnews*, December (1990): 101–102.

———. *Matisse: The Man and His Art, 1869–1918*. Ithaca, New York: Cornell UP, 1986.

Francis, Lisbeth. "Clone Specific Segregation in the Sea Anemone *Anthopleura elegantissima*." *Biological Bulletin* 144 (1973): 64–72.

———. "Intraspecific Aggression and Its Effect on the Distribution of *Anthopleura elegantissima* and Some Related Sea Anemones." *Biological Bulletin* 144 (1973): 73–92.

Freedberg, David. *The Power of Images: Studies in the History and Theory of Response*. Chicago: U of Chicago P, 1989.

Geertz, Clifford. *Works and Lives: The Anthropologist as Author*. Stanford, CA: Stanford UP, 1988.

Goldscheider, Frances K., and Calvin Goldscheider, "Family Structure and Conflict: Nest-leaving Expectations of Young Adults and Their Parents." *Journal of Marriage and the Family* 51 (Feb. 1989): 87–97.

Harris, Joseph. "The Idea of Community in the Study of Writing." *College Composition and Communication* 40 (Feb. 1989): 11–22.

Horowitz, Ruth. *Honor and the American Dream: Culture and Identity in a Chicano Community*. New Brunswick, NJ: Rutgers UP, 1983.

Howard, Jane. *Families*. New York: Simon & Schuster, 1978.

Johansson, S. Ryan. "Centuries of Childhood/Centuries of Parenting: Philippe Ariès and the Modernization of Privileged Infancy." *Journal of Family History* 14.4 (1987): 343–65.

Kalstone, David. *Becoming a Poet: Elizabeth Bishop with Marianne Moore and Robert Lowell*. Ed. Robert Hemenway. New York: Farrar, Straus and Giroux, 1989: 30–5, 149–60, 160–66.

Lemke, Jay. *Talking Science*. Norwood, New Jersey: Ablex, 1990.

Lewis, Oscar. *Five Families: Mexican Case Studies in the Culture of Poverty*. New York: Basic Books, 1959.

Locke, John. "Of Identity and Diversity." From "Essay Concerning Human Understanding." *Personal Identity*. 1694. Ed. J. Perry. Berkeley: U of California P, 1975.

Mann, Patricia. "Personal Identity Matters." *Social Theory and Practice* 14 (1988): 285–316.

Marshall, Donald G. "Doxography Versus Inquiry: Two Ways of Teaching Theory." *Teaching Contemporary Theory to Undergraduates.* Ed. Dianne F. Sadoff and William E. Cain. New York: Modern Language Association, 1994. 80–89.

Mazess, R., and Mather, B. "Bone Mineral Content of North Alaskan Eskimos." *American Journal of Clinical Nutrition* 27 (1974): 916–25.

Messina, V., ed. *Guide to Healthy Eating.* Washington, DC: Physicians Committee for Responsible Medicine, March–April, 1990.

Millier, Brett C. *Elizabeth Bishop: Life and the Memory of It.* Los Angeles: U of California P, 1993.

Mills, C. Wright. *The Sociological Imagination.* New York: Oxford UP, 1959.

Miner, Horace. "Body Ritual Among the Nacirema." *American Anthropologist* 58 (1956): 503–507, 1956.

Moore, Henry. "On Sculpture and Primitive Art." *Modern Artists on Art.* Ed. Robert L. Herbert. Englewood Cliffs, NJ: Prentice-Hall, 1964. 138–49.

Newberry, Todd. "Fieldtrips." *The Threepenny Review* 41 (Spring, 1990): 11–12.

Parfit, Derek. "What We Believe Ourselves to Be." *Reasons and Persons.* New York: Oxford UP, 1984.

Raynolds, Martha K., and Felix, Nancy A. "Airphoto Analysis of Winter Seismic Disturbance in Northeastern Alaska." *Arctic* 42.4 (1989): 362–67.

Rosenblatt, Louise M. *Literature as Exploration.* 1938. New York: Noble and Noble Publishers, 1968.

Ryle, Gilbert. *A Rational Animal: The Auguste Comte Memorial Lecture 5.* London: Athlone Press, 1962.

Sebens, Kenneth. "The Anemone Below." *Natural History* 3 Nov. 1986: 49–52.

Spanier, Bonnie B. "Encountering the Biological Sciences: Ideology, Language, and Learning." *Writing, Teaching, and Learning in the Disciplines.* Ed. A. Herrington and C. Moran. New York: The Modern Language Association of America, 1992. 193–212.

Spitler, Amanda. "Arctic National Wildlife Refuge: Oil Field or Wilderness?" *BioScience* 37.1 (1987): 714.

Stack, Carol. *All Our Kin: Strategies for Survival in a Black Community.* New York: Harper & Row, 1974.

Tompkins, Jane. *West of Everything.* New York: Oxford UP, 1992.

Toulmin, Stephen. *The Uses of Argument.* New York: Cambridge UP, 1958.

Toulmin, Stephen, Richard Rieke, and Allan Janik. *An Introduction to Reasoning.* 2nd ed. New York: MacMillan, 1984.

Van Maanen, John. *Tales of the Field: On Writing Ethnography.* Chicago: U of Chicago P, 1988.

Walker, D. A., et al. "Cumulative Impacts of Oil Fields on Northern Alaskan Landscapes. *Science* 238 (1987): 757–76.

Wilkes, Kathleen. *Real People: Personal Identity Without Thought Experiments.* New York: Clarendon P, 1988.

ACKNOWLEDGMENTS

Abele, G., J. Brown, M. C. Brewer. "Long-term Effects of Off-Road Vehicle Traffic on Tundra Terrain," *Journal of Terramechanics*, Vol. 21, No. 3. 1984, pp. 283–294. Reprinted by permission of the International Society for Terrain Vehicle Systems, Inc.

Ariès, Philippe. "From the Medieval Family to the Modern Family," from *Centuries of Childhood*, trans. by R. Baldick. Copyright © 1962 by Jonathan Cape Ltd. Reprinted by permission of Alfred A. Knopf., Inc.

Bishop, Elizabeth. "Gwendolyn," "In the Village," and "The Baptism," from *The Collected Prose*, edited by Robert Giroux. Copyright © 1984 by Alice Mathfessel. Reprinted by permission of Farrar, Straus, & Giroux, Inc.

Congressional Quarterly Almanac. "Arctic Refuge Bill Stalls Once Again." From *Congressional Quarterly Almanac*, Vol. xlvi: 315; 1990. Reprinted by permission.

Demos, John. "Images of the Family, Then and Now," *Past, Present, and Personal: The Life Course in American History*, Oxford University Press, 1986.

De Vos, Susan. "Leaving the Parental Home: Patterns in Six Latin American Countries," *Journal of Marriage and the Family*, 51, 615–626. Copyright © 1989 by the National Council on Family Relations, 3989 Central Avenue NE, Suite 550, Minneapolis, MN 55421. Reprinted by permission.

Egan, Timothy. "Can Oil and Water Mix?" *The New York Times Magazine*, August 4, 1991. Copyright © 1991 by The New York Times Company. Reprinted by permission.

Ellis, Frey R., Schura Holesh, John W. Ellis. "Incidents of Osteoporosis in Vegetarians and Omnivores," from *The American Journal of Clinical Nutrition*, 25: June 1972, pp. 555–558. Copyright © 1987 American Journal of Clinical Nutrition. Reprinted by permission.

Flam, Jack. "Introduction" and "About Conversation," from *Matisse: The Man and His Art, 1869–1918*. Copyright © 1994 by Jack Flam. Reprinted by permission of Georges Borchardt, Inc. for the author. "Looking at Art," by Jack Flam, originally published in *ARTNews Magazine*. Copyright © 1994 by Jack Flam. Reprinted by permission of Georges Borchardt, Inc. for the author.

Walker, D. A., P. J. Webber, E. F. Binnian, K. R. Everett, N. D. Lederer, E. A. Nordstrand, M. D. Walker. "Cumulative Impacts of Oil Fields on Northern Alaskan Landscapes," *Science* 238: 757–761. Copyright © 1987 American Association for the Advancement of Science. Reprinted with permission.

PHOTO ACKNOWLEDGMENTS

223: Scala/Art Resource, NY **225:** Eric Lessing/Art Resource, NY **237:** Courtesy George Eastman House **238:** Max Ernst. *The Couple in Lace,* 1923. Oil on canvas; 101. 5 x 142 cm. Museum Boymans-van Beuningen, Rotterdam **269:** Courtesy of Kenneth Sebens **296–298:** Courtesy of the Journal of Terramechanics **510:** *Bathers with a Turtle,* 1908 oil on canvas L.R.: Henri Matisse 08, 70 1/2 x 86 3/4 in. 179.1 x 220.3 cm. Gift of Mr. and Mrs. Joseph Pulitzer, Jr. 24: 1964. The Saint Louis Art Museum (Modern Art)

INDEX

(Continued from inside front cover)

BRIEF CONTENTS